**Keep this book. You will
need it and use it throughout
your career.**

About the American Hotel & Lodging Association (AH&LA)

Founded in 1910, AH&LA is the trade association representing the lodging industry in the United States. AH&LA is a federation of state lodging associations throughout the United States with 11,000 lodging properties worldwide as members. The association offers its members assistance with governmental affairs representation, communications, marketing, hospitality operations, training and education, technology issues, and more. For information, call 202-289-3100.

LODGING, the management magazine of AH&LA, is a "living textbook" for hospitality students that provides timely features, industry news, and vital lodging information.

About the American Hotel & Lodging Educational Institute (EI)

An affiliate of AH&LA, the Educational Institute is the world's largest source of quality training and educational materials for the lodging industry. EI develops textbooks and courses that are used in more than 1,200 colleges and universities worldwide, and also offers courses to individuals through its Distance Learning program. Hotels worldwide rely on EI for training resources that focus on every aspect of lodging operations. Industry-tested videos, CD-ROMs, seminars, and skills guides prepare employees at every skill level. EI also offers professional certification for the industry's top performers. For information about EI's products and services, call 800-349-0299 or 407-999-8100.

About the American Hotel & Lodging Educational Foundation (AH&LEF)

An affiliate of AH&LA, the American Hotel & Lodging Educational Foundation provides financial support that enhances the stability, prosperity, and growth of the lodging industry through educational and research programs. AH&LEF has awarded millions of dollars in scholarship funds for students pursuing higher education in hospitality management. AH&LEF has also funded research projects on topics important to the industry, including occupational safety and health, turnover and diversity, and best practices in the U.S. lodging industry. For more information, go to www.ahlef.org.

PLANNING and CONTROL for FOOD and BEVERAGE OPERATIONS

Seventh Edition

Educational Institute Books

UNIFORM SYSTEM OF ACCOUNTS FOR THE LODGING INDUSTRY
Tenth Revised Edition

RESORT DEVELOPMENT AND MANAGEMENT
Second Edition
Chuck Y. Gee

PLANNING AND CONTROL FOR FOOD AND BEVERAGE OPERATIONS
Seventh Edition
Jack D. Ninemeier

UNDERSTANDING HOSPITALITY LAW
Fourth Edition
Jack P. Jefferies/Banks Brown

SUPERVISION IN THE HOSPITALITY INDUSTRY
Fourth Edition
Raphael R. Kavanaugh/Jack D. Ninemeier

MANAGEMENT OF FOOD AND BEVERAGE OPERATIONS
Fourth Edition
Jack D. Ninemeier

MANAGING FRONT OFFICE OPERATIONS
Eighth Edition
Michael L. Kasavana/Richard M. Brooks

MANAGING SERVICE IN FOOD AND BEVERAGE OPERATIONS
Third Edition
Ronald F. Cichy/Philip J. Hickey, Jr.

THE LODGING AND FOOD SERVICE INDUSTRY
Seventh Edition
Gerald W. Lattin

SECURITY AND LOSS PREVENTION MANAGEMENT
Second Edition
Raymond C. Ellis, Jr./David M. Stipanuk

HOSPITALITY INDUSTRY MANAGERIAL ACCOUNTING
Sixth Edition
Raymond S. Schmidgall

PURCHASING FOR FOOD SERVICE OPERATIONS
Ronald F. Cichy/Jeffery D Elsworth

MANAGING TECHNOLOGY IN THE HOSPITALITY INDUSTRY
Fifth Edition
Michael L. Kasavana/John J. Cahill

BASIC HOTEL AND RESTAURANT ACCOUNTING
Sixth Edition
Raymond Cote

ACCOUNTING FOR HOSPITALITY MANAGERS
Fifth Edition
Raymond Cote

CONVENTION MANAGEMENT AND SERVICE
Seventh Edition
Milton T. Astroff/James R. Abbey

HOSPITALITY SALES AND MARKETING
Fifth Edition
James R. Abbey

MANAGING HOUSEKEEPING OPERATIONS
Revised Third Edition
Aleta A. Nitschke/William D. Frye

DIMENSIONS OF TOURISM
Joseph D. Fridgen

HOSPITALITY TODAY: AN INTRODUCTION
Sixth Edition
Rocco M. Angelo/Andrew N. Vladimir

MANAGING BAR AND BEVERAGE OPERATIONS
Lendal H. Kotschevar/Mary L. Tanke

HOSPITALITY FACILITIES MANAGEMENT AND DESIGN
Third Edition
David M. Stipanuk

MANAGING HOSPITALITY HUMAN RESOURCES
Fourth Edition
Robert H. Woods

RETAIL MANAGEMENT FOR SPAS

HOSPITALITY INDUSTRY FINANCIAL ACCOUNTING
Third Edition
Raymond S. Schmidgall/James W. Damitio

INTERNATIONAL HOTELS: DEVELOPMENT AND MANAGEMENT
Second Edition
Chuck Yim Gee

QUALITY SANITATION MANAGEMENT
Ronald F. Cichy

HOTEL INVESTMENTS: ISSUES & PERSPECTIVES
Fourth Edition
Edited by Lori E. Raleigh and Rachel J. Roginsky

LEADERSHIP AND MANAGEMENT IN THE HOSPITALITY INDUSTRY
Second Edition
Robert H. Woods/Judy Z. King

MARKETING IN THE HOSPITALITY INDUSTRY
Fourth Edition
Ronald A. Nykiel

CONTEMPORARY HOSPITALITY MARKETING
William Lazer/Roger Layton

UNIFORM SYSTEM OF ACCOUNTS FOR THE HEALTH, RACQUET AND SPORTSCLUB INDUSTRY

CONTEMPORARY CLUB MANAGEMENT
Second Edition
Edited by Joe Perdue for the Club Managers Association of America

RESORT CONDOMINIUM AND VACATION OWNERSHIP MANAGEMENT: A HOSPITALITY PERSPECTIVE
Robert A. Gentry/Pedro Mandoki/Jack Rush

ACCOUNTING FOR CLUB OPERATIONS
Raymond S. Schmidgall/James W. Damitio

TRAINING AND DEVELOPMENT FOR THE HOSPITALITY INDUSTRY
Debra F. Cannon/Catherine M. Gustafson

UNIFORM SYSTEM OF FINANCIAL REPORTING FOR CLUB
Sixth Revised Edition

HOTEL ASSET MANAGEMENT: PRINCIPLES & PRACTICES
Second Edition
Edited by Greg Denton, Lori E. Raleigh, and A. J. Singh

MANAGING BEVERAGE SERVICE
Lendal H. Kotschevar/Ronald F. Cichy

FOOD SAFETY: MANAGING WITH THE HACCP SYSTEM
Second Edition
Ronald F. Cichy

UNIFORM SYSTEM OF FINANCIAL REPORTING FOR SPAS

FUNDAMENTALS OF DESTINATION MANAGEMENT AND MARKETING
Edited by Rich Harrill

ETHICS IN THE HOSPITALITY AND TOURISM INDUSTRY
Second Edition
Karen Lieberman/Bruce Nissen

HOSPITALITY AND TOURISM MARKETING
William Lazer/Melissa Dallas/Carl Riegel

SPA: A COMPREHENSIVE INTRODUCTION
Elizabeth M. Johnson/Bridgette M. Redman

PLANNING and CONTROL for FOOD and BEVERAGE OPERATIONS

Seventh Edition

Jack D. Ninemeier, Ph.D., CHA

American
Hotel & Lodging
Educational Institute

Disclaimer

This publication is designed to provide accurate and authoritative information in regard to the subject matter covered. It is sold with the understanding that the publisher is not engaged in rendering legal, accounting, or other professional service. If legal advice or other expert assistance is required, the services of a competent professional person should be sought.

— *From the Declaration of Principles jointly adopted by the American Bar Association and a Committee of Publishers and Associations*

The author, Jack D. Ninemeier, is solely responsible for the contents of this publication. All views expressed herein are solely those of the author and do not necessarily reflect the views of the American Hotel & Lodging Educational Institute (the Institute) or the American Hotel & Lodging Association (AH&LA).

Nothing contained in this publication shall constitute a standard, an endorsement, or a recommendation of AH&LA or the Institute. AH&LA and the Institute disclaim any liability with respect to the use of any information, procedure, or product, or reliance thereon by any member of the hospitality industry.

©2009
By the AMERICAN HOTEL & LODGING
EDUCATIONAL INSTITUTE
2113 N. High Street
Lansing, Michigan 48906-4221

The American Hotel & Lodging
Educational Institute is a nonprofit
educational foundation.

Printed in the United States of America
1 2 3 4 5 6 7 8 9 10 13 12 11 10 09

ISBN: 978-0-86612-339-6

Contents

Preface

SOME ASPECTS OF THE FOOD SERVICE INDUSTRY have changed very little, others have changed significantly since the first edition of *Planning and Control for Food and Beverage Operations* was published in 1982. During that more than a quarter century, food and beverage managers have continued their efforts to identify and meet—or, ideally, exceed—the wants and needs of their guests. While these efforts have been constant, consumer preferences have been anything but; they have changed dramatically over these same years. Examples include the shifting expectations of what defines "excellence" in fine-dining operations; the new "eatertainment" aspects of many mid-range properties that now must deliver an "experience" in addition to the food and beverage products and services; and the ever-changing nature of the dine-in, take-out, and drive-through meals purchased in quick-service properties.

Nothing, however, has changed in the food service industry more than the technology used for operational planning and control. Thanks to computers and other technology, operations of all sizes now have more tools and information available to help decision-makers plan and control their operations in order to reach financial and other goals. While previous editions of this book have addressed technology in the context of "what was new" between publication dates, this edition attempts to more fully integrate technology information with the control processes and procedures discussed in the chapters. When illustrating points made in the text, in most cases this edition uses examples drawn from computerized rather than manual planning and control systems, in recognition of the increased role that technology plays in food and beverage operations of almost every size. Also new to this edition are "Learn More on the Web" sidebars throughout the text. These sidebars point students to web-based resources that provide the latest information for those readers who want to more fully explore the technology issues and other topics discussed.

Thankfully, some things have *not* changed for this edition. The seventh edition of *Planning and Control for Food and Beverage Operations* continues an emphasis on practical activities that managers in food service operations of all sizes can use to plan and control their operations. Because managers are extremely busy, they must make the most cost-effective use of their time as they control their always limited resources. The primary topics of this book—food and beverage products, labor, and revenue—are carefully analyzed, and the very best strategies for their management are included in this "primer" for the control of commercial and noncommercial food service operations. This book is meant to be read *and* used. Students in formal educational programs and trainees in hospitality operations may read the book from cover to cover as part of formal or informal professional development and career training activities. Others, such as managers and supervisors on the front lines, can turn to this book for "how-to-do-it" help with problem-solving tasks on the job.

The book's primary objective also remains unchanged from earlier editions: to help hospitality managers and students understand the complexities of controlling the products (food and beverages), labor, and revenue in food and beverage operations. Today's emphasis within the industry on cost reduction and quality and service optimization, along with the ever-increasing desire on the part of consumers to receive value for the dollars they spend, makes the information this book brings to the reader increasingly important.

The author would like to acknowledge the significant contributions to earlier editions of this book from members of the American Hotel & Lodging Association's Food and Beverage Committee. They, along with many others, including industry experts and the Educational Institute's editorial and support staff, have provided a solid foundation of information that has been revised again in this edition, to keep up with the ever-changing world of food and beverage operations. This new edition benefits from the guidance of George Glazer, Senior Vice President—Academic Publications; and Tim Eaton, Senior Director—Academic Publications, both of the Educational Institute. Their standards have been exacting and demanding, and their suggestions have been incorporated to help move this book along its journey toward excellence.

Food service continues to be a vast, important, and growing segment of the hospitality industry worldwide. Students and managers already working in the industry who learn the fundamentals of food and beverage planning and control will likely greatly increase their career opportunities. I sincerely hope that this book will play a role in their personal and professional success.

Students in literally hundreds of hospitality education programs worldwide are using this and other Educational Institute texts. These students, who will be tomorrow's industry leaders, are the ones to whom this book is dedicated.

Jack D. Ninemeier, Ph.D., CHA
Professor
The School of Hospitality Business
Michigan State University

Part I

Introduction to Food and Beverage Control

Chapter 1 Outline

Travel and Tourism: The Umbrella Industry
    The Hospitality Segment
Overview of Hotel Organization
    The Food and Beverage Department
Commercial and Noncommercial Food
    Services
        Important Similarities
        Important Differences
Overview of Food Service Management
    The Operating Control Cycle
    The Management System
    The Management Process
    Integrating the Process
A Common Problem: The Labor Shortage
Managing a Multi-Unit Restaurant
        Multi-Unit Restaurant Organization
        Structure
The Increasing Role of Technology

Competencies

1. Identify the components of the travel and tourism industry and describe the hospitality segment of the industry. (pp. 3–6)

2. Discuss how a hotel is organized and describe food and beverage departments within hotels. (pp. 6–11)

3. Discuss the similarities and differences between commercial and noncommercial food service operations. (pp. 11–13)

4. Describe food service management, including the operating control cycle and the management tasks of planning, organizing, coordinating, staffing, directing, controlling, and evaluating. (pp. 13–20)

5. Summarize the labor shortage challenge for food and beverage operations and how managers are meeting it. (pp. 20–21)

6. Provide an overview of multi-unit hospitality operations. (pp. 21–23)

7. Review the role and impact of technology in today's food and beverage operations. (pp. 23–27)

1

The Challenge of Food and Beverage Operations

MANAGING A FOOD AND BEVERAGE OPERATION is challenging for many reasons. Food and beverage service involves both manufacturing and service-related operations that demand that the manager have not only technical knowledge and skills, but also business knowledge and people skills. The manager must know how a product is manufactured, how it is marketed to the consumer, and numerous other operational functions and activities. Above all, the manager must be able to relate well to people and to work effectively with them.

Since food and beverage operations are part of the hospitality industry—just as the hospitality industry itself is part of the travel and tourism industry—it is helpful to view the interrelationships that exist among these related enterprises.[1]

Travel and Tourism: The Umbrella Industry

Exhibit 1 shows **travel and tourism** as an umbrella industry covering five segments—lodging operations, food and beverage operations, transportation services, retail stores, and destination activities—all of which provide products and services to the traveler. Most of these businesses also provide products and services to residents of their communities. In fact, whether a business considers itself part of the travel and tourism industry likely depends on how much of its revenue is derived from travelers, compared with how much is derived from local residents. When reviewing Exhibit 1, note that food and beverage service is an important part of each segment of the travel and tourism industry. Many lodging operations and all food and beverage outlets offer these products and services. Ships, airplanes, and trains (in transportation services); food outlets in shopping malls and markets (retail stores); and food service offered as part of recreation, entertainment, meetings, and sporting events (in destination activities) are examples.

The Hospitality Segment

The **hospitality industry** comprises two segments shown in Exhibit 1: lodging operations—hotels, motels, resorts, condo-hotels, casinos, and other facilities offering sleeping accommodations—and food and beverage operations. Again, both the traveling public and local residents are served by these segments—particularly by food and beverage operations. Consider, for example, the use of lodging properties by local businesses and organizations for meetings or special-occasion

Exhibit 1   Overview of the Travel and Tourism Industry

Travel and Tourism Industry				
Lodging Operations	**Food and Beverage Operations**	**Transportation Services**	**Retail Stores**	**Destination Activities**
Hotels	Restaurants	Ships	Gift Shops	Recreation
Motels	Lodging Properties	Airplanes	Souvenir Shops	Business
Resorts	Retail Stores	Autos	Arts/Crafts Shops	Entertainment
Timeshare Hotels	Vending	Buses	Shopping Malls	Meetings
Condominiums	Catering	Trains	Markets	Study Trips
Condo-Hotels	Snack Bars	Limousines	Convenience Stores	Sporting Events
Conference Centers	Cruise Ships			Ethnic Festivals
Camps	Bars/Taverns			Cultural Events
Parks	Banquets			Seasonal Festivals
Bed and Breakfast	Contract Food Services			Gaming
Casinos	Private Clubs			Theme Parks
Convention Hotels	Off-Site Caterers			
Cruise Ships				

dining events. Some lodging properties actively market their room accommodations to local residents. Weekend "escape" packages, which may include some meals and the use of the property's recreational facilities in addition to the guestroom, are one example.

Just as the traveling public and local resident markets overlap, so do hospitality industry segments. Consider, for example, that many lodging properties have one or more food and beverage outlets, and they may have retail shops and offer various activities as well. Similarly, food and beverage service extends to the transportation, retail, and recreation segments of the industry. Food and beverage operations are crucial to the world of hospitality, travel, and tourism.

There are two basic categories of food and beverage operations. Those in lodging properties, restaurants, and other for-profit enterprises are considered **commercial food service operations;** those in organizations such as schools, nursing homes, hospitals, and military services are considered **noncommercial** or **institutional food service operations.** Exhibit 2 shows how food and beverage operations can be separated into commercial and noncommercial categories. It also separates the noncommercial segment into **self-operated** and **contract management company–operated** facilities. As the name implies, self-operated food services are those managed by the organization that offers them. By contrast, some facilities

Exhibit 2   Overview of Food and Beverage Operations

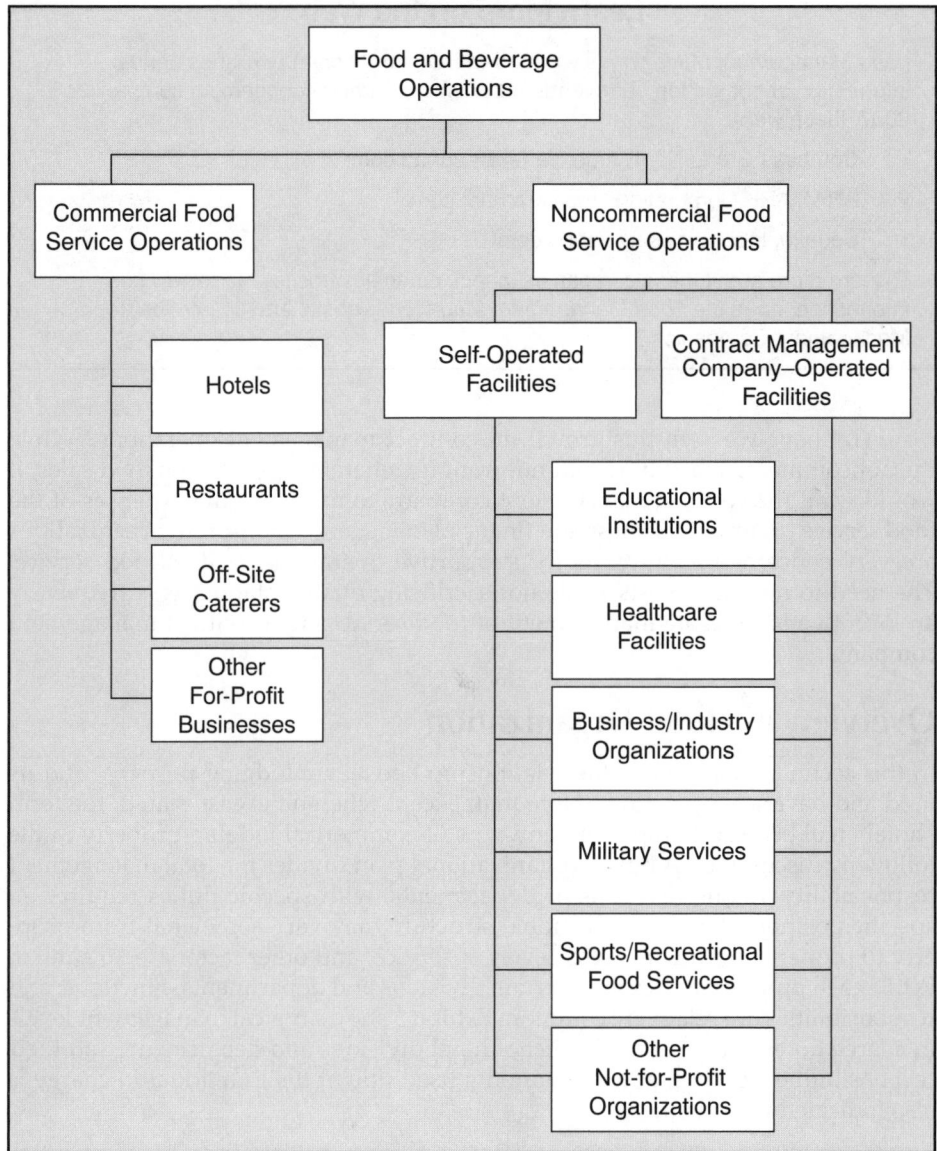

employ a contract management company to operate food services for its students, patients, residents, employees, or other constituencies.

The increase in contract management company operations is an example of the growth of multi-unit organizations. Though many people are not familiar with large management companies such as Compass Group and ARAMARK, these organizations manage food services in thousands of outlets worldwide.

Learn More on the Web

Food Management Magazine (www.food-management.com) publishes annual information about the top 50 revenue-producing contract management companies. In 2007, these were:

- Compass Group North America (www.cgnad.com)

- ARAMARK Corporation (www.aramark.com)

- Sodexo, Inc. (www.sodexousa.com)

To learn more about these companies, check out their websites. To review current information, go to the *Food Management Magazine* website and search for "Top 50 Management Companies."

Why have we seen this growth in contract management operations? While the noncommercial facility would not want to generate a profit from food sales, it would want the contract management company to minimize the expenses of the food service program. Business and financial managers of non-profit organizations are very concerned about costs for supportive operations such as food service. The need to minimize costs while not sacrificing quality standards is frequently an incentive to delegate management of food services to a contract management company.

Overview of Hotel Organization

In this section, we'll review the relationship between a lodging property and its food and beverage operation. (Note that, except when otherwise stated, the term "hotel" will be used to represent any type of commercial lodging property in the following discussion.) A hotel's organizational plan divides the total management responsibility among divisions or departments, with specific duties required in specific positions. This organizational structure may vary somewhat from property to property, even when size, levels of service, and other factors seem similar. While each property is different, certain divisions and departments, functions, and responsibilities are relatively common. Exhibit 3 shows typical management levels in a large hotel. A representative list of hotel divisions and departments and their responsibilities follows, and a commonly used title of the individual in charge is also indicated in parentheses:

- *Rooms (Rooms Division Director)*—a department that is usually responsible for several functions: reservations, front office, bell and concierge services, telephone (**PBX**) services, laundry, and housekeeping.

- *Human Resources (Human Resources Director)*—a department that assists other departments in recruiting and selecting employees and in a wide variety of other activities involved in the management of employees.

- *Accounting (Controller)*—a department responsible for accounting tasks for the entire operation. This department is often responsible for purchasing,

Exhibit 3   Typical Management Levels in a Large Hotel

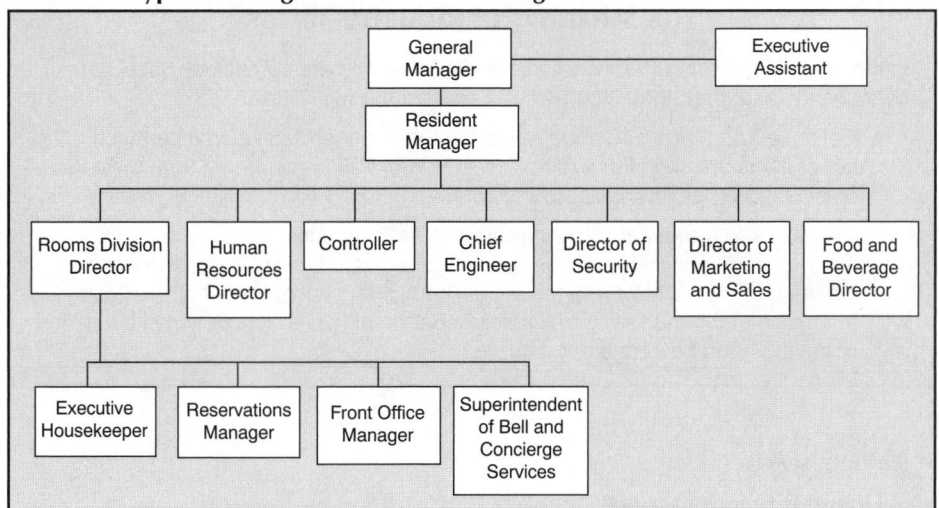

receiving, storing, and issuing food and beverage products. A food and beverage controller in a large property performs many of the property's control activities. Sometimes, in multi-unit hotel companies, the hotel's controller reports to a regional manager or other official outside the property, rather than to the hotel's general manager. This is done to provide increased control over the financial aspects of the operation.

- *Engineering and Maintenance (Chief Engineer)*—a department responsible for physical plant and equipment maintenance and repair, as well as energy conservation practices.

- *Security (Director of Security)*—a department responsible for protecting the guests, employees, property, and equipment of the hotel.

- *Marketing and Sales (Director of Marketing and Sales)*—a department responsible for attracting guests to the property, making group bookings, and handling convention services. This department is often involved with advertising and public relations.

- *Food and Beverage (Food and Beverage Director)*—a department responsible for all food and beverage services provided by the property. The operations of the food and beverage department are addressed more specifically in the following section.

The Food and Beverage Department

Separate and distinct from other hotel departments, the food and beverage department typically encompasses such diverse services and operations as:

- Coffee shops.
- Dining rooms.

The Meaning of Industry Terms

In the hospitality industry, terms with different meanings are sometimes used inter-changeably (and, therefore, incorrectly). Consider the following:

- *Revenue and Sales.* Revenue refers to money generated when a certain num-ber of items are sold. For example, *revenue* of $25 is generated from the *sales* of five chicken sandwiches costing $5 each.

- *Catering and Banquets. Catering* refers to selling public functions involving food and beverage services. *Banquets* refers to the setup, production, service, and clean-up of food and beverages in public function space. Frequently, catering is a function of the marketing and sales department, while banqueting is a function of the food and beverage department.

- Room service.
- **Hospitality suite** service.
- Lounges, bars, and other alcoholic beverage services.
- **Banquet** service.
- Other (employee cafeterias, takeout and specialty shops, within-guestroom snack/beverage centers, etc.).

The food and beverage department is an integral part of the operation of a **full-service hotel** (a hotel offering a variety of facilities and amenities, including food and beverage services). These properties generate approximately 27 percent of their total revenue from the sale of food and beverage products.[2] In some large convention hotels, food and beverage sales may account for 50 percent or more of a property's total revenue. The economic success or failure of many hotels is directly tied to the ability of the food and beverage department to effectively plan and control its operations and provide food service that will attract hotel guests.

It is important to note that the food and beverage department generally can-not survive by providing services to hotel guests only. In many properties, a sig-nificant percentage of food and beverage revenue is generated from the local area. Hotel managers can use basic marketing techniques to attract community resi-dents to the hotel's food and beverage operations.

The following sections discuss hotel food and beverage operations in more detail.

Production Facilities. Managing food production is a major responsibility in every food and beverage department. Older lodging properties were often built with sep-arate food production facilities for each food service outlet. Increased costs of space, equipment, and operations, however, have reduced the usefulness of this design concept. Many newer facilities feature centralized commissary-style kitchens that prepare many of the products used in service outlets throughout the property. For example, a central kitchen may produce bakery products, sauces, and products requiring specialized equipment or extensive labor, while **finishing kitchens** in the food service outlets prepare items requiring less equipment and labor. As a result of this newer design concept, food and beverage managers must be increasingly concerned with transport and delivery systems and with the sanitation, food quality, and production problems involved in large-volume preparation processes.

Operations Challenges. In their efforts to be profitable, food and beverage operations in lodging facilities often have to overcome several challenges that freestanding restaurants do not face. Consider the following:

- Freestanding restaurants are built in locations where food and beverage service is judged to be profitable; hotels are located in areas where the rental of guestrooms is judged to be profitable.

- Food service in hotels must operate at times convenient to hotel guests. For example, an airport hotel's restaurant may need to stay open long past "normal" restaurant operating hours to accommodate passengers from late-night flights. By contrast, a freestanding restaurant's operating hours are scheduled simply to best accommodate its guests.

- Food service in hotels must be provided to guests even on low-occupancy (and therefore low-business) days. A restaurant manager may elect to close on low-business days (for example, on all Mondays during the summer).

- Hotels often feel obligated to offer room service because many guests expect it, even though this service frequently operates at a loss. In addition, room service must generally be available at all hours of the day or night in first-class properties.

- Hotel food service operations frequently offer dining benefits for all employees—not just those in the food and beverage department. While some direct costs may be allocated to departments based on their employees' use of the dining privileges, other indirect costs are often "buried" in the food and beverage department.

- A hotel often has multiple food outlets. While some operating costs are reduced as central commissary kitchens are used, a freestanding restaurant does not incur the same costs for the transportation of food within the property. Consider also that, in some resorts, foods and beverages need to be transported by vehicle around golf courses and other recreational areas.

- Freestanding restaurants usually are highly visible to potential guests, whereas restaurants in hotels are often more difficult to see and to get to—even if a direct off-the-street entrance is provided.

- The owner and the manager of a freestanding restaurant are very involved in its operation. In a hotel, by contrast, restaurant managers must often have decisions approved by the hotel manager, who has concerns extending beyond those of the food and beverage department.

Revenue and Support Centers. A food and beverage department contributes departmental income (revenue minus direct expenses) that contributes to the hotel's overhead (fixed costs) and profit requirements. Departmental income is based on the revenue and related expenses of each separate food and beverage outlet in the property. To effectively plan for and control the operation of each outlet, food and beverage managers must know the specific revenues and expenses applicable to each outlet. The concept of dividing departments into **revenue** and **support centers** helps managers organize their planning and effectively operate each service outlet. For example, a hotel's banquet operation may generate revenue in excess of costs, and the room service operation may suffer a loss. However, since they create revenue, both the banquet and room service operations are revenue centers within the hotel's food and beverage department. The facilities and activities of the hotel's operation that support revenue centers and supply them with what they need to generate revenue are often referred to as support centers. Examples of support centers include purchasing and laundry operations.

Many properties develop accounting and control plans that separate revenue and expense by revenue center—a hotel may keep separate track of the revenue and expenses generated by each of its food service outlets, its banquet department, and its room service department, for example. In a commissary operation, such as a bakeshop or sauce/soup preparation station, revenue centers may "buy" necessary products from the production unit. The production unit, then, can be referred to as a support center. As a second example, some hotels consider the beverage storeroom to be a support center. The storeroom buys necessary products from suppliers and "sells" them to the beverage outlets, passing along labor and related costs incurred in operating the beverage storeroom.

As this need to identify and separate revenue and expenses by specific revenue and support centers within the lodging property increases, food and beverage operations, at least in large facilities, actually become "mini-multi-unit" operations. All the management principles and procedures involved in planning, coordinating, marketing, recordkeeping, and related functions of chain operations apply, on a smaller scale, to the hotel's food and beverage department.

This discussion of a typical large food and beverage department has emphasized the diversity of services for which it is responsible and the complexity of its operations. The organization necessary to provide such services is also complex.

Management Team. The overall responsibility for the food and beverage department in a typical hotel lies with the food and beverage department head, whose title may be food and beverage director or something similar. The director reports  to the hotel's general manager or resident manager and may receive help from those in other managerial positions within the department. For example, an assistant food and beverage director may be responsible for overseeing the activities of managers in each specific revenue center. Likewise, an executive chef, responsible for all food production in all outlets within the property, may report directly to the food and beverage director. In a large facility, there may be a beverage director who is responsible for all beverage operations and who reports to the director or assistant director of the food and beverage department. A food and beverage controller reporting to the accounting/controller's department may also be employed. This staff member serves in an advisory capacity to the food and beverage director and is responsible for many of the accounting/recordkeeping aspects of the food and beverage operation. Finally, because of the complexity of tasks, a wide array of

Exhibit 4   Management Positions: Sample Large Hotel Food and Beverage Department

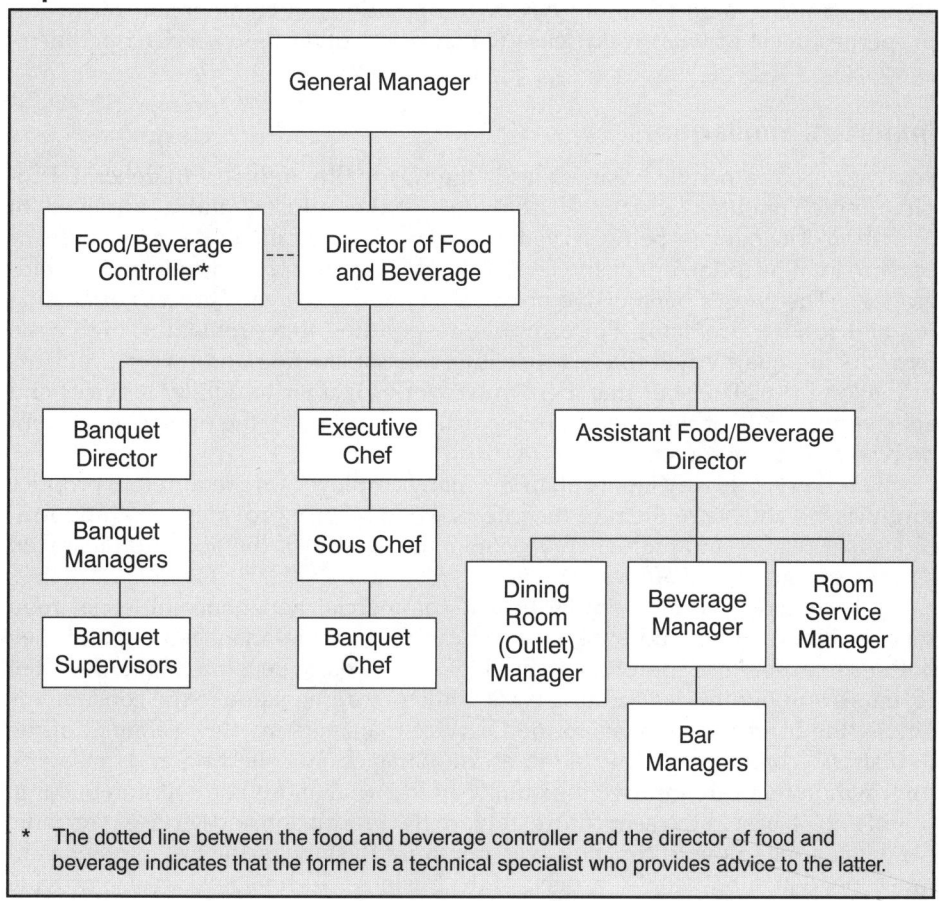

* The dotted line between the food and beverage controller and the director of food and beverage indicates that the former is a technical specialist who provides advice to the latter.

employee positions can be found within the specific revenue and support centers of the food and beverage department in a large hotel. Exhibit 4 shows selected management positions and the relationships among them in the food and beverage department of such a property.

Management System Design. The diverse services and complex organization of a food and beverage department require an effective management system. The management system must be comprehensive, encompassing all necessary management activities and all aspects of available or potential resources—people, money, products (food and beverage), time, procedures, energy, facilities, and equipment.

Commercial and Noncommercial Food Services ──────

Despite their complexity, at their most basic level, quantity food production and management systems—whether developed for commercial or noncommercial operations—are more similar than different. This common ground determines the basic requirements of a food and beverage management system. Therefore, while our focus is on food and beverage operations in commercial (for-profit) properties, most of what we discuss will apply to other food service operations as well.

Important Similarities

Food service is a people business, as is the hospitality industry in general. People are the common factor in all segments of the industry and at all levels of operation. The persons being served, whether they are called guests in a hotel or patients in a hospital, are at the center of all concerns, procedures, and considerations. The guest's perspective must be factored into every process of analyzing and solving problems. For example, responding to a problem of high costs by reducing quality will likely cause guest dissatisfaction and larger problems in the long run. The staff members must work together to deliver services and achieve the goals of the operation, regardless of whether the operation is commercial or noncommercial.

Food service is very labor-intensive; many employees are required to produce products for and serve them to the guests. Food service provides great opportunities for creative and high-energy people; the success of the operation is linked directly to consistent staff performance.

Two other important similarities of commercial and noncommercial food service should be noted: they both need careful financial management and they both increasingly use computer technology. The need to generate higher levels of revenues and minimize operating costs while providing value to the consumer is among the biggest challenges to food service managers in every segment of the industry. Technology is available to assist managers in collecting and analyzing information that can improve the quality of financial and other decision making. It will not, at least in the near future, replace the production and service personnel needed for operations. It can, however, minimize the time managers and their staff must spend in "non-people" aspects of the business. Technology can also provide managers with more information and time to resolve problems that affect their guests, their staff members, and their financial goals.

Important Differences

A major difference between commercial and noncommercial food services stems from the vocabulary used to describe management and the results of operations. For example, the language of commercial food service operations refers to "management" and "profits"; the language of noncommercial food service operations refers to "administration" and "operating surplus."

Also, among the various kinds of food and beverage operations, there are important differences in the methods used to collect revenue for services provided. For example, the typical hotel and restaurant generally collects revenue in the form of cash, checks, or payment (credit or debit) cards. Also, they typically collect this revenue when the service is provided. There may also be some house accounts that are billed separately for charges incurred during a monthly or other billing period. The "payment upon receipt of services" policy and timely billing methods make revenue collection relatively simple and straightforward.

Many hotel guests are permitted to charge food and beverage services to their guestroom folios (accounts). Guest charges complicate the revenue collection system the hotel needs to manage its operations. The hotel must use an **accounts receivable system** to handle revenue that is due but not yet collected. Gathering and channeling all the information involved in this revenue collection system can be a tedious and error-prone process, but computerized equipment—both at the point of sale and at the front office where guest folios are automatically updated—has greatly simplified the revenue collection process. Nevertheless, there is still an obvious need for an expanded revenue control and collection system for the management of hotel food and beverage operations.

Revenue from banquet sales, a large aspect of food and beverage operations in many hotels, frequently involves a combination of billing methods. To account for advance payments and to assess the amounts still due, there must be a system to accurately determine the quantity of products sold for which revenue must be collected.

Commercial operators may appreciate the special problems of noncommercial administrators in allocating and assessing operating and related costs of food services so that charges can be calculated. First, food and beverage service is only one part of the "bill" to patients, residents, students, or others being served. Also, the process of allocating expenses to each cost center, such as nutrition services, is frequently much more detailed and complicated in large hospitals and other facilities than that used by many hotel properties. Finally, noncommercial operations may collect cash, allow the use of credit or debit cards, and allow or encourage prepayments such as in colleges or universities where students pay a lump sum in advance and then draw on this amount as charges are made. As another example, private clubs typically permit or require charges by members only, who then pay amounts owed on a monthly or other basis.

Overview of Food Service Management

All food and beverage management systems begin with the menu. The operation's menu determines what production, service, and managerial responsibilities must be met. Many food and beverage operations offer a variety of menus for different meal periods and seasons of the year. The menu itself is the result of marketing efforts designed to identify the wants and needs of those being served, such as hotel or restaurant customers, hospital patients, nursing home residents, and school students. In each case, the effort is to develop strategies to satisfy the consumer's needs, while at the same time achieving the operation's own goals.

Developing the menu is only the first, and most basic, step in planning food and beverage operations. Once the menu is developed, plans and procedures for determining necessary products, equipment (purchase and maintenance), facility design and layout, and production systems must be developed and implemented. The goal is to implement an efficient operating control cycle for all revenue and support centers in the operation.

The Operating Control Cycle

An **operating control cycle** divides food and beverage operations into a series of activities. Systems must be designed to manage the flow of food and beverage products through each of the following stages of the cycle:

- Menu planning
- Purchasing
- Receiving
- Storing
- Issuing
- Production (includes preparing, cooking, and holding)
- Serving (from production to service personnel)
- Service (from service personnel to the guest)

The Management System

All food and beverage operations must develop and implement management programs and establish procedures for managing all available resources. To do this, an effective recordkeeping and accounting system is necessary. This system must be able to provide meaningful, accurate information on a timely basis so that appropriate operating and control decisions can be made and evaluated.

The basic system for managing a food and beverage operation is outlined in Exhibit 5. As the exhibit shows, the **management components**—planning, organizing, coordinating, staffing, directing, controlling, and evaluating—form the umbrella under which the entire program operates. This is true for any business enterprise. Under the umbrella, external marketing plans and strategies lead to the basic menu decisions. The menu determines what resources are needed and, therefore, what specific operating control systems are necessary. Finally, the accounting/recordkeeping system takes information from the various components in the operating control system and develops statements about the operation's current financial status. The financial statements become the measure of how well the operation is meeting its economic objectives, which can be profit enhancement or cost containment. When problems are identified, corrective action—one step in the control system—becomes necessary to ensure effective management of all resources.

The Management Process

The management process involves seven basic components: planning, organizing, coordinating, staffing, directing, controlling, and evaluating (see Exhibit 6). These management components are fundamental activities or tasks that apply to all managers, regardless of the type of food service operation for which they are responsible.

Planning. Planning is the management task of creating goals and objectives and programs of action to reach them. Goals and objectives indicate what you want

Exhibit 5   Basic Management System for Food and Beverage Operations

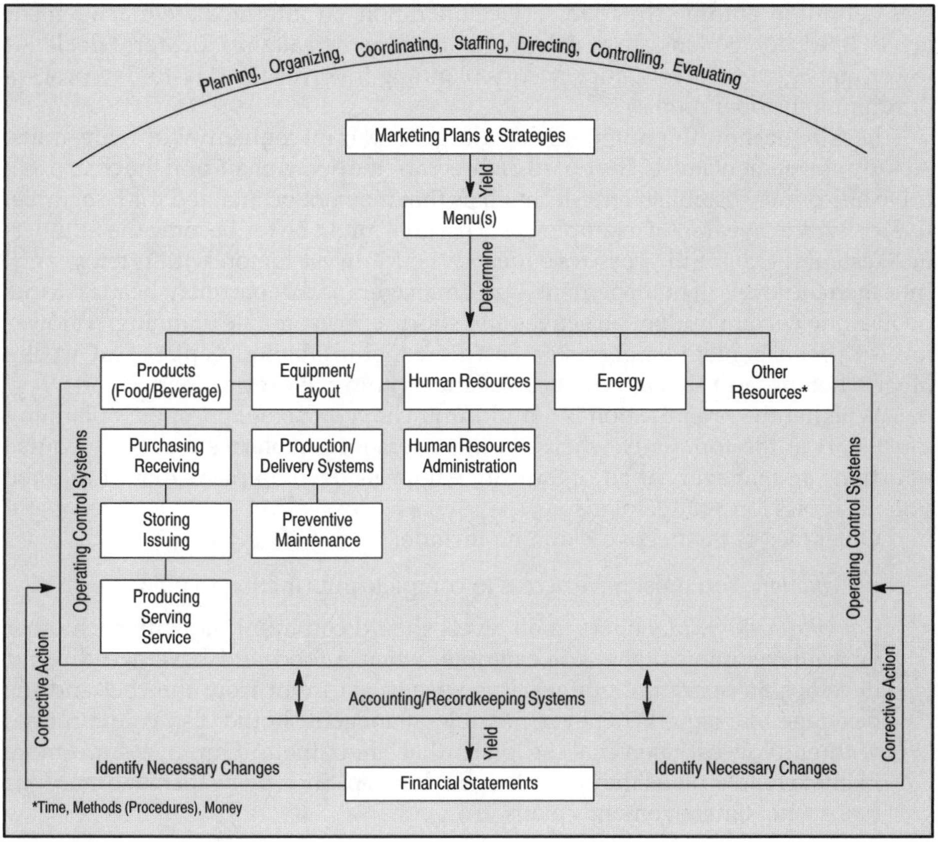

Planning, Organizing, Coordinating, Staffing, Directing, Controlling, Evaluating

Marketing Plans & Strategies

Yield

Menu(s)

Determine

| Products (Food/Beverage) | Equipment/ Layout | Human Resources | Energy | Other Resources* |

Operating Control Systems

Purchasing Receiving

Production/ Delivery Systems

Human Resources Administration

Storing Issuing

Preventive Maintenance

Producing Serving Service

Corrective Action

Accounting/Recordkeeping Systems

Operating Control Systems

Corrective Action

Yield

Identify Necessary Changes

Financial Statements

Identify Necessary Changes

*Time, Methods (Procedures), Money

Exhibit 6   The Management Process

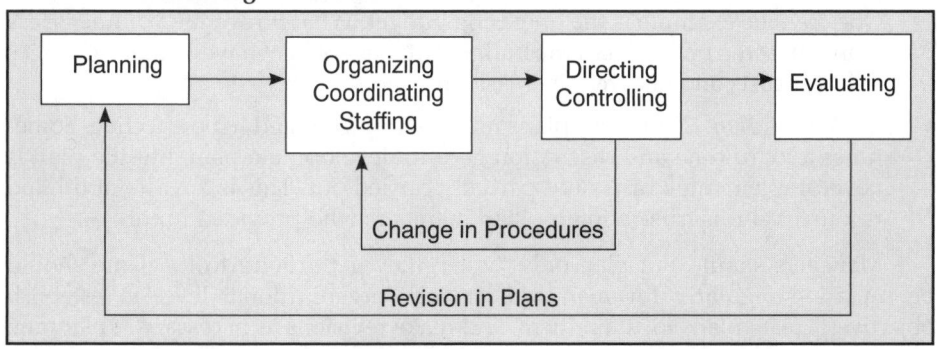

Planning → Organizing Coordinating Staffing → Directing Controlling → Evaluating

Change in Procedures

Revision in Plans

to do; action plans tell how you propose to do it. Planning should be done before other management tasks are undertaken.

Every manager, regardless of position or type of food service organization, must plan. At the highest management levels, long-range planning is undertaken by executives to develop long-term goals, visions, mission statements, and strategies helpful in guiding the food service operation. At intermediate management levels, operational plans are developed by managers to attain short-term goals. At lower management levels, supervisory planning involves the day-to-day process of running the operation.

Let's look at how this might work at a large restaurant company with many units. At top management levels, the board of directors, the board chair, and the chief executive officer may establish long-term goals that may not be attained for two, three, five, or even ten years. An example of such a goal might be to "become the number-one restaurant chain in gross revenues in the Midwest region within ten years." Intermediate levels of management—unit managers and department heads—focus on meeting current budget objectives and short-term economic planning. At lower levels of management, supervisors cost next month's banquet, plan next week's labor schedule, and set goals that can be met within a short time period.

Whether the organization is a multi-unit chain or a single property, planning must start at the top. Only when top management establishes a definite course of action can managers at all organizational levels develop plans that fit into the organization's long-range plans.

Other factors in effective planning include:

- *Information.* You must have access to complete information to plan effectively.

- *Communication.* Managers at all levels should communicate with each other when developing plans. For example, when a food and beverage director develops an operating budget, it is wise to get input from the chef and the beverage manager. Whenever possible, managers should also communicate with employees when making plans that affect them. Employees are more likely to follow plans they have helped develop. Such plans then become "our plans," not "management's plans."

- *Flexibility.* Plans should be flexible. Some food service managers develop plans and then refuse to make changes even though conditions warrant them. One obvious example is the operating budget. What if revenue volume is less than what was projected in the budget? Managers may have to make changes to lower costs and generate increased revenues.

- *Implementation.* Obviously, plans must be implemented to be effective. Sometimes a lot of time and discussion go into developing a plan, but the plan is never implemented or is only partially carried out. This is a waste of limited resources and is frustrating for staff members who provided input.

Managers should not plan only "when they get around to it." Time should be set aside regularly for managers at each organizational level to establish objectives, create plans to attain them, and make revisions as necessary. If planning time is not set aside, the organization may drift into one crisis after another, and managers may become "fire fighters," running from one unexpected situation to another to combat problems that could have been avoided through effective planning.

Organizing. The management activity of **organizing** answers the question, "How can we best assemble and use our limited human resources to attain organizational objectives?" Organizing involves establishing the flow of authority (power) and communication among people.

In any organization, care should be taken to make sure each employee has only one supervisor. If an employee has two bosses, problems can occur if conflicting orders are given.

The number of employees each supervisor should manage must be carefully determined. The right number of employees for each supervisor depends on many factors, including the supervisor's experience, the complexity of the work, the amount of supervision employees require, the frequency with which problems are liable to occur, the amount of help the supervisor can expect from higher-level managers, and other variables. What is important is that supervisors not be given responsibility for more people than they can effectively manage.

The authority to make decisions about using resources should be available at all levels. It is inefficient for a supervisor to have the responsibility to do something, but not have the authority necessary to get it done. Supervisors should not need to seek higher management approval for tasks that must be routinely done as part of the job. Increasingly, employers are **empowering** employees to make decisions as well; for example, a food server might be given the discretion to replace an incorrectly prepared meal rather than be required to check first with a manager.

Because an organization's structure evolves throughout the life of the business, many food service operations have organization charts that do not reflect current operating procedures. For example, an organization chart can indicate that the cook's supervisor is the chef, when in fact the food and beverage director has assumed the responsibility for directing the cook. Organization charts should be updated regularly so that they give a current, accurate picture of how the operation's human resources are organized.

Coordinating. Coordinating is the management task of assigning work and organizing people and resources to achieve the operation's objectives.

Coordinating depends on communication. There must be effective channels of communication to transmit messages up, down, and across the organizational structure. It is also necessary for peers (those at the same organizational level) to communicate with one another. Achieving the organization's goals can happen only if there is open communication among department heads and other department managers.

Delegation is an important aspect of coordinating. Delegation is the passing of authority down the organization. Ultimate responsibility or accountability, however, cannot be delegated. For example, the food and beverage department head is responsible to the hotel's general manager for all aspects of the food and beverage department's operating budget. He or she may delegate the authority to make some decisions about food and beverage costs to the head chef and the beverage manager, but the department head will still be responsible to the general manager for meeting budget goals.

Staffing. Staffing involves recruiting and hiring applicants. The goal of staffing is to bring the best-qualified employees into the food service operation. At large properties, you may be asked to select from applicants screened by the human resources department; at smaller properties, the general manager may give you the total responsibility for finding, screening, and hiring applicants.

Application forms, selection tests, reference checks, and other screening devices should all be parts of the recruitment and selection process. It is important to match the applicant to the job rather than hiring someone and then trying to determine what he or she can do. To do this, jobs must be defined in terms of the tasks to be performed. Job descriptions list required tasks for each position and make it easier to match applicants to jobs.

A second staffing tool, job specifications, lists the personal qualities necessary to perform jobs effectively. We all bring different amounts of knowledge, experience, and common sense to a job. A job specification indicates the personal attributes judged necessary for successful job performance.

Consider all possible sources of job applicants. Large properties may recruit from within the organization. You can also ask currently employed staff members for suggestions, work with employment service agencies, and advertise.

Some managers think that the more applicants who apply, the more work it will take to sort them out, so they try to limit the number of applicants. This is a poor strategy. The chance of finding the right person for the job increases if a large number of people are encouraged to apply.

Part of staffing is making sure new hires get off to a good start. An employee's early experiences on the job strongly affect his or her relationship with the organization. A well-planned employee orientation program is necessary to properly introduce new employees to supervisors, co-workers, and the organization in general.

Directing. Directing is a big part of most managers' jobs. Management is often defined as getting work done through other people. In the labor-intensive food service industry this is certainly true. Employees are absolutely critical to the success of every food service operation. All human beings are complex and at times difficult to understand. However, understanding the wants, needs, and expectations of your employees helps you direct them more effectively.

Directing includes supervising, scheduling, and disciplining employees. Supervising comprises all the ways you relate to your employees when work is being done. When supervising employees, you should know how to motivate, gain cooperation, give orders, and bring out the best in people. Ways to mesh organizational goals with the goals of employees become important. Employees can be motivated when their personal needs are addressed on the job. Whenever possible, employees should have input to decisions that affect them.

Scheduling employees effectively is very important. You must know exactly how much labor is needed and then be able to work within these restraints as you treat all employees fairly.

Disciplining employees is a task many managers dread. However, it can be a positive experience if you keep in mind that discipline is not a form of punishment. Rather, discipline is a way to address and correct improper behavior and help employees become productive members of the organization. Discipline can consist of informal coaching and counseling sessions, as well as more serious meetings involving the manager, employee, and perhaps a higher-level manager or (in large organizations) someone from the human resources department. Written warnings and suspensions may be used in some situations. Following a formal, written disciplinary action program is the best way to protect yourself and your organization against charges of favoritism, discrimination, and unfair practices.

Directing people is complex and sometimes difficult. In many directing situations, it is useful to think about how you would like to be treated. Chances are, your employees share many of the same concerns you have.

Controlling. There is no assurance that goals will be attained just because effective plans have been developed, resources organized, staff selected, and directions carried out. For this reason, you must attend to the **controlling** function of management, which includes developing and implementing control systems.

Many food and beverage products pass through a food service operation. Control procedures for purchasing, receiving, storing, issuing, preparing, and serving products are necessary.

But control includes much more than just the physical tasks of locking storeroom doors, checking standard recipes, or weighing incoming products on a scale. The process of control actually begins with establishing a budget. A budget indicates expected revenue and cost levels. You may look at your recent financial statements—especially income statements—and use information developed in-house electronically from sales systems and other sources as a base to project anticipated revenue and expense levels. Once the budget is established, you must measure the extent to which budget goals are met. If the variance between expected results and actual results is excessive, corrective action must be taken and the results evaluated to assess whether the corrective action was effective.

You should develop control systems that will alert you to problems on a timely basis. Obviously, it is not ideal to learn many weeks after it started that a control problem exists. Food service managers may develop daily or weekly control procedures to supplement monthly budget information provided by their accountants or bookkeepers.

Be aware that controls must be worth more than their cost. For example, to use a system that costs $50 weekly to save $35 weekly is not a good idea. On the other hand, spending $500 for a piece of equipment that will save $50 a week is reasonable because the payback period is only 10 weeks.

Evaluating. Evaluating is the management task of (1) reviewing the operation's progress toward achieving overall organizational goals, (2) measuring employee performance, and (3) assessing the effectiveness of training programs. The constant question for managers must be, "How well are we doing?"

Managers must continually evaluate whether organizational goals are being attained, because complacency can spell trouble for the future of the operation. If you are on target, you can move on to accomplish new goals. If goals are not being met, the evaluation process served its purpose: it identified a problem. Awareness of a problem is the first step toward solving it.

Managers must also evaluate themselves and their own performance. Some managers believe they always do a good job, so—in the eyes of these managers—self-evaluation is unnecessary. Others believe they are doing the best possible job and cannot do any better—again, evaluation is deemed unnecessary. Both of these approaches are unproductive. Taking an honest look at their own performance from time to time can help managers improve their professional and interpersonal skills.

Evaluating is too important to be done only "whenever there is time." Managers should regularly make time for this step in the management process.

Integrating the Process

In the previous section, we discussed each activity in the management process separately. In the real world, management activities are not so neatly categorized. Managers at all organizational levels perform many management activities each day, sometimes at the same time. For example, during a typical day, a food service manager might:

- Help develop next year's operating budget (planning, controlling).
- Deal with problems caused by improper delegation (coordinating).
- Work with a colleague in another department to plan an upcoming special event (planning, coordinating).
- Revise job descriptions and job specifications (organizing, staffing).
- Carry out routine supervisory activities (directing).
- Revise standard food and labor costs (controlling).
- Conduct employee performance reviews (evaluating).

As managers gain and learn from experience, they get better at performing all the various management activities and tasks that arise every day.

A Common Problem: The Labor Shortage

One of the most serious problems confronting all segments of the U.S. food and beverage industry is the growing labor shortage. The need for qualified and trained professionals in food and beverage operations is great. Large, rapidly expanding companies cannot find, either within or outside their organizations, enough competent staff. Basic strategies managers can adopt to address this problem are to:

- Increase productivity.
- Reduce turnover.
- Offer competitive salaries and benefits.
- Revise recruiting and hiring procedures to accommodate non-traditional workers.

Managers can also use training, cross-training, self-improvement, and other personal and professional development programs to build leadership talent and improve employees' work skills.[3] The American Hotel & Lodging Educational Institute, for example, offers courses, seminars, and certification programs, and sponsors professional development chapters for current and prospective hospitality managers and employees.

Another effective strategy for managing the labor shortage involves developing standardized procedures for routine, and even occasionally encountered, situations. This approach tries to resolve all problems in the operation by applying proven procedures and standard policies, rather than by calling on the creative problem-solving methods of ongoing managerial control and monitoring. The hope is that, after training in these procedures, more people will be qualified to work within a highly structured food and beverage operation and that most operational problems will be solved in advance by applying standard operating procedures. For example, in today's multi-unit fast-food and family restaurants, on-site managers have reduced opportunities to make decisions about menus, pricing, layout and design, purchase specifications, development of employee training programs, or wage and salary schedules. In each instance, standardized operating procedures and the decisions of district, regional, or other off-site management personnel take the place of on-site management discretion.

This standardization strategy is of less use in most hotel food and beverage operations. Although almost all hotel chains have standard operating procedure manuals, they usually provide only the most basic structure and allow a great deal of flexibility for on-site management decisions. These manuals frequently indicate that several different procedures can be used to solve various problems. Finally, standard operating procedures in most hotel food and beverage operations are often designed more to provide consistency from the guest's perspective and to allow cost comparisons among properties than to ease the tasks of managers and reduce the need for on-site problem-solving.

The labor shortage problem emphasizes that competent managers are a critical factor in determining the ultimate success or failure of all food and beverage operations. Food and beverage managers must know a great deal about many functions to offer the guidance needed at every stage of the operation. A strong educational background provides a base for analyzing and thinking about the dynamics of a large food and beverage operation, and experience must provide an understanding of exactly how the information is applied to effectively solve real and practical problems. Furthermore, management staff must have and maintain a strong positive attitude to succeed. The phrase "the business gets into your blood" reflects the sustaining interest and enthusiasm necessary to work as a food and beverage manager. The high-energy manager will accept the challenges of management problems and have the ability to direct this energy toward effective solutions.

Food and beverage managers must thoroughly understand the basic principles integral to each component of the management system for food and beverage operations illustrated in Exhibits 5 and 6. This information provides a foundation on which control aspects of the operation can be developed.

Managing a Multi-Unit Restaurant

Many restaurant managers will work in a multi-unit organization at some time (or, perhaps, all the time) during their careers. As the name implies, these organizations operate more than one restaurant and sometimes (in the case of some quick-service restaurant chains) operate in a structure of thousands of units. (The largest multi-unit hospitality organization is one that few people will recognize by its legal name—Doctor's Associates, Inc. The company conducts business as Subway and has more than 28,600 franchise units in 86 countries.)

Multi-unit organizations are structured in numerous ways. Some of the most common include the following:

- All restaurants are company-owned. An example familiar to many is Darden Restaurants, Inc., which owns/operates two large national brands (Red Lobster and Olive Garden), along with several regional brands.

- The majority of units within the organization are franchised. Quick-service restaurants such as McDonald's and Burger King are examples.

- Some units within the organization are company-owned, and others are owned/operated by someone else (franchisees, for example). Well-known brands include the Chili's and Damon's international restaurant organizations.

Why are multi-unit organizations popular in the restaurant industry? First, they provide brand recognition. Guests (or potential guests) are familiar with well-known brands and know what to expect when they see one. (An important responsibility of a franchisor is to ensure that the company's quality standards are consistently followed so public expectations are met.)

Other advantages that accrue to multi-unit hospitality organizations include:

- Opportunities to market/advertise throughout large regions (and even nationwide).

- Benefits arising from centralization, including purchase discounts, use of operating procedures, standardized building designs, and the ability to make the unit managers' jobs easier by centralizing menu planning, purchase specification development, and various other tasks.

- The ability to obtain business loans for property/equipment acquisition, building construction, and operating purposes. Most lenders are more willing to work with large, well-known multi-unit organizations than with independent restaurateurs.

- Potentially easier employee recruitment. Prospective staff members recognize "brand name" employers and may give a priority to employment with these organizations.

- The availability of specialized technical assistance. Multi-unit organizations employ experts in real estate, risk management, law, construction, and other disciplines, along with specialists in operating disciplines such as culinary, marketing, and operating control who can assist unit managers with almost every type of problem.

Multi-Unit Restaurant Organization Structure

A unit within a multi-unit organization is likely to be staffed with workers whose positions are similar to those of their counterparts that are not affiliated with a chain. Organizational differences occur outside of the individual unit. Exhibit 7 illustrates the organization of a typical multi-unit restaurant enterprise and suggests the number of managers who might be supervised by each person in each successively more responsible position.

Exhibit 7   Multi-Unit Restaurant Organization

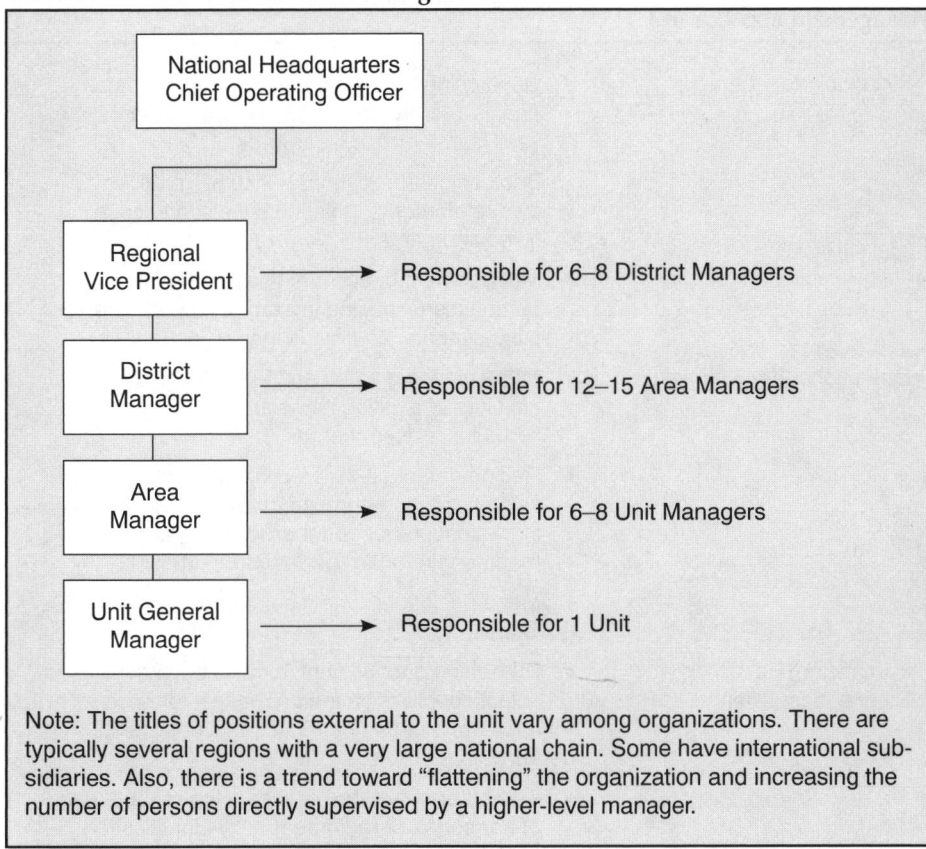

National Headquarters
Chief Operating Officer

Regional
Vice President → Responsible for 6–8 District Managers

District
Manager → Responsible for 12–15 Area Managers

Area
Manager → Responsible for 6–8 Unit Managers

Unit General
Manager → Responsible for 1 Unit

Note: The titles of positions external to the unit vary among organizations. There are typically several regions with a very large national chain. Some have international subsidiaries. Also, there is a trend toward "flattening" the organization and increasing the number of persons directly supervised by a higher-level manager.

The author thanks Dr. Jeffery Elsworth, Associate Professor, The School of Hospitality Business, Michigan State University, for his assistance in preparing this exhibit.

The Increasing Role of Technology

Not too many years ago, mechanical cash registers were the norm in all types of food and beverage operations. They did a good job of making change for customer purchases, but they did very little to collect sales information other than to track the number of items sold and the amount of revenue rung up on the machine. When electronic register (**point-of-sale, or POS**) systems were introduced in the 1980s, it took little time for large operations to adapt them to their operations, and only a short time for even relatively small operators to begin using them. The reason: the capability of these systems to track and record meaningful financial information that managers could use to better control their food and beverage operations.

Modern POS technology provides managers with access to information about almost any area of management concern, from product costs to human resources information to data helpful for product purchasing. Exhibit 8 reviews examples of management and control-related technology applications.[4]

Exhibit 8   Examples of Common Technology Applications for Food/Beverage Management and Control

Financial Management	• Developing and re-forecasting budget; data analysis (current month, year-to-date, last year [same month, year-to-date]).
	• Back office applications—income (profit and loss) statements, balance sheets, and cash flow statements.
	• Management of accounts payable for purchases (including invoice review, electronic bill payments, and credit memo control).
Operational Pre-Planning	• Menu planning data used to track sales histories of existing items and for selecting items for revised menus.
	• Recipe database for precosting to establish selling prices, determine quantities of ingredients required for production, and for menu engineering (evaluation) purposes.
	• Menu design, including composition and layout.
Purchasing, Receiving, Storing, and Issuing	• Determine quantities of items to purchase, select suppliers based on request for price quotations or use of prime supplier system, and place orders.
	• Computer-generated delivery invoices and use of bar codes or radio frequency identification (RFID) to manage items on-site.
	• Optical scanning of physical inventories and electronic updates of quantities available tied to par levels for product re-ordering.
	• Electronic issue requisitions of products from storage to production (kitchen/bar) areas.
Production	• Use of sales history information for production planning (number of items to prepare).
	• Generation of recipes for specific quantities needed for daily batch production needs.
	• Automated beverage dispensing equipment with product usage and revenue reports.
	• Kitchen printers to place guest orders that have been processed through POS systems.

Exhibit 8 *(continued)*

Service	• Guest order information, which drives production, guest service, and guest payment processes. Reservation and table status systems.
	• Wireless (hand-held) guest order systems.
	• "Open-check" systems for management control of revenue before guest payment.
Other Management Control Activities	• Calculation of food costs based on sales tallies of precosted menu items.
	• Per-check and total revenue for service employees, outlets, and the entire operation (per hour, shift, cumulative, or other time periods).
Labor Control	• Development of employee schedules using sales history data to estimate future sales that drive labor hours to be scheduled.
	• Determination of expected labor hours based on actual sales levels.
	• Use of point-of-sale systems for tracking employee hours worked.

Information is required for effective resource control. Effective resource control is the management goal that helps managers determine what information should be collected, either manually or electronically through the use of technology, to help them meet that goal. This information, along with any additional suggestions about data applications made by others within the organization (or by representatives of technology manufacturers), should be carefully evaluated. However, the emphasis should be on the "need to know," rather than "nice to know" to reduce the otherwise voluminous amount of financial data that may confuse rather than focus decision-making. Should an à la carte restaurant system calculate menu item sales and revenues on a continuous basis? Yes; this information can be very useful. Should the system at the receptionist's stand have access to details typically found in human resources files? Probably not, unless there is a unique reason for it that passes the "need-to-know" test.

It is important to reinforce the point that managers must develop control procedures that can be implemented either manually or electronically. While the mechanics of how the control process will work varies depending upon the extent that technology is used, the same basic principles of control must be incorporated. Exhibit 9 illustrates this point using one inventory management tactic (determining the quantity of items in storage areas) as an example. When reviewing Exhibit 9, note that the reason to assess inventory levels, the time of inventory assessment, the location of inventory, and the person responsible for the task is identical regardless of whether a manual or computerized inventory system is used. Only the physical procedures

Exhibit 9   Determining Product Quantities in Inventory

Factor	Manual System	Computerized System
Reason to Assess Inventory Levels	To determine food cost and verify perpetual inventory count.	To determine food cost and verify physical inventory count.
Time of Inventory Assessment	List day of month.	List day of month.
Location of Inventory	Central food and beverage storeroom.	Central food and beverage storeroom.
Person Responsible	Food and beverage controller.	Food and beverage controller.

Procedures	• Physically count unopened cases of each product and manually:
	  ○ Record information on pre-printed inventory form.
	  ○ Multiply number of cases by purchase price of cases.
	  ○ Tally information.
	  ○ Verify physical count with perpetual inventory information.
	  ○ Calculate inventory value and use in food cost calculations.
		• Optically scan bar codes on unopened cases of each product. The computerized system will electronically:
		  ○ Count cases.
		  ○ Determine purchase costs.
		  ○ Match perpetual inventory records with optical scanning data and note discrepancies.
		  ○ Calculate inventory value and include it in food cost calculations.

required for taking inventory and the amount of easily accessible and useful information differ between the alternate systems. Computerized systems allow the task to be done more quickly and perhaps more accurately, which will allow more time for the food and beverage controller to address other responsibilities.

Because technology enables managers to more quickly obtain necessary information, it often allows managers to perform important functions that would not otherwise be done because of the limited time available.

Present applications of technologies to help the food and beverage operator are significant. Future systems will likely be even more impressive. The best advice is to recognize that technology can be used to generate information and to perform repetitive tasks, but it can only support (not replace) the need for high-quality management decision-making.

Businesses of all types, including restaurants, will increasingly use **e-commerce** processes for procurement. Food and beverage managers will, therefore, need the ability and the willingness to manage within these new ways of doing business.

How can managers spend more time using current, accurate, and necessary information and devote less time to gathering it? One answer, of course, is the use of technology applications. These evolving processes will increasingly influence the way things are done in food and beverage operations.

Endnotes

1. Those interested in information about the travel, tourism, and hospitality industries should refer to Rocco Angelo and Andrew Vladimir, *Hospitality Today: An Introduction*, 6th ed. (Lansing, Mich.: American Hotel & Lodging Educational Institute, 2007).

2. *Trends in the Hotel Industry—USA Edition 2006* (PKF Hospitality Research).

3. Those interested in strategies managers can adopt to address the labor shortage problem should read Robert H. Woods's *Managing Hospitality Human Resources*, 4th ed. (Lansing, Mich.: American Hotel & Lodging Educational Institute, 2006).

4. For additional information about hospitality technology, refer to Michael Kasavana and John Cahill, *Managing Technology in the Hospitality Industry*, 5th ed. (Lansing, Mich.: Educational Institute of the American Hotel & Lodging Association, 2007).

Key Terms

accounts receivable system—A system to handle revenue that is due but not yet collected.

banquet—A group function in which guests are served a pre-determined menu.

commercial food service operations—Food service operations found in lodging properties, clubs, restaurants, and other businesses; these operations exist to make a profit from the sale of food and beverage products.

contract management company (food services)—A for-profit company that operates food services for a noncommercial (institutional) organization such as a school or hospital.

controlling—The management task of comparing actual results with expected results, as in measuring actual revenues against expected or budgeted revenues. Controlling also refers to safeguarding the operation's property and income.

coordinating—The management task of assigning work and organizing people and resources to achieve the operation's objectives.

directing—The management task of supervising, scheduling, and disciplining employees. Supervising includes such things as training and motivating employees.

e-commerce—All aspects of business and market processes enabled by the Internet and web-based technologies.

empowerment—The redistribution of power within an organization that enables managers, supervisors, and employees to perform their jobs more efficiently and effectively. The overall goal is to enhance service to guests and increase profits for the organization by releasing decision-making responsibility, authority, and accountability to every level within the organization.

evaluating—The management task of (1) reviewing the operation's progress toward overall organizational goals, (2) measuring employee performance, and (3) assessing the effectiveness of training programs.

finishing kitchen—A work area used to complete the preparation of food produced in a central kitchen and/or to re-heat food produced elsewhere.

full-service hotel—A hotel offering food and beverage services.

hospitality industry—The industry composed of lodging operations (e.g., hotels, resorts, condo-hotels, etc.) and food and beverage operations (e.g., restaurants, hotels, bars/taverns, etc.) for people when they are away from their homes.

hospitality suite—A private guestroom used for a meeting and/or food and beverage services for a small group of people.

management components—Activities for managing available resources; activities include planning, organizing, coordinating, staffing, directing, controlling, and evaluating.

noncommercial food service operations—Organizations such as schools, nursing homes, hospitals, and military services that are nonprofit and exist primarily for reasons other than to provide food or lodging services to guests. Also called institutional food service operations.

operating control cycle—A system that divides food and beverage operations into a series of activities involved in providing food and beverage products to guests.

organizing—The management activity that attempts to best assemble and use limited human resources to attain organizational objectives. It involves establishing the flow of authority and communication among people.

PBX—Short for "private branch exchange"; the hotel's telephone system.

planning—The management task of creating goals, objectives, and programs of action to reach those goals and objectives. It should be done before undertaking other management tasks.

point-of-sale (POS)—An electronic register that instantly captures information about sales transactions and manages the ordering and service of menu items in one or more restaurants/bars.

revenue center—A revenue-producing department within a hospitality operation.

self-operated food services—A food service operation in a noncommercial (institutional) organization, such as a school or hospital, that operates its own food services.

staffing—The management activity of recruiting and hiring applicants.

support center—A department within a hospitality operation that is not directly involved in generating revenue but that incurs costs as it provides support services to revenue-generating departments.

travel and tourism industry—All of the businesses that provide products and/or services to the traveling public. It is comprised of five segments: lodging operations, food and beverage operations, transportation services, retail stores, and destination activities.

 ## Review Questions

1. Why is it important for hotel food and beverage operations to market services to residents in the community as well as to hotel guests?

2. What aspects must be considered when designing a food and beverage management system?

3. What is the difference between a revenue center and a support center?

4. Why must food and beverage managers know the specific revenues and expenses related to each food and beverage outlet in the department?

5. What is the first step in planning food and beverage operations?

6. What are some examples of standard operating procedures that may be important in the management of resources available to the food and beverage manager?

7. What are some factors that complicate revenue collection systems in commercial and noncommercial food service operations?

8. What are some of the basic skills and traits a food and beverage director must have to be successful?

9. Why is an effective recordkeeping and accounting system necessary in a food and beverage operation?

10. What strategies can managers adopt to address the industry's labor shortage problem?

11. What are the potential advantages and disadvantages of serving as a unit manager in a chain (multi-unit) organization? In an independent (single-unit) restaurant?

12. What are some typical examples of ways that technology makes the work of food service managers easier, more effective, and more efficient? What factors should be considered as a manager decides whether to use a manual or computerized process to collect information for decision-making?

 ## Internet Sites

For more information, visit the following Internet sites. Remember that Internet addresses can change without notice. If the site is no longer there, you can use a search engine to look for additional sites.

Industry Associations

American Bartending Association
www.americanbartendingassociation.com

American Culinary Federation (ACF)
www.acfchefs.org

American Hotel & Lodging
Association (AH&LA)
www.ahla.com

American Hotel & Lodging
Educational Institute
www.ahlei.org

Club Managers Association of America
www.cmaa.org

The Educational Foundation of NRA
www.nraef.org

Hospitality Financial and Technology
Professionals
www.hftp.org

Institute of Hospitality
www.instituteofhospitality.org

International Association of Culinary
Professionals
www.iacp.com

International Hotel & Restaurant
Association
www.ih-ra.com

National Association of College &
University Food Services
www.nacufs.org

National Restaurant Association
www.restaurant.org

National Society for Healthcare
Foodservice Management
www.hfm.org

School Nutrition Association (SNA)
www.schoolnutrition.org

Travel Industry Association
www.tia.org

Hotels

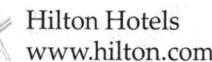

Four Seasons Hotels and Resorts
www.fourseasons.com

Hilton Hotels
www.hilton.com

Hyatt Hotels
www.hyatt.com

InterContinental Hotels Group
www.ichotelsgroup.com

Marriott International
www.marriott.com

Radisson Hotels & Resorts
www.radisson.com

Regent International Hotels
www.regenthotels.com

Starwood Hotels & Resorts
www.starwoodhotels.com

The Peninsula Hotel
www.peninsula.com

Restaurants

Burger King Restaurants
www.burgerking.com

Chili's
www.chilis.com

Commander's Palace
www.commanderspalace.com

Darden Restaurants, Inc.
www.darden.com

Damon's International
www.damons.com

Hard Rock Cafe
www.hardrock.com

Hilltop Steak House
www.hilltopsteakhouse.com

Hillstone Restaurant Group
www.hillstone.com

McDonald's
www.mcdonalds.com

Outback Steakhouse
www.outback.com

Rainforest Cafe
www.rainforestcafe.com

Steak n Shake
www.steaknshake.com

Tavern on the Green
www.tavernonthegreen.com

Taco Bell
www.tacobell.com

T.G.I. Friday's
www.tgifridays.com

Food Service Management Companies

ARAMARK Corporation
www.aramark.com

Bon Appétit Management Company
www.bamco.com

Canteen
www.canteen.com

Compass Group North America
www.cgnad.com

Sodexo, Inc.
www.sodexo.usa.com

Publications—Online and Printed

AAHOA Lodging Business
www.aahoa.com

Chef Educator Today
www.chefedtoday.com

Club Management Magazine
www.club-mgmt.com

Cornell Hospitality Quarterly
www.hotelschool.cornell.edu/research/
chr/pubs/quarterly

Electronic Gourmet Guide
www.globalgourmet.com

Food and Hospitality Magazine
www.foodserviceworld.com

Food Channel
www.foodchannel.com

Food Management Magazine
http://food-management.com

Hospitality Net
www.hospitalitynet.org

HOTELS
www.hotelsmag.com

Hotel F&B Magazine
www.hotelfandb.com

Hotel Online
www.hotel-online.com

International Journal of Hospitality Management
www.elsevier.com/locate/ijhosman

Lodging Hospitality Online
www.lhonline.com

Lodging Magazine
www.lodgingmagazine.com

Nation's Restaurant News
www.nrn.com

ONTHERAIL
www.ontherail.com

Restaurants & Institutions
www.rimag.com

Restaurant Business
www.restaurantbiz.com

Restaurant Hospitality
www.restaurant-hospitality.com

Chapter 2 Outline

Management Resources and Objectives
The Manager in the Management Process
The Control Process
    Establish Standards
    Measure Actual Operating Results
    Compare Actual Results with
        Standards
    Take Corrective Action
    Evaluate Corrective Action
    Food Service Operations Control
Considerations in Designing Control
    Systems
Responsibilities for Control
Control in Multi-Unit Operations

Competencies

1. Identify the resources managers use to attain organizational objectives, and describe what managers do, including the process and tools they use to plan for and reach organizational goals. (pp. 35–37)

2. Describe the basic steps in the control process. (pp. 38–45)

3. Identify issues that managers consider when designing control systems. (pp. 45–50)

4. Discuss people and departments that assist the food and beverage department manager with his or her control responsibilities. (pp. 50–51)

5. Outline control issues in multi-unit operations. (pp. 51–52)

2

The Control Function

CONTROL IS ONE OF THE MOST IMPORTANT FUNCTIONS of the complex system of activities referred to as "management." There are many definitions of management, reflecting the variety of concepts included within the term. For our purposes, a workable and practical definition is: Management is using what you've got to do what you want to do. A manager uses available resources to attain the organization's objectives.

Management Resources and Objectives

Resources are the assets of an operation. Food and beverage managers are responsible for eight basic types of resources:

1. People
2. Money
3. Products (food, beverages, and supplies)
4. Time
5. Procedures
6. Energy
7. Facilities
8. Equipment

All resources are in limited supply. No manager has all the people, money, products, and other resources that he or she would like to work with. Therefore, part of the manager's job is to decide how best to use the limited resources available to attain the organization's objectives. Traditionally, food and beverage operations have attempted to effectively manage resources in efforts to control (minimize) their cost of doing business. While this is of continuing importance today, managers of many **green restaurants** are increasingly concerned about the negative consequences of excessive use of natural resources. In doing so, they assume a corporate (social) responsibility to effectively manage these resources for the benefit of society in general.

Objectives are what the management of the operation wishes to accomplish. They indicate why the organization exists and what it is trying to do. The objectives of a food and beverage operation often center on such things as:

- **Profit** and **cost** levels.

Learn More on the Web

The Green Restaurant Association (www.dinegreen.com) is a non-profit organization that works to create an ecologically sustainable restaurant industry. Its website
lists environmental guidelines useful for concerned restaurant managers, provides
a quiz to help one assess the environmental responsibilities of his or her restaurant,
and offers a *Certified Green Restaurant Guide,* which lists properties that meet the
association's standards.

The Growing Greener website (www.greenrestaurants.org) presents a *Green-
ing Guide* that discusses how food service managers can effectively manage energy,
water, solid waste, cleaning, carry-out containers and disposables, food purchasing,
and design and construction. It also provides an extensive resource guide for additional information about each of these topics.

- Maintaining or increasing financial strength during changing social and economic conditions.

- Guest (marketing) concerns.

- Management and employee interests.

- Professional obligations.

- Societal concerns such as those shared by green restaurants.

Without objectives to lend direction and focus to all activities, managers can
easily become sidetracked and find themselves involved in tasks that are unim-
portant or unrelated to meeting the organization's goals.

Management's first activity must be to plan organizational objectives. Management must establish broad courses of action designed to move the operation
from where it is to where management wants it to go. Exhibit 1 shows the process
by which an initial abstract vision is organized into specific, interdependent steps
for achieving the property's goals.

The Manager in the Management Process

A manager is a staff member who (1) decides the best way to use organizational
resources to attain objectives, and (2) participates in the management tasks of planning, organizing, coordinating, staffing, supervising, **controlling**, and evaluating.

Since most managers supervise employees, they are also responsible for the
performance of those employees. To a large extent, managers are only as successful
as their employees. Said another way, managers—not employees—are responsible
for many of the problems encountered in food and beverage operations. Being
held accountable for their own work as well as the work of others is common to
those in management positions.

An effective manager not only knows basic management principles, but is
also able to put them into practice. While knowledge alone cannot replace experience and common sense, it is a vital ingredient in creative decision-making. The
remainder of this chapter focuses on basic concepts of control.

Exhibit 1   The Sequence of Planning

Planning is a process that involves the development of six management tools. Some managers incorrectly believe that these tools can be developed independently of each other. However, effective planning requires that they be developed more sequentially:

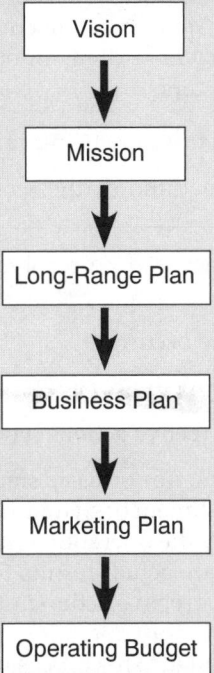

A **vision** is a broad and abstract view of what the organization should be like. (For example, a property's vision may be "to become the very best hotel in the community for the convention and business traveler.") The vision shapes the **mission,** which is a more specific statement about what the property will do and how it will do it. (For example, concepts in a mission might include "being the first choice of convention travelers by offering the finest food and beverage services.")

The **long-range plan** indicates what managers desire to accomplish in a specified time period (often five years) in relation to the mission. (Continuing our example, the property's goal may be to have 75 percent of the city's convention business within five years.) The **business plan** indicates specifically what will be done within the next year and may include revenue goals. (The property in this example may want to achieve 40 percent of the city's convention business within the next year.) After the business plan is developed, managers develop a **marketing plan,** which indicates specific procedures that will be used to accomplish guest-related aspects of the business plan. A wide range of strategies and action plans with associated schedules is included in a marketing plan.

Finally, an **operating budget** is established. An operating budget details revenue, costs associated with the products and services that are produced, and the property's financial goals.

The Control Process

A simple definition of control emphasizes its relationship with planning. **Control** is a series of coordinated activities that helps managers assess the extent to which *actual* results of operations match the *planned* results.

An effective control system is important because managers must know how the operation is doing; in other words, to be effective, a control system must be able to determine whether, and to what extent, an operation is meeting its goals. Control procedures can help managers:

- Determine whether delegated tasks are being carried out correctly.

- Assess the effect of changes required by the economy, market, and reactions to competition.

- Identify problems early so they can be resolved before they create bigger problems.

- Determine where problems are occurring.

- Identify mistakes and plan **corrective action** tactics to correct the mistakes.

- Assess the extent to which corrective actions have resolved the mistakes.

The control process follows a series of basic steps as illustrated in Exhibit 2. The process begins with the establishment of standards. Next, accurate information about the actual results achieved by the operation must be gathered. The food and beverage manager can then compare actual results to standards. If actual results do not conform to the standards, corrective action must be taken. The action taken will probably be a change in one or more operating procedures. Finally, results of the corrective action must be evaluated. This process may lead to a revision of the standards. By repeating the cycle, the effects of implementing corrective action can be evaluated. Though all resources must be controlled, remember that throughout the process, the primary resources—food, beverage, labor (taken together, these three are called **prime costs**), and revenue—have highest priority.

Let's look more closely at each of the steps in the control process.

Establish Standards

The first step in the control process is the establishment of **standards**. There are several types of standards:

- *Quality standards.* **Quality** is the consistent delivery of products and services according to expected **benchmarks** that help define when and how quality is attained. For example, the quality of dining service might be judged by the extent to which basic standard operating procedures are followed. A review of comment cards from guests and **mystery shoppers** might be used to assess whether and to what extent quality service is consistently attained.

- *Quantity standards.* The volume of output can reflect a benchmark of expected productivity. For example, the number of guests served per labor hour or number of minutes per guest meal are examples of quantity standards.

Exhibit 2   Basic Steps in the Control Process

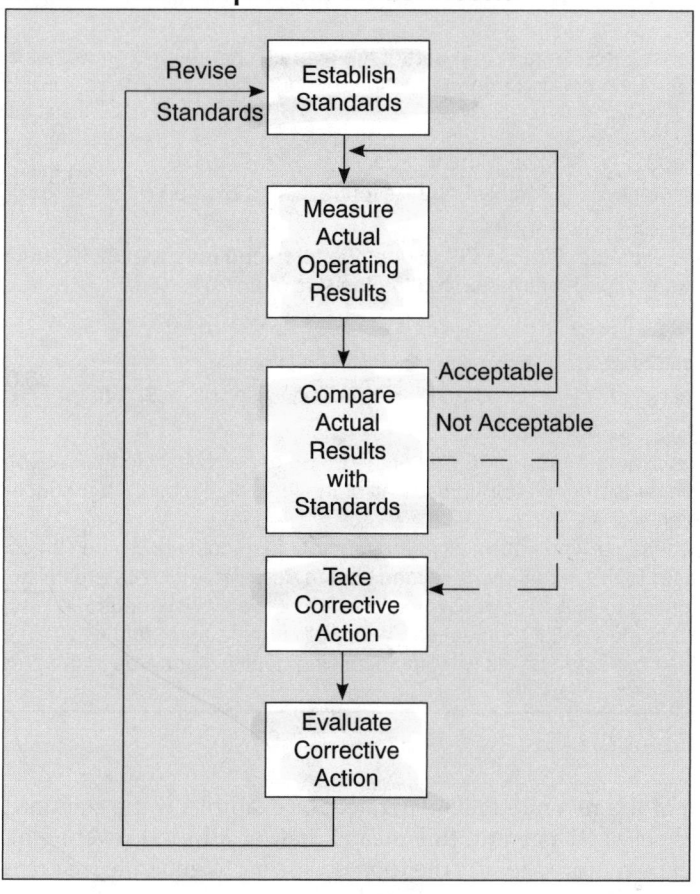

- *Control standards.* In the context of control, standards are the planned or expected results of the operation and are expressed as a level of performance. For example, a restaurant may establish control standards that permit a variance of no more than 1.0 percent between planned and actual food costs.

It is important to recognize that standards are not limited to expected levels of performance for individual employees. Depending on the resource to be controlled, standards might involve anything from revenue goals to menu item sales and production targets to employee attendance and safety records. Consequently, the unit of measurement in which the standard is expressed changes from one situation to another. Most operations establish standards for each of the key services or products that they provide.

In general, establishing financial standards involves determining the expected amounts of revenue and the allowable costs of the resources that should be used to generate that revenue. Standards often express the costs of resources in terms of a

Exhibit 3   Calculating Food Cost Percentages

The food cost percentage is that part of the overall food item revenue that is used to purchase the food needed to generate the revenue.

Example 1:

$$\frac{\text{Monthly Food}}{\text{Cost Percentage}} = \frac{\text{Monthly Food cost}}{\text{Monthly Food Revenue}} = \frac{\$79,450}{\$271,400} = \underline{29.3\%} \text{ (rounded)}$$

In this example, 29.3% ($79,450) of the total food revenue ($271,400) was used to purchase the food that generated the food revenue.

Example 2:

$$\frac{\text{Menu Item Food}}{\text{Cost Percentage}} = \frac{\text{Food Cost for Chicken Dinner}}{\text{Chicken Dinner Selling Price}} = \frac{\$3.15}{\$8.55} = \underline{36.8\%}$$

In this example, $3.15 (36.8%) of the $8.55 generated from the sale of one chicken dinner is needed to purchase all of the ingredients used to produce one chicken dinner.

The manager who knows what the monthly food cost should be can compare this standard to the actual monthly food cost to determine if costs are in line with expectations. If they are, corrective actions are probably not needed. If they are not, knowledge of a potential problem can prompt the manager to find ways to reduce costs to their expected levels without sacrificing quality standards in the process.

percentage of the revenue they generate. For example, if the standard (expected) food cost is set at 31 percent, this means that, of all food revenue generated, 31 percent will be required to buy the food necessary to generate that revenue. (Food cost percentage is determined by dividing total food cost by total food revenue.) Exhibit 3 shows basic calculations to establish food cost percentages.

In noncommercial food service operations, expenses are often stated as a percentage of the total expense. For example, a 35-percent food cost means that, of the total expense incurred by the food service operation, 35 percent is required to purchase food products.

Sources of Control Information. One reason that it is so difficult to establish effective standards is that it is hard to find reliable information to use as the basis for setting the standards. There are several readily available sources of control information:

- *Averages* developed by the industry nationally, statewide, and even locally. For example, the National Restaurant Association may collect and publish statistics about the food, beverage, or labor cost percentages realized by its members.

- A property's own *financial statements*, especially the **income statements**, from past fiscal periods.

<table>
<tr><td>

Learn More on the Web

The National Restaurant Association (www.restaurant.org) publishes an annual *Restaurant Industry Operations Report.* While a fee is charged for this document, you can learn more about the report on the National Restaurant Association website. When you reach the site, click on "Industry Research," then "Research Reports," and then "Restaurant Industry Operations Report."
</td></tr>
</table>

- Property *operating budgets* that specify anticipated levels of revenue and expenses for a current fiscal period.

- *In-house measurements* that consider potential costs matched with anticipated revenue. Managers of multi-unit operations have the advantage of an additional source of control information that is not available to their single-unit counterparts: data from other units in the organization. If several properties within the organization are located in the same general area and use the same menu, ingredients, and supplies, they likely incur the same basic labor costs. Therefore, operating data from these properties can provide benchmarks for comparison with other units in the organization.

The two best sources of information are operating budgets and in-house measurements. Basing standards on information obtained from these sources will provide numbers that are most directly relevant to the specific food and beverage operation. Using industry averages presumes (probably incorrectly) that one food and beverage operation is enough like another that the numbers will mutually apply. In fact, average costs (in dollars and as a percentage of revenue) vary significantly among segments of the food service industry and even dramatically within the same segment and the same geographic area. For example, properties that use a significant amount of **convenience foods** (those that have some or all of the labor built into them that otherwise would need to be provided on site) tend to have higher food costs and lower labor costs. By contrast, properties that make a large amount of food "from scratch" will likely have lower food costs and higher labor costs. A property's past financial statements provide information that is relevant to the particular food and beverage operation, but using them to establish standards assumes the company is satisfied with past performance and content that they were managed effectively. If this is not the case, past financial statements are much less useful as a source for measurement information because they, in effect, use ineffective operating results as a benchmark for future operations.

In-house measurements that assess potential costs based on actual unit sales are an excellent source of control information. Such information today is easily gathered and generated by high-tech point-of-sale (POS) equipment. Consider, for example, the effectiveness of common POS systems that can inform managers about estimated food costs (number of each menu item sold, multiplied by its food cost, and summed for all menu items) and then compare the estimate to actual food costs. These systems create excellent control benchmarks by enabling managers to compare what food costs should be (from calculations based on unit sales) with actual results of operations.

Effective Standards. To be effective, standards must accurately reflect results desired by the manager, based on the expectations of the target markets. Standards must also be high enough to offer a challenge and encourage excellence, but not so high as to be unattainable and result in frustration. Effective standards must also:

- *Be specific and measurable.* For example, "Food revenue will be $225,000, food costs will not exceed $75,000 for the first three months of operation, and the quality of food service will not drop below the following minimum requirements" is a much better statement of standards than "Food costs will be kept as low as possible while ensuring maximum food revenue and without sacrificing quality."

- *Encourage further creativity and challenge.* For example, if a desired labor cost of 31 percent of revenue is attained, a future goal might be to reduce it to 30 percent with no reduction in quality. (Or, in times of rising labor and benefit costs, the 31-percent cost goal might be continued in a future fiscal period.)

- *Include feedback as part of the control system.* Affected employees must know how they are doing. When staff members are in the information loop, they are better equipped and more likely to come up with practical suggestions about how control procedures can be made more effective.

Measure Actual Operating Results

After standards are established, management must develop procedures for collecting and assessing actual operating information. For example, if the standard food cost is set at 31 percent, how close to this goal is the actual food cost?

At this point, some basic principles for assessing information about actual operating performance are helpful:

- *Information about actual operating performance must be simple and easy to collect.* Most managers are very busy, so time-consuming activities are impractical. A system must be cost-effective; the information collected must be worth more than the cost to collect it. Very accurate data requiring a great deal of time to generate is not practical. The perceived practicality of a system correlates directly with the extent to which it is used.

- *Actual information must be collected in a manner consistent with the procedures and formats used to establish performance standards.* For example, to include values of food and beverage transfers or salaried labor in standard costs and to exclude them in the calculation of actual costs does not permit meaningful comparisons. Actual information should be expressed in the same format as standard information. One would not, for example, determine standard costs as a percentage of revenue and actual costs as dollars per day or per meal.

- *Actual information generated for control purposes should be compatible with the formats used in accounting systems.* Since the source documents for control and accounting purposes are often the same, the problems of keeping two sets of figures can be avoided if control information is compatible with the accounting system.

- *Information must be collected consistently for each fiscal period.* This ensures that trending, indexing, and other measures can be used to identify problems. If this is not done, the meaning of comparisons between fiscal periods is difficult to interpret.

- *Checks on the controls should be part of the control system itself.* Normally, those responsible for attaining a standard should not collect actual information. While collusion is still possible and any control system is more vulnerable when collusion is present, one person working alone cannot "beat" a good control system.

Compare Actual Results with Standards

After collecting actual operating information, the next step in the control process is to compare it with the standards that have been established. This comparison measures how well actual performance meets planned or desired results. Then, food and beverage managers can determine the extent to which operational goals are being met (or missed). It is important that comparisons be made:

- Frequently, so that observed problems can be corrected as soon as possible.

- Routinely, not just when problems are suspected.

- During different time frames, so, for example, standard and actual costs can be compared both daily and monthly.

- As soon as possible after actual costs are known.

Comparisons should be analyzed by top management, as well as other managers responsible for attaining cost goals.

Take Corrective Action

The comparison of actual to expected results may reveal a significant variance that requires corrective action. A small variation may be permitted; for example, if standard food costs are set at 31 percent of food revenue, corrective action might not be required unless actual food costs exceed 32 percent of food revenue. On the other hand, a "small" variation may represent significant drains on profits (see Exhibit 4). Food and beverage managers often consider corrective action to be the only or most important part of the control process. However, control is more than just taking corrective action. If the variance between standard and actual costs is excessive, reasons for the higher cost must be discovered before corrective action can be determined. In some cases, the cause of the variance is obvious and can be quickly brought under control. For example, higher-than-expected food costs may mean that changes in inventory management, product purchasing, portion control, and other aspects of the operation are needed.

However, some variances are not easily explained, and these call for special analysis. For example, while a greater-than-expected labor cost may be identified in the comparison step, some basic potential causes of increased labor cost, such as decreasing productivity or fraud in reporting labor hours, are often not readily detected. These situations can be discovered only by a thorough review of operating practices and procedures.

Exhibit 4   Small Variances Can Yield Significant Losses

Assume the following:

- Monthly food costs are budgeted at 32.5%.
- Actual food costs for the month are 33.1%.
- Food revenues were $740,000 for the month.

In this example, a variance of only 0.6% (33.1% – 32.5%) reduced profits by $4,440, calculated as follows:

Food Revenue	=	$ 740,000	Food Revenue	=	$ 740,000
Actual Food Cost (%)		33.1%	Budgeted Food Cost (%)		32.5%
Actual Food Cost		$ 244,940	Budgeted Food Cost		$ 240,500

Actual Food Cost	$ 244,940
Budgeted Food Cost	$ 240,500
Excessive Food Cost	$ 4,440

Once the cause of an unacceptable variance between standard and actual results is determined, corrective action must be taken. That action may lead to a change in operating procedures.

Evaluate Corrective Action

After corrective action has been taken, it is important to evaluate the effects of the changes. Careful evaluation is necessary to determine whether the corrective action has, in fact, resolved the problem(s) that caused an unacceptable variance between expected and actual costs. Furthermore, it is necessary to determine whether any changes in operating procedures as a result of corrective action have themselves caused unforeseen problems in other areas.

Evaluation ensures that corrective procedures are acceptable, reveals whether additional decisions are needed, and indicates whether more problems need to be resolved. Several principles guide the evaluation process:

- *Clearly identify the desired outcome of corrective actions.* Without clear goals, managers will have no way to know if their actions actually corrected the problems. The answer to the question, "How will we know whether the corrective action is successful?" helps define what the situation should be after successful corrective action has been taken.

- *Timing of the evaluation is important.* Begin the evaluation as soon as practical after corrective actions are implemented. Often staff must first become familiar with changes, or new procedures must be revised slightly. This may delay the impact of the corrective actions on the original problem. An evaluation performed too soon may not accurately measure the results of the actions that were taken for problem resolution.

- *The evaluation should be objective and rational.* Has the problem been resolved, and is it more likely that organizational goals will be attained? While these may seem obvious questions to consider, evaluations often focus incorrectly on such concerns as: What is the easiest? Which way has my department always used? Which way makes us look the best? Which way will meet with the least resistance from employees? Which method will my boss like the best? Which process is the cheapest and fastest?

- *If the evaluation identifies other problems or indicates that corrective action has not been successful, reconsider the corrective action.* The cycle of control procedures may need to be repeated. New corrective action(s) may be required, or standards may need to be revised. It is extremely important that management take great care when considering revisions to standards. It is far too easy to rationalize the inability to achieve a standard by saying that the standard is too high. Consequently, revisions of standards should be considered only after a complete examination of operating procedures.

Food Service Operations Control

The control process to address costs that we have described can also be used to identify and correct problems of other types. Consider, for example, the use of a mystery shopper to help a manager identify product- and service-related issues in public areas of a food service operation. With this approach, a "mystery shopper" retained by the manager pretends to be a guest. This person visits the property to experience the extent to which its food and beverages, service, and cleanliness standards are being met. The mystery shopper completes a report, forwards it to the manager, and potential problems become known. Corrective actions can be taken, and a subsequent evaluation visit can be planned to determine whether the problems have been resolved. Exhibit 5 shows factors and evaluation points used by an organization that conducted mystery shopper visits to a full-service restaurant.

Considerations in Designing Control Systems ———————

In this discussion of the control steps used by a food and beverage operation, it is obvious that the manager's role is critical. To help ensure that management's time spent in the control function is productive, several factors should be considered in the design of a control system.

Accuracy. While the control system must provide a reasonably accurate assessment of whether goals are being attained, accuracy must be balanced against the time spent developing control systems. For example, it would be impractical for most operations to determine and monitor the expected cost per meal for meats and poultry, even though today's POS technology could make these calculations. In the not-too-distant future, it will also be possible (and fast and easy) to calculate actual food costs on a by-category (meats/poultry, for example) basis. The unit manager, however, must determine whether this increased level of control will be useful. Remember that all procedures must be cost-effective; they must be worth the time necessary to carry out the control procedure.

Exhibit 5   Mystery Shopper's Report for Full-Service Restaurant

FULL SERVICE RESTAURANT / Region 1 / District 13 - Dining

Location: 125 - Boynton Beach, Boynton Beach, FL -- SCORE = 88

Visit Information	Response	Points Available	Points Awarded
1.Dollar Amount Spent Include Tip (do not use dollar sign):	40.57		
2.Day of Week:	Saturday		
3.Date of Visit ie 2/19/2001:	08/11/2001		
4.Time of Visit:	07:05 PM		
5.Business Volume:	Heavy		
6.Transaction / Receipt #:	129 and F-0014 (Bar)		
7.Servers Name (or description)	Heather		

Telephone 6 of 6 Points - 100%	Response	Points Available	Points Awarded
1.Was the telephone answered promptly and professionally?	YES	2	2
2.Was the telephone answered in a friendly and enthusiastic manner?	YES	2	2
3.Were all of your questions answered accurately?	YES	2	2

Facility 6 of 8 Points - 75%	Response	Points Available	Points Awarded
1.Did the exterior of the restaurant appear clean and well maintained?	YES	2	2
2.Did the interior of the restaurant appear clean and well maintained?	YES	2	2
3.Were the restrooms clean and well stocked?	NO	2	
4.Was the table top, menus, silverware and fixtures clean?	YES	2	2

Host 24 of 26 Points - 92%	Response	Points Available	Points Awarded
1.Were you greeted promptly upon entering?	YES	4	4
2.Were you given a proper welcoming greeting?	YES	3	3
3.Were you offered a seating preference?	YES	2	2
4.If there was a wait, were you quoted a waiting time?	YES	2	2
5.If quoted a waiting time, was it accurate within 5 min?	NO	2	
6.If not how long was the quote off in minutes:	Early by 24 minutes		
7.Did the greeting host seem genuinely friendly and make good eye contact with you?	YES	3	3
8.Were you offered a proper greeting upon leaving the restaurant?	YES	3	3
9.Did the host that seated you ask you to follow?	YES	2	2
10.Were you graciously seated?	YES	2	2
11.Did the seating host appear genuinely friendly and make good eye contact with you?	YES	2	2
12.Were you informed of who your server would be?	YES	1	1

Service 29 of 37 Points - 78%	Response	Points Available	Points Awarded
1.Were you greeted promptly by your server?	YES	3	3
2.Did your server suggest a specific drink or appetizer?	NO	4	
3.Were your beverages served promptly?	YES	2	2
4.Did your server mention the daily special?	NO	2	
5.Did your server have good menu knowledge?	YES	2	2
6.Was your order taken in a timely manner after being seated?	YES	2	2
7.Were there appetizer/bread plates available?	YES	1	1
8.Were the correct food and drink items delivered?	YES	2	2
9.Did your server check back within three minutes?	YES	3	3
10.Did your server offer you additional beverages in a timely manner?	YES	1	1

Exhibit 5   *(continued)*

	Response	Points Available	Points Awarded
11. Did your server anticipate your needs?	YES	3	3
12. Did your server honor your request on a timely basis?	YES	2	2
13. Was your table manicured in a timely manner?	YES	2	2
14. Were you offered dessert or coffee?	NO	2	
15. Was your check accurate and delivered promptly?	YES	1	1
16. Did you recieve genuinely friendly service?	YES	5	5

Food 10 of 10 Points - 100%	Response	Points Available	Points Awarded
1. Was the hot food hot/cold food cold?	YES	3	3
2. Did all food meet your expectations?	YES	3	3
3. Was all food served promptly?	YES	4	4

Runners 3 of 3 Points - 100%	Response	Points Available	Points Awarded
1. Did the food runner appear genuinely friendly?	YES	1	1
2. Did the food runner contribute to the manicure of your table?	YES	1	1
3. Did the runner honor your requests on a timely basis?	YES	1	1

Management 10 of 10 Points - 100%	Response	Points Available	Points Awarded
1. Based on this visit would you return to FULL SERVICE RESTAURANT?	YES	5	5
2. Would you recommend FULL SERVICE RESTAURANT?	YES	5	5

Evaluation Information	Response	Points Available	Points Awarded
1. Greeting Host (name or description):	Tera at the door/Amy at the podium		
2. Seating Host (name or description):	Ryan		
3. Bartenders (names or descriptions) if applicable:	Jeff W.		
4. Server (name or description)	Heather G		
5. Food Runner(s) (name(s) or descriptions)	M-drk brwn hair.reg.or med. lgnth 19-21 (2 others)		
6. Food & Drink items ordered:	Pork BBQ Sandwich, Scallop Platter, 2 Iced Teas		
7. Was the manager visible and interacting with guests?	YES		
8. Did anyone recognize you by name or try to learn your name?	NO		
9. If you asked to take some of your food with you, was it packaged by a staff member in a positive manner?	NO		
10. Was the noise level comfortable?	YES		
11. Was the temperature comfortable?	YES		
12. How would you rate your overall visit?	Positive		

When we arrived at the very festive restaurant we noticed the grand opening appearance. There was an area outside for customers to get beverages. We were greeted by Tera who held the waiting list at the opened door. Though she did not smile, she was pleasant and efficient asking us our seating preference. She then told us that the wait would be 45 minutes. After we entered we were greeted by Amy who gave us our disk and she said that it would light up when they were ready for us. She did not recommend an area to wait so we decided since the wait was so long that we would get a beverage at the bar. Every seat at the bar was filled and customers were standing, waiting for their tables, as well. It took about 5 minutes to get Jeff W's attention because we had to keep moving out of the way from the food coming through from the kitchen. Jeff W. asked what we would like to order. We asked if there were any special beer offers for the night and he named off some light beers that were $1.00. For our beverages we chose a Coor's light and a diet coke. When he brought them, he said that it would be $3.00. I gave him the money and he brought back 26 cents. I gave him $1.00 tip. A minute later, he rang up our order as well as some others that he had in his hand and I got his attention and asked for a receipt since "I am from out of town on business". He rang something up and then gave me my receipt after attaching two receipts together. He just rang up the total amount, not the way the transaction had happened. In other words he rang up $2.74 including tax but not that I had given him $3.00 and he had given me 26 cents change. I did not see anything untoward, any underage people at the bar nor any who appeared to be intoxicated. The cash registers were busy the entire time that we were there with three bartenders preparing beverages and then putting them in the register. Later, another bartender came back from the kitchen area and he worked mainly where the servers were placing their orders. We were called much sooner for our table. It was approximately 20 minutes instead of 44 minutes. Ryan greeted us and took

(continued)

Exhibit 5   *(continued)*

us to our table at an easy pace. He made eye contact and told us that Heather would be our server. In one minute a very friendly, perky Heather arrived with a sunshine smile. She passed a moment of small talk though she did not ask us if we had been to FULL SERVICE RESTAURANT previously. She knew the menu well, though she did not mention any specials. She did, however, mention specials at other tables. She took our order for two iced teas and did not make any special recommendations for the beverages. She returned in three minutes with two very tasty, full bodied glasses of sweetened tea that we had requested and we then talked about the menu. My dining partner was considering the BBq pork sandwich. She pointed out to him that there was also a platter but she thought that the sandwich was so good in that it was piled high with strings. She said it was very good!! I was still having trouble making a decision which she noticed and she told us of two chicken platters, one being the Okeechobee chicken that she especially liked and we talked about the coconut shrimp which she said was out of this world! I decided on the scallop platter since she still had not mentioned any specials. Heather said that was an excellent decision, as well. Since she was ready to leave, I said that the wings looked good but I did not know if we could eat them all and have dinner, as well. She said that they also had an order of 5 but it just wasn't on the menu. We talked about the wonderful sweet island sauce and we chose those. We had also asked if salads were served with the meal and she said, no, they did not but she pointed us to where the salads were only $1.95 with the meal so we decided to get one each. She left us at 7:40 with the order and she brought the salads at 7:44. They were crisp and fresh. I had ordered the gorgonzola salad and the gorgonzola was sprinkled on top of the salad so that it looked like snow on top of a mountain with the salad piled high and beautiful on it's plate. They were wonderful! The five wings arrived at 7:53. We were well into our salads. A runner, male, described above brought them. He made eye contact, smiled and placed them inbetween our salad plates and said enjoy! They, too were a good choice. They were served piping hot and were on top of a delicious light, sweet nectar. Our entrees arrived at 8:05 by two runners. The scallop plate was very hot and it was obvious that the runner who brought the scallops was quite uncomfortable with hot fingers. He had a clean white cloth but it apparently did not help very much. Male: 18 years of age, short black or dark brown hair, 5'6-5'7" tall. The other runner was a female with dark hair pulled back into a pony tail. Both made eye contact, smiled and the female said to enjoy our dinner. My dining partners salad plate had been removed but my salad plate was not removed when they left. Our server moved it a few minutes later. There were 8 beautiful, succulent scallops prepared to perfection on top of safron rice. It was also served with a generous portion of mixed vegetables. While the vegetables were very tasty they were a little overcooked. They were broccoli, carrots, cauliflower, squash (green and yellow). The pork sandwich was huge, topped with strings and was generously accompanied with crisp hot fries and what appeared to be a red cabbage leaf topped with cold,crispy, delicious cole slaw. During the entire night, we were not able to pick our a manager. No one stood out as being "in charge" and we did not see anyone dressed any differently from the servers. If there was a manager, he or she worked just as hard as the servers and all of them were working well on their own. All patrons seemed to be happy and enjoying themselves and their meals. We also did not see anyone leaving with an unhappy face. After our meal, Heather asked if we would like to take our meals home with us since we had not eaten very much of them. She said that she would bring the take-home boxes which she did, leaving them for us to fill. She did not ask us if we would like to have coffee or would like to try a dessert. She quickly brought our bill. Returned for it in a minute and returned within two minutes with our receipt. Heather thanked us sincerely and thanked us very much for coming in and to please come back again. We left at 8:23 The restrooms were both very neat and clean with a fresh aroma. There was, however, no paper towels in the dispenser and there were none anywhere else. The floor in front of the sinks was very wet since there were no towels. The check list on back of the door was as new as the restaurant. Nothing had been filled in. The restaurant was very jovial and festive and all of the employees were in good spirits. We left in a jovial, festive mood as well having enjoyed our dinner and good service. We would very much like to return.

Source: Satisfaction Services, Inc. (www.satisfactionservices.com).

Timeliness. To be useful, control systems must provide evidence of performance as soon as possible after business activities occur. Food and beverage managers may design control procedures to provide information on a daily basis about actual food and beverage costs. Other systems use "to-date" data to tally information as a fiscal period progresses. Most food and beverage operations provide reports, such as a monthly financial statement giving actual operating results, at the conclusion of a fiscal period. Many properties now use computer-based systems to provide complete and accurate daily financial reports.

Objectivity. To be objective, measurements of the level of performance must accurately reflect the desired results that control procedures are designed to monitor. For example, if profit is incorrectly defined as a desired percentage of revenue rather than as a required return on investment, control procedures may indicate satisfactory performance during a time of declining revenue when bottom-line profits are actually lower. Objectivity requires designing the best control system, not necessarily the one that is the easiest to implement. Objectivity is more likely to be achieved when control systems are designed by a team of managers with help from all affected staff. Recall once again the control advantage that accrues to multi-unit managers: they can pool the collective array of tactics used by management peers to yield the best control system.

Consistency. When actual results are measured, management must assess the performance in a manner consistent with what is expected. A number of elements may or may not be included when determining a particular standard. When a control system is designed, the manager should decide whether those elements will be included or excluded in the definition of that standard. For example, a manager working with the accountant (food and beverage controller) may decide to include (or exclude) food in work station storage areas when calculating the value of food inventory. From that point, this value should be consistently included (or excluded) from inventory value calculations.

Priority. The control system must give priority to those factors that are most relevant to attaining the operation's goals. For example, control systems for food costs or revenue should be developed before those for lower-cost supplies.

Cost. A well-designed control system is cost-effective. This can be measured by comparing the cost of implementing the control system with the cost reductions achieved by using it. A system costing $5,000 annually that reduces costs by $2,000 annually probably indicates management did not wisely design its control procedures.

Realism. A realistic control system is first of all a practical system. This involves all the considerations that we have been discussing, such as cost-effectiveness and accuracy. Another realistic consideration has to do with the chain of command. A junior staff member cannot be responsible for controlling operations managed by a senior department head. Also, control systems need a reward/motivation system that acknowledges high levels of performance when identified.

Appropriateness. The control system must fit into the work flow. If the use of control procedures decreases productivity, reduces guest acceptance, or in other ways hinders the operation, then that system is inappropriate and new control procedures must be designed.

Flexibility. A food and beverage operation is always changing, and organizational goals are continually evolving. For instance, new ways of doing things will affect what and how control procedures are used. The control system must be flexible enough to adapt to these changes.

Specificity. The main purpose of a control system is to help identify what corrective action is necessary to bring actual results closer to management expectations. Well-designed control systems provide specific information. For example, there is a big difference between a labor control system that merely indicates "labor costs are too high" and one that says "in the lunch shift, dishwashing labor is 15 percent over budget."

Acceptability. Staff members must understand and accept the controls that are implemented, and they must be trained in using those procedures. Where possible, all affected staff members should participate in designing the control systems to facilitate acceptance and use of the system. All procedures should be fully explained and justified in writing. This not only helps the staff understand and appreciate the rationale behind the procedures, but it also is useful when the control procedures are evaluated. It is important for staff members to view the procedures as beneficial to both themselves and the food and beverage operation.

Responsibilities for Control

The food and beverage manager who has ultimate responsibility for the department or operation should provide significant input to the design of data collection systems and to the interpretation of actual operating results. The manager should make control decisions based on information supplied by other departments, managers, and food and beverage personnel.

In many food and beverage operations (especially large ones), the accounting department is responsible for determining how costs should be assessed. For example, someone must determine whether food and beverage transfers and/or salaried labor are to be included in the calculation of costs. In most operations, the accounting department determines the recordkeeping forms to be used to assemble financial information for income statements, balance sheets, and other financial reports.

In addition, after actual income and cost levels are assessed and reported on income statements, the controller in the accounting department may provide observations about the meaning of the numbers. For example, if actual food costs are higher than those estimated in the operating budget, the controller will point this out and may make suggestions about why cost variances are excessive and even what strategies might be helpful in reducing the problem.

The food and beverage manager should consider the information from the controller to be advice—not a dictate about what must be done. Rather, the food and beverage manager should consider input from other sources, such as his or her own staff and higher management levels, and additional facts when making a decision about whether corrective action is necessary and what that action should be.

An example will illustrate the point. Based on the small amount of revenue generated after 9:00 P.M. in a hotel's restaurant, the controller may suggest that the operation should close at this time because costs to remain open exceed revenue generated. However, the property's general manager may recognize the restaurant's need to stay open to serve guests arriving from late airline flights. In fact, these guests may choose that particular hotel primarily because of its dining service after 9:00 P.M.; revenue from room rentals must be considered when making the decision. The manager with knowledge of the "big picture" (what's best for the entire property) would likely choose to keep the restaurant open, even if the restaurant-related costs for doing so exceed the revenue the restaurant generates.

Large hospitality operations frequently have a **food and beverage controller** employed by the accounting department. The responsibilities of this person may include developing food and beverage cost estimates, assisting in budget development, analyzing income statements, directly supervising receiving and storeroom personnel, and participating in end-of-period inventory valuations. The food and beverage controller may also be responsible for supervising cashiers in restaurants and lounges. This person often becomes the accounting representative with whom

Exhibit 6   Responsibility for Financial Reconciliation

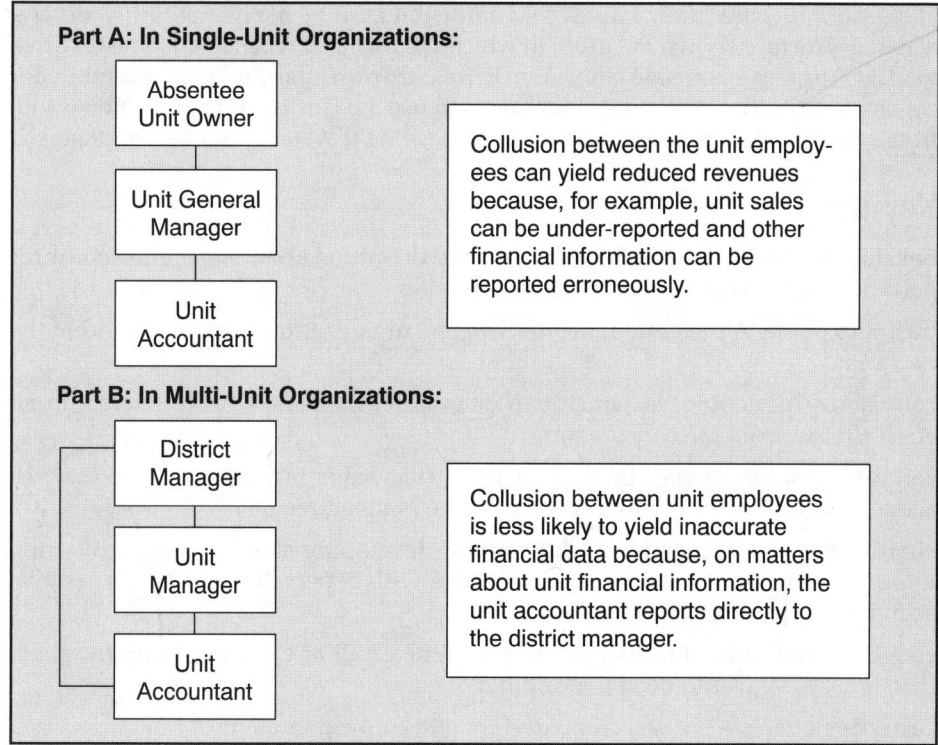

Part A: In Single-Unit Organizations:

Absentee Unit Owner
Unit General Manager
Unit Accountant

Collusion between the unit employ-ees can yield reduced revenues because, for example, unit sales can be under-reported and other financial information can be reported erroneously.

Part B: In Multi-Unit Organizations:

District Manager
Unit Manager
Unit Accountant

Collusion between unit employees is less likely to yield inaccurate financial data because, on matters about unit financial information, the unit accountant reports directly to the district manager.

the food and beverage manager has the most contact. However, the role of the food and beverage controller should still be one of providing assistance and advice—not making operational decisions that bind the food and beverage department.

It is often noted that the management of a food and beverage operation is complex, and a great deal of teamwork involving personnel in a number of different departments is required.

Control in Multi-Unit Operations

We have already noted two potential control tactics employed by managers of multi-unit operations:

- They can compare their unit's actual operating results with benchmark data from other units within their chain.

- A team of unit managers (and those at organizational levels above them) can work together to develop initial and revised operating procedures and control systems to best manage resources.

From a control perspective, there is another dimension to the control process that can be very significant: financial reconciliations can bypass the unit manager. This is illustrated in Exhibit 6; Part A shows the unit manager's line responsibility to the accountant in an independent operation with an absentee owner. Since these managers work together daily and closely, **collusion** is more likely than in the organizational structure shown in Part B, in which the financial reconciliation rests with a manager inside and outside of the unit. In this structure, there is less opportunity for collusion. Note that absentee owners also can use the Part B model in Exhibit 6 and, from a control perspective, the financial management system can be strengthened.

Key Terms

benchmark—A pre-established statement or definition about what must occur for performance to be considered acceptable.

business plan—A plan that indicates what an organization plans to do within the next year.

collusion—An activity in which two or more employees secretly interact in an effort to steal from the corporation.

control—A series of coordinated activities that helps managers ensure that the actual results of operations closely match the planned results.

controlling—The management function of developing standards and collecting information to compare actual performance with expectations so that corrective action(s) can be taken, if necessary.

convenience foods—Products that have some or all of the labor built into them that, otherwise, would need to be added on-site.

corrective action—The selection, design, and implementation of new or revised procedures or policies to reduce the level of variance between standards and actual operating results.

cost—An expense (reduction of an asset) generally incurred for the purpose of increasing revenues.

food and beverage controller—An accounting department employee who develops food and beverage standard costs, assists in budget development, analyzes income statements, directly supervises receiving and/or storeroom personnel, and participates in end-of-period inventory valuations.

green restaurants—Restaurants and other food and beverage operations that implement systems to conserve water, energy, and other natural resources.

income statement—A report of the organization's profitability that indicates revenues earned and expenses incurred for a specific time period; also called a "profit and loss" or "P and L" statement.

long-range plan—A plan that indicates what managers desire to accomplish within a specified time period (often five years).

marketing plan—A plan that indicates specific procedures to accomplish guest-related aspects of the organization's business plan.

mission—A specific statement about what an organization will do and how it will do it.

mystery shopper—A control tactic that involves the use of an individual posing as a guest, who assesses the extent to which a property's food, beverage, service, and cleanliness standards are attained.

objectives—Statements that indicate why a business exists and what it is trying to do.

operating budget—A financial plan that details estimated revenues, costs associated with the products and services that are produced, and the organization's financial goals.

profit—The difference between revenue and expense when there is more revenue than expense.

prime costs—Those costs—product (food and beverage) and labor—that comprise the most significant costs in a food and beverage operation.

quality—The consistent delivery of products and services according to expected standards.

standards—Planned or expected results of the operation expressed as a level of performance.

vision—A broad and abstract view of what an organization believes it should ideally be like.

 # Review Questions ————————————————

1. What resources are necessary to successfully operate a food and beverage operation?

2. Why is it important to have objectives?

3. What is control? Why is it important? What does control mean to many food and beverage managers? What control elements are missing in the traditional definition?

4. How can an effective control system reduce daily operating problems?

5. What are the four basic sources of standard control information? Which are the easiest to use? Which are the best to use?

6. When might a variance be permitted between standard plans and actual operating results?

7. What factors should be considered when implementing a control system?

8. What are some of the duties typically assigned to a food and beverage controller?

9. Why must managers be careful when deciding to revise a standard?

10. With regard to control systems, what advantages do managers in multi-unit food and beverage operations enjoy that their counterparts in single-unit operations do not?

Internet Sites

For more information, visit the following Internet sites. Remember that Internet addresses can change without notice. If the site is no longer there, you can use a search engine to look for additional sites.

Small Business Resources

(Enter "operating control" in the following websites' search fields.)

About Management
www.management.about.com

Entrepreneur.com
www.entrepreneur.com

Business Know-How
www.businessknowhow.com

MoreBusiness.com
www.morebusiness.com

Food Service Management Trade Publications

Foodservice.com
www.foodservice.com

Restaurant Business
www.restaurantbiz.com

Hotel F&B Magazine
www.hfbexecutive.com

Restaurants & Institutions
www.rimag.com

Nation's Restaurant News
www.nrn.com

Restaurant Evaluation Mystery Shopper Organizations

The Insight Group International
www.theinsightgroupintl.com

Restaurant Cops
www.restaurant-cops.com

Mini-Case Studies

Case One—The New General Manager

You are the newly employed general manager of a relatively large ($750,000 annual revenue) restaurant owned by an investor in another city. There has been a rapid succession of managers within the past two years because of financial losses.

During the first several weeks on the job, you learn that:

- Financial information (including bank deposits, invoices, time sheets, and miscellaneous bills) is sent directly to the owner's accountant for payment. The accountant pays the bills, completes the basic bookkeeping, and compiles the financial reports. Copies are then sent to the owner and you, the restaurant manager.

- Labor schedules are completed by the chef, bar manager, and restaurant (dining) manager, based on expected business volumes. However, they are not approved in advance by the general manager.

- While the general manager has always worked with the chef in planning the menu, the manager's input has historically been considered suggestion only; final authority rests with the chef, who purchases products, establishes selling prices, and determines actual food costs, which are summarized for the general manager.

- Amounts budgeted for food and labor costs in your restaurant are, according to a current state restaurant association publication, several percentage points higher than the state average costs.

What are some tactics you would implement immediately to establish a basic control system at the restaurant?

Case Two—The Unit Manager

You are the unit manager in a chain restaurant organization. The budget is created by the area manager with some input by you. All bills are paid at corporate headquarters based on payroll information (for labor) sent electronically from your unit and on hard-copy delivery invoices (for food and other items) routed from delivery personnel through you to corporate headquarters. Other bills received by the unit are forwarded to corporate headquarters. You receive an income statement that is hand-delivered by the district manager during the second week after the month to which it pertains.

Until recently, your unit was performing at about average in relation to the seven units in the area. During the past three months, however, the food, beverage, and labor costs have risen, and your unit is now ranked as a below-average performer in the district. You have implemented or revised no operating changes that can account for the higher food/labor percentages. What are some possible causes of this problem? What can you do about them?

Case Three—Using the Five-Step Control Process

For the past two months, beverage revenues have been lower and beverage cost percentages have been higher than those budgeted at the restaurant you manage. There have been no personnel changes. (The bar manager and bartender staff have been with the restaurant for more than a year.) Use the five-step control process discussed in this chapter to illustrate how you might address this problem.

Part II

Planning for Food and Beverage Control

Chapter 3 Outline

Competencies

1. Explain how managers use standard purchase specifications as cost control tools. (pp. 59–60)

2. Explain how managers use standard recipes and portion control techniques as cost control tools. (pp. 60–67)

3. Determine standard yields for food products. (pp. 67–69)

4. Calculate the cost per servable pound of a food product. (pp. 69–70)

5. Use an adjustment factor to increase or decrease the yield from a standard recipe. (pp. 70–72)

6. Calculate standard portion costs and standard menu item costs for food items on the basis of standard recipes and standard portion sizes, and calculate standard portion costs and describe standard cost tools for beverages. (pp. 72–79)

7. Identify the functions of files typically maintained by recipe management software applications. (pp. 79–81)

8. Explain how managers use standard food and beverage costs and ideal food and beverage costs to evaluate actual results of operations. (pp. 81–86)

3

Determining Food and Beverage Standards

DEVELOPING STANDARDS (levels of expected performance) is the first step in the process of controlling food and beverage costs. Once developed, standards can be compared against actual operating results to determine whether variances exist and, if so, which variances are excessive. Standards specific to the property's current plans will better indicate problems (variances from planned cost levels) than will standards based on industry averages or standards developed from the property's past operating statistics.

The usefulness of control information can be increased by establishing standards for each revenue center within the food and beverage operation. For example, instead of computing a standard (expected) food cost for all outlets combined, a hotel might establish separate standard cost levels for its coffee shop, dining room, room service, and banquet operations. An advantage of this approach is that each outlet can be evaluated separately, based on its own set of anticipated costs.

Unfortunately, it takes time to develop and monitor specific standards. The longer the time needed to collect information on which to base the standard (or later to measure actual results), the less likely it is that managers will take the time to do it. In addition, the more complex the development of standard costs becomes, the more likely the task will be met with resistance by those who must collect the information.

Therefore, an ideal control system must strike a balance between the time and effort spent developing it and the usefulness of the results it provides. Simplified time- and cost-effective systems for determining food and beverage standards are offered in this chapter. The principles for establishing standards are the same regardless of whether the property is commercial or noncommercial, large or small, fast-food or gourmet, hotel restaurant or freestanding restaurant. Managers in any kind of operation who want to develop in-house food and beverage standards can use the procedures discussed in this chapter.

Systems for developing food and beverage standards must begin with the menu. Because it establishes which food and beverage items will be served, the menu is the most basic and important control tool. Once a menu is created, five standard cost tools can be developed:

1. Standard purchase specifications

2. Standard recipes

3. Standard yields

4. Standard portion sizes

5. Standard portion costs

As shown in Exhibit 1, the development and use of each of these tools is sequential; effective managers develop them in order and use the previous cost tool to develop the next cost tool.

Let's look at each of these standard cost tools very carefully.

Standard Purchase Specifications

A **purchase specification** is a concise description of the quality, size, weight, count, and other factors needed to describe a desired item. The specified factors should be described in sufficient detail to properly guide the company's suppliers and receiving personnel in the delivery and receipt of the desired products.

Management, working with purchasing personnel if available, should establish standard purchase specifications based on menu requirements and the operation's merchandising and pricing policies. Once developed, standard purchase specifications should be given to the property's suppliers and receiving personnel. In this way, all of the parties involved in ordering, supplying, and receiving will have the necessary written guides to permit the operation to consistently obtain the quality and kind of food and beverage items desired.

In addition to describing what the operation requires, standard purchase specifications offer several other advantages:

- Fewer products may be required. Analyzing the menu may suggest ways to use an ingredient for several menu items so that fewer ingredients have to be purchased. For example, size 36–42-count shrimp (36–42 headless shrimp per pound) may be used both for a seafood platter and a shrimp sandwich rather than purchasing shrimp of two different sizes for the two menu items.

- Reduced purchase costs may be possible. Purchase specifications based on the needs of the menu will keep the property from buying higher-quality products than it needs for its purposes.

- If purchase specifications are properly established, more than one supplier will likely be able to quote prices and compete for the operation's business.

The development and use of specifications involves time and effort. However, considering the many advantages purchase specifications offer relative to the few disadvantages, they are clearly a critical standard cost control tool. Carefully developed and rigidly enforced specifications help the operation ensure that the right quality product is consistently available for production and service. Remember, however, that standard purchase specifications call for effective receiving control procedures to assure that what is ordered (products meeting specification agreements) is, in fact, delivered.

Standard Recipes

A **standard recipe** is a formula for producing a food or beverage item. It provides a summary of ingredients, the required quantity of each, specific preparation

Exhibit 1   Sequential Development of Standard Cost Tools

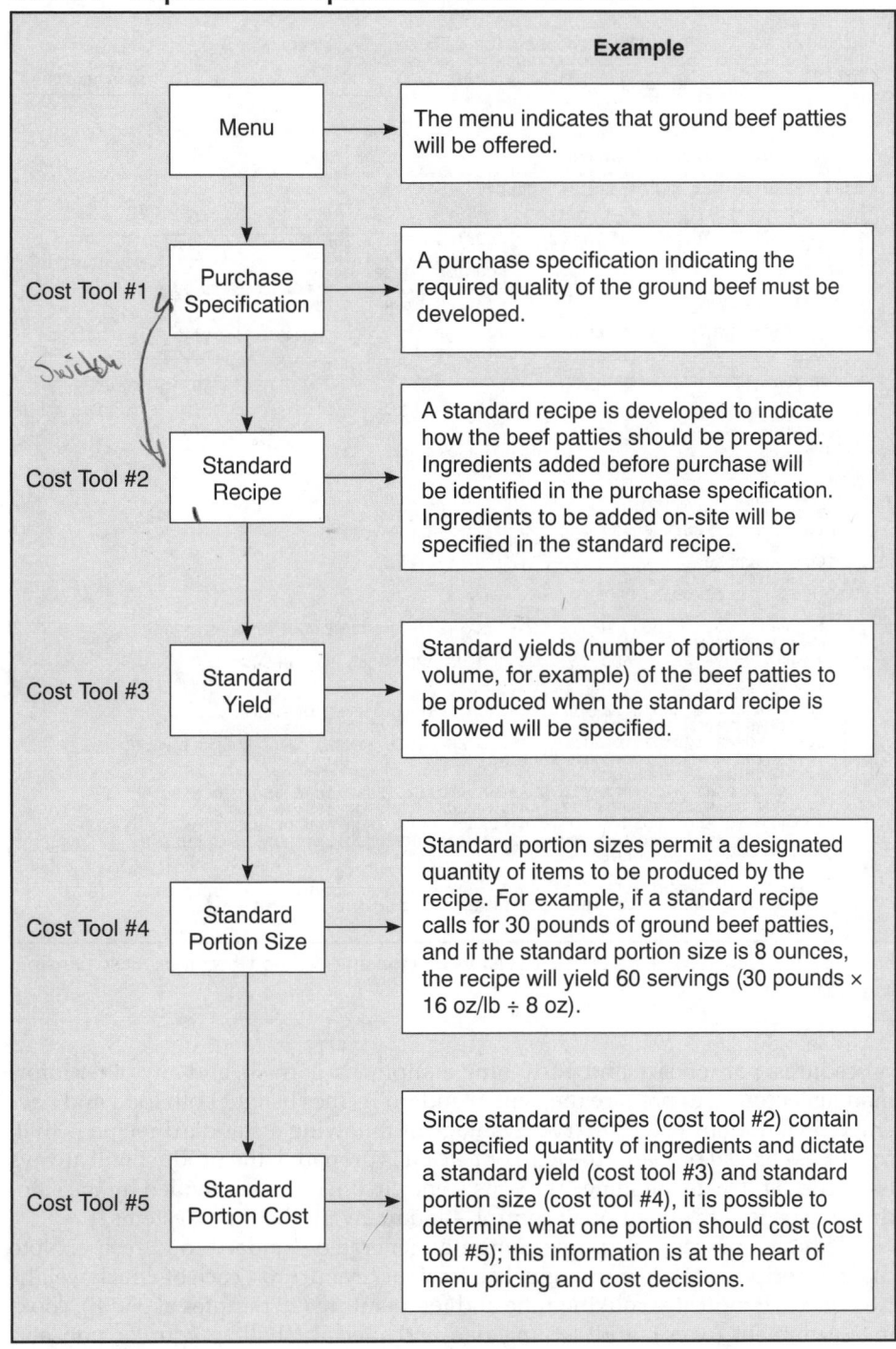

Exhibit 2   Computer-Generated Standard Recipe

```
REPORT#: 90    * * * CBORD FOODSERVICE MANAGEMENT SYSTEMS * * *      PAGE:   4
OPTION : 3.5.8.          MENU MANAGEMENT SYSTEM - V6.23              MAY 09
USER#  : 28          MSU Residence Halls Fall - LCode 1             1540 HOURS
                 PRODUCTION RECIPE

 FUNCTION NAME:
         UNIT:
         DATE: FRIDAY    05/09
===============================================================================
 0084  BURRITO WET MEAT (BEEF & TURKEY)
                                                 YIELD    :      1.80 SCP

 PORTIONS :      30.00     8.30 OZ    COOKING TIME : 25MIN
 PORTION DESC : 1 BURRITO            COOKING TEMP : 350F
 PREP TIME:                          COOKING EQUIP: Oven
                                     SERVING PAN  : SHALLOW COUNTER PAN
 PREPARE MAIN BATCH  1 TIME(S)       SERVING UTEN : SPATULA

      INGREDIENT          ------- MAIN BATCH -------- ------ PARTIAL BATCH ------
                                QUANTITY                     QUANTITY

      REVISED 12-20

 GROUND TURKEY                2 LBS     8     OZS
 GROUND BEEF                  1 LBS     4     OZS
 ONIONS                                 4 3/4 OZS
 TACO SEASONING                         1 3/4 OZS
 SALT                                   1 1/4 OZS
 REFRIED BEANS                1 QT      3 1/2 CUP
 10" DIE CUT TORTILLA                  30     EACH
 ENCHILADA SAUCE SUBR 2643              3 3/4 CUP
      **GARNISH**
 LETTUCE SHREDDED                       7 1/4 OZS
 TOMATOES DICED                        14 1/2 OZS
 MILD SHREDDED CHEDDAR                  7 1/4 OZS

     1. BROWN BOTH GROUND MEATS TOGETHER (BE SURE THEY ARE WELL MIXED.)
        WITH ONIONS.
     2. DRAIN OFF FAT.  ADD TACO SEASONING AND SALT, MIX WELL.
        ADJUST SEASONING IF NECESSARY.
     3. ADD BEANS TO SEASONED MEAT AND MIX WELL.
     4. MAKE SAUCE AND HOLD AT A MINIMUM INTERNAL TEMP OF 145.
     5. TO ASSEMBLE BURRITOS: PLACE A #12 SCOOP OF FILLING (4OZ)
        ON LOWER 1/3 OF TORTILLA.  FOLD IN SIDES FIRST, THEN ROLL STARTING
        AT THE BOTTOM TO COVER FILLING.
     6. PLACE 16 IN EACH SCP.
     7. COVER PANS WITH PLASTIC WRAP AND FOIL.  BAKE IN A 350 DEG OVEN
    CCP>FOR 25 MINUTES OR UNTIL AN INTERNAL TEMP OF 155 IS REACHED.
     8. UNCOVER AND LADLE 16 OZS. OF SAUCE OVER EACH PAN OF BURRITOS.
     9. JUST BEFORE SERVICE SPRINKLE ON 4OZ SHREDDED LETTUCE, 4OZ CHEESE
        AND 8OZ DICED TOMATOES.

     NOTE:   HEAT FLOUR TORTILLAS ON A 300F GRILL FOR APPROX. 30 SECONDS.
             THIS WILL MAKE THE TORTILLAS FLEXIBLE AND EASY TO FOLD.
```

Source: Michigan State University, Division of Housing & Food Services, East Lansing, Michigan.

procedures, portion size and portioning equipment, garnish, and any other information necessary to prepare the item. Standard recipes benefit both food and beverage preparation. The primary advantage of following a standard recipe is that, regardless of *who* prepares the item or *when* it is prepared, the product will always look, cost, and taste the same. The consistency in operations provided by the standard recipe is at the heart of all control—and many marketing—systems.

Exhibit 2 presents a sample computer-generated standard food recipe. Note that this recipe yields 30 portions of beef and turkey burritos, each of which weighs 8.3 ounces. It indicates cooking time and temperature (25 minutes at 350°F), cooking equipment (oven), and serving pan and utensil (shallow counter pan and

Exhibit 3   Computer-Generated Sub-Recipe

```
REPORT#: 90    * * * CBORD FOODSERVICE MANAGEMENT SYSTEMS * * *      PAGE:   5
OPTION : 3.5.8.              MENU MANAGEMENT SYSTEM - V6.23           MAY 09
USER#  : 28            MSU Residence Halls Fall - LCode 1            1540 HOURS
                   PRODUCTION RECIPE

FUNCTION NAME:
          UNIT:
          DATE: FRIDAY    05/09
==============================================================================
2643   SAUCE ENCHILADA HOMEMADE
                                          YIELD    :     0.23 GALLONS

PORTIONS :      9.98    3.00 OZ    COOKING TIME :
PORTION DESC : SERVING             COOKING TEMP :
PREP TIME:                         COOKING EQUIP:
                                   SERVING PAN  :
PREPARE MAIN BATCH  1 TIME(S)      SERVING UTEN :

       INGREDIENT         ------- MAIN BATCH -------- ------ PARTIAL BATCH ------
                                  QUANTITY                   QUANTITY

    NEW RECIPE 2-29

MARGARINE                            1 1/4 OZS
ALL PURPOSE FLOUR-GOLDMED            1 1/4 OZS
VEGETARIAN CHICKEN BASE                3/4 OZS
LAWREY SEASONING SALT                  1/2 TSP
GROUND CHILI POWDER        1 TBSP      3/4 TSP
GROUND CUMIN SEED           2          TSP
GARLIC POWDER                          1/2 TSP
GROUND RED PEPPER                      1/8 TSP
TOMATO PUREE                           1/8 #10 CAN
WATER                       3          CUP

    1. MELT MARGARINE IN KETTLE.  ADD FLOUR TO MAKE ROUX.
    2. COOL SLIGHTLY, ADD WATER AND SPICES. WHIP UNTIL SMOOTH.  SIMMER
       10 MINUTES.
    3. ADD PUREE AND SIMMER 5 MINUTES.
    4. ADJUST SEASONING IF NEEDED.
    5. SERVE ON WET BURRITOS.
```

Source: Michigan State University, Division of Housing & Food Services, East Lansing, Michigan.

spatula). It also provides details about ingredients, quantities of ingredients, and production procedures.

Exhibit 2 also illustrates another interesting use of standard recipes: one recipe (a **sub-recipe**) can yield an ingredient for another recipe. Note that one ingredient (3¾ cups of enchilada sauce) is required, and it is listed as "SUBR 2643" (sub-recipe #2643). Exhibit 3 shows the sub-recipe for the enchilada sauce required by the burrito recipe.

Sub-recipe #2643 yields 0.23 gallons (the approximately 3¾ cups required by the recipe shown in Exhibit 2).[1] If the enchilada recipe is adjusted to yield a different number of portions, the computer-generated sub-recipe can easily be revised to yield the correct amount for the adjusted recipe. Alternatively, operations requiring large quantities of a sub-recipe item may produce large quantities at one time. Production personnel can then use the batch produced for all the different recipes requiring the sub-recipe ingredient.

There are several other reasons to use standard recipes in addition to the advantages of consistency in appearance, cost, and taste:

- When managers know that the standard recipe will yield a specific number of standard-size portions, it is less likely that too many or too few items will be prepared. They can estimate the number of portions required and adjust a standard recipe to yield the number of portions needed. This tactic helps to control food costs.

- Since standard recipes indicate needed equipment and required production times, managers can more effectively schedule food production employees and necessary equipment.

- Less supervision is required, since standard recipes tell the employees the quantity and preparation method for each item. Guesswork is eliminated; employees need only follow recipe procedures. Of course, managers should routinely evaluate the quality of items produced to ensure that standard recipes are followed correctly.

- If the chef is ill or the bartender doesn't show up, a product of appropriate quality can be produced if a standard recipe is available. Granted, inexperienced employees will be slow and may make mistakes, but if the recipe resides only "in the head" of an absent employee, instead of on a standard recipe card or available for printout, management will be in an even more awkward position.

Standard recipes are also critical to controlling the consistency (quality and cost) of beverages. Today in the United States, it is critical to use standard recipes specifying ingredient and portion sizes of alcoholic beverages for reasons other than to control beverage costs and assure consistency to meet guests' preferences. Liquor liability concerns often arise when standard recipes are not available or when standard portion controls are not in use. Those who sell alcohol must be able to verify the actual quantity of alcohol (not just number of drinks) that a guest has consumed, and this will be indicated in the standard recipe.

Using a standard recipe does not require that the recipe be physically in the work area during production times. After a cook prepares a menu item several times, or a bartender mixes a drink several times, he or she will remember ingredients, quantities, and procedures. It would obviously be impractical if, before preparing a drink, a busy bartender had to refer to a standard recipe. *A standard recipe must always be followed and must always be available, but it does not always need to be read before every preparation.*

Developing Standard Recipes

Developing standard recipes does not require throwing out existing recipes and starting over. Rather, it often requires standardizing existing recipes according to a series of steps.

Select a time period for standard recipe development. For example, you may choose to standardize one recipe at each weekly cooks' meeting, or spend one hour each week with the head bartender to develop standard beverage recipes. At these meetings, ask the cook or head bartender to talk through the preparation of the item. What are the ingredients and how much of each ingredient is needed? What are the exact procedures? What are cooking/baking temperatures and times? What portion control tools are, or can be, used? On what plate or in what glassware is the item served? What garnish is used? Double-check the recipe by closely observing the cook or bartender as the item is actually prepared.

Record the recipes in a standard format that will be helpful to those preparing the items. For example:

- Decide on the desirable yield. If 25 portions of a food item are normally prepared for slow periods and 60 portions are needed for busy times, recipes should be designed to produce these two different yields.

- List all ingredients in the order they are used.

- Decide whether to use weights or measures or both. Weighing is always more precise than measuring, and it is just as practical to weigh liquids, flour, etc., as it is to measure them. Avoid confusion by using consistent abbreviations throughout all the standard recipes you are developing. For example, you may decide to use "t," "tsp," or "tea" as the abbreviation for teaspoon.

- When possible, express all quantities in amounts that are practical for those preparing the item. For example, convert all measures into the largest possible units. Change ⅛ cup to ½ cup, four cups to one quart, or three teaspoons to one tablespoon. At this point you need to be sure that the proper equipment is available. It does little good to specify a three-ounce quantity of sugar when an accurate scale to weigh the sugar is not available. Also, when applicable, ensure that the recipes you develop call for standard-size pans and other equipment that you have available.

- Record procedures in detailed, concise, and exact terms. Avoid confusing statements. For example, what does "one cup whipping cream" mean? Does it mean one cup of cream that has been whipped, or does it mean one cup of cream that must be whipped? When mixing is called for, tell how to mix (by hand or by machine) and provide the approximate time and exact speed if a machine is used. State the size and type of equipment and small wares such as pans or bowls needed, and always list exact temperatures, cooking times, and other necessary controls.

- Carefully consider potential sanitation problems that can arise in each step of recipe production; note these and incorporate food-handling precautions directly into the recipe. For example, if the operation uses a hollandaise sauce, which is potentially hazardous and highly susceptible to contamination by microorganisms, a last step in the recipe might state: "Hollandaise sauce is a potentially dangerous food that can become contaminated by microorganisms; always prepare in small batches and do not hold on the serving line for more than one hour. Do not store (refrigerate) for later use or use as a leftover. Discard all remaining sauce at the end of each shift."

- Provide directions for portioning. Indicate the type and size of the serving dish. Also, indicate portioning equipment, such as ladle or scoop, and specify the expected number and size of portions. Be sure all required portioning equipment is available for use. If garnishes or sauces are needed, these should be listed, and recipes, if applicable, should be referenced.

Learn More on the Web

Recipe software for quantity food production operations is available from many sources, and the technology provided can assist managers and chefs in numerous ways. For example, consider Star Chef (www.chef365.com). Depending upon the system selected, users of this recipe software can:

- Store information about cost, purchase unit size, and issue unit size (volume or weight) for thousands of ingredients.
- Store pictures of each ingredient.
- Store standard recipes built upon ingredients in a database. Recipes can be associated with categories, regions, special occasions, users, and outlets.
- Include (nest) sub-recipes when required as an ingredient in another recipe.
- Specify critical control points for each recipe.
- Utilize photos of the items produced by the recipes.
- Automatically adjust (scale or re-size) recipes based on desired yields.

Those developing recipes can save significant time and better assure accuracy in the development of recipe-related information by using recipe software.

After the standard recipes have been developed, share them with other production staff. Solicit their ideas about accuracy and possible refinements. Finally, test the recipes to be certain that they yield products of the desired quantity and quality. After successful testing, the recipe may be considered standardized and should then be used without variation.

Despite the advantages of using standard recipes, some difficulties may be encountered in implementing them. Cooks or bartenders, for example, may feel that they can no longer be creative in the kitchen or behind the bar. They may resent the need to put things down on paper or to print them out from the computer for each day's use. Other potential difficulties relating to staff may be about time or even about whether their positions are in jeopardy ("If anyone can do it, why am I still needed?"). Also, it takes time to standardize existing recipes, and it takes time to train production employees to follow them precisely.

These concerns, however, are minor when compared to the points already noted in favor of using standard recipes. In addition, managers can minimize any difficulties in implementing standard recipes by explaining to employees why standard recipes are necessary and by involving them in developing and implementing the recipes.

Sources of Recipes

Chefs typically pride themselves on their ability to both develop new recipes and modify existing ones. Many have accumulated large numbers of cooking-related resources through years of collecting, exchanging with fellow chefs, and creating their own libraries of materials—including recipes—from numerous sources such as publications, professional chefs' associations, and equipment/product manufacturers and suppliers.

In addition, today's chefs have an additional source of standard recipes: the Internet. A quick search can uncover countless large-volume and family-oriented recipes that can provide creative chefs with opportunities to revise menus, plan daily "specials," and meet the needs of a special banquet menu. For example, the RecipeSource (www.recipesource.com) website includes more than 70,000 recipes sorted into two major groups: those primarily identified with an **ethnic cuisine** and others categorized by type of dish. While the recipes yield small quantities, their value lies in the suggestion of ideas, after which recipes can be adjusted for larger-volume needs using procedures described later in this chapter.

There are excellent sources of recipes from professional chefs available as well. See, for example, Global Chefs (www.globalchefs.com), AskaChef.com (www. askachef.com), and famous chefs' recipes (www.topsecretrecipes.ivillage.com/ food), or simply type "chefs recipes" into your favorite search engine. Many food service distributors such as Sysco Corporation (www.sysco.com) and Gordon Food Service (www.gfs.com) also feature recipes on their home pages. Food manufacturers are still another source of recipes on the Internet—for example, Kraft Foodservice (www.kraftfoodservice.com) and the J. M. Smucker Company, the marketer of jams, jellies, preserves, and other food spreads (www.smucker.com).

Associations representing specialized food manufacturers, processors, and growers are another good source of recipes. See, for example, the website of the American Dairy Association (www.ilovecheese.com) and the California Dried Plum Board (www.californiadriedplums.org).

Recipes for alcoholic beverages are also readily available from electronic sources, including iDRINK (www.idrink.com), Recipe Goldmine (www.recipegoldmine.com), and Drinks Mixer.com (www.drinksmixer.com). These types of websites can be of great interest to properties developing a specialty drink list and even to bartenders who have been asked to prepare an unknown drink for a guest.

Standard Yields

The term **yield** means the net weight or volume of a food item after it has been processed and made ready for sale to the guest. The difference between the raw or "as purchased" (AP) weight and the prepared or "edible portion" (EP) weight is termed a **production loss.** For example, if 25 pounds (AP weight) of pork tenderloin are purchased and, after trimming and baking, 22.5 pounds remain, there is a production loss of 2.5 pounds (25 pounds AP weight minus 22.5 pounds EP weight).

In general, there are three steps in the **production** process for many foods. The first is preparation, which includes such activities as meat trimming and vegetable cleaning. The second is cooking. Holding, the third step, includes the portioning of those products that have not been pre-portioned. A "loss" can occur in any of these steps.

A **standard yield** results when an item is produced according to established standard production procedures outlined in the standard recipe. It serves as a base against which to compare actual yields. For example, if the standard purchase

Exhibit 4   Summary of Yield Test Results

#109

Item: *Oven Prepared Beef Rib*   Grade: *USDA Choice*
Pieces: *8*   Total Weight: *162 lb*   Average Weight: *20 lb, 4 oz*
Average Item Cost: *$120.49 at $5.95/lb*
Supplier: *Various*

Summary of Yield Test Results

Cooking and Portioning Details	Weight	% of Original Weight	Cost Per Servable Lb	Cost Factor
Edible Portion (EP) Weight	11 lb 3 oz	55.25%	$10.77	1.81
Loss due to fat trim & bones	5 lb 3 oz	25.62		
Loss due to cooking	3 lb 14 oz	19.13		
As Purchased (AP) Weight	20 lb 4 oz	100.00%		

Other Data:
   Cooked at 300°F for 4 hrs, 45 min

specifications are followed, and a meat item is properly trimmed, cooked, and portioned, the actual yield should closely approximate the standard yield.

Determining Standard Yield

Standard yields are determined by conducting a **yield test.** Ideally, everything that does not have a 100-percent yield should be tested. Examples of items with 100-percent yield (100-percent edible portion) are some portion-controlled products such as meats and those convenience foods that only need to be plated. However, from a practical standpoint, yield tests are typically performed only on higher-cost items or on lower-cost products used in large quantities.

The yield from a product depends on several factors, including the grade, original weight, and preparation and cooking methods. Therefore, it is helpful for a food and beverage purchaser to compare the yields for similar products from different suppliers. It may be possible to substitute a raw product with a lower cost per unit that provides a yield similar to that of a higher-cost product, without compromising the operation's quality standards.

An example of the results of a yield test (sometimes called a butcher test when done for meat) is shown in Exhibit 4. In this example, eight oven-prepared beef rib sections averaging 20 pounds, 4 ounces each (162 pounds ÷ 8 pieces) were cooked and trimmed, and the bones were removed according to a property's standard recipe and standard preparation and cooking procedures. (Eight rib pieces were used in this example to provide a more accurate base for the yield calculations.) By weighing the meat at each step, the loss due to cooking and trimming can be assessed.

Since the AP weight is already known (162 pounds), the meat is next weighed when it is removed from the oven after cooking. By subtracting the cooked weight from the original weight, you can determine the loss in cooking—in this example, an average of 3 pounds, 14 ounces per rib section. Next, the fat cap and bones must be removed and the remaining meat weighed. This is the edible portion or servable weight—assume in this example it averages 11 pounds, 3 ounces per rib section. Subtracting the edible portion (servable) weight from the cooked weight indicates that the loss in carving and bones averaged 5 pounds, 3 ounces.

Cost per Servable Pound

Once the edible (servable) portion weight is determined, a **cost per servable pound** can be determined. To find the cost per servable pound, first establish the yield percentage. The **yield percentage** (sometimes called **yield factor**) is the ratio of servable weight to original weight. It is calculated by dividing the servable weight by the original weight (normally both weights are expressed in ounces; there are 16 ounces in one pound) and multiplying the result by 100 to convert the decimal to a percentage. For example, the yield percentage of the beef rib recipe shown in Exhibit 4 is calculated as follows:

$$\frac{\text{Servable Weight}}{\text{Original Weight}} \times 100 = \text{Ratio of Servable Weight to Original Weight}$$

$$\frac{11 \text{ lb} \times 16 \text{ oz per lb} + 3 \text{ oz}}{20 \text{ lb} \times 16 \text{ oz per lb} + 4 \text{ oz}} = \frac{179 \text{ oz}}{324 \text{ oz}} \times 100 = 55.25\% \text{ (rounded)}$$

This means that 55.25 percent of the purchase weight of the beef ribs will be available for service to guests.

The cost per servable pound is found by dividing the AP price by the yield percentage. For example, continuing with our beef rib recipe, the cost per servable pound is calculated as follows:

$$\frac{\text{AP Price}}{\text{Yield Percentage}} = \text{Cost per Servable Pound}$$

$$\frac{\$5.95}{0.5525} = \$10.77 \text{ (rounded)}$$

In other words, if beef ribs cost $5.95 per pound, $10.77 will be required to produce one pound of product that can be plated and served to guests.

The cost per servable pound is the information needed to calculate standard portion costs, which is discussed later in the chapter.

One can make a similar calculation to determine the total AP quantity needed once the yield percentage is known. Assume that fifty 8-ounce edible portions of beef ribs in the above example are required for a banquet and that there is a 55.25-percent yield. What quantity of beef ribs will be needed to yield the 25 pounds (50 portions at 8 ounces per portion) that are requested?

$$\frac{\text{Quantity Needed} \times \text{Edible Portion}}{\text{Yield Percentage}} = \text{Quantity to Purchase/Prepare}$$

$$\frac{50 \text{ portions} \times 8 \text{ oz/portion}}{0.5525} = 724 \text{ oz (rounded)}$$

The cook will have to prepare approximately 45.25 pounds (724 ounces divided by 16 ounces per pound) to yield the 25 servable pounds that are needed for the banquet.

The Cost Factor

The **cost factor** is a constant value that may be used to convert new AP prices into a revised cost per servable pound when purchase prices change. The cost factor assumes that the standard purchase specifications, standard recipe, and standard yield remain the same. The cost factor is obtained by dividing the cost per servable pound, calculated as part of the yield test, by the original AP cost per pound. For example:

$$\frac{\text{Cost per Servable Pound}}{\text{AP Price}} = \text{Cost Factor}$$

$$\frac{\$10.77}{\$5.95} = 1.81$$

Any time the AP cost changes from the amount used to calculate the original cost per servable pound in the yield test, a new cost per servable pound can be computed by multiplying the cost factor by the new AP price. For example, if the AP price for the beef rib increased to $6.29 per pound, the new cost per servable pound would be:

New AP Price	×	Cost Factor	=	New Cost per Servable Pound
$6.29	×	1.81	=	$11.38

One final note: it is critical that all established standards remain the same. The proper use of the cost factor is dependent on the operation adhering to the same standard purchase specifications and following the preparation and cooking methods used in the yield test.

Adjusting Standard Recipe Yields

The yield from a standard recipe can be easily increased or decreased by using an **adjustment factor.** An adjustment factor is found by dividing the desired yield by the original yield. For example, if a recipe yields 100 portions, and you want 225 portions of the same size, the adjustment factor would be:

$$\frac{\text{Desired Yield}}{\text{Original Yield}} = \text{Adjustment Factor}$$

$$\frac{225 \text{ portions}}{100 \text{ portions}} = 2.25$$

Each recipe ingredient is then multiplied by the adjustment factor to determine the amount needed for the desired yield. For example, if the original recipe required 8 ounces of sugar, the adjusted quantity would be:

Original Amount	×	Adjustment Factor	=	New Amount
8 oz	×	2.25	=	18 oz (1 lb, 2 oz)

The quantity of ingredients to be included in the recipe should be that which is easiest to apply in the preparation area. In the example above, if the kitchen had a 2-pound (32-ounce) scale, the amount (18 ounces) will probably be appropriate. If, however, only a 1-pound scale is available, it would probably be best to specify "1 pound (16 ounces) plus 2 ounces."

A similar procedure can be used to determine the new amount required if the portion size is altered. For example, if a recipe yields forty 12-ounce servings and you want forty 8-ounce servings, the adjustment factor would be:

$$\frac{\text{Desired Amount}}{\text{Original Amount}} = \text{Adjustment Factor}$$

$$\frac{8 \text{ oz}}{12 \text{ oz}} = 0.67 \text{ (rounded)}$$

Each recipe ingredient must then be multiplied by this factor to determine the amount of the ingredient required for the recipe. For example, if a recipe required 30 pounds of ground beef to yield forty 12-ounce servings, to prepare forty 8-ounce servings, you would need approximately 20 pounds of ground beef.

Original Amount	×	Adjustment Factor	=	New Amount
30 lb	×	0.67	=	20.1 lb

A recipe can also be adjusted if both the number of portions *and* the portion size change. First, determine the total volume of the original and desired amounts, then calculate the adjustment factor. For example, if a recipe yields fifty 4-ounce servings and the desired yield is seventy-five 6-ounce servings, the adjustment factor would be:

$$\frac{\text{Total Volume of Desired Yield}}{\text{Total Volume of Original Yield}} = \text{Adjustment Factor}$$

Total Volume of Desired Yield	=	75 portions × 6 oz/portion	=	450 oz
Total Volume of Original Yield	=	50 portions × 4 oz/portion	=	200 oz

$$\frac{450 \text{ oz}}{200 \text{ oz}} = 2.25$$

Using an adjustment factor can provide very accurate ingredient quantities when the total volume of a recipe's yield does not change significantly. However, the use of an adjustment factor for a recipe in which the yield changes substantially must be done carefully. For example, it is unlikely that a recipe yielding 10 portions of a specific size can merely be multiplied by an adjustment factor of 100 to yield 1,000 portions of the same size. In such situations, it is best to start with the indicated adjustment factor and then carefully modify it until the recipe yields the desired volume. Likewise, one must be careful when calculating revised quantities for spices and herbs. Some chefs, for instance, use the calculation just described as a base to determine the necessary amount of herbs and spices. Then they begin with 50 percent of the quantity and add additional amounts on a "to-taste" basis until they are certain about the exact quantity needed.

Numerous recipe software packages can automatically adjust standard recipes to increase or decrease the number of portions and/or portion sizes, and they do so quickly and with great accuracy.

There is one potential disadvantage to electronic adjustments of recipes, however: the quantity (weight or volume) of each ingredient needed may be rounded to a relatively unusable amount, and some slight adjustment to the quantities may be needed. For example, it is likely difficult for a cook to accurately measure "1.63 pounds" and "2.17 teaspoons." For most recipes, it is probably appropriate to round up or round down to the approximate quantity needed. However, when precision measurements are required, some attention to electronic calculations may be necessary.

Standard Portion Sizes

Each food and beverage standard recipe indicates a **standard portion size.** This is the fourth standard cost tool for ensuring consistency in operations. Because a given menu item or drink will be the same size each time it is portioned, no guest will get a larger or smaller portion or a stronger or weaker drink. The benefit is twofold: portion costs for the same food and beverage items will be consistent, and the guests will always receive the same value for the dollars they spend.

Value is the relationship between price and quality. Basing the selling price of the food or beverage item, at least in part, on its product cost will help to establish a fair selling price, or value, from the guest's perspective. Assume that an operation does not provide a standard portion size. On one occasion, a guest may receive a very large portion—a great value. Returning at a later time, the same guest may receive a smaller portion at the same selling price—a lesser value and a disappointment. Consistency, in terms of value perceived by guests, is a primary advantage of standard portion sizes.

Portion control tools must be available and used every time a recipe or beverage is prepared. Portion control tools include such items as weighing and measuring equipment, ladles and scoops to portion food, jiggers and shot glasses for beverages, and automated beverage-dispensing equipment.

Employees must know about portion sizes if they are expected to follow them. Required portion sizes from each standard recipe should be posted in production areas for cooks and bartenders to refer to. A sample standard portion-size sheet for food and a standard drink size list are shown in Exhibits 5 and 6, respectively. In addition to these lists, some operations use pictures of each item. When these are posted in serving line stations, employees can see how the item should look and how it is placed on the plate.

Standard Portion Costs

After standard recipes and standard portion sizes have been developed, a **standard portion cost**—the fifth standard cost tool—can be calculated. A standard

Exhibit 5 Sample Standard Portion-Size Sheet—Food

Items	Portion Size	Product Form	Other Data	Work-Station Responsible
APPETIZERS				
Shrimp Cocktail	5 ea	AP	21–25 Count	Cold
Fruit Cup	5 oz	EP	See Recipe No. P12	Cold
Marinated Herring	2½ oz	AP		Cold
Half Grapefruit	½ ea	AP	27 Count	Cold
Soup, Cup	6 oz	EP	6¾ oz Cup	Hot
ENTREES				
Sirloin Steak	14 oz	AP	AP—Bone-in	Hot
Prime Rib of Beef	9 oz	EP		Hot
Lobster	1½ lb	AP		Hot
Ragout of Lamb	4 oz	EP		Hot
Chicken	½ ea	AP	2 lb Average	Hot
VEGETABLES & SALADS				
Whipped Potatoes	3 oz	EP		Hot
Baked Potato	1 ea	AP	90 Count	Hot
Asparagus Spears	3 ea	AP	Jumbo Spears	Hot
Half Tomato	½ ea	AP	4 × 5's	Hot
Garden Salad	2½ oz	EP		Cold
Hearts of Lettuce	¼ head	EP	5's	Cold

AP—As Purchased; EP—Edible Portion

portion cost is the cost of preparing and serving one portion of food or one drink item according to the standard recipe. The process of establishing this cost is called **precosting.**

A standard portion cost is determined by dividing the recipe's total ingredient costs by the number of portions the standard recipe yields. For example, if the cost to prepare a recipe is $75.00, and if it yields 50 portions, then the standard portion cost for one item is $1.50 ($75.00 ÷ 50 portions).

The prices for ingredients listed in standard recipes can be obtained from current invoices. Today, many operations use computerized precosting systems to keep the per-portion cost of standard recipes current. For example, if the price of ground beef increases, the new cost is entered into the menu management system, and the costs of all recipes in which ground beef is an ingredient are automatically adjusted to reflect the price increase.

Exhibit 6   Sample Standard Drink-Size List

Beverage	Drink Size in Ounces	Glass Used
Whiskies (Bourbons & Ryes)	1¼ oz	Highball (8 oz)
Canadians	1¼ oz	Highball (8 oz)
Irish	1¼ oz	Highball (8 oz)
Scotch	1¼ oz	Highball (8 oz)
Rum	1¼ oz	Highball (8 oz)
Brandies	1¼ oz	Line Brandy (2 oz)
Cordials	⅞ oz	Cordial (1 oz)
Wines (by the glass)		
Appetizers	1¾ oz	Sherry (2 oz)
Desserts	2¼ oz	Port (2½ oz)
Cocktails	See Standard Recipe Manual	

Exhibit 7   Example of a Computer-Generated Precosted Recipe

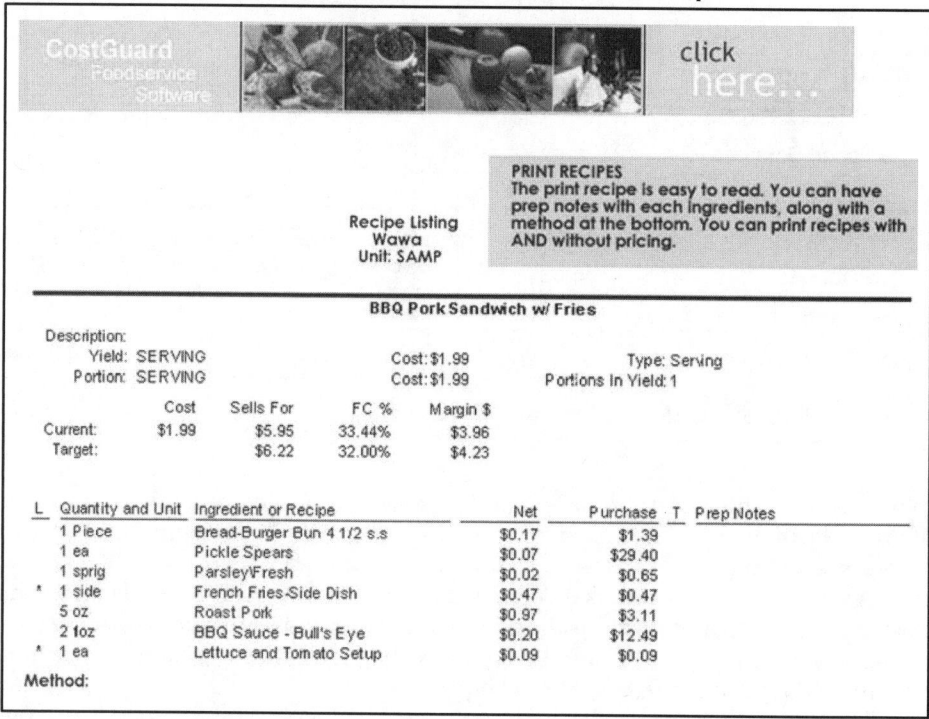

Courtesy of CostGuard Foodservice Software (www.costguard.com).

Exhibit 7 presents a precosted recipe generated by computer that shows the standard portion cost as calculated by the software. Note that the recipe for BBQ pork sandwich with fries indicates the standard recipe cost (the sum of all the costs

Exhibit 8   Building the Cost of a Menu Item

Item	Qty	UOM	Cost
Hamburger Patty-Beef	1.00	ea.	$0.4167
Napkins	1.00	ea.	$0.0085
Ketchup	0.50	oz.	$0.0291
Mayonnaise	1.00	oz.	$0.0913
Mustard	0.50	oz.	$0.0165
Buns-Hamburger	1.00	ea.	$0.1661
Wraps-Burger	1.00	ea.	$0.0110
Pickles-sliced	3.00	Slice	$0.0057
Lettuce-Shredded	1.00	oz.	$0.0588
Tomatoes-Sliced	2.00	Slice	$0.0510

Courtesy of TracRite Software, Inc. (www.tracrite.net).

of all ingredients) is $1.99. It also includes the purchase unit price for each ingredient. Consider roast pork; it is purchased for $3.11 per pound and 5 ounces are to be used in the sandwich. The cost for the pork used is, therefore, $0.97 ($3.11/lb ÷ 16 oz × 5 oz = $0.97). It is impractical—or, at least, not useful—to cost some ingredients, especially a small amount of an inexpensive item. For example, no costs might be included in a precosted recipe for salt and pepper.

A change in the portion size will also affect the standard portion cost. Any time the portion size is altered, a new standard portion cost must be calculated.

Calculating Standard Menu Item Costs

Some operations such as cafeterias offer items à la carte—each item individually priced. However, many food service operations combine individual food items to create dinners or other meals that are costed, priced, and sold as one selection. For example, a guest ordering an entrée may be able to select other items (salad, dressing choice, and vegetable accompaniment and may also receive bread, butter, and a range of condiments) at no additional charge.

Exhibit 8 shows how individual food items (and even supplies) can be summed to determine a total menu item cost. In Exhibit 8, the item being costed is a hamburger. However, this software could also be used to determine the cost of a steak dinner comprising the entrée, one or more vegetables, salad with choice of dressing, rolls and butter, and other items. As individual menu items are costed, they can be electronically added to the entrée cost by use of the "product recipe" window.

Because vegetables offered may vary from day to day (the term "du jour" means "of the day") and because guests may have choices of potato, salad dressing, or other items, it would take an impractical amount of time to determine the standard menu item cost for all the different dinner combinations that are possible, even with the use of point-of-sale systems or other computer applications. For the categories in which the guests have a choice, managers can choose the cost of the most popular item in the category to determine the dinner cost. For example, if guests most often choose baked potatoes, the portion cost of baked potatoes might be used when calculating the standard menu item cost. It is also possible to select the item with the highest portion cost in a category and use this when determining the standard dinner cost. In addition, managers can track the actual number of each item chosen for several days, and then calculate an average cost that can be used when determining the standard dinner cost. Regardless of the method used, planners should be aware of the item cost that is used in calculating the standard menu item cost. Then, when additional items are considered, they can better ensure that the per-portion cost of the new item will be in line with that used in earlier cost calculations.

Calculating Standard Portion Cost: Beverage

Establishing a standard drink cost for beverages is relatively simple because usually there are few ingredients. A standard recipe form, such as the one shown in Exhibit 9, can provide space for listing ingredient costs and calculating the standard drink cost.

All ingredients required are listed, and the bottle size for each liquor ingredient is noted. (Bear in mind that most alcoholic beverages are sold by the liter rather than by the ounce. Therefore, because recipes and bar equipment typically use ounces as a unit of measure, it is usually necessary to convert liters to ounces before making recipe extensions or costing calculations.)

How are ingredient costs calculated? To determine the cost of rye whiskey used in a Manhattan, for example, the price of the bottle of rye whiskey first must be divided by the number of ounces in the bottle to obtain the cost per ounce:

$$\text{Cost per Ounce} \quad = \quad \frac{\$9.65 \text{ (price per liter bottle)}}{33.8 \text{ (ounces per liter bottle)}} \quad = \quad \$0.286 \text{ (rounded)}$$

When calculating a bottle's cost per ounce, some beverage managers deduct an ounce or so before dividing to allow for evaporation or spillage. This will increase the cost per ounce.

If 1.5 ounces of rye whiskey are used in the Manhattan described above, the ingredient cost for rye whiskey is \$0.43 (\$0.286 × 1.5 ounces = \$0.429, or \$0.43 rounded).

The costs of the rye whiskey and the other ingredients used to make the Manhattan are added to calculate the total drink cost.

A drink cost percentage expresses how much of the drink sales price is needed to purchase the ingredients required to prepare the drink. The drink cost percentage is calculated by dividing the cost of the drink by the drink's selling price and

Exhibit 9   Sample Standard Beverage Recipe

ITEM: Manhattan

	Date	Date	Date	Date
	6/19/—			
A) Drink Sales Price	$4.00	$ _____	$ _____	$ _____
B) Drink Cost	.530	$ _____	$ _____	$ _____
C) Drink Cost Percentage	13.3%	_____ %	_____ %	_____ %

Ingredients	Size	Bottle Data 6/19— Cost	Cost	Cost	Cost	Drink Data Size	6/19			
1	2	3	3	3	3	4	5	5	5	5
Whiskey, Rye	L (33.8 oz)	9.65				1.50 oz	.430			
Vermouth, Sweet	750 ML (25.4 oz)	2.69				.75 oz	.080			
Angostura Bitters	16 oz	4.56				dash	.010			
Cherry (stem maraschino)						1 ea.	.010			
Water (Ice)						.75 oz	—			
TOTALS						3 oz	.530			

PREPARATION PROCEDURE:
Place ingredients into a mixing glass. Add ice and stir long enough
to chill. Strain into cocktail glass. Garnish with a stem maraschino
cherry.

GLASS USED: 3^{1}/$_{2}$ oz Line Cocktail.

multiplying by 100. The drink cost percentage for the Manhattan drink in our
example is calculated as follows (assume its selling price is $4.00):

$$\text{Drink Cost Percentage} = \frac{\$0.530 \text{ (drink cost)}}{\$4.00 \text{ (selling price)}} \times 100 = 13.3\%$$

Special Standard Cost Tools for Beverage Control

The five standard cost tools we have discussed—standard purchase specifications,
standard recipes, standard yields, standard portion sizes, and standard portion
costs—are necessary to establish performance standards for both food and beverages. However, two additional standard cost tools are important to the beverage
operation: standard glassware and standard ice size.

Exhibit 10   Sample Review Sheet for Standard Beverage Glassware

Line Cocktail
(4½ oz. lines at 3 oz.)

Collins
(12 oz.)

Champagne
(5½ oz.)

Highball
(8 oz.)

Old Fashioned
(6 oz.)

Line Whiskey
(1½ oz. line at 1¼ oz.)

Red and White
Table Wine
and Champagne
(8½ oz.)

Aperitif or
Dessert Wine
(3 to 5 oz.)

Line Brandy
(2 oz.)

Cordial
(1 oz.)

Whiskey Sour
(6 oz.)

On-the-Rocks
(7 oz.)

Port Wine
(4 oz.)

Brandy Snifter
(5 oz.)

Beer Pilsner
(8 oz.)

Standard Glassware. Glassware obviously affects portion size, quality, and perceived value. In too small a glass, highballs made with mixers such as soda, tonic, or water will be too strong, since less mixer can be added to the standard portion of liquor. Conversely, in too large a glass, the drink will taste weak, since the greater amount of mixer dilutes the standard portion of liquor. Therefore, the standard drink recipe should specify a standard glass size, which should be determined when the beverage recipe is standardized. A standard glassware sheet such as the one shown in Exhibit 10 should be posted in the work area. The same style and size of glass should be used every time the drink is prepared. This means, of course, that sufficient quantities of all necessary glassware must be available at all times.

Glassware is also important in marketing to help carry out a themed atmosphere and enhance the appearance and presentation of the drink. However, while glassware affects presentation (marketing) concerns, it is wise to limit the number of different glasses in inventory. For example, the same glass might be used for ice water, soft drinks, milk, and highballs. If this can be done, problems with the costs of glassware, storage space behind the bar, and training time for bartenders and servers may be reduced.

Standard Ice Size. It is easy to ignore the effect of ice size on drink quality. Although any size ice is suitable for most food service purposes, drink standardization must consider ice cube size. Bigger cubes leave more empty space in the glass because they do not clump together as smaller cubes do. This space must be filled with something. In a liquor-only drink, such as a martini, the amount of beverage appears smaller, unless a larger portion is served. In a mixed drink, the drink will be diluted by adding more mix. On the other hand, small cubes or shaved ice fill up a glass more completely before a beverage is added, but both melt more quickly. Therefore, a delay in serving or consuming the drink may create a diluted taste. Management must therefore consider operating procedures to determine the proper size of ice cubes for the operation.

Recipe Management Software

Throughout this chapter, we have presented some information about the use of computers for establishing food and beverage cost standards. Details about how recipes can be electronically managed will help clarify how technology assists menu planners and recipe writers. Recipe management software maintains three of the most important files used by an integrated food service computer system: an ingredient file, a standard recipe file, and a menu item file. Most other management software programs must access data contained in these files to produce special reports for management.[2]

Ingredient File

Some information about **ingredient files** was presented in an earlier discussion about standard recipes. You learned that they contain important data about each purchased ingredient. In addition to providing the basic information required for recipe development and adjustment, they provide data needed for product purchasing, receiving, storing, and issuing applications.

Ingredient file reports detail usage at current costs and monitor relationships among various product units (such as purchase, issue, and recipe units of the same ingredient). Some ingredient files may specify more than one recipe unit. For example, the recipe unit for bread used for French toast is by the slice; the recipe unit for bread used for stuffing may be by the ounce.

Creating an initial file for each ingredient and making file updates as ingredients are added and purchase prices change (among other reasons) can be challenging, but the benefits outweigh the cost of creating and maintaining the file. The best systems allow the ingredient file to be accessed through other management software programs (especially through inventory software), so ingredient data can

---

Learn More on the Web

While the uses for information contained in ingredient files do not change, the format for them does vary between software providers. For examples of electronic ingredient files and a further explanation of their importance and uses, check out:

- Star Chef (www.chef365.com) – When you reach the site, click on "Products," then "Features," and then "View Demo" within the "Ingredient Database" box.

- CostGuard Foodservice Software (www.costguard.com) – When you reach the site, click on "Products," then "Inventory," then "Tutorial." When you click on "Inventory," you can advance through several screen shots of CostGuard windows applicable to ingredient information.

---

easily be transferred (rather than re-input) to appropriate management software programs.

Since other management software programs rely on data maintained by the ingredient file, it is important that the data contained in the file be accurate. If errors are made when initially entering data, all subsequent processing will be unreliable, and system reports will be relatively worthless.

Standard Recipe File

Computers assist in generating standard recipes by simplifying many of the calculations needed. Numerous software programs are available that both calculate recipe quantities based on estimated unit sales and then print the standard recipe. Exhibit 2 of this chapter illustrates a standard recipe generated by computer.

Standard recipe conversion software converts recipe ingredient amounts to weights and then to ingredient costs. It can also determine nutritional information for an entire meal and define applicable preparation areas (for example, whether ingredients are to be issued or delivered to specific work stations).

Few restaurants purchase all menu item ingredients in ready-to-use or pre-portioned form. Some ingredients are made on the premises. This means that the ingredients within a **standard recipe file** may be either inventory items or references to other recipe files.

Including sub-recipes as ingredients for a particular standard recipe is called **chaining recipes.** Chaining recipes enables the food service computer system to maintain a single record for a particular menu item that includes a number of sub-recipes. When ingredient costs change, recipe management software programs automatically update not only the costs of standard recipes, but also the costs of sub-recipes that are used as ingredients in other standard recipes.

Menu Item File

A **menu item file** consists of information related to the menu items tracked by the **point-of-sale (POS) system.** Important data maintained by this file may include the menu's identification number, descriptor, recipe code number, selling price, ingredient quantities for inventory reporting, and sales totals (by unit).

This file also stores historical information about the actual number of items sold. After a meal period, the actual number of menu items served can be manually entered into the menu item file. Increasingly, however, sales data is automatically transferred from an electronic cash register (ECR) or POS system through an interface to the restaurant's management system. This data can be accessed by management or by sophisticated forecasting programs to project future unit sales, determine the number of ingredient quantities to purchase, and schedule needed personnel. In addition, computer-based sales analysis applications access data in the menu item file to produce various sales analysis reports for management. When menu items, prices, or tax tables need to be changed, the menu item file is accessed, and appropriate changes are entered.

Precost and Postcost Analysis

Precosting yields a standard cost that enables an operator to accurately evaluate a meal plan relative to budgetary plans before service. The precost analysis produces projected cost data based on the application of ingredient costs across recipe offerings. For example, assume a four-entrée menu: tenderloin tips, steak, spaghetti, and lobster tail. Forecasted servings for each are 25, 57, 63, and 23, respectively. After determining each recipe's standard portion cost, the computer will report a food precost for this sales mix. This precost is the result of multiplying the number of projected servings for each entrée by its standard recipe cost and then summing the results.

Computer speed and accuracy assure management of sufficient planning time. Manual equivalent procedures are tedious, cumbersome, and, in many cases, tardy (at best, completed just prior to service).

After meal service, actual sales counts taken from POS tallies are multiplied by standard recipe costs (the same costs as in precost analysis) to produce an ideal food cost. Ideal food cost data can be summed for all meals/days in an accounting period. Then, when an end-of-period physical inventory is taken and actual usage is known, expected product costs based upon POS records can be compared to actual product usage based upon inventory information. Excessive variances suggest the need for tighter control to more effectively manage product costs.

In addition to cost reports, precost and postcost systems can be used as a base to produce purchase orders, stockroom breakout quantities, labor scheduling forecasts, production area reports, and the like. Many operators also elect to use pre- and postcosting for meal period simulations, ingredient substitution evaluation, and potential menu-item trending.

Standard Food Costs

The best sources of information for establishing food cost standards are the property's operating budgets for the current fiscal period and in-house measurements that consider potential costs such as the process described in the previous section.

When standard food costs are known, management is able to compare the cost of food with the revenue it generates. There are several ways to measure food cost. One way expresses costs in terms of total dollars spent on food per day, week, month, or other time period. The more common method of measuring food cost in commercial food and beverage operations is the **food cost percentage.** This expresses cost as a percentage of food revenue, and it is calculated by dividing food costs by food revenue and multiplying by 100. In noncommercial, non-pricing operations, the food cost percentage often measures food cost differently by expressing it as a percentage of total operating expenses rather than as a percentage of revenue. For example, a hospital operating with a 31-percent food cost spends 31 percent of all its allocated operating costs on food purchases. In all cases, the **standard food cost percentage** represents the planned food cost percentage against which actual food costs are measured.

The procedure for calculating food cost percentage begins by first implementing all standard cost tools: standard purchase specifications, recipes, yields, portion sizes, and portion costs. With these tools, the standard food cost for each item is developed following the process discussed earlier.

As you've learned, most POS software tracks the number of each menu item sold and tallies this information for any time period desired. The total of each item sold can then be multiplied by its per-portion standard food cost to arrive at the ideal (theoretical) cost for serving all of that item during the period analyzed. When this process is repeated for all menu items served, and when resulting costs are summed, an ideal cost for the entire period under study can be determined. This is especially appropriate when, for example, the ideal cost (expected cost based on the actual number of each menu item sold) can be compared to the food costs that are actually incurred.

Exhibit 11 shows an abbreviated version of a report that determines the ideal food cost based on actual sales mix. Note that, for each menu item, information about sales (weighted average net sales price, total quantity, total net sales, and percentage of total sales by category) is presented. Also reported is ideal cost information, including cost percentage (total cost divided by total net sales), total food cost (total item cost times quantity sold), and total margin (total net sales minus total cost).

In Exhibit 11, the *Total Food* line represents the sale of all appetizers and soups. The report would normally be expanded to show total sales for all categories of food. You will note that the ideal (theoretical) cost in Exhibit 11 is 28.66 percent (see the *Total FOOD* row where it meets the *Cost %* column). This should represent the correct ideal cost percent if:

- All items sold were recorded and if the applicable revenue was collected.

- Each item was prepared according to the standard recipe.

- Each standard recipe was accurately precosted with current ingredient costs.

Current technology provides food service managers with great cost control benchmarks that are helpful in meeting budget goals. They can easily determine what food costs should be (the ideal cost), which they then can compare with the actual food costs that have been incurred.

Exhibit 11   Calculation of Ideal (Theoretical) Food Costs

Menu Item Theoretical Cost of Sales
Mike Rose Cafe - Beltsville, MD

Report Date: 02/01/1998 to 02/06/1998
Filter: All Groups

M. Bruno
Printed on 02/13/1998 - 12:30 PM

Menu Item Number	Item Name	Sales					Theoretical Costs			
		Weighted Average Net Sales Price	Total Quantity	Total Net Sales	% of Total		Weighted Average Item Cost	Cost %	Total Cost	Total Margin
3	Quesadilla	5.95	42.00	249.90	92.59%		1.67	28.07%	70.14	179.76
4	Beef Ques	5.75	2.00	11.50	4.26%		1.78	30.96%	3.56	7.94
5	Chix Nachos	4.50	1.00	4.50	1.67%		1.78	39.56%	1.78	2.72
6	Chix Ques	4.00	1.00	4.00	1.48%		1.78	44.50%	1.78	2.22
	Appetizers			**$269.90**	**95.83%**			**28.63%**	**$77.26**	**$192.64**
8	French Onion	4.25	1.00	4.25	36.17%		1.15	27.06%	1.15	3.10
10	White Chix Chili	4.25	1.00	4.25	36.17%		1.23	28.94%	1.23	3.02
11	Clam Chowder	3.25	1.00	3.25	27.66%		1.07	32.92%	1.07	2.18
	Soups			**$11.75**	**4.17%**			**29.36%**	**$3.45**	**$8.30**
	Total Food			**$281.65**	**100.00%**			**28.66%**	**$80.71**	**$200.94**
	Total FOOD			**$281.65**	**88.81%**			**28.66%**	**$80.71**	**$200.94**
103	Budweiser	2.75	3.00	8.25	23.24%		0.53	19.27%	1.59	6.66
190	Coors Light	2.75	4.00	11.00	30.99%		0.51	18.55%	2.04	8.96
210	Bass Ale	3.25	5.00	16.25	45.77%		0.63	19.38%	3.15	13.10
	Draft Beer			**$35.50**	**100.00%**			**19.10%**	**$6.78**	**$28.72**
	Total Beer			**$35.50**	**100.00%**			**19.10%**	**$6.78**	**$28.72**
	Total BEVERAGE			**$35.50**	**11.19%**			**19.10%**	**$6.78**	**$28.72**
	Total			**$317.15**	**100.00%**			**27.59%**	**$87.49**	**$229.66**
	Subtotal Discounts			$27.50						$27.50
	Adjusted Total			**$289.65**						**$202.16**

Total net sales in the Food Item

Total net sales in the Beverage

Total net sales in the Food and Beverages

Sales price

Total number of items sold

Total amount in net sales of all items

Percentage of total of items

Total discounts applied to these items

Cost to make the menu item

Total dollar amount made on the menu item

Total dollar amount of food cost per item

Percent cost; total cost divided by total net sales

Courtesy of MICROS Systems, Inc., Columbia, Maryland (www.micros.com).

Calculating Standard Costs per Meal

One final comment about developing standard food costs must be made. Properties offering more than one menu, such as lunch and dinner, must decide whether to develop standard food costs by meal or across all meals. If by-meal food costs are desired, calculations for each meal can be easily done by almost any popular software package. There are two advantages to a separate listing. First, when food cost standards are separated by meals, it is easier to compare any differences between standard and actual costs. Second, since corrective action can focus specifically on the meal period contributing higher-than-expected food costs, the reasons for losses can more quickly be identified and brought under control.

However, there is one serious disadvantage to overcome when standards are established for each separate meal period: actual food costs must also be assessed separately for each meal. The process of determining how much of each food item is actually used for breakfast, lunch, or dinner is very time-consuming. The *actual* cost of food used is based upon inventory-based calculations, which are time-consuming to determine (especially if usage must be separated by meal periods). Most food and beverage managers, therefore, find it more helpful to spend time identifying problems common to all meal periods, such as ineffective purchasing, receiving, storing, and issuing, or problems in production and service, rather than searching for problems applicable to a specific meal period.

Standard Beverage Costs

Standard beverage costs are calculated for exactly the same reason as standard food costs. The manager wants to establish a goal—a base of comparison—against which to measure actual results. Unfortunately, it is difficult to accurately determine expected beverage costs for several reasons:

- There are, literally, tens of thousands of different drinks that can be prepared. While effective bar control systems may classify these drinks into several types (for example, one-ounce drinks, two-ounce drinks, etc.), it is typically necessary for bartenders to properly record each type of drink that is sold if more specific records of drink sales are required.

- Electronic beverage dispensing systems do not typically dispense all types of alcoholic beverages (for example, frozen drinks and bottled beer). When mistakes or abuses in the sale of non-controlled items occur, they can create errors in tallies of expected beverage costs.

- There are a wide variety of food-related products used to prepare many alcoholic drinks, including juices, ice cream, and food garnishes. These food products should be considered part of beverage costs because they generate beverage-related revenue. However, the cost of these items is frequently managed with less caution in beverage operations than in food production areas.

For these and related reasons, most beverage managers base their expected beverage cost on budgets developed from actual information generated from previous sales periods. At the same time, they closely monitor ongoing operations to ensure that required basic operating procedures are consistently followed:

- Standard beverage recipes are used whenever drinks are prepared.

- Portion control tools (shot glasses, jiggers) and standard glassware are used in preparing every drink.

- Managers must approve all complimentary drinks. Staff must save all drinks returned because of mistakes. Special precautions to minimize the possibility of guest "walkouts" and errors in guest checks are used.

Managers sometimes work behind the bar to ensure that required procedures are followed consistently. When not working the bar, they carefully supervise operations to ensure compliance with all standard operating procedures.

Exhibit 12 shows how a beverage cost percentage is calculated. Because actual beverage costs typically include inventory calculations, beverage managers—especially in operations with more than one bar—have a challenge similar to that of food production managers in serving menus for different meal periods. When actual beverage costs are based upon changes in beverage inventories, it is not possible to determine actual beverage costs for specific bar outlets. This is because bar outlets typically share the same central beverage storage areas. Therefore, the tally

Exhibit 12   Calculation of Beverage Cost Percentage

Value of Inventory Behind Bar at the Beginning of Period
+ Value of Issues to the Bar During the Period
− Value of Inventory Behind Bar at the End of Period
= Gross Beverage Cost

+ Value of Transfers to Bar During the Period
− Value of Transfers from Bar During the Period
− Cost of Complimentary Drinks (if any)
= Net Beverage Cost

$$\frac{\textbf{Net Beverage Cost}}{\textbf{Beverage Revenue During Period}} \times 100 = \begin{array}{c}\textbf{Standard}\\ \textbf{Beverage Cost}\\ \textbf{Percentage}\end{array}$$

of issues to specific bar outlets during a specific counting period becomes even more important.

As with the standard food cost percentage, the standard beverage cost percentage is a goal that managers of the beverage operation should work toward. Unfortunately, many factors affect actual practice. Errors may occur, beverage operation controls may gradually become looser, or changes in policy may require revised procedures. These and other factors (the potential for theft of product and/ or beverage revenue, for example) reinforce the value of emphasizing standard beverage cost expectations when examining actual operating results. The beverage manager should understand that when actual beverage costs exceed standard beverage costs, a problem may exist.

Computerized Standard Beverage Cost Calculations

Revenues from beverage sales and the products themselves are both theft-prone. Special attention is required to control these resources. Once again, the first step in the control process is to establish standards. Computerized standard beverage cost calculations are increasingly used to determine the expected beverage cost. Point-of-sale technology makes this simple.

With many systems, sales of each liquor type (bar whiskey, Bombay Sapphire gin, frozen daiquiri, etc.) are tracked as part of the process by which the bartender rings up a sale. At the end of the shift, the total ounces of each type of liquor that should have been dispensed according to standard recipes/portion sizes are determined. Also, the total beverage cost for the shift can be determined, and the standard beverage cost percentage can be assessed. Since the POS system tracks both sales (number of ounces) and revenues (charges for the drinks), this calculation can be made easily and quickly.

Information about ideal (theoretical) beverage cost, beverage revenues, and beverage cost percentages can be carried forward for whatever time period the manager desires. It then becomes possible to compare the theoretical or expected results with the actual results from the period.

> ### Learn More on the Web
>
> Beverage revenues are best controlled when dispensing devices are interfaced with the property's POS system. Then portion sizes can be measured at the same time sales are tallied, and the revenues that should have been generated will be known.
>
> Berg Controls (www.berg-controls.com) is a leading manufacturer of electronic beverage dispensing systems. Its website provides an overview of the liquor and draft beer dispensing systems developed by the company. Additionally, the website includes the company's manuals and brochures.

Use of Standard Costs in Multi-Unit Operations

Unit managers in chain organizations typically have much less discretion in establishing food and beverage cost standards than do their counterparts in independently owned and operated properties. In a multi-unit operation, menus are typically established at the corporate level; this practice affects standard recipes, including the ingredients used. Purchase specifications for the ingredients are likely developed by chefs or skilled food technicians, a practice that affects both the quality and cost of the products prepared from the recipes. In the case of company-owned units, suppliers for the units may also be selected at the corporate level. Multi-unit chains often negotiate national contracts with manufacturers/distributors who are then responsible to supply applicable items to individual units. U.S. law prohibits franchisers from requiring that franchisees purchase products from the franchisers' commissaries or other specified sources, thus allowing franchisees to purchase from whomever they desire. However, no matter what supplier is selected, the items purchased must meet specifications established by the franchiser.

At times, a franchisee or a unit manager may suggest a new menu item or develop a new recipe deemed appropriate for the menu. In most organizations, this item would be evaluated at a corporate-level test kitchen facility and field-tested in one or more units before being added to the menu chain-wide.

Automated systems such as those discussed throughout this chapter will likely be specified by the organization for local use. Large organizations may develop their own system for use by unit managers and higher-level organization officials to plan standards and monitor subsequent results.

The food standards points noted also apply to beverage standards. For example, multi-unit organizations likely specify brands of alcoholic beverages to be offered at each unit, develop promotional campaigns that influence the beverages sold at each unit, and require the use of specific data collection systems to monitor actual operating results.

Endnotes

1. 16 cups (in gallon) × 0.23 gallons = 3.68 cups (approximately 3.75 [3¾] cups).

2. For a detailed explanation of computer applications and recipe management software, see Michael L. Kasavana and John J. Cahill, *Managing Technology in the Hospitality Industry*, 5th ed. (Lansing, Mich.: American Hotel & Lodging Educational Institute, 2007).

 **Key Terms**

adjustment factor—The number by which the amount of each ingredient indicated in a standard recipe is multiplied to increase or decrease the recipe's yield, determined by dividing the desired yield by the original yield.

chaining recipes—Including sub-recipes as ingredients for a particular standard recipe. This enables the food service computer system to maintain a single record for a particular menu item that includes a number of sub-recipes.

cost factor—A constant value that may be used to convert new "as purchased" (AP) prices into a revised cost per servable pound, assuming that the standard purchase specifications, standard recipe, and standard yield remain the same. The cost factor is determined by dividing the cost per servable pound by the original "as purchased" (AP) cost per pound.

cost per servable pound—Information needed to calculate standard portion costs, determined by dividing the "as purchased" (AP) price by the yield percentage as a decimal.

ethnic cuisine—Food (menu items) that are popular with a group of persons who share a common and distinctive national, religious, or cultural heritage.

food cost percentage—In relation to commercial food and beverage operations, food cost percentage expresses cost as a percentage of revenue and is calculated by dividing food costs by food revenue and multiplying by 100; in relation to institutional food and beverage operations, the food cost percentage expresses cost as a percentage of expenses and is calculated by dividing food costs by total operating expenses and multiplying by 100.

ingredient file—An electronic record that contains important data on each purchased ingredient, such as ingredient code number, description, purchase unit, purchase unit cost, issue unit, issue unit cost, and recipe unit cost.

menu item file—A file containing information related to the menu items tracked by the point-of-sale (POS) system.

point-of-sale (POS) system—A computerized system that records sales, prints guest checks, and tallies sales and related information, including numerous reports for management use.

portion control tools—Items such as weighing and measuring equipment, ladles and scoops to portion food, jiggers and shot glasses for beverages, and automated beverage-dispensing equipment. These tools must be available and used every time a recipe or beverage is prepared.

precosting—The process of determining the costs of ingredients used in a standard recipe to arrive at a standard portion cost for one item yielded by the recipe.

production (food)—The process of getting food ready for service, which is comprised of three steps: preparation, cooking, and holding.

production loss—The difference between the raw or "as purchased" (AP) weight and the prepared or "edible portion" (EP) weight.

purchase specification—A concise description of the quality, size, weight, count, and other quality factors desired for a particular item.

standard food cost percentage—The planned food cost percentage against which actual food costs are measured.

standard portion cost—The cost of preparing and serving one portion of food or one drink item according to the standard recipe.

standard portion size—The quantity (for example, weight, number of ounces, or cost) of a menu item to be derived from a standard recipe.

standard recipe—A formula for producing a food or beverage item. The formula provides a summary of ingredients, the required quantity of each, specific preparation procedures, portion size and portioning equipment, garnish information, and any other information necessary to prepare the item.

standard recipe file—An electronic record that contains recipes for menu items. Important data included are recipe code number, recipe name, ingredients, preparation instructions, number of portions, portion size, cost of ingredients, menu selling price, and food cost percentage.

standard yield—Results when an item is produced according to established standard production procedures outlined in the standard recipe; for example, if the standard purchase specifications are followed and a meat item is properly trimmed, cooked, and portioned, the actual yield should closely approximate the standard yield.

sub-recipe—A recipe that yields an ingredient, such as sauce, that is used for another recipe.

value—The relationship between price and quality.

yield—The net weight or volume of a food item after it has been processed and made ready for sale to the guest.

yield factor—See yield percentage.

yield percentage—The ratio of servable weight to original weight, calculated by dividing the servable weight by the original weight and multiplying by 100.

yield test—A test performed on products to determine their standard yield.

 # Review Questions

1. What problems arise when standard food purchase specifications are not used?

2. How can existing procedures for preparing foods be incorporated into standard recipes?

3. How can knowledge of standard yields assist food buyers in determining which products are the "best" buy?

4. What is a standard portion size? What are advantages to its use?

5. Why are standard portion costs important?

6. How are standard portion costs developed?

7. What is meant by "chaining recipes"?

8. What can (should) be done if ingredient costs for standard recipes increase significantly? How does this increase affect standard portion costs?

9. How are the standard food costs for a complete dinner developed?

10. What is the primary advantage of using ideal costs for calculating standard food costs?

11. How can managers use ideal cost information to monitor and control their operation?

12. How is sales information for beverage operations the same as for food operations? What information is different?

13. What are ways in which technology has made it easier for managers to plan for and monitor food and beverage standards?

Internet Sites

For more information, visit the following Internet sites. Remember that Internet addresses can change without notice. If the site is no longer there, you can use a search engine to look for additional sites.

Recipe Management Software

CALCMENU
www.calcmenu.com

Comus Restaurant Systems
www.comus.com

CostGuard Foodservice Software
www.costguard.com

Culinary Software Services
www.culinarysoftware.com

Eatec Corporation
www.eatec.com

FoodSoftware.com
www.foodsoftware.com

FOOD-TRAK Software
www.foodtrak.com

MenuLink Computer Solutions
www.menulinkinc.com

Radiant Systems Inc.
www.radiantsystems.com

Hospitality Glassware

Libbey, Inc.
www.libbey.com

Bar Supply Warehouse
www.barsupplywarehouse.com

Beverage Dispensing Equipment

Berg Company
www.berg-controls.com

Easybar Liquor Systems
www.easybar.com

Other Culinary-Related Websites

American Culinary Federation
www.acfchefs.org

Chef Talk
www.cheftalk.com

ChefDesk
www.chefdesk.com

Society of Mad Chefs
www.madchefs.com

 Problems ———————————————————————————

Problem 1

Several yield tests for roasting rounds of beef have been carefully undertaken. A summary of results (average per round) follows:

As purchased (AP) Weight = 22 lb 7 oz *359*
Servable Weight = 17 lb 10 oz *282*
Cost (AP) = $6.95 per lb

a. What is the cost per servable pound?

b. Use the above information to determine the number of pounds of rounds to purchase for a weekend buffet being planned for 275 guests (six [EP—on the plate] ounces will be served to each guest)

c. Use the above information to calculate a cost factor and then use the cost factor to determine the revised cost per servable pound when the AP price of the round rises to $7.45 per pound.

d. Using the revised cost per servable pound, calculate the per portion cost for the six-ounce portion that will be provided on the buffet.

Problem 2

A yield test is done on three beef rounds. The as-purchased (AP) and edible portion (EP) data is shown below:

	AP (Original) Weight	EP (Servable) Weight
round #1	19 lb 12 oz	16 lb 2 oz
round #2	21 lb 13 oz	17 lb 15 oz
round #3	20 lb 9 oz	16 lb 14 oz

1. What is the yield ratio (ratio of servable weight to original weight) for each round?

2. What do the percentage numbers generated in the above calculations mean?

3. What is the *average* yield ratio (ratio of servable weight to original weight) for the three rounds calculated above?   *82 %*

4. What is the cost per servable pound for each of the above rounds if the purchase (AP) cost is $6.15 per pound?

5. What do the costs per servable pound for the three rounds in question 4 actually represent?

6. What is the *average* cost per servable pound in question 4?

7. How many pounds of round must be purchased to serve five ounces (edible portion—on the plate) to 300 guests using the average yield ratio calculated in question 3?

8. How many rounds must be purchased to prepare the required number of portions needed for the banquet?

Problem 3

Following is cost per servable pound and AP price information for rounds of beef purchased by three restaurants.

Restaurant	Cost per Servable Pound	AP Price	
A	$8.95	$5.95	1.50
B	$10.12	$6.10	1.65
C	$11.70	$6.20	1.88

a. What is the cost factor for each restaurant?

b. How can a restaurant manager use the cost factor?

Problem 4

What is the new cost per servable pound using cost factors in Problem 3 above when the AP price changes in each restaurant?

Restaurant	New AP Price		Cost Factor	
A	$6.20	✗	1.50	= 9.30
B	$6.35	✗	1.66	10.54
C	$6.75	✗	1.89	12.75

Problem 5

The original recipe yields 75 five-ounce servings; the chef desires 100 six-ounce servings. What is the new quantity for each of the following ingredients in the recipe? Express the revised quantities in amounts that are easiest for the cooks to weigh/measure.

Ingredient	Original Quantity
Brown Sugar	2 pounds
Fluid Milk	3 quarts
Dry Mustard	1 tablespoon

3.2 32 oz
1 gallon 30+ 4.8
1.6

3 lb 2 oz   75, 5 ounce servings

$$\frac{100 \times 6\ oz}{75 \times 5\ oz} = \frac{600\ oz}{375\ oz} = 1.6$$

Problem 6

What is the easiest way to express each of the following in a standard recipe?

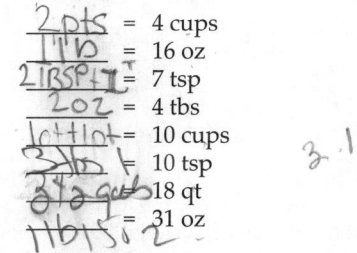

2 pts	= 4 cups
1 lb	= 16 oz
2 TBSP + 1 =	7 tsp
2 oz	= 4 tbs
10 ttlnt =	10 cups
3 tb =	10 tsp
3 gct = 18 qt	
1 lb 15 oz 2 =	31 oz

3.1

Problem 7

What is the adjustment factor in each of the following situations?

Original Recipe	**New Recipe (Desired Yield)**
60 3-oz servings	80 3-oz servings
70 5-oz servings	45 5-oz servings
80 ½-cup servings	100 ½-cup servings
50 ¾-cup servings	35 ¾-cup servings

Problem 8

What is the adjustment factor in each of the following situations?

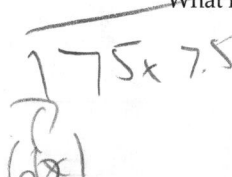

Original Recipe	**New Recipe (Desired Yield)**
60 1-cup servings	75 ¾-cup servings
45 ¾-cup servings	30 ½-cup servings
90 4-oz servings	80 6-oz servings
125 3-oz servings	200 4-oz servings

Problem 9

What is the quantity of each ingredient required to produce the desired recipes?

Ingredient	Original Quantity	Desired Recipe Adjustment Factor
Brown Sugar	3 pounds 12 oz	1.4
Fluid Whole Milk	2 quarts	1.4
Salt	1½ tablespoons	1.4

Problem 10

Cost the following recipe and calculate the per portion cost:

Recipe: Baked Lasagna
Yield: 30 servings

Ingredient	Amount Needed	Purchase Unit	Cost/ Purchase Unit
Lasagna Noodles	3 lb	10-lb box	$11.71
Garlic Cloves	6 cloves	lb	1.01
Olive Oil	¾ cup	4 1-gal/case	62.09
Onion, diced	3 cups	20 lb	14.33
Ground Beef	3 lb	10-lb poly bag	22.17
Tomato Sauce	3 qt	6 #10/case	16.25
Oregano	1½ tsp	5-oz can	1.93
Ricotta cheese	3 cup	2 5-lb/case	13.70
Mozzarella cheese	2¼ lb	5 lb	14.55
Romano cheese	¾ cup	5 lb	22.97
Hints:			

Conversions are available from: Francis T. Lynch, *The Book of Yields: Accuracy in Food Costing and Purchasing,* 7th ed. (Hoboken, N.J.: Wiley, 2007).

Onion   3.72 cups per pound
Garlic   15 cloves per head; 1.85 ounces per head = 0.04
Oregano   one tablespoon = $^1/_{10}$ ounce
Ricotta cheese 8.68 ounces per cup
Romano cheese (assume similar to parmesan)   4.7 cups per pound

Chapter Appendix

Weight and measurement conversions can be used for chapter problems and for questions that arise in food and beverage operations. An excellent website that assists with many types of conversion is www.onlineconversion.com.

Weight & Measurement Conversions

kilogram × 2.204 = pounds (1 kg = 2.2 lb)
grams × 0.035 = ounces (100 g = 3.5 oz)
ounce × 28 = grams (1 oz = 28 g)
liter × 2.1 = pints (1 liter = 2.1 pt)
liter × 1.06 = quarts (1 liter = 1.06 qt)
cups × 0.24 = liters (5 c = 1.05 liters)
gallons × 3.8 = liters (1 gal = 3.8 liters)

Celsius temperature × 9/5, add 32 = ° Fahrenheit   Note: ⅘ = 1.8
Fahrenheit temperature minus 32, × 5/9 = ° Celsius   Note: ⅝ = 0.55
0° Celsius = 32° Fahrenheit
100° Celsius = 212° Fahrenheit

3 teaspoons = 1 tablespoon	2 cups = 1 pint
4 tablespoons = ¼ cup	4 cups = 1 quart
8 tablespoons = ½ cup	4 quarts = 1 U.S. gallon
16 tablespoons = 1 cup	8 quarts = 1 peck (dry)
1 cup = 8 fluid ounces	16 ounces = 1 pound

200°F to 205°F = 95°C
220°F to 225°F = 105°C
245°F to 250°F = 120°C
275°F to 275°F = 135°C
300°F to 305°F = 150°C
325°F to 330°F = 165°C
345°F to 350°F = 175°C
370°F to 375°F = 190°C
400°F to 405°F = 205°C
425°F to 430°F = 220°C
445°F to 450°F = 230°C
470°F to 475°F = 245°C
500°F = 260°C

WEIGHT

grams/pounds/ounces
1 kilogram = 2.204 pounds
1 gram = 0.035 ounces
1 pound = 0.454 kilograms
1 ounce = 28 grams

VOLUME

liters/gallons/quarts/pints/cups/ounces
1 milliliter = 0.03 ounce
1 liter = 4.4 cups
1 liter = 2.1 pints
1 liter = 1.06 quarts
1 liter = 0.26 gallon
1 teaspoon = 5 milliliters
1 tablespoon = 15 milliliters
1 fluid ounce = 28 milliliters
1 cup = 0.24 liter
1 pint = 0.47 liter
1 quart = 0.95 liter
1 gallon = 3.8 liters

¼ tsp = 1.25 ml
½ tsp = 2.5 ml
¾ tsp = 3.75 m
1 tsp = 5 ml
1 ½ tsp = 7.5 ml
1 ¼ tsp = 6.25 ml
1 ¾ tsp = 8.75 ml
2 tsp = 10 ml
1 tablespoon (tbs) = 15 ml
2 tbs = 30 ml
1 fluid ounces (fl oz) = 30 ml
¼ cup (c) = 0.06 liter
½ c = 0.12 liter
¾ c = 0.18 liter

1 c = 0.24 liter
1¼ c = 0.3 liter
1½ c = 0.36 liter
1 pint (pt) = 0.47 liter
2 c = 0.48 liter
2½ c = 0.6 liter
3 c = 0.72 liter
3½ c = 0.84 liter
1 quart (qt) = 0.95 liter
4 c = 0.96 liter
4½ c = 1.08 liters
5 c = 1.2 liters
5½ c = 1.32 liters
1 ounce (oz) = 28 grams (g)
1 lb = 0.45 kg

Chapter 4 Outline

Competencies

1. Describe the importance and function of an operating budget as a planning and control tool. (pp. 97–99)

2. Distinguish bottom-up budgeting from top-down budgeting, and discuss budget reforecasting. (pp. 99–102)

3. Identify factors that managers consider when projecting revenues in the budgeting process. (pp. 102–104)

4. Describe the two basic ways profit can be treated when budgeting, and identify how fixed, variable, and mixed costs change in response to changes in the sales volume of a food and beverage operation. (pp. 104–106)

5. Distinguish the mark-up method from the percentage method of estimating expenses in the budgeting process, describe zero-based budgeting, and discuss special concerns when estimating beverage expenses. (pp. 106–108)

6. Calculate and interpret variances for revenue and expense items for food and beverage operations. (pp. 108–117)

7. Describe how computers help with the budget process. (pp. 117–120)

8. Given relevant cost factors, use a cost-volume-profit equation to calculate the revenues required to reach desired profit levels. (pp. 120–125)

Operations Budgeting and Cost-Volume-Profit Analysis

IN COMMERCIAL FOOD AND BEVERAGE OPERATIONS, budgets are planning and control tools because managers use them to forecast future revenues, expenses, and profits. In noncommercial food and beverage operations, budgets are just as important. They help to ensure that planned expenses do not exceed anticipated revenues and, if required, that an operating surplus ("profit") can be generated. An operating budget is not an obstacle to efficient performance to be prepared and followed only when top management insists. In fact, operating budgets are critical for planning the profit requirements of food and beverage operations. The budget is your best forecast for the future.

Operating budgets are an excellent source of estimated revenue and cost information that can represent planned performance standards. Actual operating data can then be compared against budgeted information to determine the extent to which financial plans are attained and whether corrective action is required to improve performance.

But establishing cost standards is only one use of this important control tool. In this chapter we will see that an operating budget is necessary for many other reasons. This chapter also examines an important financial planning tool—cost-volume-profit (CVP) analysis. Managers can use CVP analysis to determine the revenues required at any desired profit level. Sometimes referred to as "break-even analysis," CVP reviews the relationships among costs, revenue, and profits associated with alternative plans.

The Budget Process: An Overview

An **operating budget** is a plan that estimates how much revenue will be generated and what expenses will be incurred to meet financial requirements and goals. There are several different types of budgets—long-term, short-term, capital, and cash, for example. The type of budget most useful to a food and beverage operation is a short-term (one-year) operating budget that covers items affecting the income statement. The budget is a constant reminder of the amount of revenue planned. And, just as crucial for purposes of control, information stemming from the budget defines the amount of allowable expenses. If these limits are exceeded, budgeted profits decrease unless expenses are reduced in other areas and/or revenue increases beyond the anticipated level.

Exhibit 1   How the Operating Budget Drives the Control Process

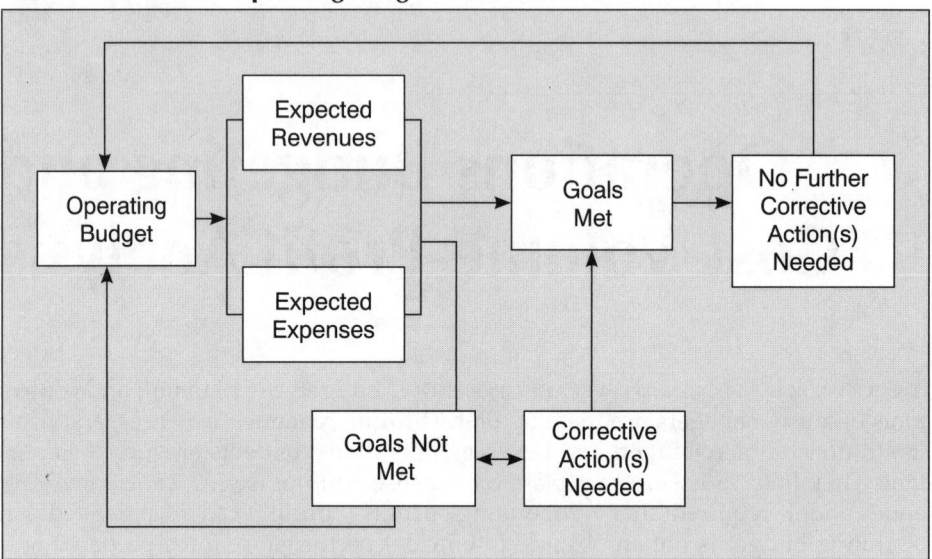

Once developed, the budget becomes an important part of the control process. The budget plan tells managers how much money can be spent in each expense category. When actual revenue falls below forecasted levels or when actual expenses exceed budget estimates, managers know there may be problems. Corrective action can then be implemented on a timely basis.

Because the budget provides anticipated revenue and cost figures, it enables the calculation of a budgeted food cost percentage (budgeted food cost divided by budgeted food revenue multiplied by 100) and a budgeted beverage cost percentage (budgeted beverage cost divided by budgeted beverage revenue multiplied by 100). In a similar way, benchmarks for all other expenses—such as labor and energy costs—can also be calculated. These budget percentages can later be compared with percentages representing actual operating results to measure the food and beverage manager's effectiveness in meeting budget goals. An overview of the process by which the operating budget drives the control process is presented in Exhibit 1.

Note that the operating budget indicates expected revenues and expenses. If goals are met, no further corrective action is needed. However, if budget goals are not met, corrective action is needed until budget goals are met, after which no further corrective action is needed. If budget goals are met, the actual operating results will have a direct influence on the development of the next operating budget. Also, even if budget goals are not met, those areas that fail to meet the manager's expectations must be considered when the new budget is developed (for example, budget standards that perhaps were set too high and must be revised downward).

Managers have two special concerns when they establish operating budget standards. The goals set for revenue, profit requirements, and operating expenses (1) must be attainable and (2) must not compromise established quality requirements. If standards are impossible to attain, personnel may become frustrated, and the operation could deteriorate. For example, if food costs have averaged 45 percent, achieving a budgeted goal of 38 percent may not be possible, at least within a single fiscal period. Moreover, food and beverage managers must also be concerned about quality standards. In our example, the options available to achieve the 38-percent projected food cost include raising prices, reducing portion sizes, or purchasing lower-quality products. However, these options will likely be unacceptable because they will reduce perceived value for the operation's guests. Management should set minimum quality standards based on the expectations of the target markets. This helps ensure that standards will not be compromised as the budget plan is developed and implemented.

When necessary, management can use the budget not only to evaluate past efforts but to plan corrective action for the future as well. A current period's budget is often used to develop the budgets for the next fiscal period. Information from the current budget can be the basis for beginning the budget process for the next fiscal year. Also, since the budget helps define responsibilities, management personnel can be held responsible for meeting revenue goals and keeping all operating costs within budgeted limits. When actual figures are over or under budget, responsibility can correctly be assigned to the manager in charge.

In small food and beverage operations, the owner/manager generally develops the budget. In larger operations, other staff members provide important help. For example, department heads, whose performance will be judged by the extent to which they attain budget goals, might be assigned to plan expense levels for their areas of responsibility, in consultation with senior management personnel. In still larger operations, a budget committee may review department revenue and expense plans before a final property-wide budget is approved.

Budgeting in Multi-Unit Operations

The budget development process described in this chapter works well in a single-unit operation, where all profit must be generated by a single property. But how should budgets be developed in multi-unit operations, where ownership is concerned about total profits from all operations?

There are basically two methods for developing operating budgets in multi-unit operations. One method uses a **bottom-up budgeting** approach in which operating budgets are assembled at the unit level and are "rolled" up the organization. Another approach is referred to as **top-down budgeting**. With this plan, budgets are developed at the corporate level and passed down to lower organizational levels, with each successively lower level becoming responsible for a specific segment of the budget.

The main advantage of using bottom-up budgeting is that budget plans are geared specifically toward the individual operation. When budgets are developed for a specific operation by the unit manager, the lower-level participation yields a budget that is "our plan," not a plan thrust upon lower management by higher organizational levels. The "ownership" this creates helps the unit manager recognize the importance—and feasibility—of the operating budget, and it provides an incentive for the unit manager and his or her team to meet budget goals. Likewise,

---

Multi-Unit Budgets

How much input does the unit manager have in developing the operating budget? The answer really depends on the corporate culture of the organization. The operating budget of a single unit will likely need to be approved not only by the area manager but also by others at higher levels in the organization. Frequently, the unit manager and area manager work together to create a budget. After agreement, it is then moved forward to the corporate level, at which point the proposed budget is accepted, modified, or rejected. If it is not accepted, a negotiation process is typically used to arrive at consensus about the "numbers."

Technology helps immeasurably with the budgeting process; details about actual operating results are tracked, stored, and readily available at all organizational levels, and this is important input in the budgeting process.

The unit manager should be best informed about how to estimate controllable costs such as food (within the parameters established by the menu planned at the corporate level), labor, and supplies. The area manager typically has a better ability to look at the "bigger" picture, such as the impact of corporate requirements. He or she will also know benchmark revenues and expenses based on data from the other properties for which he or she is responsible. Top-level (corporate) managers will likely have the best knowledge about fixed costs, benefits, advertising and marketing plans, and overall profitability expectations.

---

bottom-up budgeting enables budget planners to focus on specific units and the unique challenges likely to be encountered in them.

Unfortunately, corporate-level managers encounter a problem when the sum of profits planned by individual units generating their own operating budgets does not equal the profit requirements of the corporation. For example, a restaurant may be owned by a parent organization that mandates a profit contribution larger than that planned to be generated by the individual units. This points to an advantage of top-down budgeting.

In addition to helping plan for corporate-level profit expectations, top-down budgeting has other potential advantages. For example, unit managers in specific properties may not be aware of marketing commitments, advertising campaigns, menu changes, and other factors that can have a significant impact on operating budgets within an individual unit.

In practice, budget planners in multi-unit organizations often use a give-and-take method that first develops tentative budget plans and then modifies them to yield realistic expectations for individual properties. Psychological aspects of budget development must also be considered and incorporated into budget development strategies. For example, unit managers may wish to send conservative estimates "up the organization," and, conversely, top-level managers may wish to suggest more aggressive budget goals.

Budget Reforecasting

Budgets are developed several months before the start of the food and beverage operation's fiscal year. As such, future events that could affect revenue and expense levels cannot be accurately forecasted. Consider, for example, that an operating budget for November of a specific year was likely planned 12 months or longer before the period to which it applies. Since the operating budget is a critical control tool, it is important to have updated information against which to compare actual operating results.

Many food and beverage operations use a method called **reforecasting** to update budgets. For example, if revenue trends during the budget year are significantly different than expected, revised revenue estimates for the budget may be developed. This same approach is used to consider realistic expense estimates based on actual performance during the earlier parts of the budget year.

Reforecasting is most easily accomplished when all expenses are expressed as a percentage of revenue. Then, as revenue estimates increase or decrease, affected operating expenses can be adjusted accordingly. Assume the following, for example:

Expense	Original Budget (Revenue = $740,000)		Reforecasted Budget (Revenue = $680,000)
Direct operating expense	(5%)	$37,000	$34,000
Advertising	(2%)	$14,800	$13,600
Administrative/general	(4%)	$29,600	$27,200
Repairs/materials	(1%)	$ 7,400	$ 6,800

The original budget estimated revenue at $740,000 and established percentages of this revenue as targets for the four categories of expenses illustrated. For example, 5 percent of the original revenue was allocated to direct expenses ($740,000 × 0.05 = $37,000). If the actual level of revenue is now forecasted downward to $680,000, only $34,000 ($680,000 × 0.05) should be spent on direct operating expenses.

It is important to note, however, that some costs such as salaries, rent, and insurance are considered **fixed costs** and cannot be changed when revenue levels vary. Therefore, as revenue levels decrease, these costs will require a larger percentage of total revenue. Some adjustments in other cost categories will be required to compensate for the larger share of revenue required by the fixed costs. The resulting lower profits can create significant financial challenges for owners and investors who rely on profits for financial commitments. Wise managers recognizing the need for long-term survival and the growth of their business do not cut costs in the short term to increase profit dollars unless they can do so without affecting guest perceptions of the business. Many managers have tried to defer maintenance costs, eliminate training hours, and find other shortcuts to reduce costs. Often, however, these tactics lead to a spiraling downturn in quality standards from which the operation may never recover.

It is a better strategy to develop creative plans to increase revenues, if possible, while at the same time examining ways to reduce costs without affecting guest value. Operators serving alcoholic beverages recognize that food and beverage services are interrelated. Successful efforts to increase revenues and/or to reduce costs in one segment (such as the beverage operation) can help the business during times of decreased profits in the other (food) business segment.

When reforecasting has been completed, food and beverage managers can use information from income statements to compare actual operating results with:

- Budgeted revenue and expense levels—both for the current period and for to-date results during the budget year.

- Reforecasted revenue and expense information—both for the month and fiscal year-to-date.

Three Steps of Budget Development

There are three major steps in the process of developing a budget: forecasting expected revenue, calculating required profit levels, and calculating projected costs incurred in generating the forecasted revenue. Although it is useful to divide the process of budget development into these three steps, the last two steps really belong to the same phase of budget development, because the profit requirement can really be considered as one of the "costs" assessed in calculating expenses. This concept of treating profit as a cost is explained later in the chapter. Fortunately, technology provides increasing assistance in the budget development process, and we will explore its role after discussing the basics of budget development.

Step 1: Calculate Projected Revenue Levels

The first step in the budget development process is to estimate revenue levels. In hotel and restaurant operations, forecasts are normally made separately for food and beverage revenues. This helps managers pinpoint operating problems during the budget period. (If budgets are based on combined food and beverage revenues, it will not be as easy for managers to assess whether revenues from both sources are on- or off-target.) When accurate **guest check averages** are available, some managers combine food and beverage revenues when developing budgets. In this case, revenue forecasts are based on the number of guests anticipated for the period covered by the budget. Revenue forecasts are determined by multiplying the number of anticipated guests by the amount of the average guest check. Then, as other factors are considered, this forecast may be increased (for example, if selling prices are planned to increase during the period covered by the budget) or decreased (for example, if fewer guests are anticipated because of major road construction in front of the restaurant).

Projected revenue calculations should be made on at least a monthly basis. Calculating revenue projections on a weekly basis would provide even more specific information and perhaps increased accuracy. Individual estimates can then be combined into an annual revenue forecast. Using either monthly or weekly projections, managers can later compare actual revenue with budgeted revenue and actual expenses against budgeted expenses as part of the corrective action process. Generally, figures for past revenue levels can be obtained from monthly income statements. Collecting revenue figures is made relatively easy by today's common use of computerized systems that list monthly to-date and other statistics that yield revenue data of any type managers require. This also makes it easy to note and track trends between fiscal periods.

Many factors affect the development of revenue forecasts. In fact, anything that affects revenue levels affects the development of revenue forecasts. For instance, internal sales promotion plans or scheduled remodeling could have a strong impact on revenue. Consequently, projected revenue for the coming fiscal period may need to be adjusted to account for these plans. Important elements to consider in determining revenue estimates include revenue histories, current factors, economic variables, and other factors.

Revenue Histories. Useful forecasts for the new budget period can be developed by analyzing past revenue levels and identifying trends. For example, if revenue histories show that food and beverage revenue has increased by an average of eight percent for each of the past five years, then revenue for the upcoming period could be estimated by simply adding eight percent to the current revenue level. This assumes that the revenue growth of the past will continue in the future.

Current Factors. There are many factors over which the property has little or no control that may affect revenue during the new budget period. New competition, street improvement projects, or even the weather can have a strong impact on revenue levels. Social issues, such as liability laws regarding the sale and service of alcoholic beverages, can affect alcoholic beverage revenue.[1] Budgeted revenue figures based on revenue histories and trend studies would need to be adjusted if any of these factors will affect the business.

Economic Variables. As costs increase during periods of inflation, selling prices for food and beverage products must also be increased. At the same time, the public's habits and lifestyles are affected by economic conditions. When inflation rises, guests often demand greater value for their money. Some guests may "trade down" and replace their usual dining experiences with less expensive meals in lower-priced restaurants. Other guests may simply "trade out" and enjoy more meals at home with their families.

Other Factors. Properties offering both food and beverages must estimate total revenue levels for both services. As noted previously, when making projections for food and beverage operations, revenue and expenses should normally be kept separate so that each can be controlled separately. Many lodging properties use the concept of **derived demand**, in which estimates of room revenue are used to help project revenue from food, beverages, and other revenue centers based on guest spending patterns that have been developed from in-house studies. The hotel food and beverage manager must still calculate the impact of banquet operations and local community spending patterns separately to determine the total operating budget for the food and beverage department.

Special Concerns in Forecasting Beverage Revenue. Few small beverage operations develop specific budget revenue estimates for individual beverage products such as beer, wine, liquor, and soft drinks. Rather, they assume that each beverage product will generate the same percentage of total beverage revenue in each budget period. For example, if liquor has been responsible for 70 percent of beverage revenue in past years, beverage managers may assume that it will continue to contribute 70 percent of future beverage revenue. However, beverage managers should carefully review trends in these percentage-of-revenue statistics. Wine, sparkling water, and non-alcoholic specialty drinks are generating an increased proportion of beverage revenue in many places. Where this is true, other products, such as liquor, will contribute a reduced percentage of revenue.

Decisions regarding the percentage of total beverage revenue applicable to each product are relatively easy to make when electronic cash registers or other point-of-sale devices are used to record information about beverage revenue by category. In operations that do not use such computerized equipment, it may be necessary to base product revenue percentages on administrative judgment. In such a case, perhaps a trial period for keeping careful product revenue records may provide some hard data to back up estimates of product revenue percentages.

Step 2: Determine Profit Requirements

There are two basic ways to treat profit when budgets are developed: (1) regarding profit as "what is left over from revenue after subtracting expenses" and (2) treating profit as if it were a "cost." The traditional approach determines profit by deducting estimated expenses from forecasted revenue:

$$Profit = Revenue - Expenses$$

A better approach treats profit as a "cost." This approach determines profit requirements before estimating expenses so that, in effect, the property pays itself first. Money remaining after profit requirements have been deducted from revenue is used to pay for the operation's expenses. While the traditional method uses estimated expense levels to determine profit, this approach uses forecasted revenue and required profit levels to determine allowable expenses:

$$Revenue - Required Profit = Allowable Operating Expenses$$

With this strategy, the food and beverage manager is concerned about achieving budgeted profit levels while at the same time ensuring that there will be sufficient revenue to meet expenses. Using this plan for developing a budget, the food and beverage manager wants to:

1. Generate revenue.
2. Plan for the desired operating profit.
3. Have sufficient money remaining to meet the expenses required to generate the revenue.
4. Achieve all this without sacrificing quality requirements.

The "profit as cost" approach to budget development requires that profit levels be assessed after revenue is determined. How should profit levels be determined? The answer to this question depends on the specific nature of each food and beverage operation.

For a freestanding restaurant or other food service operation, the principles behind the determination of profit can be understood in terms of the accounting concepts of "return on investment" or "return on assets." Investors require that the property provide them with a reasonable return on their investment and that management safeguard the assets they have invested in the operation. This entitles investors to require additional profit to help compensate for the risk of their invest-ment. In light of the high rate of restaurant failures, this risk is often great and, therefore, required returns are often high.

In lodging operations, investment requirements can be generated from the rooms department, food and beverage department, and perhaps other revenue centers as well. The owner, working with the general manager, must first deter-mine the amount of profit required from the lodging operation. Then, the staff must allocate profit responsibilities among the different departments based on expected levels of departmental revenue. The food and beverage manager will ultimately be responsible for generating a required amount of profit and will spread this responsibility among revenue-producing centers such as á la carte din-ing, banquets, beverage operations, and room service.

What happens when it is not possible to generate the required profit levels given the amount of estimated revenue? Does this mean that this method of treat-ing profit is incorrect? On the contrary; this situation proves that the method works very well! Instead of waiting until the budget year is almost over to discover a profit problem, food and beverage managers using this method can learn when the bud-get is being developed whether required profit levels can be generated. If they can-not, alternatives can be considered early in the planning process. If profit require-ments are known at the time the budget is developed, plans to generate required profit (such as increasing revenue or reducing expenses) can be formulated.

Step 3: Calculate Projected Expense Levels

Once revenue volumes are estimated and profit requirements are determined, expenses required to generate the projected level of revenue can be estimated. These expenses include cost of food sold, labor, supplies, utilities, marketing, rent, depre-ciation, insurance, and many others. Budget planning requires that management examine how these expenses are affected by changes in revenue. In this context, costs can be seen as fixed, variable, or mixed (partly fixed and partly variable).

As noted earlier, fixed costs are costs that remain constant in the short run, even though revenue may vary. Common examples of fixed costs are management salaries, rent, insurance, property taxes, depreciation, and interest.

Variable costs are costs that vary in relation to changes in the volume of busi-ness. If variable costs are strictly defined as costs that vary in exact proportion to total revenue, then few costs are truly variable. However, several costs come close to this definition and may be legitimately considered variable costs. For example, food and beverage costs increase as revenue volume increases simply because more food and beverage products must be purchased to prepare and serve the additional meals and drinks. Other examples of variable costs are labor costs for hourly per-sonnel and the cost of some supplies used in food production and service areas.

Mixed costs are costs that contain both fixed and variable cost elements. These costs are also referred to as semi-variable or semi-fixed costs. Although, in practice, the variable element of a mixed cost may not be directly proportional to usage or rev-enue volume, this assumption is generally accepted. An example of a mixed cost is telephone expense. One portion of this expense would be the fixed cost of the system; the other portion would be the variable cost of calls made during a specified period.[2]

More about Profits

Budgets are developed as a tactic to generate desired profits, which, in turn, measure the operation's financial results. Profits can be expressed in several ways:

$$\text{Profit Margin Ratio:} \quad \frac{\text{Net Income}}{\text{Total Revenue}}$$

This profitability ratio expresses the net income ("bottom line") relative to the operation's total revenues. Its best use is to measure the property's ability to manage revenue and expenses.

$$\text{Return on Investment (ROI):} \quad \frac{\text{Net Income}}{\text{Average Owners' Equity}}$$

This profitability ratio measures the amount (percentage) of owners' equity that has been recovered by the net income. In other words, it can be used to compare the amount of money earned to the owners' other investment alternatives.

$$\text{Return on Assets (ROA):} \quad \frac{\text{Net Income}}{\text{Average Total Assets}}$$

This profitability ratio indicates the profitability of the property's assets. When owners have only a small investment in the business, the ROI ratio becomes less useful, and the ROA ratio enables owners to determine how well managers have used the property's assets to generate profits.

Those developing operating budgets must understand their organization's profit requirements and recognize that dollars, not percentages, are required to meet the owners' financial expectations and obligations.

Managers must consider each of these types of expenses as the budget is developed. The best method for estimating expense levels is, of course, the one that is most useful to the individual operation. Several widely used methods are described in the following sections.

Simple Mark-Up Method. Perhaps the most common method of estimating food and beverage operating expenses for the budget is the **mark-up method,** which is based on the current expense level. This amount is then increased (or perhaps decreased, though this is rare) to arrive at the expense level for the new operating budget. For example, if the current month's food cost is $135,000, and a 12-percent cost increase is anticipated for the same month in the next budget period, the adjusted food cost for the new budget period is:

Current Month's Food Cost	×	Cost Increase	=	Anticipated Cost Increase
$135,000	×	0.12	=	$16,200

Current Month's Food Cost	+	Anticipated Cost Increase	=	Anticipated Cost Increase
$135,000	+	$16,200	=	$151,200

Note that the above calculations are the same as estimating a 112-percent food cost for the new period: current month's cost ($135,000) × anticipated cost (112%) = $151,200.

Budgeted food costs for each month in the budget year are totaled to arrive at the estimated food cost for the new budget year. Total projected costs for the entire food and beverage operation are then determined by combining similar calculations for beverage and all other expense categories.

One problem with this method is that, by basing projections on current expense levels, it assumes all costs were reasonable during the current year. If, in fact, some costs were too high because of inefficiency from waste, theft, or for another reason, that inefficiency is extended into the new budget.

Percentage Method. Another frequently used method of estimating food and beverage operating expenses is the **percentage method**, which is based on the current percentage of each expense relative to revenue. Food and beverage cost percentages are calculated by dividing food or beverage cost by food or beverage revenue and multiplying by 100. The percentage method for forecasting food and beverage expenses assumes that the same cost percentages from the current period will continue to apply to the projected revenue for the new budget period. For example, if the current beverage cost percentage is 24 percent, when the new budget is developed, 24 percent of the estimated beverage revenue will be allocated to beverage costs.

Like the mark-up method, the percentage method assumes that the current situation is reasonable. This has the potential disadvantage of continuing an inefficient operation if the current budgeted cost percentage is higher than it should be. Close analysis to ensure that the budget allows for the planned profit goal can offset this disadvantage.

Zero-Based Budget Calculations. A third method, **zero-based budgeting**, avoids the disadvantages of the other two methods by starting over from zero instead of using costs or cost percentages from the current period. This method takes more time and involves starting at a zero expense level for each category of cost and building up to new budgeted expense levels, justifying each step along the way. As a result, it yields expense information designed specifically for the period covered by the new operating budget. Forecasting costs in this way provides a very useful control tool for later comparing budgeted costs with actual costs. However, because it requires a significant commitment of time, the zero-based budget is not frequently used in commercial food and beverage operations.

Special Concerns in Estimating Beverage Expenses. Separate costs for different beverage products may be considered in budget development. For example, suppose 70 percent of beverage revenue is estimated to be from liquor, and the beverage cost for liquor is 28 percent of its revenue. If beverage revenue equals $100,000, the total cost of liquor is:

% of Beverage Revenue (Liqour)		Total Beverage Revenue		Beverage Cost (Liquor)		Total Liquor Cost
0.70	×	$100,000	×	0.28	=	$19,600

The same process is used for estimating costs of beer, wine, and soft drinks. The sum of the costs for the separate beverage products will be the total beverage cost to be used for budget calculations.

Estimating Other Expenses. So far, our discussion of budget development has emphasized calculating the allowable food and beverage costs based on forecasted revenue. However, management must also consider the impact that other expenses such as labor, supplies, and advertising have on the entire budget.

The same basic procedures can be used to estimate costs for all other expenses allocated to the food and beverage department. For example, labor costs represent a significant expense for all types of food service operations. Managers must take the time to objectively assess likely labor cost levels based on estimated revenue. Energy and advertising expenses are other examples of costs that are generally significant and, therefore, demand attention during budget development. However, some categories of expense, such as office supplies, may have little financial impact on the food and beverage operation. Simple mark-ups are likely to be a fast and reasonably accurate way to budget for these expenses.

Budget Development: An Example

The following example illustrates a step-by-step process for developing a budget. Although the example focuses on developing a budget for the food operation, the same procedures can be used to plan a beverage budget. Where applicable, the example includes completed sample budget worksheets accompanied by a discussion reviewing the role of the worksheets in developing operating budget information.

Step 1: Calculate Projected Revenue Levels

The first step of the budget development process is to forecast revenue levels for the new budget period. As explained earlier, these projections can be based initially on the operation's history.

Assume that the food and beverage operation in this example is in its third year. Further assume that this operation maintains revenue history records electronically. The monthly food revenue information is copied to Budget Worksheet A: Food Revenue History Analysis, which is shown in Exhibit 2. Notice that since next year's budget is being developed in October of the current year, revenue figures for October, November, and December are estimates. The worksheet reports revenue for each month and indicates the amount of change in dollars and percentages over the same month in the previous year.

Determining Monthly Revenue Differences. To calculate the amount of change in January revenue from Year 2 to Year 3, subtract January revenue for Year 2 (column 4) from the January revenue for Year 3 (column 7):

Year 3 January (column 7)	–	Year 2 January (column 4)	=	Change in Revenue Dollars (column 8)
$129,600	–	$118,420	=	$11,180

Exhibit 2   Budget Worksheet A: Food Revenue History Analysis

Food Revenue History Analysis									
	YEAR 1			**YEAR 2**			**YEAR 3 (Current Year)**		
Month	**Revenue**	**Difference (Previous Year)**		**Revenue**	**Difference (Previous Year)**		**Revenue**	**Difference (Previous Year)**	
		$	**%**		**$**	**%**		**$**	**%**
	1	2	3	4	5	6	7	8	9
Jan.	$ 112,550			$ 118,420	$ 5,870	5%	$ 129,600	$ 11,180	9%
Feb.	112,430			116,550	4,120	4	125,400	8,850	8
Mar.	112,220			121,375	9,155	8	126,350	4,975	4
Apr.	113,050			119,000	5,950	5	127,450	8,450	7
May	112,975			119,800	6,825	6	126,575	6,775	6
June	112,490			117,550	5,060	4	124,300	6,750	6
July	112,200			122,400	10,200	9	128,500	6,100	5
Aug.	112,950			119,900	6,950	6	124,375	4,475	4
Sept.	112,490			121,540	9,050	8	129,500	7,960	7
Oct.	112,420			122,410	9,990	9	124,650*	2,240	2
Nov.	112,310			121,450	9,140	8	131,150*	9,700	8
Dec.	112,300			120,400	8,100	7	129,200*	8,800	7
Totals	**$1,350,385**			**$1,440,795**	**$90,410**	**7%****	**$1,527,050**	**$86,255**	**6%****

* Estimates (the operating budget is being developed in October for the coming calendar year).
** Percents are rounded.

Note that column 8 shows that January revenue has increased by $11,180.

To calculate the monthly percentage of revenue increase, divide the $11,180 increase (column 8) by January revenue for Year 2, $118,420 (column 4), and multiply by 100. This percentage (column 9) is:

$$\frac{\text{Increase in January Revenue Year 2 to Year 3 (col. 8)}}{\text{Year 2 January Revenue (column 4)}} \times 100 = \text{Monthly \% of Revenue Increase (column 9)}$$

$$\frac{\$11,180}{\$118,420} = 0.09 \text{ (rounded)} \times 100 = 9\%$$

Determining Annual Revenue Differences. To calculate the annual percentage of revenue differences, perform the same type of calculation using totals at the bottom of the columns. To calculate the current year increase over the previous year:

$$\frac{\text{Increase in Revenue from Year 2 to Year 3 (col. 8)}}{\text{Year 2 Revenue (col. 4)}} \times 100 = \text{Annual \% of Revenue Increase (column 9)}$$

$$\frac{\$86,255}{\$1,440,795} = 0.06 \text{ (rounded)} \times 100 = 6\%$$

To calculate the percentage revenue increase in the second year over the first year:

Increase in Revenue from

$$\frac{\text{Year 1 to Year 2 (col. 5)}}{\text{Year 1 Revenue (col. 1)}} \quad \times \quad 100 \quad = \quad \text{Annual \% of Revenue Increase}$$
$$\text{(column 6)}$$

$$\frac{\$90,410}{\$1,350,385} = 0.07 \text{ (rounded)} \times 100 = 7\%$$

Revenue History Analysis. Analysis of the revenue history shows that the total food revenue in Year 2 increased 7 percent over Year 1, while food revenue in the current year (Year 3) increased 6 percent over Year 2. With this knowledge, the food service manager should study current economic and other factors to estimate revenue for the next year. Suppose the manager believes the downward trend can be reversed and that revenue will increase by 10 percent during the coming year. The manager can then distribute monthly food revenue projections on Budget Worksheet B: Estimated Monthly Food Revenue for Operating Budget (Exhibit 3) by adding 10 percent to each month's revenue. Some food and beverage operations are much more seasonal than the one in this example. A property in a seasonal location may generate 80 percent of its revenue in three or four months and be closed for several months. That is why it is important to study and budget revenue and expenses on a by-month basis.

While using Worksheet B to distribute revenue, the budget planner can analyze monthly trends and operations. The manager of the food and beverage operation in this example should consider why the increase in percentage of revenue declined in some months, such as March, August, and especially October (see column 9 in Exhibit 2). The manager can also ask what can be done to continue the high revenue growth in January, February, and November. Furthermore, the manager must determine how much of the revenue increase is real growth and how much is due only to an increase in selling prices.

The total estimated revenue of $1,679,756 for the operating budget in Budget Worksheet B is a 10-percent increase in food revenue over the current year. This revenue of $1,679,756 is the base from which to generate required profits and meet expenses incurred in producing that revenue from food operations. The next two steps show how to estimate profits and expenses.

Step 2: Determine Profit Requirements

Determining the amount of profit expected from the food and beverage operation involves separating required profit levels for the food operation from the profit required from the beverage operation.

To understand how profit is determined, you need to know how costs are allocated within a food and beverage operation. Although details of cost allocation are beyond the scope of this chapter, some basic principles of cost allocation are discussed in the following section.[3]

Cost Allocation Principles. Food and beverage costs are charged to food and beverage departments, respectively. The application of this principle requires correct assigning of food transfers to the beverage department and beverage transfers to the kitchen.

Other large expenses are divided between the food and beverage departments and prorated according to how much expense each incurs. For example, wages for

Exhibit 3   Budget Worksheet B: Estimated Monthly Food Revenue for Operating Budget

	Estimated Monthly Food Revenue for Operating Budget		
Month	**Revenue in Current Year**	**Increase by 10%**	**Estimated Revenue: New Operating Budget**
January	$ 129,600	$ 12,960	$ 142,560
February	125,400	12,540	137,940
March	126,350	12,635	138,985
April	127,450	12,745	140,195
May	126,575	12,658	139,233
June	124,300	12,430	136,730
July	128,500	12,850	141,350
August	124,375	12,438	136,813
September	129,500	12,950	142,450
October	124,650*	12,465	137,115
November	131,150*	13,115	144,265
December	129,200*	12,920	142,120
Totals	**$ 1,527,050**	**$ 152,706**	**$1,679,756**

* Estimates

employees involved in both food and beverage operations, such as the bookkeeper and purchasing agent, can be prorated based on the percentage of revenue. If 75 percent of the total food and beverage revenue comes from food, then 75 percent of these indirect labor costs could be allocated to the food department. Smaller expenses, such as supplies or equipment, can also be allocated on the basis of a simple revenue percentage.

Budget Worksheet C: Recap and Allocation of Current Costs Between Food and Beverage Operations (Exhibit 4) shows the total amount (column 2) of each cost (column 1) identified in the restaurant's accounting system. Each cost is then divided between the food and beverage operations according to the applicable revenue percentages. (To simplify the example, no allocations based on transfers to and from the food and beverage operation are included.)

The figures at the top of columns 3 and 5 on Worksheet C are the current food revenue and beverage revenue, respectively. The current food revenue total of $1,527,050 is transferred from Budget Worksheet B (Exhibit 3), which we just reviewed. Percentage of revenue (columns 4 and 6) is calculated for each cost by dividing the amount of cost allocated to the operation in the current budget by the total revenue for the operation and multiplying by 100.

Calculating Profit. Profit before taxes for the current year of the food and beverage operation is calculated as follows: total revenue of $1,908,810 minus total costs

Exhibit 4   Budget Worksheet C: Recap and Allocation of Current Costs between Food and Beverage Operations

		Recap and Allocation of Current Costs Between Food and Beverage Operations				
			Amount Prorated To			
	Total Annual Current Cost	**Food**		**Beverage**		
Type of Cost		**Revenue = $1,527,050**	**Percent of Revenue**	**Revenue = $381,760**	**Percent of Revenue**	
1	2	3	4	5	6	
Food	$534,468	$534,468	35%	—	—	
Beverage	99,258	—	—	$99,258	26%	
Payroll	419,938	366,492	24	53,446	14	
Payroll Taxes and Employee Benefits	34,359	30,541	2	3,818	1	
Direct Operating Expenses	95,441	76,353	5	19,088	5	
Music/Entertainment	61,082	—	—	61,082	16	
Advertising	38,176	30,541	2	7,635	2	
Utilities	83,988	76,353	5	7,635	2	
Administration/General	76,352	61,082	4	15,270	4	
Repairs/Maintenance	22,906	15,271	1	7,635	2	
Rent	141,252	106,894	7	34,358	9	
Real Estate/Property Taxes	22,906	15,271	1	7,635	2	
Insurance	38,176	30,541	2	7,635	2	
Interest Expense	68,717	61,082	4	7,635	2	
Depreciation	57,265	45,812	3	11,453	3	
Totals	$1,794,284	$1,450,701	95%	$343,583	90%	

Recap	Total	Food Operation	Beverage Operation
Revenue	$1,908,810	$1,527,050	$381,760
Product Cost	633,726	534,468	99,258
Non-Product Cost	1,160,558	916,233	244,325
Total Cost	(1,794,284)	(1,450,701)	(343,583)
Profit Before Tax (Revenue Minus Total Cost)	$ 114,526	$ 76,349	$ 38,177

of $1,794,284 equals $114,526. The profit percentage for the current year is determined by dividing the profit before taxes by total revenue and multiplying by 100 ($114,526 ÷ $1,908,810 = 0.06 [rounded] × 100 = 6 percent. This means that profit before taxes for the current year is 6 percent of total revenue.

Let's suppose that, for next year, the owner wants to realize a before-tax profit of 10 percent of total revenue. Worksheet B (Exhibit 3) calculates food revenue for the next year at $1,679,756. Let's assume that a similar worksheet was prepared for beverage revenue and it estimates next year's beverage revenue at $385,580. Total projected revenue amounts to $2,065,336 ($1,679,756 + $385,580). The dollar amount of the owner's required profit for the next year would then be calculated as $206,534 ($2,065,336 × 0.10).

To reach this new profit requirement, the food and beverage manager will have to operate the food and beverage program more effectively. The manager will have to increase revenue from the current year and also work to reduce operating costs. Moreover, the manager will have to take the needed steps to achieve the required profit goal without sacrificing quality requirements. This is the control process in action.

Two points should be made about the required profit level. First, determining profit requirements on the basis of revenue alone is not always appropriate. As stated earlier, it may be better to express profit requirements as a specified percentage of return on investments or assets. Second, although the required amount of profit can be generated by either food or beverages or both, normally the beverage operation yields a higher profit per dollar of revenue. One approach to spreading required profit between food and beverage operations includes the following:

1. Charge the food operation for direct product costs (food costs).

2. Allocate non-product costs between the food and beverage operations by percentage, as was done for the current year in Budget Worksheet C.

3. Calculate profit required from food revenue:

$$\text{Food Revenue} - \left[\text{Food Costs} + \frac{\text{Allocated Share of}}{\text{Non-Product Costs}}\right] = \frac{\text{Profit Required}}{\text{from Food Revenue}}$$

4. Calculate profit required from beverage revenue:

$$\text{Total Required Profit} - \text{Profit from Food Revenue} = \frac{\text{Profit Required from}}{\text{Beverage Revenue}}$$

Step 3: Calculate Projected Expense Levels

The next step in the budget development process is to estimate the expenses that the food and beverage operation will incur in generating the estimated revenue. Some of these expenses, such as food, beverage, and labor costs, can be considered "variable" in that the amount of the expense changes proportionately with the level of revenue. To project these costs, the planner multiplies each cost's current percentage of revenue from Budget Worksheet C by the estimated revenue for the new budget period ($1,679,756 in Exhibit 3).

Other expenses, such as interest and depreciation, are considered fixed because they do not vary with the level of revenue. These expenses are estimated for the budget year using the actual dollar amount for the current year. The estimated cost is then divided by the estimated revenue to determine the budgeted percentage.

The calculations for both variable and fixed budgeted costs are done on Budget Worksheet D: Calculation of Food Operation Costs for Budget (Exhibit 5). Note that the forecasted percent of food revenue (column 2) is multiplied by the budgeted food revenue for the new budget. Note also that the dollar amounts for rent, real estate/property taxes, insurance, interest, and depreciation did not change from the current year's expenses shown on Budget Worksheet C.

The Operating Budget as a Control Tool

For the operating budget to be a meaningful and workable control tool, it must be in an easy-to-use format, such as Budget Worksheet E: Food Operation Budget

Exhibit 5   Budget Worksheet D: Calculation of Food Operation Costs for Budget

Calculation of Food Operation Costs for Budget			
Category of Cost	**Percent of Food Revenue**	**Estimated Revenue: Budget Year**	**Estimated Cost: Budget Year**
1	2	3	4
Food Cost	35%	$1,679,756	$587,915
Payroll	24	$1,679,756	403,141
Payroll Taxes/Employee Benefits	2	$1,679,756	33,595
Direct Operating Expenses	5	$1,679,756	83,988
Music/Entertainment	—	$1,679,756	—
Advertising	2	$1,679,756	33,595
Utilities	5	$1,679,756	83,988
Administration/General	4	$1,679,756	67,190
Repairs/Maintenance	1	$1,679,756	16,798
Rent	6*	$1,679,756	106,894
Real Estate/Property Taxes	1*	$1,679,756	15,271
Insurance	2*	$1,679,756	30,541
Interest Expense	4*	$1,679,756	61,082
Depreciation	3*	$1,679,756	45,812
Other (Specify):	—	$1,679,756	—
		Total Estimated Cost:	**$1,569,810**

*These percentages are for fixed costs and are calculated by dividing cost (see Exhibit 4) by estimated food revenue for the new budget year. All percentages are rounded.

(Exhibit 6). Worksheet E is generated each month. The sample shown in Exhibit 6 is for January, the first month of the new budget year.

1. Column 1 lists food revenue, cost of goods sold (food cost), individual operating expenses, total operating expenses, and profit before taxes in a format similar to an income statement.

2. Column 2 shows the percentage of food revenue represented by each item as indicated in Budget Worksheet D.

3. Column 3 lists budgeted revenue, expenses, and the before-tax profit goal of the month. Total food revenue of $142,560 is obtained directly from Budget Worksheet B. To calculate the amount for each variable expense listed in column 1, multiply the budget percentage (column 2) as a decimal by the total monthly revenue of $142,560 (column 3). For example, the monthly payroll expense is:

Exhibit 6   Budget Worksheet E: Food Operation Budget

		Budget		Actual			
Item	Budget Percent	Month	Year	Month	Year	Variance	Actual Percent
1	2	3	4	5	6	7	8
Food Revenue	100%	$142,560	$1,679,756	$155,440	$155,440	$12,880	100%
Cost of Goods Sold Food Cost	35	49,896	587,915	51,750	51,750	-1,854	33
Operating Expenses Payroll	24	34,214	403,141	36,400	36,400	-2,186	23
Payroll Tax/Benefits	2	2,851	33,595	3,000	3,000	-149	2
Direct Operating Expenses	5	7,128	83,988	7,900	7,900	-772	5
Music/Entertainment	—	—	—	—	—	—	—
Advertising	2	2,851	33,595	2,851	2,851	0	2
Utilities	5	7,128	83,988	7,190	7,190	-62	5
Administration/General	4	5,702	67,190	5,800	5,800	-98	4
Repairs/Maintenance	1	1,426	16,798	1,400	1,400	26	1
Rent	6	8,908	106,894	8,908	8,908	0	6
Real Estate/Property Taxes	1	1,273	15,271	1,273	1,273	0	1
Insurance	2	2,545	30,541	2,545	2,545	0	2
Interest Expense	4	5,090	61,082	5,090	5,090	0	3
Depreciation	3	3,818	45,812	3,818	3,818	0	2
Other (Specify)	—	—	—	—	—	—	—
Total Operating Expenses	60%*	$82,934	$981,895	$86,175	$86,175	$-3,241	55%*
Profit (Before Tax)	7%	$ 9,730	$109,946	$17,515	$17,515	$ 7,785	11%

Food Operation Budget
Month: *January*

*Because of the rounding of percentages for fixed costs (see Exhibit 5), the sum of the percentages for individual operating expenses is one percentage point higher than this figure.

Budget Percentage	×	Food Revenue	=	Monthly Payroll Expense
0.24	×	$142,560	=	$34,214 (rounded)

To calculate the monthly amount for fixed expenses, divide the budgeted amount for the entire year (column 4) by 12. For example, the monthly interest expense is calculated as follows:

$$\frac{\$61,082}{12} = \$5,090$$

To find the monthly profit before taxes, subtract food and operating costs from revenue:

$	142,560	Budgeted Monthly Revenue
$	– 49,896	Budgeted Monthly Food Costs
$	– 82,934	Budgeted Monthly Operating Costs
$	9,730	Budgeted Monthly Profit Before Taxes

4. Column 4 lists budgeted revenue, expenses, and the before-tax profit goal for the entire year. Total food revenue of $1,679,756 is obtained directly from

Budget Worksheet B (see Exhibit 3). Each operating expense—for example, payroll of $403,141—is obtained directly from Budget Worksheet D (see Exhibit 5).

5. Column 5 lists the actual revenue, expenses, and before-tax profit for the month. Information in this column is entered every month during the time covered by the operating budget. Data is obtained from the same source documents used to develop information for monthly accounting statements.

6. Column 6 tallies information about actual revenue, expenses, and before-tax profit on a year-to-date basis. Since January is the first month of the new budget period, the figures in column 6 are the same as those recorded in column 5.

7. Column 7 shows the variance between budgeted and actual amounts. To calculate the variance for a revenue item, subtract budget from actual. Classify the variance as favorable if it is positive or unfavorable if it is negative. For example, the variance in food revenue for January is:

$$\text{Actual} \quad - \quad \text{Budget} \quad = \quad \text{Revenue Variance}$$
$$\$155{,}440 \quad - \quad \$142{,}560 \quad = \quad +\$12{,}880 \text{ (favorable)}$$

The variance for an expense item is determined by subtracting actual from budget. A favorable variance is positive; an unfavorable variance is negative. For example, the variance for direct operating expenses is:

$$\text{Budget} \quad - \quad \text{Actual} \quad = \quad \text{Expense Variance}$$
$$\$7{,}128 \quad - \quad \$7{,}900 \quad = \quad -\$772 \text{ (unfavorable)}$$

8. Column 8 provides information about each expense as a percentage of actual food revenue. For example, the actual food cost percentage for January is:

$$\frac{\text{Food Cost}}{\text{Food Revenue}} \quad \times \quad 100 \quad = \quad \text{Food Cost Percentage}$$

$$\frac{\$51{,}750}{\$155{,}440} = 0.33 \times 100 = 33\%$$

Assessing Results. Information in Budget Worksheet E tells the food manager:

- What food revenue, costs, and profits *should be.*

- What food revenue, costs, and profits *actually are.*

A simple analysis of the variance column on Budget Worksheet E yields important information:

- The actual food revenue for January was greater than anticipated. The favorable variance, actual food revenue of $155,440 minus $142,560 in planned food revenue, represents an increase in revenue of $12,880.

- Food costs were $1,854 greater than planned ($49,896 budgeted food cost minus $51,750 actual food cost). This is an unfavorable variance.

- Although the dollar amount for food costs is expected to be greater, since food revenue was also greater than planned, the actual food cost percentage

(33 percent, as shown in column 8) is less than the planned food cost percentage (35 percent, as shown in column 2). This indicates that there is a potential problem with food quality, portion control, or another area; it is unlikely that food cost percentage could be reduced this much unless there was an obvious reason (such as a much lower purchase cost for a high-volume entrée).

- Operating expenses were $3,241 greater than planned ($82,934 budgeted operating expenses minus $86,175 actual operating expenses). This is an unfavorable variance, but it might be explained, at least in part, by the much higher revenue volume.

- Profit was $7,785 more than planned ($17,515 actual profit minus $9,730 planned profit). This variance is favorable.

In reviewing these results of operations, the most important feature is that actual profit is higher than expected. Not only are the dollars greater, but so is the percentage of profit to total revenue. This means that, while total expenses were higher due to increased revenue, they increased at a smaller percentage of revenue than was budgeted.

A word of caution must be expressed. You might want to question the increases in the budgeted expenses. Can higher revenue alone explain the higher-than-budgeted costs, or are there other explanations? Recall that food costs were slightly greater than anticipated. Some further analysis may be appropriate here.

Finally, recognize that it is difficult to generalize about variances after only one month. More accurate and meaningful analysis becomes possible with data from several months.

Computers and the Budget Process

Computers are now in common use for both routine and advanced budgeting applications in all but the smallest operations.[4] The programs designed to best perform these activities are termed electronic spreadsheet software. Electronic spreadsheets are simple in concept, but possess powerful computation capabilities.

Electronic Spreadsheets

Electronic spreadsheets resemble a traditional accounting worksheet organized by rows and columns. The border along the worksheet's left margin typically contains numbers to designate row locations, while the top margin contains letters depicting column locations. The intersection of a row and column forms a **cell**. A cell address is defined by its respective row and column indicators (see Exhibit 7).

Unlike an accountant's worksheet, which is very limited in size, electronic spreadsheets are often so large that their size prohibits them from being displayed in their entirety on a display screen or monitor. At any point in time, the user views only a section (a window) of an otherwise enormous spreadsheet. The terminal keyboard contains cursor (arrow) keys enabling the user to move from cell to cell and from window to window.

Exhibit 7   Electronic Spreadsheet Format

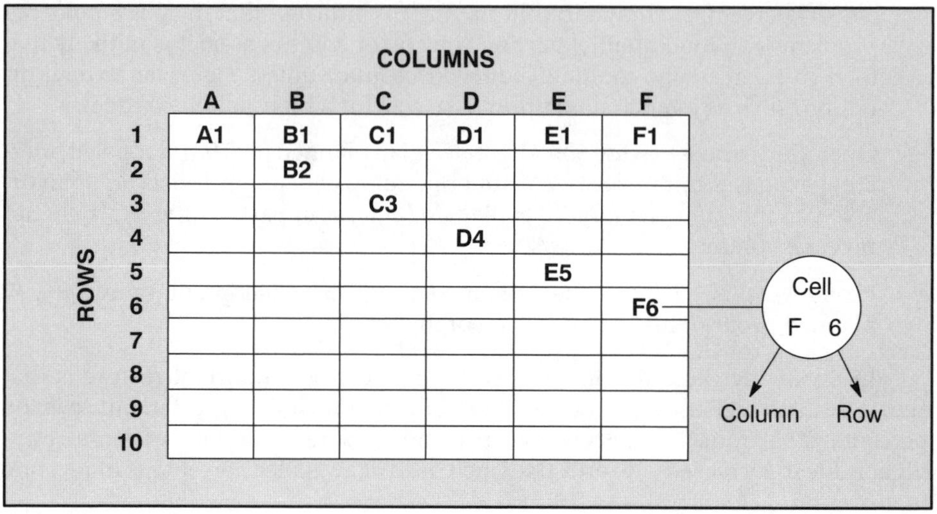

Cell Contents

The food and beverage manager customizes a generic spreadsheet by defining the content of its cells. Electronic spreadsheet cells can contain a label, a number, or a formula. When textual information is entered into a cell it is referred to as a label. Spreadsheet software automatically identifies labels, since they are entered from the terminal's keyboard. Labels assist in the organization of data input and in the comprehensibility of output information. Headings, titles, chart of account lists, etc., typify budgeting labels.

Numeric values, used to produce calculated results, are entered into cells from the keyboard's number keys. The software is capable of identifying numeric input (coming from the numeric keys) similar to the manner in which it recognizes text characters for labels.

Formulas are preceded by special characters (for example, +) or words (for example, sum). These are used so that only the results and not the formula will appear in the addressed cell.

Perhaps the most important benefit of spreadsheet software is its ability to maintain a formula that relates specific cells. To illustrate, consider the spreadsheet in Exhibit 8, which contains labels in rows 3, 4, 5, 7, and 9. Numeric values appear in cells B4, C4, D4, E4, B5, C5, D5, and E5. The results of stored formulas are presented in cells B7, C7, D7, E7, and B9. The formula used to produce the output in B7 is + B4/B5. Cell C7 is generated from formula + C4/C5 (D7 and E7 are similarly derived). The calculated average food cost percentage found in B9 is computed from this formula: + B7 + C7 + D7 + E7/4.

Formulas, capable of referencing various cells and constants, illustrate the usefulness of spreadsheet programs. They enable someone who has only basic computer skills to direct the computational efforts of a powerful machine.

Exhibit 8   Sample Food Cost Spreadsheet

	A	B	C	D	E
		Food Cost Spreadsheet			
1					
2					
3		Week 1	Week 2	Week 3	Week 4
4	Food Cost	2500	3000	2750	3275
5	Food Revenue	6500	8000	7775	8400
6					
7	Food Cost %	0.3846	0.3750	0.3537	0.3899
8					
9	Average FC%	0.3758			
10					

Recalculation Feature

The budgeting process generally requires many calculations. Moreover, whenever data is altered or extended, numerous recalculations are necessary. Spreadsheet software significantly enhances and streamlines this process, since it contains formulas composed of cell addresses and possesses a recalculation feature. Spreadsheets can be configured to automatically recalculate all numeric values whenever one value changes. Recalculations are performed in a chaining fashion. As a cell is modified, any and all cells related to it are also changed. In Exhibit 8, the formulas in cells B7, C7, D7, and E7 relate corresponding row 4 and 5 elements. The formula in cell B9, however, depends on the calculated outputs of B7, C7, D7, and E7. Assume week two's food cost was erroneously entered. The data in cell C4 should have been 3200, not 3000. When the cursor is moved to cell C4 and the figure 3200 is entered (replacing 3000), all subsequent computations dependent on this cell data (C7 and B9) will automatically be recalculated. In a manual process, these recalculations would require a working knowledge of the relationship among all data, and would take considerable time to accomplish. There would also be an increased opportunity for making errors in the recalculations.

As noted earlier in the chapter, budget reforecasting is becoming increasingly popular as a tool to help the food and beverage manager monitor the operation. The recalculation feature of electronic spreadsheet software enables food and beverage managers in all sizes and types of operations to quickly update budget projections by reforecasting revenue levels or expenses when necessary.

Food and beverage managers tend to appreciate spreadsheet output options as much as they do the usefulness of cell contents and automatic recalculations. Many electronic spreadsheet programs provide both text (worksheet) and graphic output formats for any portion of the spreadsheet. Text output consists of a printed copy of the spreadsheet as it appears on the display screen.

The data on a spreadsheet can also be displayed graphically. Graphic options include bar charts, pie charts, or line drawings. Often, a visual presentation of the same data improves comprehension and understanding.

Technology Helps with Budget Development

Before electronic spreadsheets became popular, food and beverage managers used calculators to manually develop budgets, income statements, and other accounting tools. These efforts required significant time and produced the real possibility of errors that could be compounded as inaccurate figures were used in subsequent calculations, making all resulting calculations inaccurate. As a result, many managers did not make detailed budget and/or income statement calculations and, in the process, they lost the opportunity to gain significant control over their operations.

Today, POS systems generate revenue information for any time period desired by the budget planner. Income statements are generated electronically as well, and technology enables managers to easily review budget and actual data (such as that shown in Exhibit 6) without the need for any additional calculation or other efforts. As with other aspects of computerized control elements, managers enjoy the benefits of accurate data and additional time that can be re-directed to other management activities.

Cost-Volume-Profit Analysis ————————————————————

Cost-volume-profit (CVP) analysis can be used to determine the revenues required at any desired profit level. Also referred to as "breakeven analysis," CVP reviews the relationships among costs, revenue, and profits associated with alternative plans. CVP analysis is used to help managers answer such questions as:

- How many guests must the operation serve to meet budgeted profit goals?

- When fixed or variable costs increase, how many additional guests must the operation serve to meet budgeted profit goals?

- How profitable would it be for the restaurant to expand its hours of operation?

- Should the restaurant remain open during predictably slow meal periods?

Graphs or equations can be used to conduct the analysis. Use of equations is likely to be faster and more accurate, and this procedure will be used in the discussion and examples that follow.[5]

CVP Assumptions and Limitations

Like all mathematical tools, CVP analysis is based on several assumptions. If these assumptions are not relevant to the actual situations being analyzed, the results of the analysis may be flawed. Some of the more basic assumptions behind CVP analysis include the following:

- Fixed costs remain constant during the period being analyzed. Over time, fixed costs do change. However, it is generally reasonable to assume that fixed costs remain constant over a short time span.

- Variable costs vary directly with revenue during the period under study. In other words, if variable costs equal a certain percentage of revenue, and revenue increases, the new level of variable expenses will still equal the same percentage of revenue.

- Revenue relates directly to volume. For example, CVP analysis assumes that as business volume (the number of guests served) increases by a certain percentage, revenue will then increase by that same percentage. This means that decisions made from CVP analyses must be reviewed if, during the time period in question, the **sales mix** changes. A change in the sales mix usually affects the amount of the guest check average. A higher guest check average results in higher revenue at the same level of business volume (number of guests served).

- All costs can be properly divided into two components: fixed costs (which do not change as revenue levels change) and variable costs (which vary directly with revenue).

- Only quantitative factors are considered by the CVP model. Qualitative factors such as employee morale, guest goodwill, and so forth are not considered. Therefore, food and beverage managers must carefully consider these qualitative factors before making any final decisions.

The Basic CVP Equation

The basic CVP analysis equation expresses the cost-volume-profit relationship at the breakeven point as follows:

Net Income ($0.00) = Total Revenues − Total Variables − Total Fixed Costs

Since there is no net income at breakeven, the value is set at zero when performing a breakeven analysis. However, the same equation can be used when an amount of desired net income is known. In these cases, the amount of desired net income is used as the value instead of zero. Variables within the basic CVP analysis equation can be broken down into the following more basic elements:

Total Revenues = Guest Check Average × Number of Guests Served

Total Variable Costs = Variable Costs per Guest × Number of Guests Served

Breaking these variables of the basic CVP equation into more basic elements allows managers the flexibility to rearrange the elements into new equations that address a number of different situations. Exhibit 9 lists a few of these equations.

CVP Example: The Lumberjack Cafe

The following information is taken from the budget being proposed for the next calendar year for the Lumberjack Cafe. The number of guests used to estimate the budgeted revenues is 133,333.

• Total annual revenues		$1,000,000
• Total annual fixed costs	$ 110,000	
• Total annual variable costs	$ 740,000	
• Total annual costs		($ 850,000)
• Total net income before taxes		$ 150,000

Exhibit 9   Variations of CVP Analysis

PROBLEM TO BE SOLVED	EQUATION TO USE
Number of guests served at breakeven point	$$\frac{\text{Total Fixed Costs}}{\text{Guest Check Average} - \text{Variable Costs per Guest}}$$
Number of guests served at desired net income level	$$\frac{\text{Total Fixed Costs} + \text{Desired Net Income}}{\text{Guest Check Average} - \text{Variable Costs per Guest}}$$
Number of additional guests needed because of new fixed costs	$$\frac{\text{New Fixed Costs}}{\text{Guest Check Average} - \text{Variable Costs per Guest}}$$
Total number of guests needed due to additional variable costs	$$\frac{\text{Total Fixed Costs} + \text{Desired Net Income}}{\text{Guest Check Average} - \left[\text{Old Variable Costs per Guest} + \text{Additional Variable Costs per Guest} \right]}$$
Number of guests needed if operating time is extended to yield a desired increase in net income	$$\frac{\text{Total Additional Fixed Costs} + \text{Desired Increase in Net Income}}{\text{Guest Check Average} - \text{Variable Costs per Guest}}$$

Given this information, we can calculate the guest check average as follows:

$$\frac{\text{Total Annual Revenues}}{\text{Total Guests}} = \text{Guest Check Avverage}$$

$$\frac{\$1,000,000}{133,333} = \$7.50$$

Variable costs per guest can also be calculated:

$$\frac{\text{Total Annual Variable Costs}}{\text{Total Guests}} = \text{Variable Costs per Guest}$$

$$\frac{\$740,000}{133,333} = \$5.55$$

Given this information, we can now determine the number of guests that must be served for the Lumberjack Cafe to break even by using one of the equations shown in Exhibit 9:

$$\frac{\text{Number of guests served}}{\text{at breakeven point}} = \frac{\text{Total Fixed Costs}}{\text{Guest Check Average} - \text{Variable Costs per Guest}}$$

$$56,410 = \frac{\$110,000}{\$7.50 - \$5.55}$$

The manager does not, of course, want to merely break even. While the operating budget states a net income goal of $150,000, let's use another equation shown in Exhibit 9 and determine the number of guests that must be served for the Lumberjack Cafe to generate a net income of $100,000:

$$\text{Number of guests served at desired net income level} = \frac{\text{Total Fixed Costs} + \text{Desired Net Income}}{\text{Guest Check Average} - \text{Variable Costs per Guest}}$$

$$107,692 = \frac{\$110,000 + \$100,000}{\$7.50 - \$5.55}$$

To generate a $100,000 net income, the Lumberjack Cafe must serve 51,282 guests more than required at the breakeven point (107,692 – 56,410 = 51,282). This is not an unreasonable goal. In fact, the manager is forecasting to serve approximately 133,333 guests during the calendar year for which planning is being done. The net income with this estimated guest count was given to be $150,000. This can be proven as follows:

Net Income	=	Total Revenues	−	Total Variable Costs	−	Total Fixed Costs
$150,000	=	$1,000,000 (133,333 guests × $7.50 guest check average)	−	$740,000 (133,333 × $5.55 variable costs per guest)	−	$110,000

To conclude this example, assume that the property is considering the need to close for extensive remodeling. Only 32,500 guests (fewer than the breakeven guest count of 56,410 noted above) are expected to be served. How much of a loss will the property suffer?

Net Income	=	Total Revenues	−	Total Variable Costs	−	Total Fixed Costs
($46,625)	=	$243,750 (32,500 guests × $7.50 guest check average)	−	$180,375 (32,500 guests × $5.55 variable costs per guest)	−	$110,000

The Lumberjack Cafe will lose $46,625 during the period in which only 32,500 guests are expected to be served.

CVP Example: The Plantation Grill

The following information is taken from the budget being proposed for the next calendar year for the Plantation Grill, a small food and beverage outlet in the Fresh Air Hotel. The number of guests used to estimate the budgeted revenues is 39,000, with a guest check average of $11.

- Total annual revenues $ 429,000
- Total annual fixed costs $ 85,000
- Total annual variable costs $ 300,000
- Total annual costs   ($ 385,000)
- Total net income before taxes $ 44,000

Given this information, we can calculate the total variable cost per guest as follows:

$$\frac{\text{Total Variable Costs}}{\text{Total Guests}} = \text{Total Variable Costs per Guest}$$

$$\frac{\$300{,}000}{39{,}000} = \$7.70$$

Variable costs as a percentage of revenue can be calculated as follows:

$$\frac{\text{Total Variable Costs}}{\text{Total Revenue}} = \text{Variable Costs as a Percentage of Revenue}$$

$$\frac{\$300{,}000}{\$429{,}000} = 0.70 \,(\text{rounded}) \times 100 = 70\%$$

The food service manager of the Plantation Grill is considering adding entertainment. The cost of the entertainment and special advertising will be $2,800 for a one-month trial period. How many additional guests will be required to break even on this entertainment test? Using another equation from Exhibit 9, we can calculate the number of additional guests as follows:

$$\begin{matrix} \text{Number of additional} \\ \text{guests needed because} \\ \text{of new fixed costs} \end{matrix} = \frac{\text{New Fixed Costs}}{\text{Guest Check Average} - \text{Variable Costs per Guest}}$$

$$848 \text{ Guests} = \frac{\$2{,}800}{\$11 - \$7.70}$$

Almost 850 additional guests will be required during the month to generate the additional revenue needed to break even on the entertainment test. Is this reasonable? The food service manager must consider this information when the entertainment decision is made.

Let's assume that the manager of the Plantation Grill is confronted by a 10-percent increase in variable costs. How many guests will be required if fixed costs do not change and the profit goal remains the same? Using another equation from Exhibit 9, we can calculate the number of additional guests as follows:

$$\begin{matrix} \text{Total number of guests} \\ \text{needed due to additional} \\ \text{variable costs} \end{matrix} = \frac{\text{Total Fixed Costs} + \text{Desired Net Income}}{\text{Guest Check Average} - \left[\begin{matrix} \text{Old Variable Costs} \\ \text{per Guest} \end{matrix} + \begin{matrix} \text{Additional} \\ \text{Variable} \\ \text{Costs per} \\ \text{Guests} \end{matrix} \right]}$$

$$50{,}988 \text{ Guests} = \frac{\$85{,}000 + \$44{,}000}{\$11 - [\$7.70 + (.10 \times \$7.70)]}$$

All told, 50,988 guests spending an average of $11.00 each will be necessary to generate revenue needed to cover fixed costs, variable costs (including increases), and profit requirements.

Can the manager find ways to increase the check average and/or number of guests served? Are there methods to reduce variable costs (or at least the variable cost *increase*)? Will profit expectations have to be reduced? These are some of the options the manager must evaluate, and CVP analysis will provide input as decisions are made.

Let's assume that the Plantation Grill is currently closed on Monday nights. How many guests will be required to generate a $500 net income level if it were to open for Monday night business? The net income goal of $500 is judged to be the minimum required to compensate for the operating challenges of keeping the facility open. Assume that additional fixed costs of $275 will be incurred to compensate for production, service, and management labor to staff the operation and pay for other costs, such as advertising, that are directly incurred by the decision to open. Using an equation from Exhibit 9, we can determine the number of guests that must be served as follows:

$$\begin{array}{l}\text{Number of guests needed} \\ \text{if operating time is} \\ \text{extended to yield a desired} \\ \text{increase in net income}\end{array} = \frac{\text{Total Additional}}{\text{Fixed Costs}} + \frac{\text{Desired Increase in}}{\text{Net Income}}$$
$$\frac{}{\text{Guest Check Average}} - \frac{}{\text{Variable Costs per Guest}}$$

$$235 \text{ Guests} = \frac{\$275 + \$500}{\$11 - \$7.70}$$

Can the Plantation Grill generate new business at this volume level? Only the manager can decide. The manager can:

- Choose to remain closed on Monday evenings.

- Accept a lower profit requirement (perhaps the "goodwill" and increased possibility of repeat business will be of interest even if there is no or very little profit generated).

- Find a way to reduce the additional fixed costs incurred by opening on Monday evenings.

- Develop procedures to reduce variable costs without reducing quality. If this can be done, variable costs for the other nights of operation also will be affected—and income might be increased significantly.

Let's assume that management is considering the purchase of a new $6,000 dishwashing machine for the Plantation Grill, to be depreciated over a 10-year period. Annual equipment cost is, therefore, $6,000 divided by 10 years = $600/year. A variation of CVP analysis will allow the manager to determine how much of an increase in revenue will be needed to cover this additional cost without reducing the profit goal. Using an equation from Exhibit 9, we can first calculate the number of guests required and then compute the additional revenue level.

$$\begin{array}{l}\text{Number of additional} \\ \text{guests needed because} \\ \text{of new fixed costs}\end{array} = \frac{\text{New Fixed Costs}}{\text{Guest Check Average} - \text{Variable Costs per Guest}}$$

$$182 \text{ Guests} = \frac{\$600}{\$11.00 - \$7.70}$$

The additional revenue can now be determined as $2,002. This is calculated by multiplying the number of additional guests by the guest check average (182 guests × $11).

Endnotes

1. For further information, see *CARE: Controlling Alcohol Risks Effectively* (Lansing, Mich.: American Hotel & Lodging Educational Institute, 2007).

2. Readers interested in a detailed explanation of determining the fixed and variable elements of mixed costs should read Raymond S. Schmidgall's *Hospitality Industry Managerial Accounting,* 6th ed. (Lansing, Mich.: American Hotel & Lodging Educational Institute, 2006).

3. Readers interested in a detailed explanation of cost allocation should read Schmidgall.

4. Readers interested in a detailed explanation of the use of computers in budgeting and financial planning should read Michael L. Kasavana and John J. Cahill's *Managing Technology in the Hospitality Industry,* 5th ed. (Lansing, Mich.: American Hotel & Lodging Educational Institute, 2007).

5. Readers interested in a more detailed explanation of cost-volume-profit analysis should read Chapter 7 of Schmidgall.

Key Terms

bottom-up budgeting—A method of budget development in multi-unit organizations in which budgets are assembled at the unit level and then "rolled" up to higher organizational levels.

cell (spreadsheet)—The intersection of a row and a column on an electronic spreadsheet.

cost-volume-profit (CVP) analysis—An analytical process used by managers to examine the relationships among various costs, revenues, and profit in either graphic or equation form, allowing one to determine the revenue required at any desired profit level. Also called breakeven analysis.

derived demand—A concept of estimating room revenue and then using this information to project revenue from food, beverages, and other revenue centers based on guest spending patterns that have been developed from in-house studies.

electronic spreadsheets—Computer terminal displays that resemble traditional accounting worksheets but possess powerful computation capabilities.

fixed costs—Costs that remain constant in the short run even though revenue volume may vary; examples of fixed costs include salaries, rent expense, insurance expense, and so on.

guest check average—Total revenue (usually assessed separately for food and beverage) divided by total guests; the average amount of revenue generated from each guest.

mark-up method—An approach to pricing goods and services that determines selling prices by adding a certain percentage to the cost of goods sold (food cost); the mark-up is designed to cover all non-product costs (labor, utilities, supplies, interest expense, taxes, etc.) and the desired profit.

operating budget—Management's detailed plans for generating revenue and incurring expenses to meet profit requirements for each department within the hospitality operation; also referred to as the revenue and expense budget.

percentage method—A method of estimating food and beverage operating expenses based on the current percentage of each expense relative to revenue.

reforecasting (budget)—The process of revising (updating) a budget to reflect factors not anticipated when the budget was initially developed.

sales mix—The number of each specific menu item that is sold during a certain time period relative to the total number of all menu items sold.

top-down budgeting—A method of budget development in multi-unit organizations in which budgets are developed at the corporate level and are then passed down to lower organizational levels, with each successively lower level becoming responsible for a specific segment of the budget.

variable costs—Costs that change proportionately with the volume of business; examples of variable costs include food costs, beverage costs, labor costs, and the cost of some supplies used in food production and service areas.

zero-based budgeting—A method of estimating food and beverage operating expenses that starts over from zero instead of extending costs or cost percentages transferred from the current budget period; it involves starting at a zero expense level for each category of cost and building up to the new budget expense level, justifying each step along the way.

 Review Questions ────────────────────────────

1. What is an operating budget and why is it important?

2. What are the basic procedures necessary to develop a budget plan?

3. Why is it important to compare budget standards with actual operating results? How often should this be done?

4. How should the required level of profit be determined?

5. What advantages does an electronic spreadsheet have over manual methods in the budgeting process?

6. What is meant by a "chained recalculation"?

7. How would you go about incorporating profit requirements into the pricing process?

8. What are the advantages and disadvantages of top-down and bottom-up budgeting in multi-unit properties? Which would you prefer if you were a unit manager? Why?

9. What are the assumptions required for CVP analysis?

10. What are some examples of the types of management issues that can be addressed by CVP analysis?

Internet Sites

For more information, visit the following Internet sites. Remember that Internet addresses can change without notice. If the site is no longer there, you can use a search engine to look for additional sites.

Budgeting

For an extensive compilation of information about operating budgets, go to the website of the U.S. Small Business Administration: www.sbaonline.sba.gov/. You may also wish to check out the following websites:

AbusinessResource
www.abusinessresource.com

Score
www.score.org

Microsoft Small Business Center
www.microsoft.com/smallbusiness/
hub.mspx

Small Business Notes
www.smallbusinessnotes.com

priZem
www.prizem.com

Cost-Volume-Profit (CVP) Analysis

Business Owner's Toolkit:
   Cost/Volume/Profit Analysis
www.toolkit.cch.com/text/PO6_7500.asp

Mira Consulting
www.miraconsulting.com/brkevn.html

Buzgate.org
www.buzgate.org

U.S. Small Business Administration
www.sba.gov
(Enter "breakeven analysis" in the site's search field.)

DinkeyTown
www.dinkeytown.net/business.html

Problems

Problem 1

a. What is the initial budgeted profit (before tax) being planned by the Spartanland Restaurant for the current year, given the following information?

   • Revenue (food) $975,000   Y. 31

   • Revenue (beverage) $135,000

   • Food cost = 31% of food revenue

   • Beverage cost = 22% of beverage revenue

   • Labor cost (payroll) = 34% of total revenue

   • Employee benefits = 18% of labor cost (payroll)

   • Other operating expenses = 14% of total revenue

   • All fixed costs = 8% of total revenue

b. The owner does not approve of the initial budget. Working together, the owner and manager believe they can accomplish the following:

- Implement marketing plans to increase the number of guests consuming food by an additional 12,000 (guest check average = $22.50)

- Increase beverage revenues by 8% over initial estimates

- Decrease food costs to 30%

- Decrease beverage costs to 20%

- Decrease payroll costs to 32% (but benefit costs will increase by 6% over the initial budget because of new payroll taxes not included in the original budget)

- Decrease operating expenses to 12% of total revenue

(Fixed costs will remain at the same *dollar* amount as in the original budget.)

c. What is the revised estimate of budgeted profit before tax?

Problem 2

The manager of the Spartanland Restaurant is developing the operating budget for next year using the following financial information from the current year:

Item	Current Year's Amount	Next Year's Percentage Increase (Decrease)	Next Year's Amount ($)
Food revenue	$973,000 $\times$ .37	4%	1011920
Beverage revenue	$112,500	2%	114750
Food cost	36%	1%	_____
Beverage cost	23%	(1%)	_____
Labor (including benefits)	$298,000	(2%)	_____
Other operating costs	16%	same	_____
Fixed costs	$70,000	same	_____

a. What is the *current year's* budgeted profit (loss)?

b. Develop next year's budget: indicate the profit (loss).

Problem 3

Assume the approved food operations budget for the Hilotown Restaurant for 20X1 is as follows:

	$	% of Revenue
Food revenue	1,400,000	100
Food cost	434,000	31
Payroll	364,000	26
Payroll taxes/benefits	42,000	3
Direct operating expenses	112,000	8
Entertainment	14,000	1
Advertising	42,000	3
Utilities	70,000	5
Administrative/general	56,000	4

fixed costs [

Repairs/maintenance	14,000	1
Rent	70,000	5
Real estate/property taxes	28,000	2
Insurance	14,000	1
Interest expense	42,000	3
Depreciation	28,000	2
Income (profit) before taxes	70,000	5

Unforeseen problems beyond the control of the owner (ongoing terrorism alerts that have significantly reduced the tourist travel on which the restaurant relies) have caused a substantial reduction in revenue. In June (the restaurant operates on a calendar year [January–December] budget), the owner reforecasted revenues down to $1,100,000.

   a.   What will be the fixed costs under the new budget?

   b.   Assuming the owner wants to maintain the original "bottom line" profit (income [profit] before taxes) of $70,000, how much in revenues will remain to be spent on variable costs?

   c.   Assuming the owner is willing to break even on the restaurant's operation, how much in revenues will remain to be spent on variable costs?

Problem 4

The Blue Ridge Café's budget for next year indicates the following:

Revenues		$765,000
Total fixed costs	$ 91,000	
Total variable costs	$512,000	
Total Costs		$603,000
Net income before tax		$162,000

Revenue estimates assume 89,470 guests will be served.

   a.   What is the guest check average?   8.55

   b.   What are the variable costs per guests?   5.72

   c.   How many guests must be served for the Blue Ridge Café to break even?   32,155

   d.   If the owner needed a net income of at least $114,000, how many guests would need to be served?   72,438

   e.   How many more guests are needed to generate a net income of $114,000 than are needed to break even?   40,283

   f.   If the Blue Ridge Café decides to close during two months that traditionally generate slow business, it will lose about 18,000 guests. If the owner chooses to do this, what will be the new net income or loss?   520,068

   g.   The manager is considering a kitchen renovation that will add $7,500 in new fixed costs (depreciation and interest) each year. How much will the café's net income (loss) be if it does this during the first year that it closes for two months? (See Question F above.)

   h.   The Blue Ridge Café closes for two months (Question F), incurs the additional fixed costs (Question G), *and* is the "victim" of a problem in the economy that results in a 14-percent increase in variable costs. How many additional guests are needed for it to maintain its net income level (Question G)?

Problem 5

The Anytown Restaurant has recorded the following financial information:

Food costs	$365,000
Labor costs	$315,000
All other costs (including fixed costs)	$224,000
Net income (profit)	$76,000
Number of guests served	89,000

a. What is Anytown Restaurant's revenue?

b. What is Anytown Restaurant's guest check average?

c. Assume the Anytown Restaurant has fixed costs of $95,000; what are its variable costs? (Hint: all costs — fixed costs = variable costs.)

d. What is the variable cost per guest?

e. How many guests must the restaurant serve to break even?

f. How many guests must be served to have a net income (profit) of $105,000?

g. Assume that Anytown Restaurant serves only 84,000 guests. What will be its net income (loss)?

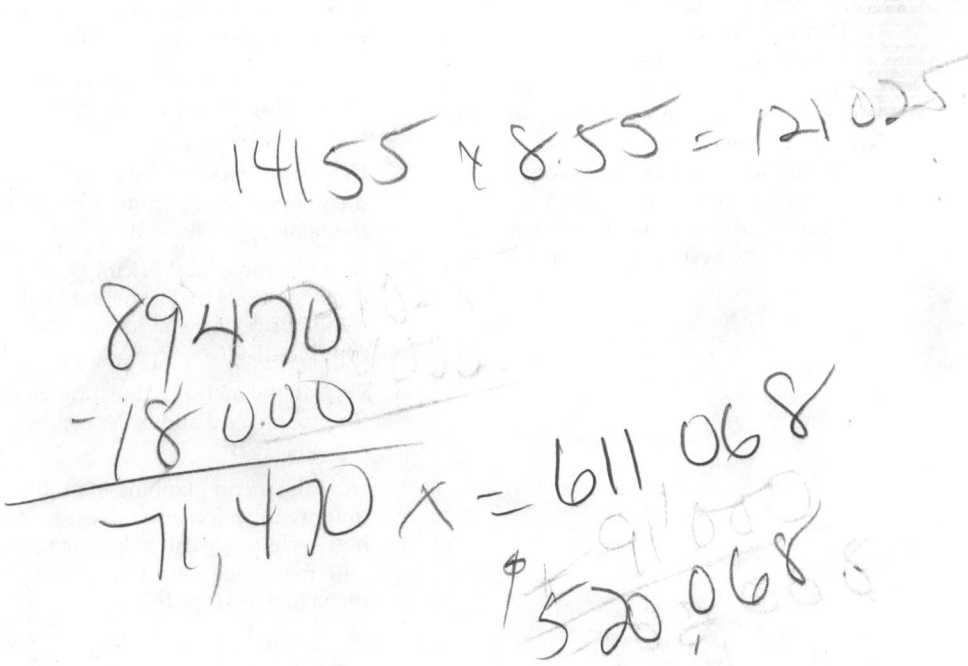

Chapter 5 Outline

Competencies

1. Explain how a system of food service control points helps managers carry out critical functions on a daily basis. (pp. 133–134)

2. Describe factors that influence menu planning strategies and identify external and internal factors that influence menu changes. (pp. 134–141)

3. Discuss subjective methods for pricing menu items, and calculate a base selling price for menu items using simple mark-up pricing methods. (pp. 142–147)

4. Calculate a base selling price for menu items using the contribution margin pricing method. (pp. 147–148)

5. Calculate a base selling price for menu items using the ratio pricing method. (pp. 148–149)

6. Calculate a base selling price for menu items using prime costs pricing methods. (pp. 149–153)

7. Describe important pricing considerations that affect the final selling price of menu items. (pp. 153–154)

8. Explain the menu engineering method for pricing food and beverage items. (pp. 154–162)

9. Describe menu planning in multi-unit organizations, and discuss how technology can help managers with menu planning, design, and management. (pp. 162–170)

5

The Menu:
The Foundation for Control

THE MENU IS THE FOUNDATION for the control process in every food and beverage operation, and menu planning begins the control process. This chapter focuses on the menu and presents an overview of other control points that play crucial roles in determining the success or failure of a food and beverage operation. The chapter contains practical, objective techniques for effective menu planning, pricing, and evaluation. The final section of the chapter examines technological aspects of menu management.

Food Service Control Points

Control points are basic operating activities that must be performed in any food service establishment. Exhibit 1 illustrates the ten main control points leading to guest satisfaction. The flow chart begins with menu planning at the base, since it is the foundation for control. The arrows between boxes indicate a flow of products and, in some cases, a transfer of paperwork or a movement of personnel. For example, the arrow between the holding and **serving** control points represents the flow of food products from the production staff to the service staff. The arrow between the serving and **service** control points indicates the movement of products from the servers to the guests. Notice that three control points—preparing, cooking, and holding—are grouped together as production activities. They normally take place in the kitchen (although cafeteria and self-serve buffet operations typically hold food in public-access areas).

Beginning with menu planning, each control point plays a crucial role in determining the success or failure of a food and beverage operation. Each control point is a miniature system with its own structure and functions. Each basic operating activity has specific objectives, guidelines, standards, and internal processes that contribute to the success of the operation and the ultimate goal of guest satisfaction.

When a food and beverage operation is seen as a system of control points, the control activities associated with each function are easier to identify and carry out on a daily basis. This systems approach permits the manager to establish an audit trail of control activities. It is then easier to separate, identify, and take corrective action to resolve problems. The manager can then undertake short- and long-range planning in the effort to control future events, rather than waiting for crises to develop and then taking a "fire-fighting" approach.

133

Exhibit 1   Flow Chart of Basic Operating Activities (Control Points) in a Food and Beverage Operation

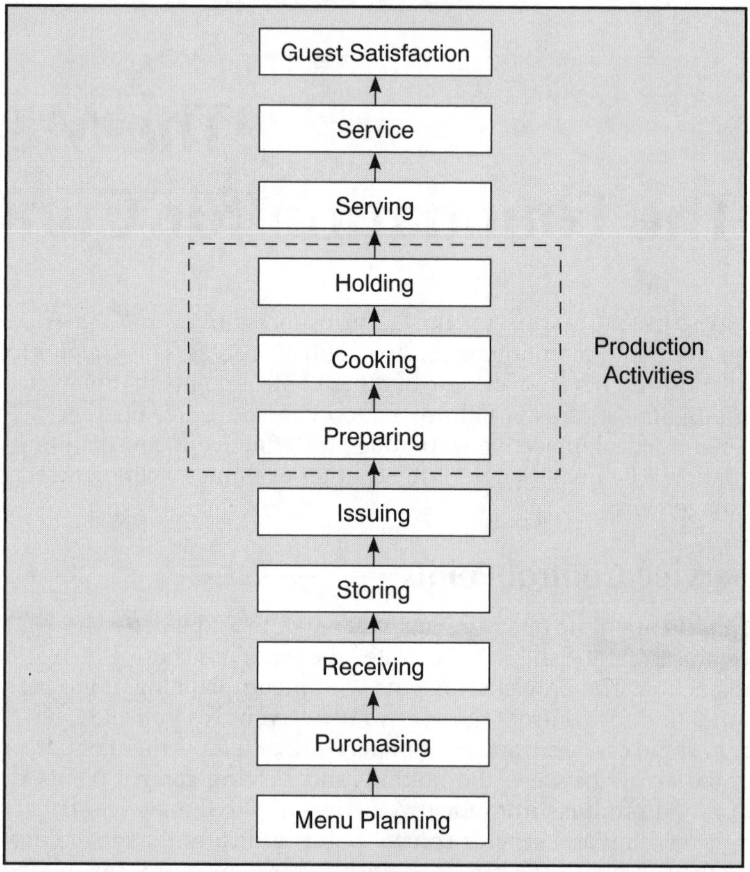

Source: Adapted from Ronald F. Cichy, *Quality Sanitation Management* (Lansing, Mich.: American Hotel & Lodging Educational Institute, 1994), p. 3.

The Menu's Influence

The process of planning a menu never ends; the final menu is never achieved. Rather, the process is ongoing, dynamic, and based on the expectations of the operation's present and potential guests. From creating an image to communicating a plan for satisfying the guests, influencing the guests' purchase decisions, **merchandising** the correct products, and more, the menu has a continuous impact on all aspects of an operation. A properly planned and well-designed menu stimulates revenue and increases the guest check average because, whenever a menu is presented to a guest, a sales transaction begins. And the menu not only creates the operation's image but reflects it. The image may be elegant, businesslike, fun, ethnic, or trendy, depending on what the target markets desire.

The menu has an impact on every aspect of a food and beverage manager's job as well as the operation itself. The following paragraphs identify some of the important areas of a food service operation that are directly affected by the menu.

Product Control Procedures. The food and beverage products must be controlled. If an operation needs shrimp to produce a menu item, shrimp must be purchased, received, stored, issued, prepared, cooked, held, served, and accounted for.

Cost Control Procedures. Careful cost control procedures must be followed as more expensive products are served, as service styles dictated by the menu become more complex, and as guests increasingly demand a "dining experience" as opposed to "just a meal."

Production Requirements. Food items required by the menu must be produced consistently. Product quality, staff productivity and skills, timing and scheduling, and other kitchen (back- or heart-of-the-house) functions are all dictated by the menu.

Nutritional Content of Meals. Noncommercial food service programs and, increasingly, commercial food service operations are concerned about the nutritional content of food served to consumers. The menu offerings can have an impact on the health and well-being of those to whom they are offered.

Equipment Needs. Equipment must be available to prepare products offered on the menu. The menu must be balanced and based on available equipment resources so that no one workstation is overloaded or underutilized.

Sanitation Management. Since the menu sets the stage for the remaining control points, management must consider menu items in light of possible sanitation hazards. Once the potential hazards are identified, the risks can be reduced.

Layout and Space Requirements. There must be adequate facilities for the staff and equipment required to produce items listed on the menu. The layout and design of facilities establish the physical space within which food production, serving, and service take place. The physical facilities must be adequate for the purchasing, receiving, storing, issuing, production, and serving of every menu item.

Staffing Needs. Employees must be available to produce and serve all items offered on the menu. As a menu becomes more complex, greater demands may be placed on the staff. Staffing needs are also influenced by the degree to which the menu uses **convenience food** items (products that have some or all of the labor built into them that otherwise would need to be added on site).

Service Requirements. The food and beverage manager must carefully plan how products will be served to the guest. The menu affects the skill levels required for service personnel, along with equipment, inventory, and facilities needed in the front of the house.

Revenue Control Procedures. When a simple menu is used in a fast-food operation and guests pay before they are served, the potential for revenue control problems is not as great as the problem potential in a table service restaurant offering an elaborate menu.

Exhibit 2   Priority Concerns of the Menu Planner

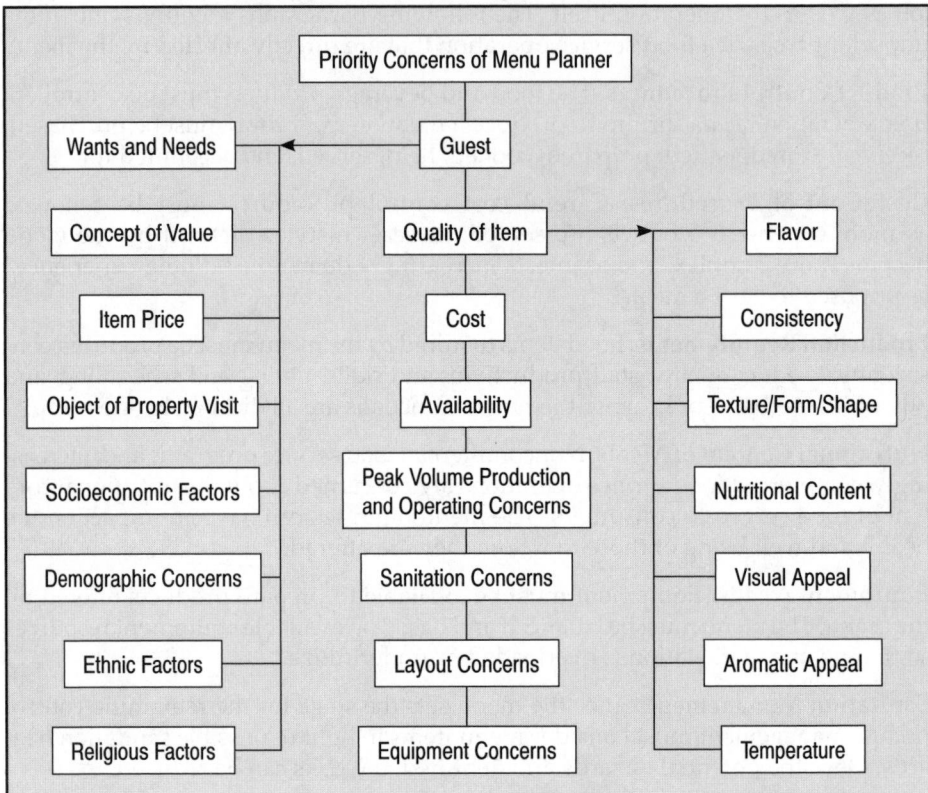

Menu Planning

The menu is not only an important control tool, it is also a sales, advertising, merchandising, and marketing tool. In this respect, the menu addresses both control- and marketing-related concerns and blends them into a workable system.

Marketing Implications of the Menu

Because it lists the items an operation is offering for sale, a menu, in effect, communicates a property's food and beverage marketing plans. In developing its marketing plans, a property needs to assess the products, service, **ambience** (theme and atmosphere), and perceived value that its target market(s) expect. Items selected for inclusion on the menu should be based on the needs and desires of the operation's target market(s). In carrying out its marketing plans, the food and beverage operation must strive to meet or exceed the expectations of the guests being served.

Management must never forget the marketing implications of the menu planning process. Exhibit 2 illustrates factors to consider in planning the menu. Notice that the most important and numerous concerns involve the guest and the quality of menu items. These are also the most complex concerns. Other factors include cost, availability, and production/operation issues.

In addition, menu planners should study the competition and the types of menu items offered by both direct and indirect competitors in the area. It is especially necessary to consider items offered by competitors who are trying to attract the same target market(s). What are guests of other properties purchasing? Why? What are the selling prices? What can be done to make the property's own products and services special—and more attractive to guests? These and related questions with marketing implications constitute a primary source of information for menu planners in all types of food and beverage operations.

Theme and Atmosphere

The complexity of menu planning in commercial properties depends on the ambience of the operation. Menu planning for table service restaurants is different from menu planning for banquet or buffet service operations. Ambience, the guest check average, and marketing concerns are prime examples of these differences.

Many food and beverage operations have a specific theme and atmosphere. French, Italian, and Chinese restaurants are examples of operations with ethnic themes. Others feature the cuisine of the American Southwest (for example, chili rellenos, tortillas, enchiladas) or Cajun cuisine (for example, jambalaya, gumbo, blackened redfish). Still others create a healthy ambience by capitalizing on an atmosphere and theme built on open, airy, plant-filled facilities that serve high-quality, light, fresh foods. In any case, menu items offered must be compatible with the theme and atmosphere of the operation.

Menu Planning Strategies

In the past, food service managers often attempted to diversify their menus by adding new menu items. Since most items were made "from scratch" (an industry term meaning on-site food preparation), the number and variety of raw ingredients increased correspondingly.

Another strategy, called "rationalization," works to simplify the operation to make it more efficient. For example, a restaurant can offer several menu items that use the same raw ingredients. This cross-utilization enables an operation to prepare and serve many menu selections with a limited number of raw ingredients.

When the menu is carefully planned to ensure a balance of menu selections in each category, the results of these new strategies can be a streamlining of the purchasing, receiving, storing, issuing, production, and serving control points.

Today, as in the past, food service managers are searching for new menu item alternatives. The increasing number of high-quality convenience foods has made it easier to offer new items without having to buy additional raw ingredients or elaborate equipment. High-quality convenience products can be purchased in semi-prepared or fully prepared forms. Because they have built-in labor, they also reduce in-house labor requirements. Of course, convenience food products usually have a higher as-purchased (AP) price than the raw ingredients from which they are made.

It is always best to base initial menu plans on the needs and desires of the target market(s). However, several other factors may influence the menu selection. Among these factors are the recommended storage conditions (time and temperature); personnel skill levels; the product's availability and seasonality; the stability of quality and price levels; and the operation's ability to purchase, produce, and serve the menu items in a safe, sanitary, and cost-effective way.

Building the Menu

Entrées are typically selected first in the menu planning process. It is important to consider not only the types of entrées, but also their costs, preparation methods, and compatibility with the operation's theme and atmosphere. A basic decision in planning the entrée concerns the number of entrées to offer. Some managers feel they should have something for everyone and, therefore, provide a wide range of choices. This approach can create a number of problems that require careful planning and control to resolve.

The variety of entrées also affects the types and quantities of ingredients (each with its own standard purchase specifications) that must be received, stored, issued, produced, and served. A corresponding amount of preparation equipment and number of skilled personnel must also be available, and production and service problems are more likely to occur. In summary, control becomes more complex as the number of "scratch" entrées offered on the menu increases.

The reverse approach—making available only a limited number of entrées—reduces these types of problems considerably. In the United States, there are many specialty/theme restaurants that offer relatively few entrées. By focusing on a specific market segment, these operations simplify marketing techniques and minimize many in-house production, serving, and control problems.

After selecting entrées, menu planners must choose menu items to complement the entrées. A common procedure is to plan, in sequence, appetizers and soups, followed by high-starch items and vegetables (if not part of the entrée), then accompanying salads, and, finally, other menu components such as breads, desserts, and beverages. Trends in entrée consumption affect the other items added to the menu.

Dining Trends

A current trend in dining that is compatible with many lifestyles is "grazing." Grazers are unlikely to select a full meal, but rather choose appetizers, salads, and desserts to complete their menu selections. Grazers are more likely to choose smaller portions of more menu items than select a larger portion single entrée. Therefore, menus featuring a wide selection of appetizers, salads, and desserts are popular with grazers. As a consequence, menus are being designed with interchangeable courses, sometimes referred to as "modular cuisine."

The grazing trend may grow as guests change their eating habits and focus on the perceived high value of making multiple menu selections to "build their own" meals. The grazing trend seems to be particularly popular with health- and fitness-conscious guests, whose lifestyles reflect their desire for variety.

If a food and beverage operation's business is transient and the clientele changes frequently, the menu may be static (remain the same). Generally, menus that change are preferable to static menus. However, menu variability depends on the seasonal availability of raw ingredients at reasonable costs, the number and types of courses offered, the potential for using leftovers and local ingredients, the preferences of the guests, the operation's image, and the desires of the target market(s).

When the business is highly repetitive and involves regular guests such as businesspeople and others who work and reside in the local area, there is a greater need for daily specials that change regularly. Often, daily specials feature local or regional fresh ingredients and permit the menu planner to take advantage of reduced costs and increased availability to add interest to a menu. A trend today in daily specials is to announce their availability on attractive, eye-catching iridescent or colorfully lighted menu boards and train service staff to merchandise them to guests.

Menu Design

As noted, the design of the menu can influence the guest's purchase decisions, stimulate sales of additional or preferable menu items, and increase the guest check average. Guests are influenced by visual cues provided by the menu. Readability, artwork, type styles, physical design, and layout play an important role in merchandising the food and beverage products that are both profitable to the operation and satisfying to the guests.

Exhibits 3, 4, and 5 show the focal points of single-sheet, single-fold, and two-fold menus. Menu items featured in these positions often draw the reader's attention because of their location. Of course, other devices such as art, pictures, and graphics can be used to draw the reader's attention elsewhere. You'll learn more about the importance of using menu space effectively in the discussion of menu engineering later in this chapter.

Menu Changes ~~Guest #4~~

Because conditions change, a food service operation's menu must also change. Menu changes are influenced by both external and internal factors.

External Factors. External factors include consumer demands, economic conditions, the competition, supply levels, and industry trends. Consumer demands are perhaps the most important factor to consider in changing a menu. Management should first decide which potential market(s) it wants to attract with the modified menu, and then evaluate the proposed menu changes in light of the negative and positive effects they may have on current guests.

Economic conditions include the cost of ingredients and the potential profitability of new menu items. Menu items offered by the competition may dictate choices to be made available. For example, a hotel food service located next to a restaurant offering the "best Chinese food in town" may elect not to serve Chinese cuisine. Supply levels relate the price to the quality and quantity of the proposed menu items. Supply levels are highly variable for some seasonal raw ingredients such as fresh fruits and vegetables. Industry trends provide general information about how the industry is responding to new demands.

Exhibit 3   Focal Point of Single-Sheet Menu

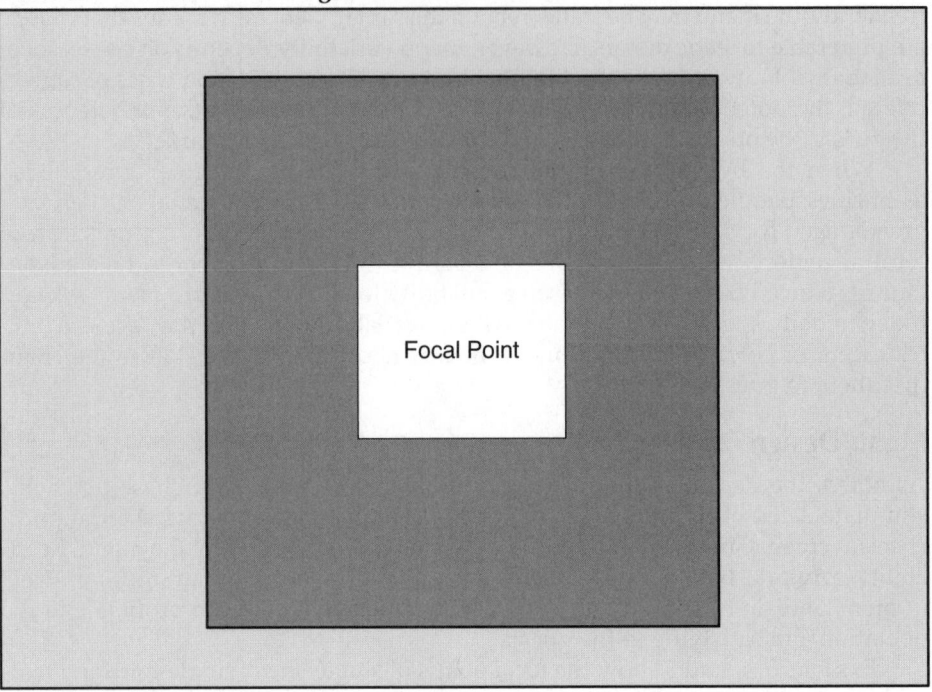

Exhibit 4   Focal Point of Single-Fold Menu

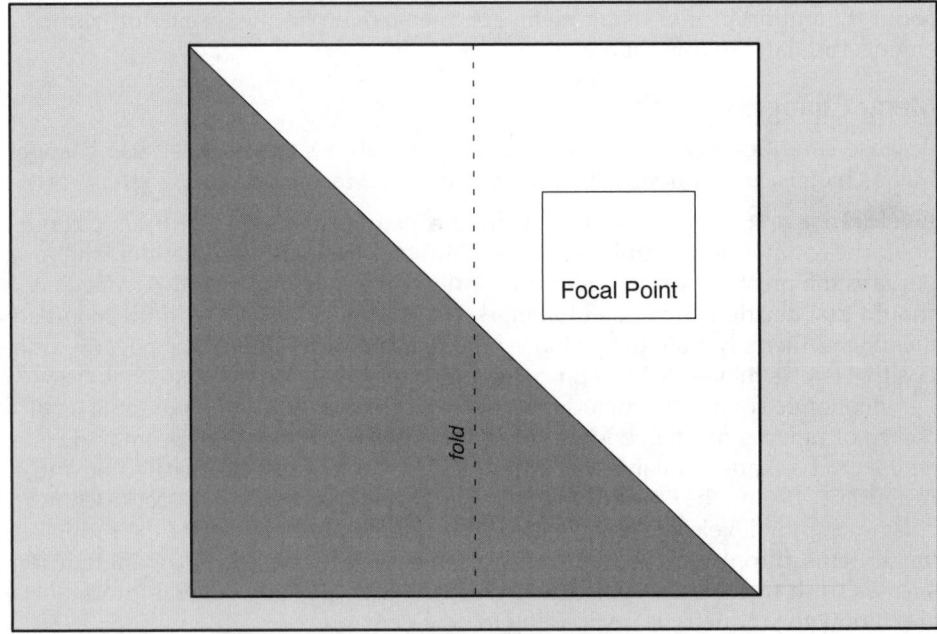

Exhibit 5   Focal Point of Two-Fold Menu

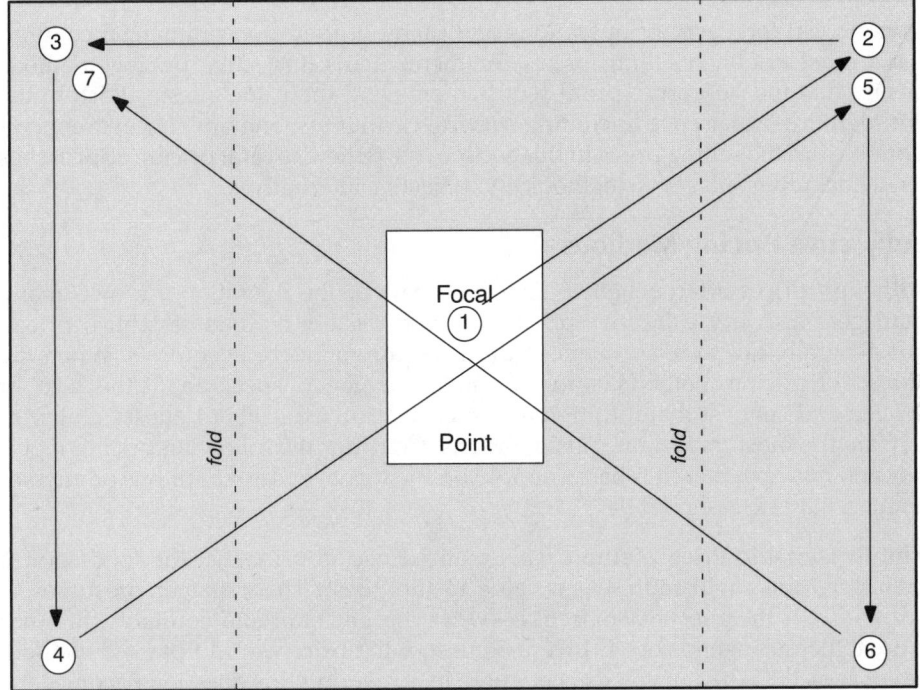

The numbers indicate the order of eye movement when no special graphics are used.

Internal Factors. Internal factors that may result in a proposed menu change include the facility's meal pattern, concept and theme, operational system, and menu mix. The typical meal pattern is breakfast, lunch, and dinner. Management must decide if existing meal periods should be continued or altered, and the decision is heavily influenced by expectations of guests. Any change must fit with the establishment's concept and theme. A restaurant that is known as the best steakhouse in the city may do itself a disservice by adding an extensive variety of seafood to the menu. An establishment's image may also rule out certain foods that do not blend with its theme and decor. For example, even though ethnic foods are growing in popularity, a hotel restaurant may find it difficult to fit ethnic foods into its projected image.

Menu changes are also modified by the establishment's operational system. For example, if extensive new equipment purchases are crucial to the introduction of a new menu item, the change may be too costly. Also, the change may raise both food and labor costs to unacceptable levels. Or, in some cases, the skill levels of production and service personnel may not be adequate to produce the new menu item. The operation's existing menu has a certain overall combination or mix of items. This menu mix will be affected by any change in individual items. All of these factors should be evaluated before menu changes are finalized and implemented.

Calculating Menu Selling Prices

Commercial food service operations and many of their noncommercial counterparts must establish selling prices for menu items. Objective pricing methods ensure that the property's profit requirements and the value guests attach to the entire dining experience (including service, cleanliness, and ambience) are incorporated into the selling price. In this section, we review several pricing approaches used, including subjective methods and objective alternatives.

Subjective Pricing Methods

Although prices affect whether financial goals of the operation are met, many managers use very subjective pricing methods. These methods establish prices, but generally fail to relate them to profit requirements or even costs. When the subject of pricing methods comes up, many managers speak about the "art" of pricing and suggest that intuition and special knowledge about guests' ability to pay are the most important considerations. Consider the following pricing methods and notice that each is based simply on the manager's assumptions or guesses about what prices should be.

The Reasonable Price Method. This method uses a price that the food service manager thinks will represent a value to the guest. The manager presumes to know—from the guest's perspective—what charge is fair and equitable. In other words, the manager asks, "If I were a guest, what price would I pay for the item being served?" The manager's best guess in answering this question becomes the product's selling price.

The Highest Price Method. Using this plan, a manager sets the highest price that he or she thinks guests are willing to pay. The concept of value is stretched to the maximum and is then "backed off" to provide a margin of error in the manager's estimate.

The Loss Leader Method. With this plan, an unusually low price is set for an item (or items). The manager assumes that guests will be attracted to the property to purchase the low-priced item(s) and that they will then select other items while they are there. Beverage or food prices on some items are set low to bring guests into the property, but purchases of other items are necessary for the operation to meet profit requirements. This pricing method is sometimes used as an "early bird" or senior citizen discount to attract specific segments of the market.

The Intuitive Price Method. When prices are set by intuition alone, the manager takes little more than a wild guess about the selling price. Closely related to this approach is a trial-and-error pricing plan: if one price doesn't work, another is tested. The intuitive price method differs from the reasonable price method in that there is less effort to determine what represents value from the guests' perspective.

These pricing methods are based on assumptions, hunches, and guesses. Such methods are generally ineffective because they do not consider profit requirements and the product costs necessary to put the item on the table.

Subjective pricing methods may be common in the food service industry simply because they have been used in the past, because the manager setting prices has no information about product costs or profit requirements to work with, and/or because the manager is not familiar with more objective methods. In today's market, with increased consumer demands for value in dining, and with higher purchase prices for products needed by the property, these plans seldom work.

Objective Pricing Methods

If the reasonable price, highest price, loss leader, and intuitive price methods are subjective and should not be used, what are better alternatives? Objective methods based on data in the approved operating budget help the manager transfer budget plans into selling prices that help generate revenue required by the operating budget. Each of the methods that follow, to some extent at least, helps the manager to ensure that selling prices incorporate budget requirements.

Before any objective pricing method can be used, however, three basic cost procedures must be in place and consistently used:

- *Standard recipes.* A standard recipe must be available for each item when a selling price is being developed. For example, if the manager is pricing an oyster platter, standard recipes must be available for the oyster entrée, its garnish, salad with dressing choice, potato or other starch, vegetable choice, bread and butter, and any other items included in the "oyster platter."

- *Precosting with current costs.* Each affected recipe must be precosted with current market cost data to determine the cost to produce one portion when carefully following the standard recipe for each component of the menu item being priced.

- *Standard recipes must be used.* While this may be obvious, many operations have standard recipes available but do not consistently use them. Too often, because of labor turnover and other reasons, production personnel deviate from recipes that have historically dictated the quantity, methodology, and cost of food production. If recipes are not used, there is no reason to have them or to cost them.

Simple Mark-Up (Multiplier) Pricing Methods. Some pricing methods use a mark-up (multiplier) based on food costs for menu items. The methods are designed to cover all costs and to yield the desired profit. The following paragraphs examine the ingredients mark-up, prime-ingredient mark-up, and mark-up with accompaniment costs pricing methods.

Ingredients mark-up method. The **ingredients mark-up pricing method** attempts to consider all product costs: food costs when pricing food items and beverage costs when pricing beverages. The three steps of this method are:

1. Determine the ingredients' costs from all applicable standard recipes.

2. Determine the multiplier to use in marking up the ingredients' costs.

3. Establish a base selling price by multiplying the ingredients' costs by the multiplier.

A **base selling price** is not necessarily the final selling price, because the simple output from formulas may not yield an appropriate final selling price. Rather, a base selling price is a starting point, after which other factors are assessed and the price adjusted accordingly. These other factors are important pricing considerations and will be addressed later in the chapter.

The multiplier determined in step 2 is generally based on the desired food (or beverage) cost percentage, which can be established by the approved budget. For example, if the desired food cost percentage is 40 percent, the multiplier would be 2.5:

$$\text{Multiplier} = \frac{1}{\text{Desired Food Cost Percentage}}$$

$$2.5 = \frac{1}{0.40}$$

Assume that an oyster platter offered on the lunch menu has a standard food cost of $5.32 (the total per-portion cost of the standard recipes for all items constituting the platter). If a 40-percent food cost is desired, the price of the oyster platter is determined as follows:

$$\text{Base Selling Price} = \text{Ingredient Cost} \times \text{Multiplier}$$

$$\$13.30 = \$5.32 \times 2.5$$

If this price appears reasonable based on the market for oyster platters, then the item is sold for about $13.30.

Prime-ingredient mark-up method. The **prime-ingredient mark-up pricing method** differs from the ingredients mark-up method because only the cost of the prime ingredient is considered. Therefore, the multiplier must be greater than the multiplier used when considering the total cost of all ingredients.

Using the same oyster platter example, assume the prime ingredient cost is $2.65 (one portion of oysters). If a multiplier of 5.02 is used, the oyster platter is priced at $13.30. The price is calculated as follows:

$$\text{Base Selling Price} = \text{Prime Ingredient's Cost} \times \text{Multiplier}$$

$$\$13.30 = \$2.65 \times 5.02$$

If the cost of the oysters in this example increases to $2.75 for the larger dinner portion, the new base selling price would be $13.81 ($2.75 × 5.02).

The prime-ingredient approach assumes that the costs of all ingredients change in proportion to the prime ingredient. For example, when the prime ingredient's cost increases by 10 percent, other ingredient costs are assumed to increase by 10 percent also.

Mark-up with accompaniment costs method. Using the **mark-up with accompaniment costs pricing method**, managers determine ingredient costs based only on entrée items and then add a standard accompaniment or "plate" cost to this amount before multiplying by a multiplier. This plate cost is an average cost for all non-entrée and other relatively inexpensive items, including salad, vegetables, bread, butter, and non-alcoholic beverages. For example:

Entrée Costs	$ 3.15
Plate Cost	+ $ 1.25
Estimated Food Cost	$ 4.40
Multiplier	× 3.3
Base Selling Price	$14.52

Note that the plate cost covering the estimated food cost of all non-entrée food costs is added to the entrée cost before the multiplier is used.

An advantage of this method is its simplicity. Careful calculations for only the expensive entrée costs are necessary. Time can be saved by combining all other food costs into an estimated plate cost.

A disadvantage may be that plate costs are not truly representative of food costs associated with these other items. How is the plate cost determined? How often is it adjusted? Also, managers must establish a reasonable and objective multiplier that relates to profit requirements. If this is not done, the mark-up with accompaniment costs pricing method is no better than the subjective pricing methods discussed earlier.

Determining the multiplier. The three basic mark-up pricing methods just discussed are simple to use and, for that reason, are commonly used in the food service industry. A significant disadvantage, however, involves determining the multiplier. How does a manager decide this? For many managers, it is a subjective decision based primarily on experience and "rule of thumb" (such as the traditional 40-percent food cost). Should managers use last year's average food cost percentage? Should they use a statistic supplied by a national, state, or other food service association or consulting firm?

It is possible, of course, to use a multiplier based on the planned food and other costs from the operating budget. If, on the average, menu items are priced to yield the food cost percentage dictated by the budget, planners have developed a simple foundation for generating revenue sufficient to cover food costs and to yield a **contribution margin** (food revenue minus food costs) sufficient for other expenses and profit requirements. The little time required to generate and use a multiplier based on the operating budget may make it especially cost-effective for many small-volume operations.

However, the impact of sales mix cannot be overlooked. If, for example, increased unit sales of a higher food cost percentage item replace sales of its counterparts with lower food cost percentages, the average food cost percentage can be made according to budget—but with undesirable financial results. Note, though, that use of an ideal (theoretical) food cost percentage—easily calculated with point-of-sale (POS) technology—addresses this concern by using data based on the actual (not historical) sales mix.

There are other potential disadvantages of using simple multiplier pricing methods. For example, these methods do not reflect higher or lower labor, energy, or other costs associated with production of specific menu items. Rather, they either assume that all operating costs relate in some direct way to food costs or that these cost differences can be ignored. These assumptions may not be warranted when, for example, one considers the extensive amount of labor required to prepare some items relative to others.

It's Easy to Calculate Menu Pricing Mark-Ups

How to Establish Multipliers

The mark-up by multiplier pricing methods arrive at a base selling price by multiplying a factor (multiplier) by the ingredient food cost. How are the multipliers established?

I. Ingredients Mark-Up Method

$$\text{Multiplier} = \frac{1}{\text{Desired (Budgeted)} \atop \text{Food Cost Percentage}}$$

Example:
Assume budgeted
food cost percentage = 33%: $\frac{1}{33}$ = 3.03 (multiplier)

II. Prime Ingredient Mark-Up Method

$$\text{Multiplier} = \frac{\text{Total Food Revenue}}{\text{Total Entrée Costs}}$$

Example:

Assume:	Total food costs	=	$ 1,000,000
	Total entrée costs	=	$ 350,000
	Total revenue	=	$ 2,025,000

$$\text{Multiplier} = \frac{\$2,025,000}{\$350,000} = 5.79 \text{ (multiplier)}$$

III. Mark-Up with Accompaniment Method

Step A: Calculate per-meal accompaniment costs

Assume:	Total food costs	=	$ 1,000,000
	Total entrée costs	=	$ (350,000)
	Total accompaniment costs	=	$ 650,000
	Number of guests	=	125,000

$$\frac{\$5.20}{\text{Per meal} \atop \text{accompaniment costs}} = \frac{\$650,000 \text{ (accompaniment costs)}}{125,000 \text{ (guests)}}$$

(continued)

Step B: Calculate total per-meal food costs

Entrée costs	$ 5.75
Accompaniment costs	$ 5.20
Total per meal food costs	$ 10.95

Step C: Calculate multiplier
Use same method as for Method 1

$$\text{Multiplier} = \frac{1}{\text{Desired (Budgeted)}\ \text{Food Cost Percentage}}$$

Example:
Assume budgeted
food cost percentage = 33%: $\frac{1}{33}$ = 3.03 (multiplier for all entrées)

The mark-up pricing methods using a multiplier also assume that all food costs associated with producing a menu item are known. In fact, many other costs may be excluded from the cost of ingredients used as the base for the multiplier. For example, operators not adjusting cost of goods sold by values of transfers to and from the food department would ignore these costs. Also, how are theft, pilferage, overportioning, and spoilage addressed when standard recipe costs alone are used as the base for the multiplier? What about minor costs such as herbs and spices—often ignored in price calculations but relatively expensive when a year's worth of purchases is considered? Problems with calculating costs of "help yourself" salad or dessert bars, and all-you-can-eat buffets also emphasize the point that multipliers applied to partial food costs may not yield accurate base selling prices.

Contribution Margin Pricing Method. The term *contribution margin* refers to the amount left after a menu item's food cost is subtracted from its selling price. The contribution margin is the amount that the sale of a menu item "contributes" to pay for all non-food costs allocated to the food service operation and to help with profit requirements. With a **contribution margin pricing method**, managers can set base selling prices for menu items by following two steps:

1. Determine the average contribution margin required per guest by dividing all non-food costs plus required profit by the number of expected guests.

2. Determine the base selling price for a menu item by adding the average contribution margin required per guest to the item's standard food cost.

Let's assume that the approved operating budget provides that all non-food costs are $695,000, required profit is set at $74,000, and 135,000 guests are expected to be served. With this information, the manager can calculate a base selling price for a menu item with a standard food cost of $4.60 as follows:

- **Step #1: Determine the average contribution margin required per guest.** This can be accomplished by using the following formula:

$$\frac{\text{Non-Food Costs} + \text{Required Profit}}{\text{Number of Expected Guests}} = \frac{\text{Average Contribution}}{\text{Margin Required per Guest}}$$

$$\frac{\$695,000 + \$74,000}{135,000} = \$5.70$$

- **Step #2: Determine the base selling price for a menu item.** This is done by adding the average contribution margin required per guest to the item's standard food cost. The base selling price for a menu item with a $4.60 food cost would be $4.60 + $5.70, or $10.30.

Advantages of this method are its ease of use and practicality when reasonably accurate information is available from the operating budget. It is also useful in those operations where costs associated with serving each guest are basically the same, with the exception of varying food costs. Also, this method tends to reduce the range of selling prices on the menu, since the only difference is reflected in the actual food cost incorporated in the selling price. This method also assumes that each guest should pay the same share of the property's non-food costs and profit requirements (sometimes called the "seat tax").

Ratio Pricing Method. The **ratio pricing method** determines the relationship between food costs and all non-food costs plus profit requirements (contribution margin). It uses this ratio to develop base selling prices for menu items. The three steps to ratio pricing are:

1. Determine the ratio of food costs to all non-food costs plus required profit by dividing all non-food costs plus profit by food costs.

2. Calculate the amount of non-food costs plus profit required for a menu item by multiplying the standard food cost of the menu item by the ratio calculated in step 1.

3. Determine the base selling price of a menu item by adding the result of step 2 to the standard food cost of the menu item.

Assume that the approved operating budget of a family-style restaurant (with no alcoholic beverage sales) provides the following information: food costs are $435,000, all non-food costs (labor and other costs) are $790,000, and required profit is $95,000. Using the ratio pricing method, the manager establishes a base selling price for a menu item with a standard food cost of $4.75 as follows:

- **Step #1: Determine the ratio of food costs to all other costs plus profit requirements.** This is calculated with the following formula:

$$\frac{\text{All Non-Food Costs} + \text{Required Profit}}{\text{Food Costs}} = \text{Ratio}$$

$$\frac{\$790,000 + \$95,000}{\$435,000} = \$2.03$$

This ratio means that for each $1 of revenue required to cover food costs, $2.03 of additional revenue is needed to pay for non-food costs and meet profit requirements.

- **Step #2: Calculate the amount of non-food costs and profit required for a menu item.** This is accomplished by multiplying the standard food cost of the menu item by the ratio calculated in step 1. Therefore, if the standard food cost of the menu item is $4.75, the amount of non-food costs and profit required is $9.64 ($4.75 × 2.03).

- **Step #3: Determine the base selling price for the menu item.** This is done by adding the result of step 2 to the standard food cost of the menu item. The base selling price for the item with a $4.75 food cost would be $14.39 ($4.75 food cost + $9.64 for non-food costs and profit requirement).

The ratio method of menu pricing is simple to use and can be based on operating budget requirements. However, it does have several disadvantages. In an operation offering both food and beverages, it is necessary to separate non-food costs and profit requirements between the two revenue centers. Also, with this pricing method, each meal assumes an equal share of non-food costs and profit. The ratio pricing method does not compensate for higher labor costs associated with the preparation of labor-intensive menu items.

Simple Prime Costs Method. The term **prime costs** refers to the most significant costs in a food service operation: product (food and beverage) and labor. A **simple prime costs pricing method** involves assessing the labor costs for the food service operation and factoring these costs into the pricing equation. The three steps to simple prime costs pricing are as follows:

1. Determine the labor cost per guest by dividing labor costs by the number of expected guests.

2. Determine the prime costs per guest by adding the labor cost per guest to the menu item's food cost.

3. Determine the menu item's base selling price by dividing the prime costs per guest by the desired prime costs percentage (food cost percentage plus labor cost percentage).

The following example demonstrates the simple prime costs pricing method. Let's assume that the food service manager has obtained the following data:

Menu Item Food Cost	$3.75
Labor Costs	$210,000
Number of Expected Guests	75,000
Desired Prime Costs Percentage	62%
(Food Cost Percentage + Labor Cost Percentage)	

The food cost for the menu item is the standard cost derived by costing the item's standard recipe. Labor costs and estimated guests are obtained from the approved operating budget. The desired prime costs percentage combines projected food and labor cost percentages, also from the operating budget.

- **Step #1: Determine the labor cost per guest.** The labor cost per guest is determined by dividing labor costs by the number of expected guests:

$$\text{Labor Cost per Guest} = \frac{\text{Labor Costs}}{\text{Number of Expected Guests}}$$

$$\$2.80 = \frac{\$210,000}{75,000}$$

- **Step #2: Determine the prime costs per guest.** The labor cost per guest ($2.80) added to the menu item's food cost ($3.75) equals $6.55.

- **Step #3: Determine the menu item's base selling price.** This is calculated by dividing the prime costs per guest (the result of step 2) by the desired prime costs percentage:

$$\text{Base Selling Price} = \frac{\text{Prime Costs per Guest}}{\text{Desired Prime Cost Percentage}}$$

$$\$10.56 = \frac{\$6.55}{0.62}$$

The food service manager would then adjust this base selling price in relation to other factors, such as the operation's target markets and the competition. Advantages of this method are its focus on both food and labor costs and its ease of use. An obvious disadvantage is the need to assign an equal labor cost to each menu item, even though the actual labor costs for menu items may vary greatly. The specific prime costs pricing method attempts to overcome this problem.

Specific Prime Costs Method. With the **specific prime costs pricing method**, the food service manager develops multipliers for menu items so that the base selling prices for the items cover their food costs and their share of labor costs. Items with extensive preparation have higher labor costs and should have higher mark-ups and, consequently, higher selling prices. Conversely, items not requiring extensive preparation have lower labor costs that can be reflected in a lower mark-up and lower selling prices.

The manager first divides all menu items into two categories: those that do and those that do not involve extensive preparation labor. The definition of extensive preparation labor is left to the manager to determine. For example, perhaps stew made from scratch is considered labor-intensive to prepare, while a steak that only has to be broiled is considered non-labor-intensive. Typically, all items are assumed to require approximately the same amount of labor for service and cleanup; these labor costs are shared by both categories of menu items.

Next, the manager allocates appropriate percentages of total food costs and labor costs to each category of menu items. Let's assume that the manager's analysis of menu items sold during a recent period showed that:

Exhibit 6   Calculations for Specific Prime Costs Pricing

Budget Item	Operating Budget Percentage	Category A (Extensive Preparation) Items	Category B (Non–Extensive Preparation) Items
(1)	(2)	(3)	(4)
Food Cost	35%	60% of 35% = 21%	40% of 35% = 14%
Labor Cost	30%	55% of 30% = 17%	40% of 13% = 5%
		60% of 13% = 8%	
All Other Costs	20%	60% of 20% = 12%	40% of 20% = 8%
Profit	15%	60% of 15% = 9%	40% of 15% = 6%
Total	100%		67%	33%
Multiplier	$\dfrac{100\%}{35\%} = 2.9$	$\dfrac{67\%}{21\%} = 3.2$	$\dfrac{33\%}{14\%} = 2.4$

- 60 percent of the total food cost is expended for items requiring extensive preparation (Category A items).

- 40 percent of total food cost is expended for items requiring little preparation (Category B items).

- 55 percent of all labor costs is incurred for preparation of all menu items (both Category A and Category B items).

- 45 percent of all labor costs is incurred for service, cleanup, and other non-preparation activities.

Exhibit 6 shows the calculations to be made using the specific prime costs pricing method based on the cost percentages above.

Note that line items from the approved operating budget are listed in column 1. These line items include food cost, labor cost, all other costs, and profit. Operating budget percentages for each line item are noted in column 2. These figures represent percentages of forecasted revenue. For example, the operating budget specifies a 35-percent food cost—35 percent of expected revenue will go toward paying food costs. These percentages are re-allocated in column 3 for menu items that involve extensive preparation labor (Category A) and in column 4 for items that do not involve extensive preparation labor (Category B).

Recall that the manager's previous analysis of menu items sold during a recent period showed that the food costs required to produce Category A items (involving extensive preparation) represented 60 percent of the food costs incurred for the period. An adjusted food cost percentage for labor-intensive menu items of 21 percent can be calculated by multiplying the 35-percent total food cost by 60 percent ($0.35 \times 0.6 = 0.21 \times 100 = 21$ percent). Similarly, an adjusted food cost percentage for non-labor-intensive menu items of 14 percent is calculated by multiplying the 35-percent total food cost by 40 percent ($0.35 \times 0.4 = 0.14 \times 100 = 14$ percent).

The manager now needs to allocate the total labor cost percentage (30 percent as shown in column 2) between preparation and non-preparation labor activities. In this particular case, the manager decides to allocate all of the preparation labor to Category A menu items because little or no labor expense is incurred for Category B menu items. Recall that the manager's previous analysis showed that 55 percent of all labor cost is incurred for the preparation of menu items. Since all of this labor cost will be allocated to Category A menu items, the manager multiplies 30 percent (the percentage of revenue representing total labor costs) by 55 percent (the percentage of total labor costs for preparing menu items). Exhibit 6 shows that 17 percent ($0.30 \times 0.55 = 0.17$ [rounded] $\times 100 = 17$ percent) of the total labor cost is charged to menu items involving extensive preparation.

The remaining 13 percent of the total labor costs (30-percent labor costs from the operating budget, minus 17-percent labor costs for preparation of menu items) is allocated between both Category A and Category B menu items, since this is the cost of labor incurred for service, cleanup, and other activities that should be shared equally. However, sharing equally does not necessarily mean a 50/50 split. Because food costs have been allocated on the 60/40 basis, this approach is also used to allocate non-preparation labor. Therefore, 8 percent of labor costs is charged to Category A menu items ($0.60 \times 0.13 = 0.08$ [rounded] $\times 100 = 8$ percent). This labor cost is identified in column 3. The remaining 5 percent of non-preparation labor cost (13 percent $-$ 8 percent $=$ 5 percent) is allocated to Category B menu items. This labor cost is identified in column 4.

All other costs (20 percent of forecasted revenue as shown in column 2) and profit (15 percent of forecasted revenue as noted in column 2) are also allocated on the 60/40 basis between Category A and Category B menu items.

At this point in the process, the manager can determine several multipliers. Multipliers are set by adding the individual cost percentages (food cost, labor cost, all other costs, and profit) and dividing by the desired food cost percentage.

For example, a multiplier based on the 35-percent desired food cost from the current operating budget (column 2) is 2.9. This is calculated by dividing 100 percent (the total cost and profit percentage shown at the bottom of column 2) by the budgeted food cost percentage of 35 percent ($1 \div 0.35 = 2.9$ [rounded]).

The multiplier for menu items requiring extensive preparation (column 3) is calculated by dividing 67 percent (the total cost and profit percentage shown at the bottom of column 3) by the desired food cost percentage of 21 percent for this category of menu items ($0.67 \div 0.21 = 3.2$ [rounded]).

The multiplier for menu items requiring little preparation (column 4) is calculated by dividing 33 percent (the total cost and profit percentage shown at the bottom of column 4) by the desired food cost percentage of 14 percent for this category of menu items ($0.33 \div 0.14 = 2.4$ [rounded]).

Note that the multiplier for items involving extensive preparation (3.2) is higher than that for items in the non-extensive preparation category (2.4). Let's assume that the food cost of a menu item involving extensive preparation is $4.75. The food service manager determines a base selling price for that item by multiplying $4.75 by 3.2. This yields a base selling price for the menu item of $15.20.

Note that a menu item costing $4.75 that does *not* require extensive preparation would be marked up by only 2.4, which would yield an $11.40 base selling price. This lower price reflects the fact that there is much less labor required to produce the menu item.

While the specific prime costs pricing method establishes base selling prices for the items to cover their share of labor costs, there are several disadvantages to this pricing method. Managers may spend a significant amount of time classifying menu items into extensive-preparation and non-extensive-preparation categories. They will also spend time performing the necessary calculations. Also, this pricing method requires managers to assume that the relationships among all other operating costs vary in the same proportion as food costs. While this is often a reasonable assumption, there may be costs, including those for energy usage, associated with preparing some items that reduce the accuracy of this method.

Important Pricing Considerations

Throughout this section, we have suggested that the result of menu pricing calculations is a base selling price. While objective formulas reflect financial factors, they do not take into account various non-financial factors that are also considered in determining final selling prices for menu items. The base selling price is a starting point from which these other factors must be assessed.

The concept of value (price relative to quality) is always important. Guests pay for more than just the product (food and beverage) when they visit the operation. Quality of service, cleanliness of the facility, and atmosphere are also part of the dining experience and should, even if subjectively, be factored into the selling-price decision.

The basic law of supply and demand is another factor to be considered. Ultimately, the price that can be charged is established by the guests themselves as they decide whether to return to the property or whether to order a specific menu item.

Volume concerns must also be considered. As fewer guests are served, overhead charges per guest increase, and selling prices must be higher. The reverse is also true: more guests may allow the manager to reduce overhead costs in the pricing decision.

The price charged by the competition for a similar product is another concern. The more an operation can differentiate its products from those of the competition, the more freedom it has in setting a selling price that reflects a desired contribution margin.

For example, assume that two properties offer a similar steak dinner. While the price charged for the steak is important, there are other factors that may influence people to visit one property or the other. Perhaps one property provides entertainment, while the other offers an attractive atmosphere. Emphasizing the differences between the property's own products, services, and ambience and those offered by other businesses is one way to remain competitive.

One technique that can be used to attract guests from competitors is lowering menu prices. This may succeed in bringing more people into an operation, but only if the lower-priced items are considered by guests as substitutes for what the competition offers. If there are no significant differences between what one operation offers and what the competition offers, then guests may see price as the determining factor in selecting one property over the others. However, if there are non-price-related differences that are important to guests, such as atmosphere, location, and entertainment, this technique may not work.

Raising prices is also a way of responding to pressures from the competition. With higher prices, fewer menu items will need to be sold for the operation to meet profit requirements. However, raising a menu item's selling price may be effective only if the increased revenue from the price increase makes up for the revenue lost as demand falls off and current guests begin to buy other menu items as substitutes. In fact, in some cases, a more effective strategy for increasing total revenue may be lowering a menu item's selling price. Lowering prices may increase the volume of unit sales, and this increase may produce an increase in total revenue.

What we are really talking about here is the concept of **elasticity of demand**. Elasticity is a term economists use to describe how the quantity demanded responds to changes in price. If a certain percentage price change creates a larger percentage change in the quantity demanded, the demand is elastic, and the item is considered to be price-sensitive. If, on the other hand, the percentage change in quantity demanded is less than the percentage change in price, the demand is inelastic. Before changing the established price of a menu item, it is important to know the elasticity of demand for that item—the extent to which demand changes as the price changes.

Evaluating the Menu

You have learned that the menu is a most important tool influencing the success or failure of a food and beverage operation. But how should menus be evaluated to determine whether the most profitable menu items are being sold? The process of **menu engineering** is an increasingly popular approach to the need for menu evaluation.

What is a "good" menu item? There are two measures of how good a menu item is: its popularity and its profitability. A popular menu item is ordered frequently by guests. A profitable menu item generates a high contribution margin. Menu items can be evaluated in terms of both their popularity and profitability.

Basically, the menu engineering process uses information readily available to the food and beverage manager to classify menu items into four types:

- Stars—items that are popular and profitable
- Plowhorses—items that are not profitable but are popular
- Puzzles—items that are profitable but are not popular
- Dogs—items that are neither profitable nor popular

To classify each menu item into one of the four basic categories, managers must develop a practical way to define and measure the relative profitability and popularity of each menu item. This can be accomplished by using information about standard food costs and frequency of menu item sales.

Earlier, we noted that the basis of a menu item's profitability is *not* the level of its food cost, but its contribution margin. Some managers assume that the lower a menu item's food cost percentage, the more profitable the sale of the item is to the operation. In other words, the lower the percentage of revenue needed to pay for the food needed for the menu item, the larger the percentage of revenue available for all other expenses and profit. While this theory sounds good, it can be easily disproved. Consider the following example:

Menu Item	Food Cost	Menu Selling Price	Food Cost %	Contribution Margin
Chicken	$2.48	$ 7.50	33%	$5.02
Steak	$6.02	$14.00	43%	$7.98

In this example, chicken has the lower food cost percentage (33 percent compared to 43-percent food cost for steak). According to the traditional view, the sale of chicken should help the operation more than the sale of steak. However, as shown by the contribution margin (menu selling price minus food cost), only $5.02 is left from the sale of chicken to pay for all other costs and to make a contribution to the property's profit requirements. In the case of steak, $7.98 remains for this purpose.

This example illustrates a very important point: the goal of effective menu planning and evaluation should be to increase the contribution margin of each menu item—not to decrease its food cost percentage. There is truth in the old saying, "You can't bank percentages!"

Information about frequency of unit sales for each menu item can be gathered by tallying the number of each item sold during some specified time period (such as two weeks). This information can be abstracted manually from guest checks or production records indicating leftovers or, more frequently, by analysis of unit sales information from the POS system. Popular items have a relatively high menu mix percentage. Accordingly, "star" menu items are those with relatively high contribution margins and high menu mix percentages, while items classified as "dogs" score relatively low on both measures.

When performing a menu engineering analysis, it is not enough to consider menu items individually. Each item's contribution margin and menu mix percentage will provide measures for the item's levels of profitability and popularity. However, the challenge is to evaluate how high or low these levels are in comparison with all other menu items. What constitutes a "high" level of profitability or popularity? For example, suppose that unit sales of a particular menu item represent ten percent of total unit sales. Is this a "high" menu mix? Should this item be classified as a "popular" menu item? The answer depends on the menu mix percentages of all other menu items and on the total number of items on the menu. For instance, if the menu in question contains ten different items, ten percent of total unit sales may be regarded as a high level of popularity, but if there are only four items on the menu, this figure would represent a low level of popularity. Likewise, by itself, a menu item's contribution margin tells us very little about how profitable unit sales of this item are when compared with other menu items.

Defining Profitability

The basis for measuring the degree of profitability of each menu item is the average contribution margin. A "high" contribution margin for an individual menu item would be one that is equal to or greater than the average contribution margin for all menu items. The concept of the menu's average contribution margin provides managers with a precise measure of each menu item's profitability, and it is easily calculated from readily available information. Recall that the contribution margin of a menu item is calculated by subtracting its food cost from its selling price.

Since the manager knows the costs incurred and the revenue generated for each individual menu item, the total menu (food) costs and the total menu revenues generated can be determined by simply summing the figures for each menu item. The total contribution margin for all menu items is calculated by subtracting total menu costs from total menu revenues.

Finally, the average item contribution margin is calculated by dividing the total menu contribution margin by the total number of menu items sold during the specified time period in which sales data was collected:

$$\text{Average Item Contribution Margin} \ = \ \frac{\text{Total Contribution Margin}}{\text{Total Number of Items Sold}}$$

Individual contribution margins for each menu item can now be compared to the average contribution margin for all menu items to assess each item's level of profitability. A profitable menu item is one whose individual contribution margin equals or exceeds the average contribution margin. The concept of average contribution margin is further illustrated in an example of menu engineering analysis presented shortly.

Defining Popularity

The basis for measuring the degree of popularity of each menu item is called the popularity index, which is based on the notion of "expected popularity." For the purpose of analysis, each menu item is assumed to be equally popular. This means that each item is "expected" to contribute an equal share of total menu unit sales. Therefore, the expected popularity of each menu item is calculated by simply dividing 100 percent (i.e., total unit sales) by the number of items on the menu. For example, if there are only four items on a menu and each item is assumed to be equally popular, the unit sales of each item would be expected to represent 25 percent of total unit sales (100 percent ÷ 4). On the other hand, if there were ten items on the menu, each item would be expected to represent 10 percent of total unit sales (100 percent ÷ 10).

Menu engineering assumes that an item is popular if its unit sales equal 70 percent of what is expected.[1] Thus, the popularity index for items on a given menu is defined as 70 percent of the expected popularity of each item on that menu. (The popularity index for a specific property can be adjusted to a higher or lower level depending on the manager's emphasis on selling popular and profitable items.)

For example, a food item on a four-item menu would be considered popular if its unit sales represented 17.5 percent of total unit sales (100 percent ÷ 4 items = 25 percent × 70 percent = 17.5 percent). On the other hand, a food item on a ten-item menu would be considered popular if it accounted for only 7 percent of total unit sales (100 percent ÷ 10 items = 10 percent × 70 percent = 7 percent). The concept of a popularity index makes it possible to measure the relative degree of popularity of each item on a given menu.

With these tools of menu engineering, managers can evaluate the profitability and popularity of menu items and classify them as either stars, plowhorses, puzzles, or dogs. The results of this evaluation should be used to improve the menu.

Evaluating Menu Items

Exhibit 7 depicts an analysis for a food and beverage operation offering only four menu items. Each of these is listed in column A of Exhibit 7. Assume that this operation collected sales information for each menu item over a two-week period. This information is recorded in column B. Note at the bottom of column B (box N) that a total of 1,000 menu items were sold during the two-week period.

The menu mix (percentage of menu items represented by each menu item) is calculated in column C. For example, 42 percent of all menu items sold were chicken dinners (420 chicken dinners sold ÷ 1,000 total dinners sold).

The menu items' food cost is recorded in column D. For example, the total ingredient cost of all items (entrée, potato choice, etc.) in the chicken dinner is calculated to be $5.21.

Each menu item's selling price is listed in column E. This information is taken directly from the menu. You will note that the chicken dinner sells for $7.95.

Column F (*Item CM*) lists the contribution margin of the menu item. To calculate the contribution margin for the chicken dinner, we subtract the menu item's food cost from its selling price. For example, for chicken dinners: $7.95 − $5.21 = $2.74.

The total menu cost (column G) is calculated by multiplying the number of each item sold (column B) by the item's food cost (column D). The total menu cost for the chicken dinner is calculated as follows: 420 chicken dinners × $5.21 food cost = $2,188.20.

Menu revenues (column H) are calculated by multiplying the number of each menu item sold by its selling price. The menu revenue for chicken dinners ($3,339) is calculated by multiplying the number of chicken dinners sold by the selling price: 420 chicken dinners × $7.95 = $3,339.

The contribution margin for the total sales of the menu item (column L) is calculated by subtracting the menu costs from the menu revenues. For example, the menu contribution for the chicken dinner ($1,150.80) is calculated by deducting the chicken dinner's menu cost ($2,188.20) in column G from its revenues ($3,339) in column H.

It is now possible to determine the average contribution margin (the basis for profitability) and the popularity index (the basis for popularity). In Exhibit 7, the total menu cost of $7,230.70 is recorded at the bottom of column G (box I) and is calculated by summing the menu costs for each item. Likewise, the total menu revenues are calculated by summing the individual revenues for each item in column H. The total revenues of $10,675.50 are noted at the bottom of column H in box J.

The next step is to calculate the total contribution margin for all menu items by subtracting menu costs (box I) from menu revenues (box J). Because 1,000 menu items were sold (box N) and because the total menu contribution margin is $3,444.80 (box M), the average contribution margin is $3.44 (box O):

Exhibit 7   Menu Engineering Worksheet

Menu Engineering Worksheet

Restaurant: _Terrace Cafe_

Date: _6/10/XX_

Meal Period: _Dinner_

(A) Menu Item Name	(B) Number Sold (MM)	(C) Menu Mix %	(D) Item Food Cost	(E) Item Selling Price	(F) Item CM (E − D)	(G) Menu Costs (B × D)	(H) Menu Revenues (B × E)	(L) Menu CM (H − G)	(P) CM Category	(R) MM% Category	(S) Menu Item Classification
Chicken Dinner	420	42%	$5.21	$7.95	$2.74	$ 2,188.20	$3,339.00	$1,150.80	Low	High	Plowhorse
Shrimp Plate	360	36%	8.50	12.50	4.00	3,060.00	4,500.00	1,440.00	High	High	Star
Sirloin Steak	150	15%	9.95	14.50	4.55	1,492.50	2,175.00	682.50	High	Low	Puzzle
Tenderloin Tips	70	7%	7.00	9.45	2.45	490.00	661.50	171.50	Low	Low	Dog
Column Totals:	N 1,000					I $7,230.70	J $10,675.50	M $3,444.80			
				Additional Computations:			O = M/N $3,444.80		O = M/N $3.44	Q = (100%/items) (70%) 17.5%	

(Box O = Average Contribution Margin)

Source: Adapted from Michael L. Kasanava and Donald I. Smith, *Menu Engineering* (Okemos, Mich: Hospitality Publicataions, 1982), p. 64.

$$\text{Average Contribution Margin} \quad = \quad \frac{\text{Total Contribution Margin}}{\text{Total Number of Items Sold}}$$

$$\$3.44 \quad = \quad \frac{\$3,444.80}{1,000}$$

Those items that are profitable (those with a high contribution margin) are those whose contribution margin is equal to or greater than the average contribution margin for all menu items ($3.44). Items with a contribution margin above this amount are, then, those items the property most wishes to sell. Column P shows that the most profitable menu items are the shrimp plate and sirloin steak.

Column R in Exhibit 7 indicates each item's popularity. Each item's menu mix percentage (percentage of total menu item sales indicated in column C) is compared with the popularity index calculated for this particular menu. Because there are only four items, each item has an expected popularity of 25 percent (100 percent ÷ 4 = 25 percent). Since unit sales of a popular item should equal 70 percent of what is expected for it, the popularity index is 17.5 percent (70 percent × 25 percent = 17.5 percent). In Exhibit 7, then, popular items are those whose unit sales represent 17.5 percent or more of total sales (see box Q). For example, because the menu mix percentage (column C) for the chicken dinner is 42 percent, its menu mix category is rated as high (column R). In contrast, consider the tenderloin tips dinner: its menu mix (7 percent) is much lower than the 17.5 percent required for an item to be classified as popular. Therefore, its menu mix category is rated as low (column R).

Given this information, it is possible to classify menu items. Consider the chicken dinner again. We just noted that this is a popular item. Is it also profitable? Its contribution margin is $2.74 (column F). This is less than the average contribution margin and is classified as a relatively low contribution margin item (column P). The chicken dinner is popular but not very profitable. Therefore, this menu item is classified as a plowhorse (column S).

As a second example, consider the sirloin steak in Exhibit 7. Its contribution margin category (column P) is rated as high, since its individual contribution margin (column F) is $4.55, which is significantly more than the $3.44 required for an item to be classified as profitable. However, its menu mix category (column R) is low. Its menu mix percentage of 15 percent (column C) is lower than the 17.5 percent required for the item to be classified as popular. Therefore, this menu item is classified as a puzzle (column S). It is a profitable item that the property wishes to sell, but it is not popular with guests.

Improving the Menu

The benefits of menu engineering can only accrue if information gained from the menu engineering analysis is used to improve the menu. What can a food and beverage manager do with this knowledge about the various food item classifications?

Managing Plowhorses. First, let's consider plowhorses (those items low in contribution margin but high in popularity). Guests like these items, but, unfortunately, plowhorses do not contribute their share of contribution margin. Possible strategies for managing a plowhorse menu item include:

- *Increase prices carefully.* Perhaps the item is popular because it represents a great value to guests. If prices could be increased, the item may still represent a good value, may remain popular, and may generate a higher contribution margin. This alternative may be most effective when the item is unique to the property and cannot be obtained elsewhere.

- *Test for demand.* If there is no strong resistance to price increases, it may be useful to complement an increased price with other strategies, such as repackaging the item or repositioning it on the menu. These other strategies may be designed to maintain or increase the item's popularity while generating a higher contribution margin through the increase in selling price. If prices are to be increased, this should probably be done in several stages rather than all at once.

- *Relocate the item to a lower profile on the menu.* Depending on the menu layout, certain areas of a menu represent a better location than others. A plowhorse can be relocated to a less desirable area of the menu. Since the item is popular, some guests will search it out. Others will be drawn to higher profile areas of the menu with more profitable items the property wishes to sell.

- *Shift demand to more desirable items.* Menu engineering allows the manager to determine which items to sell (those high in popularity and high in contribution margin). Servers using suggestive selling techniques, for example, would *not* recommend plowhorses. Table tents and other point-of-sale tools would, likewise, suggest stars and puzzles (because of their high contribution margins); they would not suggest plowhorses.

- *Combine with lower-cost products.* The contribution margin of a plowhorse can be increased if lower-cost meal accompaniments are offered with the entrée. Perhaps higher-priced vegetables and dessert accompaniments can be replaced with other, less expensive items without reducing the item's popularity. If this can be done, the contribution margin will increase.

- *Assess the direct labor factor.* The food and beverage manager should know if there is a significant amount of direct labor required to produce the plowhorse item. If the production of an item with a low contribution margin does not require a significant amount of direct labor (the item is a convenience food product, for example), the manager may be able to justify the lower contribution margin, since fewer revenue dollars will be required to cover labor cost.

- *Consider portion reduction.* If the portion size is reduced, the product cost will be decreased and the contribution margin will increase. This alternative must be viewed with caution, since the guest's perception of value may decrease when the portion size is reduced.

Managing Puzzles. Puzzles are items that are high in contribution margin but low in popularity. They are items the food and beverage manager desires to sell, since their contribution margin is relatively high. The challenge is to find ways to increase the number of guests ordering these items. Options include:

- *Shifting demand to these items.* Techniques include repositioning the items to more visible areas of the menu, renaming them, using suggestive selling techniques, developing advertising campaigns, using table tents, using buttons and badges on server uniforms, highlighting the items on menu boards at the entrance to the dining area, and other strategies to increase the items' popularity.

- *Reducing the price.* Perhaps an item is low in popularity because it does not represent a value to guests. If this is the case, the selling price might be decreased with the contribution margin still remaining higher than average. This could lead to increased popularity, since a reduced selling price represents a greater value to the guest.

- *Adding value to the item.* Offering a larger portion size, adding more expensive meal accompaniments or garnishes, and using higher-quality ingredients are among the ways that value can be increased. These techniques may lead to increased popularity and to a contribution margin that is lower, but still higher than the average generated by the menu.

Managing Stars. Stars are items that are high in contribution margin and high in popularity. The best advice for managing stars is to:

- *Maintain rigid specifications.* Do not attempt to alter the quality of the product being served.

- *Place the item in a highly visible location on the menu.* Stars are items that the food and beverage operator wants to sell. Therefore, make sure guests are aware of them.

- *Test for selling price inelasticity.* Perhaps the star is popular because it is a significant value to the guest. Or, perhaps the star is not available in its existing form ("packaged" with the service, ambience, and location, for example) elsewhere in the marketplace. These might be two sound reasons for increasing the price without the risk of a decrease in popularity.

- *Use suggestive selling techniques.* Some of the techniques for shifting demand to puzzles might also be useful for stars.

Managing Dogs. Dogs (items that are low in contribution margin and low in popularity) are obvious candidates for removal from the menu. After all, they do not contribute their share of contribution margin, and they are not popular. Alternatively, the selling price could be increased, since this would at least generate a higher contribution margin. When a "dog" requires a significant amount of direct labor, does not permit sufficient use of leftovers, and has a relatively short storage life, the reasons for removing the item from the menu become more compelling.

Managing the Menu. To this point, we have suggested how a menu item classification system lends itself to the development of improved menus by more effective management of individual menu items. Are there other advantages to the use of the menu engineering process? Yes; it can be used to evaluate the worth of the entire menu. Consider, for example, the current practice in the industry when a menu is revised. The manager, guests, employees, and others may offer their opinions about the revisions. They may subjectively assess the menu's "worth" and offer their views about its improvements over earlier versions. If the guests seem to like it and if there are no overt employee problems with the revised menu, it is judged to be acceptable.

By contrast, menu engineering can be used to evaluate menu revisions in an objective manner. For example, if the popularity of an individual menu remains stable (or increases) while its contribution margin increases, the revised menu is a good one. With the tools of menu engineering, the worth of a revised menu can be objectively assessed. If, for example, a previous menu generated an average contribution margin of $2.50 and a new menu generates an average contribution margin of $2.75 without a subsequent decrease in guest count, the new menu is better: the average guest leaves 25 cents more in contribution margin than when the previous menu was in use.

Menu Planning in Multi-Unit Organizations

Consumers and owners/managers of multi-unit food service organizations favor consistency and believe consistency to be a significant advantage that multi-unit organizations have over individually owned and operated restaurants. From the guests' perspective, consistency means the same menu, with each menu item prepared in the same way, regardless of the location they visit. Owners/managers like the consistent purchase specifications, operating procedures, and the similar workstations, layout and design, and other factors that promote reduced costs and the prospect of higher profit levels.

However, as suggested earlier, managers of individual units within these organizations have little, if any, opportunity for menu planning, because such planning is done at the corporate level for use by the units at the local level. (There are some departures from this approach, though. Large national/international organizations may offer standard menu items in all units and, in addition, offer unique items on a by-region basis. For example, McDonald's restaurants in Hawaii offer Saimin Noodles and Spam and Rice with eggs, two items not found in its mainland restaurants.)

Many multi-unit organizations have a corporate menu planning team with an executive chef and culinary specialists who create ideas for menu items. They also have research and development teams that provide input to the menu planning team on consumer trends. There may also be a panel of menu "tasters" who evaluate and make suggestions about potential menu items. As should be true for independent operators, multi-unit-organization menu planners are concerned about variety and work toward creating menus that include items having appeal to the taste preferences of the persons in their market.

Like their unit manager counterparts, area managers for multi-unit organizations also have little input to or influence on the menu, even though they are encouraged to make suggestions about new items and provide feedback about existing items.

In a manner similar to independent restaurants, multi-unit organizations establish menu-item selling prices on the basis of targeted food costs and on the perception of what guests are willing to pay for the items.

Menu selling prices may differ in different parts of the country, just as the cost of living varies. For example, selling prices are typically higher in large metropolitan areas and along the east and west coasts. Extensive marketing analysis is conducted before a unit opens to determine the extent to which a specific area can support a unit. Even then, however, selling prices might be lower in a unit with, for example, retired persons on a fixed income located relatively close to a unit than in another area with higher personal income levels.

Many multi-unit food service organizations plan menu promotions that feature selected items for a relatively short period of time. Consider, for example, a nationwide restaurant organization that features an "all-you-can-eat" lobster or shrimp special. Planning for such a promotion must begin months ahead of time to ensure that the product will be available in the quantities needed when they are needed. Contracts must be negotiated with suppliers, national advertising campaigns must be developed, and media time and space must be purchased. Also, in-unit point-of-sale advertising materials must be designed and made available to the participating stores. Careful analysis is required to determine the extent to which the promotion will bring in incremental (additional) revenue or, alternatively, whether a significant amount of sales generated by the promotion will, instead, merely replace sales that otherwise would have been generated. Sometimes these promotions lead to menu changes in which items are made a permanent part of the menu. In many other instances, however, promotions run for a specified time and, if successful, may be offered later in evolving efforts to keep the public interested in visiting the organization's restaurants.

While unit managers may not have opportunities to address the challenges of menu planning and standard recipe development, they are able to use their creative talents as they manage employees, interact with guests, control food costs, and work to meet or exceed financial and other goals.

Menus and Technology

Technology can help busy food service managers with their menu planning, menu design, and menu management. In this section, we explore these topics.

Menu Planning and Technology

The same basic steps must be followed by all menu planners, regardless of the extent to which they use technology in the process. However, there are some important ways that technology can assist. For instance:

- *Determining what should be offered.* Marketing surveys can provide consumer input helpful to answering the question, "What items should be on the menu?" Perhaps current guests are asked to complete a survey addressing this and related questions. Software can be used for electronic tabulation and analysis. Increasingly, food service operators use home pages accessible through the Internet. Existing menus are typically posted on websites, and questions addressing prospective guests' comments and recommendations (including those about menu items) may also be included. When these tactics are used, menu planners can learn significant information about demographics, food preferences, and other meaningful information helpful to the menu-planning task.

+/3

Computers Can Almost Do It All

Food service managers make some of their most critical decisions as they plan their menus. An important resource in the decision-making process is the information available from computerized systems. Menu planners want to offer items that guests like. Computerized sales history information available from revenue management software provides this information. Managers are concerned that the items included in their menu can be offered within specific financial limitations. Technology helps by precosting recipes, computing each item's ideal contribution margin and food cost percentage, and—if selling price mark-ups are known—accurately calculating the selling prices electronically.

In many noncommercial food service operations, nutrition is a principal concern. Numerous software applications are available that calculate the nutritional content of proposed menus and allow menu planners the flexibility to make menu-item and portion-size adjustments as necessary to accommodate the consumers' nutritional needs. Operators using cycle menus and those providing menus in multiple outlets located throughout a large university campus, for example, appreciate the speed, flexibility, and accuracy of computerized menu-planning systems.

- *Selecting menu items.* Computerized input from current and prospective guests and from evaluation of the existing menu are important when selecting potential menu items. When new items are identified, the Internet can be used to not only identify recipes but learn about new preparation methods/techniques as well. Managers and chefs can also learn about and stay abreast of quality standards important to purchasing the ingredients required by new recipes.

Food service managers have a choice of menu planning software that is "stand-alone," which can interface with other food service software packages or, alternatively, can be integrated into systems with wider application related to purchasing, inventory, and cost control (among other functions).

Menu Design and Technology

Traditionally, menu planners interacted with an off-site designer and printer. The planners' ideas would be adapted into potential menu copy that evolved through numerous drafts in the menu-design process.

Menu planners today rely increasingly on desktop publishing software to produce menus for food service operators of all types, from independents operating small-volume properties to very large multi-unit operations.

Menu design software typically assists with:

- *Layout*—The placement and amount of space allocated to each part of the menu can be easily and quickly manipulated with design software.

- *Type style*—Hundreds of type styles and sizes (fonts) are available.

- *Size*—Menus ranging from very small to very large can be easily designed with readily available software.

- *Color*—Today's computer graphics software can create type, background, and illustrations of any color.

- *Photos and illustrations*—Computer programs today enable designers to select and place photos, whether from stock photo archives or from photo shoots created specifically for the operation.

- *Other graphics*—Artwork, line drawings, shading of specific colors, symbols, and menu highlight boxes can all add appeal to menus and can be easily done with the most simple desktop publishing software.

- *Menu copy*—Word-processing software allows menus to be printed directly in-house or, alternatively, to be sent by e-mail or delivered on compact disc to an off-site printer. Opportunities to print menus very inexpensively in-house allow menu planners to change menus frequently (even daily) without sacrificing the quality of this important sales tool.

Menu Production and Technology

Once designed, menus must be printed. Desktop publishing systems allow menus to be printed in-house or at a retail printing location. High-quality color printers can now be purchased at a very low cost. They enable the in-house duplication of menus at a very acceptable quality level for operations not requiring specific applications such as **dye-cut menus**, **lamination**, and specialty papers.

Menu design software assists with easy reprinting of menus when, for example, there are price changes and even menu item changes. Menu size can be changed when, for example, managers wish to develop take-home copies and/or others for mail distribution. Existing electronic copies are also used when menus are replicated on the operation's website.

Traditionally, menus were produced primarily for on-site distribution, with some limited external distribution opportunities as well. Today, however, many operations make their menus available for Internet distribution on their home pages.

Quick-service restaurants and commercial and noncommercial food service operations are among those that frequently do not offer printed menus. Digital menu display technology uses display boards or screens that can display and change content automatically using video, audio, and text messages. Programming these new "electronic menus" (which can even be done off-site—for example, for multi-unit operations) allows menu changes to be made much more quickly and less expensively than with traditional menus.

Menu Engineering and Technology

Menu engineering computer applications help management answer such questions as:

- What is the most profitable price to assign a menu item?

- At what price level and sales mix does a food service operation maximize its profits?

- Which current menu items require repricing, retention, replacement, or repositioning on the menu?

- How should daily specials and new items be priced?

- How can the success of a menu change be evaluated?

Data for analysis can be entered into the program's database manually, automatically (from an integrated restaurant management applications package), or electronically. A stand-alone version of menu engineering requires that the user input each menu item's product cost, selling price, and sales history. This minimal input is sufficient to generate a complete menu engineering analysis. Food service operators who use computer-based recipe management applications to provide accurate product cost data can program a menu engineering application to read this data from a file, rather than rely on user input.

Following data input and selection of the analysis option, the menu engineering application begins its work. As the analysis progresses, a menu item's contribution margin and unit sales activity are categorized as relatively high or low. Procedures performed here are identical to those described earlier for the manual analysis. Eventually, each item will be further classified for both its marketing and pricing success. The menu engineering output is composed of five reports:

- Menu item analysis

- Menu mix analysis

- Menu engineering summary

- Four-box analysis

- Menu engineering graph

Menu Item Analysis. Exhibit 8 illustrates the initial report in the menu engineering analysis. This is an item-by-item listing accompanied by selling price, portion cost, contribution margin, and item count (number sold). The primary purpose of this report is to provide the user with a means by which he or she can verify the data that is to be analyzed. This is especially helpful when data has been manually entered into the program.

Menu Mix Analysis. Exhibit 9 depicts a menu mix analysis report. This report evaluates each item's participation in the overall menu's performance. The percentage of menu mix (% *MM Share*) is based on each item's count, divided by the total number of items sold. Each percentage is then ranked as high or low, depending on its comparison with the menu engineering rule for menu mix sufficiency. The percentage each item has contributed to the menu's total contribution margin is found in the column labeled % *CM Share*. Each item's contribution margin is then ranked according to how it compares with the menu's weighted average contribution margin (ACM). A menu classification for each item is determined by considering its MM group rank and CM group rank together.

Menu Engineering Summary. A menu engineering summary report is shown in Exhibit 10. Perhaps the most informative report produced by the menu engineering application, this analysis presents important information in capsule form

Exhibit 8   Menu Item Analysis

	Item Analysis			
Item Name	Item Price	Portion Cost	Contr. Margin	Item Count
Fried Shrimp	7.95	4.85	3.10	210
Fried Chicken	4.95	2.21	2.74	420
Chopped Sirloin	4.50	1.95	2.55	90
Prime Rib	7.95	4.95	3.00	600
King Prime Rib	9.95	5.65	4.30	60
NY Strip Steak	8.50	4.50	4.00	360
Top Sirloin	7.95	4.30	3.65	510
Red Snapper	6.95	3.95	3.00	240
Lobster Tail	9.50	4.95	4.55	150
Tenderloin Tips	6.45	4.00	2.45	360

Source: Adapted from Michael L. Kasanava and Donald I. Smith, *Menu Engineering* (Okemos, Mich: Hospitality Publicataions, 1982), p. 77.

Exhibit 9   Menu Mix Analysis

	Menu Mix Analysis						
Item Name	MM Count	% MM Share	Group Rank	% CM Share	Contr. Margin	Group Rank	Menu Class
Fried Shrimp	210	7.00	HIGH	6.73	3.10	LOW	PLOWHORSE
Fried Chicken	420	14.00	HIGH	11.89	2.74	LOW	PLOWHORSE
Chopped Sirloin	90	3.00	LOW	2.37	2.55	LOW	<< DOG >>
Prime Rib	600	20.00	HIGH	18.60	3.00	LOW	PLOWHORSE
King Prime Rib	60	2.00	LOW	2.67	4.30	HIGH	?PUZZLE?
NY Strip Steak	360	12.00	HIGH	14.88	4.00	HIGH	**STAR**
Top Sirloin	510	17.00	HIGH	19.24	3.65	HIGH	**STAR**
Red Snapper	240	8.00	HIGH	7.44	3.00	LOW	PLOWHORSE
Lobster Tail	150	5.00	LOW	7.05	4.55	HIGH	?PUZZLE?
Tenderloin Tips	360	12.00	HIGH	9.12	2.45	LOW	PLOWHORSE

Source: Adapted from Michael L. Kasanava and Donald I. Smith, *Menu Engineering* (Okemos, Mich: Hospitality Publicataions, 1982), p. 77.

to produce a concise statement of operations. The row labeled *Price* shows total menu revenue, average item selling price, lowest selling price, and highest selling price. The *Food Cost* row contains total menu costs, average item food cost, lowest-cost item, and highest-cost item. The *Contribution Margin* row shows total menu CM, average-item CM, lowest-item CM, and highest-item CM. The *Demand Factor* row lists total number of covers (guests), average number of covers, lowest item count, and highest item count. Much of the information in the body of this report

Exhibit 10   Menu Engineering Summary

Menu Engineering Summary				
	Total	Average	Low	High
Price	22050.00	7.35	4.50	9.95
Food Cost	12374.70	4.12	1.95	5.65
Contribution Margin ...	9675.30	3.23	2.45	4.55
Demand Factor	3000	300	60	600
Food Cost Percentage	56.12%			
Number of Items	10			

Source: Adapted from Michael L. Kasanava and Donald I. Smith, *Menu Engineering* (Okemos, Mich: Hospitality Publicataions, 1982), p. 78.

Exhibit 11   Four-Box Analysis

PLOWHORSE	STAR
Fried Shrimp Fried Chicken Prime Rib Red Snapper Tenderloin Tips	NY Strip Top Sirloin
DOG	PUZZLE
Chopped Sirloin	King Prime Rib Lobster Tail

Source: Adapted from Michael L. Kasanava and Donald I. Smith, *Menu Engineering* (Okemos, Mich: Hospitality Publicataions, 1982), p. 78.

is used elsewhere in the overall menu engineering system. For example, the lowest and highest selling prices on the menu are termed *price points* and can be used to help identify target market success. This report also contains the menu's food cost percentage and number of items sold.

Four-Box Analysis. Exhibit 11 illustrates a four-box analysis that indexes the menu classifications developed in the menu mix analysis report. Since menu engineering leads to a series of decision strategies specific to each menu classification, this report provides the user with insight about the number of items found in each category. For example, Exhibit 11 displays a menu composed of five plowhorses, two stars, two puzzles, and one dog. Are five plowhorses too many? This type of evaluation

Exhibit 12   Menu Engineering Graph

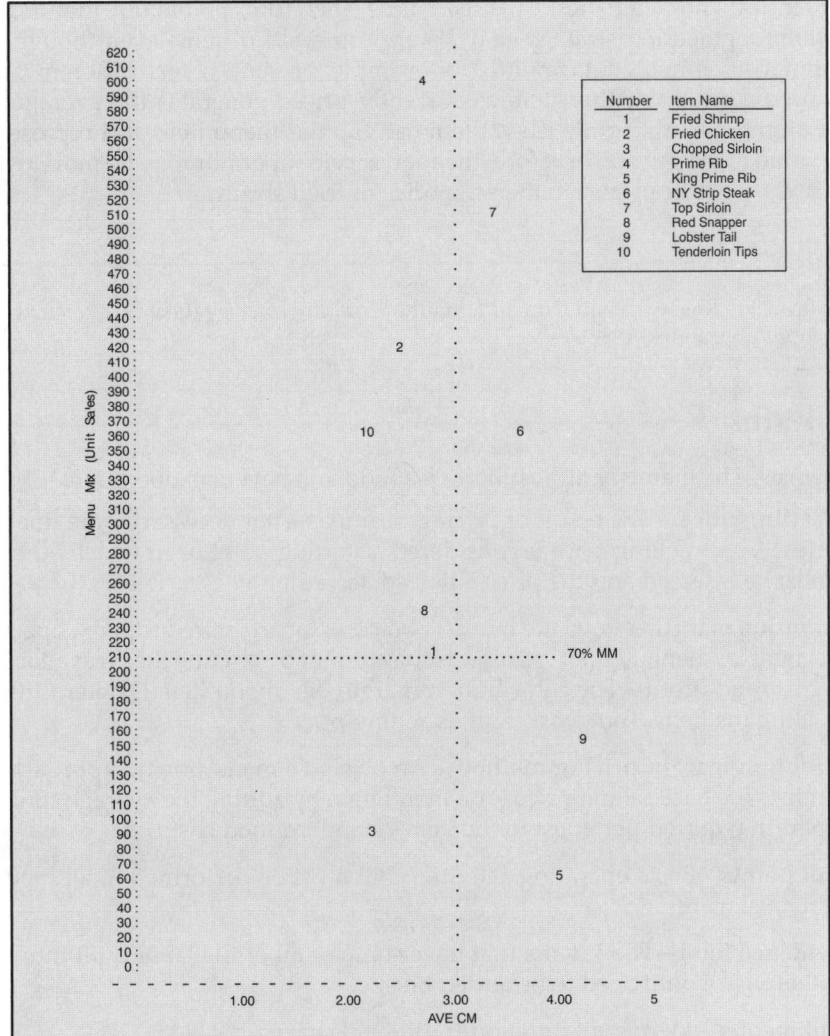

Number	Item Name
1	Fried Shrimp
2	Fried Chicken
3	Chopped Sirloin
4	Prime Rib
5	King Prime Rib
6	NY Strip Steak
7	Top Sirloin
8	Red Snapper
9	Lobster Tail
10	Tenderloin Tips

Source: Adapted from Michael L. Kasanava and Donald I. Smith, *Menu Engineering* (Okemos, Mich: Hospitality Publicataions, 1982), p. 80.

process begins with the four-box matrix and continues through the menu engineering graph.

Menu Engineering Graph. A menu engineering graph (see Exhibit 12) is a useful tool when evaluating decision strategies. Because it indicates each competing menu item's position relative to all others, the menu engineering graph is the most powerful report produced by a menu engineering application. The vertical axis of the graph positions menu mix and the horizontal axis positions contribution margin. Each item is then graphed according to its CM and MM coordinates.

It is especially important to note that not all items in the same classification possess identical characteristics. This technique, therefore, points out that a different menu engineering strategy may be appropriate for items even though they are similarly segmented. Prime rib, for example, presents a very different profile from fried shrimp. Neither item as currently priced generates the average contribution margin. Yet prime rib is the most popular menu item and represents a great value to the guest. Therefore, the food service operator may be more willing to raise the price of prime rib than the price of fried shrimp.

Endnote

1. Michael L. Kasavana and Donald I. Smith, *Menu Engineering* (Okemos, Mich.: Hospitality Publications, 1982).

Key Terms

ambience—The theme or atmosphere of a food and beverage operation.

base selling price—The result of pricing formulas—not necessarily the final selling price. A base selling price is considered a starting point from which other factors must be assessed and the price adjusted accordingly.

contribution margin—Revenue minus food costs for an entire property, operating department, or menu item. It represents the amount of revenue that is available for fixed costs and profits. The contribution margin of a menu item is determined by subtracting the item's food cost from its selling price.

contribution margin pricing method—An objective menu pricing approach that determines the base selling price for a menu item by adding the average contribution margin required per guest to the item's standard food cost.

control points—Basic operating activities that must be performed in all food service establishments.

convenience food—Food items that have some or all of the labor built into them that otherwise would need to be added on site.

die-cut menus—Menus cut into non-traditional shapes.

elasticity of demand—A term used to describe how the quantity demanded responds to changes in price. If a price change of a certain percentage creates a larger percentage change in the quantity demanded, the demand is elastic, and the item is considered to be price-sensitive. If the percentage change in the quantity demanded is less than the percentage change in price, the demand is inelastic.

ingredients mark-up pricing method—An objective menu pricing approach that considers all food costs. A base selling price is established by multiplying the ingredients' costs by a multiplier.

laminate (menus)—Menus covered with a plastic or other film that makes them easy to clean.

mark-up with accompaniment costs pricing method—An objective menu pricing approach that establishes a base selling price by determining ingredient costs based only upon the entrée and then adding a standard accompaniment or "plate" cost to this amount before multiplying by a multiplier.

menu engineering—A manual or computerized method of menu analysis and item pricing that considers both the profitability and popularity of competing menu items.

merchandising—Activities developed to promote the sale of desired food and beverage items.

prime costs—The most significant costs in a food service operation: product costs (food and beverage) and labor costs.

prime-ingredient mark-up pricing method—An objective menu pricing method in which the cost of the entrée, rather than the total cost of all ingredients, is multiplied by a mark-up value (multiplier).

ratio pricing method—An objective menu pricing method that determines the relationship between food costs and all non-food costs plus profit requirements (contribution margin) and uses this ratio to develop base selling prices for menu items.

service—The movement of food and beverage products from serving staff to guests.

serving—The movement of food and beverage products from production staff to service personnel.

simple prime costs pricing method—An objective menu pricing approach that determines a menu item's base selling price by dividing the prime costs per guest by the desired prime costs percentage.

specific prime costs pricing method—An objective menu pricing approach in which multipliers for menu items are determined in such a way that the base selling prices for the items cover their fair share of labor costs.

 # Review Questions

1. In what ways can a system of control points help the food and beverage manager consistently identify and carry out control functions on a daily basis?

2. What are some important planning and control activities directly affected by the menu?

3. What are some marketing implications of menu planning?

4. How are menu changes modified by external and internal factors?

5. How is the multiplier determined for simple mark-up menu pricing methods?

6. How does the contribution margin pricing method differ from the ratio pricing method?

7. How does the simple prime costs pricing method differ from the specific prime costs pricing method?

8. What factors other than the base selling price established by pricing formulas must managers consider when setting menu prices?

9. How would you as a manager determine which, if any, menu pricing method should be used?

10. How does menu engineering define the profitability and popularity of a menu item?

11. What actions can managers take to improve the menu by managing items identified as plowhorses? puzzles? stars? dogs?

12. How does menu planning in a multi-unit organization differ from that in an individually owned and operated restaurant?

13. How can computer technology assist in the menu planning process?

Internet Sites

For more information, visit the following Internet sites. Remember that Internet addresses can change without notice. If the site is no longer there, you can use a search engine to look for additional sites.

Restaurant Menu Planning Software

Barrington Software, Inc.
www.cooken.com/menu_planning.htm

Cost Genie
www.costgenie.com

Enggist & Grandjean Software
www.eg-software.com

Food Service Solutions, Inc.
www.foodserve.com

Food Software.com
www.foodsoftware.com

StarChef
www.chef365.com

The CBORD Group, Inc.
www.cbord.com

Menu Evaluation

Resort Software
www.resortsoftware.com

Fourth Hospitality
www.fourthhospitality.com

Commercial Menus

Many (if not most) restaurants and many full-service hotels post current menus on their websites. Just type the name of properties you would like to visit into your favorite search engine.

Case Study

The Perils of Menu Planning

Until six months ago, the Madison Avenue Grill was a thriving 300-unit casual-dining chain with restaurants stretching from Seattle, Washington, to London,

England. But lately the news has not been so good. Karen Seaton, financial officer for the chain, has discovered that customer counts are falling off, with sales down 2.9 percent.

All signs pointed to the menu. Although Madison Avenue Grill has established a strong reputation as a quality restaurant serving upscale burgers, ribs, and fish, the novelty of their offerings has faded. In many markets, fresher, trendier concepts have taken hold. If the Grill is to withstand the competition, the menu has to change. And the sooner the better.

After consulting with COO and company cofounder Marcus Turner, Karen has gained the opportunity to test a new menu concept. To help develop that concept, she has called a 9:00 A.M. meeting with Marcus and three other company leaders: Jorge Estrada, director of marketing; Anne Hudson, director of operations/service; and Chef Charles Gustafsen. Her instructions to each: Come prepared to suggest one new menu item that can be launched immediately to turn the situation around—and be prepared to offer a rationale for the recommendation.

The five met around a large conference table in Marcus Turner's office. Karen made certain there were financial reports at each place.

"Since you're all aware of why we're meeting today, I'll keep the preliminaries brief. In a nutshell, our current numbers do not look good," she said. "The bottom line's in jeopardy, people, and if we don't do something fast, it's going to look even worse. Since the problems all seem to point to our menu, that's where I suggest we look for solutions. You're all here because I think we'll be able to come to some creative solutions if we work together. Input from each of you is important, because any change we make to the menu affects a number of key control points—purchasing, receiving, storing, issuing, production, service, and, of course, guest satisfaction. We need the one solution that will work best for everyone in the operation."

"So what's your new menu idea?" Anne Hudson asked, looking up from her notepad.

"I think we need something that takes relatively little prep time, offers a high margin, and brings people through the doors," Karen said. "A profitable convenience food, if you will."

At the words *convenience food,* Chef Gustafsen's jaw tightened. "And your recommendation?"

"Prime rib."

"Done to death," Jorge Estrada sighed. "And haven't you heard that beef is out?"

"If you want convenience," the chef interjected, "you couldn't pick a more inconvenient cut. It's too easy to overcook. Of course, with the proper slow-cooking equipment, it can be managed, but—"

Karen held up her hands. "Okay, okay. Given the current financials, I'm certainly not going to recommend new equipment in every unit. I know *I* like prime rib and I thought it would be a big hit."

COO Marcus Turner leaned forward, rubbing his hands. "You know what I like? I think—"

"If you want to bring people through the door, you have to give them what they want," Jorge interrupted. "All of my market research is pointing to one thing:

pita wraps. They're very hot right now. They capture people's fondness for lighter, healthier food; you can make them any way you want—Tex-Mex, Greek, stir-fry, whatever; and they are guaranteed to pull people into our operations. If you want even more reasons, they're fast and easy to prepare, so we can turn more tables at lunch and dinner."

"Wraps have a very low margin, Jorge," Karen said, frowning.

"But we'll make it up through increased traffic."

"I'm not so sure," Anne said. "I can tell you right now that my servers are not going to be happy pushing $4 or $5 wraps all the time. To bring their tips up, they're going to be recommending higher-priced items. And frankly, wraps can be messy. That may mean my bussers have to spend a little more time cleaning up at each table, and that may cut into your fast-turning tables theory."

"Not to mention the additional prep time," Charles said. "Suddenly we're doing a lot of cutting and chopping we didn't need to do before." He paused before adding, "And for what? So we can jump on the latest sandwich bandwagon. Where's the creativity in that?"

"Speaking of creativity—" Marcus began.

Karen cleared her throat and turned to Anne Hudson. "What's your menu solution?"

Anne flipped through her notepad, searching for her notes. "To be honest, I'm not all that particular about what we decide. I just need something my people can sell easily, that generates a good-size check, and that guests will enjoy. I, uh—" at last she found her notes—"I'm recommending some kind of dessert special, offered either nightly or weekly. I think people will come out to see what the specials are—that addresses your traffic concerns, Jorge—and $4 and $5 desserts represent a good profit for the company while boosting the check average nicely for our servers," she said, nodding at Karen. "We could even make our kitchen staff happy by purchasing brand-name desserts that require minimal prepping and can be easily stored, garnished, and served."

Chef Charles, who had been looking increasingly hopeful as Anne described her idea, suddenly reddened. "Why does the Grill even pay me a salary! Here I am, a classically trained chef who could help turn things around for us, and you recommend that we throw something on a plate that our guests could just as easily pick up at the supermarket. And when do we get to show our customers we know how to prepare food? Oh, I forgot. We get to decide which side of the cheesecake to place our little sprig of mint on."

"Chef—"

"Why not let me do what I am trained to do? Give me the freedom to create true culinary specialties, not serve up some store-bought concoctions. I can create one for every day of the week, signature dishes of the Madison Avenue Grill, and guests will come back day after day to experience them. Besides, if we prepare it ourselves, we can take advantage of special buys and seasonal specials and increase value. I am certain that with my unique creations on the menu, all it would take is a little marketing expertise to bring people through the door and keep them coming back."

"I know what keeps people coming back," Marcus ventured.

"What about quality, Chef?" Anne asked. "How are our hundreds of cooks going to maintain quality for a recipe they prepare only once a week? How will servers be able to develop strong product knowledge? And how do we justify purchasing and storing specialized ingredients in all of our locations for seven one-of-a-kind dishes?"

"You talk about marketing like it's some kind of cure-all," Jorge added, feeling his own temper rising. "Even if every one of your recipes was incredible, the fact is, that's not what people are saying they want. What's wrong with giving guests what they want?"

"I have to admit I have some concerns about profitability issues, as well," Karen said.

Then, no longer able to put him off, she glanced up at her boss. Marcus Turner was poised on the edge of his seat, looking suspiciously as if he had something to add.

"Mr. Turner?"

Marcus smiled broadly. "Finally, someone wants to hear my idea." He leaned back in his chair, a faraway look filling his eyes. "As some of you may know, I recently spent a couple weeks fly-fishing in Maine."

Jorge leaned over to Anne. "While we were up to our necks in extra work," he whispered.

Marcus ignored him. "You know what they love in Maine?" he asked the ceiling. "Fresh Maine lobster. Now, I know I've been out of operations for a while, but I can recognize a hit when I see one."

Karen buried her head in her hands. "Fresh Maine lobster."

"Exactly. Now, I hate to just jump in and give you the *answer* like this, but my instincts are telling me—"

"How do you suggest we get fresh Maine lobster to our units in Montana?" Anne asked. "Or, say, North Dakota?"

"Airplanes."

"And do you know what air delivery adds to the final price? We'd be talking 25 to 35 dollars for a lobster—"

"Well, the servers would love it," Marcus interjected.

"—in restaurants with a check average of $6 for lunch and $12 for dinner. Who's going to buy them?"

"Well, now, if marketing just did their job," Marcus said, his voice trailing off.

"Marketing?" Jorge said, incredulous. "Marketing's been telling you what people want, and it isn't Maine lobster. Not in Las Vegas, not in Louisiana, and certainly not in London."

"And what about storage? We'd need lobster tanks in every store."

"We'd have to buy bibs, cookers, crackers …"

"We'd need to establish receiving procedures to process live animals."

"Okay, okay," Marcus said, his smile fading fast. "But if lobster's definitely out of the question, where does that leave us? Assuming we have some truly workable ideas already on the table, how do we determine which is the right one for Madison Avenue Grill?"

Discussion Questions

1. What rationale did each member of the management team present in support of the menu item he or she recommended?

2. What are some of the advantages and disadvantages of each suggested menu item based on the control points of purchasing, receiving/storing/issuing, production, and service?

3. Use the information you gathered in answering Discussion Question #2 to complete the following decision matrix. Place a "+" in the appropriate column/row intersection if the advantages seem to outweigh the disadvantages, place a "–" if the disadvantages seem to outweigh the advantages, and place a "?" if you cannot decide which outweighs the other.

Menu Item	Purchasing	Receiving/Storing/Issuing	Production	Service
Prime Rib				
Pita Wraps				
Dessert Specials				
Signature Items				
Maine Lobster				
Other				

4. Of all the suggested menu items, which would you choose as the best solution to the Madison Avenue Grill's declining customer base? Why?

5. Keeping in mind the chain's desire for a new high-profit, popular, convenient menu item, what item would you suggest? What would be the advantages and disadvantages of your suggested item in terms of the control points of purchasing, receiving/storing/issuing, production, and service? Add your suggested menu item to the decision matrix you completed above, and, of all the suggested menu items, which would you now choose as the best solution to the chain's declining customer base? Why?

Case Number: 4655CA

Helping to generate and develop this case study were industry experts Timothy J. Pugh, East Lansing, Michigan, and Lawrence E. Ross, Professor, Florida Southern College.

Problems

Problem 1

The total ingredient cost in a recipe is $4.73; the manager desires a 37.5-percent food cost. What is the base selling price of the item using the ingredients mark-up method? Should the manager price the item in the above example at the base selling price you calculated? Why or why not?

Problem 2

The chef has precosted the recipe for an entrée and a sauce, which is one item on the menu; the food cost is $6.34. A prime ingredient multiplier of 3.72 has been established. What is the base selling price when the prime ingredient mark-up method is used?

Problem 3

The Prairie Town Grill does not serve alcoholic beverages. Its operating budget reveals the following:

- Revenue $1,375,000
- Food cost $585,000
- Non-food costs $710,000
- Profit $80,000
- Number of guests   161,580
- Guest check average $8.51
- Contribution margin $790,000   (revenue − food costs)

Using the above information, calculate the base selling price of a menu item with a total ingredient cost of $4.85 using:

    a.   The contribution margin pricing method.

    b.   The ratio pricing method.

    c.   The simple prime costs method (note: the non-food costs *include* $426,250 in labor costs).

Problem 4

The manager uses the mark-up with accompaniment cost method to establish a base selling price. What is that price when the entrée cost is $2.12, the plate cost is $1.70, and the mark-up multiplier is 2.1?

Problem 5

The manager of the University Square Bistro has the following operating data available:

- Revenue $1,187,000
- Food cost $3°\|$ $403,580   (includes entrée costs of $274,434)
- Labor cost 3% $367,970
- Other non-food costs $316,550   (excludes labor)
- Desired profit $98,900
- Number of guests   107,900

Use the above information to establish the base selling price of a menu item with alternative pricing methods. Note: the item to be priced has a food cost of $4.57 (entrée cost = $3.12; plate cost = $1.45)

    a.   What is the approximate base selling price using the ingredients mark-up method?

   b. What is the approximate base selling price using the prime ingredient mark-up method?

   c. What is the approximate base selling price using the mark-up with accompaniment costs method?

   d. What is the approximate base selling price using the contribution margin pricing method?

   e. What is the approximate base price using the ratio pricing method?

   f. What is the approximate base selling price using the simple prime costs method?

   g. What is the base selling price using the specific price cost method? Assume that (a) 70 percent of food cost is for items involving extensive preparation, (b) 60 percent of labor cost is for preparation activities, and (c) the item to be priced involves significant preparation.

Problem 6

Complete the menu engineering worksheet on the following page. Suggest strategies to effectively manage each item after the worksheet is completed.

Problem 6 Worksheet

Menu Engineering Worksheet

Restaurant: Terry's Overland Grill

Date: 7/10/XX

Meal Period: Dinner

(A) Menu Item Name	(B) Number Sold (MM)	(C) Menu Mix %	(D) Item Food Cost	(E) Item Selling Price	(F) Item CM	(G) Menu Costs D×B	(H) Menu Revenues E×B	(L) Menu CM F×B	(P) CM Category	(R) MM% Category	(S) Menu Item Classification
A Chicken	481	40%	4.90	12.50	7.60	2357	6013	3656	Low	High	Plow
B Beef	190	16%	6.50	14.75	8.25	1235	2803	1568	High	Low	Puzzle
C Seafood	205	17%	5.20	10.60	5.40	1066	2173	1107	Low	Low	Dog
D Vegan	340	28%	7.00	16.80	9.80	2380	5712	3332	High	High	Star
Column Totals:	N 1216					I 7,038	J 16,701	M 9,663			

guest check average

Additional Computations:

$\dfrac{100}{4}$

O = M/N   7.95

$\dfrac{\text{Food Cost}}{\text{Food Revenue}}$ 42%   Contrib margin menu

Q = (100%/items)(70%)   25(70%)

17.50

Part III

Designing Effective Food and Beverage Control Systems

Competencies

1. Explain how effective purchasing practices affect the bottom line of a food and beverage operation. (p. 183)

2. Describe procedures related to the purchasing cycle and identify purchasing responsibilities within a food and beverage operation. (pp. 184–185)

3. Identify factors that food and beverage managers should consider when selecting a supplier. (pp. 185–186)

4. Identify factors that food and beverage managers should assess when purchasing food products, and calculate the quantities of food products to purchase using the minimum/maximum ordering system. (pp. 186–193)

5. Identify the elements and explain the functions of a purchase order system. (pp. 193–198)

6. Identify security concerns related to the purchasing function. (pp. 198–200)

7. Describe actions that managers can take to reduce the cost of the purchasing function, and discuss purchasing in multi-unit organizations. (pp. 201–202)

8. Describe receiving control procedures. (pp. 202–211)

6

Purchasing and Receiving Controls

Many aspects of managing a food and beverage operation, including those related to purchasing and receiving, begin with the menu. The menu determines products that must be purchased. If items are not needed, they should not be purchased. While this seems obvious, the rusty, dusty cans in some storerooms and the boxes of frozen products stored month after month in freezers suggest that this principle is not always followed. Likewise, in beverage operations, purchasing needs are determined by the menu. Some managers feel they must offer an extremely large selection of various call brand products, which may spend most of their time on the shelf. A better approach may be to offer a limited range of popular call brands while only keeping other call brands on hand as needed for regular guests.

While the menu's impact on the control system is obvious, cost control also depends on the skills and abilities of purchasing personnel and others who work within the food and beverage operation. If ineffective management and staff personnel are employed, no amount of planning and control can ensure success.

Since cost savings in food and beverage purchasing go directly to the bottom line, no hospitality operation can afford inefficient purchasing procedures. Assume that the profits earned by a food and beverage operation are eight percent of the revenue generated. This means that for every dollar of revenue, the operation earns a profit of eight cents. Let's assume that poor purchasing practices waste $500 every week. How much must the operation generate in additional revenue to pay for the wasted $500?

The answer is *not* $500 dollars. Revenue must also be used to pay for food costs, beverage costs, necessary labor costs, mortgage payments, taxes, and many other types of costs as well. The wasted $500 must come out of the operation's *profits*. To make up for $500 of lost profit, the operation must generate an equal amount of additional profit. With an eight-percent profit margin, the operation must generate additional weekly revenue of $6,250 ($500 ÷ 0.08). No operation can afford to allocate its first $6,250 in revenue each week to offset higher-than-necessary costs that could have been reduced by effective purchasing.

Although the control process is affected by decisions made in all areas of the complex food and beverage management system, it is convenient to begin discussing physical aspects of food and beverage cost control where the physical cycle of the operation begins—at the purchasing and receiving control points. However, actual cost control begins when goals for purchasing and receiving are established. Many plans and procedures are already in place before the physical cycle begins.

Exhibit 1   The Purchasing Cycle: An Audit Trail

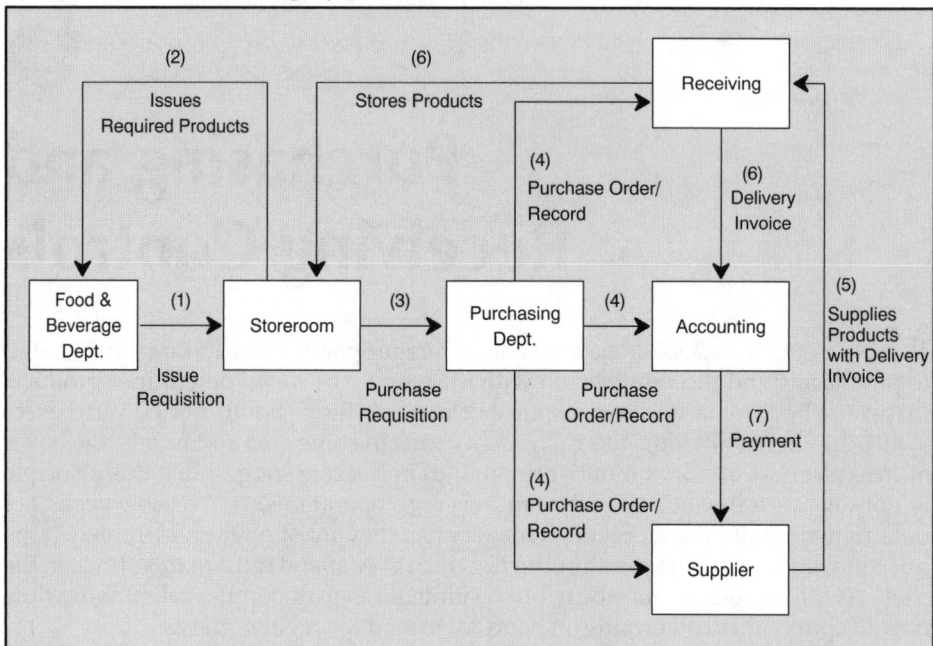

Purchasing Objectives and Procedures

Purchasing is the series of activities designed to obtain products of the right quality and quantity, at the right price and time, and from the right source. These simple-to-state objectives can be difficult to achieve. Since the purchasing cycle involves a variety of different procedures, many activities must be controlled when designing and managing purchasing tasks. The complexity of purchasing is illustrated in Exhibit 1. Notice that the purchasing cycle involves the following activities:

1. The chef in the food department and the bartender (or bar manager) in the beverage department complete an issue requisition when items are needed.

2. The storeroom responds by issuing required products to the user department.

3. When products in inventory reach a predetermined reorder point, the storeroom forwards a purchase requisition to the purchasing department.

4. The purchasing department orders required products from the proper supplier, perhaps using a purchase order or a purchase record. Increasingly, food service operators place orders with suppliers using **e-commerce** technology. Purchasing personnel send or transmit the purchase order or purchase record information to the receiving and accounting departments. (Purchase orders, purchase records, and e-commerce procedures are discussed later in this chapter.)

5. The supplier delivers the products to the receiving department along with a delivery invoice.

6. The receiving clerk moves products to the proper storage area and forwards the delivery invoice, perhaps with other documents, to the accounting department. In some properties, these documents are reviewed by the food and beverage management staff before being routed to accounting personnel.

7. After further processing of necessary documents, accounting department personnel send payment to the supplier and file copies of the purchasing/receiving forms for accounting and control purposes.

This purchasing cycle is repeated every time products are ordered. You can see that purchasing is more than "picking up the phone and calling in an order." It is a complex cycle of activities requiring special planning and control procedures that create an **audit trail** (a series of records, documents, and reports that trace the flow of resources through an operation).

Like most other aspects of food service management, technology has dramatically impacted procedures used for purchasing in even relatively small operations. After a discussion of basic principles, illustrated by some manual system components, we'll explain details of automated purchasing systems.

Purchasing Responsibilities

Ultimate responsibility for purchasing decisions generally lies with the food and beverage manager. In small operations, the general manager may function as a food and beverage manager. In very small properties, the owner, manager, food and beverage manager, and chef are frequently the same individual.

As properties increase in size, positions become more specialized. In a small hotel, for example, the food and beverage manager (who may perform many duties frequently done by individuals in different positions in larger properties) may be responsible for purchasing. In large food and beverage operations, a purchasing agent may be assigned to perform the many activities that may be necessary. The purchasing agent is in a staff (advisory) relationship to the food and beverage manager. As such, the purchasing agent should not make decisions involving, for example, the definition of required quality, whether items should be purchased in convenience form or be prepared on-site, or whether purchase quantities should be increased or decreased to reflect price trends. These and numerous other decisions applicable to purchasing should be made by line managers. In this regard, the purchasing agent functions in much the same way a personnel officer, accountant, or public relations official does; the purchasing agent studies problems and gives advice, but does not make purchasing decisions. Generally, it is the food and beverage manager who bears ultimate responsibility for purchasing decisions.

Selecting Suppliers

Managers of food and beverage operations should choose suppliers carefully. Detailed purchase specifications and objective calculations of quantities to order are ineffective without professional suppliers. Essentially, supplier evaluations should be based on the consistency of:

- Correct quality products.
- Reasonable prices.
- Prompt delivery.
- Service, including product information.

When selecting suppliers, a purchaser must consider a number of factors. Not every supplier who carries the needed product is appropriate for the food and beverage operation. The supplier with the lowest price may not be right for the operation, either. The following are important factors to consider when selecting a supplier:

- *Location.* Delivery time, transportation costs, and unexpected delays may be reduced if the supplier's facility is close to the food and beverage operation.
- *Quality of the supplier's operation.* Such things as sanitation, in-house processing, handling of orders, and the quantity and quality of items in stock must be assessed.
- *Technical ability of the supplier's staff.* Good salespersons are more than order-takers. They know their products and can help the operation resolve problems involving the products they supply.
- *Value.* The purchaser must carefully assess the supplier's prices in relation to the quality of products needed by, and the level of service given to, the operation.
- *Compatibility.* A good working relationship between the food and beverage purchaser and the supplier requires mutual beliefs about ethics and the fair treatment of both the guests and the supplier.
- *Honesty and fairness.* These traits must be part of the ongoing business relationship and the supplier's reputation.
- *Delivery personnel.* The appearance, attitude, and courtesy of the supplier's personnel contribute to the impression formed by personnel in the food and beverage operation.

The person responsible for purchasing should identify possible sources for all items needed, determine the most appropriate suppliers, and choose from among them. While longstanding relationships with suppliers can help in future dealings, managers should be careful not to get too comfortable with their suppliers. There is the danger of allowing standards to slip, with the result that the property does not receive the most from its purchasing dollar. Therefore, it is appropriate to periodically review the selection of suppliers and assess the performance of each in meeting the operation's expectations.

Purchasing the Proper Quality

Quality in the purchasing function refers to the suitability of a product for its intended use. The more suitable a product, the higher (better) its quality. For example, a super colossal olive may represent the right quality product for garnish or salad purposes. It will not, however, typically be the proper quality if it is chopped and used as a salad bar topping.

Decisions about quality requirements are first made when the goals of the business are established and subsequent marketing plans are developed. At that time, the spirit and intent of the food and beverage operation's quality standards are determined. Later, **standard purchase specifications** are documented in detail to indicate the requirements for products suitable for their intended purpose. These specifications provide detailed descriptions of the quality, size, and weight desired for particular items.

The relationship between quality and price is referred to as value. Just as the guest considers value when deciding what to order in the restaurant or lounge, food and beverage managers must also consider value when choosing products to purchase. To purchase products of optimal value for the food and beverage operation, the purchaser must carefully evaluate each product's quality (suitability for intended use) in relation to its cost.

The format for purchase specifications illustrated in Exhibit 2 indicates specific quality requirements. Notice that the specifications not only describe the desired product, but also specify how the product will be used. In addition, a specification tells the supplier about the operation's procedures for ensuring that the delivered item does, in fact, meet the required quality specifications. Standard purchase specifications must:

- Accurately describe minimum quality requirements.

- Clearly and simply indicate the food and beverage operation's needs.

- Realistically define needs, yet not limit the number of acceptable suppliers.

Generally, specifications should be developed for most products purchased. However, there is a need to be practical in following this principle. Developing detailed specifications for products such as salt and other seasonings or bar swizzle sticks may not be justified. Instead, managers involved with the purchasing function should first develop specifications for expensive, high-volume items and then formalize quality requirements for other products as time permits. In some operations, 75 percent of all product dollars are spent for only 25 percent of all products. These relatively few items require purchase specifications.

When items are purchased by brand, such as liquor or ketchup, the brand itself becomes the specification. However, it is still necessary to specify container size and special instructions.

Quality concerns are important when purchasing alcoholic beverages as well as when purchasing foods. However, liquor, wines, and beers are generally purchased by brand name and, as noted above, the brand then becomes the specification. Many food and beverage operations feature a range of quality and, therefore, a range of prices for the alcoholic beverages being served. Liquor may be available in a **house brand** (also called pour brand, well brand, or speed-rail brand [named after the shelf typically located close to the bartender for quick access]) and a **call brand**. Other properties offer very high quality brands referred to as **premium brands**. Many beverage consumers prefer a specific brand, and the manager must make a marketing decision to determine the call and premium brands to be offered.

Exhibit 2   Purchase Specification Format

<u>(Name of food and beverage operation)</u>

1. Product name: _____

2. Product used for:

> Clearly indicate product use (such as olive garnish for beverage and hamburger patty to be grilled for sandwich).

3. Product general description:

> Provide general quality information about desired product. For example, "iceberg lettuce; heads to be green, firm without spoilage, excessive dirt, or damage. No more than 10 outer leaves; packed 24 heads per case."

4. Detailed description:

> Purchaser should state other factors that help to clearly identify desired product. Examples of specific factors, which vary by product being described, may include:
>
> - Geographic origin
> - Variety
> - Type
> - Style
> - Grade
>
> - Product size
> - Portion size
> - Brand name
> - Density
>
> - Medium of pack
> - Specific gravity
> - Container size
> - Edible yield, trim

5. Product test procedures:

> Test procedures occur when products are received and as or after products are prepared or used. For example, products to be at a refrigerated temperature upon delivery can be tested with a thermometer. Portion-cut meat patties can be randomly weighed. Lettuce packed 24 heads per case can be counted.

6. Special instructions and requirements:

> Any additional information needed to clearly indicate quality expectations can be included here. Examples include bidding procedures, if applicable, labeling and packaging requirements, and special delivery and service requirements.

In addition, many guests judge the overall quality of the restaurant in part by the quality of house brands available. For example, a high-check restaurant will not likely offer a low-quality house brand. In fact, some food and beverage operations offer only call or premium brands as a statement about the quality of all products offered by the property.

Exhibit 3   Food Sample Data Sheet

1. Product: _____

2. Brand Name: _____

3. Presented By: _____   Date: _____

4. Varieties Available: _____

5. Shelf Life: (Frozen) _____ (Thawed, Refrigerated, Dry) _____

6. Preparation and Sanitation Considerations: _____

   _____

   _____

   _____

7. Menu Suggestions: _____

8. Merchandising Help Available (Posters, Table Tents, etc.):_____

9. Case Size (Number of Portions): _____

10. Portion Size: _____

11. Distributed By: _____

12. Minimum Order: _____

13. Any Additional Ordering Information: _____

    _____

14. Lead Time: _____

15. Approximate Price Per Serving: _____

NOTE: Were the following information sheets received with products?

    a. Nutritional and Ingredient Analysis: Yes _____   No _____

    b. Specification Sheet: Yes _____   No _____

Source: Ronald F. Cichy, *Food Safety: Managing with the HACCP System,* Second Edition (Lansing, Mich:. American Hotel & Lodging Educational Institute, 2008), p. 81.

Wine is also purchased with the same types of concerns. Many properties offer a house brand and numerous better-known and higher-quality wines on their list. House brands may be available by the glass or carafe (sometimes in different sizes). Today, a wide number of microbreweries produce beers that are very popular with many guests. Food and beverage managers may offer several brands at different prices. The history of the label, the guest's experience with the brand, and the amount of advertising run by beverage manufacturers and distributors all influence the perceived quality and popularity of alcoholic beverages offered by the food service operation.

Another purchasing tool is the **food sample data sheet** (Exhibit 3). This sheet helps standardize the evaluation of a product. It can be used to record purchasing, storing, preparing, and serving information about products that the operation is sampling and considering for purchase. The food sample data sheet makes product selection more objective.

Purchasing the Proper Quantities

Purchasing the proper quantities of items is just as important as developing correct quality specifications. Typical problems that can arise when too much of a product is ordered are:

- Cash flow problems resulting from excessive money tied up in inventory.
- Increased storage costs for interest, insurance, and sometimes rented storage space.
- Deterioration of product quality or damaged products.
- Increased potential for theft and pilferage.

Purchasing insufficient quantities also has potential disadvantages—dissatisfied guests not able to order what they want because of stockouts, emergency and rush orders that are frequently expensive and time-consuming, and lost discounts from volume purchases.

To avoid these problems, food and beverage managers must periodically assess a number of factors that affect the purchase of proper quantities, including the following:

- *Popularity of menu items.* As unit sales of menu items increase, additional quantities of ingredients are obviously needed.
- *Product cost concerns.* Higher product costs may result in increased selling prices, which, in turn, may result in decreased sales levels. In this case, the need for continued purchase of the product should be evaluated. Also, management may make judgments about future prices and buy more if prices are expected to increase or buy less if prices are expected to decrease. This is called **speculative purchasing** and should be done only by management, based on information provided by the purchaser.
- *Available storage space.* Available space may limit quantities purchased. Storage space in dry, frozen, and refrigerated areas may not be adequate to accommodate quantity purchases.
- *Safety level.* **Safety level** refers to a minimum quantity of product that should always be available in inventory to help ensure that stockouts do not occur. Maintaining a safety level of products in inventory may require buying a quantity above that actually needed to allow for delivery delays, increased usage, or other unexpected developments.
- *Supplier constraints.* Suppliers may specify minimum dollar or poundage requirements for delivery. Also, some suppliers may refuse to break cases, bags, or other packing containers to meet overly specific order quantities (or if they do break cases, there is likely to be a significant increase in per-unit price). Therefore, the standard commercial units of the packaging influence quantities purchased.

Exhibit 4   Perishable Product Quotation/Call Sheet (Manual System)

Item	Amount			Supplier		
	Needed	On Hand	Order	A & B Co.	Green Produce	Local Supplier
1	2	3	4	5	6	7
Spinach	6 cs	$2^1/_2$ cs	4 cs	$22^{00}/_{cs}$ = $88.00	$14^{85}/_{cs}$ = $59.40	$21^{70}/_{cs}$ = $86.80
Ice Lettuce	8 cs	1 cs	7 cs	$17^{00}/_{cs}$ = $119.00	$16^{75}/_{cs}$ = $117.25	$18^{10}/_{cs}$ = $126.70
Carrots	3-20#	20#	2-20#	$14^{70}/_{bag}$ = $29.40	$13^{90}/_{bag}$ = $27.80	$13^{80}/_{bag}$ = $27.60
Tomatoes	2 lugs	$^1/_2$ lug	2 lugs	$18^{60}/_{lug}$ = $37.20	$18^{00}/_{lug}$ = $36.00	$18^{10}/_{lug}$ = $36.20
			Totals	$861.40	$799.25	$842.15

Perishable Products

Perishable items such as fresh produce, bakery, and dairy products should be used as soon as possible after receipt. These types of products are normally purchased several times weekly to minimize in-house storage time according to the following formula:

Quantity Needed − Quantity Available = Quantity to Purchase for Immediate Use

Sample procedures for purchasing perishable products are as follows:

1. Determine normal usage rates. For a normal two-day purchasing period, for example, assess the specific number of cases of selected produce items, pounds of fresh meat, fresh poultry fryers, and other perishable products the property typically uses.

2. Assess the amount of each item currently in inventory.

3. Calculate the quantity to purchase by subtracting the quantity available (step 2) from the quantity needed (step 1).

4. Adjust routine quantities as necessary for special functions, holidays, or other non-routine events.

When purchasing items for immediate use, some properties that use manual purchasing systems use a form such as the one illustrated in Exhibit 4. When reviewing the perishable product quotation/call sheet, note that the perishable items needed are listed in column 1 and the quantity of each item needed for the time covered by the order is in column 2. The inventory amount noted in column 3 is determined by an actual physical count of the quantity on hand. The amount to order (column 4) is determined by subtracting the amount on hand (column 3) from the amount needed (column 2). In the first example, only 3½ cases of spinach are needed (6 cases − 2½ cases = 3½ cases), but 4 cases should be purchased if suppliers will not break cases or if the increased broken case price is judged excessive.

The prices quoted by eligible suppliers are listed in columns 5, 6, and 7. Each supplier has copies of the food and beverage operation's quality specifications on which to base the price for each item. The buyer can either select the supplier with the lowest total price for everything required or use several suppliers, depending on who has the lowest price item by item. However, minimum delivery requirements may limit this purchasing option. Also, the in-house processing cost for each order (usually not assessed but frequently expensive) should be considered. E-commerce, discussed later in this chapter, can reduce the paperwork required to collect the required information. In addition, large operations may subscribe to electronic newspapers that provide real-time price information.

Non-Perishable Products

To determine the quantity of non-perishable products to purchase, it is often practical to use a minimum/maximum system of inventory management. This system is based on a concept discussed earlier: only a few of all items purchased represent high-cost or high-volume items. Minimum/maximum ordering systems give first attention to these high-priority items and help managers determine when products must be purchased and how much of each product to order.

For each purchase item, the **minimum/maximum ordering system** assesses the minimum quantity below which inventory levels should not fall and the maximum quantity above which inventory levels should not rise. The **minimum inventory level** is the safety level: the number of purchase units that must always remain in inventory. The **maximum inventory level** is the greatest number of purchase units permitted in storage. The maximum inventory level of purchase units permitted in storage is the usage rate plus the minimum (safety) level.

The most important factor for determining when more purchase units must be ordered is the rate at which they are used by the operation. The **usage rate** is the number of purchase units used per order period. Purchase units are counted in terms of the number of shipping containers of normal size for each product. For example, if ten cases (six #10 cans in each) of green peas are normally used between deliveries, the usage rate for green peas is ten cases.

In addition to usage rates, managers must determine a lead-time quantity for each purchase item. The **lead-time quantity** is the number of purchase units withdrawn from inventory between the time an order is placed and when it is delivered. Again, purchase units are counted in terms of normal size shipping containers. For example, if two cases of green peas are used between ordering and receiving, the lead-time quantity is two cases. This lead-time quantity is separate from the safety (minimum) level of purchase units kept in inventory. The safety level must allow for such things as late deliveries and greater-than-normal usage.

The **order point** is the number of purchase units in stock when an order is placed. The order point is reached when the number of purchase units in inventory equals the lead-time quantity plus the safety level:

$$\begin{array}{ccc} \text{Purchase Units at} & = & \text{Purchase Units in} \\ \text{Order Point} & & \text{Lead Time} \end{array} + \begin{array}{c} \text{Purchase Units in} \\ \text{Safety Level} \end{array}$$

If products are ordered at the order point, the quantity in inventory will be reduced to the safety (minimum) level by the time products are received. When the order arrives, the inventory level for the product will again be brought back to the maximum level. Examples of the minimum/maximum order inventory system are found in Exhibit 5.

The Purchase Order System

To this point, we have discussed control procedures that apply before the actual purchasing task. Before the purchasing process begins, the food and beverage operation should have established minimum quality standards and provided them to potential suppliers, calculated quantities of products to be purchased, determined order points for each purchase item, and considered eligible suppliers. It is important that control procedures be built into the actual purchasing process as well. For this purpose, large food and beverage operations use a purchase order system.

With a **purchase order system**, a purchase order is sent (by mail, by fax, or electronically) to the supplier awarded the order. Information about the order is retained in the purchasing department and is also circulated internally among the receiving and accounting departments. The purchase order formally identifies the product, quantity, unit cost, and total cost that both the supplier and purchaser have agreed to. In addition, the purchase order may include guarantees, warranties, payment requirements, inspection rights, "hold harmless" provisions, and other legal and contractual concerns.

A purchase order, such as the example shown in Exhibit 6 for a manual purchasing system, is the food and beverage operation's record of the specifics of all incoming shipments. The property must pay the agreed-to price for no less than the agreed-to quality for the amount ordered. Higher-than-necessary food and beverage costs are frequently traced to communication and coordination problems among the several departments or personnel involved in purchasing. Properly used, the purchase order minimizes these problems.

Rather than using a purchase order system, smaller food and beverage operations may simply summarize purchase order information by using an in-house purchase record form, such as that shown in Exhibit 7. The **purchase record** performs the same functions as the purchase order, except that it is not given to suppliers. It provides the food and beverage operation with a detailed record of all incoming shipments. Affected personnel and departments must know all the specifics about incoming food and beverage products. Without a written record, busy management staff may forget the details. Properly used, the purchase record helps to control food and beverage costs.

Exhibit 5   Minimum/Maximum Order System

Example 1. Assume:
  Purchase unit = case (6 #10 cans)
  Usage rate = 2 cases per day
  Order period = monthly (30 days)
  Monthly usage rate = 2 cases/day × 30 days = 60 cases
  Lead time = 4 days
  Lead-time usage rate = 4 days at 2 cases/day = 8 cases
  Safety level = 4 days at 2 cases/day = 8 cases
  Order point = lead time + safety level
    16 cases = 8 cases + 8 cases
  Maximum level = usage rate + safety level
    68 cases = 60 cases + 8 cases
When ordering at the order point, the quantity to order is the monthly usage rate.
This is shown by the following calculation:

Order point	16 cases
Monthly usage rate	60 cases
Total cases available	76
Lead-time usage rate	− 8
Maximum level	68 cases

So the maximum level is maintained.

Example 2. When placing an order before the order point is reached, such as when putting together an order for numerous products from a supplier, first determine the number of cases in storage, then subtract the order point from the amount in storage.

Amount in storage	25 cases
Order point	− 16 cases
Excess over order point	9 cases

The amount to order is the usage rate minus the number of cases in excess of the order point:
  51 cases = 60 cases − 9 cases

The decision to order 51 cases can be proved:

Cases ordered	51
Amount available	25
Total	76
Lead-time usage rate	− 8
Maximum level	68

Again, the maximum inventory level is maintained.

Technological Purchasing Systems

As is true with all control points, basic management principles must be used regardless of whether manual or electronic systems are in place to perform required

Exhibit 6   Purchase Order (Manual System)

| Purchase Order Number: _____ | Order Date: _____ |
| | Payment Terms: _____ |

To: _____ From/Ship to: _____
(supplier)   (name of food service operation)

_____   _____

(address)   (address)

Delivery Date: _____

Please Ship:

Quantity Ordered	Description	✓	Units Shipped	Unit Cost	Total Cost

Total Cost _____

Important: This Purchase Order expressly limits acceptance to the terms and conditions stated above, noted on the reverse side hereof, and any additional terms and conditions affixed hereto or otherwise referenced. Any additional terms and conditions proposed by seller are objected to and rejected.

_____
Authorized Signature

activities. We have just reviewed some of the most important principles in the context of manual procedures. We will now explain basics in their electronic counterparts.

As with all other aspects of technology and control, managers do not make purchasing decisions using either all or no technology. In some operations, for example, electronic price quotations, bid acceptance, and supplier notification (purchase order) procedures may be the only assistance provided by technology. In others, purchasing is entirely "paperless" from the determination of purchase

Exhibit 7   In-House Purchase Record (Manual System)

Date Ordered: _____							
Delivery Date: _____			Supplier: _____				
Item Description	**Unit**	**Price**	**No. of Units**	**Total Cost**	**Invoice No.**	**Comments**	

quantities to the issuing of storeroom ingredients, which depletes inventory and begins the purchasing process all over again.

Computer-generated shopping lists can be produced by any of several kitchen management systems available today. These offer a software package with numerous modules to maintain **ingredient files, recipe files, menu item files,** and **inventory files**. For example, sales of each menu item can be forecasted for a specific period. The quantity of each ingredient needed to produce the estimated number of portions based on standard recipes can then be determined. If ingredients such as tomato paste or ground beef are used in more than one recipe, the total quantity of each duplicate ingredient is calculated as the shopping list is generated. Some systems can electronically sort needed items by suppliers who are approved by the operation to provide the item. If specific items such as dairy products or baked goods are provided by a single supplier, a purchase order can be generated and electronically sent to the supplier. Requests for price quotations (RFPs) can be sent to eligible suppliers when multiple suppliers are used, and purchase orders can be generated for those who are awarded the order. In operations that do not use RFPs, purchase orders can be generated directly from the by-supplier market lists.

In the system just described, purchase quantities are based upon sales estimates. Alternatively, with other systems, a property's purchasing needs can be estimated by noting the decreasing amounts of products in inventory (a minimum/maximum inventory process such as that described earlier). Systems can also allow managers to determine purchase quantities based upon actual menu item sales. Instead of determining ingredient quantities that should be necessary based upon estimated sales, they use data about ingredient usage based upon actual sales to determine purchase amounts needed to replenish inventories.

Depending upon the extent of automation and the purchase process desired, quantities for "shopping carts" or purchase requisition lists can be generated manually by inventory counts and estimates of par level requirements, or electronically by studying standard recipe–required product usage. Purchase needs can also be imported electronically from hand-held devices as actual inventory quantities are

Exhibit 8   Requisition List of Ingredients

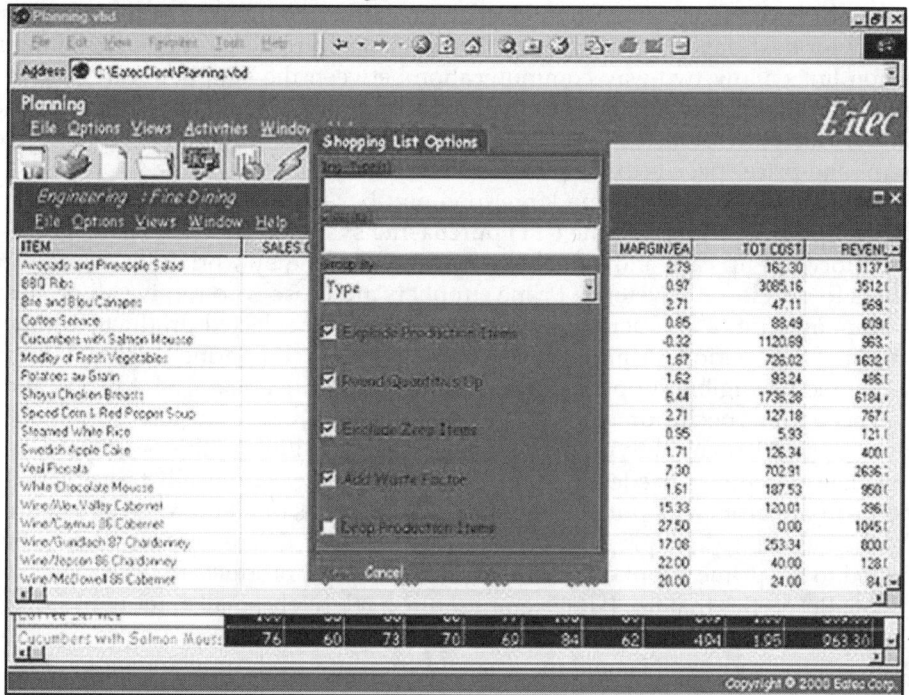

Courtesy of Eatec Corporation, Emeryville, California (www.eatec.com).

assessed. Exhibit 8 illustrates part of a requisition (market) list of ingredients to be purchased. Systems enable requisition lists to be combined for multiple outlets, such as in a hotel or multi-unit organization within a selected geographic area. Orders needed for special functions and catered events can be combined into a single list as well. Quantities to be ordered can be adjusted automatically to account for such factors as quantities on order and minimum/maximum systems.

After suppliers are selected and purchase orders are generated, purchase orders can be printed (hard copy), faxed directly to the supplier, or transferred by custom **electronic data interchange** (EDI). Reports to track products on order but not yet delivered can be generated as desired.

Properties purchasing ingredients from more than one supplier may receive competitive bids for items meeting specifications and store them in a bid specification file. These can be entered into the system, and the purchasing module can sort items to be purchased by supplier and lowest bid. Purchasing modules provide override options that enable management to alter items and quantities before the final preparation and distribution of purchase orders.

The increasing use of telephone communication links between food service operations and suppliers continues to have a significant impact on the ordering process. Order-entry telephone lines can be used to send purchase orders directly from properties to the supplier's computer system. The purchaser files the purchase orders and maintains them by number and date.

Some suppliers allow clients to use autodial modems. An **autodial modem** functions without user intervention, enabling late-night transmission of purchase orders for next-day processing. Some sophisticated purchase order telecommunication links allow two-way communication between the supplier and the property. This allows the purchaser to make online inquiries about current prices and stock availability. It also allows the supplier to send information about featured items and price specials to the purchaser.

Today, managers of some large food and beverage operations are developing computerized **just-in-time (JIT) purchasing systems**. They realize that excess inventory ties up cash and valuable storage space, so they work with **prime suppliers** to develop JIT systems. Prime suppliers are those who receive all or a significant amount of an operation's purchase orders for selected products during a specified time period. Prime suppliers are selected by comparing price quotations submitted by eligible suppliers for the estimated product quantities the operation will need for a specific time period.

In one JIT plan, individual food and beverage outlets within a property can calculate ingredients needed for daily production and electronically transmit those needs to the property's purchasing office. There, totals of all ingredients required for the following day's preparation needs are assessed. These totals are then transmitted to the prime supplier, who delivers the needed products in time for preparation. Properties that use JIT systems require a relatively small amount of storage space for back-up supplies because products are supplied according to need. As purchasing processes become increasingly computerized, implementation of JIT systems becomes more practical.

Security Concerns in Purchasing

In small food and beverage operations, where owners/managers may purchase and receive the products themselves, control procedures are less concerned with theft than with obtaining the best value. In larger operations, where other personnel take on purchasing tasks, security becomes an increasingly important concern. The control process must guard against several types of theft that are possible during the purchasing process. Owners and managers of any type of food service operation must develop and implement purchase specifications that define quality requirements. In their absence, there is less assurance that value goals can be attained.

Kickbacks. In several common types of kickbacks, the buyer for the food and beverage operation works in collusion with someone from the supplier's company. The kickback can be money or gifts. Either way, the owner of the operation is the loser. In one kickback scheme, products are purchased at prices that are higher than those currently being charged. The two thieves then split the difference between the real and inflated prices. To best control this type of theft, the owner/manager can routinely review invoices and ask such questions as, "Why are so many products purchased from the same supplier?" The manager can also periodically review the selection of suppliers and solicit price quotations randomly to ensure that prices paid are the best—or, at least, competitive—for the quality

---

Electronic Purchasing:
A Case Study in Supplier Assistance

Suppliers have done much to assist purchasers with electronic purchasing options. They can benefit from the same advantages (cost reductions, better service, and faster, more accurate information) as do food service managers implementing automated systems.

Many suppliers offer online ordering systems so that orders can be placed at any hour of any day on any computer with Internet access. It is even possible to develop an order electronically and then select a future date to transmit it to the supplier.

Suppliers encourage purchasers to develop custom "templates" (packages of items to be ordered at the same time), such as ingredients required for an ongoing Saturday night dinner special. Quantities can be established at a specific par level, or changes in quantities needed can be revised each time the template orders are placed.

Suppliers may provide online information about a food service operator's account. Account balances and details about paid and outstanding invoices and previous payment, for example, are included. Reviews of payment history are very important for multi-unit managers making numerous purchases from the same supplier for multiple outlets.

Many suppliers offer debit payment programs in which, after pre-authorization of payments from a business bank account, payment withdrawals are automatically made. (Hospitality operators are increasingly adopting this payment mode to reduce the costs of in-house payment processing.) With one system, the supplier notifies food service purchasers twice (by fax or e-mail). A pre-notification report is sent the day after a delivery is made to review details about the delivery. The day before the account debit is made, a final notification report is sent. The supplier can then make the transaction directly to the property's bank account.

---

and quantity of products being purchased. Another tactic is to require the use of competitive bids.

In another kickback scheme, the delivery invoice is padded by adding items that were not received, or it is increased by adding unreasonable charges for handling or some other service. This scheme works well when the same employee does the receiving and the purchasing. Therefore, if it is possible to use a system that separates the purchasing and receiving tasks, this type of kickback could be prevented.

In large hotels, purchasing may be the responsibility of a staff purchasing department. Receiving and storing activities may be performed by persons in the accounting department. Under this system, products do not come under the control of production staff until they are issued. This system helps reduce the possibility that one person, working alone, can implement a kickback scheme.

Fictitious Companies. Purchasing personnel can steal by setting up a nonexistent company that submits invoices for products never received. Managers can periodically review the selection of suppliers by examining the names of payees on company checks. Unless the manager is familiar with the supplier, checks should never be sent to companies with only post office box addresses.

Reprocessing Invoices. Suppliers may try to send an invoice to the food and beverage operation for processing a second time. To avoid this type of theft, operations need an internal system to verify which invoices have not been paid and to cancel invoices when they are paid.

Delivery Invoice Errors. Intentional arithmetic errors, short weight or counts, wrong quality, and similar "mistakes" can cost the operation money. Management or office personnel must check all arithmetic on invoices and statements (even when they are computer-generated) and follow proper receiving practices such as those reviewed later in this chapter to catch these mistakes. Whether they are innocent mistakes or fraud, the bottom line is the same: the operation loses money.

Credit Memo Problems. When products are not delivered or when deliveries are short of the quantities ordered, a request-for-credit memo should be issued to reduce the original delivery invoice by the value of the items not delivered. The supplier should then issue a credit memo to adjust the account. Managers and receiving staff should never accept a "we'll deliver it later and not charge you" comment from the truck driver. A request-for-credit memo should be written and attached to the delivery invoice. The manager should also alert the property's accounting department to ensure that the supplier properly processes the credit to the buyer's account. Normally, credit memo forms in multiple parts are provided by the delivery person. It is helpful for the property to also have blank copies of a generic form available in case the delivery person does not have copies.

Quality Substitutions. Quality substitutions occur when a price is quoted for the proper quality item but a lower-quality item is delivered. Proper receiving practices can help prevent paying more for a lower-quality product. Brand or label substitutions are also possible if receiving personnel are not familiar with products ordered. If alert staff do recognize product problems, the supplier can "allege" a mistake and exchange the products for those of proper quality. This problem occurs more frequently than some purchasers may suspect and requires close attention to both purchasing and receiving duties.

Purchaser Theft. Purchasers might practice a variety of other thefts: purchasing for their own use, reciprocal purchasing for their own benefit, or purchasing products wholesale with the intention of reselling them to selected employees or to others. Using an effectively designed purchasing system can help reduce these types of potential problems.

There is a gray area of purchasing ethics in which purchasing personnel may be offered gifts or free meals, invitations to parties, or other inducements designed to increase the supplier's business. Buyers must put the property first and make decisions based on what is best for the property rather than for themselves. Many food and beverage operations develop codes of ethics that, in part, detail policies about what purchasers can (and cannot) do in their relationships with suppliers.

Reducing the Cost of the Purchasing Function

Professional food and beverage managers adopt a number of techniques to make certain that purchase dollars are spent wisely. They know that there are many tactics that can be used besides increasing selling prices or reducing product quality levels.

Negotiate Prices. Some food and beverage managers mistakenly believe that an initial price quoted by the supplier is "fixed" and that purchasing involves simply soliciting price quotations and then accepting the lowest price quoted for the specified quality. In fact, discussions with sales managers (not the distributor sales representative who calls on the buyer) may yield lower prices.

Review Quality Standards. Be sure that the proper quality of products is being purchased. If, for example, products of higher-than-necessary quality are being used, purchase prices can be reduced by purchasing items of the correct quality.

Evaluate the Need to Purchase Convenience Products. Sometimes, employees can prepare products of acceptable quality at a lower cost than that required for purchasing the products in a convenience (prepared) form. Only a careful **make-buy analysis** can reveal which form of product should be used.

Discontinue Unnecessary Supplier Services. Costs incurred by suppliers for such services as storage, handling, delivery, and "grace" periods for the payment of bills may be included in product purchase costs. Purchasers should carefully consider exactly what services are desired and assess whether purchase prices can be reduced if unneeded services are discontinued.

Combine Orders. Sometimes purchase costs can be reduced if a larger order is placed with a supplier. The concept of "one-stop" shopping, which involves buying a wide range of products from one supplier, recognizes this principle.

Purchase in Larger Quantities. If practical, a larger number of units of required products can be purchased. It is necessary to weigh potential savings from volume purchases against costs incurred in tying up money and inventory space. With large volume purchases, there is also an increased possibility of theft and a potential increase in spoilage and other quality problems.

Pay Cash. Some suppliers will quote a lower price if products are paid for at the time of delivery.

Change Purchase Unit Size. For example, if flour is purchased in a 50-pound bag rather than a 10-pound bag, the cost per pound is likely to be less.

Consider Cooperative Purchasing. Consider the use of cooperative (pool) purchasing, in which several properties combine orders to increase the volume of items ordered. Cooperative purchasing systems may be coordinated by professional associations or for-profit companies.

Consider Promotional Discounts. If "opportunity buys" (for example, discontinued or overstocked products) can be used by the operation, they can represent significant savings over regular prices.

Purchasing in Multi-Unit Organizations

Unit managers in many chain organizations typically are not involved in significant purchasing activities. Large organizations with company-operated units frequently negotiate national contracts for nonperishable products (frozen and canned foods, condiments, and paper-related supplies, for example). The manufacturer who is awarded the contract must then locate distributors to provide the products to the units in all locations. While franchisors cannot require their franchisees to purchase products from specific sources such as company commissaries or specified suppliers, they can (and do) require that company-developed specifications be adhered to for products purchased from any supplier.

Franchisees may form purchasing cooperatives based on geographic regions or advertising markets. By centralizing purchases, they are able to receive lower prices because of the large volume of goods purchased. Items purchased are delivered to individual units as part of the negotiated contract.

Perishable products such as fresh produce, dairy items, and bakery products may be purchased locally by unit managers, or local suppliers of these items may be selected by corporate officials.

Multi-unit organizations take advantage of computerized systems in much the same way their single-unit counterparts do. Product quantity needs based on sales forecasts are accumulated for all units, individual items are separated into categories based on suppliers, and purchase orders are electronically generated. (Typically, large organizations negotiate product prices with suppliers for several months or longer. By so doing, suppliers are known, and RFPs become unnecessary for the length of the contract.)

Most—if not all—multi-unit organizations recognize the significant advantages that accrue to them from automated purchasing. Some multi-unit organizations (especially the smaller ones) modify generic systems to meet their specific needs. Larger organizations are more likely to use custom applications as necessary to ensure that the system's features meet their specific needs.

Receiving Controls

The planning and control that goes into the purchasing process is wasted if no one ensures that the products delivered meet the operation's standard purchase specifications. In too many operations, the person who signs the invoice is someone who happens to be available when a delivery is made. Great care must be taken to ensure an effective receiving process. Receiving is an important part of the product cost control system. Many managers, unfortunately, have learned an important lesson the hard way: it is very likely that you will *pay* for the quality of product you order; however, it is not certain that you will *receive* the quality ordered and paid for unless an effective receiving system is in use. Except as noted, controls related to receiving discussed in this section are applicable to both food and beverage products.

Receiving Personnel

Effective receiving requires knowledgeable receiving personnel. Staff must be trained to receive properly. They must know product quality standards and be able to recognize them when products are delivered. They must also understand all receiving procedures and know how to complete internal receiving records.

The number of persons who receive products varies among food service operations. In a relatively small operation, the manager or the assistant manager may be in charge of receiving. In a larger operation, full- or part-time staff typically receive products, and the person in charge of receiving may be called a receiving or storeroom clerk or steward. This individual usually reports either to the food controller (accounting department), the assistant manager, or the food and beverage manager.

Regardless of the operation's size, the general requirements for a receiver are the same. Good health and personal cleanliness are essential for the receiver (and for all others in the food service operation). To protect the health of guests and employees alike, strict sanitation standards should be part of every aspect of food handling.

Receiving personnel should be able to use all required equipment, facilities, and forms. Increasingly, computerized receiving systems require someone who is able to work with highly technical equipment and systems. Because of the volume of written information to be processed, receiving staff must be able to read and write well. They must be able to check the actual products delivered against the written purchase specifications, written purchase orders, and the delivery invoice.

Also, many incoming products will be in heavy cases and a large volume of products will likely be lifted and moved on each shift. A receiving clerk must be able to perform these physical tasks.

Receiving personnel must be committed to protecting the interests of the operation. While food production experience is invaluable, that alone does not make for a good receiver. Only selected and trained employees should be permitted to receive food and beverage products.

Properly trained receivers know what to do when there are delivery problems. The receiving function is just as important as the purchasing function; when the receiver signs the invoice, the merchandise legally becomes the property of the food and beverage operation and is no longer the responsibility of the supplier.

Finally, receiving personnel need cooperation from those in other departments. They must coordinate purchase requisitions from the departments with the delivery schedules of suppliers. Ideally, receiving should take place during slow periods in the operation's daily business cycle. Then the receiver's undivided attention can be given to required duties. The property's delivery hours should be posted, and the receiver should always be available when deliveries are expected. A supplier's ability to accommodate an operation's delivery hours should be a major consideration in the supplier selection process.

The receiving area should be near the delivery door. Delivery personnel should be allowed only in restricted back-of-the-house areas and should not be permitted in food production or storage areas, access corridors, or other off-limits areas. Since proper receiving requires that most items be weighed or counted, accurate, conveniently located scales are necessary, along with other equipment, such as calculators, marking pens, rulers, files, thermometers, and transportation equipment.

Receiving Procedures

Control procedures adopted by food and beverage operations are described in the following paragraphs.

Check Incoming Products against Purchase Orders or Purchase Records. The property does not want to accept and pay for items not ordered, receive partial or no deliveries of required products, receive items of unacceptable quality, or pay a price higher than agreed to. These problems can be prevented by comparing incoming products against an in-house copy of the purchase order or other record.

Check Incoming Products against Purchase Specifications. Knowledgeable and skilled receiving personnel are needed for this procedure to ensure that deliveries meet specifications. They should not allow themselves to be rushed by delivery persons. Sometimes suppliers will agree to deliver products at their risk, allowing the buyer to sign and send invoices after inspecting deliveries. Cooperation in receiving is important when assessing suppliers. Whether receiving 96-count (to the case) lemons, chilled poultry, or fresh seafood, receiving staff must know how to confirm that the correct product is being delivered and that the operation is getting what it pays for.

Check Incoming Products against Delivery Invoices. The supplier provides the delivery invoice, which becomes the basis for subsequent payment claims. A definite policy must be developed, implemented, and enforced for the measuring, weighing, or counting of incoming products to ensure that the proper quantity of product is delivered and billed. It is not generally practical to weigh every item or count every case of product being delivered. It is helpful, however, to routinely weigh/count selected cases on a random basis. Suppliers or delivery persons are less likely to short-weigh a count if they expect random inspections. Likewise, price information on the invoice should be verified by reviewing the purchase order or purchase record. Any discrepancies should be handled by a request-for-credit memo. A sample delivery invoice is shown in Exhibit 9.

Accept Incoming Products. Acceptance of deliveries is normally completed when the receiving person signs the delivery invoice. At this point, ownership of the products is transferred to the property, and the products become the responsibility of the food and beverage operation.

Move Accepted Products to Storage Immediately. Security to minimize employee theft is a concern. Likewise, the quality of products needing low-temperature storage will deteriorate if they are left at room temperatures, which are frequently very warm in back-of-the-house areas. Use a stock rotation process; incoming items should be placed behind or beneath items already in inventory.

Complete Necessary Receiving Documents. A typical receiving document is a daily receiving report such as that shown in Exhibit 10. The daily receiving report is used to:

- Separate beverage costs—liquor, beer, wine, soda—from food costs. This information is needed for income statements that isolate revenue and costs of goods sold categories for these items.

Exhibit 9   Sample Delivery Invoice

Delivery Invoice

**ABC Club, Restaurant, Institution,
and Hotel Supplier**

Route: _____

Invoice No.: _____

Customer No.: _____

Stop: _____

Sold To: XYZ Hotel
Street Address
City/State/Zip

Ship To: XYZ Hotel
Street Address
City/State/Zip

Salesperson	Terms	Customer P.O.	Our Order #	Order Date	Invoice Date

Ordered	Shipped	Item Description	Pack	Weight (lb.)	Unit Price	Amount
6/15	x	L.O. Bacon 18/22	15#	90.00	2.0700LB	186.30
2/6	x	Link Sausage 8/1	6#	12.00	1.5300LB	18.36
1/12	x	Sausage Patties 1.5 oz	12#	12.00	2.3900LB	28.68
1cs	x	Crepe Cheese Blintz 3 oz	24#	1.00	77.860CS	77.86
2 bxs	x	Franks in a Blanket	100PC	2.00	34.500BX	69.00
2/10	x	AB Franks 4/1	10#	10.00	1.8200LB	18.20

Total Items:	Total Boxes:	Total Weight:	Total Due: $398.40

Received On Account: Date:

_____   _____   _____
            Delivered By   **Received By**

Before signing this receipt, be sure all items are accounted for and are in satisfactory condition. ABC will not be responsible for any shortages or damages after the delivery driver leaves. Service Charge: 1.5 Percent Per Month on Unpaid Balance—18 Percent Annual Rate.

- Determine the value of "directs" if daily food costs are assessed.

- Transfer responsibility for product control from receiving to storeroom personnel (in large operations with different receiving and storeroom personnel).

In examining the daily receiving report, note that information about all incoming products received during the shift can be recorded on one form (with additional pages as needed). Columns 1 to 3 list the supplier's name, invoice number, and items received, respectively.

Exhibit 10   Daily Receiving Report

| Date: | 8/1/00 | | | | | | | | | | | | Page _1_ of _2_ |

Supplier	Invoice No.	Item	Purchase Unit	No. of Purchase Units	Purchase Unit Price	Total Cost	Food		Beverages				Transfer to Storage
							Directs	Stores	Liquor	Beer	Wine	Soda	
1	2	3	4	5	6	7	8	9	10	11	12	13	14
AJAX	10111	Gr. Beef	10#	6	$28.50	$171.00		$171.00					Bill
ABC Liquor	6281	B. Scotch	cs (750)	2	$71.80	$143.60			$143.60				Bill
		XYZ Chablis	cs (750)	1	$95.00	$95.00					$95.00		Bill
B/E Produce	70666	Lettuce	cs	2	$21.00	$42.00	$42.00						
						Totals	$351.00	$475.00	$683.50	—	$275.00		

Columns 4 to 7 indicate—for each item—the purchase unit (size of the shipping container—ground beef 10-pound bags, for example); number of purchase units (the property received six 10-pound bags of ground beef); cost per unit (a 10-pound bag of ground beef costs $28.50, or $2.85 per pound); and total cost of the item (six 10-pound bags of ground beef at $28.50 equals $171.00). In columns 8 to 13—the distribution columns—the total cost in column 7 of each item is carried over by category. Food items can be classified as "directs" or "stores" when daily food costs are calculated. ("Directs" are charged to food costs on the day of receipt; "stores" enter storage records, such as perpetual inventory forms, and are charged to food costs when issued.) Each beverage item is classified as liquor, beer, wine, or soda.

Column 14—Transfer to Storage—is used in larger operations with separate receiving and storage staff to indicate that all products received actually enter storeroom areas.

Request-for-Credit Memos

Each time a delivery invoice is modified during receiving, a request-for-credit memo such as that shown in Exhibit 11 becomes necessary. If deliveries do not include the full quantity specified on the delivery invoice, are refused because of quality problems, or are rejected for any other reason, this is noted on the request-for-credit memo. The receiver should never agree to accept delivery "free" next time for items shorted on the current delivery but appearing on the invoice. The following procedures should be used to process a request-for-credit memo:

Exhibit 11   Request-for-Credit Memo

Request-for-Credit Memo

(prepare in duplicate)   Number: _____

From: _____   To: _____
                                                                    (supplier)
          _____   _____

          _____   _____

          _____

Credit should be given on the following:

Invoice Number: _____   Invoice Date: _____

Product	Unit	Number	Price/Unit	Total Price

Reason: Total: _____

_____   _____
      (delivery person)   (authorizing signature)

---

1. Note invoice problems.

2. Complete the request-for-credit memo, have the delivery person sign it, and return a copy to the supplier, along with the delivery invoice.

3. Attach the property's copy of the memo to its copy of the delivery invoice. Note the correct amount of the invoice on the face of the invoice.

4. Advise the supplier that the original invoice has been amended by a request-for-credit memo.

5. If short or refused products are subsequently delivered, a separate invoice should accompany the items, and the new invoice can be processed in the usual manner.

6. Do not file any invoices affected by credit memos. Instead, hold them in a separate file until all problems, such as a supplier's confirmation of a credit, are resolved.

Marking Procedures

Marking is used to place invoice information directly on items. For example, marking case goods or bottles of liquor with the delivery date makes it easier to judge whether stock rotation plans are effective. When valuing inventory with a manual system, cost data can be taken directly from the cases or bottles if this information is transferred from delivery invoices to storage containers. This eliminates the time needed to search for the information on the daily receiving report, delivery invoice, or in the computerized database. Recording the unit price on products makes it more likely that the operation's staff members will think about them as alternative forms of cash. Therefore, they may be more careful in handling and portioning products and controlling waste.

Security Concerns in Receiving

Examples of supplier theft possibilities when products are received include the following:

- The supplier may deliver lesser-quality items than those ordered, such as inexpensive domestic wines instead of the proper higher-quality wines, or 30-percent fat content ground beef instead of 20-percent. The operation then pays the price for the higher-quality product it did not receive.

- Short-weight or short-count products may be delivered, and the food service operation pays for more products than it receives.

- Thawed products may be represented as fresh, while the operation pays the higher price for fresh.

- Ice may be ground into ground meat products, fillers such as soy products or non-fat dry milk extenders may be added, and meat may be sold with excess fat trim.

- The weight of ice and packaging may be included in the product weight on which the product's price is based.

- "Slacked out" seafood—frozen fish, thawed and packed in ice—may be sold as fresh.

- Expensive steaks and inexpensive meat may be combined in one container, and when the entire container is weighed, the operation may be billed for more expensive steaks than are actually in the container.

- An empty liquor bottle may be included in a case of 12 bottles.

These are just a few of the many ways that suppliers can steal from the property by overcharging for amount and quality. To help guard against theft at the receiving control point, some basic principles should be followed:

- Different people should receive and purchase products, unless the owner/manager performs both duties.

- Train employees to receive properly. Receiving is too important to leave to whomever happens to be handy.

Exhibit 12   Purchase Alert Report

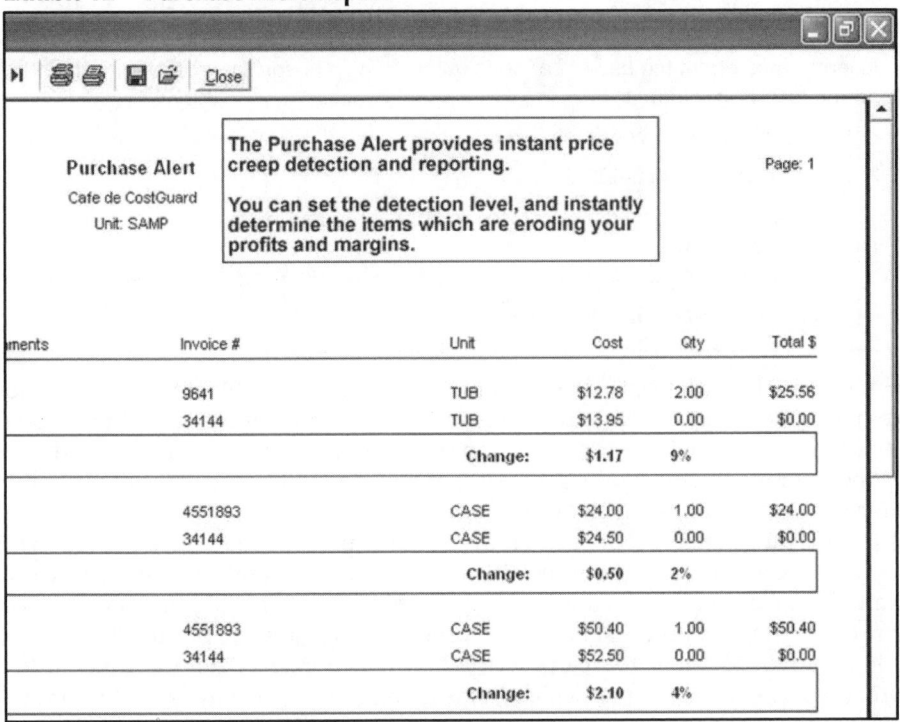

Courtesy of CostGuard Foodservice Software, Bronxville, New York (www.costguard.com).

- To the extent possible, schedule product deliveries at slow times so that receiving personnel with other duties will have time to receive correctly.

- Require deliveries to be made to a specified area of the facility, and make sure that accurately calibrated receiving scales and other equipment are available and consistently used.

- After receipt, immediately move products to storage. Chances for employee theft increase the longer products remain unattended.

- Do not permit salespersons or delivery/route persons access to back-of-the-house production or storage areas. To the extent possible, the receiving area should be close to an outside exit and visible to management personnel.

- Lock the outside door. Install an audio signal so delivery persons can ring when they arrive. With this practice, receiving personnel have delivery persons in sight during their entire visit.

Technology and Receiving Systems

Computer technology can assist food and beverage operations with the receiving task. Packing cases containing food and beverage products often have universal product code/bar code information attached. Such data indicates product code

---

Learn More on the Web

To learn more about the use of bar code technology in hospitality operations, check out the following references:

- Barcoding, Inc. (www.barcoding.com)

- intelliTrack (www.intelliTrack.net)

Both of the above websites also provide information about radio frequency identification (RFID) software.
The following reference provides detailed information about bar coding hardware:

- eBarcode (www.eBarcode.com)

(name), purchase/delivery date, product price, and possibly other information. An optical scanner is used to read this information and, at the same time, update perpetual inventory levels and develop daily receiving and other reports desired by the operation. This process allows for rapid generation of important control information with minimal chances of error.

Some automated product receiving systems provide managers with information that is difficult and time-consuming to generate manually. Price increases, for example, are easy to detect and track electronically. Exhibit 12 illustrates part of a "Purchase Alert" report that notes different costs for the same product on different delivery invoices. Managers can specify the "detection level" for these alerts. They can determine, for example, which items increased in price by 2 percent or more during the past month.

At properties operating multiple outlets, items on a single delivery invoice may be received at a central location and transported to separate outlets with associated product costs transferred (assigned) automatically to those outlets. This eliminates the paperwork often required in manual systems to record all items in central inventory and to then issue products to each separate outlet. Alternatively, if items are ordered centrally and delivered to each outlet by the supplier, electronic copies of delivery invoices can be sent to the central purchasing office for match-up with original purchase orders.

One interesting variation of the electronic routing of delivery invoices for multiple outlets to a centralized purchasing department occurs when a *blind receiving system* is used. For example, delivery invoices that accompany orders to individual outlets may include all information except the quantity and/or weight of each product being received. Receiving personnel at the unit must properly receive the products, including weighing and counting the quantities, before accepting them. Completed copies of delivery invoices can then be routed to the central purchasing office, where personnel can compare them with invoices sent directly to the central office by the supplier that include quantity amounts.

Technology can help the property to reduce receiving paperwork. For example, purchase specifications describing quality requirements can be available on a computer at the receiving site. Likewise, supplier delivery schedules can be electronically routed from purchasing to receiving personnel, and communication between departments and between the property and suppliers is facilitated.

Information from delivery invoices can be electronically summarized on daily receiving reports such as that illustrated in Exhibit 10.

Automated systems require the same basic procedures to verify incoming products as their manual system counterparts. Incoming products are checked by receiving personnel against a hard or electronic copy of the original purchase order. At least one of the several automated systems available has a feature that addresses an important sanitation concern; if there are items for which temperatures should be recorded at time of receipt, a window opens on the screen to facilitate this entry.

 ## Key Terms

audit trail—A series of records, documents, and reports that traces the flow of resources through an operation.

autodial modem—An electronic communications device that functions without user intervention, enabling late-night transmission of purchase orders for next-day processing.

call brand—A brand of liquor offered that is of higher quality and price than the property's house brand liquor.

e-commerce—Business and marketing enabled by the Internet and web-based technologies.

electronic data interchange—Transfer of data between businesses using the Internet some or other network; abbreviated EDI.

food sample data sheet—A form that helps standardize the evaluation of a product by recording purchasing, storing, preparing, and serving information about the product the operation is sampling and considering for purchase.

house brand—A brand of liquor that is served to guests when a call brand is not specified (also called pour brand, well brand, or speed-rail brand).

ingredient file—An automated file containing information about each ingredient that is purchased, including code number, description, purchase unit and cost, issue unit and cost, and recipe unit and cost.

inventory file — An automated file containing product information for all purchased ingredients, including name, description, product and storage location codes, purchase unit and price, issue unit, product group code, supplier identification number, order lead time, minimum-maximum stack level, and last purchase date.

just-in-time (purchasing system)—A process designed to minimize inventory costs by purchasing small quantities more frequently.

lead-time quantity—The number of purchase units, such as pounds or cases, withdrawn from inventory between the time the order is placed and when it is delivered.

make/buy analysis—An objective process used to determine whether to prepare a food product on-site or purchase it from an off-site supplier.

maximum inventory level—The greatest number of product purchase units, such as pounds or cases, permitted in storage. It is calculated by adding the minimum (safety) level to the usage rate.

menu item file—An automated file containing sales data for menu items sold during all meal periods.

minimum inventory level—The number of product purchase units, such as pounds or cases, that must always remain in inventory. It is also referred to as the safety level.

minimum/maximum ordering system—A system to help managers determine when products must be purchased and how much of each to order by assessing the minimum quantity below which inventory levels should not fall and the maximum quantity above which inventory levels should not rise.

order point—The number of purchase units, such as pounds or cases, in stock when an order is placed.

premium brand—A liquor of very high quality that is sold at a higher price than a property's call brand.

prime supplier—A vendor who receives the order to supply all or much of a property's need for specific product(s) for a specified period of time.

purchase order system—An ordering system requiring that formal purchase orders be sent to suppliers awarded orders. Purchase orders identify the products, quantities, unit costs, and total costs that both the suppliers and the purchaser have agreed to. In addition, the purchase order may include guarantees, warranties, payment requirements, inspection rights, "hold harmless" provisions, and other legal and contractual concerns. The purchase order is the food and beverage operation's record of the specifics of all incoming shipments. Copies are retained in the purchasing department and circulated internally among the receiving and accounting departments.

purchase record—Documentation that provides a small food and beverage operation with an in-house, detailed record of all incoming shipments. It performs the same functions as a purchase order.

purchasing—The series of activities designed to obtain products of the right quality and quantity, at the right price and time, and from the right source.

quality—As it pertains to the purchasing function, the suitability of a product for its intended use; the more suitable a product, the greater its quality.

recipe file—An automated file containing a list of ingredients, quantities of ingredients, and production procedures for menu items produced by the operation.

safety level (inventory)—A minimum quantity of product that should always be available in inventory to reduce the potential for stockouts.

speculative purchasing—A system wherein management makes judgments about future prices of products and purchases more products if prices are expected to increase and fewer products if prices are expected to decrease.

standard purchase specifications—A list providing detailed descriptions of the quality, size, and weight desired for particular items to be purchased.

usage rate—The number of purchase units used per order period.

 ## Review Questions

1. What are the purposes of an effective purchasing system?

2. What forms are necessary for effective purchasing if a manual system is in use? Why are they important? How are they used?

3. What are standard purchase specifications? Why are they important?

4. Why should a purchaser avoid ordering more products than necessary?

5. What factors should be considered when selecting suppliers?

6. What are some of the ways in which theft can occur at the time of purchase?

7. What are the basic steps in the receiving process?

8. Why is the daily receiving report important?

9. When should a request-for-credit memo be used?

10. What are common examples of theft during receiving, and what can be done to reduce the opportunities for these problems to occur?

11. How has technology simplified the purchasing and receiving processes?

12. What are special purchasing and receiving concerns that must be effectively managed by multi-unit organizations?

 ## Internet Sites

For more information, visit the following Internet sites. Remember that Internet addresses can change without notice. If the site is no longer there, you can use a search engine to look for additional sites.

Green Purchasing

Federal Environment Executive
www.ofee.gov/gp/gp.asp

General Purchasing Articles

CIO
www.cio.com
(Enter "e-procurement" in site's search field.)

Looksmart
www.looksmart.com

National Federation of Independent Businesses
www.nfib.com
(Enter "purchasing" in site's search field.)

Food Purchase Specifications

Fresh Food Group
www.freshfoodgroup.com

U.S. Department of Agriculture
www.usda.gov
(Enter "purchase specifications" in the site's search field.)

Purchase Quantities

About.com
www.logistics.about.com
(Click on "Inventory Management.")

Inventoryops.com
www.inventoryops.com
(Click on "Articles" and then "Inventory Safety Levels.")

Supplier (Electronic Ordering)

Sysco
www.sysco.com
(Click on "Order Entry.")

General Receiving Practices

HiEnd Security.com
www.hiendsecurity.com

Restaurants & Institutions
www.rimag.com
(Enter "receiving" in the site's search field.)

Restaurant Report
www.restaurantreport.com
(Enter "receiving" in the site's search field.)

Food Service Software

The following websites provide comprehensive demonstrations of software features applicable to purchasing and receiving.

Adaco Services, Inc
www.adacoservices.com

Comtrex Systems Corporation
www.comtrex.com

CostGuard
www.costguard.com

Culinary Software
www.culinarysoftware.com

Eatec Corporation
www.eatec.com

Enggist & Grandjean Software
www.eg-software.com

FoodSoftware.com
www.foodsoftware.com/default.asp

Food Trak
www.foodtrak.com

MenuLink Computer Solutions, Inc.
www.menulinkinc.com

Micros Systems, Inc.
www.micros.com

Case Study

When Life Hands You Lemons ... Better Check the Specs

Thursday, 4 P.M.

Sue, the kitchen manager at the Wagon Wheel Restaurant, glanced at the clock. Pierson's Produce would be calling soon for the weekend order. She pulled out a notepad and began to make a quick list. It was going to be a busy weekend—the homecoming game at the college would be bringing in lots of business. She'd better order an extra case of lemons for iced tea and lettuce for salads.

Sue didn't have time to take inventory, so she tried to picture the storeroom as it looked when she last peeked in. She was sure they had lettuce—or was that cabbage she saw? No, it had to be lettuce. Maybe she'd only order one case for the weekend. They were fine on parsley; no need to order that. But kiwis—that new fruit salad on the menu was popular, so she added kiwis to the list.

Sue was putting the final items on her list when George, the general manager, tapped at her office door. He carried a report in his hand and he didn't look happy.

"Have you seen this report, Sue?" he asked. "Our food costs are on the high side, and it looks like produce is the culprit. It's up to 9.5 percent, and it should be down around 7.5 percent. We really need to do something about that."

"I'll take care of it," she said.

Just then the phone rang. It was Alan from Pierson's Produce, calling for the order.

"Just the man I wanted to talk to," said Sue. She explained George's concern about the produce costs and wondered what Alan could do to help. She could hear him tapping away at his computer keyboard.

"Well, you know, it's the end of the season and prices are higher now, Sue," he said. "But, looking at your past orders, I see you've been paying $22 a case for fancy lemons. If you like, I can get you lemons for ... how does $14 a case sound?"

Sue didn't even stop to ask what she might be getting for that price. Saving $8 a case was just what she wanted to hear. She agreed and ordered three cases of lemons, a case of lettuce—yes, only one, she told him—and two cases of kiwis. She checked the items off her notepad as Alan read back her order. She thanked him and hung up the phone. Then she turned her attention to other matters.

Monday, 4 P.M.

Sue looked up in surprise as George came into her office. He looked even more unhappy than he had last week, if that was possible. He shook a report under her nose.

"I thought you were going to take care of these produce costs," he said. "These figures are even higher—11 percent! How could that happen?"

Sue looked confused. "I don't know," she stammered.

At that moment, Adrian, the chef, who had happened to hear George's question as he was walking by, stuck his head in the door.

"I know how it happened," Adrian said. "We ran out of lemons, lettuce, and parsley this past weekend and I had to send my people down to the grocery store to pick up produce—at retail prices! That's what drove our costs up."

"But I ordered lemons and lettuce on Thursday afternoon," Sue replied. She showed him the torn-off page from her notepad. "Didn't they get delivered?"

Adrian thought back. Yes, three cases of lemons had been received, but they were small and unattractive, obviously not the fancy lemons that the restaurant used to garnish its drinks. "I told the receiving clerk that the produce company must have sent us the wrong lemons and told him to send them back," Adrian said. "They definitely weren't the lemons on our specifications."

Sue groaned. So much for the $8 a case savings on lemons. She guessed she should have told the receiving clerk what to expect.

Adrian continued. "As for the rest of the order, the restaurant got only half the lettuce it needed, and no parsley at all. We had to garnish the Eggs Benedict with scallions until someone could get to the market and buy some parsley." He laughed. "But boy, do we have kiwis to spare. We already had one case. I don't know how we're going to use up two more cases before they go bad."

George looked at Sue for an explanation. "I'm sure this is an isolated incident," he began.

Adrian laughed again and said, "It happens more often than you think. Why don't you ask her about the time we ended up with Florida oranges for our garnishes instead of California oranges?"

Sue glared at Adrian, and George looked at both of them.

"I think it's time we sat down and reviewed some purchasing procedures around here," he said.

Discussion Questions

1. What standard purchasing control practices could Sue have followed that would have prevented the high produce costs?

2. What was right or wrong about the chef's actions to remedy the situation?

3. What steps can Sue take to reduce produce costs in the future?

Case Number: 4656CA

The following industry experts helped generate and develop this case: Timothy J. Pugh, East Lansing, Michigan; and Lawrence E. Ross, Professor, Florida Southern College, Lakeland, Florida.

 Problems ――――――――――――――――――――――――――――――――――――

Problem 1

Complete the following perishable product quotation/call sheet. Indicate the preferred supplier:

a. If each item is purchased from the supplier quoting the lowest price for that item.

b. If all items are purchased from the supplier submitting the lowest total price quotation (suppliers A and B will provide a three-percent discount if all products are purchased from them).

Explain any special concerns you may have about the price quotations.

	Amount			Supplier		
Item	Needed	On Hand	Order	1	2	3
Lettuce	12 cases	4½ cases		$19.90 cs =	$21.10 cs =	$18.90 cs =
Spinach	6 cases	1½ cases		$23.40 cs =	$20.10 cs =	$24.10 cs =
Cabbage	4 cases	1 case		$12.90 cs =	$ 9.80 cs =	$11.15 cs =
Escarole	7 cases	3 cases		$27.50 cs =	$21.00 cs =	$29.50 cs =
			Total			

Problem 2

Use the information below to answer the following questions:

- Purchase unit = 10-lb poly bag (ground beef)
- Usage rate = 170 lb per day
- Order period = 4 days
- Lead time = 1 day
- Safety level = 1 day

a. How many *pounds* should be ordered at the order point? How many 10-pound poly bags should be purchased?

b. The order is placed when there are 390 pounds available. How many *purchase units* should be ordered?

c. What is the usage rate in the four-day order period?

d. How many 10-pound poly bags are used daily and during the order period?

e. How many purchase units are included in the lead time and safety level factors?

f. What is the maximum number of pounds to be available?

g. How many purchase units should be purchased at the order point?

Problem 3

The following information is provided on a delivery invoice. Use this information to answer the following questions:

Item	Ordered	Pack	Weight (lb)	Unit Price	Amount
Ground Beef	25	10 lb	250 lb	$2.30	
Green Beans	12	6 #10 cs		$28.10	
Tomato Sauce	6	6 #10 cs		$26.75	
Shrimp	6	10 5-lb cs	300 lb	$8.45	

   a. What is the total amount due?

   b. The sharp-eyed employee who received the order noticed the following:

- Only 23 10-pound bags of ground beef were received.
- One case of green beans appeared damaged (the corner of the case was crushed; the cardboard case looked like it had been wet and then had dried).
- There were 7 cases of tomato sauce.
- There were only 5 cases (10 5-lb) of shrimp.

     What is the amount that should be entered on the request-for-credit memo?

     What is the adjusted amount of the delivery invoice?

   c. The supplier will give a 10-percent discount if the invoice is paid within 10 days. What is the total amount of the invoice to be paid, assuming that this discount is taken?

Chapter 7 Outline

Competencies

1. Identify the objectives of a storage system for food service operations. (pp. 221–222)

2. Explain how an inventory classification system helps food service managers design cost-effective inventory control procedures. (pp. 222–223)

3. Distinguish between "directs" and "stores" in relation to the inventory systems of food and beverage operations. (p. 223)

4. Summarize security concerns in storage areas, and describe procedures for maintaining product quality during storage. (pp. 223–226)

5. Calculate an inventory turnover rate. (pp. 227–228)

6. Distinguish a physical inventory system from a perpetual inventory system. (pp. 228–232)

7. Identify and describe automated technology applications designed for inventory management. (pp. 232–240)

8. Identify the objectives of issuing systems for food service operations and describe issuing-control procedures. (pp. 240–247)

7

Storing and Issuing Controls

THE STORING AND ISSUING CONTROL POINTS play an important role in linking product receiving and production. Food and beverage managers must recognize that product costs and quality are affected by storing and issuing systems. Unfortunately, many food and beverage operations lack adequate control procedures for these functions. Products are simply placed in the storeroom when received and taken out when needed.

Food and beverage managers should think of the storeroom as a bank vault. Products in storage represent money. If the storeroom contains, for example, $5,000 worth of food and beverage products, it is the same as having 5,000 one-dollar bills in storage. Stored products represent money in terms of both their initial cost and the cost to replace them if they are stolen, spoiled, or damaged because of improper storage practices. The same care and concern used for controlling stored cash should go into the procedures for controlling stored foods and beverages.

There are many sound reasons why strict storage and issuing controls are needed in food and beverage operations. Products can be stolen while in storage and when they are issued from storage to production areas. Also, mistakes in issuing can result in more products being used in production than necessary. This results in waste and unnecessarily high product costs. Moreover, since systems for assessing daily food and beverage costs are based, in part, on the quantity and value of daily issues, it is essential to know exactly how much of each product leaves storage areas.

In the first part of this chapter, we discuss principles of control for effective storage systems. Then we review control practices relating to issuing products from storage to production areas.

Storing Control: General Procedures

It is important to move food and beverage products into storage areas as soon as they are received. In addition, delivery personnel should have only limited access to back-of-the-house areas. This means that staff from the property (not delivery persons) should be responsible for transferring the product from the receiving to the storage area. If deliveries are left unattended in receiving areas, refrigerated and frozen products can deteriorate in quality, and dishonest employees may steal. As soon as received products are placed in storage areas, their quality and security can be better ensured by the control procedures built into the property's storage system. The principles of effective storage systems for both food and beverage products focus on the following three primary concerns:

Exhibit 1   ABCD Classification Scheme for Foods in Inventory

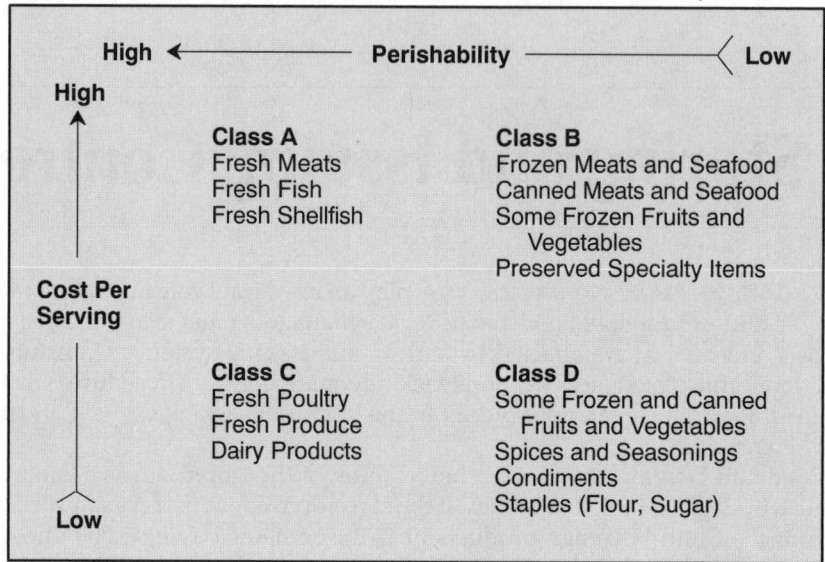

Source: Ronald F. Cichy, *Food Safety: Managing with the HACCP System*, Second Ed. (Lansing, Mich.: American Hotel & Lodging Educational Institute, 2008), p. 107.

1. Keeping products secure from theft
2. Retaining product quality
3. Providing information necessary for the financial accounting system

Inventory Control Policy

Every control procedure must be cost-effective. It is generally not practical for managers to manage all food and beverage products under a strict system of tight controls. Some properties may not justify a perpetual inventory system for any but the most expensive items. (Perpetual inventory systems are discussed later in this chapter.) Many food and beverage operations, especially smaller ones, maintain tight control over meats, seafood, liquor, and wine, but not as much control over less expensive and less theft-prone items such as produce and dairy products. Others may expand the list of items needing special controls because of specific concerns. Each property is different, and managers must develop basic control procedures that recognize their operation's unique situation.

One useful approach is based on an **ABCD inventory classification system** that categorizes products according to their perishability and cost per serving. Category A items are those high in both perishability and cost per serving, while category B items are relatively high in cost but low in perishability. Exhibit 1 presents the ABCD approach, indicating the categories and showing examples of inventory items in each category.

One advantage of using this system is the ability to regulate the products needing the tightest control—usually those in categories A and B. Storage procedures and controls for these products should be designed and implemented first. Then, as time permits and practices require, other products in lower-priority categories can be brought under tighter control.

Separating Directs from Stores

For inventory purposes, food products are often separated into two categories: directs and stores.

Directs are usually relatively inexpensive, perishable products generally purchased several times a week for more or less immediate use. Examples are fresh produce, baked goods, and dairy products. Directs may be received and transferred immediately to production areas for preparation or may be held in workstation storage areas. Alternatively, they can be received and placed in central storage areas for withdrawal as needed. However, in either case, directs are not entered into any storage records, and they are not considered part of the inventory system. Instead, if daily food cost information is being collected, they are considered part of food costs for the day on which they are received. The primary recordkeeping concern associated with these products lies with receiving, rather than storage, procedures.

Stores are relatively expensive items, may be purchased less often than directs, and are procured in quantities necessary to rebuild inventory levels. Examples are fresh and frozen meats and seafood and frozen and canned products. Food and beverage operations may purchase stores as often as once a day or as seldom as once every several months, depending on usage rates, inventory levels, and type of product. A minimum/maximum purchasing and inventory system for these items should be in place. Stores must be tightly controlled, usually by recording them in inventory records and using an issuing system to remove them from inventory. These procedures are discussed later in this chapter.

Defining Storage Areas

When products are "in storage" they have been entered into inventory records and should be under tight storage control. Each food and beverage operation must define its storage areas. For example, central storerooms and walk-in refrigerators and freezers are obviously storage areas. However, are items still "in storage" when they are in workstation storage areas such as reach-in refrigerators, pantry shelves, broken-case storage areas, and behind the bar? Managers must designate:

- Which locations are considered storage areas.
- Which items are to be tightly controlled.
- The specific procedures to be followed for keeping items secure, maintaining proper quality, taking inventory, and other accounting activities.

Security Concerns in Storage Areas

After management identifies the items that are to be tightly controlled and which locations are to be considered storage areas, security procedures can be designed to ensure that those items remain in those locations until they are issued to production areas. The following paragraphs describe measures that can help keep storage areas secure.

Limit Access

Only authorized staff members should be permitted in storerooms. In addition to management, authorized staff in larger properties may include receiving and storage personnel. Smaller operations can keep storage areas locked and involve management directly in receiving and issuing activities. When a manager is present to unlock the storeroom door, employee theft is less likely. This procedure is more easily implemented if issuing is done only at specified times. Alternatively, category A and B items (see Exhibit 1) can be kept in locked areas, and personnel can have freer access to category C and D items.

Lock Storage Areas

The storeroom, freezer, and beverage storage areas should be completely lockable. Depending on available equipment, one section of a walk-in or reach-in refrigerator might be used to secure expensive refrigerated items. Or a lockable shelving unit (or cage) can be used in the walk-in refrigerator. In this way, expensive refrigerated products, such as fresh meats and seafood, or wines being chilled for service, can be secured. At the same time, personnel still have access to produce, dairy, and similar products that are less likely to be stolen.

Refrigerator/freezer units should be lockable with reasonably strong lock clasps and door hinges. Storeroom walls should extend to the ceiling, and there should be no way to enter through the ceiling from another room. If there are windows, they should at least be made secure and unopenable. The point is to design, within practical limits, storage areas that are difficult for unauthorized personnel to enter without being detected. (Recall our example of the bank vault. How would you design it? Your answer to this question suggests the security needed for product storage areas.)

Some properties maintain a "precious room." A precious room is a locked storage area within a locked storage area. For example, liquor and expensive buffet chafing dishes might be kept in a locked area within a locked storeroom.

The goal of all of these procedures is to reduce opportunities for pilferage. The answers to commonsense questions such as "How would I steal from my storage areas if I were a dishonest employee?" may point to security loopholes in storage areas.

Minimize Behind-Bar Storage

The quantity of alcoholic beverage products kept behind the bar should be minimal, since storage space is limited and this area is less secure than the central storage area. Liquor should be locked behind the bar when the bar is closed. Lockable cabinets, roll-down screens, or similar devices can keep beverages out of the reach of cleaning staff and other employees when the bar is closed.

Control Storeroom Keys

Only staff members who need keys should have them. Manual locks or combinations should be changed routinely and each time an employee with access to keys leaves the property's employment. An excellent policy is that all keys remain at the property at all times, securely locked in the manager's office when not in use. Some food and beverage managers may feel key control procedures are unnecessary. However, a significant number of products representing substantial dollar outlays can be lost because of inadequate key control. The potential for such losses should convince managers to emphasize this aspect of the operation's control system.

Current locking systems eliminate the need for traditional keys. Pins correlating with a "combination code" can be depressed by authorized personnel who have memorized the code. When these individuals no longer need access to lockable areas, combinations can be quickly (and inexpensively) changed. Other systems may use plastic cards, similar to credit cards, with coded information designed to operate locks. These systems are in common use for hotel guestrooms and are increasingly being used in back-of-house areas as well. Either of these or related systems may yield information about the identity of persons entering lockable areas, time of entry, and length of time that the individual was in the area. Moreover, they make the process of changing the locks fast and easy, and busy managers are more likely to do so.

Increasingly, these and related systems provide more specific control information to help ensure that only persons authorized to enter storage areas do, in fact, gain access to these locations.

Maintaining Quality during Storage

Improper storage practices can reduce the quality of products in storage. In fact, most food products, including frozen foods, experience a loss in quality if stored too long. While this is especially true for foods, it also applies to some wines and most beers. It is important that control procedures designed to minimize the loss of quality of products in storage be strictly followed. Food costs increase as items judged unfit for use are discarded and replaced. If, because of pressure to keep food costs down, lower-quality products are served to guests, there may be serious marketing implications. Procedures for maintaining quality during storage are discussed in the following paragraphs.

Rotate Products

Implement the **first-in, first-out (FIFO) inventory rotation** method. The products held in inventory the longest should be the first issued to production areas. When newly received products enter storage areas, they should be placed under or behind products already in storage. Marking the date of receipt on every item makes it possible to compare dates of products used in production with those of items in storage areas. Items in production should have been received at an earlier date than those remaining in storage. This method helps management ensure that stock rotation practices are followed.

Ensure a Properly Controlled Environment

Maintain proper temperature, humidity, and ventilation. Use accurate thermometers and check them routinely. Unless otherwise regulated, proper temperatures are:

- Dry storage: 50° to 70°F (10° to 21°C)
- Refrigerated storage: 41°F (5°C) or lower
- Freezer storage: 0°F (–18°C) or lower

Staff members should be required to seek a manager's permission before discarding spoiled items. If this policy is followed, managers have the opportunity to judge the effectiveness of their purchasing and quality control methods and assess the costs of failing to follow proper storage procedures.

Implement Effective Sanitation Practices

Establish and follow regular cleaning schedules for all storage facilities (as opposed to cleaning only when time becomes available).[1] This applies not only to storerooms and storage spaces, but also to walk-in and reach-in refrigerators and storage equipment. Facilities and equipment should be made of nonporous, easily cleaned materials. Shelving units should be louvered or slotted to permit air circulation. They should not be covered with aluminum foil or any other material that impedes airflow. (Sometimes production personnel cover shelving to reduce the need to clean it. This is an example of misguided decision-making, because sanitation concerns are more important than cost-reduction tactics.) Shelves, drainage racks, and similar storage equipment should be at least two inches from walls and their lowest shelves at least six inches above the floor to permit cleaning with mops and brooms and to discourage rodent and insect infestation and nesting.

When following proper sanitation practices, it is important to use professional pest control services. In light of the many exotic chemicals and poisons on the market, probably very few food and beverage managers are qualified to plan and manage rodent and insect control programs. It is too dangerous for a well-intentioned but untrained person to spray and spread chemicals in food production and service areas.

Ensure Proper Storage

Store products properly in their original packaging and away from the walls (to allow for air circulation). Store items that absorb odors, such as flour, away from products that give off odors, such as onions. Store opened products in clean, labeled, covered containers designed for food storage, rather than using empty glass jars (which can break) or empty #10 cans (which cannot be properly cleaned).

Generally, products should be stored in quantities that can be used within a reasonable time period. There are exceptions to this rule, such as investments in wines and volume purchases made as hedges against price increases. However, these speculative purchase decisions should be made by top management, not by purchasing staff. Beverage products are generally stored for less than one month. Food items classified as stores are generally used within an even shorter time period. Perishable products are purchased two or more times weekly.

Inventory Control Procedures

The third major concern in storage, after security and minimizing quality losses, is recordkeeping. We have already mentioned that inventory procedures play an important role in the security concerns of the control system. There are several other reasons for designing and implementing effective inventory recordkeeping systems:

- Financial accounting systems need inventory values to generate monthly statements. The value of products in inventory is considered part of the property's current assets (for the balance sheet) and is also used to assess costs (for the income statement).

- Daily control procedures may require knowing the quantity of products currently available. For example, a food and beverage manager may wish to keep a perpetual inventory record of selected expensive items to allow frequent and quick assessment of any differences between the quantity that should be in storage and how much is actually there.

- Inventory records help managers determine when to order new products and how much of each product to order.

Inventory Turnover

One important function of keeping accurate inventory records is to allow managers to assess how much money is being invested in inventory. The value of goods in inventory is typically calculated on a monthly basis to provide information such as cost of sales for financial accounting systems. **Non-productive inventory** refers to products in storage that are not issued to production areas during the time period (usually monthly) covered by financial records. To determine how much money is tied up in non-productive inventory, managers measure the inventory turnover rate. The **inventory turnover rate** shows the number of times in a given period that inventory is converted or turned into revenue. In financial terms, it measures the rate at which inventory is turned into food or beverage costs required to generate food or beverage revenue.

Inventory turnover rates can be determined for food or beverage products in storage. The inventory turnover is calculated by dividing the cost of food (or beverages) used by the average food (or beverage) inventory (in dollars). The **average inventory** value is determined by adding the value of inventory at the beginning of the time period in question (usually a month) to the value of inventory at the end of that period, and then dividing the sum by two.

For example, to calculate the inventory turnover rate for food products for a month, assume the following data:

- Food Inventory Value at Beginning of Month = $18,500

- Food Inventory Value at End of Month = $19,500

- Cost of Food Used = $122,750

$$\text{Average Food Inventory for Month} = \frac{\text{Beginning Inventory} + \text{Ending Inventory}}{2}$$

$$\text{Average Food Inventory for Month} = \frac{\$18,500 + \$19,500}{2} = \$19,000$$

$$\text{Food Inventory Turnover} = \frac{\text{Cost of Food Used for Month}}{\text{Average Food Inventory for Month}}$$

$$\text{Food Inventory Turnover} = \frac{\$122,750}{\$19,000} = 6.46 \text{ times}$$

In this example, the cost of food products in inventory is turned into revenue on an average of 6.46 times during the month. This means that 6.46 times the average amount of daily inventory must be purchased sometime during the month to keep the operation supplied. It also means that the average time products remain in inventory is 4.6 days (30 days per month divided by 6.46 inventory turns equals 4.6).

The inventory turnover rate is an important tool to use in managing inventory levels. As this rate decreases, more money is being invested in inventory. If too much of the property's funds are being used to purchase excess products for inventory, cash flow problems may result and create other difficulties for the operation. Products may spoil or otherwise deteriorate in quality because of excessive inventory levels, and the possibility of theft can increase. Also, lack of storage space is a problem in many operations. On the other hand, as the turnover rate increases, less money is being invested in inventory. As average inventory levels are reduced, however, a point will be reached at which stockouts begin to occur, and guest dissatisfaction and operating problems can result.

Therefore, to properly control the property's investment in inventory, food and beverage managers must determine the best turnover rate for their particular operations. This process requires monitoring. If the turnover rate is calculated monthly, the food and beverage manager can learn of any increases or decreases in inventory turnover and respond accordingly. It may also be a good idea to calculate turnover rates for specific product categories. One would normally expect highly perishable items (such as fresh meats and seafood, fruits, and vegetables) to turn over more rapidly than less perishable items (such as spices, staples, and frozen or canned products).

Inventory Recordkeeping Systems

There are two basic kinds of recordkeeping systems for products in storage: physical inventory and perpetual inventory. A **physical inventory system** involves actual observation and counting of stored products on a periodic basis. A **perpetual inventory system** involves keeping a running balance of the quantity of stored products by recording all newly purchased items as they enter storage areas and all quantities issued from storage to production areas.

Physical Inventory System

A physical inventory system is used to periodically assess the value of food and beverage products in inventory. This is done at least monthly to develop information needed for the balance sheet and income statement. Inventory value is counted as a current asset, and inventory values, both at the beginning and end of the financial period, are a factor in assessing food and beverage costs (cost of sales).

Before a physical inventory of stored products can be taken, the food and beverage manager must make several decisions about the design of the physical inventory system by answering such questions as:

- *Which products should be considered when making an inventory count?* This decision is partially related to the question of which areas are to be considered storage areas under the control of the inventory system. For example, does inventory include products in broken-case and workstation storage areas? What about products in process, such as frozen poultry thawing in the refrigerator? What items are "stores" and included in inventory, and what items are "directs" and excluded from inventory?

- *How should monetary value be assigned to products in inventory?* One method is to calculate the actual cost of stored products at the time the physical inventory is made. Another method is to use the average costs of stored products over several inventory counts. Others include the **last-in, first-out (LIFO) inventory valuation** system and the **first-in, first-out (FIFO) inventory valuation** system.[2] Under the LIFO system, the costs of the products most recently added to inventory (last in) are the costs assigned when products are issued (first out). This leads to cost of sales figures that more accurately reflect current replacement costs. In times of inflation, it also tends to create a smaller total inventory value. That is, since the most recent (and usually most expensive) costs are the first to be "issued," the remaining inventory is made up of the earlier (and usually lower) costs. Conversely, under the FIFO system, the oldest (and usually lowest) costs are "issued" first, leaving the more recent (and usually higher) costs remaining in inventory. This creates a higher total inventory value and a lower cost of sales. Note, however, that seasonal price variations (for example, for fresh fruit) will sometimes cause recent purchases to cost *less* than earlier purchases. Typically, an accountant helps determine the best inventory valuation system for the property. This is because inventory values affect food costs that affect profitability and, therefore, tax obligations. (Do not confuse the FIFO and LIFO inventory *valuation* methods with the FIFO inventory *rotation* method. Inventory valuation deals with "issuing" or assigning *costs*; inventory rotation deals with the actual *products* removed from storage and issued. You should always issue the oldest products in storage areas first; the value that you assign to those products can vary based on the valuation method used.)

- *How should costs of such items as opened containers of spices in production areas and opened bottles of liquor at the bar be handled?* Often, the cost of such opened, unused items is assumed to average out. In other words, their value is thought to remain approximately the same from month to month. So, once an estimated cost is established, it can be used monthly.

- *What procedures should be used to count products in inventory?* Persons involved in managing storage areas should not take inventory counts alone. Perhaps the food inventory can be taken by the food manager (not the chef),

Exhibit 2   Physical Inventory Form (Manual System)

		Physical Inventory					
Type of Product: _____		Month _____			Month _____		
Product	Unit	Amount in Storage	Purchase Price	Total Price	Amount in Storage	Purchase Price	Total Price
Col. 1	Col. 2	Col. 3	Col. 4	Col. 5	Col. 6	Col. 7	Col. 8
Applesauce	6 #10	4 ⅓	$15.85	$68.63			
Green Beans	6 #10	3 ⅝	18.95	72.58			
Flour	25-lb bag	3	4.85	14.55			
Rice	50-lb bag	1	12.50	12.50			
			Total	$486.55			

while the beverage manager (not the bar manager) takes the beverage inventory. In both situations, a representative from the accounting office can assist in conducting the physical inventory.

As stored products are observed and counted in a manual inventory system, a physical inventory form (Exhibit 2) can be used to record inventory information. When reviewing the form, note:

1. Products (column 1) can be listed in the same order as they are found in the storage area (or on the perpetual inventory form). Listing products in this sequence makes the task of locating items on the form easier when taking the inventory count. It also reduces the likelihood that products will be missed when inventory is taken.

2. The storage unit (column 2) is the basis on which products are purchased and costs are assessed. For example, in the inventory shown in Exhibit 2, applesauce is purchased and stored in cases containing six #10 cans each, while flour comes in 25-pound bags.

3. The amount in storage (column 3) is determined by actually counting the items in storage. With one technique, one person counts while a second person records the quantities on the inventory form. In another, two people can make independent counts and compare results before entering information on the inventory form.

4. Purchase price (column 4) is the cost per storage unit (column 2) of the product. Price information is easier to record if products are marked with their unit prices at the time they are received and stored.

5. Total price (column 5) is the total cost of the amount of each product in inventory. It is calculated by multiplying the number of stored items (column 3) by the purchase price per storage unit (column 4).

6. Columns 6 through 8 are used to repeat the above inventory valuation procedures for a second month.

7. The total food and beverage costs (recorded at the bottom of column 5) calculated by the physical inventory are used by accounting personnel to develop financial statements. They can also be used by food and beverage managers to calculate inventory turnover rates.

A physical inventory indicates only how much of each product is in inventory and the actual value of all stored products. One limitation of a physical inventory system is that it does not indicate how much of each product *should* be available. A perpetual inventory system compensates for this shortcoming.

Perpetual Inventory System

A perpetual inventory system keeps a running balance of the quantity of food and beverage products in inventory. It operates like a bank checking account. When more food or beverages are put in the storage area (the bank), the balance is increased. As products are removed (issued), the balance decreases. At any time, then, the amount of products that should be currently available is known.

Large properties with specialized storage and accounting personnel may use a perpetual inventory system for all, or almost all, products in storage. Small food and beverage operations may find it more practical to use perpetual inventory control only for expensive items and those purchased in large quantities.

A sample perpetual inventory form used with a manual system is shown in Exhibit 3. Note the following when studying the form:

1. Information about each product under perpetual inventory control is recorded on a separate form/inventory card.

2. Each time a product enters inventory (column 2) or is removed from inventory (column 3), the balance in inventory (column 4) is adjusted.

3. Columns are repeated on the right so the form can be used for a longer time period.

4. The form does not have information about product cost. With this system, control is based on the number of units, not their cost. Costs can be assessed when taking physical inventories and recorded on the form in Exhibit 2.

A physical count is still necessary with a perpetual inventory system to verify the accuracy of the inventory balances. When using a perpetual inventory system, someone other than the staff members who maintain the perpetual inventory records should perform the physical inventory used for verification.

When the physical count of a product differs from the quantity indicated on the perpetual record, a control problem may exist, and management must determine the reason for the variance. Perhaps products are not being recorded at the time of receipt or issue, or perhaps theft is occurring. The purpose of control procedures is

Exhibit 3   Perpetual Inventory Form (Manual System)

	Perpetual Inventory							
Product Name:	*P.D.Q. Shrimp*				**Purchase Unit Size:**		*5 lb bag*	
Date	**In** **Carried Forward**	**Out**	**Balance** 15		**Date**	**In** **Carried Forward**	**Out**	**Balance**
Col. 1	Col. 2	Col. 3	Col. 4		Col. 1	Col. 2	Col. 3	Col. 4
5/16		3	12					
5/17		3	9					
5/18	6		15					
5/19		2	13					

to indicate *when* such problems exist. Management's task is to discover *why* a problem exists and to correct it.

Technology and Inventory Management

Increasingly, technology is being used to provide inventory management information and to physically determine product quantities in inventory.

Inventory Management Information

Ideally, inventory software will integrate an ingredient file for food and non-food items and an inventory file. The ingredient file contains all necessary information to define the ingredients. The inventory file contains information about inventory stock levels and reorder points and is used for computing usage, variances, and product valuations.

The initial creation of a food and beverage ingredient file and ongoing file updates to record changes in the costs and supplies can be time-consuming tasks. For example, if a restaurant offers 30 (or more) menu items and 50 (or more) beverage products, an inventory of 1,500 ingredients may need to be purchased. If errors are made when data is initially entered, all subsequent processing will be unreliable and system reports will be relatively worthless. However, the benefits to be gained from an automated inventory system are significant and, increasingly, many even relatively small operations are using automated systems.

Some inventory applications provide file space for more than one ingredient designation, such as item file code number, inventory sequence number, and internal customer code. The ability to work with additional designations can increase the efficiency of the inventory control system. For example, a user may be able

Exhibit 4   Screen Showing Inventory Purchase Units and Dollar Values

Select Locations   Enter Counts

Count Information

Count Date 05/15/20XX ▾

Location REFRIG

Count whenever you want; there are no limits or restrictions.

Count Detail

Sub	Item Name	Count Purch\Pack	Purch\Pack Units	Purch\Pack Cost	Extension $
123	Banana\Fresh	50	lb\LB	$0.61\$0.61	$30.50
DAI	Cheese\Swiss	23	lb\LB	$2.96\$2.96	$68.08
GRC	Pickle Spears	3.5	TUB\tub	$29.40\$29.40	$102.90
MT	Breaded Chicken	25	case\LB	$32.50\$3.25	$81.25
MT	Ham	43	lb\LB	$1.66\$1.66	$71.38
MT	Pork, roast	78	LB\lb	$3.11\$3.11	$242.58
PRE	Lettuce and Tomato Setup	50	EA\ea	$0.09\$0.09	$4.69
PRC	Avocado	2\6	CASE\ea	$68.00\$2.43	$150.57
PRC	Lettuce\Iceberg	2	CASE\head	$24.00\$1.00	$48.00
PRC	Parsley\Fresh	15	bunch\BUNCH	$0.65\$0.65	$9.75
PRC	Tomatoes\5x6	3	CASE\ea	$20.00\$0.67	$60.00

Sub-locations sort these items in the same order as your actual location.

Broken counts are not a problem. Enter cases and packs with a slash, and the extenstions are calculated for you.

| ◄ | ◄ | ► | ►| | + | — | | × | ⟲ |

Courtesy of CostGuard Foodservice Software, Bronxville, New York (www.costguard.com).

to print ingredients on a physical inventory worksheet according to the order in which they are shelved.

Managers must decide how usage is to be charted by the inventory application: by unit, by cost, or by both unit and cost. A system that charts items by unit may be able to report changes in stock levels, but may not be able to provide financial data necessary for food costing. The most effective inventory applications are those that track items in terms of both unit and cost. Exhibit 4 illustrates a sample screen from an inventory module that details usage in terms of both purchase units and dollar amounts.

Conversion tables can be used to track ingredients by unit and cost as they pass through the purchasing/receiving, storing/issuing, and production/service control points. To efficiently maintain a perpetual inventory record, a computerized inventory management system must be able to automatically convert purchase units into issue units and recipe units. Inventory data must be specific to each of these control points, because purchase units (case or 50-pound bag, for example) may differ from storeroom inventory units (#10 can, or pound, for example). Storeroom inventory units, in turn, differ from standard recipe units (such as cup or ounce).

Assume that an ingredient such as ground beef is purchased, issued, and used in different units. When a shipment of the ingredient arrives, it should be easy to update the inventory record by entering the purchase unit received (case of five 10-pound poly bags). The system should then automatically convert this entry into issue units (10-pound poly bags). Similarly, at the end of a meal period, the system should be capable of updating the inventory record by entering the standard recipe units (8-ounce ground beef patties) that should have been used to prepare the menu items served.

The system should also be able to track the costs associated with these various ingredient units. For example, assume that tomato sauce is purchased by the case (six #10 cans), issued from the storeroom to the kitchen by the #10 can, and used in recipes by the ounce. Given the information about the purchase unit's net weight and cost, the system should be able to automatically extend costs for issue and recipe unit(s). An integrated package can perform these calculations in fractions of a second. However, care must be taken to ensure that the ingredient file contains the necessary current data and conversion definitions.

Management should clarify how basic food service concepts are defined within the inventory application design. While the terms "inventory usage," "inventory variance," and "inventory valuation" are common, they do not have the same meaning in all computer systems. For example, inventory usage identifies changes in inventory level (depletion of stock on hand) from one point in time to another. However, is an inventory item considered "used" when it is received, when it is issued to the kitchen, or at the time of service? Each of these possible times presents a different usage result and cost computation. The point in time that is most desirable for a particular food service operation may not be the time frame built into the application's design. Also, since methods of inventory valuation vary, management must be careful to clarify which methods a particular food service inventory package should support.

Automated inventory management systems can quickly and accurately provide information that would be impractical to gather in a manual system. For example, all food service managers would like to know the quantity of products that were used and that should have been used to prepare items sold during a specific time period.

As discussed earlier, physical inventory counts are typically taken monthly. Some food service operations with limited menus, such as quick-service restaurants, may take physical counts more often (even daily) when there are unusual variances between ideal and actual costs. The physical inventory tells how much (number of items and dollar value) of each item is on hand. However, how much *should* be available, based on actual sales during the period?

Automated systems can tally the total number of all menu items sold during the period under analysis and "extend" the quantities of ingredients specified in standard recipes for that quantity of sales. For example, assume a restaurant offers two items containing ground beef: hamburger on bun and meat loaf platter. Assume also that 375 hamburgers and 125 meat loaf platters were sold during the time period of analysis. If the standard recipes for hamburgers and meat

Exhibit 5   Ideal Inventory Usage Report

Ideal Inventory Usage Report							
Date: 8/21/20XX	This details how much inventory you SHOULD have used. This						Page: 1
Time: 4:10 PM	includes any Sales Mix depletions and Requisitions.						
From 1/1/20XX to 12/31/20XX							
Details: Yes						Total Sales: $2651.65	

	Item		Ideal Usage		% of	Food
Item Name	Unit	$	Unit	$	Group	Cost %
DAIRY						
Cheese\Swiss	LB	2.96	6.1	18.00	2.7	0.7
Ice Cream /Sherbert	TUB	12.78	1.7	21.36	3.2	0.8
Oleo Blend Margarine	LB	1.08	2.4	2.57	0.4	0.1
Whipped Topping	5 GAL	38.95	0.3	9.98	1.5	0.4
** Total for DAIRY			10.4	51.90	7.7	2.0
GROCERY						
Almonds, Diced	CASE	92.58	0.0	2.47	0.4	0.1
BBQ Sauce - Bull's Eye	CASE	49.97	0.3	12.49	1.9	0.5
Bread-Burger Bun 4 1/2 s.s	PACKAG	1.39	8.0	11.12	1.7	0.4
Bread-Rye Bread	LOAF	2.30	5.6	12.95	1.9	0.5
Bread-White Bread 5x5	LOAF	1.91	16.5	31.43	4.7	1.2
Chocolate Syrup	CASE	42.09	0.1	2.66	0.4	0.1
French Fries	CASE	18.67	4.7	87.90	13.1	3.3
Ketchup-Heinz	CASE	27.98	2.0	56.46	8.4	2.1
Liquid Fry Shortening	CASE	15.40	0.9	13.98	2.1	0.5
Maraschino Cherries	CASE	50.40	0.4	21.52	3.2	0.8
Mayonnaise\Bulk	BOX	16.58	0.1	1.79	0.3	0.1
Onions - Sliced	LB	1.18	4.8	5.61	0.8	0.2
Ortega Peppers	CASE	30.21	0.5	14.72	2.2	0.6
Pickle Spears	TUB	20.40	0.6	16.05	2.6	0.6

Courtesy of CostGuard Foodservice Software, Bronxville, New York (www.costguard.com).

loaf require 4 ounces and 6 ounces of ground beef, respectively, 140.6 pounds of ground beef should have been used to produce these two items in the quantities sold (375 hamburgers × 4 oz = 1500 oz; 125 meat loaf platters × 6 oz = 750 oz; 1500 oz + 750 oz = 2250 oz; 2250 ÷ 16 oz/lb = 140.6 lb). Similarly, a system can track and extend all ingredients from the sales of all other items, and then a report indicating the *ideal* inventory usage can be generated (see Exhibit 5).

By contrast, Exhibit 6 shows an *actual* inventory usage report that indicates the actual quantity of inventory items that has been used (as noted in the exhibit, usage is based on the quantity in inventory at the beginning of the period, plus purchases, plus or minus adjustments, and minus closing inventory quantities). Any difference between ideal and actual usage represents a potential control problem (why and where are excess products being used?) and represents lost profits to the food and beverage operation.

Managers can use automated inventory management systems to learn where **inventory shrinkage** is occurring. They can review control procedures to determine where, if at all, corrective actions can be implemented. As this occurs, they can reduce variances between actual and ideal inventories and, in the process, better control costs.

Exhibit 6   Actual Inventory Usage Report

		Item	Opening		Purchases/Builds		Adjustments		Closing		Last	Usage		% of	Food
Item Name	Unit	$	Unit	$	Unit	$	Unit	$	Unit	$	Counted	Unit	$	Group	Cost %
DAIRY															
Cheese/Swiss	LB	2.98	12.0	35.82	0.0	0.00	0.0	0.00	5.0	14.90	01/21	7.0	20.72	2.1	0.8
Ice Cream/Sherbet	TUB	12.78	3.0	41.85	2.0	25.58	0.0	0.00	0.0	0.00	01/21	5.0	87.41	8.9	2.5
Oleo Blend Margarine	LB	1.09	45.0	49.60	25.0	27.00	0.0	0.00	0.0	0.00	01/21	70.0	75.60	7.7	2.9
Whipped Topping	5 GAL	38.95	3.0	116.85	3.0	116.85	0.0	0.00	0.0	0.00	01/21	6.0	233.70	23.9	8.8
'' Total for DAIRY			63.0	242.82	30.0	169.41	0.0	0.00	5.0	14.90		89.0	397.43	40.7	15.0
GROCERY															
Almonds, Diced	CASE	92.59	0.5	46.29	1.0	92.59	0.0	0.00	1.3	115.72	01/21	0.3	23.15	2.4	0.9
BBQ Sauce - Bull's Eye	CASE	49.97									1/21	0.5	24.99	2.8	0.9
Bread-Burger Bun 4 1/2 5.5	PACKAGE	1.39									1/21	18.0	25.02	2.8	0.9
Bread-Rye Bread	LOAF	2.30									1/21	7.0	16.10	1.8	0.6
Bread-White Bread 5x5	LOAF	1.91									1/21	7.0	13.37	1.4	0.5
Chocolate Syrup	CASE	42.09									1/21	0.2	7.02	0.7	0.3
French Fries	CASE	18.67									1/21	7.0	126.89	13.0	4.8
Ketchup-Heinz	CASE	27.99									1/21	1.8	41.81	4.3	1.8
Liquid Fry Shortening	CASE	15.40									1/21	1.8	27.72	2.8	1.0
Maraschino Cherries	CASE	50.40									1/21	0.1	7.17	0.7	0.3
Mayonnaise Bulk	BOX	18.59									1/21	1.1	19.11	2.0	0.7
Ortega Peppers	CASE	30.21									1/21	0.5	15.55	1.8	0.6
Pickle Spears	TUB	29.40									1/21	-5.5	-161.70	-16.5	-6.1
Pineapple Topping	CASE	35.55	0.8	29.83	1.0	35.55	0.0	0.00	1.3	35.12	01/21	0.3	11.85	1.2	0.4
Strawberry Topping	CASE	42.95	0.8	33.72	1.0	42.95	0.0	0.00	0.8	35.79	01/21	1.0	40.89	4.2	1.5
'' Total for GROCERY			106.9	739.74	94.0	787.89	0.0	0.00	180.1	1,269.51		40.8	209.92	24.4	9.0
MEAT															
Breaded Chicken	CASE	32.50	3.0	97.50	2.0	65.00	0.0	0.00	0.2	6.50	01/21	4.8	156.00	16.0	5.9
Ham	LB	1.66	26.0	43.16	25.0	41.50	0.0	0.00	52.0	86.32	01/21	-1.0	-1.66	-0.2	-0.1
Roast Port	LB	3.11	17.0	52.87	25.0	77.75	0.0	0.00	59.0	180.38	01/21	-16.0	-49.78	-5.1	-1.9
'' Total for MEAT			46.0	193.53	52.0	184.25	0.0	0.00	110.2	273.20		-12.2	104.58	10.7	3.9
PRODUCE															

Actual Inventory Usage Report

Date: 8/21/20XX
Time: 3:50 PM
From 1/1/20XX to 12/31/20XX (# of days: 365)
Sort by: Group
Details: Yes

Actual Inventory Usage Report
Your Company Name Here
Unit: SRMP
Page: 1
Total Sales: $2651.85

Actual Inventory Usage Report

This report provides your ACTUAL cost of goods for any period of time. It's calculated by taking opening inventory + purchases +/- adjustments - closing inventory.

There are many sorting options; in this case, we sorted by group.

Note: we included the entire report on this screen, so it looks very small.

Courtesy of CostGuard Foodservice Software, Bronxville, New York (www.costguard.com).

Technology and Inventory Counting

Accurate counting of products in inventory allows managers to be more effective purchasers because they know quantity usage rates and can maintain perpetual inventory balances. They can also be aware of upcoming expiration dates for inventory items.

Technology can also assist in the inventory valuation process through optical scanning. Universal product code (UPC) information on product packages can be scanned to quickly and accurately assess the quantity of unopened product packages in inventory. Scanning results can provide helpful information for verifying perpetual inventories and for calculating cost-of-goods-sold data when actual food and beverage costs are calculated.

The use of bar code technology has been relatively slow to catch on in food and beverage operations. In fact, bar code applications were available in the commercial marketplace for many years before systems were developed and adapted for use in the hospitality industry. Hand-held wireless bar code scanning equipment allows fast and accurate counting of items in inventory. Bar code information labels can be provided by suppliers on incoming containers or they can be printed in-house for items lacking the supplier labels. Information regarding quantity, unit cost, and total cost of items in inventory can be quickly assessed and transferred to inventory records. For example, manual counts can be entered into a personal digital assistant

---

Full Integration of Computer Applications

The development and use of wireless technology strongly suggests the possibility of an almost total integration of all product management tasks. Let's see how: A server enters a guest's order at tableside using a wireless hand-held device. The order is transferred through the wireless network to the kitchen. Inventory records for all ingredients required for the items that have been ordered are updated in the inventory database. If the ingredients for some items required for production must be retrieved from the storage area, a requisition can be wirelessly transmitted to the storeroom employee's hand-held device. The item can be accurately and quickly located in the storeroom using the hand-held device with a built-in RFID receiver.

A "smart" shelf from which the item is retrieved records the removal of the item, and the quantity of the product still available in inventory is updated. As the inventory level for the item reaches a predetermined order point, a reorder is developed. This request becomes a purchase order transmitted electronically to potential suppliers. The electronic bids submitted are evaluated, and the order is electronically placed with the appropriate supplier. As the incoming ingredients are received, receiving/storing staff scan the items with a wireless bar code reader to confirm that what was ordered was, in fact, received. RFID tags are placed on incoming cases and the cases are stored on smart shelves for future consumption. The smart shelf does a double-check of the quantity in inventory and reports any discrepancies. At this point, the cycle of electronic control can repeat itself.

(PDA) with wireless connection to a centralized computer. Alternatively, data can be transferred when the PDA is connected to the computer. It is possible for multi-unit operators to receive inventory information on a by-unit basis via the Internet. Hotels and other hospitality operations with multiple outlets/kitchens/storerooms can optically scan specific inventories; information can then be summarized for all outlets.

Even though bar code technology has numerous advantages over the hand-written entry of inventory data, it is still not fully automatic; the items to be counted must still be manually scanned. Another technology, radio frequency identification (RFID), may be used in the future to fully automate inventory recordkeeping. RFID technology uses transponder tags to wirelessly transmit electronic product codes (EPCs) to other devices using radio frequency waves. The tags are attached to shipping containers and identify the contents. EPC "readers" communicate with the tag through the use of radio frequencies.

A key difference between RFID and bar code technology is that RFID eliminates the need for the line-of-sight reading on which bar coding depends. Moreover, RFID scanning can be done at greater distances (up to 90 feet, as opposed to just a few inches with a bar code reader).

RFID readers can be placed in storage shelves or racks, and each time an item is removed from the shelf and whenever the level of product inventory falls below a predetermined point, a notice is sent to the automated inventory tracking system. The system also detects items stored at an incorrect location.

Special Beverage Inventory Concerns

The basic control procedures already noted apply to both food and beverage products. However, since beverages, especially liquor and wine, are expensive and popular targets of theft, they require special control precautions.

Even small food and beverage operations normally use a perpetual inventory system for alcoholic beverages. While important for many stored food products, control procedures such as locked storage areas, controlled access, and management of storeroom access are especially critical to the control of alcoholic beverages. The inventory task is easier if prices are marked on the bottles or cases when they are originally placed in storage.

An important consideration in designing inventory control procedures for beverages is whether beverage inventory values will include items currently behind the bar as well as beverage items in the central storeroom. Consistency is the key here. Items behind the bar should either always be included or never be included in inventory recordkeeping procedures. Some beverage managers believe it is unnecessary to include items behind the bar in inventories because the bar quantities will average out. Others believe that the increased accuracy gained from including behind-the-bar items in inventory records and the tighter control this provides are worthwhile.

If only central storeroom beverage products are to be counted, the physical count of bottles can be done in the same manner as that for food products. If a manual inventory system is in use, the same inventory form (Exhibit 2) can be used for both food and beverage items. However, when both central storeroom and behind-the-bar inventory costs are assessed, the system must be modified.

Behind-Bar Inventory Costs

When beverage items behind the bar are valued for inventory purposes, the following procedures can be used to manually assess costs:

1. Count the number of unopened bottles of each type of beverage product.

2. Determine the quantity of beverage products in opened bottles. This can be done either by visually estimating (for example, to the nearest tenth of a bottle) or by weighing.

3. Add the number of unopened bottles of each type of beverage to the amount remaining in opened bottles to assess the total volume of product available behind the bar.

4. Add the amount in the central storeroom to the behind-the-bar amount to determine the total beverage inventory.

5. Calculate the total cost of beverage items in inventory.

Exhibit 7 shows a beverage inventory cost record that can be used in a manual system.

Technology can also be used to ease the task of assessing beverage inventory. For example, automated beverage dispensing systems can track the quantity of each beverage dispensed. Then, much like POS technology for food item sales,

Exhibit 7   Beverage Inventory Cost Record

Beverage Inventory Cost Card							
		Quantity Available					
		Bottles Behind Bar					
Beverage Item	**Storage Unit**	**Open**	**Unopened**	**In Central Storage**	**Total**	**Cost Per Storage Unit**	**Total Cost**
Col. 1	Col. 2	Col. 3	Col. 4	Col. 5	Col. 6	Col. 7	Col. 8
Bar Scotch	*750 ml*	*¾*	*3*	*12*	*15 ¾*	*$12.50*	*$196.88*
Bar Gin	*750 ml*	*½*	*3*	*24*	*27 ½*	*11.75*	*323.13*

electronically generated reports can detail the quantity of each alcoholic beverage that should have been used (dispensed) and the amount of product that should be remaining in inventory. When interfaced with the POS system (a definite recommendation!), information relating to the amount of revenues that should have been generated from the sale of each beverage will also be known. Exhibit 8 shows a product usage report that has been electronically generated.

Managers have traditionally counted full bottles and cases of alcoholic beverages in central beverage storage areas in much the same way that food products are counted and accounted for. However, the task of counting opened bottles behind the bar has been challenging because of the subjectivity (i.e., how much is in the bottle?) that has been required. Today, however, technology can ease this task and provide information helpful for accountability, beverage inventory, and counting purposes.

Learn More on the Web

Accubar (www.accubar.com) is one company that offers technology to determine the quantity of alcoholic beverages in open bottles. (It also includes full bottles in inventory assessments.) When users scan a bottle's bar code information into a hand-held unit, an outline of the bottle appears. Then a manager can draw a line at the approximate bottle content level. The system will then automatically calculate the amount of beverage and its available value, the quantity used since the time of the last behind-bar inventory, and numerous reports can be generated.

The system can also be used to track other items, such as expensive meats, glassware, and any other item that can be counted.

The website has extensive information, including a demonstration.

Exhibit 8   Product Usage Report

Ring Off #22	—2:52 a.m.	1/06
Accumulators Cleared	—8:01 a.m.	1/05

Product Usage	Bottle Size	Ounces Poured	Bottles Emptied				
				Almond	Liter	4	
				Cacao Dark	Liter	3	
				Cacao Light	Liter	1	
Scotch	1.75 L	77	1	Menthe Green	Liter	1	
Chivas Regal	1.75 L	7		Menthe Light	Liter	15	
Cutty Sark	1.75 L	2					
Dewar's	1.75 L	82	1	Midori	Liter	2	
J&B	1.75 L	24		Peach Schnaps	1.75 L	68	1
JWalker Black	1.75 L	17		Sloe Gin	Liter	1	
				Triple Sec	1.75 L	42	1
Bourbon	1.75 L	54	1				
Jack Daniels	1.75 L	130	2	Di Saronna	1.75 L	3	
Jim Beam	1.75 L			Amorita	Liter	27	
Makers Mark	1.75 L	17		Drambuie	1.75 L	12	1
Old Granddad	1.75 L	3		Frangelico	750ml	1	
Wild Turkey	1.75 L	6		Grand Marnier	1.75 L	19	1
Canadian Club	1.75 L	64	1	Kahlua	1.75 L	4	
Crown Royal	1.75 L	17		Kamora	Liter	29	1
Irish Whiskey	1.75 L	1		Sambuca	750ml	28	1
Seagram's 7	1.75 L	60	1	Tia Maria	Liter	15	1
Seagram's VO	1.75 L	73	2				
				Chablis	1 Gal	234	1
Gin	1.75 L	43	1	Chardonnay	1 Gal	10	
Beefeater	1.75 L	6		Wht Zinfandel	1 Gal	159	1
Bombay	1.75 L	5					
Tanqueray	1.75 L	92	1	Margarita Mix	5 Gal	2	1
				Sour Mix	5 Gal	138	
Vodka	1.75 L	414	7				
Absolut	1.75 L	34	1	LemLime Syrup	1 Gal	32	
Smirnoff	1.75 L	18		Seagrams Coolr	1 Gal	7	
Stolichnaya	Liter	111	3	Cola Syrup	1 Gal	36	1
				Tonic Syrup	1 Gal	40	1
Rum	1.75 L	66	1	Diet Syrup	1 Gal	9	
Bacardi	1.75 L	5					
Myers's	1.75 L			Soda	1 Gal	799	6
				Water	1 Gal	42	
Tequilla	1.75 L	15					
Cuervo Gold	1.75 L	15					
Brandy	1.75 L	15	1				
Apricot	Liter						

continued

Issuing Control: General Procedures

At some point, products are removed from storage and transferred to production areas—the kitchen and bar. Unfortunately, some properties have very informal, if any, issuing procedures and exert little control over this process. An "open-door" policy may even be in effect: whenever anyone needs something, the person simply walks into the storage area and takes it. However, if a food and beverage operation does not limit access to storage areas and keep records of items removed, it is not possible to control the quantity of products removed from storage. Then the quantity of items produced or the levels of revenue generated are less likely to relate to the quantity of products purchased and available in inventory. Limited access to storage areas and special procedures for issuing products from storage to production are essential for effective food and beverage controls.

The objectives of a well-designed issuing system are to:

- Limit access to storage areas to authorized staff members.

- Match items removed from storage with actual production requirements and items sold.

- Assess quantities and costs of products removed from storage. This record-keeping becomes important when updating perpetual inventory records and assessing costs of issues to calculate daily food and beverage costs.

Issuing Procedures

Any food and beverage operation, regardless of size, can use a formalized issuing system. Large hotels and restaurants often have full-time storeroom staff who assemble products to be issued and sign them over to production unit employees who retrieve them. Smaller properties may assign issuing responsibilities to employees who work in storerooms at specified times only, or, alternatively, may require managers to be present when items are removed from storage. If the ABCD approach is used, some requisition forms should be used, at least for the priority items. All of these methods succeed in limiting access to storage areas and assigning responsibility for issuing to a specific person.

By planning ahead, small operations can limit issuing to specified times. For example, products for making breakfast might be issued from 6:00 to 6:30 A.M. Items needed for lunch could be issued from 10:30 to 11:00 A.M., and similarly for dinner or late evening shifts. Normally, beverages to replenish bar inventories are issued either at the beginning or end of each bar shift. (Beverage issuing is discussed later in this chapter.) By limiting issuing to specified times, even the smallest food and beverage operation can use many of the control procedures described in this chapter.

The Food Issue Requisition Process

The food issue requisition form (an example is shown in Exhibit 9) can be used by properties with manual issuing systems. It identifies the type and amount of each food item necessary for production during a given shift or other time period. The steps for its use follow:

1. The form identifies each item to be withdrawn from storage in column 1. Studying the standard recipes to be prepared helps ensure that nothing is forgotten.

2. The issue unit size of each item needed is entered in column 2, and the quantity needed is entered in column 3. The quantity of each item needed is based on the recipes to be used during the shift (or other time period) minus any products already withdrawn from inventory and available in production, broken-case storage, or other storage areas.

3. After production personnel complete the form, it then goes to the chef, kitchen manager, or other responsible employee who should approve the products for withdrawal from inventory (upper right corner).

Exhibit 9   Food Issue Requisition Form (Manual System)

Food Requisition

Storage Type (check one):   Date: 10/6/XX

Refrigerated _____

Frozen _____   Workstation: Production

Dry _____✓_____   Approved for Withdrawal: L. Sill

| | | | | | Employee Initials | |
Item	Issue Unit	No. of Units	Unit Price	Total Cost	Received By	Withdrawn By
Col. 1	Col. 2	Col. 3	Col. 4	Col. 5	Col. 6	Col. 7
Tomato Paste	CS-6 #10	2 ½	$28.50	$71.25	JC	Ken
Salad Oil	gal.	1	22.75	22.75	JC	Ken
				Total	$596.17	

4. Next, the form is routed to the appropriate storage area. The form can be designed to distinguish whether products are from refrigerated, frozen, or dry storage areas. Smaller properties may not need this classification system. Completing the unit price (column 4) is simple if costs from the delivery invoice are marked on cases and packages when they are received and placed in storage. Alternatively, costs may be transferred from the daily receiving report to containers as the items are shelved. To complete total cost (column 5), the number of purchase units (column 3) is multiplied by the cost per unit (column 4). It is not necessary to calculate total cost at the time of issuing, nor does the storeroom employee have to do so before signing products over to production areas.

5. The storage or management employee responsible for issuing verifies that items listed were indeed withdrawn by signing or initialing column 7. The employee accepting the issued products can also initial the requisition form (in column 6). This transfers responsibility for the products from the issuing person to the production employee withdrawing the products. If there is a discrepancy between the amount taken from storage and the amount delivered to production areas, documentation helps determine who is responsible and where and when the problem occurred.

6. After issuing is completed, the items should be transferred promptly to the appropriate production areas.

Depending on the operation, issue requisition forms may be processed in any of a number of ways. When all daily issues are completed, the manager, the storeroom clerk, or secretarial/bookkeeping personnel may use the forms to update perpetual inventory records. Since the perpetual inventory form (Exhibit 3) does not carry cost information, column 5 need not be completed for this task.

The food issue requisition forms for the day can be forwarded to the manager or secretary/bookkeeper to review and to use in calculating the daily food cost information. If total cost (column 5) is not yet completed, it is calculated now. If it was calculated by storage personnel, other personnel should verify the calculation before completing daily food cost records.

Computer-Generated Issue Quantities

Computer software enables managers to apply a projected sales mix across a standard recipe file to produce a "prior-to-service" cost report. A by-product of this costing tactic is a complete list of all ingredient quantities required to satisfy the demand for a planned menu. In other words, if four items on a given menu each require ketchup as a recipe ingredient, the quantity of ketchup to be issued would be the total amount needed to produce all four items for the meal period. Ingredient totals are typically contained in a breakout quantities report. The computer system lists all items (by issue unit) requiring requisition to produce a projected sales mix of menu items.

In addition to issuing on the basis of sales forecasts, quantities to issue can be based on par levels for separate workstations or standard quantities regardless of sales forecasts.

Requisition information is electronically transferred from user departments to the storage area(s). No paperwork is required. Exhibit 10 shows an electronic issue (transfer) requisition. To justify quantities in excess of par, a comment ("CHS Reunion," "Playoffs") is provided.

Some software packages split breakout quantities by preparation area. In this case, ingredients are summed by preparation area only and reported accordingly. Therefore, although the fryer, broiler, and pantry stations may all use the same ingredient, individual breakout lists will contain only the appropriate total for each workstation. This approach helps tighten inventory control and, over time, may provide a basis for a highly reliable forecasting system. Projected sales mixes, which yield breakout quantities, are easily assessed based on whether sufficient quantities were issued. If secondary requisitioning is necessary, the forecasting methods must be refined.

After electronic issue requisitions are received in the storage area, a hard copy can be printed as a "pick list" to help storeroom personnel recall what is needed. Alternatively, information can be transferred to a palm device or a tablet PC to assist the storeroom clerk with product selection. Similar procedures can be used when multi-unit operators request items from a central commissary, for example, or a hotel outlet "orders" baked goods from a bakeshop in the property.

Exhibit 10   Electronic Issue Requisition

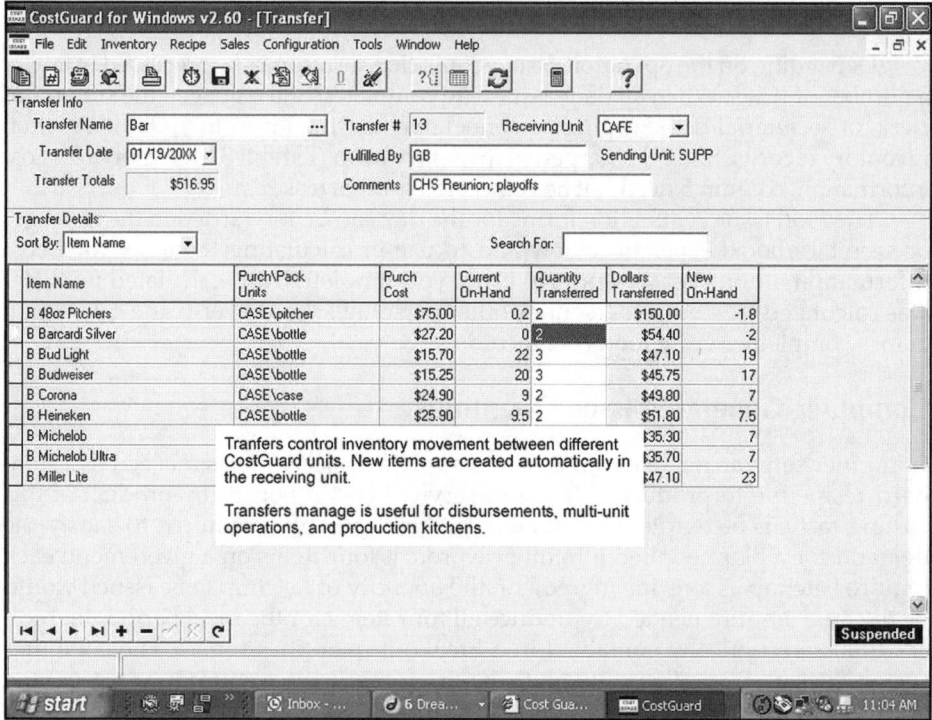

Courtesy of CostGuard Foodservice Software, Bronxville, New York (www.costguard.com).

The Beverage Issue Requisition Process

The basic procedures for issuing food also apply to beverages. However, since beverages, by their nature, are very susceptible to employee theft, there are several additional concerns in transferring beverages from storage to production areas. Special procedures incorporated into beverage issuing can reduce the possibility or frequency of employee theft.

Establishing Bar Par Inventory Levels

Normally, beverages should be issued only in quantities needed to re-establish bar par inventory levels. A **bar par** is an established number of bottles of each type of beverage that is always kept in behind-bar storage areas. A bar par is established for each type of liquor and wine kept behind the bar. Some food and beverage operations also set pars for bottled beer. Bar pars are established on the basis of the number of bottles of each beverage type used during a busy shift. For example, if an average busy shift uses four bottles of house brand scotch, the beverage manager may be conservative and set the bar par at five bottles: four full bottles in behind-bar storage and one opened bottle in the speedrail or back-bar display area. In operations such as a hotel with multiple outlets, pars are independently established for each bar.

Exhibit 11   Beverage Issue Requisition Form (Manual System)

Beverage Requisition

Shift: _A.M. (Lunch)_   Date: _8/1/XX_

Bar: _Main_   Bartender: _John Smith_

Beverage	Number of Bottles	Size	Unit Cost	Total Cost
Col. 1	Col. 2	Col. 3	Col. 4	Col. 5
B. Scotch	3	750 ml	$12.50	$37.50
B. Gin	2	750 ml	11.75	23.50

Total Bottles: _12_   Total Cost: _$118.75_

Check one:

OK to Issue: _JN_   ☐ low price

Issued by: _GC_   ☑ reg. price

Received by: _JS_   ☐ high price

$118.75 (cost) ÷ $593.75 (revenue) = 20% (beverage percent)

The number of empty bottles at the beginning or end of each shift (preferably the end) determines the number of full bottles needed to replenish the bar par. If, for example, the bar par is five bottles for house scotch and two bottles are empty, then two bottles will be issued to maintain the bar par. An important rule is that empty bottles must be presented before full bottles are issued.

Beverage Issuing Steps

The beverage issuing process typically includes the following steps:

1. At the end of each shift, the bartender places the bottles emptied during the shift on top of the bar.

2. The bartender completes a beverage issue requisition form (a sample for a manual system is shown in Exhibit 11), recording the name of each type of beverage emptied (column 1), the number of empty bottles (column 2), and the size of the bottle (column 3). Depending on the property, the bartender may also record the unit cost (column 4). Information for this column comes

from the invoice (purchase) cost marked on the bottle when it was placed in storage (if less than case lots are purchased) or when the bottle is issued (when a specific brand is purchased by the case).

3. The beverage manager checks the number and type of empty bottles on the bar against the information on the beverage issue requisition form. If there are no problems, he or she signs or initials the "OK to Issue" section of the sheet.

4. The bartender or manager takes the empty bottles and the beverage issue requisition form to the beverage storage area. The person responsible for issuing compares empty bottles with the issue requisition; replaces empty bottles with full ones, bottle-for-bottle; and signs or initials the issue requisition. At the same time, the bartender or manager, who returns full bottles to the bar, signs or initials the "received by" section.

5. Empty bottles are disposed of according to local or state laws, if applicable, or as specified by the property's control requirements.

6. Total cost calculations (column 5) and the beverage cost percent calculations at the bottom of the issue requisition form are normally completed by management or accounting/bookkeeping personnel, not the bartender or storeroom issuing staff. Except in large properties with storeroom personnel, management office staff should maintain perpetual inventory records for beverage products.

Bottle Marking

Bottle marking identifies a bottle of liquor or wine as house property, and it may also note information about the bottle's cost and date of issue. If there is only one bar, the bottle can be marked when it is placed in storage if it is purchased in less-than-case lots. If a beverage is purchased in case quantities, bottle marking is best done when the bottle is removed from the case when issued to avoid double handling of the bottle. If there is more than one bar, bottles can also be marked with the site to which they are issued.

Frequently, the bottle mark is an adhesive-backed label or hard-to-remove ink stamp, with a logo or symbol difficult to duplicate. Since the **bottle mark** identifies the bottle as house property, it helps supervisory staff ensure that all bottles behind a bar belong to the property. There is less likelihood that bartenders can bring in bottles and steal from the operation by selling their own liquor and keeping the revenue.

Bottle marking is important for other reasons. First, if the cost from the daily receiving report or delivery invoice is recorded on the bottle, it not only is easier to complete the issue requisition form, but inventory valuation will also be easier. Also, if the date of issue is recorded on the bottle, it is easier to track rotation of bottles behind the bar.

The bottle mark, or at least the cost and date of issue, should not be easy to notice. Certain situations require making exceptions to bottle-marking practices, such as liquor bottles going to the table for flaming or wine served for dining. In these cases, bottles might be marked on the bottom.

Additional Beverage Control Concerns

Several additional control concerns about issuing beverages should be noted. When beverages behind the bar run out regularly, bar par levels must be re-examined and increased. Guests do not want to wait while another bottle is brought from the storeroom. Similarly, there may not be time to complete a beverage issue requisition in the middle of a rush period, so information about beverage costs and inventory balances is lost. To avoid these problems, managers should carefully assess the need for behind-the-bar inventories during the operation's busy periods, and issuing times and bar par quantities should be planned accordingly.

When the bar is not in operation, all bar par inventories should be locked to discourage employee theft. In addition, keys to beverage storeroom areas should not be left with bartenders. In small operations, the key can be sealed in an envelope placed behind the bar. If it must be used when a manager is not immediately available, it will be available. However, the opened envelope will show that the storeroom has been entered. An immediate comparison of perpetual inventory records with a physical count may then be in order.

Endnotes

1. For more information, see Ronald F. Cichy, *Food Safety: Managing with the HACCP System*, 2d ed. (Lansing, Mich.: American Hotel & Lodging Educational Institute, 2008), Chapters 7 and 8.

2. For more information about inventory valuation, see Raymond S. Schmidgall, *Hospitality Industry Managerial Accounting*, 6th ed. (Lansing, Mich.: American Hotel & Lodging Educational Institute, 2006).

 # Key Terms

ABCD inventory classification system—A system of categorizing products according to their perishability and cost per serving; category A includes those products that are high in both perishability and cost per serving; category B items are relatively high in cost but low in perishability; category C items are relatively low in cost but high in perishability; category D items are low in both perishability and cost per serving.

average inventory—A valuation determined by adding the value of inventory at the beginning of the time period in question (usually a month) to the value of inventory at the end of that period and then dividing the sum by two; this value is used when calculating the inventory turnover rate.

bar par—An established number of bottles of each type of beverage that is always kept in behind-the-bar storage areas.

bottle mark—An adhesive-backed label or hard-to-remove ink stamp, with a logo or symbol that is difficult to duplicate; the bottle mark identifies the bottle as house property and helps supervisory staff ensure that all bottles behind the bar belong to the property.

directs—Usually relatively inexpensive, perishable products purchased several times a week for more or less immediate use; examples include fresh produce, baked goods, and dairy products.

first-in, first-out (FIFO) inventory rotation—Products held in inventory the longest are the first to be issued to production areas; when newly received products enter storage areas, they are placed under or behind products already in storage.

first-in, first-out (FIFO) inventory valuation—The earliest inventory costs incurred are assigned when products are issued.

inventory shrinkage—An industry term relative to unexplained inventory reductions.

inventory turnover rate—Shows the number of times in a given period that inventory is converted or turned into revenue; calculated by dividing the cost of food (or beverages) used by the average food (or beverage) inventory (in dollars).

last-in, first-out (LIFO) inventory valuation—The most recent inventory costs incurred are assigned when products are issued.

non-productive inventory—Products in storage that are not issued to production areas during the time period (usually monthly) covered by financial records.

perpetual inventory system—A running balance of the quantity of stored products kept by recording all newly purchased items as they enter storage areas and all quantities issued from storage to production areas.

physical inventory system—The practice of physically counting stored products on a periodic basis.

stores—Generally, relatively expensive items that are purchased less often than directs and in quantities necessary to rebuild inventory levels; examples include meats, seafood, frozen and canned products, and staples such as flour, sugar, and cereals.

 Review Questions ─────────────────────────────

1. Why is effective management of products in storage important?

2. What is the difference between "directs" and "stores"?

3. What are some of the ways to help ensure proper security during storage?

4. What are the key sanitation concerns during storage?

5. What records should be kept of products during storage?

6. How do you calculate inventory turnover? Why is the resulting ratio important?

7. What special procedures should be used to control the most expensive and most frequently used products in inventory?

8. How are purchase units, issue units, and recipe units related in a computer system?

9. What is a bar par? Why is it important?

10. What might be gained by using computerized issuing reports that show breakout quantities by preparation area?

11. How have computerized storing/issuing systems simplified the task of accounting for products before the time of production/usage?

12. How can effective beverage inventory and issuing procedures reduce bartender theft?

13. What characteristics and capabilities will be incorporated in inventory control systems of the future that use RFID technology?

Internet Sites

For more information, visit the following Internet sites. Remember that Internet addresses can change without notice. If the site is no longer there, you can use a search engine to look for additional sites.

Food Service Software

Comtrex Systems Corporation
www.comtrex.com

FoodSoftware.com
www.foodsoftware.com/default.asp

CostGuard
www.costguard.com

Food Trak
www.foodtrak.com

Culinary Software Services
www.culinarysoftware.com

MenuLink Computer Solutions, Inc.
www.menulinkinc.com

Eatec Corporation
www.eatec.com

Micros Systems, Inc.
www.micros.com

Enggist & Grandjean Software
www.eg-software.com

Beverage Systems and Software

Accardis Systems, Inc.
www.accardis.com

Easybar Beverage Management
  Systems
www.easybar.com

Berg Company
www.berg-controls.com

Case Study

Pushing the Envelope on Settings and Supplies

Reuben Diaz was feeling good. It was a hot Saturday night, and things were starting to heat up inside the 125-seat Fiesta Grill. The Grill had experienced an upturn in business the past couple of months, and this was the busiest night Reuben had seen since becoming the general manager four years ago.

A wedding reception was in full swing in the banquet room. The dining room was full, with people waiting in the lobby for tables. And Ted, the Fiesta Grill's new catering manager, had left 30 minutes ago with food and supplies for an off-premises catering event 20 miles away. This was the Grill's first venture into off-premises catering, and Reuben just knew it was going to be a great boon to business.

Reuben walked through the dining room, encouraging his staff. They seemed hurried, but Reuben didn't think that was unusual under the circumstances. He decided to chat with some of the guests.

"How are you folks tonight?" Reuben asked a couple sitting at a table nearby. "I'm Reuben Diaz, the general manager here at the Fiesta Grill."

There was a long pause. "Actually, we're not doing too well, Mr. Diaz," the man said icily.

Reuben was taken aback. "I'm sorry to hear that," he said. "What's the problem?"

"To start off, our salad plates were warm," the man began. "And coincidentally, so was the *iceberg* lettuce in the salads. Then we were told we couldn't get any wine because there weren't any clean wine glasses. To top it off, we waited 20 minutes for a cup of coffee."

"That's not all, Bob," the woman added, turning to her husband. "Even after our coffee came, we weren't given any cream. And then when our waitress finally brought us some, she forgot to bring spoons to stir it with."

"Let's just say it hasn't been our best night out to eat," Bob said with a forced smile.

Reuben felt his energy draining. He knew this couple was looking to him to solve their problem. "Please accept my apologies Bob, and—"

"Helen," the woman offered her name.

"—and Helen. Your dinners tonight are compliments of the Fiesta Grill. Although that won't change what happened, I hope it can be some consolation," Reuben said, trying to ease the tension a little.

"That's very nice of you," said Bob. "We appreciate it."

"Yes. Thank you very much," Helen added.

"You're welcome," Reuben said. "And please come again. I don't think you'll be disappointed."

"Yeah, we'll be back," Bob said. "But maybe next time on a slower night." He smiled.

"Well, I hope to see you again soon. Have a good night, now."

"Thanks," Bob said. "You too."

Before Reuben left Bob and Helen's table, he saw that none of their plates or smallware had been cleared, even though they were now eating dessert. On his way back to the kitchen, he noticed that several other tables hadn't been pre-bussed, either. "No wonder there weren't any spoons for their coffee," Reuben thought. He decided to ask the buspersons and Sylvia—Bob and Helen's server—about this, but as he reached the kitchen, Kevin, one of the Grill's dishwashers, raced past him toward the exit, pulling off his apron. He had a look of disgust on his face.

"Kevin, whoa—what's wrong?" Reuben stopped him.

"I'm sorry, Mr. Diaz, but it's a mess back there, and I'm sick of it," Kevin said. "Someone just asked me for the fourth time to run two coffee cups through the dishwasher, and they're getting on my case because they don't have any plates. Hey, it's not my fault. I'm outta here."

Reuben began to realize the problem wasn't confined to just Sylvia or Bob and Helen. "Kevin, it looks like we're having some problems tonight with our supply of dishes, cups, and silverware. But could you just stick it out? I'm going to talk to the servers and ask them to take it easy on you. I promise this won't happen again."

Kevin thought a moment. "I don't know …"

"Trust me, I'm going to take care of this," Reuben assured him.

"Well, all right," Kevin said. "You know, if you ask me, one thing you should do is tell the bussers to stop hoarding before their shifts."

"Hoarding? What do you mean?" Reuben asked.

"Hoarding—you know, bussers make a bunch of sets of rolled silverware and stash them in their areas so they don't run out," Kevin replied. "It's great for some servers, but a big pain for others. I don't think they should do it."

"Hoarding causes a lot of problems. Thanks for bringing it to my attention, Kevin," said Reuben.

"Okay," Kevin said, and headed back to the kitchen.

Reuben followed him and found Sylvia in the kitchen.

"Sylvia, hi."

"Hi, Reuben," Sylvia said as she garnished some plates.

"I just talked to Bob and Helen."

"Who?" Sylvia quickly placed the plates on a serving tray, hoisted the tray onto her shoulder, and started walking briskly toward the door to the dining room.

"Uh, Bob and Helen, the couple at table … let's see … A2," Reuben said as he followed Sylvia into the dining room.

Sylvia stopped and thought a moment. "Oh, yeah, A2," she said, rolling her eyes.

"What do you mean? Were they giving you a problem?" asked Reuben.

"Back in a minute," Sylvia said as she hurried off to her table.

Reuben waited until Sylvia returned.

"What was the problem with A2?" Reuben asked her when she came back.

"Oh, they were just kinda rude when they didn't get their coffee or their spoons."

"Has there been a shortage of glasses and smallware tonight?" Reuben asked.

"Glasses have been running low, but we have plenty of smallware," Sylvia said.

"Oh yeah, why's that?" Reuben asked.

"The bussers made plenty of extras for their stations," Sylvia replied.

"I see," Reuben said. ("Hoarding …" he thought to himself.) "But glasses are low, you say?"

"Yes."

Reuben was dumbfounded. How could this have happened? "Thanks, Sylvia," he said. "Oh, by the way, comp the meals at A2, OK?"

"Sure," Sylvia said.

"Thanks."

Reuben started to recount the events of the past week: On Monday he got the call about Saturday's off-premises event. Sixty settings were needed. He checked inventory and determined that even with the banquet and a full dining room Saturday night, the Grill would be able to handle the off-premises event. But he knew it was going to be tight; there weren't going to be any spare settings lying around. But still, they should have had enough. Then he preset the banquet room three days ago and double-checked the inventory. Again, there were enough settings. So what was the problem?

Reuben decided to check inventory again. He was shocked when he found that the dish staff was struggling just to keep glasses, plates, cups—everything—in rotation. He shook his head. What was going on? He remembered that Ted took a cellular phone with him to the off-premises event, so Reuben went to his office, closed the door behind him, and called Ted.

"Ted? Hi. This is Reuben. How is everything?"

"Reuben—hey, everything's going great here, just great."

"Well, I'm glad to hear it. Unfortunately, I can't say the same."

"Why? What's up?"

"We don't have any settings; servers are running out of cups and plates; guests are becoming irate … I just don't understand it. I figured all this out earlier in the week. It was gonna be close, but we were going to make it."

"I'm sorry to hear you're having problems there, but we took a hundred settings, and it looks like we have just enough—"

"A hundred?" Reuben interrupted.

"Yeah. One hundred."

"But that event was only scheduled for 60."

"Well, that was before they added 40. I told you about that."

"No, you didn't."

"I must have. I told Frank, and he made sure I got the extra food. I didn't tell you?"

"No, you didn't. There's nothing we can do about it now. We'll just have to make do here."

"I'm sorry, Reuben."

"That's OK. These things happen. Keep up the good work. I'll talk to you later."

But of course Reuben knew everything *wasn't* OK. Somehow he had to solve this problem for his guests and his staff—and fast. And he had to make sure the Fiesta Grill wouldn't face this problem in two months—at which time they were again booked for a banquet and an off-premises event on the same night.

Reuben grabbed a bottle of aspirin from his desk and bravely entered the kitchen. "Here we go," he thought to himself.

Discussion Questions

1. What steps could have been taken to prevent the shortage problems at the Fiesta Grill?

2. Assuming the continued success of off-premises catering, what options does the management team have in relation to securing the stock necessary to accommodate increased business? List the advantages and disadvantages of each option.

Case Number: 4657CA

The following industry experts helped generate and develop this case: Timothy J. Pugh, East Lansing, Michigan; and Lawrence E. Ross, Professor, Florida Southern College and owner of Sago Grill, Lakeland, Florida.

 Problems

Problem 1

The following information applies to the City View Restaurant.

May 1	Food inventory value:	$73,480
May 31	Food inventory value:	$77,550
Cost of food used during May		$386,410

1. What is the inventory turnover rate for food products for the City View Restaurant?
2. What does the answer (inventory turnover ratio) in question 1 mean?

Problem 2

What is the total inventory value of the following products?

Physical Inventory				
Type of Product: _____			Month: _____	
Product	Unit	Amount in Storage	Purchase Cost	Total Cost
Ground Beef	10-lb bag	6 bags	$2.10/lb	
Canned Peaches	6 #10/cs	3-5/6 cs	$39.40/cs	
Flour	50 lb	2 bags	$22.10/bag	
Shrimp	10/5 lb per case	3-8/10 cs	$7.50/lb	
			Total	

Problem 3

Complete the following perpetual inventory form.

Perpetual Inventory			
Product Name: _____			
Purchase Unit Size: _____			
	Carried Forward: ____		
Date	**In**	**Out**	**Balance**
1/7	3		
1/9		2	
1/10		1	
1/12	5	1	
1/15		2	

Problem 4

What is the value of inventory for the following products, given the following information?

Beverage Inventory Cost Card (2 Workstations)							
		Quantity Available					
		Bottles Behind Bar				**Cost Per**	
Beverage Item	**Storage Unit**	**Opened**	**Unopened**	**In Central Storage**	**Total**	**Storage Unit**	**Total Cost**
	Col. 1	Col. 2	Col. 3	Col. 4	Col. 5	Col. 6	Col. 7
Bar Vodka	750 ml	¾ + ¾	3	5		$8.45	
Bar Scotch	750 ml	¾ + ½	2	4		$9.90	
Bar Gin	750 ml	¼ + ¼	2	6		$8.70	
Bar Rum	750 ml	¾ + ¾	3	5		$7.40	

Problem 5

What is the inventory value of each of the following items at the end of the day? Assume that (1) all items are "A" items, (2) leftovers are returned to central inventory at the end of the work day, and (3) no products were received.

Item	Unit	Cost/Unit	Begin Inventory	Amount Issued	Amount Used	Ending Inventory	Cost
Shrimp	lb	$7.35	73 lb	22 lb	18 lb		
Ground Beef	lb	$2.45	60 lb	10 lb	10 lb		
Veal Patty	each	$1.12	29 ea	12 ea	10 ea		
Pork Chops	8 oz	$2.90	51 chops	15 chops 7 chops	16 chops		

Problem 6

What is the total cost of food issue requisition, given the following?

Item	Begin Inventory	Unit Cost	No. Units Issued	Total Cost
Tomato Paste	cs-6/#10	$39.95	1-5/6	
Canned Peaches	cs-6/#10	$28.40	2-4/6	
Canned Green Beans	cs-6/#10	$21.70	3	
Tomato Juice	cs-12/#303	$42.50	7/12	

Chapter 8 Outline

Competencies

1. Analyze trends to estimate food production requirements, and use the weighted time series method to estimate food production requirements. (pp. 257–262)

2. Describe the importance and function of food production planning. (pp. 262–265)

3. Identify important control procedures for food and beverage production areas. (pp. 265–271)

4. Identify important control procedures for food and beverage service areas. (pp. 271–275)

5. Describe how technology affects the service control system and discuss POS equipment, order entry devices, and printers. (pp. 275–287)

6. Describe the features and functions of an automated beverage control system. (pp. 287–292)

8

Production and Serving Controls

Guest satisfaction depends directly on production and serving, and these control points are in many ways the most important and among the most complex. Production must ensure quality while complying with cost limitations. And serving, an art much like acting, requires proper timing, accuracy, and a host of other talents to provide a dining experience that will please guests.

Production and serving involve many more activities (and many more employees) than other control points, and the activities reviewed in this chapter demonstrate how food and beverage operations depend on people. Labor-saving equipment has not replaced people in many hospitality tasks. In food production and serving, it is difficult to separate the tasks of managing and controlling from personnel supervision.

As managers develop control procedures for production and serving, they must consider the direct impact that operating/control problems will likely have on guests. As managers plan control procedures for purchasing, receiving, storing, and issuing, it is sometimes easy (but certainly not right) to forget about the guests being served. However, managers who attempt to control their operations without considering guest response and reaction will fail to control effectively, and the organization will not be successful.

Production Planning

Production planning is the first step toward ensuring quality products and dining experiences that meet or exceed guest expectations. Production actually comprises three control points: preparing, cooking, and holding. Personnel with these responsibilities are accountable for the wholesomeness, goodness, and attractiveness of the foods and beverages served to guests. Even though the cost and quality of foods and beverages may have been expertly controlled before their arrival at production centers, control procedures to guide management and staff through production and serving are still central.

Production planning involves getting ready for production. Operations of all sizes must plan for production if they are to have food and beverage products, personnel, and equipment available when needed. Planned coordination among departments also prevents under- or overutilization of resources. While planning does not guarantee that all problems will be eliminated, it addresses many that may have serious economic and marketing consequences. Success, in most instances, correlates with successful planning.

Exhibit 1   Consolidated System Menu Item Sales Summary

Weekly Consolidated System Menu Item Sales Summary
Subtotal By Family Group
Mike Rose Cafe - Beltsville, MD

NEAL MAHAFFEY

Sunday   Friday
From : 09/22   To : 09/27

		Sales Qty	% of Ttl	Net Sales	% of Ttl			Sales Qty	% of Ttl	Net Sales	% of Ttl
						1012	CRAB DIP	151	14.49%	1,019.25	15.07%
1002	BROC/CHEESE	40	3.84%	186.00	2.75%						
						1013	BBQ SHRIMP APP	42	4.03%	287.70	4.25%
1003	QUESADILLA	13	1.25%	74.75	1.11%						
						1014	LOADED SKINS	75	7.20%	446.25	6.60%
1004	CHIX FINGER APP	111	10.65%	704.85	10.42%						
						1015	TAQUITOS	18	1.73%	107.10	1.58%
1005	WHITE PIZZA	20	1.92%	139.00	2.06%						
						1016	WINGS	236	22.65%	1,404.20	20.76%
1007	ULTIMATE NACHC	29	2.78%	172.55	2.55%						
						1017	DOUBLE WINGS	45	4.32%	492.75	7.29%
1008	SUPER COMBO	80	7.68%	716.00	10.59%	Total APPS		1,042	100.00%	6,763.40	100.00%
							Grand Total	1,042		6,763.40	
							- Other Disc			-1192.14	
1009	FRIED MOZZ	87	8.35%	430.65	6.37%		Net Sales Total			5,571.26	
1010	CHIX NACHOS	38	3.65%	226.10	3.34%						
1011	SPINACH DIP	57	5.47%	356.25	5.27%						

MI_S102.RPT

Page 1

Courtesy of MICROS Systems, Inc., Columbia, Maryland (www.micros.com).

Each food and beverage operation must develop specific procedures for production planning that are suited to its own unique needs. However, a typical strategy is to first forecast production requirements and then translate those requirements into production plans.

Forecasting Production Requirements

Quantities of products required for expected production activities during an upcoming week or other planning period must be estimated. These projections typically include sales history information. A careful analysis of previous unit sales can help control production quantities and reduce leftovers. Seasons, weather, special events within the community, and similar factors also affect production estimates. These must be taken into account in forecasting production requirements during planning sessions.[1]

Sales history records can tally sales by the hour (a frequent tactic in quick-service properties), meal periods, days, or other time periods. Commonly used is a technique that generates sales history data each day of the week. Data can be derived from guest check tallies (manual system) or, increasingly, from cumulative sales from electronic cash register/point-of-sale (ECR/POS) systems (daily sales summed for a specified period such as a week or month). Exhibit 1 shows a sales history (summary) that has been tallied for a week. This example is a subtotal for appetizers. Similar data is available for all other categories of food items offered by the restaurant. Note that the exhibit shows for all appetizers:

- The total quantity sold during the week.

- The percentage of all appetizers sold, represented by each type of appetizer.

- Net sales (revenues) generated from the sales of each appetizer.

- The percentage of net sales (revenues) from the sale of all appetizers represented by each type of appetizer.

Managers and chefs can use this sales data to help estimate sales for the next planning period.

Another forecasting technique involves comparing sales data for the past month and a selected number of months from the past year. As shown in Exhibit 2, the total number of each appetizer (selected items shown for illustrative purposes) sold in January (top line) and July (second line), February (top line) and August (second line), etc. is shown. The total unit sales and sales mix (last two columns) are also shown. Note that appetizer 1 (cup of the day [soup]) represents unit sales of 1,793 (15.85 percent of all appetizers sold) for January through September. Using sales data applicable to several (or more) months allows many variables to "average out" for production forecasting purposes. In addition, this data is very helpful input for menu revisions; managers wish to sell popular items and remove those that are unpopular.

Computers can be very useful in the projection of production requirements. Electronic files can store historical data, and computer software can be developed to apply these records for future use. Computer systems typically employ time series analysis to make necessary calculations.

Time series analysis allows for weighting of historic data with respect to its recency. This forecasting method assigns more importance (weight) to recent occurrences (trends). In other words, if we are attempting to forecast how many prime rib dinners will be ordered this Saturday night, we could base our projection on data from five previous Saturdays. For purposes of this example, assume weights of 5, 4, 3, 2, and 1 for the prior Saturdays, with 5 representing the most recent Saturday. Last Saturday 220 portions were sold; the previous week, 200; before that, 110; before that, 200; and prior to that, 150. To project this Saturday's portions, follow these steps:

1. Multiply each week's number of portions sold by its respective weight, and total the values:

$$(220 \times 5) + (200 \times 4) + (110 \times 3) + (200 \times 2) + (150 \times 1) = 2,780$$

2. Divide the computed total by the sum of its weights. This will yield the weighted projection:

$$\frac{2,780}{5 + 4 + 3 + 2 + 1} = \frac{2,780}{15} = 185.3$$

Time series analysis projects that approximately 185 portions will be consumed this Saturday. The computer may develop its forecasted projections based

Exhibit 2   Gross Menu Item Sales Analysis: Nine-Month Period

RUN DATE 10/30/XX   PAGE 1
TIME 14:09   GROSS SALES ANALYSIS   VERSION 3.22d
STORE # 1   Volume Detail for All Depts
                                  SEP25–30 20XX   SALES REPORT 12

MENU ITEMS	JAN/ JULY	FEB/ AUG	MAR/ SEP	APR/ OCT	MAY/ NOV	JUNE/ DEC	TOTAL	MIX%
Apps								
1 Cup of day	242.00	244.00	237.00	174.00	188.00	157.00		
	168.00	215.00	168.00				1793.00	15.85
2 Bowl of day	38.00	30.00	26.00	21.00	25.00	25.00		
	25.00	30.00	25.00				245.00	2.17
5 Sbakd fr. onion	57.00	37.00	43.00	38.00	49.00	58.00		
	51.00	67.00	49.00				449.00	3.97
7 Lgbakd fr. onion	14.00	9.00	13.00	15.00	10.00	9.00		
	14.00	22.00	10.00				116.00	1.03
11 Cupsoup subst	38.00	23.00	33.00	17.00	28.00	24.00		
	14.00	37.00	24.00				238.00	2.10
12 Bowlsoup subst	3.00	1.00		1.00				
		1.00	2.00				8.00	0.07
26 Portobello stix				1.00				
							1.00	0.01
27 Smked salmon				2.00				
							2.00	0.02
28 Hamburger								
		100.00	24.00				124.00	1.10
30 Cup soup		2.00		2.00				
							4.00	0.04
31 Calamari		2.00		2.00				
							4.00	0.04
40 Bowl soup					1.00			
							1.00	0.01
41 Shrmp cktl		1.00		1.00	1.00			
							3.00	0.03
50 Portobello stix								
		1.00	1.00				2.00	0.02
51 Shrimp cocktail								
	3.00	6.00	5.00				14.00	0.12
56 Shrimp cocktail			6.00	6.00	5.00	25.00		
	27.00	17.00	6.00				92.00	0.81
60 Fruit cup								
			1.00				1.00	0.01
65 Chicken skewers	8.00	7.00	5.00	6.00	6.00	11.00		
	8.00	12.00	7.00				70.00	0.62
67 Coleslaw						3.00		
	3.00	2.00					8.00	0.07
68 Portobello stick	5.00	5.00	20.00	11.00	8.00	8.00		
	17.00	1.00					75.00	.66
104 Smked salmon	11.00	17.00	10.00	5.00	5.00	9.00		
	20.00	14.00	9.00				100.00	0.88

Courtesy of the University Club, Michigan State University, East Lansing, Michigan.

Technology Helps with Production Planning

As is true with manual systems used to forecast production requirements, automated planning systems begin by generating and analyzing sales history information. Point-of-sales systems can collect unit sales information on any historical period, such as by day of the week for the past six weeks, the last three years' college homecoming weekends, or the last three months. Information can also be summed for any length of time within that historical period, such as by the hour, meal period, day, or week. Data for the historical period can be separated by outlet (such as a hotel with several dining venues) or by unit (as in the case of a multi-unit organization). Sales data can be based on total units sold or on average number of units sold during the time period.

After the historical sales data is reviewed, a forecast of future sales based on the historical benchmark can be made. This will yield the estimated number of portions of each menu item to be sold during the period for which plans are being developed. Some systems use spreadsheet technology, which enables the planner to easily modify the estimated number of portions to be sold and, therefore, the estimated revenue to be generated. For example, a property may be gearing up for a Saturday night prime rib promotion, and the number of unit sales for this item is expected to be well above the average for the previous periods analyzed. Some systems allow managers to modify sales forecasts by additional factors such as quantities of items needed for off-site catering and on-site operations.

As a result of this data analysis, managers can finalize their sales forecasts. It is then possible to consider the profitability of each item for the planning period. Kitchen management software can easily and quickly calculate profitability on a by-menu-item and total-sales basis by multiplying the estimated number of items to be sold by the item's food cost (from precosted standard recipes). It also calculates estimated revenues by multiplying the number of items sold by each item's selling price. The difference between total selling price and total food cost represents the estimated contribution margin from the sale of each item and from the sales of all items. Some software programs even conduct a pre-sale menu engineering analysis that, based on forecasted sales, reflects the profitability/popularity status of each item. This type of analysis can help planners to identify, before the planning period even begins, those items requiring special attention if planning is on target.

When sales forecasts are completed, production planners know the total number of items to be produced and, therefore, the quantities of ingredients that will need to be requisitioned and purchased. For example, the quantity of ground beef that will be needed to produce all menu items using ground beef can be determined, based on the number of portions the planner believes will be sold. This amount can be compared to quantities currently available in storage, and additional quantities needed, if any, will be known. A shopping list of ingredients to be purchased can be generated and the ingredients can be ordered using manual or computerized purchasing systems.

on stored data, manually inputted data, or data transferred from an ECR/POS system. Its output can also be helpful in developing purchase order requirements and forecasting labor needs and for providing additional assistance to management.

Exhibit 3   Sample Equipment Schedule

Equipment Schedule: Banquet															
Time: **Equipment Available:**	2:00	2:15	2:30	2:45	3:00	3:15	3:30	3:45	4:00	4:15	4:30	4:45	5:00	5:15	5:30
Convection Oven															
1							Bake Batch #1			Bake Batch #2			Buns		
2							Bake Batch #1			Bake Batch #2			Buns		
Electric Oven															
1							Bake Batch #1			Bake Batch #2				Buns	
2							Bake Batch #1			Bake Batch #2				Buns	
3							Bake Batch #1			Bake Batch #2				Buns	
Gas Range													Buns*		
60 Qt. Mixer (2 Bowls)	Mix Batch #2				Mix Buns										
Proof Box															
1		Pan, Proof Batch #1						Pan, Proof Buns							
2				Pan, Proof Batch #2											
Dough Divider							Hamburger Buns								

*Depending upon the number of buns per 18" × 26" pans, there may be as many as four pans that cannot be baked by 5:30. Should this occur, they are panned, stacked, and refrigerated. The following morning they can be proofed and baked before ovens are in full use. Desserts prepared on the prior day may need to be baked at this time also.

Computer forecasts are performed quickly and accurately, which increases their value to the operation.

Formulating Production Plans

Regularly scheduled planning meetings should be held with personnel most directly involved with production activities attending. For example, in a small operation, the manager and head cook may meet every Wednesday to review production plans for the week beginning on Friday or Saturday.

During these meetings, estimates of production needs derived from a study of sales histories and similar information must be adjusted and converted into production plans. Sales history records using data from manual or computer tallies can be used to produce a planning sheet. Food production personnel can then determine the amount of each menu item ingredient to purchase. Automated systems make these calculations electronically, prepare shopping lists and, if desired, even generate purchase orders for supplies.

Other matters must be considered at the production planning meeting. Based on the estimated production needs, labor and equipment can be scheduled at this meeting. For example, perhaps a special catered event requires items to be produced in especially large quantities. The sample equipment schedule shown in Exhibit 3 relates how to use existing equipment to produce a large quantity of bread products for a special banquet.

Exhibit 4   Special Event Notice

Special Event Notice			
Event: _____			
Date: _____		Date of Notice: _____	
No. of Guests: _____			
Special Requirements: _____			
Authorizing Official: _____			
The following items are needed for the above event:			

Item	Purchase Unit	Quantity	Estimated Price

After the production planning meeting, the required number of each menu item for the forecast period is known. Therefore, food issue requisition forms for some days or items also can be partially completed. For catered events, it is possible that these requisition forms might be completed in their entirety if these costs are charged to a separate revenue center.

Production Planning and Food Purchasing

Typically, food purchase decisions are not made during production planning sessions. Perishable products are normally purchased several times weekly according to forecasted needs. Non-perishable items can be purchased according to a minimum/maximum inventory system that takes into account normal usage rates.

When these inventory/ordering systems are used, specific purchase decisions need not be based on normal fluctuations in the number of guests expected. Since these purchase decisions are based on typical usage rates, the experience factor is incorporated into the procedures for estimating purchase quantities.

The number of guests estimated during production planning meetings is important when making purchase decisions for banquet functions. These activities may greatly increase the quantity of items needed, or may require special products not normally carried in inventory. It is important, then, that there be effective communication between planners and purchasers. Although specific procedures will vary, a good policy is to provide purchasing staff with two weeks' notice of special events that will significantly increase the number of meals served or that have special purchase requirements. A special event notice (Exhibit 4) can be used to inform purchasing personnel about special purchasing requirements.

Exhibit 5   What about Convenience Foods?

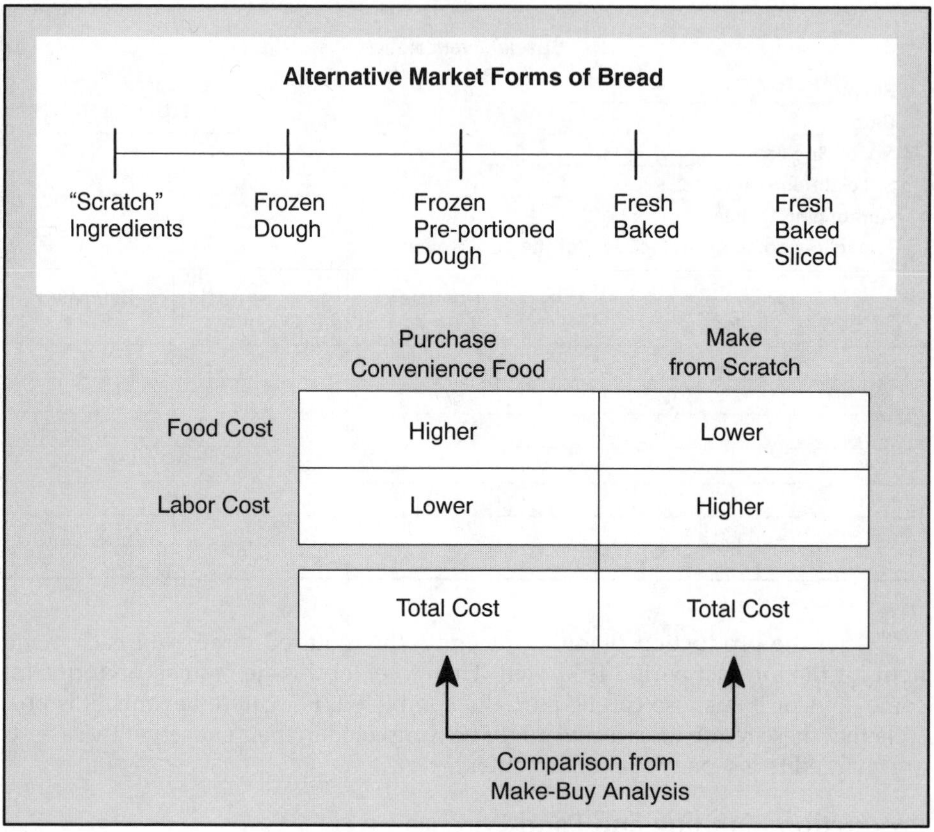

Alternative Market Forms of Bread

| "Scratch" Ingredients | Frozen Dough | Frozen Pre-portioned Dough | Fresh Baked | Fresh Baked Sliced |

	Purchase Convenience Food	Make from Scratch
Food Cost	Higher	Lower
Labor Cost	Lower	Higher
	Total Cost	Total Cost

Comparison from
Make-Buy Analysis

Production Planning: Convenience Foods

Convenience foods are items with some or all of the labor built into them that would otherwise need to be provided on-site. Typically, the use of convenience foods is not an "all or nothing" decision. Rather, it is necessary to conduct a make-buy analysis to determine whether items should be produced on-site or purchased in a readily available convenience food alternative. Let's look, for example, at the Apple Jack Restaurant, which offers bread on its menu. Exhibit 5 illustrates how bread can be purchased. It can be made from scratch; the operation can purchase the flour, shortening, yeast, sugar, salt, and other ingredients needed to bake bread on-site. Alternatively, frozen dough can be purchased and pre-portioned before proofing and baking. A third alternative, frozen dough pre-portioned in the correct weight, also is available. Bread can also be purchased fresh-baked or fresh-baked and sliced. With so many options, how should an operation needing bread make the best decision?

Exhibit 5 also illustrates the relationship between food costs and labor costs when convenience foods are used. Managers expect food costs to be higher when convenience foods are used because of extra processing costs incurred by the manufacturer. These costs are offset, either wholly or partially, by reduced on-site labor costs. Conversely, when items are prepared on-site (from scratch), food costs are expected to be lower, because these extra processing steps are not performed by the manufacturer. However, on-site labor costs will then be higher, because labor hours not needed when the convenience food is used *will* be needed for on-site production. This points out the importance of taking into account the total cost (food cost plus labor cost) of both alternatives when making a make-buy analysis.

A make-buy analysis allows the operator to first assess the quality of each alternative and consider the costs associated with acceptable alternatives. Quality should always be the first consideration; if a convenience food meeting the necessary quality levels is not available, there are only two alternatives: prepare the item on-site or do not offer it on the menu.

Managers must address another concern when evaluating the use of convenience foods. Suppose the manager decides that significant labor savings are possible if hamburger patties are purchased pre-portioned rather than in the current bulk package that requires on-site portioning. A careful study may determine that the labor hours saved more than offset the higher cost of the pre-portioned patties; savings can result if pre-portioned products are purchased. However, unless the labor hours that will be saved are actually eliminated from the schedule, the labor cost will remain the same, food costs will increase, and the manager will not realize the forecasted savings. All too often, labor savings "on paper" are not realized in the kitchen, and negative financial consequences arise.

Special Beverage Production Planning Requirements

It is important to maintain adequate bar par inventory levels and establish an effective minimum/maximum beverage purchase and inventory system for central storage areas. When these systems are used, little production planning is normally needed for beverage products. Therefore, much of the preceding discussion of production planning procedures does not relate specifically to beverage production. With regard to beverage operations, production planning generally focuses on employee scheduling and expediting. **Expediting** is frequently necessary to maintain constant supplies of some brand liquors and required wines. A special event notice (Exhibit 4) is quite helpful whenever planners deem that special event circumstances will affect purchase and inventory requirements for beverages.

Production Control

You have learned that food and beverage control begins with the menu. The menu dictates what items are to be prepared and is a major marketing tool that describes the plan for meeting or exceeding guests' expectations.

Many books have been written about managing food and beverage products during production. In them are discussions about the details of menu planning, equipment, layout, and design; personnel management; principles of food production; and other topics related to production activities. At some level, all these discussions deal with controlling products during production. In this chapter, we focus on several basic management concerns that are at the core of controlling the production process.

Quality Requirements

Managers must consider quality requirements in several different ways. These range from the detailed quality requirements of specific operating standards to the general perspectives of management policy and guest expectations. It is important to remember that control procedures must enhance the operation's ability to meet its required standards.

Control during production begins with meeting established operating standards. These include using standard food purchase specifications, standard recipes, standard yields, standard portion sizes, standard portion costs for food production, and standard glass and ice sizes for beverage production. These control tools provide procedures for uniformly purchasing, producing, and serving products that meet quality requirements. Likewise, standard operating procedures (SOPs) dictate quality standards when, for example, they describe how to thaw frozen products, evaluate convenience foods, and develop production plans.

In more general terms, quality requirements are reflected in the property's marketing plans and strategies. Some managers may wish to serve an inexpensive hamburger of minimal quality. Others might offer an inexpensive but high-quality hamburger. Still others attempt to meet a need for "a hamburger dining experience" and offer gourmet hamburgers. Marketing position statements, operating goals, and management philosophies all express requirements to be built into the control system. Management must use control procedures to ensure that the property's plans, based on guests' needs and desires, are attained.

Even though operators may not have formally evaluated marketing concerns or established written operating standards, their properties still have quality requirements. For example, many chefs are concerned that only the finest products be served. Managers want to be proud of all items being served. Over time, these implicit standards are revealed to observant and returning guests. Also, the chefs and managers become role models as they consistently emphasize the importance of meeting quality standards.

A property's history also shapes the level of quality that guests will perceive as adequate and come to expect. The status quo ("how we've always done things") often influences how things will be done in the future. In this situation it is difficult to reduce quality standards and to increase quality requirements. Quality is not a fixed standard; it evolves as market expectations change. Guests have expectations of the food and beverage operation. Successful food and beverage managers know their guests' quality standards. They train and **empower** their staff to address and, it is hoped, to exceed the guests' wants and needs.

Maintaining Standards

You've learned that control during production starts with meeting established operating standards. Food and beverage cost standards are guides to planned or expected results and cannot be developed until standard cost control tools are in use in production areas. Several factors—training, information, tools and equipment, and supervision—make it possible for employees to comply with production standards.

Standard Recipes as Production Tools

Standard recipes are critical for an operation's control system. When they are developed and consistently followed, product costs can be estimated realistically. Standard recipes are the foundation for establishing budgeting and menu pricing procedures.

Standard recipes specify the ingredients and applicable quantities and help determine the required amount of production time. If an employee closely follows the procedures outlined in a standard recipe, it should be possible to predict the time required to produce a given number of menu items.

Properly developed standard recipes can also help define effective work practices. They can remind cooks to select all necessary pots, pans, and other utensils on one trip to the pot and pan rack; they can also suggest when production equipment should be turned on and off, which can yield energy savings. Safety considerations can also be built into standard recipes. For example, recipes can warn employees not to open a vertical cutter mixer until the blade has stopped or remind them to set the wheel brakes on mobile equipment.

Planners should have standard recipes readily available during planning sessions, and supervisors should confirm that standard recipes are consistently used by all food and beverage production personnel.

Training. Employees must understand the standards. Training programs for new staff and ongoing professional development sessions for experienced workers are needed. Seasoned employees often forget about, or find shortcuts to, operating procedures. New menu items, new equipment, and revised procedures are among the numerous everyday changes that point to the need for ongoing training for all staff members.

Information. Information must be available at workstations. For example, standard recipes can be put together into readily available files or books for reference. When computerized systems are in place, recipes can be printed out and placed in workstations daily. Portion sizes should also be posted in production areas. Photographs of food items can be posted in food preparation areas (in manual systems) or printed directly on the recipe (in automated systems).

Tools and Equipment. Tools and equipment needed for food production must be available to staff members so that they can follow the standards. It does little good if a standard recipe calls for six ounces of an ingredient and an accurate portion scale is not available (or not used, if one is available). Likewise, if a recipe requires portioning with a number 8 scoop, compliance is impossible unless the operation has a number 8 scoop on hand (a number 8 scoop yields 8 level servings per quart). Operating and control problems will result if proper equipment is unavailable or is improperly used. Suppose a bar recipe specifies a certain glass for a highball. What does the bartender do when, during a rush, not enough of the specified glasses are available? Incorrect substitutions can jeopardize the control system, and, in this example, the manager, not the bartender, has created the problem.

Supervision. Management must routinely supervise personnel to ensure compliance with all production and serving control requirements. Managers must be alert to and watchful of production practices. Food and beverage managers must be able to perform more than one task at a time. For example, when walking past the bar on the way to the office, the manager can observe whether the bartender is using a shot glass or a jigger in preparing a drink. When passing a table in the dining room or the serving line in the kitchen, the manager can quickly judge the portion size of an entrée, even though there may be other important concerns at the moment.

Production Cost Control Procedures

Food production involves preparing, cooking, and holding. The purpose of production controls is to ensure quality while complying with cost limitations. What follows are some general cost control procedures:

- Require that all standard cost control tools be used consistently.

- Issue food items only in those amounts needed to meet production requirements forecasted on the basis of past sales data adjusted by current factors, including scheduled special events.

- Ensure that all personnel are trained in and constantly follow food production procedures.

- Minimize food waste through continuous improvement. How are salad greens processed? How is meat trimmed and cut? Can these processes be improved?

- Use the proper quality items. For example, if the property uses both canned whole and diced tomatoes, select the correct type for the recipe being prepared.

- Monitor employee eating and drinking practices. If a long-stem maraschino cherry costs 6 cents and each shrimp costs 20 cents, an employee working with one hand and eating with the other can quickly raise food costs. (This problem is in addition to obvious violations of established sanitation practices that prohibit employees from eating at their workstations.)

- Put unused food items withdrawn from storage back in storage (where there will be tighter control), and reissue the products when necessary. Make sure that food inventory forms are properly adjusted.

- Require that no food item be discarded without prior approval of management. This applies to items spoiled in storage as well as items improperly prepared.

- Compare issue and production records with sales records to assess the extent to which issued products generate revenue. For example, portion-controlled steaks can be issued to the workstation on the basis of production estimates for a particular shift. At the end of the work shift, compare the number of steaks sold (from the ECR/POS system sales data) with the number of steaks available in the workstation. After adjusting for any overcooked and returned steaks, the remaining steaks can be accounted for and returned to secure storage. (Perpetual inventory records, if used, can then be adjusted accordingly.)

- Look for production bottlenecks during busy periods and resolve them. Often the staff involved will have ideas about how to improve procedures and reduce costs.

- Be sure measuring and weighing tools and equipment are always used to prepare food and beverage items. Make sure staff use portion-control tools (such as scoops and ladles) when portioning food items for service.

- Carefully study the systems that manage equipment, facility layout and design, and energy usage. Management of these resources is important and has an impact on overall profitability.

- Recognize the importance of communication and coordination among work sections and departments when developing and implementing plans.

- Keep records during production to help guide further planning and to provide data for accounting use. The design of recordkeeping systems, their accuracy, and the timeliness of information and reports all have control implications.

- Be sure labor-saving convenience food or equipment is actually saving labor. Labor costs must decrease at least enough to cover the increased food or equipment costs. If not, food or equipment costs will be higher and profits will be lower than before the labor-saving food or equipment was purchased.

- Be sure production employees understand the principles of food preparation and can apply or modify them to meet quantity food production needs of the operation. Food preparation principles and resulting quality control are basically the same, whatever the quantity of food prepared. However, procedures for handling and processing large volumes of food are different.

- The cooks and managers must have a genuine concern for and appreciation of good food to apply quality control principles. Look for personnel genuinely concerned about preparing and offering the highest quality food products possible within the property's standards.

- Accurately complete leftover reports and use them to fine-tune the quantities of items prepared. Use leftovers creatively. However, remember that quality decreases over time, such as when hot items are held for service, cooled, stored, and then reheated. In addition, there are sanitation concerns that override cost control considerations. Potentially hazardous leftovers can create sanitation problems if improperly handled and re-served. Balance controlling food costs with maintaining established food quality levels.

Special Beverage Cost Control Procedures

Many control concerns in food production also apply to beverage production. Certainly, maintaining quality and cost standards is just as important. However, there are specific cost control procedures for beverage production:

- Use standard beverage recipes. Through supervision, ensure that required beverage production procedures are consistently followed. Make sure that the proper amounts of preparation ingredients are portioned into the proper glass with the proper amount and size of ice.

What about Equipment Technology?

Technology has improved the equipment used in food production. Deep-fryer baskets can be programmed to raise products from frying fat after a specified immersion time. Audio signals in the manager's office can notify him or her when there are problems with refrigerators or freezers. District managers can receive electronic reports about the maintenance needs of production equipment in geographically dispersed units. Vending route drivers can use wireless technology to determine product refill needs for vending machines before they leave their trucks, and equipment technicians can learn about vending machine repair needs directly from machine transmitters in remote locations.

When considering the purchase of such food and beverage equipment, of course, one should always make sure that the technology is worth more to the operation than it costs.

- Use portion-control tools such as shot glasses and jiggers. Automated beverage systems, which dispense measured quantities of alcoholic beverages, offer more control, but study is necessary to cost-justify the equipment's purchase. (This is reviewed later in this chapter.)

- Ensure that all beverage control procedures are being followed.

- Train beverage staff to produce drinks according to the property's quality and cost requirements.

- Bartenders, especially during rush periods, must be able to work quickly. Knowledge of work simplification principles and a properly designed bar significantly affect production volume.

- Encourage an attitude of concern for guests and other staff members among beverage staff.

- Control of employee eating and drinking practices requires special emphasis for the bar. Employees should not accept drinks from guests or from other staff members. Establish and enforce policies for employee conduct on and off the clock while at the property.

- Have returned drinks or "mistakes" saved for management review. An excessive number of such drinks is probably a sign that more training or a change in procedures is required.

- Lock bar par inventories when the bar is not in use.

- Compare the amount of beverages used based on issues to replace empty bottles with revenue generated and develop an actual beverage cost percentage. Use it as one basis for beverage control. Note that automated beverage dispensing systems interfaced with the POS system can perform this control task electronically for those beverages dispensed through the system.

- Hold the bartender responsible for cash.

- Hold the bartender responsible for behind-bar inventory. At the start of the shift, the manager and bartender can count all bottles to ensure that the required number of each type of beverage is available in inventory. A similar count of full and empty bottles at the end of the shift should show the bar par still complete.

- Ensure that adequate supplies of garnishes, drink mixes, paper supplies, and glassware are on hand to enhance production speed and efficiency. Establish procedures to estimate necessary quantities of these and related items according to sales forecasts.

Food Serving and Service

After food and beverage products are produced, they must be served to the guests. For the purposes of our discussion, we will define "serving" as moving the product from production staff to service staff, and "service" as transferring products from service staff to guests.

The serving activity is critical from a cost control standpoint because the responsibility for menu items transfers from kitchen/bar personnel to dining room/lounge or other service area personnel. This activity may enhance or detract from the quality of food and beverage products. Standards of service vary greatly with the type of establishment. Management is responsible for standardizing ordering procedures and serving procedures, sanitation practices, and personnel requirements. As with the other control points, the serving function requires sanitation, quality, and cost controls.

Food service assumes many forms today. Besides the traditional forms of table service found in many lodging and freestanding food service operations, other types of service are becoming increasingly popular in hospitality establishments. Each requires slightly different standards. For example, special functions and banquets are served differently than cooked-to-order meals. Also, when food products are prepared and transported to a catered event off the premises, product holding becomes a critical control point. Similarly, hotel room service and carry-out service can be profitable and safe if designed and executed properly.

The Server and the Guest

Control procedures are important to the relationship between the server and the guest. Fundamentally, guests' concerns dictate control procedures. The server must realize that the guest has needs, wants, desires, and expectations that must be addressed during the dining experience. Important components of dining, including timing, accuracy, merchandising, and work practices, affect guests' experience and satisfaction.

What do guests want? Among other things, they want courteous and attentive service, product information, cleanliness, and no problems. In addition:

- The serving process must be accurate; the right products must be delivered.

- Serving must be properly timed. At breakfast and lunch, this may mean faster service. At a leisurely dinner, timing means a proper flow of products and services throughout the meal, without awkward waits.

- Service staff must know the menu, the daily specials, the brands of beverages in stock, and the ingredients and production methods for the food and beverage products offered.

- Service staff must know how to properly serve. They must match guests with orders, and use standardized procedures for serving and removing food and beverages.

- Service staff must deal with people in a tactful, courteous, and friendly but professional manner while being helpful but not overbearing.

Ironically, service personnel are often the lowest paid and most poorly trained of all employees in a food and beverage operation. The high turnover rates among servers at many properties illustrate these points. However, from the guest's perspective, servers represent the property, and they may be the only employees with whom the guests come in contact. They represent management and the food service operation to the guests. The best plans and goals of management are often met (or not met) according to how the guest feels about the property, and this feeling is in large measure influenced by the service staff.

As with most other phases of food and beverage management, staff can think about how they would like to be treated if they visited the property as guests. The answer to this question may establish the parameters within which food and beverage service should operate.

Server Responsibilities

Food servers must meet and greet the guests. They are really the property's salespersons, using the most powerful in-house marketing tool—the menu—to please the guests and generate revenue for the property and, often, for themselves (in the form of tips). Following are several procedures that are basic to the control of the food and beverage service system.

Order-Taking and Placement. The correct order must be taken and served. Poor communication between service personnel and guests has the same consequences as poor communication between production and service staff: higher costs and guest dissatisfaction. Effective communication can be helped by such techniques as reviewing orders with guests and using the bin number, if available, rather than pronouncing difficult names of foreign wines. The use of POS technology, discussed later in this chapter, also helps to ensure the accuracy of order placement by servers. As already noted, servers must be prompt, courteous, and tactful while interacting with guests. Invariably, guests expect a certain quality of service relative to cost. If they are disappointed, revenues will be lost, guests will not return, and word-of-mouth reports will be negative.

Suggestive Selling. Servers should know which menu items to recommend—generally those with the higher contribution margins because they are more profitable for the property. (The contribution margin represents money used to cover other costs and to contribute to required profit levels after product cost is deducted from the selling price.) If, through suggestive selling techniques, a server sells a bottle of

---

Work Simplification in Action

Simplifying work practices can reduce labor costs and increase guest satisfaction. Many servers waste steps by walking to or from the dining room empty-handed or without trays. When refilling water glasses or coffee cups at one table, servers should do so for other guests who, invariably, will also ask for water or coffee refills a few moments later. Similarly, a server removing an empty glass from one table can remove used dishes from other tables on the way to the dish return area.

---

wine, an appetizer, or a dessert that guests would not have purchased otherwise, then all three parties benefit:

- Guests have enjoyed products that they otherwise might not have ordered.

- The server has increased the check size and, probably, the tip.

- The food and beverage operation has generated increased revenue.

General Service Procedures. Control procedures designed for food and beverage service systems must be correlated with the property's priorities and must constantly focus on the guest's concerns. For example, when the manager designs systems to ensure that all revenue is collected from all sales, lengthy procedures may result. Reducing the quality of guest service (speed, in this case) is not acceptable. Also, consider a beverage charge transfer system that transfers pre-meal beverage charges in the lounge to the dining room for payment at the end of the meal. This system may be cumbersome from the manager's perspective, but it might be implemented because guests appreciate the convenience it affords.[2]

How should the property handle these and similar situations involving concerns of both the property and the guest? Each property will find its own answer to this question, and resulting procedures will reflect the extent to which the manager's perspective of guest service is built into operating plans.

Since servers greatly influence guests' perceptions of the property, rules for service personnel must be developed and used. This information can be included in employee handbooks, and it may also be the basis for employee training sessions.

The food and beverage server must be alert to the guest's needs. If the guest seems in a hurry or wants a more leisurely dining experience, the server should react accordingly. Likewise, the server must know when to present the check (bill). If servers remain alert and cooperate, they can reduce the possibility of guests leaving without paying.

Servers and bartenders must make sure that they enter each food and beverage order onto guest checks or into the automated system and that they write or print clearly and comply with all in-house rules relating to product orders and revenue collection.

After guests leave, the tables must be cleared and reset quickly for other guests. Revenue is lost when tables are not occupied. Reservation systems depend on the ability to get tables ready quickly. Guests sitting next to soiled tables throughout their meal do not enjoy the atmosphere that management intends. For this and similar reasons, the front-of-the-house control system must pay close attention to ways that servers and dining room attendants prepare tables for reuse.

Service Control Factors

Service involves the activities of transferring products from serving staff to the guests. In a **public bar**, guests may order beverages directly from the bartender while they are sitting or standing at the bar. In a **service bar**, the bartender prepares drinks ordered by serving staff, who then serve the drinks to guests. In bars that function as both public and service bars, the bartender prepares drinks directly for guests as well as for servers to deliver to guests. The following paragraphs examine factors managers should consider when establishing service control procedures.

Timing of Service. Many aspects of food and beverage service must be taken into account when designing service control systems. Timing systems for placing orders are needed. At the same table, one guest may want a well-done filet mignon, while another wants a rare portion of prime rib. When should the order be turned in? What if these guests are in a hurry or, conversely, are lingering over a salad? Many things can happen to increase costs. For example, if the prime rib comes out medium instead of rare, it must be replaced. Complimentary meals or portions of meals may have to be given ("comped") to dissatisfied guests. Other guests may leave without paying because they are in a hurry and servers do not present the check in time. Therefore, procedures specifying time limits for specific orders, the sequence for turning in orders, and other server-related concerns are needed.

Staff Communication. Production and service staff must communicate effectively. Does "SP" on a guest check (manual system) or server note pad mean shrimp platter or seafood platter? Does the notation "martini" tell whether it is to be served with ice or straight up? Do service personnel know an item is sold out before placing an order for it? Communication problems increase costs and create dissatisfied guests. Such problems can be resolved, however, by requiring the use of specified abbreviations for food and beverage orders and constantly updating portions left and items sold out. **Workstation printers** help to avoid communication difficulties between production and service staff if order information is entered correctly.

Effects of Favoritism. Favoritism may disrupt service. For example, a production person (bartender or cook) may show favoritism toward a service employee. If one server receives orders out of sequence and before others, guests are affected; they are not concerned or interested in these inter-staff relationships.

Adequate Supplies. Backup supplies must be sufficient. Service, cost, and guest satisfaction are affected by the availability of food items or beverage mixes made in advance of actual production orders. Likewise, plates and glassware, disposable or washable guest supplies, and other materials must be available in the correct quantities. The common production term *"mise en place"* refers to the need to get ready; it applies to both front- and back-of-the-house areas. Serving plans must include supplying service areas such as buffet lines, banquet setups, and portable bars. Consider both the speed factor and the costs involved in using service areas. Excess labor may be needed to continually keep them supplied.

Temperature and Holding Time. Foods must be kept hot (above 135°F/57°C) or cold (below 41°F/5°C), as appropriate, until served. Not only is palatability (taste and appearance) affected, but poor sanitation practices can create other problems. Excessive holding times can result in reduced product quality and make the food item unservable. What could damage a food and beverage operation's reputation more than an outbreak of foodborne illness caused by food-holding equipment not being available or staff not trained to work safely and maintain cleanliness around foods?

Updated Job Descriptions. All staff members must clearly understand the exact duties of service personnel. Job descriptions listing required tasks, responsibilities, and other concerns for each position can accomplish this. Job descriptions are helpful management tools. Exhibit 6 shows a sample job description for a server in a coffee shop.

Food Appearance. Do not neglect food appearance. Food and beverages should look attractive when served. Creative garnishes, how food is placed on plates, and wiping plate rims to remove spilled sauce all influence appearance. The product's appearance and presentation influence the guests' perceptions of value and willingness to pay the prices set for menu items.

Expediters. Consider using a food expediter during busy serving times. An **expediter** helps communication between production and service personnel. This staff member (often a manager) controls the process of turning in orders and picking up food items. In some properties using manual systems, the food server turns in the order to the expediter, who enters the order into a time recorder to monitor production times. In other operations, the expediter manages the orders generated by a workstation printer. The expediter also resolves disputes about orders and calls out or gives order information to cooks or servers. The expediter can coordinate order pickups to help ensure that the entire order is ready at the same time and that the server picks up the complete order when it is ready. The expediter may also check portion size and appearance, ensure that all items on the server's tray have been entered into the revenue control system, and verify the prices of items (on manual guest checks). However, even when an expediter is used, the executive chef or kitchen manager still should have control over and responsibility for the quality and appearance of all food items served.

Technology and Service

As you've seen in our discussions about other control points, technology is available to provide significant assistance to managers as they develop and implement effective control systems. Automated systems also provide many ways to achieve control over the production-to-serving-to-service link.[3] These systems are composed of hardware and software designed for operational efficiency. Point-of-sale (POS) system terminals are connected to local and workstation printers to form a communication network between production work areas and service stations. The server enters a food or beverage order through a terminal that, in turn, relays the recorded items to the proper workstation for preparation.

Exhibit 6   Sample Job Description for a Coffee Shop Server

JOB TITLE: Coffee Shop Server

IMMEDIATE SUPERVISOR: Coffee Shop Manager

JOB SUMMARY:

Assists coffee shop guests, takes their orders, and serves them immediately when orders are prepared. When guests have departed, quickly cleans and resets tables. Responsible for knowing the menu items, prices, and daily specials. Must perform side work as required.

DUTIES:

Greets guests at assigned tables or dining counter, gives them menus, and pours water. When guests are ready, takes order. Places food orders with kitchen personnel; portions and serves nonalcoholic beverage orders. Serves food orders immediately when prepared.

Watches assigned tables carefully to anticipate guests' needs; checks back with guests regularly for additional orders or requests. When guests complete courses, removes used cutlery and dishes. Presents menu so that guests may order dessert; presents check when guests have been served their final orders.

Places dishes and cutlery removed from the guests' tables in proper bus trays.

Wipes table clean and dries it; decrumbs chair seats; resets table with placemats, cutlery wrapped in a napkin, and glassware; places condiments in proper place.

Side work such as stocking condiments, filling salt and pepper shakers, and organizing side stands is done as needed by server during shift. At end of shift, all condiments should be completely full.

SPECIFICATIONS AND PREREQUISITES:

Requires a basic knowledge of composition of food and beverage items on menu as well as menu prices.

Requires familiarity with daily specials and proper table cleaning and setting procedures. Must be able to speak and write basic English.

SKILLS:

Must have the special skills necessary to make guests feel welcome, must have legible handwriting and basic mathematical skills, must be able to operate the point-of-sale system, and provide courteous, efficient service.

PHYSICAL:

Must be neat in appearance, possess a pleasant personality, and be able to carry loaded service trays.

Computerized systems ensure that no food or beverage items are produced unless they have first been recorded (accounted for) in a pre-check file. The elimination of the need for servers to physically turn in guest checks for orders to kitchen personnel or bartenders helps assure management that production will not begin without a sale being entered into the property's revenue and cost management systems. Automated systems enable managers to randomly review guest checks while in process by using the **open check file**. This helps managers verify that items ordered are in fact being served and that revenues from their sale will be collected and accounted for.

POS Technology

Some properties use an **electronic cash register (ECR)** to generate sales information. An ECR is an independent (stand-alone) computer system. This means that all required hardware components are located in the same unit. The register's keyboard serves as an input device, the operator display unit provides output, and the storage (memory) unit and central processor are located within the terminal housing. Therefore, an ECR is a complete computer that does not need to be connected to any other device to function.

A **point-of-sale (POS) terminal**, on the other hand, contains its own input/ output units and may even possess a small storage (memory) capacity, but it does not contain its own central processing unit. To process POS transactions, the terminal must be connected to a central processing unit located outside the terminal unit. Since the central processing unit is the most expensive component of a computer system, increasingly food service properties are reducing the cost of automation by interfacing several POS terminals located throughout the restaurant and lounge areas with one large central processing unit.

Because ECR and POS devices are generally sold as modular units, all components except the basic terminal are considered optional equipment. The cash drawer is no exception. Management may choose not to have a cash drawer at all, or to have several cash drawers connected to a single register. Multiple cash drawers may enhance management's cash control system when several cashiers or bartenders work at the same register during the same shift. Each employee can be assigned a separate cash drawer so that, at the end of the shift, cash drawer receipts can be individually accounted for.

A terminal without a cash drawer is commonly referred to as a **pre-check terminal**. Pre-check terminals are used to enter orders, not to settle accounts. For example, a server can use a pre-check terminal located in the dining room to relay orders to the appropriate kitchen and bar production areas but generally cannot use this device for guest check settlement. An ECR/POS device with a cash drawer is commonly referred to as a **cashier terminal**. This device can normally handle both pre-checking and cashiering functions.

In addition to terminals, food service computer systems generally require hardware components for order entry and output devices for printing.

Order Entry Devices

Order entry devices include traditional POS terminals, touchscreen terminals, hand-held server terminals, and self-service terminals (kiosks). Historically, the most common order entry device has been the keyboard, but touchscreen terminals are now replacing them in even relatively small operations.

Traditional POS Terminals. A traditional POS terminal consists of a keyboard and monitor. Two primary types of keyboard surfaces are micro-motion and reed style. The micro-motion design has a flat, spill-resistant mask. Reed styling involves

Exhibit 7   Sample Menu Keyboard

CARAFE WHITE WINE	CARAFE RED WINE	BOURBON	VODKA	DECAF COFFEE	COFFEE	SALAD	BAKED POTATO	HASH BROWNS	FRENCH FRIES	SOUR CREAM	TIME IN
CARAFE ROSE WINE	SCOTCH	SODA	WATER	BLOODY MARY	TEA	WITH	WITHOUT	BREAD	STEWED TOMATO	VEGETAB	TIME OUT
RARE	GIN	TONIC	COLA	SCREWDRIVER	MILK	HOUSE DRESS	FRENCH DRESS	VINEGAR & OIL	EXTRA BUTTER	MUSHRM SAUCE	ACCOUNT #
MEDIUM	WELL	SAUTEED MUSHRMS	SHRIMP COCKTAIL	FRENCH ONION SOUP	CRAB MEAT COCKTAIL	OYSTERS ON 1/2 SHELL	ITALIAN DRESS	BLEU CHEESE DRESS	COUPON 1	COUPON 2	COUPON 3
PRIME RIB	T-BONE	SHRIMP	LOBSTER	CIGARS	CASH BAR	CLEAR	ERROR CORRECT	CANCEL TRANS	CHECK TRANSFER	PAID OUT	TIPS PAID OUT
CHATEAU-BRIAND	FILET	CLAMS	TROUT	CANDY	SERVER #	TRAN CODE	SCREEN	NO SALE	CASHIER #	EMPL DISC	MGR DISC
TOP SIRLOIN 16 OZ	TOP SIRLOIN 12 OZ	SEA BASS	SCALLOPS	SNACKS	VOID ITEM	7	8	9	QUANTITY	ADD CHECK	CREDIT CARD 2
PORTER-HOUSE	CHOPPED SIRLOIN	OYSTERS	ALASKAN KING CRAB	# PERSONS ADD ON	REVERSE RECEIPT	4	5	6	VOID TRANS	CHARGE TIPS	CREDIT CARD 1
STEAK & CHICKEN	SURF & TURF	RED SNAPPER	SEA FOOD PLATTER	DINING ROOM SERVICE	PRICE LOOK UP	1	2	3	NEW CHECK	CASH BAR TOTAL	CHARGE
LEG OF LAMB	ROAST DUCK	PORK CHOPS	CHICKEN LIVERS	LOUNGE SERVICE	MODE SWITCH	0	MENU 1	PREVIOUS BALANCE	CHECK TOTAL	CASH TEND	

liquid-proof keys raised along the keyboard's surface. Both keyboard designs are usually capable of supporting interchangeable menu boards.

A **menu board** overlays the keyboard surface and identifies the function performed by each key during a specific meal period (see Exhibit 7). Types of keyboard keys identified by a menu board include:

- Pre-set keys.
- Price look-up keys or screen icons.
- Modifier keys.
- Function keys.
- Settlement keys.
- Numeric keypad.

A **pre-set key**, which can be a name ("hamburger") or a drawing of the item, is programmed to access the price, descriptor, department code, tax, and inventory status for a specific menu item. Automatic menu pricing makes faster guest service possible and eliminates price and tax errors by servers during busy meal periods. The term "descriptor" refers to the abbreviated description of a menu item, such as SHRMPCKT for shrimp cocktail or PRIME for prime rib. A department code refers to the menu category to which the pre-set item belongs. Typical department codes are appetizer, entrée, and dessert.

Once a pre-set key is pressed, descriptions of the item and its price are retrieved from the system's memory and appear on the operator's monitor. This data may also be relayed with preparation instructions to the appropriate production station or be retained for later printing or printed on a guest check. In addition, the dollars represented by this transaction are retained for revenue reporting and the sales units are maintained to track inventory levels. Sales data information for individual items is important for guest check totaling and for producing management reports.

Because terminals generally have a limited number of pre-set keys, **price look-up (PLU) keys** are used to supplement pre-set keys. Price look-up keys operate similarly to pre-set keys, except that they require the user to identify a menu item by its reference code number (up to five digits) rather than by its name or descriptor. For example, if a server wants to record the sale of a cheeseburger and there is no pre-set key for that item, the server must enter the code number for cheeseburgers (706, for example) and press the PLU key. Once activated, PLU keys perform the same functions as pre-set keys.

Modifier keys allow servers to relay preparation instructions (such as rare, medium, or well-done for a steak) to remote workstation printers or monitors located in food and beverage production areas. Typically, a server enters the item ordered and then presses the appropriate preparation modifier key. Modifier keys can also be used to alter menu item prices. For example, they may be useful to a restaurant that sells house wine by the carafe and half-carafe. Instead of tying up one pre-set key for carafes and another for half-carafes, a single pre-set key can be designated for house wine by the carafe and a modifier key can be programmed as a half-portion modifier. When a half-carafe is sold, the server presses the carafe pre-set key and half-portion modifier key to register the sale. The system adds the price of a half-carafe to its running total of wine revenues and adjusts its inventory records accordingly.

While pre-set and PLU keys are used for order entry, **function keys** assist the operator in processing transactions. Sample function keys are *Clear*, *Discount*, *Void*, and *No Sale*. These keys are important for error correction (*Clear* and *Void*), legitimate price alteration (*Discount*), and proper cash handling (*No Sale*).

Settlement keys are used to record the methods by which accounts are settled: cash, credit card, house account, charge transfer to the guest's folio (in a hotel), debit card, smart card, or other payment method.

The keys in the **numeric keypad** are used to ring up menu items by price, access PLU data by menu item code number, access open guest check accounts by serial number, record the number of items sold, and perform other data entry operations. For example, if the register or terminal is used to record and store payroll data, the numeric keypad can be used to enter employee identification numbers as employees begin and end their work shifts. The numeric keypad may also be used to enter report codes that initiate the production of management reports.

As mentioned earlier, in addition to a keyboard, POS terminals contain an operator display unit (monitor) so the user can review and edit entries. The monitor helps the user check transactions in progress and respond to prompts necessary for carrying out various system procedures.

Some POS terminals with cash drawers support a customer display unit. In food service operations where guests view settlement transactions, this can be very useful. Managers who do not use customer display units lose an excellent method of tracking cashier and bartender recordings. A cashier may charge a guest for a $3.45 purchase and make change from a $10 bill. How does one prove that $3.45 was actually rung? Suppose the cashier had rung only $0.45 and later removed and pocketed $3.00 from the cash drawer? How can this act be detected and corrected? By after-the-fact audit trails, perhaps. However, a display of settlement amounts is a simple means of control at the point of order entry.

Video monitors are used in many food service and other operations to enable order takers to more effectively communicate with preparation personnel. Most orders are entered by the server directly into the POS system for transfer to remote video display units in applicable production areas.

Touchscreen Terminals. Touchscreen terminals simplify data entry procedures and are increasingly used in place of POS terminals with traditional keyboards. A special microprocessor within the terminal is programmed to display data on areas of the screen that are sensitive to touch. Touching one of the sensitized areas produces an electronic charge, which is translated into signals processed by the terminal in much the same way that a terminal would process signals from a conventional keyboard. This signal also instructs the microprocessor to display the next screen.

Terminal designs vary. Flat, color touchscreen terminals require significantly less space than the traditional POS terminals that they replace. Flat screens measure only a few inches thick and can be mounted from walls, ceilings, counters, or shelving units. The design offers restaurants flexibility in determining where to locate the terminals.

Touchscreen terminals are also interactive. The system provides on-screen prompts guiding servers through order-entry or settlement procedures. For example, after a server enters an order for a menu item that needs preparation instructions (such as a New York strip steak), the screen shifts to display the appropriate modifiers (rare, medium rare, medium, medium well done, well done). Forced modifiers will not allow the user to proceed with order entry until a response is indicated. This eliminates the possibility of servers sending incomplete orders to production areas. The interactive nature of these systems decreases the time it takes to train new employees.

Magnetic strip readers can also be used to capture credit or debit card information so transactions can be handled by the POS system without the need for special processing.

Hand-Held Server Terminals. Hand-held server terminals are remote (wireless) palm-size devices that may replace traditional server order entry systems in many operations. They perform most of the functions of a pre-check terminal and enable servers to enter orders at tableside. This technology can be a major advantage for large establishments with long distances between server stations and outdoor dining areas or with very busy lounges where it is difficult to reach a stationary pre-check terminal. Service is faster during peak business periods when servers do not have to walk to the server station, kitchen, or bar areas to place orders or wait in line with other servers to use a pre-check terminal. In some cases, appetizers and drinks may be ready to serve just seconds after a server has finished entering the orders and has left the guest's table.

A two-way communications capability allows a server to deliver special instructions to production areas—"no salt" or "medium rare," for example—when entering an order. Production employees can also communicate with the server. For example, they can immediately alert a server if an item is out of stock and when it is ready for pickup.

Because all items must be entered through the server's hand-held unit, the common problem of coffee and desserts being inadvertently left off guest checks can be reduced. In addition, some units enable managers to monitor service through their own hand-held devices.

Hand-held server terminals use low-frequency FM radio transmission and receiving technology. As orders are entered at guest tables, signals are first sent to antenna units in the dining area. These, in turn, relay signals to a radio base station were they are sent to remote workstation printers or kitchen monitors. Hand-held server units are powered by a battery pack.

Touchscreen hand-held devices have color touch-sensitive screens. When a server touches a sensitized area, an electric charge is produced. This is translated into digital signals that identify the area touched to a microprocessor. The signal also instructs the microprocessor to display the next screen. Write-on hand-held terminals use a digital pad and pencil system with handwriting recognition. With these terminals, servers can write orders in the same way they would with a paper and pencil (manual guest check system) and then transmit the order to the kitchen or bar through the property's wireless network.

Self-Service Terminals (Kiosks). Some quick-service and casual-service restaurants use customer-activated ordering systems that enable guests to order foods and beverages without interacting with counter employees. This self-service is designed to reduce labor costs and increase the speed of service. Some systems incorporate color graphic components, including photos and character drawings representing chicken, fish, french fries, and other items. With one system, guests place orders by:

- Pressing a "start" icon on the screen.

- Indicating whether the order is take-out or dine-in.

- Touching desired items on the screen. (As items are ordered, a "video receipt" appears on the screen to keep a running total of the order.)

- Touching a "finish" box when the order is complete.

- Paying the amount due per the final screen display. (Credit, debit, and gift cards are accepted.)

After payment is authorized, the order is produced in the food preparation area for pick-up by the guest. The system also uses suggestive selling to increase check averages. For example, if the guest has not ordered beverages or desserts, a screen will appear prompting the guest to order if these items are desired.

Additional features of this system include informing guests about out-of-stock and on-sale items and the estimated preparation time for their food. The

---

Learn More on the Web

Information about current features of alternative order entry devices is readily available on the Internet from manufacturers of this hardware. To view examples of this information, check-out the following websites:

Touchscreen Terminals

- Tyco Electronics: www.elotouch.com
- Radiant Systems: www.radiantsystems.com (click on "Point of Sale" under "Hospitality" and then "Industry Brochures")
- Squirrel Systems: www.squirrelsystems.com
- Comus.com: www.comus.com
- PC America: www.pcamerica.com

Hand-Held Server Terminals

- Ameranth Wireless: www.ameranth.com (click on "Products" and then "21st Century Restaurant")
- Action Systems, Inc.: www.actionsystems.com
- DirectPOS.com: www.directpos.com

Self-Service Terminals (Kiosks)

- NCR Corporation: www.infoamerica.com (you can interact ["order"] in a demo on this site)
- Kiosk Information Systems, Inc.: www.kis-kiosk.com (click on "Quick Jump To" drop-down tab and then click on any of the kiosks listed in the drop down display)
- Radiant Systems: www.radiantsystems.com (enter "Kiosk" in the site's search field)

---

system even generates coupons for use by guests. Also, multi-language voice prompts are available.

Printers

Output devices include guest check, workstation, and receipt printers. **Guest check printers** are standard POS output devices. Many guest check printers have **automatic form number reader** capability to facilitate order entry procedures. To access a guest check account, a server places the guest check into the terminal's automatic form number reader unit. A bar code on the check contains the check's serial number in a machine-readable format and provides rapid access to the correct guest check account.

Unless a printer has **automatic slip feed** capability, overprinting items and amounts on guest checks can be a problem. Servers using a printer without this feature must manually align the printer's ribbon with the next blank printing line on the guest check. If the alignment is not correct, the guest check appears disorganized and messy, with lines printed over one another or with large gaps between lines of print.

Printers with automatic slip feed capability prevent overprinting by retaining the number of the last line printed for each open guest check. The server simply aligns the top edge of the guest check with the top edge of the printer's slot and the terminal automatically moves the check to the next available printing line and prints the order entry data. Some properties use mobile printers to accept guest payments and issue receipts at tableside and at remote locations such as a hotel's snack bar at poolside. This technology will be discussed more fully later in this chapter.

Workstation printers are usually placed in kitchen preparation areas and service bars. As orders are entered at POS terminals, they are sent to a remote printer to initiate production. This communication system enables servers to spend more time meeting the needs of guests, while significantly reducing traffic in kitchen and bar areas.

If the need for hard-copy output in production areas is not critical, remote display units (kitchen monitors) are alternatives to workstation printers. Because these units can display several orders on a single screen, kitchen employees do not have to handle numerous pieces of paper. A cursor control keypad enables kitchen employees to easily review previously submitted orders.

Receipt printers produce hard copies on thin, narrow register tape. These devices may help control the production of menu items that are not prepared in departments receiving orders through workstation printers or remote display units. For example, when servers prepare or pick up desserts in a pantry area not equipped with a workstation printer, desserts could be served without being recorded in the POS system. It is also possible that desserts could be served without ever being posted to guest checks, and revenue could be lost. Use of receipt printers helps prevent these problems. Servers preparing desserts can be required to deliver a receipt tape to the dessert pantry area as proof that the desserts are properly posted to guest checks for settlement. This procedure enhances management's internal control by ensuring that a record of every menu item served is stored in the POS system.

Managing Guest Accounts

Managing guest accounts[4] involves either a **hard check** POS system, which uses guest checks made of stiff paper cards stored outside the cashier terminal system, or a **soft check** system, which uses guest checks made of very lightweight receipt paper. Before entering an order, the server "opens" the guest check within the system by inputting an identification number. Once the system recognizes the server and opens a new guest check, orders are entered and, if applicable, relayed to remote printers or monitors at production areas. The same items with selling prices are printed on the server's guest check.

When a guest check is opened, it becomes part of the system's open check file, which may contain the following data:

- Terminal number where the guest check was opened
- Guest check serial number (if applicable)

Learn More on the Web

Want to learn more about POS printers, mobile printers, workstation printers, and remote kitchen display units? If so, check out the following:

POS Printers

- Semicron Systems: www.semicron.com

- Epson: www.epson.com (click on "North America," "USA," and then enter "restaurant printers" in the site's search box)

Mobile Printers

- Zebra: www.zebra.com (click on "Industry Solutions," then "Hospitality," and then "Restaurants")

Workstation Printers

- DED Limited: www.ded.co.uk (enter "kitchen printers" under "Quick Search")

- Star Micronics: www.starmicronics.com (click on "Americas," "Food Service Solutions," and "Kitchen")

Remote Kitchen Display Units

- Micros: www.micros.com (click on "Industries," "Restaurants," "Table Service," and "Kitchen Display Systems")

- CRS, Inc.: www.crs-usa.com/kdsvideo.asp

- QSR Automations: www.qsrautomations.com

- Radiant Systems: www.radiantsystems.com (enter "Kitchen Display System" in the site's search field)

- Server identification number
- Time guest check was created
- Menu items ordered
- Selling prices of items ordered
- Applicable tax
- Total amount due

A server adds orders to the guest check at the terminal by first inputting the guest check's serial number (or other identifier) and then entering the additional items.

There are many variations of this automated system. Some systems use guest checks with bar codes corresponding to the pre-printed serial numbers. This eliminates the need for servers to input the guest check's serial number when opening a guest check or when adding items to guest checks already in use. When the guest check is placed in the guest check printer, the system reads the bar code and immediately accesses the appropriate file.

Soft check systems eliminate the traditional externally stored guest check and maintain only an electronic file for each open guest check. A receipt-like guest check can be printed at any time during service, but is usually not printed until the server presents a final version of the check to the guest for settlement. Since no paper forms are used during service, the table number often is the tracking identifier for the order. With some systems, seat numbers are used for tracking multiple checks per table. When presenting soft checks to guests for settlement, the receipt-like guest checks can be inserted in high-quality paper, vinyl, or leather presentation jackets.

Most POS systems feature a soft guest check that also serves as a credit card or debit voucher. This often reduces the time it takes servers to settle guest checks. Instead of presenting the guest check, collecting the guest's credit or debit card, printing a voucher, transferring information from the guest check to the voucher, and then presenting the voucher to the guest to sign, servers can present the guest check and the credit or debit card voucher simultaneously.

Other Automated Service Applications

Our discussion of the technology of service would be incomplete without discussing several additional concepts.

Automated Reservation and Table Management Systems. Several guest reservations (dining room management) systems are available. When guests call in, their names are entered into the system by keyboard, mouse, or touchscreen and displayed on a screen grid that corresponds to the desired (or closest available) dining time. If the guests have visited before, a "look-up" feature allows information to be quickly entered.

When guests arrive (with or without reservations), the host or hostess accesses a screen showing dining room table layout and the status of each. With some systems, color coding is used to indicate tables that are available, reserved, in use, and being cleaned. Information about each server (number of tables and total guests) can also be shown to help determine whether an additional table can be assigned to a specific server. With some systems, information about each table (number of guests seated, server number assigned to the table, and number of minutes the guests have been seated) is provided.

During busy dining periods and for restaurants that do not accept reservations, information about guests waiting (length of time since they registered and the approximate wait time based on the party size) can be tracked.

Automated reservations systems can create database information such as frequency of guest dining, total number of persons dining with the guest, birthday and anniversary information, preferred table and server, and other information useful for a frequent diner program. These systems are capable of generating a wide variety of management reports, including statistics about average guests per table, average waiting time, and average time spent at a table, based on number of guests in a party. Data showing peak and valley times of guest dining can be helpful when scheduling employees. Special screens are frequently included as part of an automated table management system.

Learn More on the Web

Check out the following websites for detailed information about these automated service applications:

Automated Reservation and Table Management Systems

- Ameranth: www.ameranth.com (click on "Products" "21st Century Restaurant," and "Host Alert")
- OpenTable.com: www.opentable.com

Online Ordering Systems

- Big Holler: www.bigholler.com
- Delphis Software: www.delphissoftware.com

Digital Menus

- IDS Menus: www.idsmenus.com
- Epicure Digital Systems: www.epicuredigital.com

Online Ordering Systems. Many casual-service restaurants generate significant revenues from carry-out/take-home food services. Guests can place orders when visiting the property or by telephone, fax, e-mail, or online ordering. When orders arrive by fax or come from guests waiting in-house, the order information is entered into the existing POS system. However, when orders arrive via the Internet, special software is required. Customer advantages to online ordering include reduced time and greater convenience. The operation can use high-quality marketing information and no-cost advertising messages to encourage increased sales. Reductions in incorrect or lost orders can yield increased business and greater levels of guest satisfaction.

Online ordering is simple for customers. They can review the menu on the property's website, select the items to order, and enter their name, address, and other demographic information that is automatically sent to the property. Online ordering systems may validate the customers' payment card numbers and allow them to place the order at any time of the day or even several (or more) days before the preparation date. Systems can display images of menu items and allow for easy duplication of previous orders.

As orders are placed, price differences for items offered at both lunch and dinner will automatically be posted, and food options and choices such as type of salad dressing and items presenting additional charges will be displayed. There may be a special text area that enables customers to add special ordering instructions.

Call Centers. Technology is also increasingly involved in another method of customer ordering: the use of call centers. Large food service operations may have centralized call centers serving perhaps hundreds of units. Some operators create call centers in which staff members enter customer orders into the restaurant's website. However, most call centers use call center employees and some use of voice recognition technology to reduce labor costs. It is also possible to use independent, home-based agents to manage customer calls. Call centers can affect customer ordering in unusual ways. For example, some quick-service restaurant orders placed from an automobile in a drive-through lane are processed at call centers hundreds or even thousands of miles from the unit before being routed back to the property for preparation and customer pick-up after payment.

Digital Menus. Digital menus involve display boards or screens that can be programmed to display and change content at pre-set times. High resolution and high-definition video provide graphics that can catch the customers' attention. Innovative programmers find numerous ways to suggestively sell high-profit menu items on their display boards. Other advantages to digital menus include the ability to quickly change an item, photo, and/or price on the display without having to change or revise the entire menu board. Multi-unit operations can make specific changes at central locations.

Automated Beverage Control Systems

Automated beverage control systems are designed to enhance production and service capabilities, while improving accounting and operational controls. A beverage control unit is the brain of an automated system. Generally located close to a beverage storage area, this control unit is primarily responsible for regulating all essential mechanisms within the system. The unit communicates requests from order entry terminals to the system's delivery network and directs the flow of beverages from a storage area to a dispensing unit.

Automated beverage control systems can generate projected beverage sales and revenue data based on forecasts for future planning periods. Beverage dispensing stations may be connected to a guest check printer that records transaction data as drinks are dispensed. Some systems require that a hard copy guest check be inserted in the printer before the drink is dispensed. When soft guest check systems are used, a roll of paper must be in the printing unit. The goal is to automatically track all sales generated through the dispensing equipment.

Revenue control is best achieved when the dispensing equipment is interfaced with the property's POS system. Then managers know the quantity of drinks that have been dispensed (from the dispensing system data) and the amount of revenue that should be generated (as recorded in the POS system).

With one type of automated system, liquor is stored at the bar, and price-coded pourers (nozzles) are inserted into each bottle. When a drink is ordered, the bartender slips a special activator ring over the neck of the liquor bottle and hand-pours the beverage. The activator ring is connected to a master control panel by a cord, and the liquor flow is measured so the number of drinks poured at each price level can be determined and recorded. This system is typically connected to a POS terminal for control.

Another type of beverage dispensing system uses liquor stored in a locked storage area away from the bar. The bartender "prepares" the drink by pushing a key on the dispensing device. Liquor and mixes, if any, required by the recipe travel to the bar dispensing location through plastic tubing. The system pours the drink when the glass is held under the dispensing device. The drink can then be manually garnished and given to the server or guest.

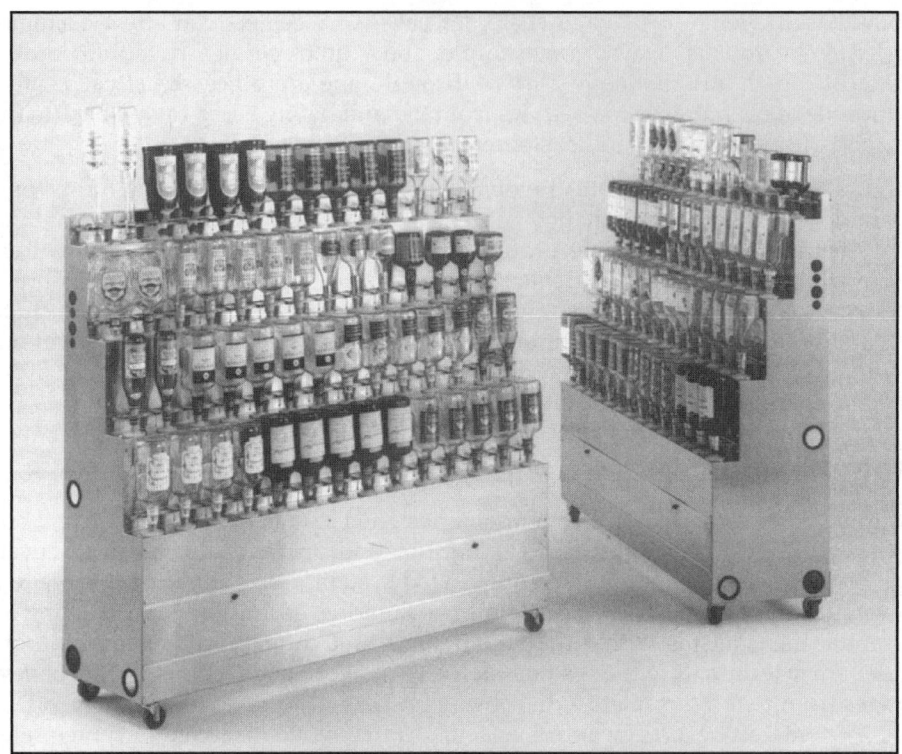

Bottle racks from an automated beverage control system in a storage area.

Automated beverage control systems use different kinds of sensing devices to increase operational controls within the system. Glass sensors are electronic mechanisms located in a bar dispensing unit that will not permit liquid to flow from the dispensing unit unless there is a glass positioned below the dispensing head to catch the liquid. Guest check sensors prevent the system from fulfilling beverage orders unless they are first recorded on a guest check or entered into the POS system. When a server or bartender places a beverage order whose ingredients are out of stock, an empty bottle sensor relays a signal to the order entry device.

Sophisticated systems can record data input through order entry devices, transport beverage ingredients through a controlled delivery network, dispense ingredients for ordered items, and track important service, sales, and revenue data to produce various management reports. The following sections examine the basic components of an automated beverage control system: an order entry device, a delivery network, and dispensing units.

Order Entry Devices

In an automated beverage control system, the primary function of an order entry device is to initiate activities involved with recording, producing, and pricing beverage items requested by guests. There are two order entry devices in common use today: a group of pre-set buttons located on a dispensing unit, and keyboard units.

A group of pre-set buttons on a dispensing unit is the most popular order entry device. These devices may result in lower system costs because the dispensing unit serves as both an order taker and a delivery unit. However, since dispensing units have a limited number of pre-set buttons, the number of beverage items under the control of the automated beverage system is limited.

Keyboard units (which can be touchscreen) function like pre-check terminals, with beverage dispensing performed by a separate piece of hardware. Because they support a full range of keys (including pre-set keys, price look-up keys, and modifier keys), keyboard units place a large number of beverage items under the control of the automated system. Keyboard units may be equipped with a guest check or receipt printer and may feature a colorful array of keys or icons.

Delivery Networks

An automated beverage control system relies on a delivery network to transport beverage item ingredients from storage areas to dispensing units. The delivery network must be a closed system capable of regulating temperature and pressure conditions at various locations and stages of delivery. To maintain proper temperature conditions, the delivery network typically uses a cooling subsystem that controls such mechanisms as cold plates, cold boxes, and cold storage rooms.

Most automated beverage control systems can deliver beverage ingredients by controlling pressure sources such as gravity, compressed air, carbon dioxide, and nitrous oxide. Gravity and compressed air are used for delivering liquor, nitrogen or nitrous oxide for delivering wine, compressed air for draft beer, and a carbon dioxide regulator for dispensing post-mixes. A post-mix soft drink dispenser combines syrup and carbonated water at the dispenser instead of storing, transporting, and distributing the soft drink as a finished product.

The type of pressure source selected to transport a specific ingredient affects the taste and wholesomeness of the finished beverage item. For example, if carbon dioxide is attached to a wine dispenser, the wine would become carbonated and spoiled. If compressed air is connected to a post-mix soft drink dispenser, the finished beverage item will not be carbonated. Pressure sources affect the quality of finished beverage items and the timing, flow of mixture, portion size, and desired foaming.

Almost any type of liquor and accompanying liquor ingredient can be stored, transported, and dispensed by an automated beverage control system. Portion sizes of liquor can be controlled with remarkable accuracy. Typically, systems can be calibrated to maintain portion sizes ranging from one-half ounce to three-and-one-half ounces.

Dispensing Units

After beverage item ingredients are removed from storage and transported by the delivery network to production areas, they are ready for dispensing. Automated beverage control systems can be configured with a variety of dispensing units.

Touch-Bar Faucets. A **touch-bar faucet** can be located under the bar, behind the bar, on top of an ice machine, or on a pedestal stand. These devices do not have the versatility, flexibility, or expandability of other dispensing units. Typically, touch-bar faucets are dedicated to only a single beverage type and are pre-set for one specific portion size output per push on the bar lever. For example, to obtain a double shot of bourbon, the bartender must push twice on the bar lever.

Console Faucets. Console faucet dispensing units are similar to touch-bar faucet devices in that they can be located in almost any part of the bar area. In addition, these units may be located up to 300 feet from beverage storage areas. Unlike touch-bar faucet devices, however, console faucet units are able to dispense various beverages in a number of portion sizes. Using buttons located above the faucet unit, a bartender can trigger up to four different portion sizes from the same faucet head. An optional feature of this dispensing device is a double-hose faucet unit that can transport large quantities of liquids in short amounts of time.

Hose-and-Gun Devices. The **hose-and-gun device** has control buttons on the handle of the gun, which is connected by hoses to liquors, carbonated beverages, water, and wine tanks. This dispenser can be installed anywhere along the bar and is frequently included as standard equipment on portable bars and at service bar locations. Pressing a control button produces a pre-measured flow of the desired beverage. The number of beverage items under the control of a hose-and-gun dispensing unit is limited to the number of control buttons the device supports.

Mini-Tower Pedestals. The **mini-tower pedestal** dispensing unit combines the portion-size capabilities of console faucet units with the button selection technique of hose-and-gun devices. In addition, the mini-tower concept offers increased control of bar operations. For a beverage to be dispensed, the mini-tower unit requires that a button be pressed and a glass-sensing device requires that a glass be in place directly under the dispensing head. This dispensing unit is popular for dispensing beverage items such as wine and beer that need no additional ingredients prior to service. A mini-tower unit can be located on a wall, ice machine, or pedestal base in the bar area.

Bundled Tower Units. The most sophisticated and flexible dispensing unit is the **bundled tower unit**, also referred to as a tube tower unit. It is designed to dispense a variety of beverage items. Beverage orders must be entered on a POS device. Bundled tower units can support more than 110 beverage products and contain a glass-sensing element. Each liquor type has its own line to the tower unit and a variety of pressurized systems can be used to enhance delivery from storage areas. While other units sequentially dispense beverage item ingredients, the bundled tower unit simultaneously dispenses all required ingredients, and the bartender merely garnishes the finished product. This dispensing unit can be located up to 300 feet from beverage storage areas.

Management Considerations

There are several advantages to be gained from using automated equipment, including detailed information about unit sales and revenue control and faster drink preparation. Sales control is possible because the number of ounces sold and potential revenue are known.

Bartender errors, including spillage, over- or under-pouring, and pricing, are eliminated or reduced. Also, it is more difficult for bartenders to "beat the system." Bartender supervision and the bartender's work are made easier. Training time is reduced, and turnover can be easier to manage.

Other advantages include faster drink preparation; the potential for lower per-ounce cost through purchase of large bottles; less need for large quantities of liquor to be stored behind the bar; and fewer employees needed if drinks are prepared more quickly.

There are also disadvantages associated with automated equipment. Equipment malfunctions create crises: supplies must be brought to the bar, a non-operative cash drawer must be used, and untrained bartenders must hand-pour drinks. Also, costs of maintenance, operation, and repair may add to the already high capital purchase costs of automated beverage equipment.

When patrons see the equipment in use, they may feel they are receiving a smaller portion or lower-quality drink than they ordered. This may affect both revenue and customer perception of value. Another disadvantage is that it is difficult to objectively evaluate the payback period and, therefore, the cost-effectiveness of the equipment. Also, many types of equipment still require experienced and trained bartenders to prepare drinks that cannot be produced by the system.

Along with the advantages and disadvantages of automated beverage equipment, there are other considerations, including:

- *Meeting guest expectations of quality and value.* If guests believe that the equipment is impersonal or that it reduces portion size or quality, this may be a good reason not to install the equipment. On the other hand, these problems can be reduced or eliminated if the equipment is used only in non-public service bars.

- *The availability of pertinent data.* When determining cost implications, use data applicable to the specific property rather than statistics for an "average" operation supplied by the equipment manufacturer or dealer.

- *Employee resistance.* Change can generate resistance. It must be dealt with effectively.

- *Changes to existing systems.* Before purchasing an automated beverage system, determine what changes in the existing control systems will be required. The manager will have to revise control systems in light of the automated beverage equipment.

- *Installation issues.* Physical changes may be required. These include such things as installation of dispensing equipment and bottle dispensing racks, and running beverage lines to equipment locations.

- *Scheduled servicing, and breakdowns.* An effective working relationship with the supplier/dealer must be established as equipment is installed and employees are trained. Automated equipment needs routine maintenance and repair and will probably break down at times. When this happens, an effective supplier relationship is helpful.

Automated beverage equipment undergoes constant change and improvement. Managers must attempt to stay abreast of advancements in the state of the art of these systems, while remaining sensitive to the needs of their properties. With this knowledge, effective decisions can be made. And if it is found that automated beverage equipment is desirable, managers will be able to select that system that is most compatible with the property's existing control system and other requirements.

Endnotes

1. For a detailed explanation of forecasting techniques used in the hospitality industry, see Raymond S. Schmidgall, *Hospitality Industry Managerial Accounting*, 6th ed. (Lansing, Mich.: American Hotel & Lodging Educational Institute, 2006).

2. For a more detailed discussion of food and beverage service procedures, see Ronald F. Cichy and Phillip J. Hickey, Jr., *Managing Service in Food and Beverage Operations*, 3d ed. (Lansing, Mich.: American Hotel & Lodging Educational Institute, 2005).

3. Materials in this chapter relating to computerized pre-check systems and automated beverage systems are adapted from Michael L. Kasavana and John J. Cahill, *Managing Technology in the Hospitality Industry*, 5th ed. (Lansing, Mich.: American Hotel & Lodging Educational Institute, 2007).

4. This section is excerpted from Kasavana and Cahill.

Key Terms

automatic form number reader—A feature of a guest check printer that facilitates order entry procedures; instead of a server manually inputting a guest check's serial number to access the account, a bar code imprinted on the guest check presents the check's serial number in a machine-readable format.

automatic slip feed—A feature of a guest check printer that prevents overprinting of items and amounts on guest checks.

bundled tower unit—Part of one kind of automated beverage control system incorporating a dispensing unit designed to dispense a variety of beverage items; it is also referred to as a tube tower unit.

cashier terminal—A POS device with a cash drawer that supports purchasing and cashiering functions.

console faucet dispensing unit—Part of one kind of automated beverage control system that can dispense various beverages in different portion sizes and can be located up to 300 feet from beverage storage areas. Using buttons located above the faucet unit, a bartender can trigger up to four different portion sizes from the same faucet head.

digital menu—An electronic display screen that is programmed to display a menu using video, audio, and/or print.

electronic cash register (ECR)—An independent (stand-alone) computer system that incorporates all the necessary components of a computer system: an input/output device, a central processing unit, and storage (memory) capacity.

empower—To delegate to or authorize employees to make their own decisions about how to meet the guests' wants and needs.

expediting—The process of facilitating and emphasizing the urgency of a pending purchase.

expediter—One who helps communication between production and service personnel by controlling the process of turning in orders and picking up food items.

function key—An element in a POS keyboard that helps to process a transaction; function key examples are "clear," "void," "discount," and "no sale."

guest check printers—Sometimes referred to as slip printers, guest check printers may be equipped with automatic form number readers. Many have automatic slip feed capabilities.

hand-held server terminals—Also referred to as portable server terminals, these units perform most of the functions of a pre-check terminal and enable servers to enter orders at tableside.

hard checks—Guest checks that are made of stiff paper cards. Hard checks are stored outside the cashier terminal system.

hose-and-gun device—A beverage-dispensing unit that has control buttons connected by hoses to liquors, carbonated beverages, water, and wine tanks.

magnetic strip readers—An input device connected to a POS terminal that collects data stored on the magnetized strip on the back of a payment or gift card.

menu board—A keyboard overlay for a POS terminal that identifies the function performed by each key during a specific meal period.

mini-tower pedestal—A beverage-dispensing unit that combines the portion-size capabilities of console faucet units with the button selection technique of hose-and-gun devices.

modifier key—An element in a POS keyboard that works with pre-set and price look-up keys to provide preparation instructions (e.g., rare or medium) and to change prices based upon portion size (e.g., small or medium); see also "price look-up (PLU) key" and "pre-set key."

numeric keypad—Numbers in a POS keyboard used to ring up menu items by price, access price look-up (PLU) data by menu item code number, and perform numerous other data entry tasks.

open check file—A file incorporated in many POS systems that maintains current data for all open guest checks; it is accessed to monitor items on a guest check, add items to a guest check after initial order entry, and close a guest check at the time of settlement.

point-of-sale (POS) terminal—An electronic unit that contains its own input/output component and may possess a small storage (memory) capacity, but usually does not contain its own central processing unit.

pre-check terminal—A POS device without a cash drawer that is used to enter guests' orders, but not to settle guests' checks.

pre-set key—An element in a POS keyboard that maintains the price, item description, tax, and inventory status of a menu item.

price look-up (PLU) key—An element in a POS keyboard used to identify a menu item by a code number rather than a name or description.

production planning—Designing or determining food and beverage preparation requirements in advance of actual production.

public bar—A bar where bartenders directly serve drinks to guests.

receipt printers—A device that prints hard copies on thin, narrow register tape. It helps control the production of menu items that are not prepared in departments receiving orders through workstation printers.

service bar—A bar where bartenders provide drinks to servers who deliver them to guests.

settlement key—An element in a POS keyboard used to record the method by which a guest's account is settled, such as cash, credit or debit card, house account, or transfer to guest's folio (in a hotel).

soft checks—Guest checks made of flimsy receipt paper.

time series analysis—A forecasting method that assigns more importance (weight) to recent occurrences (trends).

touch-bar faucet—A beverage-dispensing unit that is dedicated to only a single beverage type and is pre-set for one specific portion-size output per push on the bar lever.

touchscreen terminal—A unit containing a special microprocessor within the terminal that is programmed to display data on areas of the screen that are sensitive to touch.

workstation printer—A unit usually placed at kitchen preparation areas and service bars that relays orders submitted from POS terminals to production personnel.

Review Questions

1. Why is it difficult to control food production and service procedures?

2. Why is the menu an important element in controlling food and beverage production?

3. Why must quality requirements be considered as food and beverage products are produced?

4. Why are standard recipes important? How do automated recipe management systems work?

5. What are some ways to control beverage production?

6. What is an expediter? Why would a food and beverage operation use an expediter?

7. How do POS systems enhance management's control of production and service areas?

8. What are the different order entry devices used by POS systems?

9. What functions are performed by modifier and numeric keys?

10. How can hand-held server terminals assist with dining room service?

11. What control factors should management consider when automating bar operations? What are the pros and cons from the guests' perspective?

 Internet Sites

For more information, visit the following Internet sites. Remember that Internet addresses can change without notice. If the site is no longer there, you can use a search engine to look for additional sites.

POS Systems

Action Systems, Inc.
www.actionsystems.com

AM PM Service
www.ampmservice.com

Comtrex Systems Corporation
www.comtrex.com

Digital Dining
www.digitaldining.com

Geac Restaurant Systems
www.rsd.geac.com

Infogenesis
www.infogenesis.com

Integrated Restaurant Software
www.rmstouch.com

Micros Systems, Inc.
www.micros.com

National Cash Register Company
www.ncr.com

Nationwide POS
www.nationwidepos.com

NextPOS Corporation
www.nextpos.com

Posera
www.posera.com

POSitouch
www.positouch.com

Squirrel Systems
www.squirrelsystems.com

Production Control Software

Adaco Services, Inc.
www.adacoservices.com

Eatec Corporation
www.eatec.com

CostGuard
www.costguard.com

HyperActive Technologies
www.hyperactivetechnologies.com

Culinary Software Services
www.culinarysoftware.com

Customer Service Assistance

CrossFire Software, Inc.
www.crossfirereservations.com

MAI Systems Corporation
www.maisystems.com

Guestware
www.guestware.com

 # Mini-Case Studies

In the two following mini-case studies, you are the manager of food service operations. What initiatives would you take to resolve the problems cited?

Mini-Case One—The Need for Production Planning

As the new manager of the Anytown Restaurant, you quickly observe problems relating to stockouts and numerous occurrences of too many or too few production and service employees available on the job. Review the basics of a production planning system that you would establish for the restaurant to address these problems.

Mini-Case Two—Should You Automate?

As the manager of the Kahuku Restaurant, you are trying to assess the advantages, if any, that would accrue to your operation from implementing an automated guest reservations system. You are open for lunch and dinner each day of the week. The current restaurant policy is to accept reservations for any meal except those on Friday and Saturday nights and Sunday brunch (because these shifts are so busy) and for guest parties of more than eight persons. However, many of your regular guests have been asking about whether "special arrangements" can be made for them.

The restaurant seats approximately 175 persons, it enjoys a relatively high check average, and table turns are approximately 1.25 during the week and 2.5 during the busy weekend periods.

How does an automated guest reservation system "work"? Would such a system be advantageous to your operation? If so, what would be its advantages? If you should decide to install such a system, how might it be implemented?

Problems

Problem 1

The following data recaps the number of portions of each menu item sold on Friday evening for the past five weeks:

	Week 1	Week 2	Week 3	Week 4	Week 5 Last Friday
Chicken	71	60	55	59	90
Pork Chops	60	43	57	61	81
Prime Rib	90	71	51	59	107
Lobster	82	63	75	80	91
Veal Cutlet	79	40	68	79	90
	382	277	306	338	459

a. What is the percentage of total items sold for each menu item averaged over the past five Fridays?

b. The manager notes that sales on the second Friday were lower than normal because of a weather problem. Sales on the last Friday were higher than normal because of an in-town sporting event. He believes the number of menu items to be sold this Friday will be about "average"; that is, they will exclude the one lower-than-normal Friday and one higher-than-normal Friday.

1. What is the total number of entrées expected to be served this Friday?

2. Assume that the manager believes sales of each entrée this Friday will approximate those on the three "average" Fridays over the past three weeks; what is the expected sales of each entrée?

3. The manager is introducing entertainment during the dinner shift. This is expected to generate 20 additional sales of each menu item each Friday evening. Assuming that these additional guests select entrées in the same proportion as those over the last three "average" Fridays, what is the expected number of entrées to be sold?

Problem 2

What is the percentage of total sales represented by each of the following menu items during "average" Friday and Saturday evenings at the Green Pastures Restaurant?

Menu Item	Total Sales (Portions)	Percentage of Total Sales
Chicken	175	
Beef Stew	137	
Pork Chops	112	
Vegetarian Dinner	62	
Veal Cutlets	98	
Filet Mignon	128	

Problem 3

The manager of the Green Pastures Restaurant is expecting a busy weekend; the local college is celebrating homecoming with a football game against its big rival. The expected number of guests on Friday and Saturday night is, respectively, 950 and 1,100 guests. Assuming the percentage of total sales remains the same as in Problem 2, what is the total number of each menu item that is expected to be sold over the two-night period?

Problem 4

What is the total increase in expected meals to be served on Friday and Saturday nights at the Green Pastures Restaurant because of the college homecoming celebration?

Part IV

Using Information from the Control System

Chapter 9 Outline

Competencies

1. Calculate the basic monthly cost of sales for food and beverages. (pp. 301–308)

2. Use the FIFO method to calculate the value of products in inventory. (pp. 308–309)

3. Use the LIFO method to calculate the value of products in inventory, and describe the actual cost method. (pp. 309–310)

4. Use the weighted average method to calculate the value of products in inventory, and discuss inventory counting procedures. (pp. 310–311)

5. Identify adjustments used to calculate a monthly net cost of sales for food and beverages. (pp. 311–315)

6. Describe daily calculations of actual food and beverage costs, and explain how the daily beverage cost percentage worksheet can be used to assess a bartender's performance. (pp. 315–323)

7. Describe how current technology helps managers monitor food and beverage costs. (pp. 323–325)

9

Calculating Actual Food and Beverage Costs

AFTER A FOOD AND BEVERAGE manager has developed standards, constructed the operating budget, and designed effective control procedures, the next task in the control cycle is to assess the actual operating results. The reason: to compare expected revenues and costs against the revenues actually generated and the costs actually incurred. This comparison process will help the manager to determine if plans were successful or, alternatively, whether corrective actions are necessary. One part of this process is calculating the actual food and beverage costs incurred to generate revenues during a specified period of time. This chapter discusses procedures for accomplishing these calculations.

To ensure that actual operating costs are comparable to standard or planned costs, several general rules must be followed. First, **actual costs** must be stated in the same manner as standard costs so managers can analyze the differences between them. For example, if standard food costs are stated as a specified percentage of revenues, then actual food costs must also be stated as a percentage of revenues. It is very difficult to compare a standard food cost expressed as a percentage with an actual food cost expressed in dollars.

A second rule for relating actual costs to standard costs is that both actual cost calculations and standard cost estimates must cover the same meal periods. The reason for this rule is the same as for the first: to make actual and standard costs truly comparable. For example, if actual costs are expressed as a specified percentage of revenue across all meal periods, standard costs should not be determined separately for breakfast, lunch, and dinner.

Third, all factors used to estimate standard costs must be included in the calculation of actual costs. For example, if food transfers, beverage transfers, employee meals, and complimentary meals are excluded from standard cost estimates, then they must also be excluded from the calculation of actual costs.

Finally, actual costs must be assessed on a timely basis. Decision-makers must know as soon as possible if (and to what extent) actual costs differ from planned standard costs.

Calculations of actual costs must be accurate. Good decisions cannot be based on inaccurate cost information. Accuracy, however, is partially related to the time spent collecting the information. If the development of extremely accurate cost information requires an excessive amount of time, then the assessment procedures are not practical and, most likely, will not be done.

There is a cost-benefit consideration here. Managers must be able to justify the time they spend generating increasingly more accurate information. A decision needs to be made about how much time should be spent collecting accounting information used to develop financial statements. Information collected during this process generally becomes the basis for assessing actual costs.

Actual Food and Beverage Costs: Monthly Calculations ——

Calculations of **actual food and beverage costs** are based on the same set of information used to develop financial operating statements. Generally, financial statements for food and beverage operations are developed monthly. (Some properties, however, even out the days in the months by establishing 13 four-week accounting cycles within the fiscal year, each containing 28 days.)

A strict accounting definition of the concept of "cost of sales" is beyond the scope of our current discussion. For our purposes, **cost of sales** is defined as the food or beverage cost incurred to produce all food or beverage items sold during a specific accounting period (a month or a year, for example).

Generally, the income statement expresses cost of sales as total dollars and as a percentage of revenue (or total sales). The National Restaurant Association's *Uniform System of Accounts for Restaurants*[1] includes a sample income statement (see Exhibit 1). Note that total revenue, called "total sales" in Exhibit 1, is food sales (revenue) plus beverage sales (revenue):

Food Sales	+	Beverage Sales	=	Total Food and Beverage Sales
$1,030,000	+	$257,500	=	$1,287,500

To calculate the percentage of total sales by revenue center, divide sales for the revenue center by total food and beverage sales and multiply by 100:

$$\frac{\text{Food Sales}}{\text{Total Food and Beverage Sales}} \times 100 = \text{Percentage of Sales (Food)}$$

$$\frac{\$1,030,000}{\$1,287,500} \times 100 = 80\%$$

In this example, 80 percent of all sales (revenue) accrued from the food operations, while 20 percent (100 percent − 80 percent) was generated by the beverage operation.

To calculate the cost percentage for each food or beverage revenue source, divide the cost of sales by sales and multiply by 100:

$$\frac{\text{Cost of Sales (Food)}}{\text{Food Sales}} \times 100 = \text{Food Cost Percentage}$$

$$\frac{\$360,500}{\$1,030,000} \times 100 = 35.0\%$$

In Exhibit 1, 35 percent of food sales was used to purchase food products necessary to generate the food revenue. A similar calculation ($68,240 ÷ $257,500)

Exhibit 1   Sample Restaurant Income Statement

Statement of Income
for Full Service Restaurant
Serving Food and Beverages

	Amount	Percentages*
SALES		
Food	$1,030,000	80%
Beverage	257,500	20
Total Sales	1,287,500	100
COST OF SALES		
Food	360,500	35
Beverage	68,240	27
Total Cost of Sales	428,740	33
GROSS PROFIT		
Food	669,500	65
Beverage	189,260	73
Total Gross Profit	858,760	67
OPERATING EXPENSES		
Salaries and Wages	386,250	30%
Employee Benefits	51,500	4
Direct Operating Expenses	77,250	6
Music and Entertainment	1,300	00.1
Marketing	25,750	2
Utility Services	38,600	3
Repairs and Maintenance	25,800	2
Occupancy	90,200	7
Depreciation	25,500	2
General and Administrative	39,000	3
Other Income	(6,440)	00.5
Total Operating Expenses	$ 754,710	59
OPERATING INCOME	104,050	10
INTEREST	6,500	00.5
INCOME BEFORE INCOME TAXES	$ 97,550	8%

*   All ratios are calculated as a percentage of total sales except food and beverage cost
   of sale and gross profit which are based on their respective sales.

Source: *Uniform System of Accounts for Restaurants,* 7th rev. ed. (Washington, D.C.: National Restaurant
Association, 1996).

shows that 27 percent of beverage sales was used to purchase beverage products
necessary to generate the beverage revenue.

Continuing with our review of Exhibit 1, note that the total cost of sales is
$428,740, which is the sum of the cost of food sales ($360,500) and the cost of beverage sales ($68,240). The total cost of sales expressed as a percentage is calculated
as follows:

$$\frac{\text{Total Cost of Sales}}{\text{Total Sales}} = \frac{\$428,740}{\$1,287,500} \times 100 = \frac{33\%}{(\text{rounded})}$$

Total gross profit and gross profit for each revenue center is calculated by deducting food and beverage product costs from product revenue:

Gross Profit (Food) = $1,030,000 − $360,500 = $669,500
       (Total Food Sales) (Total Food Cost) (Gross Profit: Food)

$$\text{Gross Profit Percent (Food)} = \frac{\text{Gross Profit (Food)}}{\text{Food Sales}} = \frac{\$669,500}{\$1,030,000} \times 100 = 65\%$$

Gross Profit (Beverage) = $257,500 − $68,240 = $189,260
           (Total   (Total   (Gross Profit:
        Beverage Sales) Beverage Costs)   Beverage)

$$\begin{array}{l}\text{Gross Profit Percent} \\ \text{(Beverage)}\end{array} = \frac{\text{Gross Profit (Beverage)}}{\text{Beverage Sales}} = \frac{\$189,260}{\$257,500} \times 100 = \begin{array}{l}73\% \\ \text{(rounded)}\end{array}$$

$858,760 = $669,500 + $189,260
(Total Gross Profit) (Gross Profit Food) (Gross Profit: Beverage)

$$\begin{array}{l}\text{Total Gross Profit} \\ \text{Percentage}\end{array} = \frac{\text{Total Gross Profit}}{\text{Total Sales}} = \frac{\$858,760}{\$1,287,500} \times 100 = \begin{array}{l}67\% \\ \text{(rounded)}\end{array}$$

All other percentages in Exhibit 1 are calculated as a percentage of total sales. For example:

$$\begin{array}{l}\text{Salaries and Wage} \\ \text{Percentage}\end{array} = \frac{\text{Salaries/Wages Cost}}{\text{Total Sales}} = \frac{\$386,250}{\$1,287,500} \times 100 = 30\%$$

and

$$\begin{array}{l}\text{Income Before} \\ \text{Income Taxes}\end{array} = \frac{\text{Income Before Income Taxes}}{\text{Total Sales}} = \frac{\$97,550}{\$1,287,500} \times 100 = \begin{array}{l}8\% \\ \text{(rounded)}\end{array}$$

The *Uniform System of Accounts for the Lodging Industry*[2] recommends a format (Exhibit 2) that a food department in a lodging property can use to gain relevant financial information. Notice in Exhibit 2 that:

- The form includes food and beverage data. Note the numerous types of revenues and expenses that are listed.

- Observe that the "bottom line" at the bottom of Exhibit 2 is called "Departmental Income (Loss)." This reflects the financial results of the food and beverage department for the month and is the amount that is moved forward to the property's summary operating statement.

- Note that the suggested format of the statement allows readers to note, for each line on the statement, the actual, forecast (budget), and prior year's actual results for the current month and year-to-date.

Exhibit 2   Food and Beverage Department Operating Statement Format

	CURRENT MONTH						YEAR-TO-DATE					
	ACTUAL		FORECAST		PRIOR YEAR		ACTUAL		FORECAST		PRIOR YEAR	
	$	%	$	%	$	%	$	%	$	%	$	%
REVENUE												
Outlet Food Revenue												
Outlet Beverage Revenue												
In-Room Dining Food Revenue												
In-Room Dining Beverage Revenue												
Banquet/Catering Food Revenue												
Banquet/Catering Beverage Revenue												
Mini Bar Food Revenue												
Mini Bar Beverage Revenue												
Other Food Revenue												
Other Beverage Revenue												
Less: Allowances												
Total Food and Beverage Revenue												
OTHER REVENUE												
Audiovisual												
Public Room Rentals												
Cover Charges												
Service Charges												
Miscellaneous Other Revenue												
Less: Allowances												
Total Other Revenue												
TOTAL REVENUE												
COST OF FOOD AND BEVERAGE SALES												
Cost of Food Sales												
Cost of Beverage Sales												
Total Cost of Food and Beverage Sales												
COST OF OTHER REVENUE												
Audiovisual Cost												
Miscellaneous Cost												
Total Cost of Other Revenue												
TOTAL COST OF SALES AND OTHER REVENUE												
GROSS PROFIT (LOSS)												
EXPENSES												
Payroll and Related Expenses												
Salaries, Wages, and Bonuses												
Salaries and Wages												
Bonuses and Incentives												
Total Salaries, Wages, and Bonuses												
Payroll-Related Expenses												
Payroll Taxes												
Supplemental Pay												
Employee Benefits												
Total Payroll-Related Expenses												
Total Payroll and Related Expenses												

(continued)

Exhibit 2 *(continued)*

	CURRENT MONTH			YEAR-TO-DATE		
	ACTUAL	FORECAST	PRIOR YEAR	ACTUAL	FORECAST	PRIOR YEAR
	$ %	$ %	$ %	$ %	$ %	$ %
Other Expenses						
Banquet Expense						
China						
Cleaning Supplies						
Complimentary Services and Gifts						
Contract Services						
Corporate Office Reimbursables						
Decorations						
Dishwashing Supplies						
Dues and Subscriptions						
Equipment Rental						
Flatware						
Glassware						
Ice						
Kitchen Fuel						
Laundry and Dry Cleaning						
Licenses and Permits						
Linen						
Management Fees						
Menus and Beverage Lists						
Miscellaneous						
Music and Entertainment						
Operating Supplies						
Paper and Plastics						
Printing and Stationery						
Royalty Fees						
Telecommunications						
Training						
Travel-Meals and Entertainment						
Travel-Other						
Uniform Laundry						
Uniforms						
Utensils						
Total Other Expenses						
TOTAL EXPENSES						
DEPARTMENTAL INCOME (LOSS)						

Source: *Uniform System of Accounts for the Lodging Industry*, 10th rev. ed. (Lansing, Mich: American Hotel & Lodging Educational Institute, 2006), pp. 51–52.

These examples illustrate the kind of information food and beverage managers use to calculate actual food and beverage costs and to state them in ways that allow them to compare these actual costs to standard or budgeted costs.

Exhibit 3   Information for Basic Cost of Sales Calculation

Required Information	Cost of Sales: Food	Cost of Sales: Beverage
Beginning Inventory	Physical Inventory Forms (last month)	Physical Inventory Forms (last month)
+ Purchases	Delivery Invoice*	Delivery Invoice*
Amount Available – Ending Inventory	Physical Inventory Forms (end of current month)	Physical Inventory Forms (end of current month)
Basic Cost of Sales	Basic Cost of Sales: Food	Basic Cost of Sales: Beverage

* Larger operations with formal accounting procedures may post information from the delivery invoices to a "purchase journal" after payment. This source, representing invoices for products received and paid for during the month plus delivery invoices representing products received but not paid during the month, may also be totaled to determine the value of purchases for the month. (Note: the value of credit memos, if any, which represent items on delivery invoices that are rejected/returned, must be deducted from the value of purchase noted on delivery invoices.)

Note that the suggested format of the statement allows readers to note, for each line on the statement, the actual, estimated (budgeted), and prior year's actual results for the current month and year-to-date.

Actual Cost of Sales: The Basic Calculation

What is the actual amount of money used to purchase the food and beverage products that were sold during the month? The basic actual monthly cost of sales for food and beverages is calculated as follows:

$$\text{Cost of Sales } = \text{ Beginning Inventory } + \text{ Purchases } - \text{ Ending Inventory}$$

For example, assume:

	Food	Beverage
Beginning Inventory	$ 124,500	$ 36,800
Purchases	+ 85,000	+ 29,500
Ending Inventory	– 112,250	– 27,500
Cost of Sales	$ 97,250	$ 38,800

Sources of Information for Basic Cost of Sales

Exhibit 3 illustrates the sources of information for calculating the basic cost of sales. As you review these sources, note that the value of product inventory is calculated only once monthly. The value of ending inventory on the last day of one fiscal period (such as July 31) is the same as the value of beginning inventory on the first day of the next fiscal period (August 1).

When manual accounting systems are used, the value of food and beverage purchases for the month can be obtained from the sum of the daily receiving reports for the period. Delivery invoices may be attached to these documents. If all the daily receiving reports are completed correctly, they will separate all food and beverage purchases, thus reducing the time needed to make these calculations. If a daily receiving report is not used, the value of purchases will be the sum of delivery invoices, adjusted by applicable request-for-credit memos. Often invoice items are separated into food and beverage categories.

The use of integrated purchasing, receiving, and accounts payable software eases the tasks of manual "paper shuffling" and routing. Managers can still pay suppliers based on individual delivery invoices or from statements that summarize one or more invoices. As part of the payment process, items can be sorted into food and beverage categories, tallies for the period can be made, and the total purchase cost of food and beverage products can be easily and accurately calculated on a timely basis.

Values of ending inventories for food and beverage items can be taken directly from the physical inventory system. Remember the importance of consistency in:

- The method used to calculate the cost of inventory items (inventory valuation methods are discussed in the next section).

- Decisions such as how to treat the value of food supplies in workstations and the value of opened bottles behind the bar.

- Whether items in broken (open) cases, in miscellaneous storage areas, or in process are to be considered "in storage" and under inventory control, or whether they are considered issued and are to be included as part of the costs incurred during the accounting period.

Calculating Inventory Value

The value of inventory is a critical element in calculating the cost of sales. We have also noted the importance of using a consistent method to calculate inventory. There are four generally accepted methods for calculating inventory:

- *First-in, first-out (FIFO).* The **first-in, first-out (FIFO)** approach assigns the first, or earliest, product costs to *issues,* so the most recent, or latest, product costs are applied to the products left in inventory.

- *Last-in, first-out (LIFO).* The **last-in, first-out (LIFO)** approach assigns the last, or most recent, product costs to *issues,* so the earliest product costs are applied to the products left in inventory.

- *Actual cost.* The value of stored products is the total value represented by the individual costs of the units in storage when the inventory is taken.

- *Weighted average.* The quantity of products purchased at different unit costs is considered by "weighting" the prices to be averaged based on the quantity of products in storage at each price when the inventory is taken.

To explain further and clarify the differences among these methods of inventory valuation, let's assume that, among the items in inventory at the end of the month, there are 28 cases of applesauce with a cost of $22.00 per case. Therefore, at the beginning of the next month, there are also 28 cases of applesauce available as part of the beginning inventory for that month. Now, assume that this month's delivery invoice shows that 15 cases of applesauce with a cost of $23.80 per case were purchased. Finally, suppose that at the end of this current month, the inventory count reveals there are now 20 cases available. From this, we know that 23 cases were issued (28 cases in beginning inventory + 15 cases purchased − 20 cases in ending inventory = 23 cases issued). What is the value of the applesauce in inventory?

Let's see how the different inventory valuation methods are applied to this example.[3] Notice that the four methods yield different values for the same amount of applesauce in inventory.

FIFO Method. Using the FIFO method, we value issues by assigning costs in the order in which they were incurred; consequently, we value inventory by assigning the most recent costs before earlier costs. As stated above, 23 cases were issued. Since 28 cases at the earlier cost of $22.00 were available, it is possible to assign this earlier cost to all 23 cases issued during the month. After we have done this, we have 5 remaining cases valued at the earlier cost and all 15 of the cases purchased at $23.80. The calculated value of the applesauce in inventory is:

Most Recent Costs:	15 Cases
	× $23.80/Case
	$357.00
Beginning Inventory Costs:	5 Cases
	× $22.00/Case
	$110.00
Value of Applesauce in Inventory:	$357.00
	+ 110.00
	$467.00

LIFO Method. Using the LIFO method, we value issues by assigning the most recent costs first. Since 23 cases were issued, we must assign the cost of all 15 of the more recently purchased cases *and* 8 from the earlier purchase. The 20 cases remaining in inventory are valued at the earlier cost. The calculated value of the applesauce in inventory is:

$$\text{Earlier Cost} = 20 \text{ Cases} \times \$22.00/\text{Case} = \$440.00$$

Suppose that only 10 cases had been issued during the month. In this situation, we would have 33 cases left in inventory (28 + 15 − 10). Under the LIFO system, the 10 cases that had been issued would be costed at $23.80 each. Of the 33 remaining in inventory, 28 would be costed at $22.00 each and the other 5 at $23.80 each.

Actual Cost Method. If the actual cost method were used, each case of applesauce would be dated and marked with its actual purchase price when it was received and entered into storage. (This marking system should be used regardless of the inventory valuation method in use for inventory control purposes.) To calculate inventory costs, the number of cases of applesauce available at each purchase price would be counted. Let's assume that, according to an actual count made at the end of the month, there are 14 cases that were purchased at $23.80 per case and 6 cases that were purchased at $22.00 per case currently available in inventory. (In other words, for whatever reason, one of the new cases was issued before all of the older cases had been issued.) The actual cost method of calculating inventory value would determine the actual value of applesauce in inventory to be:

$$14 \text{ Cases} \times \$23.80/\text{Case} = \$333.20$$
$$6 \text{ Cases} \times \$22.00/\text{Case} = \$132.00$$
$$\text{Value of Applesauce in Inventory} = \$465.20$$

Weighted Average Method. The **weighted average** method for inventory valuation also takes into account the actual number of cases acquired at each price. However, this method determines the value of inventory by multiplying the number of cases remaining in inventory at the end of the month by the average case price paid during the month. According to this method, the value of applesauce in inventory is calculated as follows:

$$\text{Beginning Inventory} = 28 \text{ Cases} \times \$22.00/\text{Case} = \$616.00$$
$$\text{Purchases During Month} = 15 \text{ Cases} \times \$23.80/\text{Case} = \$357.00$$
$$43 \text{ Cases} \qquad\qquad = \$973.00$$

$$\text{Average Case Price} = \$973.00 \div 43 \text{ Cases} = \$22.63/\text{Case}$$

$$\frac{\text{Number of Cases}}{\text{in Inventory}} \times \text{Average Case Price} = \frac{\text{Value of Applesauce}}{\text{in Ending Inventory}}$$

$$20 \text{ Cases} \qquad \times \qquad \$22.63/\text{Case} \qquad = \qquad \$452.60$$

Clearly, the method used to measure inventory can have a significant effect on the calculated value. In our example, the value of applesauce in inventory could be any of the following:

$467.00 — FIFO method
$440.00 — LIFO method
$465.20 — Actual cost method
$452.60 — Weighted average method

There is a range from $467.00 (FIFO method) to $440.00 (LIFO method). This difference of $27.00 represents only a small quantity of one product in inventory. When the values of large quantities of different products are assessed, the difference between the results obtained by the various inventory valuation methods can be several thousand dollars or more.

The inventory valuation method chosen should be used consistently. There are tax implications and restrictions placed on changing inventory valuation methods. Also, consistent information is needed for accounting purposes. The value of inventory will affect the operation's subsequent profit level. As the value of inventory increases, the value of actual product cost (cost of sales) will decrease. As this occurs, profit levels increase, and the income tax paid on profits will also increase. The reverse is also true. As the value of inventory decreases, actual product cost

(cost of sales) will increase. As this occurs, profit levels will decrease because there is an increase in total costs, and tax liabilities on profits will decrease. It is very important that managers obtain advice from an accountant knowledgeable about current tax laws when deciding which inventory valuation method would be appropriate for the specific food and beverage operation.

Inventory Counting Procedures. As a control measure, it is important that the task of assigning inventory values be given to someone not responsible for storage. Perhaps the food service manager or head cook can work with the accountant/controller/bookkeeper to determine the value of food products in inventory. Similarly, the manager or beverage manager might work with an accounting representative to determine inventory values in beverage storage areas. Of course, in small properties the manager/owner, perhaps working alone, will be responsible for determining the value of inventory.

Policies and procedures for counting inventory should be carefully developed and consistently followed. Also, to obtain ending inventory values for the fiscal period (which will be the beginning inventory values for the next fiscal period), inventory counts should be taken at the close of the last day of the fiscal period.

Adjustments to Basic Cost of Sales

One reason to calculate the cost of sales is to determine the product cost incurred in generating revenues. However, to make the information more meaningful and useful, some adjustments to the basic cost of sales may be helpful. This is because the unadjusted basic cost of sales will include costs not directly related to generating revenue. For example, in operations where meals are provided free of charge or at a reduced charge to employees, the food cost (and food cost percentage) will be overstated if the cost of sales is not adjusted (reduced) to compensate for employee meals. These food expenses were incurred to feed employees, not to generate revenue. The cost of meals to employees is properly considered a labor or benefits cost rather than a food cost.

Some food and beverage managers use the unadjusted cost of sales as their monthly food and beverage costs because they believe that the increased degree of accuracy does not warrant the increased amount of time it takes to make adjustments. However, even food and beverage operations with relatively small annual revenue levels (less than $500,000) may note a significant difference in product costs when adjustments are made to yield a more accurate picture of the cost of generating revenues.

When adjustments are made to the basic cost of sales, the amount deducted must be charged to some other expense category. Managers who want a more accurate identification of the costs of food and beverage products that generated revenue may make any or all of the adjustments listed in Exhibit 4. These adjustments are examined in the following sections. If any of these adjustments are made to the actual cost of sales, they also must be reflected in how standard food costs are calculated for comparisons to be meaningful. In other words, if, for example, employee meal costs are excluded from actual food cost calculations, they should also be excluded when determining standard (expected) food costs. Note, however, that computerized systems generating ideal (theoretical) costs based on number of

Exhibit 4   Adjustments to Basic Cost of Sales

Cost of Sales: Food	Charge to:	Cost of Sales: Beverage	Charge to:
Value of Beginning Inventory + Purchases − Value of Ending Inventory		Value of Beginning Inventory + Purchases − Value of Ending Inventory	
Unadjusted Cost of Sales: Food		Unadjusted Cost of Sales: Beverage	
+ Transfers to Kitchen	Food Cost	− Transfers to Kitchen	Food Cost
− Transfers from Kitchen	Bev. Cost	+ Transfers from Kitchen	Bev. Cost
− Employees' Meal Cost	Labor Cost		
− Value of Complimentary Meals	Promotion Expense	− Value of Complimentary Drinks	Promotion Expense
Net Cost of Sales: Food		Net Cost of Sales: Beverage	

items sold times recipe costs already exclude irrelevant costs, so no adjustments are needed. Once calculated, the actual monthly cost of food or beverages should be compared with standard costs, budgeted performance expectations, and, if useful, past financial statements.

Food Transfers. Transfers from the kitchen to the bar decrease the cost of food sales. Examples of food transfers are fruits from the kitchen taken to the bar to be used as drink garnishes, and ice cream taken from the kitchen to be used to prepare after-dinner drinks at the bar. Food served in bars during "cocktail hours" or at other times can be a large cost, which, more appropriately, should not be charged to the food costs. Because these transfers generate beverage revenue, they are more appropriately charged to the beverage operation. This adjustment would decrease the operation's food expense and increase its beverage expense.

Beverage Transfers. Transfers to the kitchen from the bar increase the cost of food sales. Examples of beverage transfers are wine used for cooking in the kitchen and **liqueurs** used for tableside flaming of desserts in the dining room. Although these expenses were initially charged to the beverage operation, they did not generate beverage revenue, but were used to increase food revenues. Therefore, these costs are more appropriately charged to food. This adjustment would increase food costs and decrease beverage costs.

Transfer Memo. When adjustments are made for the cost of transfers, a beverage and food transfer memo (Exhibit 5) can be used as the **source document**. A memo is completed each time products are transferred between the food department and the beverage department. The forms can be hard copy or electronic. Once transferred, they can be held (hard copy) or electronically summed through the accounting period, after which the bookkeeper can total all transfers and make the adjustments in the cost of sales. Transfers to the beverage department will increase beverage costs and decrease food costs by the same amount. Transfers to the food department will increase food costs and decrease beverage costs by the same amount.

Food and beverage departments in large hotels can use transfer memos in another way. Some large properties set up support centers, such as bake shops,

Exhibit 5   Sample Beverage and Food Transfer Memo

Date: _____		Memo Number: _____107801_____		
Issued to: ☑ Food ☐ Beverage		**Name of Employee**		
		Issuing Food/Beverage: _____Joe_____		
Issued from: ☐ Food ☑ Beverage		**Receiving Food/Beverage:** _____Sam_____		

Item	Unit	No. of Units	Cost/Unit	Total Unit
House Burgundy	3L	2	8.15	16.30
Sauterne	L	1	3.90	3.90
			Total	$20.20

production kitchens, and even beverage storerooms. As revenue centers (restaurants or bars) requisition products from these support centers, costs for the products are charged to the revenue centers that requisition them. Charges may even include an allocated share of administrative and overhead costs incurred by the support center.

Employee Meals. Employee meal costs are usually calculated by multiplying a fixed amount (the property's food cost per meal) by the number of employee meals served. This food cost may be deducted from the cost of food sales and charged to the labor or employee benefits account. (Procedures for calculating employee meal costs are beyond the scope of this chapter. They can be complicated and have both legal [wage and hour law] and income tax implications. Interested readers can contact their state restaurant association, Department of Labor, or accountant for current information.)

Complimentary Food and Beverages. Complimentary meals and drinks—for example, those provided to prospective guests touring the operation or for other purposes—might reasonably be considered a marketing (promotion) cost. If so, the cost of food or beverage sales can be reduced by their value, and the costs can be transferred to the appropriate marketing account.

Sample Calculations

Now that we have reviewed procedures to calculate actual food and beverage costs, let's look at an example. The manager of the Sunny Seaview Restaurant has recorded the following information for July:

July 31 inventory (food)	$ 78,500
July 31 inventory (beverage)	$ 28,500
Food purchases	$387,000
Beverage purchases	$109,350
Food revenues	$975,000
Beverage revenues	$410,250
Transfers to kitchen	$ 19,475
Transfers from kitchen	$ 10,775
Employees' meal cost	$ 17,400
Complimentary food	$ 6,400
Complimentary beverages	$ 4,800

Assume that the June 30 (end-of-month) food and beverage inventory values were $57,400 and $34,750, respectively.

To determine the cost of sales for food and beverage for July, the manager makes the following calculations:

Factor	Food		Beverage	
Beginning inventory *	$ 57,400		$ 34,750	
Purchases	387,000		109,350	
Total food/beverage available	444,000		144,100	
Less ending inventory	(78,500)		(28,500)	
Unadjusted cost of sales		$ 365,500		$ 115,600
Transfers to kitchen	19,455		(19,455)	
Transfers from kitchen	(10,775)		10,775	
Employees' meal cost	(17,400)			
Complimentary food	(6,400)			
Complimentary beverages			(4,800)	
Total adjustments		(15,120)		(13,480)
Net cost of sales		$ 350,380		$ 102,120

*The July 1 beginning inventory value is the same as the June 30 ending inventory value.

As seen above, net costs of sales for food and beverage are $350,380 and $102,120, respectively. If the manager had not made the adjustments, the product costs would have been overstated by the amount of the total adjustments ($15,120 for food plus $13,480 for beverages).

Now let's calculate the food and beverage cost percentages:

Industry Leaders Recognize the Importance of Adjustments

The lodging industry's uniform system of accounts* notes that "Cost of Food Sales" includes the cost of food served to guests, including the cost of beverage items transferred from the beverage department and used for food preparation and service. It also notes that spoilage, waste, and spillage are included in the cost of food sales, and these costs are not charged to another expense account. It also emphasizes the importance of adjustments when it indicates that the cost of food sales does not include the cost of food items that can be transferred to other departments, and that these transfers should be charged to the cost accounts in the departments receiving the food items. The *Uniform System of Accounts for the Lodging Industry* also notes that "cost of food sales" does not include the cost of food used to prepare employee meals, and that these costs should instead be allocated to each employee's department. Finally, the "cost of food sales" does not include food items used for gratis (free) purposes; complimentary foods should instead be charged to the department providing these gifts.

* *Uniform System of Accounts for the Lodging Industry,* Tenth Revised Edition (Lansing, Mich.: American Hotel & Lodging Educational Institute, 2006). Information about cost of food sales appears on page 58.

Unadjusted Cost			Net Cost		

$$\text{Cost of sales: food} \quad \frac{\text{Unadjusted cost of sales}}{\text{Food revenues}} = \frac{\$365,000}{\$975,000} = \frac{37.5\%}{\text{(rounded)}} \qquad \frac{\text{Net cost of sales}}{\text{Food revenues}} = \frac{\$350,380}{\$975,000} = 35.9\%$$

$$\text{Cost of sales: beverage} \quad \frac{\text{Unadjusted cost of sales}}{\text{Beverage revenues}} = \frac{\$115,600}{\$410,250} = \frac{28.2\%}{\text{(rounded)}} \qquad \frac{\text{Net cost of sales}}{\text{Beverage revenues}} = \frac{\$102,120}{\$410,250} = \frac{24.9\%}{\text{(rounded)}}$$

Since managers made the appropriate adjustments to the food and beverage cost, the actual food cost percentage was lowered to 35.9 percent (from the unadjusted cost of 37.5 percent), and the actual beverage cost percentage was lowered to 24.9 percent (from its unadjusted counterpart of 28.2 percent).

Actual Food Costs: Daily Calculations

Monthly calculations of actual food and beverage costs are sufficient to yield information required for monthly accounting statements. However, for control purposes, some food and beverage operators require more timely information about actual costs against which to compare standard cost estimates. Suppose something goes wrong early in a month and continues to the end of the month. Another several days may elapse while actual operating data is developed into formal accounting reports. When these reports are then compared with standard costs, the problem is finally discovered. However, several weeks may now have passed since the problem first developed, and more time will be needed to resolve the problem. Many dollars might have been saved if the problem had been detected earlier. Therefore, some properties use a practical daily food cost control system to help reduce this kind of problem.

Components of Daily Food Costs

The two components of daily food costs are directs and stores. **Directs** are typically inexpensive and perishable items, such as fresh produce, bakery, and dairy products, which are purchased on a frequent basis for immediate use; they are not entered into perpetual inventory records. Directs are charged to daily food costs on the day they are received, even if they are not used on that day. Because directs are considered a food cost when received, they can be assessed daily. When received, directs are entered into manual or electronic daily receiving reports like all other items. They then can be sent to production immediately or to a storage area for later use. For example, fresh bread may be sent to the pantry as soon as it is received. By contrast, fresh produce may be placed in the refrigerator for use over the next one or two days. However, because it is classified as a direct, it will not be entered into perpetual inventory records even though it is physically stored in an inventory area.

Stores are charged to food costs when they are issued. All food items are ultimately perishable, but some items (frozen meats and seafood, for example) may be stored for a longer period of time than perishable directs. Since they are purchased on the basis of anticipated rather than immediate need, they may be purchased, in effect, for inventory. When received, they are entered into the daily receiving report and perpetual inventory records. When needed for production, they are withdrawn from inventory using the property's issuing process, and perpetual inventory information is adjusted accordingly. Food items removed from inventory are first listed on a food issue requisition form. Food items frequently classified as stores include frozen products, grocery (canned) items, and, sometimes, staples such as flour and sugar. Some fresh items, such as meats, poultry, and seafood, while extremely perishable, are also often considered stores, since they are expensive and would otherwise significantly overstate food costs on daily records.

Sources of Actual Daily Food Cost Information

Two source documents provide reasonably accurate information for calculating actual daily food costs. Cost of daily directs comes from the daily receiving report. Cost of daily stores used in production comes from food issue requisitions. If an operation's standard and actual food cost calculations include adjustments for food and beverage transfers, employee meals, and complimentary food and beverages (as discussed earlier), these adjustments should also be made to daily food cost calculations.

Calculating Actual Daily Food Costs

If daily receiving report and issue requisition information from manual or electronic systems is gathered daily, it is easy to assess the actual daily food cost. While reviewing the actual daily food cost worksheet (Exhibit 6), note that information for each day is listed separately. The date is indicated in column 1. The unadjusted

Exhibit 6   Daily Food Cost Worksheet

	Cost of					Daily Food Cost		Food Revenue		Food Cost Percent	
Date	Store-room Issues (Stores)	Directs	Total Food Cost	Add Adjust-ments	Less Adjust-ments	Today	To Date	Today	To Date	Today	To Date
Col. 1	Col. 2	Col. 3	Col. 4	Col. 5	Col. 6	Col. 7	Col. 8	Col. 9	Col. 10	Col. 11	Col. 12
8/1	$385.15	$176.85	$562.00	+42.50	−18.75	$585.75	$ 585.75	$1,425.00	$1,425.00	41.1%	41.1%
8/2	370.80	110.15	480.95	+31.80	−36.15	476.60	1,062.35	1,218.50	2,643.50	39.1%	40.2%

Month: August

daily food cost (column 4) is calculated by adding the value of all issues for the day (the sum of costs of all food issue requisition forms reported in column 2) to the value of all directs (calculated by adding the directs column from daily receiving report information and recorded in column 3).

Any factors that increase food cost, such as transfers to food from beverage, are listed in column 5. Similarly, factors that reduce food costs, such as transfers from food to beverage, cost of employee meals, and complimentary meals, are listed in column 6.

Daily food cost (column 7) is calculated by adding "total food cost" (column 4) to "add adjustments" (column 5) and subtracting "less adjustments" (column 6). For example, for 8/1, the calculation is:

$$\begin{matrix} \text{Total food} \\ \text{cost} \end{matrix} + \begin{matrix} \text{Add} \\ \text{adjustments} \end{matrix} - \begin{matrix} \text{Less} \\ \text{adjustments} \end{matrix} = \begin{matrix} \text{Total daily} \\ \text{food cost} \end{matrix}$$

$$\$562.00 \quad + \quad \$42.50 \quad - \quad \$18.75 \quad = \quad \$585.75$$

In column 8, the food and beverage manager, accountant, and area manager (in multi-unit operations) can keep a running total of daily food costs throughout the month. This is important, because, for a single day, the total daily food cost is not likely to reflect actual costs. Suppose that a large shipment of fresh produce—which is classified as a direct—is received on 8/1. Even though some is used on 8/1 and the remainder is used on 8/2, the cost of all this produce is charged to food cost on 8/1 (column 3). This practice, while easy and fast, overstates the daily food cost (column 7) for 8/1. On the following day, the value of directs (column 3) is less, because no fresh produce is received, and total food cost (column 7) is reduced accordingly. A running total food cost, then, allows these factors to even out. As the number of days increases, the food cost total in column 8 becomes more accurate. Column 8 is calculated by adding that day's food cost (column 7) to the previous day's to-date food cost (column 8). In the worksheet for 8/1, food cost (column 7) equals column 8, since it is the first day of the month. However, on 8/2 the to-date cost (column 8) is:

$$\begin{array}{ccccc} \text{Food Cost} & + & \text{Food Cost} & = & \text{To-Date Food Cost} \\ (8/2) & & (8/1) & & (8/2) \end{array}$$

$$\$476.60 \quad + \quad \$585.75 \quad = \quad \$1,062.35$$

Column 9—food revenue today—is the revenue generated from the sale of the food in column 7. The source of this information depends on the revenue control system used. It may be the sum of food revenue from guest checks, POS system (sales journal records) reports, or daily food revenue reports.

Column 10—food revenue to date—is the food revenue generated to date during the month. It is the sum of today's revenue plus yesterday's to-date revenue. For example, on 8/2:

$$\begin{array}{ccccc} \text{Food Revenue} & + & \text{Food Revenue} & = & \text{To-Date Food Revenue} \\ (8/2) & & (8/1) & & (8/2) \end{array}$$

$$\$1,218.50 \quad + \quad \$1,425.00 \quad = \quad \$2,643.50$$

The day's food cost percentage is in column 11. It is calculated by dividing today's food cost (column 7) by today's food revenues (column 9) and multiplying by 100. For example, on 8/2:

$$\frac{\$476.60}{\$1,218.50} = 0.391 \times 100 = 39.1\%$$

The food cost percentage to date (column 12) is calculated by dividing the food cost to date (column 8) by the food revenue to date (column 10) and multiplying by 100. For example, on 8/2:

$$\frac{\$1,062.35}{\$2,643.50} = 0.402 \times 100 = 40.2\%$$

The food cost percentage is the actual food cost percentage to date for the month. This actual food cost can be compared with standard (expected) food costs (for example, from ideal data generated by the POS system) and budgeted performance expectations, as well as—if useful—past financial statements. If, as the month continues, daily actual food cost percentages are higher (or lower) than standard food cost percentages, some immediate corrective action may be needed. With a daily food cost system in place, identifying problems and taking corrective action to resolve them can occur much earlier in the process.

Actual Beverage Costs: Daily Calculations

The beverage manager, like the food manager, has access to monthly cost of sales information reported on the income statement. However, the beverage manager, like the food manager, may also want more timely information to make decisions as soon as possible after observing a problem. If a practical system to assess actual daily beverage costs is available that will provide reasonably accurate information without requiring a significant amount of time to develop, implement, and utilize, it would be a very useful control tool to beverage management. This section explains how to develop such a system. Once developed and implemented, it can be used to collect daily beverage cost information as an integral part of the control process.

Principles for Calculating Actual Daily Beverage Costs

The cost of beverages issued to each bar in a hotel or restaurant at either the end or the beginning of a shift can be used to represent the actual beverage costs for the just-completed shift. If a bar par inventory is developed, and if issues are made only to restore the bar par on a bottle-for-bottle replacement basis, it is simple to collect beverage cost information based on the cost of issues. Beverage managers must decide whether to collect beverage cost information by shift or by day. When information is collected by shift, beverages are issued to the bar at the end or beginning of each shift. The cost of issues reported on the beverage issue requisition form to replenish bottles emptied during the shift represents the cost of beverages used for the shift. If beverage cost information is collected on a per-day basis, the cost of all bottles issued to the bar during the day represents the daily beverage costs.

Beverage Cost per Shift. Several factors influence the decision to collect beverage cost information by shift or by day. As more accuracy is desired, more specific data by shift is necessary. Also, as explained later in the chapter, collecting information by shift makes it very easy to assess beverage costs both by shift and by bartender, since the required data can be easily summarized. In this way, detailed beverage control plans can identify and help correct problems on a very specific (by-bar and by-bartender) basis.

As the volume of revenue increases, it becomes even more important to collect beverage cost information by shift. Unless storage space behind the bar is very large, some issuing during the day may be necessary. Also, increased quantities of issued products and higher revenue levels may make it more difficult to identify causes of problems when only per-day data is available.

With more beverage outlets, the difficulty of identifying and correcting operational problems increases. If, for example, the beverage cost is too high, how does the beverage manager determine which bar and which bartender are responsible and when the problem(s) occurred?

As suggested, beverage costs can be represented by the costs of issues to the bar or bars at the end or the beginning of the shift or day. With this plan, no cost or inventory count is needed for central beverage storerooms, bar inventories, or changes in opened bottles behind the bar. Obviously, this is a simple procedure, but how much accuracy is sacrificed?

Behind-the-Bar Bottle Cost. On average, each opened bottle behind the bar is half full. Some bottles are almost full or almost empty; others may be one-quarter or three-quarters full. But the average bottle (and the average becomes more accurate as both the number of bottles and the number of observations increase) is half full. Therefore, unless extreme accuracy is desired, there is little need to calculate the quantities and costs of opened bottles behind the bar when taking inventory. A one-time cost of the opened-bottle inventory can be established based on the bar par, subject to increases over time as costs (inventory values) rise. This constant cost can be added to the value of beginning and ending inventories when calculating cost of sales. (Alternatively, no value can be assigned to opened-bottle inventory since, on average, it is the same at the time of beginning and ending inventory counts.)

When calculating daily beverage costs, changes in opened-bottle inventories become even less important. It is usually not practical to inventory opened bottles each shift or each day. Sometimes at the beginning of a shift, most of the bottles are almost full. Since few bottles may be emptied by the end of the shift, beverage cost, based on issues to replace empty bottles, is low. However, at the beginning of the next shift, most of the bottles may be almost empty. With the same amount of drinks produced, more bottles will be emptied during this shift, and the resulting beverage costs will be high. Again, since the volume of opened-bottle inventory will even out over time, there is little need to account for these differences. Eliminating the cost of opened-bottle inventory allows reasonably accurate daily or shift beverage costs to be developed speedily and practically in a manual beverage control system.

Procedures for Calculating Daily Beverage Costs: Manual System

The following procedures can be used to calculate daily beverage costs when a manual control system is in place:

1. At the beginning of a shift, the bartender reviews the inventory of bottles behind the bar to ensure that the bar par is complete. If the bar par is replenished at the beginning of a shift, the bar is now restocked on a full-bottle for empty-bottle basis.

2. During the shift, the bartender prepares drinks and collects revenue according to required procedures.

3. At the end of the shift, bottles emptied during the shift are listed on the beverage issue requisition form. (The bar par can be replenished if restocking is done at the end of the shift.) If costs were marked on the bottles at the time of receiving, storing, or issuing, the bartender can easily record the unit costs.

4. The operation's procedures for issuing the bottles from the beverage storeroom should be followed.

5. The actual beverage cost for the shift (the cost of bottles issued at the end of the shift) is calculated by completing the beverage issue requisition form.

6. Revenue information is obtained from the POS system (or guest checks if a manual revenue control system is used). The beverage cost of sales percentage is calculated by dividing the beverage cost by the beverage revenue during the shift and multiplying by 100:

Exhibit 7   Daily Beverage Cost Percentage Worksheet: Manual System

	Bar: Lunch		Bar: Main		Bar: Service		Bar: French		Beverage Cost		Beverage Revenue		Beverage Cost Percent	
Date	Cost	Rev.	Cost	Rev.	Cost	Rev.	Cost	Rev.	Today	To Date	Today	To Date	Today	To Date
1	2	3	4	5	6	7	8	9	10	11	12	13	14	15
2/1	$82.15	$410.75	$125.15	$585.75	$88.00	$465.00	$215.25	$1,052.35	$510.55	$510.55	$2,513.85	$2,513.85	20.3%	20.3%
2/2	$98.50	$415.80	$165.35	$625.00	$110.00	$565.35	$263.15	$1,182.30	$637.00	$1,147.55	$2,788.45	$5,302.30	22.8%	21.6%

$$\frac{\text{Beverage Cost/Shift}}{\text{Beverage Revenue/Shift}} \times 100 = \text{Beverage Cost of Sales Percentage/Shift}$$

While it may be useful to compare the actual beverage costs with expected beverage costs, it is better to compare one shift's actual costs with those from previous shifts. A daily beverage cost percentage worksheet can help:

1. In the sample form shown in Exhibit 7, only one bar is open during the lunch shift. In the evening, that bar, the main and service bars, and a second public bar (the French Bar) are open.

2. Each date of beverage operation is shown in column 1. The next eight columns list cost and revenue (in dollars) for each shift and each bar. Information is taken directly from applicable beverage issue requisition forms.

3. To find today's total beverage cost (column 10), add the beverage costs for all bars for the day. On 2/1, the beverage costs are:

$$\$82.15 + \$125.15 + \$88.00 + \$215.25 = \$510.55$$

4. The beverage cost to date and beverage revenue to date (columns 11 and 13, respectively) are calculated by adding the daily cost and revenue to yesterday's to-date cost and revenue. On 2/2, the beverage cost to date is calculated as follows:

$$\$637.00 + \$510.55 = \$1,147.55$$

5. Today's beverage cost of sales percentage (column 14) is calculated by dividing the beverage cost today by beverage revenue today and multiplying by 100. For 2/1:

$$\frac{\$510.55}{\$2,513.85} \times 100 = 20.3\%$$

Exhibit 8   Bartender Performance Review Form

					Bartender Name								
Joe			Sam			Jack			Relief Only			Weekly Average	
Date	Bar	%	Date	Bar	%	Date	Bar	%	Date	Bar		%	
2/1	Lunch	20.0	2/1	Main	21.4	2/1	Service	18.9	N	O	N	E	
2/2	Lunch	23.7	2/2	Service	19.5	2/2	French	22.3	N	O	N	E	
2/7	Lunch	22.8	2/8	Main	21.2	—	—	—	N	O	N	E	
		22.3			20.5			21.5				—	21.4%

6. The to-date beverage cost of sales percentage (column 15) is calculated by dividing the beverage cost to date by the beverage revenue to date and multiplying by 100. For 2/2:

$$\frac{\$1,147.55}{\$5,302.30} \times 100 = 21.6\%$$

The to-date beverage cost of sales percentage (column 15) is the actual beverage cost of sales percentage to date for the month. If, as the month continues, the actual daily beverage costs are higher than the standard beverage costs, immediate corrective action may be in order.

Bartender Performance Review

Information from the daily beverage cost percentage worksheet also can be used to assess each bartender's performance. This is desirable, because some bartenders may fail to use standard beverage control tools (standard recipes, standard portion tools, and standard ice size) or not consistently comply with revenue control procedures. When reviewing the bartender performance review form (Exhibit 8), note that:

1. Beverage cost information from the beverage issue requisition form is transferred directly to this form. Cost and revenue data were listed for each bar and bartender in Exhibit 7, but the by-bar beverage cost of sales percentages were not calculated.

2. Each time a bartender works, his or her name, the bar worked, and resulting beverage cost of sales percentage are noted. Information comes from the beverage issue requisition form.

3. The average beverage cost of sales percentage for each bartender can be easily calculated. Assume that bartender Joe incurred the following beverage cost of sales percentages during the six shifts he worked during the week:

Date	Percentage
2/1	20.0
2/2	23.7
2/3	22.8
2/4	24.5
2/6	19.8
2/7	22.8

The average beverage cost of sales percentage is determined by adding each percentage and dividing by the number of days worked:

$$\frac{133.6\%}{6} = 22.3\%$$

The process can be used to compare each bartender's performance with the percentage recap form (Exhibit 7, column 15).

Comparisons may show a bartender's cost of sales percentage to be high or low. Perhaps the bartender is over-pouring or stealing, or perhaps the bartender is under-pouring or finding creative ways to bypass the property's revenue security system. In these cases, the bartender may require additional training or closer supervision to better ensure that quality and control requirements are consistently met. Note: bartenders who always work on special shifts (for example, during low-price cocktail hours or high-price entertainment periods) will typically have, respectively, higher and lower beverage cost percentages, since revenue levels affect beverage cost percentages.

Technology and Actual Product Cost Calculations

As with most other aspects of food and beverage control, technology can assist in the calculation of actual product costs. A special challenge is created, however, because accurate assessment of actual food and beverage cost requires information about changes in inventory volumes. (Recall from our discussion earlier in the chapter that actual cost of sales is determined by considering the costs of products in beginning inventories, plus those purchased, reduced by the cost of products still in storage.) While the use of bar coding and radio frequency identification (RFID) systems eases the inventory counting task, some time is still required, and relatively few properties with extensive menus requiring a large number of ingredients conduct daily inventory counts. (Some quick-service restaurants with limited menus [and, therefore, fewer ingredients] do take daily inventories, especially during times when food costs appear excessive.)

You learned that the ideal (theoretical) food costs can be determined by POS systems that consider the food cost that should have been incurred from the sale of all menu items. (This is calculated by multiplying the number of each menu item sold by its standard food cost per portion when standard recipes have been pre-costed with current market costs.) While this cost can (and should) be considered an actual cost that should be compared with the budgeted or other expected cost, the element of inventory change is still not considered, and unacceptable variances may not be identified until inventory counts are taken at the end of the month.

Multi-units organizations may transmit daily (or more frequent) sales information to central locations where cost of sales and numerous other calculations are made to compare estimated and actual cost data.

Technology is increasingly helpful in providing information that summarizes the actual cost of alcoholic beverages served. For example, automated beverage dispensing systems count (meter) the number of portions of each beverage dispensed through the system. Assume 37 drinks containing bar (well) whiskey are dispensed during a specific shift. The count of each will be recorded, and the total quantity of bar whiskey dispensed will be summed, as will the total amount of all other beverages dispensed through the system. These systems provide extra security when, for example, bottles are housed in a controlled-access area away from the bar.

Technology can be helpful in addressing the actual inventory count challenge noted earlier in the discussion about actual food costs. Wireless scanning technology can identify the beverage in each bottle behind the bar when a scanner reads a bar code placed on the bottle. If the bottle is opened, the manager can use a palm-type hand-held device to measure liquor level. With a stylus, the manager taps the liquor level observed to be in the bottle on an outline of a generic bottle showing on the palm device's screen. This process is repeated for all bottles behind the bar. When the inventory is taken, data is transmitted to a special server for report processing. Numerous reports can be created, including those that record quantities of liquor used and potential revenue that should have been generated. These are e-mailed to the manager's computer for viewing, printing, and analysis.

Digital scales are also available that weigh the contents of individual bottles of liquor, taking into account (deducting) the weight of the bottles themselves. This process yields information about the weight of liquor dispensed and remaining. Digital scales can be interfaced with a POS terminal at the bar or into a notebook PC. Revenues are downloaded from the POS system to produce variance reports that, among other factors, record the revenues that should have been generated based on the actual quantities of beverages dispensed.

A third example of technology developed to provide more precise beverage costing is a system of sensors designed to measure the amount of draught beer drawn by bartenders. Information generated by the system is sent to a personal computer where it can be compared with revenue figures downloaded from the POS system. The technology takes into account spillage, promotional discounts, foam, and the amount of predetermined shortage allowed by the manager. Information is available on a by-shift or other basis that managers deem to be most appropriate.

You have learned about the use of technology for receiving, storing, and issuing. Information about incoming products can be electronically summarized for receiving clerks' daily reports and food issue requisitions. Therefore, daily food cost worksheets such as the one shown in Exhibit 6 can be generated by the property's automated systems. How? The value of storeroom issues (stores) can be determined from computerized food issue requisitions, and the value of directs can be summarized from electronic receiving reports, which provides the input necessary for the daily food cost worksheet. Similarly, electronic versions of issue requisitions can be used to generate information required for the daily beverage cost percentage worksheet and bartender performance review forms illustrated in Exhibits 7 and 8, respectively.

Endnotes

1. *Uniform System of Accounts for Restaurants*, 7th rev. ed. (Washington, D.C.: National Restaurant Association, 1996).

2. *Uniform System of Accounts for the Lodging Industry*, 10th rev. ed. (Lansing, Mich.: American Hotel & Lodging Educational Institute, 2006).

3. This inventory valuation example is adapted from Raymond S. Schmidgall et al., *Restaurant Financial Basics* (New York: Wiley, 2002).

Key Terms

actual cost—A method of valuing inventory that considers the actual cost paid for all products in inventory; the value of stored products is the total value represented by summing the individual unit costs.

actual food and beverage cost—The cost of items sold, as determined by a factual weekly or monthly record.

cost of sales—The food or beverage cost incurred to produce all food and beverage items generating revenue during an accounting period.

directs (daily food cost components)—Inexpensive and typically perishable products charged to food costs on the day they are received.

first-in, first-out (FIFO)—A method of valuing inventory; the products in storage areas are valued at the level of the most recently purchased items to be placed in inventory.

last-in, first-out (LIFO)—A method of valuing inventory; the inventory value is assumed to be represented by the cost of items that were placed into inventory the earliest.

liqueurs—Sweet alcoholic beverages made with spices, fruits, nuts, seeds, or herbs.

source document—The point of original entry of financial data into the accounting or control system.

stores (daily food cost components)—Relatively expensive products charged to food costs when issued.

weighted average—A method of valuing inventory in which the quantity of products purchased at different unit costs is considered by "weighting" the prices based on the quantity of products in storage at each price.

Review Questions

1. Why is it important to compare standard and actual food and beverage costs?

2. Why are revenues and product costs determined separately for food and beverage revenue centers?

3. How are food cost percentages and beverage cost percentages determined?

4. How is the cost of sales (for food and for beverage) calculated?

5. What is the process for making adjustments to transfer food and beverage costs among revenue centers?

6. How would you decide on the method of inventory valuation to be used for a given property?

7. To what account should employee meals be allocated?

8. How are actual daily food costs and actual daily beverage costs calculated?

9. Why can it be important to separate beverage cost information by bartender?

10. How has technology eased the task of assessing actual food costs? actual beverage costs?

Internet Sites

For more information, visit the following Internet sites. Remember that Internet addresses can change without notice. If the site is no longer there, you can use a search engine to look for additional sites.

Actual Food Cost Calculations

Cyberchefs Electronic Union
www.marscafe.com/php/foodcost/
cost.html

Schiff's Food Service, Inc.
www.schiffs.com

Food Reference
www.foodreference.com/html/
artfoodcost.html

Automated Beverage Control Systems

Accubar
www.accubar.com

FreePour Controls, Inc.
www.freepour.com

Azbar Inc.
www.azbarusa.com

iBar Control, Inc.
www.ibarcontrol.com

Berg Company
www.berg-controls.com

USBeveragenet.com
www.usbeveragenet.com

Easybar Beverage Management
  Systems, Inc.
www.easybar.com

Wunder-Bar
www.wunderbar.com

Automated Food Cost Control Systems

Comus Restaurant Systems
www.comus.com

CostGuard Food Service Software
www.costguard.com

Culinary Software Services
www.culinarysoftware.com

Menulink Computer Solutions, Inc.
www.menulinkinc.net

Eatec Corporation
www.eatec.com

Optimum Control Software
www.tracrite.net

Enggist & Grandjean Software
www.eg-software.com

Radiant Systems, Inc.
www.radiantsystems.com

FoodSoftware.com
www.foodsoftware.com/default.asp

 **Problems**

Problem 1

Use the following data to answer the question below about actual food and beverage costs for the Marina Bay Grill for July:

Ending Inventory (Food)	$68,000
Ending Inventory (Beverage)	$23,470
Food Purchases	$305,000
Beverage Purchases	$24,700
Beginning Inventory (Food)	$72,400
Beginning Inventory (Beverage)	$19,700
Transfers to Bar	$3,870
Beverage Theft/Pilferage	$510
Food Over-Portioning Expense	$615
Transfers from Bar	$4,100
Complimentary Food	$2,160
Complimentary Beverages	$890
Employee Meal Cost	$11,225
Food Revenues	$878,000
Beverage Revenues	$116,500

What is the net cost of sales for food and beverage? Indicate dollar and percentage costs.

Problem 2

a. What are the unadjusted food and beverage costs for the Hillside Resort, given the following information for April? (Express your answer in dollars and percentages.)

	Food	**Beverage**
Beginning Inventory	$110,000	$38,500
Ending Inventory	$98,470	$41,000
Purchases	$488,000	$161,000
Revenues	$1,268,000	$742,000

b. The following additional information about April's food and beverage costs is also available. Use this data to calculate net costs of sales for food and beverage. (Express your answer in dollars and percentages.)

Transfers to Bar	$5,170
Transfers from Bar	$6,850
Employee Meals	$7,640
Complimentary Meals	$2,290
Complimentary Beverages	$840

c. By what amounts are the food and beverage costs over- or understated, based on comparisons between the unadjusted and net costs?

Problem 3

The Pleasant Meadows Restaurant uses frozen ground beef packed in 10-pound poly bags for many of its soup and casserole items. The per-bag purchase cost of all bags received in January was $30. Use the following information to calculate the value of ground beef inventory at the end of January:

	January 1	**January 31**
Inventory Count	17 bags	28 bags
Ending Inventory	$28.00	$30.00

There were 37 bags purchased (delivered) during January.

a. Calculate the value of ground beef inventory using the FIFO method.

b. Calculate the value of ground beef inventory using the LIFO method.

c. Calculate the value of ground beef inventory using the actual cost method. (A proper inventory rotation system was in use.)

d. Calculate the value of ground beef using the weighted average method.

Problem 4

Complete the following daily food cost worksheet:

Date	Issues	Directs	Total Cost	Add Adjust	Less Adjust	Daily Food Cost Today	Daily Food Cost To Date	Food Revenue Today	Food Revenue To Date	Food Cost % Today	Food Cost % To Date
7/1	$350.00	$210.00	560	$110.00	$120.00	550	550	$2400.00	2400	22.9	22.9
7/2	$870.00	$320.00	1190	$85.00	$55.00	1220	1770	$2900.00	53.00	42.1	33.40
7/3	$805.00	$290.00	1095	$70.00	$50.00	1115	2885	$3100.00	8400	36.00	34.3

+ ↑   + −

Problem 5

Using the worksheet below, calculate the daily food cost in dollars and percentages for three days given the following data:

Date	Issues	Directs	Trans to Bar	Trans from Bar	Employee Meals	Revenue
8/1	$410.00	$205.00	$71.00	$60.00	$81.00	$1850.00
8/2	$370.00	$175.00	$45.10	$51.00	$65.75	$1790.00
8/3	$520.00	$199.00	$50.70	$40.60	$68.00	$2150.00

Date	Issues	Directs	Total Cost	Add Adjust	Less Adjust	Daily Food Cost Today	Daily Food Cost To Date	Food Revenue Today	Food Revenue To Date	Food Cost % Today	Food Cost % To Date
8/1	$410.00	$205.00		60	152	523	1850	1850	1850	28.3	28.3
8/2	$370.00	$175.00		51	110.85	1008.15	3640	1790	3640	27.1	27.7
8/3	$520.00	$199.00		40.60	118.70	1649.05	5790	2150	5790	29.8	28.5

The desired food cost percentage is 27.8 percent. What should the manager do, based on calculations for the first three days of the month?

Problem 6

Complete the following daily beverage cost percentage worksheet:

Date	Bar 1 Cost	Bar 1 Revenue	Bar 2 Cost	Bar 2 Revenue	Beverage Cost Today	Beverage Cost To Date	Beverage Revenue Today	Beverage Revenue To Date	Beverage Cost Percentage Today	Beverage Cost Percentage To Date
(1)	(2)	(3)	(4)	(5)	(6)	(7)	(8)	(9)	(10)	(11)
7/1	$110.00	$470.00	$210.00	$840.00	320	320	1310	1310	24.4	24.4
7/2	$180.00	$710.00	$295.00	$1280.00	475	795	1990	3300	23.9	24.1
7/3	$161.00	$512.00	$300.00	$950.00	461	1256	1462	4762	31.5	26.4
7/4	$98.00	$480.00	$145.00	$615.00	243	1499	1095	5857	22.2	25.6

a. The beverage cost percentage is budgeted at 23 percent. What should the manager do, based on the first four days of the month?

b. The manager wonders whether one bar has a higher beverage cost than the other. What is the actual beverage cost of each bar?

c. Assume Bar 1 is open only at night and has a higher drink price than Bar 2. If the costs to purchase liquor (per bottle cost) are the same for Bar 1 as for Bar 2, would you expect the Bar 1 beverage cost *percentage* to be higher or lower than the beverage cost percentage for Bar 2? Why?

Problem 7

What is the beverage cost percentage for Bartenders 1 and 2, given the information in the following bartender performance review form? What is the weekly average beverage cost?

Bartender #1			Bartender #2		
Date	**Bar**	**%**	**Date**	**Service**	**%**
7/1	Main	24.1	7/1	Service	22.3
7/2	Main	23.8	7/2	Service	22.3
7/3	Main	23.4	7/3	Service	21.0
7/4	Main	24.0	7/4	Service	23.0
7/5	Main	24.6	7/5	Service	21.2

a. What is one example of an acceptable reason that Bartender 1 could have a higher beverage cost percentage than Bartender 2?

b. What is one example of an unacceptable reason for the higher beverage cost percentage of Bartender 1?

c. If prices are the same in both bars, what is an unacceptable reason for the lower beverage cost percentage of Bartender 2?

Chapter 10 Outline

Competencies

1. Explain how food and beverage managers compare standards with actual results. (pp. 333–343)

2. Identify factors food and beverage managers consider when taking corrective action to control operations. (pp. 343–349)

3. Explain how food and beverage managers evaluate the effectiveness of corrective actions. (p. 349)

4. Explain how technology has aided food and beverage managers in their control efforts. (p. 350)

10

Control: Analysis, Corrective Action, and Evaluation

THE SEQUENCE OF THE CONTROL PROCESS begins with setting standards—goals or expected results—for the food and beverage operation. The second step is measuring actual operating results. This chapter addresses the last three steps in the control process: (1) analyzing—comparing standards with actual results, (2) taking corrective action if necessary, and (3) evaluating the effectiveness of the actions taken.

Analyzing: Comparing Standards with Actual Results

Expected operating results or standards, taken from the budget or other sources, must be compared with actual results to show how successful an operation has been in meeting its goals. Any significant **variances** between expected and actual results must be analyzed.

Exhibit 1 lists four sources of standard (expected) costs and briefly describes the information each source provides. A property's management team must carefully select the source of standard food and beverage cost information against which it will compare actual operating results. As we will see later in this chapter, the method used for generating cost standards for a food and beverage operation affects the process used to compare standard and actual costs.

Sources of information for determining actual food and beverage costs are listed in Exhibit 2. Current income statements and selected management reports contain information about actual costs. The current income statement, prepared by the bookkeeper or accountant, shows the cost of sales—the food and beverage expenses incurred in generating revenue for the current month. The other internal records report daily operating information. These are developed by management staff to reflect—daily and to-date—the actual costs of food and beverages.

The Comparison Process

There are a number of methods of evaluating the actual success of a food and beverage operation in meeting its goals. Each corresponds to a different way of establishing an expected goal—a standard (also called "ideal" or "potential") cost—for the operation. The following sections examine standards based on:

- Industry averages
- Past financial statements

Exhibit 1   Sources and Information Provided for Standard (Expected) Food and Beverage Costs

Source	Information Provided
Industry averages	National or state restaurant or lodging association or other statistics on average food and beverage cost percents
Past financial statements	Previous income statements for the property that indicate food and beverage costs as a percentage of revenue for a specific period of time
Operating budgets (past or current)	Food and beverage costs in dollars or in percentage of estimated revenue for the property, based on past or current budget periods
In-house standard costs	Food and beverage costs generated specifically for the property from point-of-sale (POS) data

Exhibit 2   Sources and Information Provided for Establishing Actual Food and Beverage Costs

Source	Information Provided
Monthly income statement	Cost of food products and beverage products expressed, respectively, as a percentage of food revenue and beverage revenue
Internal Records	
a. Daily food cost worksheet	To-date food cost percent calculated by: $$\frac{\text{Issues to date} + \text{Directs to date} + \text{ or } - \text{Adjustments to date}}{\text{Food revenue to date}}$$
b. Daily beverage cost percentage recap	To-date beverage cost percent calculated by: $$\frac{\text{Issues to all bars to date}}{\text{Revenue from all bars to date}}$$
c. Bartender performance review form	Bartender's weekly beverage cost percent compared with the to-date beverage cost percent for all bartenders

- Operating budgets
- In-house standard costs

Industry Averages. The first source of information listed in Exhibit 1—industry averages—is the easiest to use. However, it provides the least reliable basis for developing cost standards because it does little to address the specific concerns of a property whose needs likely differ from the "average" property.

While the success of an individual food and beverage operation may not be accurately measured by comparing it to industry-wide averages, many operations use such averages as standards. This approach can be helpful when several units of a multi-unit chain are located near each other. Food, labor, and related costs are likely to be similar in such a case, and external-property comparisons may be more relevant.

Consider the following example of an operation comparing its actual costs against industry averages. A property's food and beverage manager learns that 38 percent is the average food cost percentage for similar types of operations (38 percent of all revenue generated from the sale of food is used to purchase the food). The manager's current income statement shows a 42-percent food cost. Since this is higher than the industry average of 38 percent, the manager worries that there may be a problem. If the property maintains internal daily records of actual food costs, such as the daily actual food cost worksheet, the manager could use these as a basis for reviewing actual costs to determine where reductions might be possible. However, note that the manager is assuming that the industry average, supplied by an association or appearing in a trade journal or on a trade website, applies to his or her property; this may not be true.

Past Financial Statements. Financial statements prepared for the property in the past can provide cost information that may be used to define standards for the property's current operations. A major disadvantage of using these records is that inefficiencies in past operations may continue unnoticed if management strives only to do as well as it did in a past financial period. Consider the situation in which a food and beverage manager bases the property's cost standards on a past income statement showing a relatively high food cost percentage. Because the cost standards are thus flawed, problems can result when using them to judge actual food costs shown in the current income statement or in daily food cost records. If there is no variance between the cost standard and the actual food cost, operational efficiency might be mistakenly assumed to be good when it really isn't, and the inefficiencies of the past are continued.

Operating Budgets. Comparing actual costs to estimates in past or current operating budgets can also result in a continuation of past inefficiencies. This may be largely avoided, however, if the property's operating budgets are developed according to procedures that incorporate specific profit requirements. If an operating budget for the current period has been developed, the food and beverage cost percentage calculated in that budget is compared with the actual cost percentages shown in the current income statement or in daily cost records.

In-House Standard Costs. The best and most accurate information about what costs should be is based on in-house cost standards developed specifically for the particular property. They incorporate the results to be expected when all aspects of the operation's control system are functioning properly. Standard costs are developed, then actual costs are compared with in-house standard costs. Actual costs can also be compared with anticipated costs based on the actual sales mix. Point-of-sale technology can help immensely with these calculations. For example:

- At the end of each shift, the ideal food cost percentage can be calculated by multiplying the number of each menu item sold by its precosted recipe (portion) cost. This yields the total expected food cost for the sale of all menu items during the shift.

- The ideal food cost for each menu item sold is tallied to yield the ideal food cost for all menu items sold during the shift.

- The ideal food cost for the shift is added to the applicable total for all other shifts during the accounting period. For example, if the manager is calculating the ideal food cost for the month, the shift's total would be added to the rest of the month's shift totals to calculate the monthly ideal food cost.

- The total monthly ideal food cost can be compared with the actual food cost calculations based on changes in inventory values. Any significant variances between the two should be investigated, using procedures developed in this chapter.

In each method of comparison described in this section, the food and beverage manager establishes an operating goal—a standard cost—and compares it with the actual results of the operation. The same process can be used to compare standard and actual costs for all other categories of expense. Many managers use several or all of these comparison methods, thus enabling them to make comparisons from different perspectives. In this way, opportunities to discover potential problems are increased and faster problem resolution becomes possible.

Questions to Consider during the Comparison Process

Regardless of the source of standard costs or the method of assessing actual results, several basic questions should be asked when comparing standard and actual costs:

- *Is the standard (expected) cost correct?* If standards have been based on average costs reported in trade journals or other industry sources, then some variance in actual costs may not be evidence of a problem. Even a standard developed specifically for the property may not be correct. Errors in calculating the standard cost may have been made, or the sales mix on which the standard was based may have changed. For example, a standard food cost developed during the summer, when many salads and light meals are eaten, may differ from one developed in the winter, when guests are more likely to choose heavier meals. (Note: Use of ideal costs from POS data that considers the specific sales mix addresses this problem.)

- *Is the actual cost correct?* Calculations and other information in the property's accounting system should be checked for accuracy.

- *Have the components of food cost changed?* Actual costs and standard costs must be calculated on the same basis, including or excluding the same factors (such as the treatment of transfers and employee meals).

- *Are there similar variances between standard and actual costs when these are compared by different methods?* If, for example, standard costs estimated from the operating budget are compared with actual costs from both the income statement and the daily food cost record, there should be some correlation in the variances exhibited.

- *Is the variance between standard and actual costs from this period significantly different from other periods?* For example, if the variance between standard and actual costs has been about 1.5 percent for six months, a variance in the current month of 4 percent may indicate an increased need to look for problems.

- *Is the amount of variance great enough to warrant corrective action?* As you will see later in the chapter, costs that represent the greatest amount of potential savings should normally receive priority for corrective action. This cost may not necessarily be the one with the largest percentage of variance between expected and actual results; rather, the costs with the largest dollar variance should be the priority for analysis.

- *Could there be theft of revenue or revenue reporting problems?* Cost percentages are based in part on revenue totals; therefore, the problem may relate to revenues rather than costs.

- *Are variances understandable?* For example, when the current sales mix has changed—more people buying higher- or lower-cost items than in the sales mix observed in an earlier period—a variance should be expected. Studying sales history records generated by the POS system may help clarify the situation.

Variances from Standards

Comparisons often reveal the actual cost to be greater than the standard cost. Does this mean that, in each instance, the manager must take corrective action? Standards, especially those developed in-house, indicate expected costs if nothing goes wrong. However, even with the best management systems, things do go wrong. Therefore, managers commonly set a predetermined variance—a difference between standard and actual costs—that is regarded as permissible and not requiring corrective action.

For example, assume a standard beverage cost of 26 percent and an actual beverage cost of 27 percent. If a variance of no more than one percent is permitted, no further analysis or corrective action may be needed. On the other hand, if the actual beverage cost is 30 percent, the variance of four percentage points (30 percent actual cost less 26 percent standard cost) clearly requires investigation.

How much of a variance is acceptable? In many operations, allowable variances are measured more often in dollars than percentages. For example, if beverage costs are $27,000 monthly, each percentage point variance represents $270 (1 percent of $27,000 = $270) of higher-than-expected costs and $270 of lost profits. In deciding when to take corrective action, management must consider profit requirements and the opportunity to reduce other expenses.

Management time and priorities must also be considered when setting variance levels. Suppose there is a 2-percent variance between standard and actual food costs and a 5-percent variance between actual and standard beverage costs. Which profit center (food or beverage) should be studied first? If food revenues are $500,000 and beverage revenues are $50,000, the amount of lost profit is:

Analysis Procedures in Multi-Unit Operations

Unit managers within multi-unit chains and their bosses (usually area managers) have information helpful for control analysis that is not available to their counterparts in single-unit properties: benchmark information from other units in the same chain. We noted earlier that industry averages (based on information from all restaurant managers responding to an association survey, for example) might be of little help, because this data represents properties of all types with different menus, pricing structures, and labor rates (among other differences).

Multi-unit operators are not confronted with this problem. They may compare their financial data, for example, to that of properties that are very similar because of the same general geographic location (keeping labor and other operation costs similar), the same menu and service style (making food costs and productivity rates comparable), and the same guest demographics (which influence pricing structures). These managers can compare their unit's financial data with the same data from other, similar units for the same time periods. Dissimilarities among units will indicate potential problems to be investigated. In addition, managers of the best-performing units can provide training and other assistance to their peers in lower-performing properties to improve their financial performance.

Food Operation:	$500,000	×	0.02	= $10,000
Beverage Operation:	$ 50,000	×	0.05	= $ 2,500

Clearly, there is a more significant problem with food costs. In this case, even though the variance percentage between standard and actual costs is lower, management should focus on controlling food expenses.

When deciding what level of variance between standard and actual costs to permit, remember that the savings realized by implementing controls must offset their cost. If it costs $500 monthly to save the $270 in excess beverage costs annually, the added control procedures are not justified. On the other hand, if it costs only $500 annually to save $270 monthly (or $3,240 annually), implementing additional control procedures may be justified.

Potential Savings (Profits)

Differences between standard and actual costs typically represent **potential savings** (profits) to the property. For example, if actual beverage costs are $270 greater than standard beverage costs, management could have saved $270, and thereby increased profits by $270, during the financial period, just by eliminating this variance. Each dollar of excess cost saved is a dollar of additional profit, provided that all other costs remain the same.

Converting percentage differences between standard and actual costs to dollar differences helps management understand when and if corrective action is in order. Exhibit 3, a potential savings worksheet, provides a format for making the necessary calculations. When reviewing the form, note that:

- The budget is the source of standard percentage information used for the worksheet comparison.

Exhibit 3   Food and Beverage Potential Savings (Profit) Worksheet

	Food Cost						Beverage Cost					
							Source of Standard Percent: Current Operating Budget					
Month	Actual			Budget Percent	Difference	Potential Savings (Profit)	Actual			Budget Percent	Difference	Potential Savings (Profit)
	Cost	Revenue	Percent				Cost	Revenue	Percent			
1	2	3	4	5	6	7	8	9	10	11	12	13
			2 ÷ 3		4 – 5	3 × 6			8 ÷ 9		10 – 11	9 × 12
Jan.	$118,545	$330,209	35.9%	33.5%	(2.4%)	$7,925	$13,875	$51,772	26.8%	21.0%	(5.8%)	$3,003
Feb.												
March												
April												
May												
June												
July												
Aug.												
Sept.												
Oct.												
Nov.												
Dec.												

- The formal worksheet comparison is made at least monthly (column 1). Quick, informal comparisons can be made daily by recalling the standard cost when reviewing forms such as the daily actual food cost worksheet and the daily beverage cost percentage recap.

- The best source of information about food costs for the month (column 2) is the cost of food sales reported in the monthly income statement. Monthly beverage costs (column 8) are reported on the income statement as the cost of beverage sales.

- Food revenue as reported on the monthly income statement is listed in column 3 and beverage revenue is noted in column 9.

- The actual food cost percentage for the month (column 4) is calculated by dividing the month's food cost (column 2) by the month's food revenue (column 3) and multiplying by 100. For example, in January:

$$\frac{\text{Month's Food Cost}}{\text{Month's Food Revenue}} \times 100 = \text{Actual Food Cost Percentage}$$

$$\frac{\$118,545}{\$330,209} \times 100 = 35.9\%$$

- Similarly, the month's actual beverage cost percentage (column 10) is determined by dividing the month's beverage cost by the month's beverage revenue and multiplying by 100. In January, the calculation is:

$$\frac{\text{Month's Beverage Cost}}{\text{Month's Beverage Revenue}} \times 100 = \text{Actual Beverage Cost Percentage}$$

$$\frac{\$13,875}{\$51,772} \times 100 = 26.8\%$$

- The food cost percentage (column 5) is taken directly from the budget for January, which was estimated when the operating budget was developed. The beverage cost percentage of 21 percent (column 11) is also taken from January's operating budget.

- The difference between the actual and standard food cost percentage (column 6) is:

Column 4	−	Column 5	=	Column 6
35.9%	−	33.5%	=	(2.4%)

- Similarly, the difference between the actual and standard beverage cost percentage (column 12) is:

Column 10	−	Column 11	=	Column 12
26.8%	−	21.0%	=	(5.8%)

Note: The 2.4 percent in column 6 and the 5.8 percent in column 12 are placed in parentheses to indicate a negative (undesirable) variance.

- It is unlikely that the standard food and beverage cost percentages will be higher than the actual food and beverage cost percentages. Recall that the standards represent expected costs if nothing goes wrong, and how often does that occur? Reasons for standard costs being higher than actual costs include an incorrect standard, smaller portions, lower-quality foods, poor recordkeeping, inadequate inventory, or some other improper practice. They all call for corrective action by management.

- The potential savings for the food operation (column 7) are determined by multiplying the difference between the actual and standard food cost percentages (as a decimal) by the food revenue. For example, consider January:

Food Revenue	×	Percentage Difference (as a decimal)	=	Potential Savings
$330,209	×	0.024	=	$7,925

In this example, the food operation spent approximately $7,925 more on food than it should have during the month. Following more closely the procedures on which the food standards were based should decrease food costs and increase profit by $7,925. The potential savings for the beverage operation are calculated in the same manner:

Beverage Revenue	×	Percentage Difference (as a decimal)	=	Potential Savings
$51,772	×	0.058	=	$3,003

Profit from the beverage operation could have been increased by up to $3,003 by more closely following the procedures on which the beverage standards were based.

Identifying the Problem

Sometimes the **variance analysis process** is relatively easy because the problems causing the variance are known. For example, increases in food and beverage purchase prices may explain a variance, and may indicate the need for improved precosting procedures and a change in menu selling prices. Revisions in recordkeeping procedures or changes in how financial reports are generated and revenue is collected might also explain differences between standard and actual costs.

If variances cannot be explained even after study, a serious problem may exist. If the actual costs are higher than planned and the manager cannot determine why, a close look at the food and beverage operation is in order. Many variances are caused by a failure to follow required procedures designed to keep costs within acceptable limits.

One problem that can frustrate managers analyzing variances relates to the difficulty in separating actual food costs by meal period (lunch and dinner, for example). They know that the more specific the standard cost, the easier it will be to identify the problem; conversely, the more general the standard cost, the more difficult it is to identify the problem. Separate food cost standards can be established for lunch and dinner based upon POS data. If the actual food cost is higher than standard for lunch while the actual and standard costs for dinner are in line, the high food cost problem is clearly within the lunch operation. On the other hand, if the food cost standard is combined for lunch and dinner, it is more difficult to identify whether a problem is caused by lunch, or dinner, or both.

Historically, the costs of all meals served during all meal periods are combined when a standard, such as the budgeted food cost percentage, is developed. While technology makes it easy to assess what food costs should be for each meal period, there is not a practical way to calculate actual food costs on a by-shift or by-meal basis. Beginning and ending inventory values are major components in the calculations of actual food costs (cost of sales). Inventory is not typically separated for use by meal period. For example, dairy products, bread, eggs, fruit, and numerous other products can be used to prepare items for breakfast, lunch and dinner. Therefore, while it is easy to estimate *standard* food costs by shift or by meal, it is not easy to determine *actual* food costs on these bases. Variances between expected and actual costs must be based on differences between expected costs, taken from the POS system and the budget, and actual food costs, which consider inventory data.

Today, it is time-consuming to calculate inventory costs because a physical inventory is needed. For this reason, these assessments are typically made only once a month; therefore, actual food cost figures are available only on a monthly basis. Optical scanning equipment (used in relatively few operations today but gaining in popularity) makes it relatively easy and fast to calculate inventory values. As the use of this equipment increases within the industry, it is likely that potential savings (profits) will begin to be calculated much more frequently, perhaps on a daily rather than a monthly basis.

Be Careful When Analyzing Variance Percentages

What should a manager think when analyzing the following information:

Food Revenue		Food Cost		Labor Cost	
Standard	**Actual**	**Standard**	**Actual**	**Standard**	**Actual**
$197,500	$181,250	36.1%	36.3%	31.4%	27.8%

Note that the actual revenues ($181,250) for the month under study are less than expected ($197,500). However, the actual food cost percent (36.3 percent) is relatively close to that which was expected (36.1 percent). Is this "good" or "bad"? In fact, food cost is a variable cost. In other words, it varies in proportion to revenues. While the number of food cost dollars will decrease as fewer revenue dollars are generated (because fewer meals are served), the food cost percentage should remain relatively close to expectations.

Now let's look at labor cost. A 31.4 percent labor cost was expected, while actual labor costs were 27.8 percent of revenues. Some managers might suggest that the manager did a good job of controlling (minimizing) labor cost in response to lowered revenues—that is, revenue labor dollars should decrease when revenues decrease, because fewer variable (non-salary) hours are needed to serve fewer guests. However, the labor cost percentage should actually increase in many cases, because the fixed (salary) labor cost must be spread over a smaller revenue base. In our example, the labor cost percentage should have increased rather than decreased, since the actual revenues are lower than those expected.

To further illustrate, assume a restaurant's budget for three consecutive months estimates revenues of $140,000 and labor costs of 28.7 percent, but the revenue goal is only achieved in month 2. Data for the three months follow:

Month	Revenue	LABOR COST(S)			Labor Cost (%)
		Salary	**Non-Salary***	**Total**	
1	$125,000	$15,000	$22,500	$37,500	30.0%
2	$140,000	$15,000	$25,200	$40,200	28.7%
3	$155,000	$15,000	$27,900	$42,900	27.7%

* Assume non-salary (variable) labor is set at 18% of revenue.

Since the $15,000 in salaried labor expense is fixed and paid each month, only the non-salaried labor can be adjusted as revenues fluctuate. Note, then, that as revenues fall below the $140,000 goal (in month 1), the labor cost percentage increases (from 28.7 percent to 30.0 percent). Conversely, when revenues increase beyond the goal (in month 3), the labor cost percentage decreases (from 28.7 percent to 27.7 percent).

Assume that traditional (monthly) comparisons are made between budgeted and actual food costs that include all meal periods. How can a manager determine the cause(s) of excessive food costs? Defining problems contributing to high costs essentially involves questioning each operating procedure. Is it done the way it is supposed to be done? Can the procedure be improved? However, it is difficult to know which procedures to review and to correct and whether changes in one will affect the others. The difficulty here is that all systems are very closely related.

Identifying the problem requires asking such questions as: Are gross revenues decreasing? Why? Is the check average (revenue dollars divided by number of guests served) decreasing? Why? Is seat turnover (number of guests served divided by number of seats in the property) changing? Is there evidence of employee theft?

If revenues are decreasing while food costs remain the same, then negative variances from standards will increase. As noted previously, high food cost percentages may result from lost revenue dollars as well as from increased food costs.

It is important to know whether product costs are increasing. Trend analysis or indexing, which shows changes over time, may help put product costs in historical perspective.[1] When questioning product costs, it is also important to ask whether procedures used to control costs are reasonable at each control point and if they are followed consistently. Can practical changes be made to procedures to reduce costs without sacrificing product quality or the property's standards?

A checklist for profitable food operations (Exhibit 4) and a similar one for profitable beverage operations (Exhibit 5) itemize specific procedures to control food and beverage costs. These may become the basis for standard operating procedures used by a property. Management should study the lists routinely, update and revise them as necessary, and ensure that the procedures are being followed consistently. Tight systems often become loose over time because employees find shortcuts and supervisors find other priorities. Without supervision, there is little assurance that procedures are being followed.

When variances between standard and actual costs are found, the checklists and standard operating procedures should be carefully reviewed. Are all the required procedures being followed? Are there any loopholes in the requirements that could cause costs to increase? Do staff, at any organizational level, have ideas about what is causing the trouble and how to correct it? Reviewing procedures may show managers which procedures are not being followed consistently or which ones need improvement. Such a review may also identify factors contributing to variances between standard and actual costs.

Taking Corrective Action

Once problems have been identified, management must determine how to correct them. Several factors become relevant when considering strategies to implement:

- The probability of success (reduction of variances) must be weighed for all possible alternatives.

- All costs of implementing the corrective action must be known; there can be no surprises.

- Knowing what has or has not worked in similar situations in the past is an excellent clue to resolving current problems.

Exhibit 4   Checklist for Profitable Food Operations

Purchasing
☐ Food purchase specifications are used. When food is purchased:
    ☐ Quality descriptions are given.
    ☐ Items sold by several suppliers are purchased wherever possible.
    ☐ Unit size is stated.
    ☐ Best product for intended use is purchased.
    ☐ Vendors know (have copies of) your quality standards (specifications).
☐ Seasonal and value buys are taken advantage of.
☐ Prices are obtained from several suppliers.
☐ Salespersons do not inventory and compute quantity needs of the operation.
☐ Lowest-priced suppliers offering quality needed are given orders.
☐ Beware of "deals."
☐ Don't buy for inventory (usually not more than for one month); weekly (or more frequently) may be much better.
☐ Bills are paid to take advantage of discounts.
☐ When possible, separate prices for food and its delivery are obtained.
☐ If it isn't needed, it isn't purchased.
☐ A list with quantities needed is available when meeting with suppliers.
☐ The chef helps determine (is aware of) quantities of food purchased.
☐ Perishable items used in small quantities are purchased in small quantities.

Receiving
☐ Foods are checked to be sure:
    ☐ Quality standards are met.
    ☐ Amount received is amount ordered (items received are counted or weighed).
    ☐ Amount received is amount charged for (per delivery invoice).
☐ Invoice extensions are verified.
☐ Foods are marked (date; cost).
☐ Proper receiving equipment is used; it is in good working condition.
☐ Deliveries are not accepted at peak business times.
☐ Someone is trained to receive food properly.
☐ Items are removed to storage promptly.
☐ Unacceptable items are refused.
☐ Spot-checking portion-controlled products is done to ensure that weight requirements are maintained.
☐ Meats, chicken, etc., are unboxed before weighing.
☐ Cartons of fruits and vegetables are checked throughout to ensure uniform quality.

Storage
☐ Oldest items are used first.
☐ Food is stored away from walls and off floor.
☐ Opened items are stored in containers with tight lids.
☐ Items giving off odors are stored away from items that absorb odors.
☐ Spoiled foods are removed promptly.
☐ Rodents and insects are professionally controlled.
☐ Proper storage temperatures are maintained.
☐ Foods in refrigerator are covered.
☐ Foods stored in freezer are in original container or in freezer bags or aluminum foil.
☐ Thawed foods are not refrozen.
☐ Storage areas are locked with limited access.
☐ Employee packages are checked.
☐ Special safeguards are in place for expensive items in storage.
☐ Inventory valuation and control recordkeeping procedures are followed.

Exhibit 4 *(continued)*

☐ Items are shelved according to inventory records.
☐ Keys to storage areas are controlled.
☐ In-kitchen storage areas are locked when not in use.
☐ Inventory valuation is done by someone other than the staff member responsible for storage.

Issuing
☐ Only items used for production are removed from storage.
☐ Oldest items are used first.
☐ Perishables are costed as a daily direct food cost.
☐ Generally, items are issued only at certain times of the day.
☐ Records are maintained for all items removed from storage.
☐ Issuing is done by the person responsible for storage.

Food Production
☐ Employees are trained to perform required tasks.
☐ Standard recipes are used and closely followed.
☐ Employees are properly supervised.
☐ Production equipment is adequate and maintained.
☐ Food production is scheduled according to need; leftovers are explained.
☐ There is agreement between the manager and chef about production needs.
☐ Leftovers are used in future production when possible.
☐ Employee meal and eating policies are enforced.
☐ Time between food production and service is minimized.
☐ High-cost convenience foods are offset with reduced labor cost.
☐ There is not an unnecessarily large variety of menu items.
☐ Proper food handling procedures result in minimum food spoilage.
☐ Amount of food left after service is reconciled with amount of food served.

Food Service
☐ Proper food ordering procedures are followed.
☐ Plate waste is analyzed.
☐ Portion size standards are maintained and followed.
☐ Food served meets the manager's quality standards.
☐ Food served is presented attractively.
☐ Proper serving equipment is available.
☐ Policies regarding returned food are followed.
☐ An effective food revenue control system is used.
  ☐ Revenue is received for all food served.
  ☐ Food and revenue control procedures minimize abuses by serving personnel.
☐ Dining room supervision prevents, or at least minimizes, guest walkouts.
☐ A system to account for food and beverage transfers has been set up and is used.
☐ Unprofitable, unpopular menu items are removed from the menu.
☐ The menu is designed to market high gross profit items.

- It must be possible to implement the chosen plan. Some food and beverage managers spend more time saying "things would be much easier if ..." than in evaluating the current problem and attempting to find the best solution within existing limitations.

- The best plan to resolve a problem is often a compromise between—or a combination of—several possible solutions.

Exhibit 5 Checklist for Profitable Beverage Operations

Purchasing

☐ Purchasing is done in quantities necessary to build up and maintain a predetermined par stock level (the minimum/maximum system).

☐ Real costs of "deals" and special discounts are evaluated.

☐ Purchasing different house brands considers guest acceptance and value.

☐ Par stock levels are reviewed occasionally to determine if levels should be changed due to a changing sales mix.

☐ Inventory levels turn over at least twice monthly on the average. (No more than one-half the monthly beverage cost is in inventory at one time.)

☐ Beverages are purchased by brand names; unit size is stated.

☐ Salespersons do not inventory and compute quantities needed.

☐ Bills are paid to take advantage of discounts.

☐ A list with quantities needed is available when meeting with suppliers.

☐ The beverage manager (if separate from purchasing official) helps determine (is aware of) quantities of beverages purchased.

☐ Purchases are made in the largest practical bottle sizes.

Receiving

☐ Incoming beverages are checked against both the purchase order and delivery invoices for brand, quantity, and cost.

☐ Invoice extensions are verified.

☐ Deliveries are not accepted at peak business times.

☐ Incoming beverages are counted/weighed.

☐ Bottle prices are marked on bottles when received.

☐ Someone is trained to receive beverages properly.

☐ Items are removed to storage promptly.

☐ Unacceptable items are refused.

☐ Wet or punctured cases are inspected very closely before acceptance.

☐ Generally, the person purchasing beverages does not receive beverages.

Storage

☐ A perpetual inventory system is used; purchases are added to and issues are subtracted from amounts of stored items.

☐ Storage areas are locked, with limited access.

☐ Employee packages are checked.

☐ Items are shelved according to inventory records.

☐ Keys to storage areas are controlled.

☐ Physical inventories assess validity of the perpetual inventory system.

☐ Locks are changed at frequent intervals, especially when personnel with access to keys leave.

☐ Bottle stamps are used to identify the property's inventory.

☐ Someone other than bartenders keeps records.

☐ Par stock levels are established, used, and changed as necessary, both in central and bar storage areas.

☐ Proper storage temperatures, especially for beer and wine, are maintained.

☐ Spot-checks of inventory levels/records are made. Reasons for discrepancies are identified.

☐ Generally, more popular brands should be readily accessible; less popular brands can be stored in less accessible areas.

Issuing

☐ Issues are in amounts sufficient only to maintain the bar par(s).

☐ Full bottles are used only in return for empty bottles; empty bottles are broken (as laws permit).

Exhibit 5   *(continued)*

☐   Beverage issue requisition forms are completed.
☐   Generally, items are issued only at certain times of the day.
☐   Issuing is done by the person responsible for storage.

Service/Revenue Control
☐   Standard recipes, glassware, portion sizes, and bar par levels are used.
☐   Portion-control tools (jigger, shot glass, etc.) are always used.
☐   Employees are properly supervised.
☐   Beverages served meet the manager's quality standards.
☐   Beverages served are presented attractively.
☐   Policies regarding employees visiting/drinking at the bar during off hours are enforced.
☐   An effective beverage revenue control system is used.
    ☐   Revenue is received for all beverages served.
    ☐   Beverage and revenue control procedures minimize abuses by personnel preparing
       and serving beverages.
☐   A system to account for food and beverage transfers has been set up and is used.
☐   Only management determines drink prices.
☐   Mystery shoppers are used as required.
☐   Only management personnel can access POS data.
☐   Policies regarding drinks on the house are strictly enforced.

- In some instances, alternatives can initially be implemented on a limited (experimental) basis rather than throughout the operation. For example, if issuing practices are judged to be at fault, a new control procedure for issuing selected high-cost items—meats or liquor—might be tried before applying it to all items in inventory.

- Studying similar operations, reviewing books and articles from trade journals and the Internet, discussing problems with peers from other properties, and attending professional association meetings and educational seminars often generate useful ideas to help solve problems.

Assigning Responsibility

Another concern when considering strategies for corrective action is assigning responsibility for the action. There are several factors to consider in making this decision. First, how important is the problem? As the variance between standard and actual costs increases, more dollars become involved, and the urgency to resolve the problem becomes greater. As the importance of the problem increases, so does the need for higher levels of management to be involved in resolving it. Also, higher-level managers generally need to be involved if the proposed solution affects several departments.

Second, how specialized is the problem? If, for example, the corrective action involves changing procedures for determining the value of directs on the daily receiving report, it may be advisable to involve the receiving clerk and his or her supervisor. Who is responsible for the area of concern? Clearly, the management staff responsible and accountable for the area should be involved in some way in resolving the problem.

Learn More on the Web

Effective food service managers realize the need for careful decision-making as they analyze variances, take corrective action, and evaluate the effectiveness of their problem-resolution tactics. How are effective decisions made? What methods and procedures can be used to help improve one's decision-making abilities? You can learn about a wide range of useful decision-making techniques at www.mindtools.com (when you reach the site, click on "Decision-Making").

Should employees help determine necessary corrective action? Many human resource specialists stress the use of a **participative management** leadership style, which permits staff affected by management actions to help determine those actions. The employees who actually work with food and beverage products and procedures may have very good ideas about problems, their causes, and how to correct them. By involving staff in making these decisions, the ideas for changing systems or procedures become the group's, as opposed to management's. This lessens the likelihood of staff resistance to revisions in operating plans as they are implemented.

Responsibility might be assigned to a person or persons in one or more of the following categories:

- Top management—those ultimately accountable to the owners; corporate-level officers; or the owners themselves

- Middle-level managers—those who have been delegated the authority and responsibility for operating specific segments of the property's activities

- Employees—those who most frequently perform or come in contact with control procedures

- External consultants—those who have special knowledge and experience

- In multi-unit operations, district or area managers outside of the unit may also be involved in corrective action decision-making activities

There are several concerns to keep in mind as corrective actions are implemented. Personnel affected by revised plans and procedures will often resist the changes; they may be more comfortable with the status quo. They may say, "We've always done things this way." This is especially true if staff members have not been involved in planning for change. Often, a situation like this is best resolved by involving affected personnel in analyzing and solving problems and by explaining, defending, and justifying the reasons for revised practices. Employees need to know how the changes will make things better from their perspective.[2]

Employees should be trained to follow the new procedures.[3] Managers are often rushed and may give their staff members incomplete or incorrect instructions, perhaps because they aren't sure how the revised plan will work. Managers may believe they have effectively communicated when, in fact, staff members are not sure what has been said. Management must understand the new procedures to train staff and evaluate staff performance. Indeed, preparing for training sessions and effectively communicating instructions to employees encourages managers to fully think through new plans and procedures. For example, managers should ensure that all tools and equipment required by the revised procedures are available. In addition, it may be necessary to teach employees the proper ways to use new tools and equipment.

Evaluating the Effectiveness of Corrective Actions

Evaluating the effectiveness of corrective actions is another step in the control system. The main concern here is assessing whether the variance between standard and actual costs has been reduced as a result of the corrective actions taken. If it has, the corrective actions may have been helpful. On the other hand, if the variance has not been reduced, it is clear that the corrective actions have not been successful. A revised plan or procedure must then be implemented and evaluated.

There are several important considerations in the evaluation process. First, evaluation should not be done too early. Staff must have time to learn what they are supposed to do. Sufficient time must elapse between implementation of revised procedures and evaluation to allow for the elimination of start-up problems with the new system. During this transitional period, costs may continue to be higher than expected, so variance levels may continue to indicate a problem.

Choose an appropriate time frame for the evaluation. For example, to measure the success of corrective actions, the reduction of variance can be evaluated for the next fiscal period. Or actual and standard costs could be compared one or two months after implementation to see whether the variance is reduced. Once the revised procedures succeed in making the operation more efficient, tightening up the standards themselves might be justified.

Evaluation of corrective actions may have spin-off effects on less obviously related parts of the food and beverage system. The evaluation itself may uncover other problems that must be resolved through further corrective action. For example, evaluation of changes in issuing procedures may uncover problems with the record-keeping system used to assess issue values or with the stock rotation process.

Because all systems within an operation are complex and interrelated, changes in one system may negatively affect another system. Suppose, for example, that to reduce food costs, new standard purchase specifications are written and new suppliers are chosen. If subsequent evaluation shows variances to be reduced, then the changes succeeded in reducing food costs. If evaluation stopped here, it would appear that the problem was resolved. However, further evaluation might reveal that quality levels have been sacrificed. A change in purchase specifications might lead to inferior products. As a result, guests may become dissatisfied. At best, they may complain. At worst, they may stop visiting the property altogether and tell others about the problems they experienced. Sooner or later, unhappy guests result in decreased revenues. Therefore, evaluation must consider not only the specific target of corrective actions (controlling costs) but also the consequences of these actions for the entire food and beverage operation.

Technology and Analysis, Corrective Action, and Evaluation

You learned that the control steps of analysis, corrective action, and evaluation require, in large measure, the development and use of information to determine (1) whether variances exist between expected and actual operating results, and (2) whether actions implemented to address them have been effective.

Expected financial results are stated in operating budgets and by point-of-sale (POS) systems, which rely on computer technology. Actual operating results such as those included on a property's income statement are generated by **back office accounting systems** that are computer-based.

When analysis indicates that negative variances exist, analysis and corrective actions frequently incorporate the use of computer-generated reports. If, for example, food costs are judged to be out of line, computer-generated food issue requisitions, daily food cost reports, and meal item production/sales reports may be analyzed to help identify problem areas. If labor costs are high, labor reports may be studied to determine potential causes. In both of these examples, computerized reports may be generated after corrective actions are implemented to assess the extent to which negative variances have been reduced.

Today, hospitality organizations, like their counterparts in other industries, take advantage of technology as "numbers are crunched" to yield information helpful in a wide range of management decision-making activities.

Endnotes

1. Though trend analysis is beyond the scope of this text, a good subject resource for interested readers is Raymond S. Schmidgall's *Hospitality Industry Managerial Accounting,* 6th ed. (Lansing, Mich.: American Hotel & Lodging Educational Institute, 2006).

2. For more information on how to manage change, interested readers are referred to Raphael R. Kavanaugh and Jack D. Ninemeier, *Supervision in the Hospitality Industry,* 4th ed. (Lansing, Mich.: American Hotel & Lodging Educational Institute, 2007).

3. Readers interested in more information on training should read Debra F. Cannon and Catherine M. Gustafson, *Training and Development for the Hospitality Industry* (Lansing, Mich.: American Hotel & Lodging Educational Institute, 2002).

Key Terms

back office accounting system—The equipment and processes used to document, collect, summarize, and report the financial activities and condition of a hospitality organization.

participative management—A leadership style that stresses input from employees as decisions are made about matters that affect them.

potential savings—The difference between expected and actual costs when the latter are greater than the former.

variance—The difference (in dollars and/or percent) between expected and actual revenues and expenses. Variances can be positive (favorable) or negative (undesirable) to the operation.

variance analysis process—Procedures used to analyze variances between expected and actual revenues and expenses in an effort to determine and correct problems.

Review Questions

1. What are the most frequently used sources of information for defining standard food or beverage costs?

2. Is corrective action always necessary when actual costs are higher than standard costs? Why or why not?

3. What is meant by the concept of "potential savings (profits)"? Why must potential savings (profits) resulting from corrective actions be considered before implementing corrective actions?

4. What questions should be asked when comparing variances between actual and standard costs?

5. How do unexplainable variances between standard and actual food costs occur? Between standard and actual beverage costs?

6. Is corrective action necessary when variances between standard and actual costs cannot be explained? Why or why not?

7. Why should a standard cost that is *higher* than an actual cost be of concern to management?

8. What are some objectives of corrective action procedures?

9. Who should managers involve in corrective action plans?

10. Why is it important to evaluate the effectiveness of corrective action plans?

11. How can technology be used to determine standard food costs? How will it help in calculating actual food costs?

12. What is the primary problem today that inhibits the opportunity to calculate actual food costs on a very frequent basis?

Internet Sites

For more information, visit the following Internet sites. Remember that Internet addresses can change without notice. If the site is no longer there, you can use a search engine to look for additional sites.

Variance Analysis

All Business
www.allbusiness.com
(Enter "operating budget variance analysis" in the site's search box.)

B Plans.com
www.bplans.com
(Click on "See more articles" and then "Growing a Business.")

Budgetary Control and Variance
  Analysis
www.financialmanagementdevelop-
ment.com/slides/handouts/213.pdf

Microsoft Office
www.office.microsoft.com
(Enter "variance analysis" in the site's
search box.)

Future Accountant
www.futureaccountant.com
(Enter "variance analysis" in the site's
search box.)

Problems

Problem 1

Financial information for a restaurant's beverage operation is as follows:

Beverage Cost Percent

Month	Beverage Revenue	Standard	Actual
January	$19,500	22%	26%
February	$21,005	22%	23.2%
March	$22,100	22%	24.7%

By what amount could profit levels have been increased if actual beverage cost percentages were on target with estimated standard costs?

Problem 2

Food revenues are $850,000; beverage revenues are $110,000. There is a 1-percent variance between standard and actual food costs and a 4-percent variance between standard and actual beverage costs. Which operation (food or beverage) likely has the most significant control problem? Why?

Problem 3

With regard to Problem 2 above:

a. How much higher would food profits have been if actual food costs were in line with standard food costs?

b. How much higher would beverage profits have been if actual beverage costs were in line with standard beverage costs?

c. What is the total amount of profit lost because actual food and beverage costs were higher than the standard costs?

Problem 4

Complete the following food and beverage potential savings worksheet:

	Food and Beverage Potential Savings											
	Food Cost						Beverage Cost					
	Actual			Standard		Potential	Actual			Standard		Potential
Month	Cost	Revenue	Percent	Percent	Difference	Savings	Cost	Revenue	Percent	Percent	Difference	Savings
Jan.	$180,015	$485,510		38.7%			$80,100	$290,000		25.8%		
Feb.	$159,850	$397,480		38.7%			$61,700	$220,500		25.8%		
March	$152,700	$381,000		38.7%			$63,000	$200,400		25.8%		
April	$158,750	$382,750		38.7%			$62,775	$193,200		25.8%		
May	$161,420	$390,770		38.7%			$61,600	$195,400		25.8%		

What is the total amount of potential savings year-to-date in the food and beverage operation?

Problem 5

a. Control procedures implemented during June have reduced the actual food cost percentage by 0.5 percent and the actual beverage cost percentage by 1.8 percent from the May levels calculated in Problem 4. If actual revenues in June were as follows, calculate the actual costs.

Data for June

Food Revenue	Actual Food Cost Percent	Actual Food Cost	Beverage Revenue	Actual Beverage Cost Percent	Actual Beverage Cost
$192,665			$74,700		

b. What is the amount of cost savings (increased profits) realized by the control measures if, in their absence, the actual product cost percentages were the same as in May?

Problem 6

Following is selected information from three units of a fast-food restaurant chain from last month. All operate in the same metropolitan area. You are the district manager analyzing these results. What are the major problem areas, if any, with each unit?

	Net Revenue		Planned Revenue Growth		Marketing (Promotion) Costs	
	Actual	Budget	Actual	Budget	Actual	Budget
Unit 1	$110,000	$108,000	1%	0	3%	3%
Unit 2	$90,050	$107,000	3%	2%	4%	4%
Unit 3	$171,100	$160,000	(2%)	1%	2%	4%

	Food Cost		Labor Cost	
	Actual	Budget	Actual	Budget
Unit 1	29.3%	29.4%	23.8%	24.1%
Unit 2	30.5%	29.4%	23.1%	24.1%
Unit 3	28.8%	29.4%	22.9%	24.1%

Part V

Controlling Revenue

Chapter 11 Outline

Revenue and Guest Check Control
  Manual Guest Check Systems
  Automated Guest Check Systems
Collecting Revenue from Guests
  Server Banking System
  Cashier Banking System
  Revenue Reports
Assessing Standard Revenue: Beverage
  Operations
  Beverage Revenue Standards: Manual
    System
  Beverage Revenue Standards:
    Automated Systems

Competencies

1. Describe revenue control procedures typical of food and beverage operations with manual guest check systems. (pp. 357–359)

2. Explain how point-of-sale technology simplifies guest check control systems. (pp. 359–360)

3. Distinguish server banking from cashier banking systems. (pp. 360–365)

4. Explain how managers use revenue reports as control tools. (pp. 365–367)

5. Explain how managers in nonautomated operations control beverage revenue, and identify the advantages and disadvantages of automated beverage control systems. (pp. 367–376)

11

Revenue Control

P LANNING FOR AND CONTROLLING REVENUE—the money received from guests for the products and services purchased—is just as important and as difficult as properly managing costs.

The first step in designing a control system for any resource, including revenue, is to set a standard: the amount of revenue that should have been generated. Then the revenue standards can be compared against actual revenue received. But how should a food and beverage operation define its revenue standards? If a properly prepared operating budget (the operation's profit plan) has been developed, it indicates the standard (expected) revenue for the fiscal period covered by the budget. As an integral part of the control process, the manager should routinely compare the expected revenue in the operating budget with the actual revenue reported in the income statement. Then he or she can implement corrective action plans, if needed. New marketing strategies may be developed, for example, to increase revenue, or new tactics might be implemented to control costs.

It is also important for the manager to accurately estimate the amount of revenue generated by the actual sale of all food and beverage products. How much revenue should be generated, for example, during a lunch or dinner shift? Historically, manual systems using guest checks were commonly used. The standard—the amount of revenue a property expected to collect—was represented by the totals from all guest checks for a specific meal period or periods. Increasingly, automated systems, even in relatively small properties, are replacing such methods. These new systems use information entered into point-of-sale (POS) equipment before menu items (food or beverages) are produced. The sum of this sales information defines revenue expectations.

This chapter begins by examining guest check control systems in relation to nonautomated and automated operations. Next, we discuss procedures that are designed to help ensure that the actual revenue collected corresponds with defined revenue standards. The final sections of the chapter examine the unique features of beverage operations that challenge revenue control systems for both nonautomated and automated operations.

Revenue and Guest Check Control

In some food and beverage operations, a guest check system is at the heart of revenue control. The standard (expected) amount of revenue is represented by the total of all amounts recorded on individual guest checks for a meal period (or periods) after all checks have been accounted for. The reliability of this standard

Exhibit 1 Guest Check Number Log (Manual System)

Guest Check Log							
		Type Ticket			Guest Check No.		
Date	Shift	Food	Bev.	Server	Start	End	Signature
8/1/00	*A.M.*	✓		*Phyllis*	*111789*	*111815*	*Phyllis*
8/1/00	*A.M.*	✓		*Joe*	*700100*	*700125*	*Joe*
8/1/00	*A.M.*		✓	*Janis*	*40010*	*40040*	*Janis*
8/1/00	*P.M.*	✓		*Joe*	*111850*	*111899*	*Joe*
8/1/00	*P.M.*	✓		*Andy*	*111900*	*111930*	*Andy*

depends on servers following strict procedures when processing individual guest checks. The effectiveness of these procedures depends on the degree of automation within the operation. The following sections examine guest check control systems for nonautomated and automated operations.

Manual Guest Check Systems

Operations using manual guest check systems typically use a **duplicate guest check system** for food orders. The server turns in the duplicate copy to the kitchen and keeps the original copy for presentation to the guest. When the guest is ready to pay, the guest check is tallied to determine the amount due.

Requisition slips and duplicate checks are useful for routine **guest check audit** functions. At the end of a meal period, or when a server completes a shift, the manager matches requisition slips (or duplicate copies of guest checks) with the corresponding guest checks for which revenue has been collected. This procedure identifies any differences between what was produced and what was served and can also reveal mistakes made by servers in pricing items on guest checks or in calculating totals.

It is best to order specially printed, hard-to-duplicate guest checks, and unused checks should be securely stored. If generic guest checks are purchased from a local restaurant supply company, anyone—including dishonest employees—can buy and use them, and there will be no record of who has them or from whom revenue is due.

Guest checks should be sequentially numbered, and beginning and ending numbers for all checks issued to servers should be listed on a guest check number log (see Exhibit 1).

All checks issued to each server must be accounted for at the end of a shift. Checks will be either used and turned in with revenue, unused and turned in as part of the server closing procedures, or in use and transferred to another server. Duplicate guest checks are helpful when a guest check is unaccounted for. If a

Exhibit 2   Return/Void Reason Code Report

Return/Void Reason Code Report

Jasper's GB -

MICROS 3 MICROS 3
From : 09/14/20XX   To : 09/14/20XX

Printed on 9/14/ 20XX 5:58 PM

Menu Item	Void Total	Reason Code	Authorizing Employee
9/14/20XX 1 - Dining Room			
1,002 - Sophia Lubin			
Check# 81			
10005 CHEESECAKE	-3.55	2 Order Time	119 MICROS3
1007 CAJUN SHRIMP	-7.35	7 Too Spicy	119 MICROS3
40902 SEA BREEZE	-3.10	8 Server Error	119 MICROS3
40551 L.I. ICED TEA	-3.75	107 Lost appetite	208 Hrarg
29003 SPEC 3	-1.95	107 Lost appetite	208 Hrarg
Employee Void Total	-$19.71		
1,004 - BOB JOHNSON			
Check# 82			
8009 SWS & BACON	-5.75	5 Foreign object	208 Hrarg
901213 MEDIUM WELL	0.00	5 Foreign object	208 Hrarg
901501 'PASS	0.00	5 Foreign object	208 Hrarg
Employee Void Total	-$5.75		

Courtesy of MICROS Systems, Inc. (www.micros.com).

copy corresponding to a missing guest check has been turned in to the kitchen or bar, management knows that the missing guest check has been used, that items listed on it have been served, and that revenue is due from the server.

Automated Guest Check Systems

Some automated systems use preprinted, hard-copy, serially numbered guest checks similar to manual guest checks. Before entering an order, the server usually inputs an identification number and the guest check's serial number. Once the system has recognized the server and "opened" the guest check, orders are entered and relayed to remote printers located at appropriate production areas. Precheck terminals are also equipped with guest check printers. As orders are relayed to production areas, the same items (with their selling prices) are printed on the server's guest check.

Point-of-sale technology simplifies guest check control functions and eliminates the need for time-consuming manual audit procedures. Automated pre-checking functions eliminate mistakes servers make in pricing items on guest checks or in calculating totals. When items must be voided, a supervisor uses a special identification number to access the system and delete the items. Generally, automated systems produce a report that lists all guest checks with voided or returned items, the servers responsible, and the supervisors who voided the items. Automated systems must distinguish voided from returned items because returned items should be included in inventory usage reports, while voided items may not. If an item is voided after it has been prepared, the item typically is classified as "returned." Exhibit 2 shows a return/void reason code report. It provides a void total for each menu item, employee void total, reason code, and authorizing staff identifier.

At any point, managers and supervisors can access the system and monitor the status of an open or closed guest check. This check-tracking capability can help identify potential walkouts, reduce server fraud, and tighten guest check and sales income control.

Exhibit 3   Employee Open Guest Checks Report

Employee Open Guest Checks									
Mike Rose Cafe - Beltsville, MD									
									NEAL MAHAFFEY
								Printed on Monday, October 14, 20XX - 8:14 PM	
Check	Tbl/Grp	Check ID	Guests	Open Date & Time Printed		Subtotal	Tax Total	Svchg	Payment Total	Amount Due
1 - Dining Room										
1027 - DELANA HARRISON										
5364	510/1		2	09/28 - 1:00am	2	21.58	0.71	3.24	0.00	25.53
4436	509/1		1	09/28 - 1:11am	1	8.40	0.42	1.26	0.00	10.08
4437	511/1		3	09/28 - 1:16am	1	18.65	0.73	2.80	0.00	22.18
	Employee Total		6		3	48.63	1.86	7.30	0.00	57.79
Dining Room Total			6		3	48.63	1.86	7.30	0.00	57.79
	Grand Total		6		3	48.63	1.86	7.30	0.00	57.79

Courtesy of MICROS Systems, Inc. (www.micros.com).

The status of a guest check changes from open to closed when payment is received from the guest and is recorded in the system. Most automated systems produce an **employee open guest checks report** (see Exhibit 3) that lists all guest checks (by server) that have not been settled. These reports may list the guest check number, server identification number, time at which the guest check was opened, number of guests, table number, and guest check total. This makes it easier for managers to determine responsibility for unsettled guest checks. Exhibit 4 presents a sample server check-out report. Note that the report lists time in, time out, hours worked, number of guests served, tables attended, net sales, and tip information.

Collecting Revenue from Guests

To this point we have been discussing procedures to assess the amount of standard (expected) revenue to be generated from sales to guests—the total amount represented by guests' checks after all have been accounted for (manual system) or the total generated by POS reports (automated systems). The next step in revenue control is to develop and implement revenue collection procedures to help ensure that the expected amount of revenue is collected. The following sections examine procedures for two types of systems: the server banking system and the cashier banking system. In addition, revenue reports produced by POS systems are examined.

Server Banking System

With a **server banking system**, servers and bartenders use their own banks of money to collect payments from guests and retain the collected revenue until they check out at the end of their shifts. In some operations, locking cash boxes are provided for each server to store collected revenue, payment card vouchers, and other sales materials.

At the end of a shift, the amount of revenue due the operation when a manual (hard-copy check) system is used is determined by tallying the totals from all guest checks assigned to each server. The tally is made by the manager in the presence of the server. Totals from guest checks settled by payment card vouchers, personal checks, gift certificates, and house account charges are subtracted from the tally to

Exhibit 4   Sample Server Check-Out Report

```
                    MRS
            DEMONSTRATION

    Server: ANNA

    Date: 11/20

        In Time    Out Time   Total
        12:36      15:23      02:47
        15:25      15:26      00:01

    Total Hours Worked: 02:48

            Persons  Tables    Net      Tips
    Lunch:    19       6      290.55    39.71
    Dinner:    0       0        0.00     0.00
    Total:    19       6      290.55    39.71

              Tips on Credit Cards:     39.71
              Credit Card Surcharge:     1.99

                   Net Total Tips:      37.72

                     Balance Due:      37.72
```

Source: Genlor Systems, Inc., Northport, New York.

arrive at the amount of cash to be collected from the server. The remaining cash represents the server's opening change bank and any cash tips earned. After the actual revenue collected by the manager balances with the tally of totals from all guest checks assigned to the server, charged tips (as recorded on credit card or house account vouchers) are paid to the server.

In nonautomated properties, these closing procedures can be very time-consuming. POS technology speeds up the process by producing a report at the end of each shift that automatically tallies the total revenue due from each server. The report generally identifies transactions opened by the server and itemizes each in terms of:

- Table number
- Number of covers
- Elapsed time from opening to closing of the transaction
- Totals for food and beverage revenue
- Tax

Technology for Settling Guest Accounts

Magnetic strip readers are input devices connected to a POS terminal that are used to collect data stored on the magnetic strip on the back of a payment (debit or credit), gift, or other card. When used, they allow authorized employees to sign into the POS system and settle the account transaction.

Wireless hand-held devices brought by the server to the tableside can also be used to process payment cards when swiped into the portable device. Current technology allows guests to push a button that automatically calculates the tip or splits the bills among diners at the table. Usage procedures are simple:

1. The server enters the table number into the hand-held terminal, and the item-ized bill is generated.

2. The terminal device is provided to the guest to review, and he or she then presses a key to indicate it is correct.

3. A screen asks if the customer wants to add a tip. If so, the customer can select a predetermined percentage to calculate the tip.

4. The customer is prompted to ask how payment will be made (credit card, debit card, cash, or gift card).

5. A receipt is printed for signature if it is a card payment.

Proponents of these devices suggest that customers are more comfortable with them over traditional payment methods because, since the customers do not lose sight of their payment card, identity theft concerns are reduced. They also note that guest service is improved because less time is required for customer payment.

Contactless payment card systems using RFID technology are also increas-ingly available in restaurants, including quick-service drive-through operations.* The wireless technology embedded into these cards allows transactions between a card and a POS terminal to be completed without the customer swiping the card. Customer signatures are not required for small-value transactions, and all the user must do is hold the card approximately one inch from the reader to activate it. One advantage is speed; transactions using contactless payment can be completed in about one-third the time of a cash transaction and about half the time of a swipe-card transaction. To learn more about contactless payment processing, check out the following websites: Ingenico—www.ingenico.com, and VeriFone—www.verifone.com (once on the VeriFone website, click on "Industry Solutions" and then "Restaurants & Hospitality").

---

* Robert Mitchell, "Swiping Your Credit Card Is So Yesterday." Retrieved June 25, 2007, from www.technewsworld.com/story/57977.html.

- Tips due

- Settlement method

Exhibit 5 presents a sample report listing details of all daily transactions of one server. Exhibit 6 summarizes unit sales, revenue totals, and related data for all

Exhibit 5   Sample Daily Server Transactions (Sales) Report

		Date	8–30											
		Time	5:31 A.M.			DAILY TRANSACTIONS								
Guest Check	Tabl/ Covrs	Employee	ID	Time In	Time Out	Elapsed Time	Food	Bar	Wine	Guest Total	Tax	Tip	Settlement Method	Settlement Amount
11378	2–2	Jones	4	8:23	9:00	0:37	13.75	0.00	3.50	17.25	0.87	2.00	CASH	20.12
11379	2–1	Jones	4	8:25	9:00	0:35	2.35	0.00	0.00	2.35	0.12	0.00	COMP 1 0004	2.47
11380	3–3	Jones	4	8:32	9:01	0:29	13.15	0.00	5.50	18.65	0.93	0.00	CASH COMP 2 0033	9.58 10.00
11381	4–4	Jones	4	8:34	9:16	0:42	9.05	0.00	0.00	9.05	0.47	0.00	MC	9.52
11382	3–2	Jones	4	8:40	9:18	0:38	6.20	0.00	5.50	11.70	0.60	0.00	Cancelled	
11383	3–2	Jones	4	8:41	9:19	0:38	4.35	0.00	0.00	4.35	0.22	0.00	COMP 1 0004	4.57
11384	4–4	Jones	4	8:43	10:16	1:33	33.80	11.00	0.00	44.80	2.25	0.00	AMEXPRESS	47.05
11385	4–2	Jones	4	8:46	10:17	1:31	0.00	9.75	0.00	9.75	0.49	0.00	VISA	10.24
11386	4–5	Jones	4	8:51	10:17	1:26	0.00	18.50	0.00	18.50	0.91	0.00	MC	19.41
11387	8–2	Jones	4	8:54	10:18	1:24	14.65	2.50	0.00	17.15	0.85	0.00	COMP 1 0004	18.00
11388	4–3	Jones	4	9:23	10:17	0:54	4.70	3.00	0.00	7.70	0.39	1.00	CASH	9.09
11389	2–2	Jones	4	9:34	10:16	0:42	4.60	0.00	0.00	4.60	0.24	0.00	CASH	4.84
11398	3–2	Jones	4	12:09	12:10	0:01	11.35	0.00	0.00	11.35	0.57	0.00	CASH	11.92
11399	3–2	Jones	4	12:20	12:21	0:01	10.25	2.00	0.00	12.25	0.61	0.00	CASH	12.86
21615	3–2	Jones	4	11:39	11:41	0:02	13.15	0.00	0.00	13.15	0.65	0.00	CASH	13.80
21616	1–2	Jones	4	11:40	11:41	0:01	7.90	0.00	3.50	11.40	0.58	0.00	CASH	11.98
	Total cancelled			11.70										
	**** Totals						143.05	46.75	12.50	202.30	10.15	3.00		215.45

servers for one shift (meal period). Exhibit 7 shows detailed sales information for all of the guest checks used by one employee during a shift. In operations with server banking systems, managers using these reports will find closing procedures greatly simplified.

Cashier Banking System

With the **cashier banking system**, guests pay the cashier, bartender, counter attendant, or food or beverage server (who then pays the cashier or the bartender with cashiering duties). Upon receiving a guest check for settlement in a manual system, the cashier keys each item listed on the check into the register. The register tallies each item and imprints the total on the check for verification with the server's handwritten total. The cashier (or bartender) then retains the money and the accompanying guest checks.

With today's revenue control systems, the cashier does not have to key in each item from every guest check. The cashier's POS terminal simply accesses the transaction number opened by the server, and the cashier closes it by collecting and recording the revenue. At the end of the shift, the cashier's cash drawer and supporting documents are accounted for.

When a nonautomated system is used, register readings are taken and summarized at the end of each shift. The cash, payment card vouchers, other types of payments, and any miscellaneous paid-outs are reconciled with the cash register readings using a **daily cashier's report**. An operation with several stations

Exhibit 6   Summary of Unit Sales, Revenue Totals, and Other Data for Meal Period

PMIX Report—All Terminals

for 5/31/XX

Page 6
06/04/XX at 8:36 a.m.
3.659

Rank	Category	Item Num	Item Name	Num Sold	Sales	Cost	Profit	Food Cost %	% Sales	% Cat Sales
	Grand Total:			4369	15147.70	0.00	15147.70	0.00	100.0	

Summary Section

	Apps			116	617.45	0.00	617.45	0.00	4.08	
	Non-Alc			172	216.00	0.00	216.00	0.00	1.43	
	Salads			15	88.85	0.00	88.85	0.00	0.59	
	Soups			5	15.35	0.00	15.35	0.00	0.10	
	Chip & Fries			77	399.25	0.00	399.25	0.00	2.64	
	Dinners			40	360.50	0.00	360.50	0.00	2.38	
	Desserts			4	15.10	0.00	15.10	0.00	0.10	
	Burgers			62	320.30	0.00	320.30	0.00	2.11	
	Sandwiches			61	343.65	0.00	343.65	0.00	2.27	
	Pizza			28	279.60	0.00	279.60	0.00	1.85	
	Liquor			1016	3125.00	0.00	3125.00	0.00	20.63	
	Kids			11	35.05	0.00	35.05	0.00	0.23	
	Beer			2580	8331.35	0.00	8331.35	0.00	55.00	
	Wine			52	145.35	0.00	145.35	0.00	0.96	
	Theater			77	462.00	0.00	462.00	0.00	3.05	
	Open Pool			1	361.65	0.00	361.65	0.00	2.39	
	Drink Mods			22	11.00	0.00	11.00	0.00	0.07	
	Food Mods			30	20.25	0.00	20.25	0.00	0.13	
	Grand Total			4369	15147.70	0.00	15147.70	0.00	100.00	

Non-Sales Categories

Summary Section—Non-Sales Categories

************ **End of Report** ************

and shifts may use several daily cashier's reports and summarize the data on a single report.

Register readings are taken by the manager or a designated individual other than the cashier. The differences between beginning and ending readings, less any "voids" (voided register entries approved by supervisors), represent food revenue and sales taxes collected.

Exhibit 8 presents a sample daily cashier's report. The "Total to Be Accounted For" section represents net register readings (food revenue and sales tax), tips entered by guests on payment cards or charge accounts, collections from guests that are to be applied to prior balances of open accounts, and the initial change fund in the register. The result of this section is a "Control Total." The "Total Accounted For"—the actual revenue received—in the next section should reconcile with this control total, except for minor cash shortages/overages due to the common minor errors staff members make when processing a food and beverage operation's numerous cash transactions (i.e., minor errors when making change). Large variances, however, should be investigated for irregularities.

Exhibit 7 Employee Guest Check Detail

Employee Closed Guest Checks
Mike Rose Cafe - Beltsville, MD

NEAL MAHAFFEY
Printed on Monday, October 14, 20XX - 8:07 PM

Check Tbl/Grp	Check ID	Printed	Guests	Subtotal	Tax	Svchg	Pymnt1	Pymnt2	Pymnt3	Pymnt4	Pymnt Ttl
1 - Dining Room											
1002 - BEV NELSON											
1759 2/1		2	1	8.30	0.00	1.25	9.55				9.55
	09/22 - 10:56pm	09/22 - 11:28pm	0:32								
4925 401/1		3	5	49.40	2.47	8.00	59.87				59.87
	09/22 - 5:31pm	09/22 - 6:51pm	1:20								
4929 405/1		3	2	29.05	1.45	0.00	30.50				30.50
	09/22 - 6:14pm	09/22 - 6:56pm	0:42								
4935 404/1		3	2	41.45	1.58	0.00	43.03				43.03
	09/22 - 6:40pm	09/22 - 7:36pm	0:55								
4950 404/1		2	2	38.15	1.91	0.00	40.06				40.06
	09/22 - 7:52pm	09/22 - 9:04pm	1:13								
4959 407/1		2	2	41.09	1.71	6.16	48.96				48.96
	09/22 - 9:39pm	09/22 - 10:36pm	0:57								
4960 401/1		2	1	3.98	0.20	0.60	4.78				4.78
	09/22 - 10:17pm	09/22 - 10:37pm	0:20								
5842 404/1		2	2	34.05	1.70	0.00	35.75				35.75
	09/22 - 4:46pm	09/22 - 5:58pm	1:12								
5845 403/1		2	2	24.35	1.22	0.00	25.57				25.57
	09/22 - 5:07pm	09/22 - 6:26pm	1:18								
5875 403/1		4	2	36.60	0.99	5.49	43.08				43.08
	09/22 - 10:10pm	09/22 - 10:56pm	0:46								
6783 401/1		3	8	95.35	4.52	14.30	114.17				114.17
	09/22 - 7:39pm	09/22 - 9:04pm	1:25								
6793 405/1		2	2	44.50	2.23	0.00	46.73				46.73
	09/22 - 8:31pm	09/22 - 9:26pm	0:55								
Employee Total		**12**	**31**	**446.27**	**19.98**	**35.80**	**502.05**				**502.05**
Dining Room Total		**12**	**31**	**446.27**	**19.98**	**35.80**	**502.05**				**502.05**
Grand Total		**12**	**31**	**446.27**	**19.98**	**35.80**	**502.05**				**502.05**

Courtesy of MICROS Systems, Inc. (www.micros.com).

Revenue Reports

Managers of automated food and beverage operations benefit from the speed at which their revenue reports are produced, the level of accuracy automation provides, and the ability to generate data for whatever specific purpose they desire. For example, revenue reports enable managers to measure the sales of individual menu items by product category within certain time frames. Managers can track individual item sales, analyze product acceptance, and monitor advertising and sales promotional efforts. The time frames are commonly referred to as **day parts**, which vary by type of food service operation. Fast-food restaurants may desire revenue analysis reports segmented by 15-minute intervals, table service restaurants by the hour, and noncommercial food service operations by meal period. The information reported is used to assess potential revenue (that which should have been collected during the time period) and to forecast revenue and determine labor requirements for future periods. A sample hourly time period summary is shown in Exhibit 9.

A **revenue summary report** generally contains detailed revenue and tax information by such categories as food items, beer, wine, and liquor. Generally, totals for each category are printed for each meal period, and totals for each meal period are shown in different sections of the report. Exhibit 10 illustrates a cashier detail for one revenue center (the main bar) for one day.

Productivity reports typically detail revenue activity for all assigned server revenue records. A **daily productivity report** may be generated for each server and cashier in terms of guest count, total revenue, and average revenue. A sample productivity report is shown in Exhibit 11. Notice that it provides information about guest check average (average/guest) and average total check. In addition, a weekly productivity report can be generated, showing average revenue amount per guest for each server.

Exhibit 8   Daily Cashier's Report

Daily Cashiers Report	Key A (Sales)		Key B (Sales Tax)	
DATE _12/8/X2_ Day: _Sat._ Weather: _Rainy + Cold_				
Z Readings	1 350	67	81	04
TOTAL TO BE ACCOUNTED FOR:				
Food Sales	1 350	67		
Sales Tax	81	04		
Tips Charged	50	00		
Customer Collections	185	00		
Change Fund (Start)	150	00		
CONTROL TOTAL	1 816	71		
TOTAL ACCOUNTED FOR:				
Cash for Deposit	1 407	06		
Purchases Paid Out	8	75		
Tips Paid Out	50	00		
Customer Charges	200	00		
Change Fund (Return)	150	00		
Total Receipts and Paid Outs	1 815	81		
Cash Short (+)		90		
Cash Over (−)				
TOTAL ACCOUNTED FOR	1 816	71		

EXPLANATION OF CUSTOMER COLLECTIONS & CHARGES:				
CUSTOMER	TAB		COLLECTION	CHARGE
DEBCO, Inc.	1812			200 00
J.R. Rickles			185 00	
TOTAL			185 00	200 00

EXPLANATION OF PURCHASES PAID OUT:		
PAID TO	PURPOSE	AMOUNT
Ted's Market	Food items for kitchen	8 75
TOTAL		8 75

Source: Raymond Cote, *Basic Hotel and Restaurant Accounting*, 6th ed. (Lansing, Mich.: American Hotel & Lodging Educational Institute, 2006), p. 333.

Exhibit 9   Sample Hourly Time Period Summary Report

Revenue Center Time Period Summary
Printed on 11/17/20XX—3:21 PM
Monday, November 17, 20XX

102- 6 AM–7AM

Net Sales	33.00
Guests	3
Average	11.00
Checks	2
Average	16.50
Tables	0
Average	0.00

103 - 7 AM–8 AM

Net Sales	228.90
Guests	21
Average	10.90
Checks	10
Average	22.89
Tables	2
Average	114.45

104 - 8 AM–9 AM

Net Sales	350.95
Guests	37
Average	9.49
Checks	19
Average	18.47
Tables	13
Average	27.00

105 - 9 AM–10 AM

Net Sales	162.40
Guests	23
Average	7.06
Checks	12
Average	13.53
Tables	5
Average	32.48

Assessing Standard Revenue: Beverage Operations

As with expected food revenue, expected beverage revenue is based on the total number of items actually sold. However, procedures for controlling beverage revenue are more complex to develop, especially when a nonautomated (manual) guest check system is in use.

In properties using manual guest check systems, useful procedures to control revenue include the following:

Exhibit 10 Sample Cashier Detail by Revenue Center Report

Cashier Detail by Revenue Center

Mike Rose Cafe - Beltsville, MD

2 - Main Bar

Shift 6 - From 09/22 - 2:38am - To 09/23 - 1:14am 2 2

NEAL MAHAFFEY

Printed on Monday, October 14, 20XX - 2:42 PM

2 - BAR 2

Net Sales	553.11									
+Service Charge	10.50	Returns	0	0.00	Mgr Voids	0	0.00	Checks Begun	57	591.28
+Tax Collected	27.67	Voids	4	-3.76	Error Corrects	4	11.15	-Checks Paid	60	626.62
=Total Revenue	591.28	Credit Total		-0.04	Cancel	1	0.00	+Transferred IN	2	35.34
		Change Grand Ttl		619.05				-Transferred OUT	0	0.00
Item Discount	0.00	Rounding Total		0.00	No Sale	6		=Outstanding	-1	0.00
+Subtotal Discoun	-23.97									
=Total Discounts	-23.97									

Order Type	Net Sales	% of Ttl	Guests	% of Ttl	Avg/Guest	Checks	% of Ttl	Avg/Chk	Tables	% of Ttl	Avg/Tbl	Turn Time
1 - Dine In	525.36	94.98%	47	95.92%	11.18	56	98.25%	9.38	6	100.00%	87.56	2.18
2 - To Go	27.75	5.02%	2	4.08%	13.88	1	1.75%	27.75	0	0.00%	0.00	0.00
Total	553.11		49		11.29	57		9.70	6		92.19	

4 - Cashier Ttl Tracking

100% Discount	2	-19.80	=Ttl Svc Chrg	0	0.00		0	0.00
60% Emp Meal	1	-4.17	Amex	2	46.62	.House Accounts	0	0.00
40% Emp Meal	0	0.00	Visa	3	54.64		0	0.00
40% Emp Comp	0	0.00	Mastercard	1	16.45	Comp 1 Customer	0	0.00
20% Coupon	0	0.00	Discover	0	0.00	Comp 2 MGMT	1	28.09
Dead Food	0	0.00	Diner's Club	1	20.40	Comp 3 Open	0	0.00
Dead Liquor	0	0.00	=Ttl Credit Cards	0	0.00	Comp 4	0	0.00
20 % Teacher	0	0.00	G/C 21 Customer	0	0.00	Comp 5 Promo	0	0.00
$1 Food Disc	0	0.00	G/C 22 Employee	0	0.00	Comp 6 To Go	0	0.00
$1 Liquor Disc	0	0.00	G/C 23 Charity	0	0.00	Comp - 50%	0	0.00
=Ttl Discounts	0	0.00	G/C 24 Advertising	0	0.00	=Ttl Comps	0	0.00
$ Charged Tip	4	10.50	G/C 25 Special Eve	0	0.00		0	0.00
Non Rev Svc Chrg	0	0.00	G/C 26 Compliment	0	0.00	Cash	52	460.42
15% Auto Tip	0	0.00	=Ttl G/C	0	0.00	-Tips Paid	4	10.50
Subtotal	7	-13.47	Subtotal	7	138.11	Subtotal	57	499.01

Courtesy of MICROS Systems, Inc. (www.micros.com).

Exhibit 11 Sample Daily Employee Productivity Report

Daily Employee Detail

Mike Rose Cafe - Beltsville, MD

NEAL MAHAFFEY

Printed on Tuesday, October 15, 20XX - 9:32 AM

Shift 6 - From 09/22 - 2:36am - To 09/23 - 1:12am

1002 - BEV NELSON

		Returns	0	0.00				Gross Receipts		446.27
Net Sales	444.02	Voids	0	0.00	Carried Over	0	0.00	Charged Receipts		49.40
+Service Charge	29.64	Credit Total		0.00	+Checks Begun	12	495.89			
+Tax Collected	22.23	Change Grand Ttl		501.86	-Checks Paid	12	502.05	Service Charges		27.80
=Total Revenue	495.89	Rounding Total		0.00	+Transferred IN	0	0.00	+Charged Tips		8.00
		Training Total		0.00	-Transferred OUT	0	0.00	+Tips Declared		0.00
Item Discount	0.00				=Outstanding	0	-6.16	=Total Tip	8.02%	35.80
+Subtotal Discoun	-5.97	Mgr Voids	0	0.00						
=Total Discounts	-5.97	Error Corrects	12	28.10	No Sale	0		Tips Paid		35.80
		Cancel	0	0.00				Tips Due		0.00

Order Type	Net Sales	% of Ttl	Guests	% of Ttl	Avg/Guest	Checks	% of Ttl	Avg/Chk	Tables	% of Ttl	Avg/Tbl	Turn Time
1 - Dine In	444.02	100.00%	31	100.00%	14.32	12	100.00%	37.00	0	0.00%	0.00	0.00
Total	444.02		31		14.32	12		37.00	0		0.00	

3 - Employee Tracking

.Insuf Bev	0	0.00	60% Emp Meal	1	-5.97	Visa	1	59.87
.Bev Added	0	0.00	40% Emp Meal	0	0.00	MasterCard	0	0.00
Food Cold	0	0.00		0	0.00	Discover/Bravo	0	0.00
Took Too Long	0	0.00	40% Emp Comp	0	0.00	Diners/CB	0	0.00
Did not want	0	0.00	20% Coupon	0	0.00	=TTL CREDIT	0	0.00
OverCooked	0	0.00	Dead Food	0	0.00	G/C 21 Customer	0	0.00
Foreign Object	0	0.00	Dead Liquor	0	0.00	G/C 22 Employee	0	0.00
Tough	0	0.00	20% Teacher	0	0.00	G/C 23 Charity	0	0.00
Too Spicy	0	0.00	=Ttl Disc	0	0.00	G/C 24 Advertising	0	0.00
Server Error	0	0.00	$ Charged Tips	1	8.00	G/C 25 Special	0	0.00
Bar Error	0	0.00	Non Rev Svc Chg	0	0.00	G/C 26 Compliment	0	0.00
Kitchen Error	0	0.00	15% Auto Tip	1	21.64	=Gift Certificate	0	0.00
=Ttl Voids	0	0.00	=TTL Srv Chrg	0	0.00	.House Accounts	0	0.00
100% Discount	0	0.00	Amex	0	0.00	.COMPS	0	0.00
Subtotal	0	0.00	Subtotal	3	23.67	Subtotal	1	59.87

Courtesy of MICROS Systems, Inc. (www.micros.com).

1. The bartender is assigned guest checks at the start of a shift and must follow all requirements regarding their use. When a guest at the bar or lounge table orders a drink, the bartender writes the order on a guest check.

Multi-Unit Organizations Use Revenue Reports

Most, if not all, multi-unit food and beverage operators use point-of-sale (POS) technology. Typically, these organizations invest significant funds to ensure that their systems are the best available and incorporate features that increase the efficiency of their operations.

Company-operated units typically use identical equipment. Franchisees may have a choice of system brands, but the equipment chosen must collect the same standardized information necessary to calculate payments to franchisers, since these payments are based on revenues.

Systems typically record the details of each guest transaction, track food costs through the point of inventory, and incorporate timekeeping functions for labor control.

Unit managers are able to conduct nightly counts of entrées and other expensive items in inventory and compare available quantities to inventory counts at the beginning of the day. By including any deliveries received during the day, they can determine the quantities of items that have been sold. Sales figures from the POS system can then be compared with actual quantities used to match expected revenues and quantities of products used with actual revenues and product usage. The availability of detailed food and labor cost information, along with tracking revenue information on a by-product basis, enables multi-unit managers to develop an income statement each day for each unit.

Unit performance information is often available to organization decision-makers on a real-time basis, if desired. It then becomes possible to compare actual operating information for each specific unit to a budget (year-, month-, or week-to-date), to the previous year's operating performance, and to applicable data for other specific units, the area, region, or entire organization. Variances can be quickly identified, and those requiring corrective action can be quickly assessed. Area managers can then begin working with unit staff to correct problems.

---

2. The bartender places the guest check in front of the guest and writes additional drink orders on the same check. If the register has an accounts receivable function, the bartender can ring the check through the machine before serving the drink.

3. When the guest is ready to pay, the bartender rings the check into the register and deposits the funds.

4. The bartender puts used guest checks in a locked check box until the end of the shift.

5. Totals from the guest checks are matched with register readings. Totals from all guest checks determine the expected revenue, which is then compared to the actual revenue collected.

An obvious disadvantage of this method is the time required for the bartender to record guest check information. During busy rush periods, the procedure slows service. This is an excellent example of control procedures clashing with the need to meet the service expectations of guests. Management must consider the unique costs and benefits of each control procedure. Increasingly, managers are using systems that can electronically track the sales of each type of liquor and other beverages so that potential revenues from the sales can be easily determined.

The basic data tracking/recording procedures of POS systems used in food operations are used in beverage operations as well. The bartender takes a drink order from the guest and enters it into the system using a keyboard or touch-screen terminal. He or she prepares and serves the drink to the guest. Payment is recorded, and a receipt printer produces a narrow register tape for the guest.

One challenge in controlling beverage revenue is the impracticality of separating preparation, service, and collection activities. Bartenders frequently take an order, prepare and serve the drink, collect revenue, register the sale, and make change for guests. The possibilities for theft of revenue are numerous. Managers have fewer opportunities to ensure that all required revenue control procedures are being followed, making single-person theft (theft without the need for **collusion** between two or more people) easier.

With these problems, how can the manager assess the expected revenue from beverage sales? Beverage cost percentages from operating budgets provide longer-range benchmarks. And data from revenue reports (in automated systems) and estimates from bottle sales (in manual systems) are useful alternatives.

Managers of nonautomated beverage operations can match the number of ounces of liquor used with the amount of revenue generated. The following sections examine the bottle revenue value method, which yields reasonably accurate information. Automated beverage control systems are also discussed in relation to beverage revenue control and the types of reports that can be produced for managers of beverage operations.

Beverage Revenue Standards: Manual System

The **bottle revenue value system** provides an estimate of revenue expected based upon the number of empty liquor bottles. This estimate is compared with the amount of actual revenue generated, and any difference indicates a variance that may be analyzed.

For example, suppose that, at the end of a shift, three bottles of bar scotch are issued in exchange for three empty bottles. If each empty bottle represents a revenue value of $40, then $120 in revenue should have been generated from the sale of scotch during the shift. This system does not account for changes in opened-bottle inventory, but instead assumes that the value of liquor in opened bottles evens out over time.

This method is easy to use, but its usefulness depends on how accurately bottle revenue values are determined. The procedure involves examining the historical sales mix to establish a weighted average revenue value per bottle. The following paragraphs describe the method step by step.

Classify All Liquor by Type. Two common classifications of spirits are house and call liquors. House liquor is served when no specific brand is ordered. Call liquor is liquor that guests order (call for) by brand. (When even more specific revenue information is desired, a third type of liquor—premium—can be classified.)

Exhibit 12   Revenue Value per Ounce Calculation

	House			Call		
	Mixed Drink	Cocktail	Total	Mixed Drink	Cocktail	Total
Drinks	1	2	3	4	5	6
A) Low Price	48	20		28	4	
B) Regular Price	+ 48	+ 2		+ 40	+ 10	
C) Total (A + B)	96 +	22	= 118	68 +	14	= 82
Ounces						
D) Oz/Drink	× 1	× 2		× 1	× 2	
E) Total (C × D)	96 +	44	= 140	68 +	28	= 96
Revenue						
F) Low Price Charge	4.00	4.50		5.00	5.50	
G) Regular Price Charge	4.25	4.75		5.25	5.75	
H) Total (Low Price) (A × F)	192.00	90.00		140.00	22.00	
I) Total (Reg. Price) (B × G)	+ 204.00	+ 9.50		+ 210.00	+ 57.50	
J) Total (H + I)	396.00 +	99.50	= 495.50	350.00 +	79.50	= 429.50
Revenue Value per Ounce						
K) Value = (J ÷ E)			3.54			4.47

revenue value = revenue value per ounce (line K) × number of ounces per bottle

Classify All Drinks by Kind. Two common classifications of bar beverages are mixed drinks and cocktails. Mixed drinks are liquor drinks to which a non-alcoholic mixer (soda, tonic, or water) is added. A cocktail is a drink made with two or more liquors, or a drink containing a large amount of a single liquor. Classifications for other kinds of drinks can help maintain consistency in the collection of revenue information during the study period.

Examine the Beverage Sales Mix. Since drinks may be sold at different prices during different periods of the day, the manager should review the proportion of drinks sold during the various pricing periods. Observing and counting actual drinks sold during the various pricing periods allows for greater accuracy in determining a revenue value per ounce of liquor. The longer the observation period, the more accurate the resulting calculation becomes.

Count the Number of Each Type and Kind of Liquor Served. During the study period, a count is kept of the number of each type (house or call) and kind (mixed drink or cocktail) of drink served. Guest checks, register data, or physical counts can be used to determine the number of drinks served.

Determine the Revenue Value per Ounce. A revenue value per ounce calculation form (Exhibit 12) can be used to determine the revenue value per ounce of house and call liquors.

When reviewing Exhibit 12, note that a count from several low-pricing periods showed that 48 mixed drinks using house liquor were served (line A, column 1). Also, 48 mixed drinks using house liquor were served at regular prices (line B, column 1). The total of all drinks served, line A plus line B, is shown in line C (96 drinks).

The number of ounces of liquor in each type of drink, line D, is multiplied by the number of drinks served (line C). There is one ounce of liquor in each mixed drink.

The sales price for each drink type is noted in lines F and G. The low price of mixed drinks with house liquor is $4.00; the regular price of house liquor cocktails is $4.50. In line H, the total revenue from low-priced drinks is reported (48 mixed drinks sold at $4.00 each [line A times line F] equals $192). This is the revenue generated from the sale of house liquor mixed drinks during low-price periods. In line I, the same process is repeated for regular-priced drink sales. In the example, 48 regular-priced mixed drinks sold at $4.25 each equals $204. In line J, the total revenue is calculated: $192 from the sale of low-priced mixed drinks (line H) plus $204 from regular-priced mixed drinks (line I) yields $396 (line J).

In line K, the revenue value per ounce for house and call liquors is calculated. This per-ounce revenue value is determined by dividing the total number of ounces of each type of liquor into the total revenue generated by the liquor type. The total amount of house liquor, 140 ounces (line E, column 3), is divided into the total revenue for house liquor, $495.50 (line J, column 3). Therefore, the weighted average revenue value per ounce of house liquor (line K, column 3) is $3.54 ($495.50 ÷ 140 = $3.54, rounded). The same process used for house liquor is repeated for call liquor. The revenue value per ounce of call liquor (line K, column 6) is $4.47 ($429.50 ÷ 96 = $4.47, rounded).

To calculate the bottle revenue value, the number of ounces of liquor in each bottle is multiplied by the revenue value per ounce. Since there are 33.8 ounces of house liquor in a liter bottle, each liter bottle has a potential revenue value of $119.65 ($3.54 × 33.8 ounces = $119.65, rounded).

The potential revenue values for each bottle of house and call liquor are multiplied by the number of empty bottles at the end of each shift. All liter bottles of house liquor, whatever type, have the same revenue value. The same is true for all liter bottles of call liquor. In the example, a liter bottle of house liquor—whether Scotch, gin, or bourbon—should generate $119.65 in revenue. A liter bottle of call liquor has a revenue value of $151.09 ($4.47 per ounce × 33.8 ounces per bottle).

This may seem strange, since each type of liquor costs a different amount. However, most operations do not charge a different amount for each house liquor. The selling price of a mixed drink made with house liquor is generally the same regardless of whether it is made of Scotch, gin, or bourbon.

After the revenue value per bottle for house and call liquors is established, standard beverage revenue for liquor can be assessed. As full bottles are issued to replace empty bottles, the revenue value of each bottle is noted. A beverage issue and revenue sheet (Exhibit 13) is a modified version of a beverage issue requisition form. The sum of revenue values for all bottles issued is the standard (expected) revenue generated during the shift.

The standard revenue can be compared with the actual revenue generated, as recorded on guest checks or register tapes. A form to compare standard with actual revenue (Exhibit 14) can be used for this purpose. When reviewing this form, note the following:

Exhibit 13   Beverage Issue and Revenue Sheet

Beverage Issue and Revenue

Shift: _P.M._   Date: _10/1/XX_
Bar: _Main_   Bartender: _BT_

Liquor	Number of Bottles		Unit Cost	Total Cost	Revenue	
	Number	Size			Unit	Total
B. Scotch	3	750 ml	$ 12.75	$ 38.25	$119.65	$ 358.95
B. Vodka	3	750 ml	11.50	34.50	119.65	358.95
B. Gin	2	liter	12.00	24.00	119.65	239.30
B. Rum	1	liter	12.50	12.50	119.65	119.65
S. Seven	1	750 ml	15.85	15.85	151.09	151.09
Tia Maria	1	750 ml	19.80	19.80	151.09	151.09
Drambuie	1	750 ml	19.75	19.75	151.09	151.09
				$164.65 (Cost)		$1530.12 (Value)

Total Bottles: _12_
OK to issue: _JN_
Issued by: _KT_
Received by: _BT_

Check one
☐ low price
☑ reg. price
☐ high price

$164.74 (Cost) ÷ $1530.12 Revenue × 100 = 10.8% (Beverage Cost Percent)

Exhibit 14   Sample Form for Comparing Standard and Actual Revenue

Standard and Actual Revenue Comparison

Month: _October_   Bar: _Main_

Date	Daily Revenue		To-Date Revenue		Percent Difference To-Date
	Standard	Actual	Standard	Actual	
1	2	3	4	5	6
10/1	$690.45	$666.28	$ 690.45	$ 666.28	96.5%
10/2	402.00	395.50	1,092.45	1,061.78	97.2

1. For each date, daily standard revenue is shown (column 2) as assessed on the beverage issue and revenue sheet (Exhibit 13). The actual revenue (column 3) is determined from sources such as the register or guest checks.

2. To-date standard and actual revenues are reported in columns 4 and 5, respectively. Column 4 is the total of daily entries in column 2. Column 5 is the total of daily entries recorded in column 3.

3. Column 6 indicates the percentage of standard revenue actually received. It is calculated by dividing actual revenue to date by standard revenue to date and multiplying by 100. For 10/2, the calculation is as follows:

$$\frac{\$1,061.78}{\$1,092.45} \times 100 = 97.2\%$$

This means that, as of 10/2, the beverage operation had actually received 97.2 percent of the revenue expected from liquor sales.

The process is repeated to calculate standard and actual revenue for the day or any future date. As the month progresses, the variance between actual revenue and standard revenue should decrease. Acceptable variances should be established, and, when they are exceeded, corrective actions may be necessary.

Beverage Revenue Standards: Automated Systems

Automated beverage systems significantly reduce many of the time-consuming management tasks for controlling beverage operations. While automated beverage systems vary, most systems can:

- Dispense drinks according to the operation's standard recipes.
- Count the number of drinks poured.
- Assess the standard (expected) revenue for beverage sales.
- Provide timely management reports. Some systems generate these reports with their own hardware/software. Others interface with POS systems to generate this information.

Extensive revenue reports can be produced by POS systems that are interfaced with automated beverage dispensing systems. For each shift and each station during a shift, separate reports can indicate:

- Revenues by major beverage category.
- Revenues by time of day.
- Revenues by server.
- Settlement methods.
- Outstanding guest checks.
- Sales mix by beverage product.

Exhibit 15 indicates the standard beverage revenue by major beverage category (liquor, beer, wine, and others) for four separate stations. Exhibit 16 indicates revenues by beverage server. When bartenders close their stations, the system generates a settlement methods report (Exhibit 17) that indicates the amounts due in the form of payment card vouchers, house account charges, and cash. Note: the total of the settlement report (the amount of revenue for which the bartenders will be held accountable) does not include revenues due from outstanding guest checks.

Unquestionably, automated beverage systems can greatly enhance management's control of beverage operations. At the least, these systems can provide accurate information about the number of drinks or ounces sold. At best, such a system will not allow a drink to be served without its being entered as a sale within the POS system.

Exhibit 15   Sales by Major Beverage Category Report

Ring Off #22	— 2:52 A.M.	1/06			
Accumulators Cleared	— 8:00 A.M.	1/05			
Sales by Major Category	Station 1 Sales	Station 2 Sales	Station 3 Sales	Station 4 Sales	Total Sales
Liquor	1,185.75	977.25	1,040.25	417.75	3,621.00
Beer	469.50	372.25	236.50	144.00	1,222.25
Wine	29.75	45.00	77.00	19.50	171.25
Soft Drinks	1.75	20.75	17.25	8.75	48.50
Misc A	34.50	61.15	88.70	117.90	302.25
Btl Wine	.00	.00	.00	.00	.00
Lookups	57.85	94.55	23.80	.00	176.20
Price Mode 1	3.00	77.00	110.25	.00	190.25
Mode 2	1,776.10	1,492.20	1,363.25	707.90	5,339.45
Mode 3	.00	1.75	10.00	.00	11.75
Tax— Mode 1	.00	.00	.00	.00	.00
Mode 2	.00	.00	.00	.00	.00
Mode 3	.00	.00	.00	.00	.00
Tips 1.50	.00	11.10	.00	12.60	
Gross Sales	1,780.60	1,570.95	1,494.60	707.90	5,554.05
Net Sales	1,779.10	1,570.95	1,483.50	707.90	5,541.45
Accumulated Sales	919,058.24	43,281.83	50,696.30	30,780.18	
Transactions	16	190	24	93	323

Exhibit 16   Revenue by Beverage Server

Ring Off #22		—2:52 a.m.	1/06							
Accumulators Cleared		—8:00 a.m.	1/05							
Server	Reported Tips	Total Sales	Cash	Visa	Dine	Amex	Prom	Comp	Disc	Dire
					(All Sales Include Tax and Tips)					
1	6.10	1252.05	1160.45	.00	.00	91.60	.00	.00	.00	.00
4	.00	197.45	197.45	.00	.00	.00	.00	.00	.00	.00
5	.00	223.40	223.40	.00	.00	.00	.00	.00	.00	.00
6	.00	493.50	493.50	.00	.00	.00	.00	.00	.00	.00
12	1.50	785.65	553.70	.00	179.70	52.25	.00	.00	.00	.00
15	.00	644.75	644.75	.00	.00	.00	.00	.00	.00	.00
16	.00	5.00	5.00	.00	.00	.00	.00	.00	.00	.00
17	.00	288.90	288.90	.00	.00	.00	.00	.00	.00	.00
27	.00	111.75	111.75	.00	.00	.00	.00	.00	.00	.00
35		21	21.00			00				00
7	.00	24.25	.00	.00	.00	24.25	.00	.00	.00	.00
78	.00	208.25	208.25	.00	.00	.00	.00	.00	.00	.00
80	.00	10.50	10.50	.00	.00	.00	.00	.00	.00	.00
93	.00	1.75	1.75	.00	.00	.00	.00	.00	.00	.00
Totals	12.60	5524.05	5140.50	10.75	179.70	173.10	.00	.00	.00	.00

Exhibit 17 Settlement Methods Report

Ring Off #22	—2:52 a.m.	1/06			
Accumulators Cleared	—8:00 a.m.	1/05			

Settlement Methods	STATION 1 SALES	STATION 2 SALES	STATION 3 SALES	STATION 4 SALES	TOTAL SALES
Cash	1548.65	1560.20	1368.00	683.65	5160.50
Visa/MC	.00	10.75	.00	.00	10.75
Diners	179.70	.00	.00	.00	179.70
Amex	52.25	.00	96.60	24.25	173.10
Promo	.00	.00	.00	.00	.00
Company	.00	.00	.00	.00	.00
Discovery	.00	.00	.00	.00	.00
Direct Bill	.00	.00	.00	.00	.00
Total Settlements	1780.60	1570.95	1464.60	707.90	5524.05

Perhaps the best approach for controlling revenue with an automated beverage system is to make sure that it complements the revenue collection system used in the food and beverage operation.

 Key Terms

bottle revenue value system—In nonautomated beverage operations, a procedure for estimating the amount of revenue expected from a bottle of liquor.

cashier banking system—A revenue collection system by which guests pay the cashier, the bartender, or the food or beverage server (who then pays the cashier or the bartender who has cashiering duties).

collusion—The instance of two or more people cooperating to steal from the hospitality operation.

daily cashier's report—A revenue collection control document used to record cash register readings, cash count, bank deposits, and other transactions handled by a cashier.

daily productivity report—A report produced by POS equipment; the report details revenue activity for all assigned server records. It can be generated for each server and cashier in terms of guest count, total revenues, and average revenues.

day part—A time interval during the day for which financial and sales information is tracked by automated revenue systems.

duplicate guest check system—A manual revenue control system in which the server turns in the duplicate copy to the kitchen and keeps the original copy for presentation to the guest.

employee open guest checks report—A report produced by the POS system that lists all open checks by server; information may include the sequence number, server identification number, time at which the transaction began, number of guests, table number, and guest check total.

guest check audit—A manual control function that identifies any differences between what was produced and what was served. At the end of a meal period, the manager matches duplicate copies of guest checks turned in to the kitchen with the corresponding guest checks for which revenue has been collected.

revenue summary report—A report produced by POS equipment containing detailed revenue and tax information by such categories as food items, beer, wine, and liquor. Generally, totals for each category are printed for each meal period, and totals for each meal period are shown in different sections of the report.

server banking system—A revenue collection system in which servers and bartenders use their own banks of change to collect payments from guests and retain the collected revenue until they check out at the end of their shifts.

Review Questions

1. How are duplicate checks useful in determining expected food revenue in nonautomated food operations?

2. How do point-of-sale (POS) systems simplify guest check control functions? How do they help simplify the collection of accurate unit sales and revenue data?

3. What is a server banking system? a cashier banking system?

4. How is a daily cashier's report used to compare standard revenue and actual revenue collected when a manual revenue system is used?

5. How are revenue and productivity reports useful to managers of automated food and beverage operations?

6. What are the advantages and disadvantages of using a guest check system to control revenue in nonautomated beverage operations?

7. How can a bottle revenue value system help managers determine standard revenue for nonautomated beverage operations?

8. How can automated beverage systems reduce many of the time-consuming tasks in controlling beverage operations?

9. What are some problems that may arise in assessing standard revenue from beverage sales in operations with automated beverage systems?

10. How should managers determine the revenue-related reports they want generated from their POS system?

Internet Sites

For more information, visit the following Internet sites. Remember that Internet addresses can change without notice. If the site is no longer there, you can use a search engine to look for additional sites.

Point-of-Sale Systems

Action Systems, Inc.
www.actionsystems.com

Agilysys
www.hospitality.agilysys.com/index.
aspx

Aldelo Systems
www.aldelo.com

AM/PM Service Ltd.
www.ampmservice.com

Comtrex Systems Corporation
www.comtrex.com

Digital Dining
www.digitaldining.com

Infor Restaurant Systems
www.rsd.geac.com

Menusoft Systems Corporation
www.menusoft.com

MICROS Systems, Inc.
www.micros.com

NCR Corporation
www.ncr.com

POSitouch
www.positouch.com

Squirrel Systems
www.squirrelsystems.com

Technology Services Corporation
www.restaurantpos.net

Problems

Problem 1

What is the potential revenue for the Marina Boulevard Café, given the following sales information from last Saturday?

Item	Number Sold	Selling Price	Potential Revenue
Chicken	94	$ 8.95	*841.30*
Veal	73	12.50	*912.50*
Pork chops	68	11.95	*812.60*
Vegetarian entrée	55	9.50	*522.50*
Lobster Newburg	38	14.75	*560.50*
Beef casserole	81	12.95	*1048.95*

Total 4698.35

a. Assume that the total food cost to prepare all the above items is $1,470.50; what is the standard food cost percentage?

b. What is the guest check average for the Saturday under study?

c.. What factors should the manager address if the actual revenue collected is less than that expected?

Problem 2

What is the total revenue expected from the sales information presented in the following table?

Item	No. Produced	No. Leftover	No. Sold	Sales Price	Total Revenue
A	28	2		$8.95	
B	45	0		$10.50	
C	64	8		$7.95	
D	55	5		$8.50	
E	49	4		$7.95	

Problem 3

Use the following information to calculate the total cost of issues and the revenue value of the bar in the Pleasant Hollow Restaurant.

Liquor	No. Bottles Issued	Unit Cost	Total Cost	Revenue Total Unit	Revenue Total Total
Bar Gin	2	$9.70		$ 69.50	
Bar Vodka	2	$8.65		69.50	
Bar Rum	1	$8.75		69.50	
Bar Scotch	3	$10.70		69.50	
Dewar's Scotch	1	$16.50		115.40	
Kahlua	1	$17.25		98.70	

   a. What is the standard beverage cost percentage?

   b. If the cost of all bottles of house (bar) liquor increased by $1.50 each, what would be the new cost of issues and beverage cost percentage?

Problem 4

Complete the standard and actual revenue comparison sheet below:

Standard and Actual Revenue Comparison					
Month: _____ July _____				Bar: _____ Main _____	
Date	Daily Revenue Standard	Daily Revenue Actual	To-Date Revenue Standard	To-Date Revenue Actual	Percent Difference To-Date
7/1	$650.10	$644.50			
7/2	712.40	703.90			
7/3	595.50	605.50			
7/4	625.10	610.10			
7/5	710.00	701.50			

If on 7/5, the actual amount of revenue received to date had been $3,140.50 instead of $3,265.50, what would be the percentage difference between standard and actual revenue?

Problem 5

What is the revenue value per ounce for house and call liquors, given the following information?

Drinks	House			Call		
	Mixed Drink	Cocktail	Total	Mixed Drink	Cocktail	Total
Low Price	155	95		110	75	
Regular Price	225	125		190	85	
Total						
Ounces						
Oz/Drink	1.0	1.75		1.0	1.25	
Total	____ + ____		= ____	____ + ____		= ____
Revenue						
Low Charge	$2.75	$3.50		$3.75	$4.25	
Regular Charge	$3.50	$4.00		$4.25	$4.75	
Total (Low)	____	____		____	____	
Total (Reg.)						
Total	____ + ____		= ____	____ + ____		= ____
Revenue Value per Ounce	____			____		

What is the revenue value for house and call liquors, given the information above? (Assume 750 ml [25.4 oz] bottles are used.)

Problem 6

Complete the food service revenue recap sheet for Joe's Café—a very small operation using a manual revenue control system.

Food Service Revenue Recap Sheet			
	Revenue		
Server	Standard	Actual	Difference
Jack	$110.50	$105.50	
Ray	$98.70	$98.70	
Mike	$125.40	$130.50	
Ron	$180.10	$177.50	

You are Joe, the owner of the café. What should you do about Jack's and Ron's shortages? What should you do about Mike's overage?

Chapter 12 Outline

Competencies

1. Describe some of the ways bartenders can steal, and identify precautions managers can take to reduce this kind of theft. (pp. 383–390)

2. Explain how shopper services work and why food and beverage operations use them. (pp. 390–391)

3. Describe some of the ways cashiers, food and beverage servers, and other staff can steal, and identify precautions managers can take to reduce this kind of theft. (pp. 391–395)

4. Describe some of the ways guests can steal, explain some of the ways employees can steal from guests, and identify precautions food and beverage managers can take to reduce this theft. (pp. 395–402)

5. Describe cash control procedures appropriate for food and beverage operations. (pp. 402–407)

12

Preventing Theft of Revenue

FOOD AND BEVERAGE CONTROL PROCEDURES require constant review of standard (expected) and actual cost percentages. When actual cost percentages exceed standards, most managers try to reduce costs. Yet, the problem often is not that costs are too high but that revenue is too low. (A product cost percentage is based on cost divided by sales; therefore, a high cost percentage can result both from costs being higher and from revenues being lower than planned.) Even though expenses may, in fact, be reasonable, theft reduces revenue levels and increases food and beverage cost percentages. Therefore, managers must consider both expenses and revenue levels when assessing the effectiveness of control systems.

A large percentage of the revenue for many food and beverage operations is in the form of cash, in contrast to payment cards, **prepayment cards**, or personal checks. (Although it should be noted that quick-service restaurants, long-time holdouts for cash-only payments, increasingly are accepting payment cards.) Without effective control systems, cash is extremely vulnerable to theft. Consider the following:

- Personnel who handle cash, including bartenders, cashiers, and service staff, often hold low-paid, entry-level positions. Many of these employees frequently move from job to job and have little identification with or loyalty to a property.

- The busy environment of a food and beverage operation and the complexity of production and service tasks provide the opportunity for personnel who handle money to take advantage of loopholes in revenue collection systems.

- To some extent, many managers are unconcerned about employee theft. Some feel that theft is inevitable and simply increase prices to cover it. Others think they employ only honest staff members (they can "tell" if a person is dishonest), and still others erroneously believe "it can't happen to me."

Guests' demands for value are increasingly important factors in establishing food and beverage selling prices. If the costs of theft are built into selling prices, the operation may lose its competitive edge in pricing. A more reasonable way to minimize the consequences of employee theft is to design and implement a system incorporating the basic principles of revenue control. However, even after a revenue control plan is in effect, it is still important to supervise operations to ensure that the system works and that staff members have not found creative ways to steal.

While not becoming unduly alarmed, food and beverage managers must realize that some employees steal, others will if they have the opportunity to do so, and all staff are likely, at times, to make mistakes. The net result of all theft and employee error is reduced profit. This cannot be tolerated when it can be controlled.

It is difficult, perhaps impossible, to design a revenue control system that will prevent clever, dishonest employees from stealing. This is especially true when we consider the possibilities for **collusion**—cooperation between two or more dishonest staff members. However, well-designed and closely supervised revenue control systems make it difficult for a single staff member, who is working alone, to steal. This chapter will address revenue management tactics managers can take to reduce the opportunities for theft by employees and guests, and to control revenue after it is collected from guests.

Theft by Bartenders

Because the bartender prepares and serves products, and—at least in public bars—also collects and records revenue, it is perhaps easier for the bartender to steal revenue than for any other employee. Bartender theft centers mostly on misuse of point-of-sale (POS) systems and improper dispensing of beverage products. The following sections discuss each of these problems separately.

Theft by Misuse of Revenue Management Equipment

POS systems are increasingly critical to the property's revenue control and record-keeping systems. Management staff should develop specific cash-handling procedures to be followed by bartenders, food service cashiers, and any other employees who collect and record transactions (for example, those who ring-up sales on POS systems). A sample of control policies and procedures for handling cash is shown in Exhibit 1. Bartenders and other employees will have fewer opportunities to steal revenue when control policies and procedures are strictly enforced.

Managers must know about procedures that should be incorporated into an effective revenue control system, and they must be aware of inappropriate procedures that would allow employees to misuse the bar's revenue equipment. There are several ways that misuse of equipment can result in errors or permit employee theft of revenue.

"No-Ring" Sales. In **no-ring sales**, the bartender collects money from guests, opens the cash drawer by pressing a "no sale" or similar key, and makes change for currency collected. In this way, the sale has not been entered into the system's revenue data. Although the collected cash has been placed in the cash drawer, this is only a temporary arrangement. The register operator does not want to remove stolen funds several times during a shift, since this increases the likelihood of being observed. So the dishonest bartender generally keeps a record of the unrecorded revenue and removes it from the register only one time near the end of the shift.

Bartenders keep track of unrecorded revenue in numerous ways. For example, a bartender may place coins under the cash drawer—ten pennies can mean ten dollars in unrecorded drink revenue. Separating or bending swizzle sticks or

Exhibit 1   Control Procedures for Handling Cash

Cash Banks:

At the beginning of each shift, bartenders and cashiers are each given a cash bank. The amount of money in the bank will be set by management and will not vary from shift to shift. A minimum amount of currency to ensure that change can be made throughout the shift should be determined.

Responsibility for securing change for cash banks should be assumed by management. Cashiers and bartenders should not bring in their own change. The bank should remain intact. No IOUs, petty cash receipts, personal loans, or other deductions from the cash balance should be carried in the bank.

Personnel receiving a cash bank should be allowed to confirm (count) it, and then sign a document showing that they have done so. Then personnel will be responsible for their own cash bank until the end of their shift.

At the end of the shift, the value of the beginning bank should be counted out first. The remaining funds in the cash drawer should equal the value of revenue collected per POS tallies. Cash handlers will be liable for any shortages in cash banks or revenue.*

Specific Operating Procedures:

The cash drawer is to be closed when not in use.

Each guest order must be rung up separately. (At no time should two or more guest orders be totaled in the bartender's head and rung as a total.)

At no time is the bartender's tip jar to be near POS equipment. It should be located away from the equipment to eliminate the possibility of the bartender making change from it or moving money from the equipment to the tip jar.

Only one bartender or cashier should have access to a single cash drawer. No one other than the employee with responsibility should use, enter, or otherwise have any contact with the equipment for any reason. Management may conduct spot audits of tapes and currency as necessary.

Bills over $20 should be placed under the currency tray. Bills collected from the guest should remain in front of the guest until the transaction is acceptable to him/her. When making change, count from the amount of the sale to the amount of money given by the guest. Call the manager on duty if there are any questions regarding cash collection or change making.

All procedures for recording transactions should be designed to provide revenue information on a department basis for greater accuracy in financial accounting.

The bartender or cashier should not be able to read or total revenue information entered into the machine.

Each bartender should have a separate key code or other access to the equipment. A separate identification number should be used to identify transactions in revenue data.

---

* Managers should check with their attorney or other officials to determine the legality of requiring employees to make up cash shortages.

(continued)

Exhibit 1   *(continued)*

Each sale must be rung up in proper sequence, in the proper amount, and without "bunching" or totaling sales. Each transaction must be rung separately.

Each bartender should have a written copy of procedures for use of the equipment.

The cash drawer should be opened only by depressing the sales price or "no sale" key. It should not be possible to enter the machine by use of a mechanical device except in case of a power outage.

Detail tapes (if used) should be replaced before they run out. (There is generally a colored strip or other marking that becomes noticeable as the tape supply diminishes.)

Equipment should be empty, unlocked, and left open when not in use (or drawers should be removed) to prevent damage to the machine during possible theft attempts.

Voids, overrings, and other problems should be reported to managers as soon as possible after they occur.

Audits, including the counting of money in the drawer(s), should be made on a random basis.

Managers should monitor the equipment and its operation closely as part of their ongoing supervisory responsibilities.

Financial information should be studied on a random basis to uncover possible fraud.

Bartenders are not allowed to accept postdated checks or IOUs in payment or as collateral for loans.

Only a minimum number of supervisory personnel should have access to financial information in the system.

Banks should be counted and exchanged each time there is a change in bartenders or cashiers; financial information should be read/totaled and cleared at each change of bartenders.

All checks accepted after appropriate verification procedures should be immediately marked "FOR DEPOSIT ONLY."

Sales data should be available for the entire day (or other period) from each item of equipment used for food and beverage service.

Financial information should be reconciled with cash receipts at least once each shift.

Revenue from miscellaneous cash sales (vending proceeds, recyclable grease, returnable bottles, etc.) must be properly recorded in business accounts if it is first deposited in a register.

Bell, alarm, or buzzer systems on the equipment should not be bypassed; a noise should be audible each time the cash drawer is opened.

The equipment should be located in a position visible to guests, employees, and management.

Equipment should be kept locked during service periods when the register operator is not at the machine.

Exhibit 1 *(continued)*

> If manual guest checks are used, audits should ensure continuity in transaction numbers. The first transaction number for a new shift should be in sequence with the last transaction number from the previous shift.
>
> Constant cash overages should be investigated. (The register user may be under-ringing and removing only part of the money to avoid a shortage that might alert management.)
>
> Random and unexpected audits should be made of the equipment. During a shift, the amount of revenue collected during the shift can be determined. This revenue, plus the amount of the beginning cash bank, should be in the register. If there is more money in the machine, it may be because the operator has not rung or has under-rung revenue and has not had time to remove the cash.
>
> No money should be paid out of cash register funds without the approval of management, and then only with a written paid-out slip; if applicable, an invoice or sales slip should be attached.
>
> The system should not contain funds for petty cash.
>
> All employees who handle cash should be bonded.

matches is another technique. Managers should go behind the bar frequently and carefully look for things out of the ordinary. Why are some bottle caps lying in the corner of the bar? Why is a napkin with several tears lying on the back bar? Why is one glass with several lemon twists or toothpicks in an unusual place?

A shopper's service, a control method discussed later in the chapter, can also help reduce the opportunity for no-ring sales.

Under-Ringing. Bartenders who use guest checks in a manual system can collect the proper amount of revenue from guests but record a lower sales value on the check. The bartender rings the lower value into the machine and steals the difference between this amount and what was actually collected from the guest. This practice is called **under-ringing**. To reduce the opportunity for under-ringing, managers need to randomly check the amount rung into the machine or printed on the check. Automated equipment using preset keys and video touch-screen monitors for data entry make under-ringing more difficult, but dishonest bartenders can still find ways to ring an inexpensive drink into the system and then prepare, serve, and collect revenue for a more expensive drink.

Bunched Sales. **Bunched sales** occur when employees add guest check totals or drink charges in their heads and enter only the totals into the equipment. Theft occurs when an employee purposely lowers the total of a guest check or drink charge, collects the full amount from the guest, and pockets the difference. This type of theft can be prevented by requiring handwritten totals on all guest checks (for properties using a manual system), and by enforcing policies that hold employees accountable for failing to follow proper procedures. POS systems and automated drink dispensing equipment require that each order be placed separately, which reduces the possibility of this problem.

Misuse of Guest Checks (Manual Systems). When guest checks are used, one guest's check can be reused when another guest places the same order. The revenue from this second guest is not recorded, and the bartender can steal it. A locked box for all used tickets (those run through the register after payment) can deter this technique, especially when supplemented with other control procedures such as routine security shopping.

Register operators can steal guest checks or purchase similar checks and use them to undermine the property's revenue control system. Increased use of automated systems that eliminate the use of hard-copy guest checks help to reduce opportunities for employee theft.

Substituting Stolen Bank Checks or Credit Card Vouchers for Cash. Register users can steal personal checks from anyone or emboss additional credit card vouchers from guests and replace cash in the register with the stolen check or charge voucher. Credit card and check acceptance procedures, discussed later in the chapter, can help prevent this type of theft.

Mixing Revenue with Tips. Bartenders might also use the tip jar to steal revenue from the property. Basically, the bartender collects revenue from guests and deposits it directly in—or makes change from—the tip jar. Suppose, for example, when paying for two beers at $2.25 each (a $4.50 charge), the guest says, "Here's a five; keep the change." The bartender can then put the entire $5 in the tip jar. The guest who does not wait for change will hardly notice what is happening. A locked tip box placed away from the register, along with regular supervision and use of a shopping service, will help prevent this method of employee theft.

"Borrowing" from the Register. The best intentions to pay back borrowed funds too often don't materialize. When the beginning cash bank is counted and removed at the end of each shift—along with the actual revenue collected—borrowing is no longer possible.

In many loosely controlled operations, bartenders simply remove cash from the income drawer. It is impossible to overemphasize the need to double-check the amount of revenue expected to be in the cash drawer. The manager must have a system in place to determine standard (expected) revenue, which can then be compared to the actual revenue collected.

Stealing from Other Bartenders. Bartenders can also ring sales on another bartender's key and pocket the revenue. The dishonest bartender can remove the "excess" cash from the register without detection, and the honest bartender may be suspect. Funds owed to the property as tallied on the victimized bartender's equipment will be overstated, and funds available will be short. The best precaution here is a separate POS register—or, at the very least, a different cash drawer—for each bartender. Modern systems requiring an employee identification number, key, key card, or other security device have made this theft method increasingly difficult.

Many beverage managers believe that an effective way to reduce the potential for bartender misuse of the cash register involves removal of the cash drawer during the bartender's shift. The manager using this technique will go to the bar at a random time during the shift and determine the amount of sales rung on the equipment to that point. He or she will remove the cash drawer and replace it with a new cash drawer having a precounted cash bank, enabling the bartender to continue working. The manager can count the amount of money in the drawer and compare it to the amount of revenue rung on the register. The amount that should be available is the amount of the beginning cash bank plus the amount of revenue from sales registered to the time the drawer was removed. This procedure is an effective control technique. If the register count indicates a shortage of funds in the cash drawer, there is clearly a problem with employee theft or errors. Beverage managers must also be concerned when the comparison shows there is too much money in the cash drawer. As noted earlier, bartenders using a no-ring theft method will typically leave unrecorded revenue in the cash drawer until the end of the shift. If the count of money in the drawer indicates that the amount of cash is greater than that which can be accounted for, it is possible that the bartender is not ringing all sales and has yet to remove unrecorded revenue from the drawer.

Theft by Misuse of Beverage Products

Bartenders can find many ways to steal revenue by misusing beverage products when they prepare drinks for guests. These theft methods often result in higher beverage cost percentages, since beverages are used but no revenue (or an incorrect amount of revenue) is collected.

Underpouring Drinks. Bartenders can underpour drinks by using an improper shot glass or jigger. **Freepouring**—not using a measured pour at all—can also result in underpoured drinks. For example, if 1-ounce drinks are underpoured by ¼ ounce, the bartender can steal the revenue from every fifth drink without affecting the beverage cost percentage. Managers can protect the property against this type of theft by requiring that portion control tools—a proper jigger or shot glass—be used every time liquor is poured, or by using a metered or computerized beverage-dispensing system.

Diluting Liquor. Diluting liquor is another technique that might be used to get more drinks out of a bottle without affecting the beverage cost percentage. The bartender steals the revenue from the "extra" drinks. To detect this problem, managers should check bottles, since liquors often become lighter in color or cloudy when water or soda is added. Frequent complaints from guests regarding beverage quality are also clues to this method of bartender theft.

Substituting Lower-Quality Liquor for Call Brands. With this method of theft, bartenders charge the higher price and pocket the difference. This practice can be prevented by requiring that orders be written on the guest checks and that the check be rung through the register (at properties using a manual system). This problem may be uncovered by random examinations of guest checks (if used) and by observing the way that orders are written and rung up. Automated systems requiring separate order entry for each drink are also helpful deterrents.

Pouring Drinks from Private Bottles. Bartenders can bring in their own bottles and pour from them. This kind of theft will not result in higher beverage cost percentages for the property because the bartender incurs all costs and collects all revenue. Essentially, the operation has a "partner" in the business—one who does not share in the payment of overhead expenses. Bottle marking can help prevent bartenders from substituting their own liquor for the property's. This is especially effective when access to the marking stamp or other marking device is controlled. As always, careful supervision, including frequent behind-the-bar checks, is an important control tool.

Misrepresenting Sales as Spilled, Complimentary, or Returned Drinks. Bartenders can sell drinks for cash, keep the revenue, and report the drinks as spilled, complimentary, or returned. Management should view all returned drinks before disposal. Policies regarding complimentary drinks should be developed and consistently followed. Bartenders reporting excessive spillage and returns should be retrained, closely supervised, or terminated.

Collusion with Beverage Servers. Bartenders can work in collusion with beverage servers. Drinks can be prepared for the server, and the unrecorded revenue split between the two employees. Supervision is needed to ensure that the procedures of the property's revenue collection system are consistently followed. Shift rotations and close comparisons of standard and actual beverage costs may help detect and prevent this problem.

Collusion with Food Production Employees. Bartenders can trade liquor for food products from the kitchen. Managers should ensure that all eating and drinking policies are consistently followed. Signs of policy violations—such as glasses in the kitchen or plates in the bar, restroom, or locker areas—should be followed up with corrective action.

Pouring Free Drinks. Bartenders can rob the property of revenue by giving away drinks to friends or employees. They also may try to promote bigger tips by providing free beverages to guests. The need for policies regarding complimentary drinks has already been stressed. An effective way to prevent and discover these problems is by regular use of a shopper service.

Preventing Theft through Shopper Services

The value of using a **shopper service** to detect bartender theft has been mentioned several times in this chapter. With this technique, the manager hires someone to pose as a guest, sit at the bar, and watch the bartender work. Many operations bring in shoppers every month or even more frequently. Bartenders or other employees should not know the shoppers. Shoppers could be friends of the management staff or employees of a professional shopping service, or even students meeting age requirements who are enrolled in local hospitality programs.

Informing the staff that a shopper service is used routinely to assess the effectiveness of the operation's revenue control system may itself help deter theft. Remember that the purpose of the control system is to prevent and reduce the opportunities for employee theft, not to "catch it" after the theft occurs.

Shopper Training. Before the on-site visit, it is important that management meet with the person who will be "shopping" the property. The usefulness of shopper services to management's control system depends on shoppers knowing what to look for.

A shopper is not simply someone looking for overt cases of employee theft. It is much more likely that a shopper will note the use of an improper procedure rather than an actual theft taking place. Therefore, the exact procedures to be followed by the bartenders and beverage servers must be fully explained to the shopper before the visit. Shoppers should be familiar with all drink preparation and revenue collection procedures established by management. This includes such things as how guest charges should be transferred (if permitted) between the lounge and restaurant, how appetizers should be accounted for in the lounge, and how guest bar tabs should be run.

During the visit, all bartenders should be randomly observed by the shopper. However, a manager can ask the shopper to more carefully observe specific staff members, such as a bartender suspected of theft, or a new bartender who may still be trying to learn the property's procedures.

With this information, the shopper can closely monitor the actual procedures during the visit. For example, the shopper may order a drink and carefully observe all procedures for taking the order, preparing and serving the drink, collecting cash, and ringing the sale on the POS equipment. The shopper generally remains at the bar and casually observes the various transactions and procedures. At the conclusion of the visit, the shopper should report all findings to the manager, perhaps using a form such as the one shown in Exhibit 2.

Shoppers as Marketing Consultants. Shoppers can and should be concerned with more than just a study of the bartender's and beverage server's handling procedures for beverages and revenue. Shoppers may also be used to view the operation from the guest's perspective. For example, they can note whether service was efficient and hospitable and whether products meet quality expectations. They can also determine whether sanitation procedures are being followed and whether facility cleanliness meets their expectations. In effect, then, the shopper can serve as a consultant to the manager, looking at procedures and facilities from the point of view of the guest.

Theft by Cashiers

Food cashiers have the same opportunities for revenue equipment misuse as bartenders. Most of the control procedures noted in Exhibit 1 apply to cashiers, but dishonest cashiers can still find creative ways to steal revenue. Exhibit 3 lists some of these methods, and also indicates preventive measures. Note that in several theft methods, the dishonest act affects employees other than the cashier. Management must actively try to prevent theft to protect honest employees. Close supervision can help ensure that required procedures are being used.

Theft by Food and Beverage Servers and Other Staff

Food and beverage servers can use a variety of common methods to steal from the operation. With some manual check and cash collection systems, servers may be able to receive cash from a guest without using a guest check and simply steal the revenue. This practice becomes difficult with an effective guest-check or automated control system.

Exhibit 2   Sample Shopper Report for Bar Operations

Shopper Report
OPERATIONAL AND SERVICE REPORT

Name of Bar: _____   Date: _____

Address: _____   Time: _____

_____

Employee Reviewed: Badge/ID _____ Sex _____ Other Age _____ Descriptive Build _____ Features: Hair Color _____ Glasses _____	**Items Purchased** Quantity Item Charge Tax _____ Amt. Paid _____

Part I—Service Details

	Yes	No
A. Was service cordial?	☐	☐
B. Were you greeted?	☐	☐
C. Was the area where you were seated clean?	☐	☐
D. Was service prompt?	☐	☐
E. Was employee neat/clean?	☐	☐
F. Was employee aware of prices/brands?	☐	☐
G. Was serviceware clean?	☐	☐

Part II—Revenue Collection
When check was issued:

	Yes	No
A. Was sales chit (check) presented immediately upon service?	☐	☐
B. Were charges/arithmetic correct?	☐	☐
C. Was bar tab run?	☐	☐
D. Check Number (if appropriate)	_____	
E. Served At: ☐ Bar ☐ Table		

Part II—Revenue Collection *(continued)*
When money was collected:

	Yes	No
A. Was payment requested upon service?	☐	☐
B. Was amount of purchase quoted?	☐	☐
C. Were charges correct?	☐	☐
D. Was charge called back?	☐	☐
E. Was revenue rung up immediately/correctly?	☐	☐
F. Were you thanked after payment?	☐	☐
G. Was tip handled properly?	☐	☐

Part III—Other Information

A. Operation

B. Production/Service Concerns

C. Interaction with Other Employees

D. Comments

(Use continuation sheet as necessary)

Exhibit 3   Common Methods of Theft by Cashiers

Theft Method	Affects	Prevention Method
1. Collect cash and void sales checks/chits	Cashier	Sales checks must be matched with duplicates in manual check systems; managers must approve all voids
2. Collect cash and record sales as a charge	Cashier	See procedures for processing credit card charges
3. Collect cash, claim guest walked out ("dine and dash" claim)	Cashier Server	Walkouts should be tallied by employee; more than very occasional walkouts call for retraining or more supervision of the affected employee
4. Remove cash; claim shortage	Cashier	Expected and actual revenue amounts must be known as the basis for the revenue control system
5. Make payments from cash drawer for personal expenses	Cashier	Imprest petty cash system must be used for all purchases
6. Understate cashier's reports	Cashier	A non-cashier employee should process or at least review all revenue reports detailing cashier transactions. POS systems address this; all financial information is available only to managers
7. Fail to record miscellaneous revenue (vending machine proceeds, grease sales, etc.)	Cashier	Miscellaneous revenue should be paid to management, not to the cashier
8. Incorrectly use revenue equipment	Cashier	All POS operating procedures reviewed in Exhibit 1 should be consistently followed
9. Ring up on another cashier's key	All Cashiers	When possible, each cashier should have a separate POS terminal, drawer, or access key
10. Collect revenue, claim guest refused to pay	Cashier	These situations should be referred to management
11. Receive cash, destroy ticket, claim ticket was not received (manual system)	Cashier Server	If problem occurs more than very occasionally, a sign-off system should require the cashier to accept responsibility for tickets/chits received from servers
12. Collect cash and change ticket to show reduced amount owed (manual system)	Cashier Server	All procedures for guest check control should be in use; match original to duplicate checks (manual systems); use automated systems as source of standard (expected) revenue

When guest checks are used, servers may receive or take products without entering the required information on the guest check. With few exceptions, the control system should prohibit production staff (cooks and bartenders) from giving products to service personnel until they present appropriate requisition slips or duplicate guest checks or until orders are entered into an automated system. Servers may use guest checks purchased at a local restaurant supply store to bypass the existing guest-check system. This cannot happen if unique, hard-to-duplicate checks are issued, used, and stored securely. The following paragraphs describe how servers may steal by abusing a manual guest-check control system. Many of these theft methods won't work if automated systems are used and required procedures are followed.

Servers may reuse a check to obtain an identical order for another guest. Servers should present requisition slips/duplicate checks to kitchen staff before receiving food. In the bar, a stamp, marking, or register imprint can certify which drinks on a guest check have already been served.

Servers may understate a check, delete items to help a friend, or overstate the check to influence the tip. Guest checks should be regularly audited. If requisition slips/duplicate checks are used, copies should be matched with the original guest check on a random basis.

Servers may collect cash and destroy a check, claiming that it was lost or that the guests left without paying. Because checks will be accounted for, the missing check will be noticed. When a server loses checks or has guests "walk," the server, at the least, needs close supervision or additional training.

A dishonest food server may collect revenue for a beverage charge transferred from the lounge, destroy the guest check, steal the money, and claim that the transfer was never received. This can be prevented by requiring that the supervisor, host, or cashier verify transactions by recording the appropriate guest check numbers alongside items that have been transferred.

A server may claim that a dissatisfied guest returned an item listed on the guest check, pocket the money, and turn in only the revenue for the other items. The manager should approve all returned menu items and approve any changes to totals recorded on guest checks.

Servers may pocket the revenue from items such as salads or nonalcoholic beverages that they can retrieve without presenting duplicate checks (in a manual system) or entering order information into a POS system. Management should design procedures that minimize the number of menu items to which servers can help themselves.

In addition to bartenders, cashiers, and food and beverage servers, other employees who do not normally come in direct contact with revenue may still present problems. Exhibit 4 lists common methods of theft used by non-cash-handling personnel, as well as corresponding methods of prevention. (Special concerns regarding embezzlement by secretarial or accounting staff are discussed later in the chapter.)

While employee theft of revenue can never be fully prevented, the consistent use of the following tactics is always in order:

- Procedures designed to minimize revenue theft should be developed and implemented. Note: Operating manuals and other information provided with POS systems may provide assistance.

Exhibit 4   Theft by Non-Cash-Handling Personnel

Theft Method	Prevention Method
1. Housekeeping personnel steal cash left unattended in cash drawer or in the office when cleaning.	Lock or empty revenue equipment when unattended. Keep cash in office areas under lock.
2. Revenue awaiting deposit in bank is stolen.	Keep revenue locked in bank bags in the safe or other secure area(s).
3. Employees pass bad checks or request loans that are difficult to collect.	Do not accept employee checks. Keep loans small, and do not make a loan if another loan remains unpaid; loan total should not exceed the amount of salary or wage due.
4. Employees misuse petty cash funds.	Follow imprest petty cash fund procedures.
5. Buspersons or other staff steal tips or revenue from service staff.	Service personnel should keep close track of their guests. Servers should keep money collected in a server banking system on his or her person or in a locked box area provided by the manager.
6. Employees intercept mail, remove checks.	Deny employee access to all incoming and outgoing mail.

- Employees should be trained to consistently follow required revenue management procedures.

- Managers should closely supervise employee performance. For example, they can "manage by walking around" and notice whether the procedures actually being used are those which should be used.

- Managers should take advantage of the "open check" feature of POS systems. They should randomly but routinely note items such as beverages, appetizers, and desserts at selected guest tables and confirm that, in fact, these items have been entered in the revenue management system for these tables.

- A policy that no food or beverage item should be given to service staff by food or production personnel without being entered into the POS system should be in place and strictly enforced.

Theft by Guests

Unfortunately, some guests will steal from the food and beverage operation if given the opportunity. Knowing ways dishonest guests can steal enables managers to incorporate practical preventive procedures into their control systems. The following paragraphs describe some methods guests may use to steal.

Guests may take advantage of staff errors. Guests can take advantage of server errors in calculating charges. This problem is reduced if servers use a calculator with a printing tape in a manual check system. Servers using such devices should carefully double-check the numbers and attach the calculator tape to the guest check before presenting it. A similar problem occurs when guests do not point out omissions on the guest check. Again, recording everything on checks and adding carefully can help reduce this type of problem. Use of automated equipment reduces the potential of simple arithmetic errors on guest transactions.

Guests may walk out before paying the bill. Service staff should present bills promptly and pay attention to guests who appear to be finishing and getting ready to leave. Service staff can also be trained to notice guests being served in other workstations who appear to be ready to leave. They can then notify the guests' server. Also, positioning the cashier or hostess station at the entrance to the dining area helps reduce the possibility of walkouts.

Guests may disclaim transfer charges. Some guests may disclaim beverage charges incurred in the lounge that are transferred to the restaurant. Staff should have guests sign transferred guest checks or slips and process them in a manner that ensures payment for all transferred checks. Errors (transferred charges that are not noticed, for example) can occur even when automated systems are in use. For this reason, many restaurants do not permit such transfers. However, procedures that make dining experiences pleasant for guests are important. Managers should focus on what is best for guests, not what is easiest for the operation, when they make transfer decisions.

Guests may steal property. Guests can also steal flatware, glassware, room furnishings, and other easily transportable items. While this is not theft of cash, there are clear cost implications. Service staff should be trained to promptly remove all soiled items from tables to reduce opportunities for this kind of theft. They should also be alert to items missing from the table or surrounding areas as guests leave and should promptly notify management if they are suspicious. Some properties make unique items available for sale to guests. In this way, the property can generate additional revenue at the same time that it reduces the potential for theft-incurred costs. Logoware (items on which the property's name is etched or embossed or otherwise attached) is especially theft-prone. Managers should consider appropriate but generic serviceware to reduce this type of guest theft.

Guests may pass worthless checks. Managers or designated staff members should approve all payments by guests using personal checks or traveler's checks. The information presented in Exhibit 5 can help those approving such payments to spot forged checks. As part of the control system, managers should maintain a list of all personal and business checks that are not to be accepted. National check approval services, which provide full payment for checks they approve that are later dishonored by the bank, should be considered. Guests wishing to pay by check should be asked to present two forms of identification, one of which should be a major credit card accepted by the property. Personal checks without the depositor's name printed on them should not be accepted. Exhibit 6 suggests steps to follow when accepting checks. Additional procedures may include the following:

- Accept checks only for the amount of the bill.

Exhibit 5   How to Spot Forged Checks

How to Spot Forged Checks

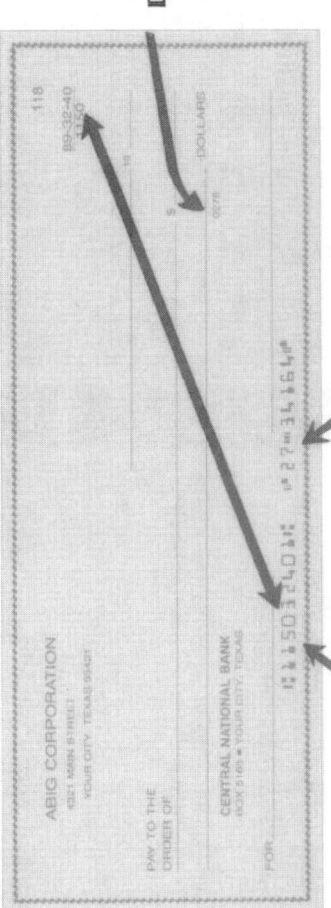

Check for Perforations

You'll be able to feel perforations on at least one edge of all legitimate checks except for government checks—printed on computer card stock. Perforation equipment is expensive and bulky, so most forgers use a regular paper cutter—leaving all four sides smooth.

Watch for Clues Revealing Color Copied Checks

Magnetic routing numbers at the bottom of a check will be raised off the surface—almost like braille—because of the dull ink's effect on the reflective light duplicating process. The numbers on the copy will be shiny instead of dull. Also, because the color is created by a chemical process rather than by ink, the moisture from your fingers will often cause them to smear an opposite color.

Date Code

Verify Federal Reserve District Numbers

The nine place number between the brackets is the routing code for the bank the check is drawn on. The first two indicate which of the 12 Federal Reserve Districts the bank is located in. Refer to the codes below. It is important that you compare this to the location of the bank since a forger will sometimes change these in order to buy more float time while the check is routed to a distant, incorrect Reserve Bank. It should also agree with the routing fraction printed in the upper right hand corner.

Federal Reserve Bank Codes

01—Massachusetts, Maine, New Hampshire, Connecticut, Vermont, Rhode Island
02—New York, New Jersey, Connecticut
03—Pennsylvania, Delaware, New Jersey
04—Ohio, Pennsylvania, Kentucky, West Virginia
05—Virginia, Maryland, North Carolina, Washington, D.C., South Carolina, West Virginia

06—Georgia, Alabama, Florida, Tennessee, Louisiana, Mississippi
07—Illinois, Michigan, Indiana, Iowa, Wisconsin
08—Missouri, Arkansas, Kentucky, Tennessee, Indiana, Illinois, Mississippi
09—Minnesota, Montana, North Dakota,

South Dakota, Wisconsin, Michigan
10—Missouri, Colorado, Oklahoma, Nebraska, Iowa, Wyoming, Kansas, New Mexico
11—Texas, Arizona, New Mexico, Louisiana
12—California, Oregon, Washington, Utah, Hawaii, Alaska, Idaho, Nevada, Arizona

Check Magnetic Numbers for Dull Finish

The special magnetic ink required for automated check sorting is extremely flat and dull. If you spot shine, or reflected light, off these numbers when you tilt the check under normal lighting, it is probably a forgery. This ink is expensive, and restricted, so the forger will usually not go to the trouble to obtain it. Being aware of the short cuts taken by forgers due to expense and unavailability of certain papers and inks, will help you to quickly and easily spot forged checks.

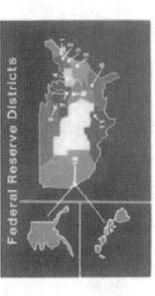

Federal Reserve Districts

Source: Frank W. Abagnale & Associates, Tulsa, Oklahoma.

Exhibit 6 Steps to Follow when Accepting Checks

Steps to Follow when Accepting Checks

1 Be cautious of new checking accounts

Of all the insufficient, "hot" checks, 90% are drawn on accounts less than a year old. The consecutive numbers in the upper right hand corner begin with 101 and you should be especially careful when taking low numbered checks. Because knowing the age of the account is so important, some banks now print a code of when the account was opened (for example, 0278 means February, 1978) on all checks.

2 Place all information on front of check

As described in Regulation CC, either write the information consecutively across the top of the front or use the cross method.

Driver's license number	Credit card number
Clerk's initials	Other ID or manager's approval

3 Examine driver's license carefully

After you have the license out of the customer's wallet and in your hand, quickly ask yourself the following questions: Is the person in the photo and in front of you the same person? Are the addresses on the check and license the same? When does the license expire? More than 60% of the forged checks last year were cashed with an expired driver's license. Also, the courts have ruled that licenses are legally worthless for identification as soon as they expire. Be sure you examine the driver's license carefully.

4 Other Negotiable Instrument Codes

On drafts issued by savings and loan institutions and mutual savings banks, magnetic bank routing numbers may start with the digit 2 or 3. Credit union drafts are honored by the bank on which they are drawn. International traveler's checks have routing numbers starting with 8000. U.S. Government checks contain the routing number 000000518.

5 Traveler's check identification

VISA—When held above eye level, a globe of the world will appear on the front left and a dove in the upper right.
MASTERCARD and THOMAS COOK—When held above eye level, on the right side of the check in a circle, a woman with short black hair will appear.
CITICORP—When held above eye level, a Greek god will appear on the right.
BANK OF AMERICA—No distinguishing watermarks.
AMERICAN EXPRESS—Turn check over. Moisten your finger tip and run it over the left denomination. If it smears it is good. Right side will not smear.

6 Be impressed with the check—not the person

Don't let a customer's appearance lull you into ignoring any of these steps. Frank Abagnale, the retired master forger, once cashed a $50 check written on a cocktail napkin, before a hidden camera for television, because the bank teller was more impressed by his appearance than by the item he presented. When you're in a hurry, or want to make an exception, think how you will defend your decision if the check is returned. Then, only the check will matter —not the circumstances in which you took it.

Developed by Frank W. Abagnale

Frank W. Abagnale & Associates/PO Box 701290, Tulsa, Oklahoma 74170/Telephone 918-492-6590

Source: Frank W. Abagnale & Associates, Tulsa, Oklahoma.

- Postdated or two-party checks are not acceptable.

- All checks should be legible and made out to the correct name of the food and beverage operation. Those showing any sign of tampering are not acceptable.

- Checks marked "For Deposit Only" are not acceptable.

- The guests must sign the check in the presence of the manager or designated staff member.

- Checks should be marked or stamped "For Deposit Only" as soon as they are accepted.

Guests may use fraudulent payment cards. Managers should ensure that before accepting payment, bartenders, servers, and cashiers follow all rules required by payment card companies regarding authorization. Operations process the guest's payment card through an automated authorization device. Additional procedures for approval of payment cards may include the following:

- Have the guest sign the payment card voucher as well as applicable guest checks or slips.

- "Loans" should not be made on payment cards. Food and beverage operations pay a discount fee for the value of these charges.

Guests may pass counterfeit currency. Food and beverage operations often serve as convenient places for dishonest guests to pass counterfeit currency. Exhibit 7 suggests how to detect counterfeit currency, what to do if counterfeit currency is detected, and pertinent facts about paper currency in the United States. Note that in many cases the passer may not have made the bills, but may be able to help police trace their origin.

Guests may shortchange cash-handling employees. The fast pace of busy meal periods presents another convenient opportunity for dishonest guests to shortchange employees handling cash payments. Exhibit 8 describes one trick of a shortchange artist and suggests how to avoid being victimized.

Employee Theft from Guests

While employee theft from guests may not immediately affect the property's revenue, it can significantly affect the property's reputation and, therefore, its long-term profitability. Guests who discover that they have been cheated will often blame the property, not the dishonest employee. This is reasonable, since the employer selects and trains employees and has an obligation to design and enforce procedures and policies to protect guests.

Staff members with the greatest opportunity to steal from guests are those who handle cash: bartenders, cashiers, and servers. Several of the methods used to steal money from guests are:

- Attempting to increase tips by padding bills—putting items guests did not order on guest checks to increase the amount of the check (since most guests base their tips on the amount of the charge).

Exhibit 7   Counterfeit Paper Currency Test

WOODROW
FEDERAL RESERVE BANK OF MINNEAPOLIS

Counterfeit Protection

Whether altering the design of ancient coins or making photocopies of bills with high-tech machines, counterfeiters have made illegal money throughout history. The Secret Service, an agency of the U.S. Treasury, has investigated suspected counterfeit operations since 1865. Over the past decade, the Secret Service has seized approximately 90 percent of all known counterfeit currency printed before it reached circulation.

In the printing process, the Bureau of Engraving and Printing uses complicated techniques to stifle counterfeiters. Beginning with the $100 bill in 1996, currency will be redesigned to include more security features. The following pictures explain how the Bureau protects your money.

Portrait
The portrait on the bill is a lifelike picture, distinctly different from the screen-like background. Each portrait is only on one denomination. For example, George Washington appears only on the $1 bill, **not** on the $100 bill. Portraits on counterfeit bills appear unclear or unnaturally white.

Feel of Paper
Money is printed on high-quality paper made of cotton and linen. It has a strong "feel" to it, different from regular paper.

Border
The artwork along the side of the bill has intricate, crisscrossing lines which are clear and unbroken. Lines in counterfeit bills are often smudged or broken.

Threads
Bills have tiny red and blue fibers that are embedded inside the bill.

Ink
The special "never-dry" ink that is used can be rubbed off. However, this isn't a fool-proof test since ink on some counterfeit bills also rubs off.

Recent Measures

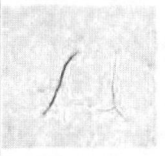

Security Thread
Beginning with series 1990, a polyester thread, which can't be reproduced by photocopiers, is woven inside $10, $20, $50 and $100 bills. USA TEN, USA TWENTY, etc. is printed on it to match the denomination.

Microprinting
"The United States of America" is printed in miniature letters around the border of the portrait. To the naked eye the words appear as a black line, which is also how photocopiers print them.

What to do if you have counterfeit currency
Since the consequences for passing counterfeit currency include fines up to $5,000 or imprisonment up to 15 years, you need to be careful. If you have a suspicious bill:

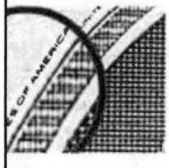

- Write your initials on the back so you can identify it later.
- On a separate sheet of paper write in detail how you got it:
  1. **Who** gave it to you.
  2. **Where** you got it.
  3. **When** you got it.
- Handle it as little as possible to preserve any fingerprints.
- Contact the nearest Secret Service office or local police.

You are not reimbursed for turning in counterfeit bills; however, you protect yourself from trouble by following proper procedures.

Source: Federal Reserve Bank of Minneapolis (www.woodrow.mpls.frb.fed.us).

Exhibit 8   Tricks of a Short-Change Artist

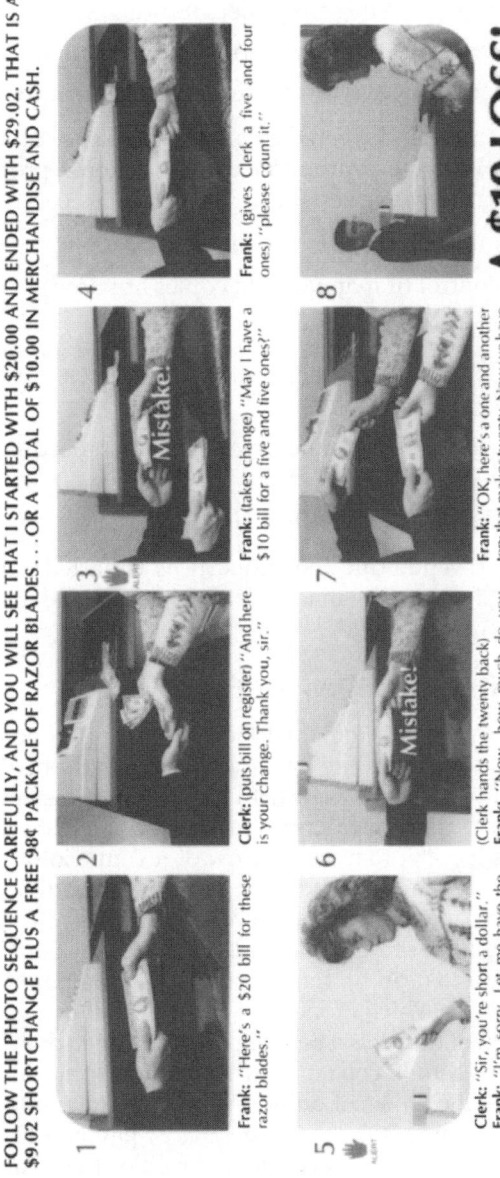

Tricks of a Short-Change Artist

The short-change artist is a master of the art of deception and persuasion. Each has a particular individual style and technique. The short-change artist may be a man, woman, teenager, even a child, but regardless of sex or age, he/she usually operates within these four basic rules:

(1) Establishes credibility and trust. (2) Gains the confidence of the prospective victim. (3) Confuses the prospective victim without making him suspicious. (4) Short changes the victim even without knowing what has happened.

FOLLOW THE PHOTO SEQUENCE CAREFULLY, AND YOU WILL SEE THAT I STARTED WITH $20.00 AND ENDED WITH $29.02. THAT IS A $9.02 SHORTCHANGE PLUS A FREE 98¢ PACKAGE OF RAZOR BLADES. . . OR A TOTAL OF $10.00 IN MERCHANDISE AND CASH.

1
Frank: "Here's a $20 bill for these razor blades."

2
Clerk: (puts bill on register) "And here is your change. Thank you, sir."

3
(hand) ALERT!

4
Frank: (gives Clerk a five and four ones) "please count it."

5
(hand) ALERT!
Clerk: "Sir, you're short a dollar."
Frank: "I'm sorry. Let me have the twenty back and we'll start over."

6
(Clerk hands the twenty back)
Frank: "Now, how much do you have?" Clerk: "Nine dollars."

7
Mistake!
Frank: (takes change) "May I have a $10 bill for a five and five ones?"

8
Frank: "OK, here's a one and another ten; that makes twenty. Now we have it. Thank you!"

A $10 LOSS!

The Answer: 1. Be Alert! 2. Have the customer's money in your hands before making change!
3. Never mix transaction A with B

Developed by Frank W. Abagnale

Frank W Abagnale & Associates/Box 701290, Tulsa, Oklahoma 74170   918-492-6590

Source: Frank W. Abagnale & Associates, Tulsa, Oklahoma.

- Charging higher prices for items than those established by management and pocketing the difference.
- Altering payment card charges after the guest leaves, or imprinting additional vouchers with the guest's payment card before returning it. The dishonest employee can then use these vouchers fraudulently.
- Altering personal checks that guests use for payment.
- Making change incorrectly by shortchanging or fast-counting.

Guests are also cheated when they are served items of lower quality than they order and pay for. With the appropriate control systems, properties can prevent or reduce employee theft from guests. The most effective control methods include:

- Proper operation of the revenue equipment.
- Guest check control (if manual hard copies are used).
- Routine but random audits.
- Close supervision.
- Use of shoppers.
- Compliance with the check and payment card procedures reviewed earlier.

Control of Cash after Collection

Even if all actual revenue due the property is collected from guests, theft may occur when bank deposits are made, when bills are paid, or when bookkeeping/accounting tasks are performed.

Preventing Theft of Bank Deposit Funds

All revenue must be deposited in the food and beverage operation's bank account. Revenue should be deposited at least daily and should be deposited intact. This means that bills should not be paid with cash from the revenue that has been collected from guests but not yet deposited. Instead, bills should be paid by check. This policy makes it easier to trace the flow of revenue into the property, on to the bank, into the proper account, and back out again through proper disbursement procedures when paying bills. (It should be noted that electronic bill payment is gaining popularity with some food and beverage operations. When electronic bill payment is used, funds can be transferred from the operation's bank account to that of the company to which money is owed without using a hard copy check.)

The separation of duties is a basic element in effective control. When possible, different employees should collect revenue, audit and account for guest checks (if used), and prepare the tallies of daily revenue. These employees should not normally be involved in preparing bank deposits or paying bills. In small properties, the manager or owner will perform many or all of these tasks. For example, the manager should be able to double-check revenue levels from source documents such as POS system data, verify the amount of revenue collected from these tallies, make adjustments, and note the amount of revenue to be deposited by way of a bank deposit slip.

In addition to the basic control policies noted, specific practices that can help control revenue at the time of deposit include the following:

- Compare the amount of each bank deposit with records of daily revenue collected.

- Cash received from miscellaneous sources, such as grease sales or bottle returns, should be in the form of a check and deposited in the bank as "other revenue," along with deposits from daily operations.

- Deposits for nonrecurring transactions, such as the sale of equipment or insurance proceeds, should be made separately from revenue deposits.

- When practical, personnel who open mail should not make bank deposits. This reduces the possibility of employees diverting revenue from checks received that should be deposited. In other words, it is less possible to replace cash from daily revenue collections with a check received in the mail.

- All persons involved with money, deposit assessment, and cash disbursements should be **bonded**.

- The person preparing the deposit should not make the deposit unless the owner/manager takes responsibility for these tasks.

- All involved personnel should be aware of and consistently follow deposit procedures. Close supervision of this task is extremely important.

- All checks should be marked "For Deposit Only," preferably at the time of receipt. Instruct local banks not to issue cash for any checks made payable to the food and beverage operation.

- Checks returned as "NSF"—Not Sufficient Funds—should be turned over to the bank to be held for collection. This way, funds later deposited in the account will first be used to meet NSF obligations.

- Checks returned as "Account Closed" should be turned over to a collection agency.

- If the bank provides a carrier service, schedule a daily pick up and implement a procedure that requires management officials to verify the amount of the deposit.

Two final rules are important for handling revenue receipts. First, change the combination of the safe periodically. As few staff members as possible should know how to open the safe. Second, require all employees who handle cash to take uninterrupted annual or more frequent vacations. This way another employee can assume the cash-handling duties and may uncover improper practices.

Preventing Theft when Bills Are Paid

To reduce the opportunities for theft, bills should be properly processed and paid. Basic procedures for paying bills should be incorporated into the cash disbursement system. The following procedures should be implemented to safeguard against theft when bills are paid:

- Pay bills by check. Do not use cash, except for minor expenses to be paid with petty cash funds.

- Use a formal purchase order system for all but the smallest petty cash purchases. When processing bills for payment, compare the in-house (hard or electronic) copies of the purchase order or purchase record, the suppliers' delivery invoices, and the in-house receiving report.

- Develop and use control procedures for issuing checks. If practical, use check protectors that imprint the check amount. Print all checks with the name of the property and mark them "void after 60 days." Never sign blank checks, and do not use rubber signature stamps or electronic signatures. Inform banks of all management staff authorized to sign checks. Checks in excess of a specified dollar value may require more than one manager's signature. Keep unused checks locked in a secure area.

- The person who signs the checks should mail them. They should not be returned to the employee who processed the bills for payment.

- Personnel who sign checks should not normally have access to petty cash funds and should not be permitted to approve cash disbursements or to record cash receipts—unless it is the manager or owner who performs all these tasks.

- Make out all checks to a specific company or person. Never make out checks to "cash" or "bearer."

- Clearly mark invoices and statements "PAID" after processing. The date, check number, invoice, and check amount should all be clearly noted on the forms. File these documents, with supporting information, by supplier.

- Investigate outstanding checks that are not promptly returned or cashed.

- Place all returned checks in sequential order and properly and immediately reconcile bank statements.

- Deface voided checks (those written out to a supplier but not used) and keep them in a special file for examination when audits are undertaken.

Although bills should be paid by check whenever possible, writing checks for minor expenses can be a nuisance. For this reason, many food and beverage operations set up a petty cash fund. Proper procedures for handling petty cash are an important aspect of the cash control system. The basic plan for using a petty cash system should include these steps:

1. Set the total of the petty cash fund at the amount normally needed for very small purchases over several weeks. To establish the fund, write a check charged to "petty cash." This amount—in dollars or in supporting receipts— should always remain in the fund. When replenishing the petty cash fund, write a second check for the total amount of receipts in the fund to bring it back up to its proper level. Make out the checks to "petty cash," not to "cash" or to the name of the person managing the fund.

2. Assign responsibility for the fund to one staff member and keep the fund in a secure place. It should not be mixed with funds in cash registers.

Exhibit 9   Sample Petty Cash Voucher

Petty Cash Voucher

Voucher Number: _____

Date: _____

Purpose: _____

_____

Account: _____   Account to Be Charged: _____

Authorized By: _____

(Attach Receipt to This Voucher)

---

3. Do not authorize the person responsible for managing the fund to write or sign a check to replenish it unless the owner/manager is responsible for the fund.

4. Develop definite policies regarding what can and cannot be purchased with funds from petty cash. These policies should also specify how often purchases can be made and a dollar limit above which checks must be written for purchases.

5. Support all purchases with a receipt for the amount of the purchased items.

6. Use a petty cash voucher (see Exhibit 9) to summarize petty cash transactions.

7. Cash advances or loans for employees should not be made from the petty cash fund.

8. Spot-check petty cash funds to ensure that the fund is at the proper level and that all purchases are for authorized purposes and supported by receipts.

Preventing Bookkeeper and Accountant Theft

Many types of theft are related to the misuse of bookkeeping and accounting procedures. Managers need to remain constantly alert to this wide range of opportunities for theft. Examples include:

- Changing revenue records to show lower daily revenue and stealing the difference between revenue reported and actual revenue collected.

- Removing cash from the petty cash fund and either allowing the fund to remain short or submitting false expense receipts to cover the shortage.

- Billing charge customers at the full amount but recording a lower amount owed and pocketing the difference.

- Showing higher than actual discounts when reimbursement checks from credit card companies are deposited.

- Claiming a guest's check was marked "NSF" (Not Sufficient Funds) or "account closed" and then converting the check to personal use.

- Preparing checks payable to oneself and forging signatures or using signed blank checks, then destroying paid checks when returned from the bank.

- Manipulating bank statement reconciliations—overstating deposits not yet recorded, understating outstanding checks, and purposely miscalculating on reconciliation worksheets—to cover cash shortages.

- Overstating expenses but paying only the supplier's correct charge.

- Overpaying a supplier's invoice and converting the supplier's refund check for personal use.

- Resubmitting invoices previously paid for a second payment and splitting payment with the suppliers in collusion with a company thief.

- Setting up a "dummy" company to submit invoices for payment. Invoices listing a post office box for the company's address are especially suspicious.

- Padding the payroll by preparing checks for employees who have been terminated or adding fictitious employees to the payroll.

- Adding overtime or additional hours to payroll records to increase wages.

- Converting unclaimed payroll checks and cashing them with forged signatures.

Employing Other Revenue Control Tactics

There are many other tactics owners and top-level managers of food and beverage operations can use to help ensure that fraud is not committed by dishonest back-of-the-house employees. For example, owners and top managers should:

- Review the property's banking activity online several times weekly and randomly verify that supporting in-house source documents are available and have been correctly processed.

- Require that bank statements be mailed directly to them and be opened by them for careful analysis.

- Eliminate the use of management credit cards for the business or implement tactics to assure that they are not improperly used. For example, detailed receipts should be required for all transactions, and statements should be sent directly to the owner or general manager.

- Require a manager's approval for voids and complimentary meals or other deductions for guest purchases greater than a specified amount.

- Review petty cash funds with the individual who is responsible for them at least monthly and at other random times.

- Review the websites of newly used vendors, and call the telephone numbers on their invoices when the invoices are received.

- Compare the addresses of office staff to the addresses of all vendors, looking for matches.

- Include reference checks as part of the hiring process for all employees.
- Run credit checks on all back-office personnel with accounting responsibilities.

The owner should approve and sign checks for all purchases made by the general manager.

 Key Terms ————————————————————————————————

bond (revenue control)—An insurance policy that reimburses a hospitality operation for loss when a covered employee commits fraud.

bunched sales—In operations using manual guest checks, a type of theft in which employees add guest check totals or drink charges in their heads and enter only the totals into the register. Theft occurs when an employee purposely lowers the total of a guest check, collects the full amount from the guest, and pockets the difference.

collusion—A relationship between two or more employees or between employees and non-employees that allows them to work together to steal revenue and products from the operation.

freepouring—A type of theft in which a bartender does not use measuring tools when pouring drinks. By underpouring 1-ounce drinks by ¼ ounce, the bartender can steal the revenue from every fifth drink without affecting the beverage cost percentage.

no-ring sales—Theft by an employee who collects revenue from guests, opens the cash drawer by pressing a "no sale" or similar key, and makes change for currency collected. Later the employee removes cash in the amount of the sale. There is no record of a transaction when "no sale" is used to access the cash drawer.

prepayment card—A device, similar in size and shape to a credit card, that contains prepaid deposits for future transactions (a gift card, for example).

shopper service—A technique to detect employee theft in which the manager hires someone to pose as a guest, sit at the bar, and watch the bartender work. The "shopper" looks for any discrepancies from established operating procedures in the bartender's performance of his or her duties, notes them, and provides a detailed report to the manager.

under-ringing—Theft by an employee in an operation that uses manual guest checks. In this theft method, the employee collects the proper amount of revenue from the guests but records a lower sales value on the check. He or she then rings the lower value into the machine and steals the difference between this amount and what was actually collected from the guest.

 Review Questions ————————————————————————————————

1. Why is it important to develop and implement specific procedures for using the point-of-sale (POS) system ?

2. What are some of the ways that a bartender can steal from a property? What procedures can be implemented to reduce opportunities for bartender theft? How can use of a POS system reduce opportunities for bartender theft when a manual hard-copy guest check system is used?

3. What is a shopper service? Why and when should this service be used?

4. What are some of the ways that food service staff can steal from a property? What procedures can be implemented to reduce these possibilities? How can use of a POS system reduce opportunities for server theft when a hard-copy guest check system is used?

5. What are some of the ways cashiers can steal from a property? What procedures can be implemented to reduce these possibilities? How can a POS system help reduce cashier theft?

6. What are some of the ways guests can steal from a property? What procedures can be implemented to reduce these possibilities?

7. What are some of the ways employees can steal from guests? What procedures can be implemented to reduce these possibilities? How do POS systems reduce opportunities for employee theft from guests?

8. When should revenue be deposited in the bank? Why?

9. What are some effective procedures for handling petty cash?

10. How can bookkeepers and accountants steal from a property? What procedures can be implemented to reduce these possibilities?

 **Internet Sites** ——————————————————————————————

For more information, visit the following Internet sites. Remember that Internet addresses can change without notice. If the site is no longer there, you can use a search engine to look for additional sites.

Theft Prevention Websites

About.com
www.about.com
(Enter "employee theft" in the site's search box.)

Allfoodbusiness.com
www.allfoodbusiness.com/
theft_management.php

Crime Doctor
www.crimedoctor.com

King County, Washington,
   Prosecuting Attorney
www.metrokc.gov/proatty/fraud/
employee.htm

QSR Magazine.com
www.qsrmagazine.com
(Enter "employee theft" in the site's search box.)

Revenue Control Software

Actions Systems, Inc.
www.actionsystems.com

Agilsys Hospitality Solutions
http://hospitality.agilysys.com/
index.aspx

Aldelo Systems
www.aldelo.com

NCR Corporation
www.ncr.com

AM/PM Service Ltd.
www.ampmservice.com

POSitouch
www.positouch.com

Comtrex
www.comtrex.com

RMS-TOUCH
www.rmstouch.com

Digital Dining
www.digitaldining.com

Squirrel Systems
www.squirrelsystems.com

Infor Restaurant Systems
www.rsd.geac.com

 # Mini-Case Studies

Mini-Case One—Employee Romance

You are the manager of a high-volume restaurant/bar. On one of your days off, you are shopping in a grocery store and notice that one of your bartenders and a beverage server are walking down a nearby aisle holding hands in what appears to be a romantic manner. Until now, you were unaware of any romantic relationship between the two. They frequently work in the bar during the same shift, and you have never noticed any actions that have suggested they have anything but a professional (on-job) relationship.

   a. Is this a potential problem that could have an impact on your business?

   b. What, if anything, should you do, now that you know about this apparent relationship?

Mini-Case Two—Deciding on a POS System

You are the owner of a small-volume restaurant and bar that has been growing in popularity. You are planning to upgrade your revenue control system by purchasing a point-of-sale system to replace your current manual guest-check system. What are some of the most important factors you should consider when deciding on a system for your operation?

Mini-Case Three—Manager Problems and Decisions

You are the manager of a restaurant. What would you do in the following situations?

   a. You are alone in your office counting cash from the day's receipts. An employee who has been employed at the property for five years enters the office and receives your permission to make a telephone call. Shortly thereafter, you must leave for a few moments to address a situation in the kitchen and the employee is still talking on the phone. What would you do? How, if at all, would your response to this situation change if the employee in your office had been with you for only two weeks?

b. Joe, a bartender, is typically "over" in his cash drawer by two or three dollars each shift. In the past, you have always thought that it is "better to be over than to be short" and have not worried about it. However, after reviewing this chapter, you recognize that there might be a problem. What would you do?

c. You walk through the bar and notice that the bartender on duty is not using a shot glass or jigger to portion liquor as procedures require. What problems can arise when portion control tools are not used? What would you do about the problem?

Part VI

Controlling
Labor Costs

Competencies

1. Describe how food and beverage managers use staffing tools such as job descriptions, job specifications, and organization charts in planning for labor cost control. (pp. 413–416)

2. Describe how food and beverage managers use recruitment and selection tools to ensure that the most qualified applicants are hired for open positions. (pp. 416–419)

3. Explain how orientation programs, training programs, proper supervision, and employee performance evaluations help control labor costs. (pp. 419–425)

4. Outline factors affecting employee work performance and productivity, and explain how food and beverage managers can increase staff productivity by simplifying work processes and revising performance standards. (pp. 425–431)

5. Explain how food and beverage managers use techniques such as job rotation, job enlargement, and job enrichment to increase productivity and employees' interest in work. (pp. 431–435)

6. Review basic tactics that food and beverage managers can use to reduce employee turnover rates. (pp. 435–437)

7. Summarize responsibilities of area managers in multi-unit organizations. (pp. 437–440)

13

Labor Cost Control

$\mathbf{F}$OOD AND BEVERAGE MANAGERS are well aware of the need to control labor costs. To put the issue in perspective, consider the following:

- Labor costs are the largest costs (or second largest, after food) in almost all food and beverage operations.

- The food service industry is labor-intensive. Technology has not found a way to replace people with equipment. Even an increased emphasis on convenience food usage in many properties has not eliminated the need for a large staff. Employees are needed to produce, serve, and clean up in food and beverage operations. And many employees occupy entry-level hourly positions, where problems of high turnover, accidents, absenteeism, tardiness, and low morale—all factors that add to labor costs—are often prevalent.

- Direct labor costs are increasing. Minimum wage scales increase periodically, and many hospitality employees are paid at rates significantly higher than minimum wage in order to attract and retain them. Competition for qualified people from other food and beverage operations and especially from other service industries raises labor rates. And, in many areas, there is a need for larger incentives to attract people to work in entry-level positions.

- Increases in labor costs are usually not balanced by increases in productivity. Labor needed just to maintain operations becomes increasingly expensive.

- Fringe benefits packages are increasingly very creative—and increasingly expensive. Not long ago, a benefits package generally included employer contributions for social security, meals, uniforms, and unemployment taxes. Today, however, employees often receive such additional benefits as dental and health insurance, education and training assistance, contributions toward retirement plans, and many others.

- It is difficult to manage people in any industry, but in the hospitality industry it is especially true that people with differing attitudes, beliefs, problems, goals, and personalities are commonly found among staff. This diversity can be a good thing; it brings different ideas for problem resolution into the decision-making process, for example. It can also create challenges, however, as managers must learn how to supervise staff members with different backgrounds, expectations, and even languages.

- In addition to economic and supervisory concerns, managers often recognize the need to help employees find meaning and satisfaction in their jobs. Labor

413

costs, then, are difficult to control because people cannot—and should not—be managed in the same way as food and beverage products.

Before labor costs can be controlled, basic human resources management concerns must be addressed. Then, once the basic personnel infrastructure is in place, planning and control tactics to manage labor effectively can be implemented. This chapter addresses labor cost control issues of importance to every food and beverage operation. Because labor costs account for such a large proportion of an operation's costs, controlling them must be at the forefront of strategies to attain an operation's financial goals.

Managing Human Resources

From management's point of view, the major human resources objective is to control labor costs while attaining the operation's financial, quality, and other goals. If employees are not skilled, knowledgeable, interested, or trainable, these goals will never be realized. All too often, managers of food and beverage operations are almost forced to hire whoever walks in the door. The reasons are varied and many: a perceived or actual "emergency" labor shortage, a failure to plan for staffing needs, a lack of knowledge about principles of human resources administration, or too few qualified applicants. Whatever the cause, considerable time and money are spent in training and closely supervising the new employee. During this orientation period, when the new staff member is learning about the job and its responsibilities, productivity is low. In addition, other problems may occur, such as less-than-ideal product quality, increases in the number of accidents and errors, misuse of equipment, and breakage. Then, after a short time of unsatisfactory job performance, the employee quits. This situation is repeated much too often in many food and beverage operations. Managers come to believe that this is to be expected: they think that high turnover is an integral part of the job and the industry.

This example emphasizes that labor cost control must begin with the procedures used to recruit, select, orient, and train employees. Managers must be concerned with each employee's reactions to human resources administration and control procedures. In addition to orienting and training new employees, the control system for labor must include procedures for the supervision and appraisal of all employees.

Basic Staffing Tools

The first step in the human resources administration process—employee recruitment—begins with writing **job descriptions** that summarize each job, list its major tasks, and identify who supervises the employee filling the job and whom the employee supervises. Exhibit 1 presents a sample job description for a dining room server.

Some properties also use a second document—a **job specification**—to list personal qualities judged necessary for successful performance on the job.

When writing job descriptions, remember that they are developed for a position, not for a particular person. A job description is task-oriented. Don't think, "I have a cook named John. What does he, or should he, do?" Instead, focus on tasks that any cook in that position might reasonably be expected to do.

Exhibit 1   Sample Job Description: Dining Room Server

POSITION DESCRIPTION

POSITION: ___*Server*___   JOB NO.: _____

REPORTS TO: ___*Restaurant Manager*___   DATE: _____

DEPARTMENT: ___*F & B*___   PREPARED BY: _____

WAGE & HOUR CLASS: ___*Hourly*___   APPROVED BY: _____
                                                        (Supervisor)

COMPANY: _____   CLASSIFICATION CODE: _____

POSITION PURPOSE:

To be responsible for the proper service of meals to guests in an assigned area of the dining room.

NATURE AND SCOPE:

This position reports to the Restaurant Manager.

Before the restaurant opens, servers set the tables in assigned areas and ensure everything is in order.

Servers may assist the hostess in seating the guests in their area. They accurately take food and beverage orders from the guests in an efficient manner and use the point-of-sale system to send the order to the kitchen or bar. Before the food or beverages are delivered to the tables, servers check the orders to see if they have been correctly filled. They serve the meals by courses, making sure that the proper orders are placed in front of the guests. If the busperson has not placed ice water, bread, and butter on the tables, this is done, and items are replenished as needed. Servers also replenish coffee or tea, and remain alert to the needs of the guests at all times.

Servers present the checks to the guests with a pleasant, "Thank you."

After the guests have left the tables, servers clear the tables and reset them if the busperson is busy.

Servers assist in training new servers and buspersons and perform other related duties as required.

Servers must perform their duties efficiently and pleasantly to ensure that the restaurant's high standards of quality and service are maintained.

PRINCIPAL ACTIVITIES:

1. Sets tables in assigned area prior to serving time.

2. Takes orders and serves food and beverages in an efficient manner to the complete satisfaction of the guests.

3. Presents tickets to the guests that have been correctly tabulated, with a pleasant, "Thank you."

4. Clears tables and resets them if the busperson is busy.

Exhibit 2   Sample Organization Chart for the Dining Room of a Large Hotel

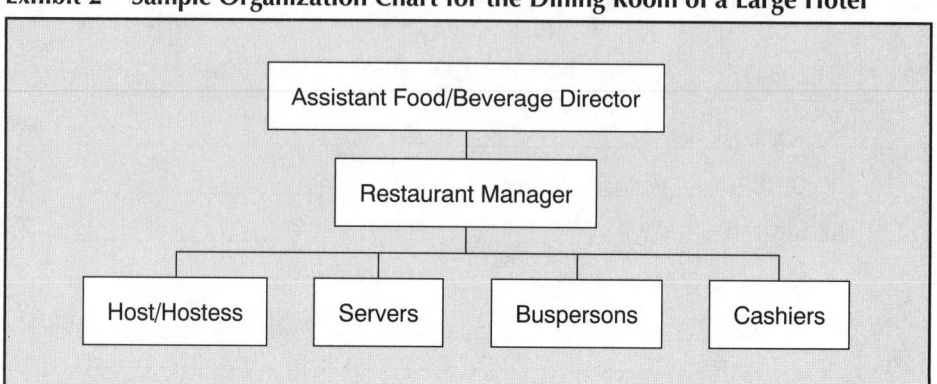

Do not overstate personal attributes needed to perform the job. As qualifications for the job increase, it becomes more difficult to find employees. As experience and other capabilities increase, so will labor costs, since employers must pay more for highly qualified employees. Finally, if overqualified applicants are hired, they may become bored because they are underemployed.

Job descriptions are useful in several ways. They help managers recruit and select job applicants. Because managers know the work to be done and the type of person generally qualified to do it, they can evaluate applicants against these requirements. Job descriptions also assist in the design of training programs. Staff members must be trained to perform each task required by the job description. Job descriptions also help with daily supervision, answering such questions as, "Who should prepare salad greens, the assistant cook or food service worker?" Finally, job descriptions also help with employee evaluation. Each staff member should be able to adequately perform the tasks included in the applicable job description.

After job descriptions are developed, an **organization chart** should be used to show the relationships among all positions in the food and beverage operation. Exhibit 2 presents an organization chart for the service-related positions in a dining room of a large hotel, while Exhibit 3 depicts the same type of chart for a bar in the large hotel. Notice that the charts do not indicate the number of individuals employed in each position; rather, they indicate only how each position relates to all others. The charts, developed to fit the needs of individual properties, let all staff members know where they fit into the organization. The charts show channels of communication and coordination by illustrating the **chain of command**. With an organization chart as a guide, specific decisions and problems can be directed to the right position and to the responsible person. Organization charts also suggest a **career ladder** of promotion, with additional responsibilities within the organization.

Recruitment and Selection Procedures

After the tools of labor control planning (job descriptions, job specifications, and the organization chart) are developed, specific procedures can be designed to

Exhibit 3   Sample Organization Chart for a Bar Operation

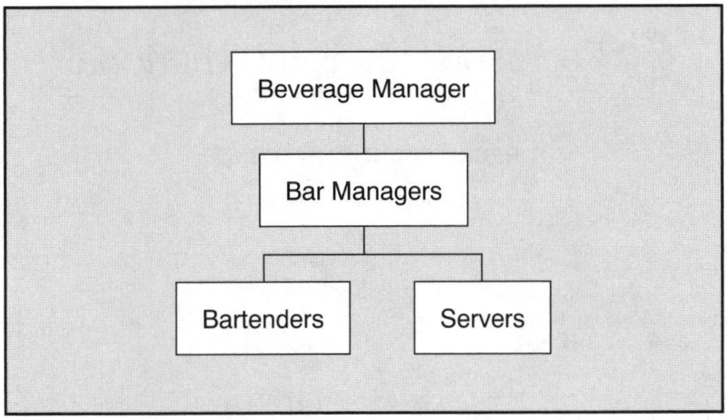

obtain the best possible employees for all positions in the operation. Recruitment begins with attracting qualified applicants for vacant positions and continues with screening procedures so that employees can be selected from a pool of the best-qualified people.

Sources of Job Applicants. The list for potential job applicants can include relatives and friends of current staff. There are both advantages and disadvantages to this source of job applicants. One advantage is that current employees can be good salespersons for attracting others. A possible disadvantage is that, if one member of a family or group of friends is disciplined or terminated, this may negatively effect the others in the family or group. In addition, collusion may occur between relatives or friends.

Promoting current employees is another way to fill vacant positions. A career ladder that indicates advancement opportunities within the food and beverage operation is often a good idea. Promotion from within may build morale, encourage existing staff to perform better, and reduce turnover.

Applicants for vacant positions may learn of openings through newspaper or trade magazine advertisements, state or private employment agencies, word of mouth, schools with education and training programs in food and beverage operations, and other sources. Exhibit 4 lists possible strategies to use in recruiting applicants. Lists of applicants may also be available from state employment services, single-parent organizations, and veterans' groups, among others.

Application Form. Once prospective employees are identified, they must be evaluated. The use of an employment application form helps determine whether the applicant meets minimum job qualifications. The form should be simple and require only information relevant to judging the applicant's suitability for the job, since federal, state, and perhaps local laws prohibit discrimination based on factors such as age or race. Employment applications, properly developed, help screen out unsuitable applicants. Information on the application can become the basis for conducting interviews. An attorney knowledgeable about applicable employment laws should review application documents before they are used.

Exhibit 4   Recruitment Strategies

Radisson Hotels International
W O R L D W I D E • W O R L D C L A S S℠

RECRUITMENT STRATEGIES

1. **Youth**
   Schools, Vo-Techs, Colleges
   — Meet with counselors
   — Speak to classes
   — Sponsor work study programs
   — Participate in career days
   — Invite classes to tour hotel

2. **Minorities**
   — Meet with representatives from minority community agencies and invite for lunch and tour of hotel
   — Advertise in minority newspapers
   — Visit schools in minority neighborhoods
   — Notices at churches in minority communities
   — Visit youth centers and place notices there

3. **Disabled Persons**
   — State Rehabilitation Agencies
   — National Alliance of Business
   — Private Industry Councils
   — National Association of Retarded Citizens
   — Goodwill Industries
   — Other local agencies

4. **Women**
   — Local organizations that assist women in transition
   — Community colleges, universities
   — Bulletin board notices in supermarkets, libraries, YWCAs, exercise centers
   — Flyers in parking lots
   — Displaced Homemakers organizations
   — Craft centers
   — Child care centers

5. **Older Workers**
   — AARP Senior Employment Services
   — Senior Citizen Centers
   — Synagogues and churches
   — Retirement communities and apartment complexes
   — Newspaper ads worded to attract
   — Retired military

6. **Individuals in Career Transition**
   — Newspaper ads
   — University evening programs
   — Referrals
   — Teachers
   — Unemployed actors
   — Laid off workers from other industries
   — Speak at community functions, e.g., Rotary, Toastmasters

7. **Lawfully Authorized Immigrants**
   — Ads in foreign language newspapers
   — Churches
   — English as a Second Language classes
   — Citizenship classes
   — Refugee resettlement centers
   — Employee referrals

Courtesy of Radisson Hotel Corporation, Minneapolis, Minnesota.

Employee Interviews. The next stage of the selection process is to conduct interviews with job candidates chosen from among the employment applications. The initial employee interview can help managers gain additional information about applicants and allows them to inform candidates about the company and the position. This is also a time to answer applicants' questions. In large operations, the human resources department conducts the opening interview; applicants judged eligible are then interviewed in the department in which the position is located. In smaller operations, the owner/manager or department head may conduct interviews personally.

Reference Checks. After the initial pool of applicants has been narrowed by the interview process, a reference check can be performed for the remaining applicants. Such a check may help verify information provided on the application form. Telephone conversations with past employers named on the application form can be a helpful start. Increasingly, however, former employers are reluctant to provide information other than to verify employment dates, because of concern over lawsuits by applicants who are rejected by firms to which they have applied.

Selection Tests. Employers may use a **selection test** to allow applicants to demonstrate skills needed on the job. For example, an applicant for a cashier's position should know how to make change, and a cook may need to know how to extend recipes.

Supervisor Interview. The staff member who will supervise the new employee should have the opportunity to interview applicants, since he or she will be directly affected by the selection. This can be a second interview, in which the supervisor asks very specific questions and, with the applicant, considers how their personalities and attitudes will mesh on the job.

All concerned parties—the human resources manager or owner/manager, department head, and position supervisor—should be involved in the hiring decision. The final decision should be based on a careful review of the information gained from the sources described previously. This requires that ample time be given to the recruitment and selection process. It also implies that as many applicants as possible should be recruited and evaluated, in contrast to the common alternative of recruiting one person at a time and using selection procedures to ensure that he or she can do the work.

Employee Orientation Procedures

An **orientation program** is needed for new employees. Although often overlooked, an orientation program is very important, because a good one can get the relationship between the new employee and the organization off to a positive start.

The new staff member's first experiences on the job affect later performance. Experienced food and beverage managers agree that employees are more likely to leave relatively soon after hiring than after many years on the job. A quick departure indicates that perhaps the employee was not a good choice. Or, it may suggest something happened soon after hiring that made the employee unsuitable or want to leave the position. Either way, the human resources administration process appears to be at fault.

Usually, new employees are eager employees or, at least, are open to being motivated. Management should build upon this attitude so that new employees will want to perform effectively. An inadequate orientation program tells new employees that the supervisor doesn't care about them and that the property may not be a good place to work.

Orientation programs should incorporate the following basic principles:

- The new staff member should receive an updated employee handbook covering the basic facts about the company and the job, including: property background, organization chart, job description/specification, company policies, and job benefits.

- All forms to be completed, including tax withholding, insurance, and similar forms, should be assembled so they can be completed during the employee's first day on the job.

- The employee should be given a job orientation that includes a tour of the property and introductions to all staff members with whom he or she will work. The work group should be informed in advance about the new employee's arrival.

- The employee's workstation should be viewed, and a locker, a uniform, and small tools (or similar items, as applicable) should be available.

- The employee(s) responsible for on-the-job training, if this technique is used, should be selected, and specific plans for training developed (see the following discussion).

- The trainer or contact person should work closely with the new staff member during the first several days. Perhaps answering the question, "How would I like to be treated if I were a new employee?" can be the guide to carrying out the orientation.

- The supervisor should check with the new staff member frequently during the first several days, then adjust the degree of supervision according to the nature of the work the employee does and the amount of person-to-person help that the employee needs.

An orientation checklist (Exhibit 5) can help ensure that a manager or other staff member does not overlook anything of importance when orienting a new employee to the job and the property.

The Training Process

Training is important for both new and current employees to help them learn and improve necessary job knowledge and skills. Properly trained employees are critical to the success of the labor cost control program and the attainment of the property's goals. The company, after all, is only as good as its employees.

When planning a training program, managers should determine exactly what trainees need to know; how to evaluate if trainees have, in fact, learned the material (at least at a minimum performance level); and the amount of training time needed. Exhibit 6 presents a general property, department, and position orientation

Exhibit 5 New Employee Orientation Checklist

New Employee Orientation Checklist

Name of New Employee: _____   Position: _____

Department: _____   Supervisor: _____

Date Hired: _____

Instructions—Initial and date when each of the following is completed.

Part I—Introduction

- ☐ _____ Welcome to new position (give your name, find out what name the employee prefers to be called, etc.)
- ☐ _____ Tour of property
- ☐ _____ Tour of department work area
- ☐ _____ Introduction to fellow employees
- ☐ _____ Introduction to trainer
- ☐ _____ Explanation of training program
- ☐ _____ Review of job description
- ☐ _____ Explanation of department

Part II—Discussion of Daily Procedures

- ☐ _____ Beginning/ending time of workshift
- ☐ _____ Break and meal periods
- ☐ _____ Uniforms (responsibilities for, cleanliness of, etc.)
- ☐ _____ Assignment of locker
- ☐ _____ Employee meals (if any)
- ☐ _____ Parking requirements
- ☐ _____ First aid and accident reporting procedures
- ☐ _____ Time clock or "sign-in log" requirements
- ☐ _____ Other (specify)

Part III—Information about Salary/Wages

- ☐ _____ Rate of pay
- ☐ _____ Deductions
- ☐ _____ Pay periods
- ☐ _____ Overtime policies
- ☐ _____ Complete all payroll withholding, insurance, and related forms
- ☐ _____ Other (specify)

Part IV—Review of Policies and Rules

- ☐ _____ Safety, fires, accidents
- ☐ _____ Maintenance and use of equipment
- ☐ _____ Punctuality
- ☐ _____ Absenteeism
- ☐ _____ Illness
- ☐ _____ Emergencies
- ☐ _____ Use of telephone/cell phone
- ☐ _____ Leaving work station
- ☐ _____ Smoking/eating/drinking
- ☐ _____ Packages
- ☐ _____ Vacations
- ☐ _____ Other (specify)

(continued)

Exhibit 5   *(continued)*

Part V—Employee Handbook/Related Information

☐ _____ Received and reviewed
☐ _____ Review of employee appraisal process
☐ _____ Review of organization chart
☐ _____ Review of job description
☐ _____ Review of department's responsibilities
☐ _____ Review of all benefit plans
☐ _____ Discuss performance standards/expectations
☐ _____ Discuss career path possibilities

Part VI—Miscellaneous Orientation Procedures (Review all other areas covered with the new employee)

_____

_____

_____

I certify that all of the above activities were completed on the date indicated.

Employee _____   Date _____

Supervisor _____   Date _____

Source: Adapted from Raphael R. Kavanaugh and Jack D. Ninemeier, *Supervision in the Hospitality Industry,* 4th ed. (Lansing, Mich.: American Hotel & Lodging Educational Institute, 2007), pp. 129–130.

and training schedule for servers. Note that the general property orientation lasts almost two days. The department and position orientation and training continues for eight more work days.

How is a training program developed and implemented? Details are beyond the scope of this chapter.[1] However, a basic outline of the process is illustrated in Exhibit 7. Note that the first step is to determine training needs.

Employee Supervision

The most important responsibility of most food and beverage managers is supervising other staff members.[2] Unless employees receive direction as they undertake their work, labor cost control goals cannot be met. Therefore, effective supervision is essential to the overall labor control system. The supervisor must accept the responsibility for directing the work of employees in addition to performing other job requirements. This means that supervisors must spend the amount of time necessary to properly direct employees as they do their jobs.

Supervisors are responsible to several groups. First, they are responsible to themselves because they want to be competent and feel satisfied that they are doing well. Responsibilities to peers and colleagues include cooperating in a team effort to meet goals. Supervisors must also help solve problems within budget and cost restrictions, provide timely and accurate information, and help higher-level managers with ongoing work.

Exhibit 6   Server Training Schedule

FOOD AND BEVERAGE TRAINING PROFILE

Department: __Beverage__   Position: __Server__

Week 1

Mon _____	Tue _____	Wed _____	Thu _____	Fri _____
8:00 A.M.–4:00 P.M. Hotel Orientation	8:00 A.M.–4:00 P.M. Hotel Orientation 3:30 P.M. Training Manual Program Handout	9:00 A.M.–4:00 P.M. 9:00 A.M. Department Introduction 1:00 P.M. Introduction to IBM	8:45 A.M.–3:30 P.M. 8:45 A.M. "Drink Presentation" 1:00 P.M. IBM Role Play	10:00 A.M.–5:00 P.M. 10:00 A.M. "Service Fundamentals Beverage Style" 12:00 NOON Floor Observation, All Outlets
4:00 P.M. Home	4:00 P.M. Home	4:00 P.M. Home	3:30 P.M. Home	5:00 P.M. Home

Off Saturday & Sunday

Week 2

Mon _____	Tue _____	Wed _____	Thu _____	Fri _____
5:00 P.M.–Closing Follow Seasoned Trainer Paperwork	5:00 P.M.–Closing Follow Seasoned Trainer Paperwork	2:00 P.M.–8:00 P.M. Follow Trainer No Paperwork	10:30 A.M.–6:00 P.M. Training Station Paperwork	10:30 A.M.–6:00 P.M. Training Station Paperwork

Courtesy of Opryland Hotel, Nashville, Tennessee.

Exhibit 7   Flow Chart of Training Program Development and Implementation

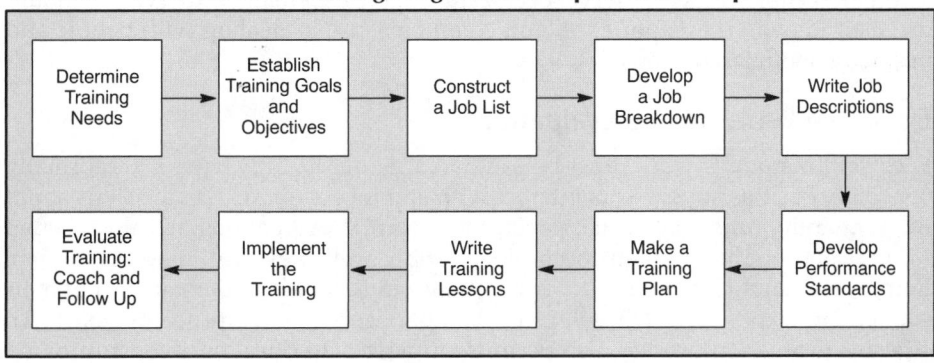

Supervisors also have some very direct responsibilities to employees. For example, they must:

- Try to understand the employee as an individual in the context of a human relations approach.

- Place people in positions according to job descriptions. Fitting jobs to employees may not benefit the property or the employee.

- Support employees when they perform as required, and provide constructive feedback when individual staff members need to improve work performance.

- Provide adequate training and appraisal.

- Be fair and reasonable in all relationships with employees.

- Be concerned about employee safety and well-being.

- Provide an example of acceptable behavior while on the job; in other words, serve as role models.

Successful supervisors want to help their employees to do the best job possible. They do not quickly write off employees as unmanageable. Effective supervisors develop ways to involve employees in the work as much as possible and to satisfy desires and needs of individual employees on the job.

Employees, in turn, must be able to accept the authority for and responsibility of completing assigned work. They must have the physical and mental ability and the desire to perform their work. Supervisors should be willing to involve staff members in designing their work to the extent they wish to be involved.

Supervisors must be able to relate to and understand employees, recognize them as individuals, and treat them accordingly in work relationships. Employees are individuals on and off the job, and their personal problems can affect their work. Supervisors should have only professional, rather than personal, relationships with staff.

Management personnel should display a positive attitude and a commitment to the food and beverage operation. They should be consistently honest and fair in all relationships with employees, peers, and superiors. Finally, supervisors should use their knowledge, experience, and common sense in dealing with people and in solving job-related problems.

Employee Performance Evaluation

Each staff member's work must be evaluated regularly. This happens informally on a daily basis as supervisors interact with employees and make decisions about work quantity and quality. However, more formal evaluations are also needed to more thoroughly explain to employees how well they are doing on the job. Employees cannot improve their performance unless they understand what their supervisors expect and where, if at all, supervisors believe problems exist. An effective evaluation process also permits employees to offer ideas for improving the operation. As training needs are identified, as bases for discipline are established, and, in general, as the labor cost control program is improved, good work can be recognized through wage increases and promotions.

Procedures for evaluating employees include the following:

- Decide what factors are to be considered and ensure that employees accept them as a way to evaluate the quality of their performance. To the extent possible, factors should be measurable and objective.

- Inform employees about the purposes and frequency of evaluations, and what will be evaluated (basic job performance, whether quality standards are being met, and so on).

- Review work daily, or at some other regular time interval, to collect information about employee performance. Note critical incidents illustrating very good or very poor performance.

- Have private meetings with each employee to discuss his or her general job performance. Critical incident information can be used to illustrate or defend the points made. Formal employee appraisals should normally take place at least every six months.

- The employee should be permitted to express views about the job, the supervisor's comments, and how job performance and relationships with others might be improved.

- When concluding the evaluation session, the supervisor should emphasize the employee's strong points and indicate a desire to help the employee improve his or her performance where needed. Finally, the supervisor should invite the employee to talk with him or her at any time about any problems or concerns. In effect, then, performance appraisal is ongoing and not just a formal once- or twice-a-year process.

Exhibit 8 presents a set of guidelines useful in conducting performance evaluations.

Employees can be evaluated with a form indicating qualities considered important in performing the job. Exhibit 9 is an example of a performance evaluation form covering an extensive period of time. It can be modified to suit individual properties and specific positions.

Benefits of properly conducted performance evaluation programs include the following:

- The employees learn about ways to improve performance.

- The supervisor learns about employees' job-related problems.

- Both the supervisor and employees become aware of the importance of achieving output of an acceptable quantity and quality.

- The process by which employees are identified for promotion and salary increases is formalized.

- Employees may offer suggestions for improving the job.

Factors Affecting Work Performance and Productivity ———

To control labor costs in food and beverage operations, it is first necessary to identify those factors that influence the required number of labor hours—and therefore labor costs. While they vary among properties, possible influences on productivity include several factors, such as the following:

Exhibit 8   Guidelines for Conducting Performance Evaluations

1. Interview in a setting that is informal, private, and free of distraction.
2. Provide a courteous, supportive atmosphere.
3. Encourage the employee to participate actively.
4. Clearly explain the purpose of the interview.
5. Explain problem areas thoroughly but tactfully.
6. Listen when the employee talks; don't interrupt.
7. Criticize job performance, not the employee.
8. Criticize while you're calm, not angry.
9. Avoid confrontation and argument.
10. Emphasize the employee's strengths, then discuss areas that need improvement.
11. To set goals for improvement, focus on future performance, not past.
12. Assume nothing; instead, ask for clarification.
13. Ask questions to gather information, not to "test" the employee.
14. Expect the employee to disagree.
15. Try to resolve differences; don't expect total agreement.
16. Avoid exaggerations such as "always" or "never."
17. Help the employee maintain self-esteem; don't threaten or belittle.
18. Keep your own biases in check.
19. Allow the employee to help you set goals for improvement.
20. Assure the employee that you will help him or her reach the goals.
21. Maintain appropriate eye contact.
22. End on a positive note.

Source: Raphael R. Kavanaugh and Jack D. Ninemeier, *Supervision in the Hospitality Industry,* 4th ed. (Lansing, Mich.: American Hotel & Lodging Educational Institute, 2007), p. 186.

- *Menu items.* Items involving difficult production techniques require more production hours. For example, a menu featuring beef Wellington, chicken Kiev, and other difficult entrées requires more labor time than a menu with several hamburger variations and other simple main dishes.

- *Convenience foods.* Menu items made on-site require more preparation time than similar menu items made with convenience foods. Convenience food products are purchased with "built-in" labor.

- *Service.* A restaurant featuring elegant tableside cooking and service requires more labor than a walk-up or drive-up fast-food operation.

- *Quantity of meals.* The number of labor hours needed for most positions varies according to the volume of meals produced and served.

Exhibit 9 Sample Performance Evaluation: Food Server

FOOD SERVER PERFORMANCE REVIEW

FOOD SERVER NAME _____

DIRECTIONS: Rate the performance level of the employee.

4 — Excellent — Usually meets established standards
3 — Good — Acceptable but could improve
2 — Fair — Definite need for improvement
1 — Unacceptable — Definite need for counseling

Performance Area	Date	Before Training	After Training	25-Day Eval.	90-Day Eval.	180-Day Eval.	270-Day Eval.	360-Day Eval.	Comments — Indicate Date by Each Comment
		/ /	/ /	/ /	/ /	/ /	/ /	/ /	
Policies and Procedures (Knowledge)									
Use of exits and entrances									
Uniform exchange/cleaning procedures									
Sign-in and sign-out sheets									
Cafeteria hours									
Restaurant hours of operation									
Employee schedules									
Fire procedures									
Accident reports									
Absenteeism, sick calls, tardiness									
Table numbers and stations									
Pre-meal meetings									
Bulletin board information									
Performance reviews and evaluations									
Rules of conduct									
Locker issue and use									
Personal phone call rules									
Transfers and promotions									
Exit interview policy									
Paycheck procedures									
Service Concept (Knowledge)									
Upper Level service standards									
Personal appearance specifications									
Restaurant safety									
Menu knowledge									
Wine knowledge									
Beverage knowledge									
Service scenario									
Opening Sidework (Knowledge/Skills)									
Preparing flowers									
Preparing butter									
Preparing sugar bowls									
Preparing salts and peppers									

(continued)

Exhibit 9 *(continued)*

Performance Area	Before Training	After Training	25-Day Eval.	90-Day Eval.	180-Day Eval.	270-Day Eval.	360-Day Eval.	Comments
Date	/ /	/ /	/ /	/ /	/ /	/ /	/ /	Indicate Date by Each Comment
Preparing gueridons								
Folding napkins								
Preparing silverware (regular/special)								
Setting up service trays								
Stocking chilled forks/plates								
Checking Benny Wafers								
Stocking ashtrays and matches								
Setting tables								
Checking overall station appearance								
Service Procedures (Knowledge/Skills)								
Greeting guests								
Taking cocktail order								
Picking up drinks								
Serving cocktails								
Presenting menus								
Taking the food order								
Presenting the seafood tray								
Suggestive selling								
Taking the wine order								
Assisting with wine selection								
Performing pre-check operation								
Ordering food								
Serving wine/champagne								
Picking up food orders								
Serving food orders								
Serving food courses								
Clearing between courses								
Preparing table for each course								
Checking tables for needs								
Changing ashtrays								
Removing soiled dishes to dishroom								
Clearing after entree course								
Crumbing the table								
Taking dessert and coffee order								
Serving dessert and coffee								
Serving hot tea and Sanka								
Selling and serving cordials								
Preparing the guest check								
Presenting the guest check								

Exhibit 9   *(continued)*

Performance Area	Before Training	After Training	25-Day Eval.	90-Day Eval.	180-Day Eval.	270-Day Eval.	360-Day Eval.	Comments
Date	/ /	/ /	/ /	/ /	/ /	/ /	/ /	Indicate Date by Each Comment
Processing payment								
Assisting guests upon departure								
Delivery of the service scenario (Server)								
Resetting tables								
Closing Sidework (Knowledge/Skills)								
Storing flowers								
Cleaning gueridons								
Taking linens to laundry								
Storing condiments								
Breaking down breads and butters								
Breaking down coffee station								
Breaking down wine buckets								
Breaking down water pitchers								
Straightening and cleaning side stands								
Setting station for next meal (w/o silver)								
Securing all silverware								
Bussing all soiled items to dishwasher								
Vacuuming carpet								
Personal Attributes								
Attitude toward work								
Appearance and uniform								
Cooperation with fellow workers								
Acceptance of directions								
Attendance								
Desire to learn in job								

RATED BY (INITIALS)

Describe specific training needs (areas with scores of 2 or below):

Source: Lewis C. Forrest, Jr., *Training for the Hospitality Industry*, 2d ed. (Lansing, Mich.: American Hotel & Lodging Educational Institute, 1990), pp. 356–357.

- *Number of meal periods.* Using different menus for different meal periods requires setup and tear-down labor time and also means a larger variety of menu items.

- *Facility layout and design.* Efficient layout of space and equipment positively affects worker productivity.

- *Production equipment.* Using equipment to do work otherwise done manually reduces labor time.

- *Labor market.* If properly skilled or experienced employees are not available, other employees will need training. During training, they will be less productive than when fully trained.

- *Allocation of labor hours.* Work performance relates to productivity levels that compare labor hours to the number of meals prepared, guests served, or revenue produced. If, for example, labor costs are allocated between food and beverage departments, or indirect labor not previously charged to a revenue center is charged to a department, it affects labor costs relative to output.

- *Human resources administration policies.* When effective human resources policies and procedures are used, work performance generally improves.

- *Supervision.* Effective supervision implies that employee output will be high. The quality of supervision influences labor costs and, in general, the quantity and quality of output.

- *Employee.* The individual worker's experience, abilities, knowledge, and attitudes affect performance. This supports the need to recruit and keep the most qualified employees.

- *Work methods.* Work simplification principles can help improve employee performance, as discussed in the following section.

- *Work environment.* An employee's work environment influences productivity. Temperature and humidity, ventilation, lighting, colors, and noise levels should add to employee comfort, not hinder performance.

- *Number of hours worked.* Long hours and hard work are common in many food service jobs. Legal restrictions and common sense are now reducing the number of hours worked, at least for non-management staff. These changes help minimize negative influences on worker performance.

- *Other worker-related factors.* Adequacy of training, staff morale, relationships among staff members, type of leadership exerted by supervisors, time pressures, the worker's health and physical condition, and similar considerations all affect work performance.

Work Simplification and Labor Cost Control

When more work is done in less time, labor costs are reduced. (However, quality standards should not be reduced in the process of reducing costs.) Certain basic procedures can simplify work and help increase productivity. The operation benefits, since labor costs are better controlled, and the employee benefits, since the job is made more efficient. There are several indicators of inefficient work procedures:[3]

- Service delays requiring guests to wait beyond reservation times or for food or beverages to be served
- Labor hours in excess of labor performance standards
- Guest and employee complaints
- Peaks and valleys in workloads
- Excessive breakage or theft
- Poor use of employee skills and knowledge
- Frequent accidents or errors
- Low employee morale and motivation
- Ineffective use of space
- Too much paperwork
- Inadequate forecasting of production and service needs
- Difficulty in meeting production and service schedules
- Poor working conditions

When supervisors observe these or similar problems, they should consider implementing work simplification procedures. Priority should go to studying jobs that can benefit the most from work simplification, such as those that:

- Involve large amounts of labor time and, therefore, labor costs.
- Directly involve food production and service, in contrast to recordkeeping or exterior maintenance tasks.
- Will continue indefinitely.
- Create bottlenecks or excessive overtime hours.
- Involve many employees performing the same tasks, such as cleaning vegetables or washing dishes.
- Consistently fail to meet quality or quantity standards.

Increasing Productivity

One of the most difficult and challenging tasks for supervisors is to create improved work methods in their departments. Too often supervisors get caught up in routine, day-to-day functions and fail to question the way things are done. One way to increase productivity is to continually review and revise performance standards. The following sections present a five-step process for increasing productivity by revising performance standards.

Step 1—Collect and Analyze Information about Current Performance Standards. Often this can be done by simple observation. If you know what must be done to meet current performance standards, observe what is actually being done and note any differences. When analyzing tasks listed in performance standards, supervisors should ask the following questions:

- *Can a task be eliminated?* Before revising a task, the supervisor must ask whether the task needs to be done in the first place.

- *Can a task be assigned to a different position?* Perhaps some food preparation duties can be assigned to dishwashers during low-volume times; if so, a part-time food preparation position might be eliminated.

- *Are the performance standards of another department decreasing the productivity of employees in your department?* For example, a hotel's on-site laundry may not be supplying all the table linen needed by the food and beverage department. Productivity suffers when dining room staff must make frequent trips to the laundry area to pick up clean linen as it becomes available.

Step 2—Generate Ideas for New Ways to Do the Job. Generally, when work problems arise, there is more than one way to resolve them. Performance standards for many hospitality positions are complex, and it is often difficult to pinpoint the exact reasons for current problems or new ideas about how to do the job more efficiently.

Employees, other supervisors, and guests are important sources of information that can help a supervisor pinpoint tasks for revision. Employees who actually perform the job are often the best source for suggested improvements. Other supervisors may be able to pass on techniques that they have used successfully to increase productivity in their areas. Networking with colleagues often results in creative ideas that can be applied to one's own area of responsibility. Completed guest comment cards and personal interviews with selected guests may reveal negative aspects of the operation that supervisors might otherwise overlook.

Step 3—Evaluate Each Idea and Select the Best Approach. The actual idea selected may be a blend of the best elements of several different suggestions. When selecting the best way to revise current performance standards, make sure that the task can be done in the time allowed. It is one thing for a "superstar" employee to clean the dining room or cook a meal within a specified time; it may not, however, be reasonable to expect that an average employee—even after training and with close supervision—can be as productive. Performance standards must be attainable to be useful.

Step 4—Test the Revised Performance Standard. Have only a few employees use the revised performance standard for a specified time so it can be determined whether the new procedures increase productivity. Remember, old habits are hard to break. Before conducting a formal evaluation of the revised performance standard, employees will need time to become familiar with the new tasks and build speed.

Step 5—Implement the Revised Performance Standard. After the trial study has demonstrated that the new performance standard increases productivity, employees must be trained in the new procedures. Continual supervision, reinforcement, and coaching during the transitional period will also be necessary. Most importantly, if the increased productivity is significant, make the necessary changes to

Technology and Employee Supervision

We have noted numerous ways that technology is increasingly used to help food and beverage managers with control activities. People, the subject of this chapter, are not like food and beverage products. They cannot be manipulated by and interpreted with financial information generated by point-of-sale computing and back office accounting systems.

However, technology is typically used to maintain a master file for each employee, calculate employee pay, develop accounting records, and generate employee- and payroll-related reports required by governmental agencies.

Examples of personal information contained in a master file include:

- Employee identification number.

- Employee name and address.

- Deductions (for taxes and the cost of benefits, for example).

- Social Security number.

- Wage rate.

- Withholding tax and deduction information.

Payroll modules allow fast and accurate calculations of gross and net pay and print employee paychecks and tax registers and reports. A payroll register file—a component of the payroll module—calculates special payments for sick leave, bonuses, tips, and expense reimbursements. Vacation, sick leave, time off taken without pay, and other data can be easily tracked and is available to help managers make decisions related to employee supervision and labor costs. Data from the payroll module can be used to generate numerous labor-related reports that can help managers determine actual labor costs by department, shift, position, or any other basis, and compare it to budget expectations. Overtime, which must always be effectively managed, can be easily identified so corrective actions can be taken.

the department's staffing guide and base scheduling practices on the new productivity standard. This will ensure that increased productivity translates to increased profits through lower labor costs.

Labor Control and Employees

The labor control system must effectively manage employees, the work to be done, and costs associated with both. Viewing the job from the perspective of the employee may help supervisors discover what employees want and provide it to the extent possible. This will reduce labor problems and associated costs.

Employee Motivation

Supervisors develop a motivated staff by creating a climate in which employees want to work *toward* rather than *against* the goals of the department and those of the organization. To help employees become motivated, supervisors must understand their needs, interests, and goals. What motivates one employee may have little effect on another, because needs, interests, and goals vary among employees. These motivational factors are a function of each individual's background, personality, intellect, attitudes, and other characteristics. The challenge is for supervisors to get to know the employees they supervise.

To be a successful motivator, supervisors need to know what it takes for employees to become motivated. This is not easy, because some employees may not know, or cannot verbalize, their needs or goals. Much motivation is subconscious. For example, some "high energy" employees may be top performers because they fear rejection from co-workers if they do not produce above-average results. They may not even be aware that they are seeking approval from other staff members.

When individuals have unmet needs that stimulate them to do something, managers have opportunities for motivation. One basic approach was advanced some years ago.[4] Researchers identified factors that must be present to some extent within the work environment before an employee can be motivated. In other words, if these factors are not present, employees will become dissatisfied. One strategy involves providing these factors on the job with the hope that employees will therefore become more committed to their jobs.

The following maintenance factors, in amounts employees individually consider necessary, are part of what employees want from their jobs:

- Acceptable company policies

- Acceptable management

- Adequate relations with supervisors, subordinates, and peers

- Adequate salary and working conditions

- Appropriate job security assurances

- Proper status

The researchers also suggested another set of factors that, when meeting employees' needs, may increase worker satisfaction and job performance. These factors are:

- Challenging work.

- A sense of personal accomplishment.

- A feeling of being appreciated for performing acceptable work.

- Increased responsibility and the opportunity to advance in the job.

- Feelings of importance and contribution.

- Participation in job-related matters that affect the worker.

Each of these is an ingredient in an answer to the question, "What does an employee want from the job?" Supervisors who feel they have something in common with their employees may use a golden rule approach: "What I want from my job is what my employees may want from their jobs. The way I want to be treated in my job is the way that my employees want to be treated in their jobs."

Increasing Interest in Work

To the extent possible, improvements in work should benefit both the organization and the employee. This assumes that people have been effectively matched with their jobs. Hiring people qualified to perform tasks outlined in the job description should help to eliminate:

- Underemployment and situations in which employees become bored because their work provides no challenge.

- Over-employment and situations in which employees are frustrated because they are not qualified to perform the work.

Assuming employees are performing adequately, several techniques may help generate increased interest in the work.

Job Rotation. Job rotation is a system of moving employees among jobs they are able to perform. The employee benefits from reduced boredom caused by constantly repeating the same tasks. Rotation may also enable the employee to discover other positions of interest and develop appropriate career tracks. When enthused rather than bored, employees may be more efficient and produce higher-quality work. Employees who can do several jobs are more valuable and can fill in as required. Also, training time for jobs reached through promotion may be lessened.

Job Enlargement. Job enlargement increases the number of tasks included in a job. The additional tasks may or may not increase the variety of the work, nor will additional tasks always be of interest to the employee. When enlarging jobs, managers should consult with affected employees to determine jointly how job tasks might be recombined.

Job Enrichment. In **job enrichment**, job tasks are changed to generate interest, involvement, and challenge. Increasing employee responsibility and making employees more accountable for their own work are examples of job enrichment. Job enrichment techniques introduce more and different types of motivation factors into the job. The approach generally involves getting workers interested in doing things they want to do within the job.

Controlling Turnover

One of the most significant challenges confronting managers in almost all food and beverage operations is the difficulty of recruiting and retaining employees. For most managers, the greatest problem relates to entry-level staff members. For some, the labor shortage challenge extends to all or almost all positions within the unit, including top-level management staff. Managing turnover is a challenge that does not go away; instead, it often seems to intensify. What can managers do to reduce the turnover rate?

Exhibit 10 identifies some reasons why employees leave an organization. Many positions, especially at the entry level, are structured so that the necessary knowledge can be quickly learned, and required skills can be quickly acquired. Young people with only a few years of work experience, and others who are not

Exhibit 10   Reasons for Employee Turnover

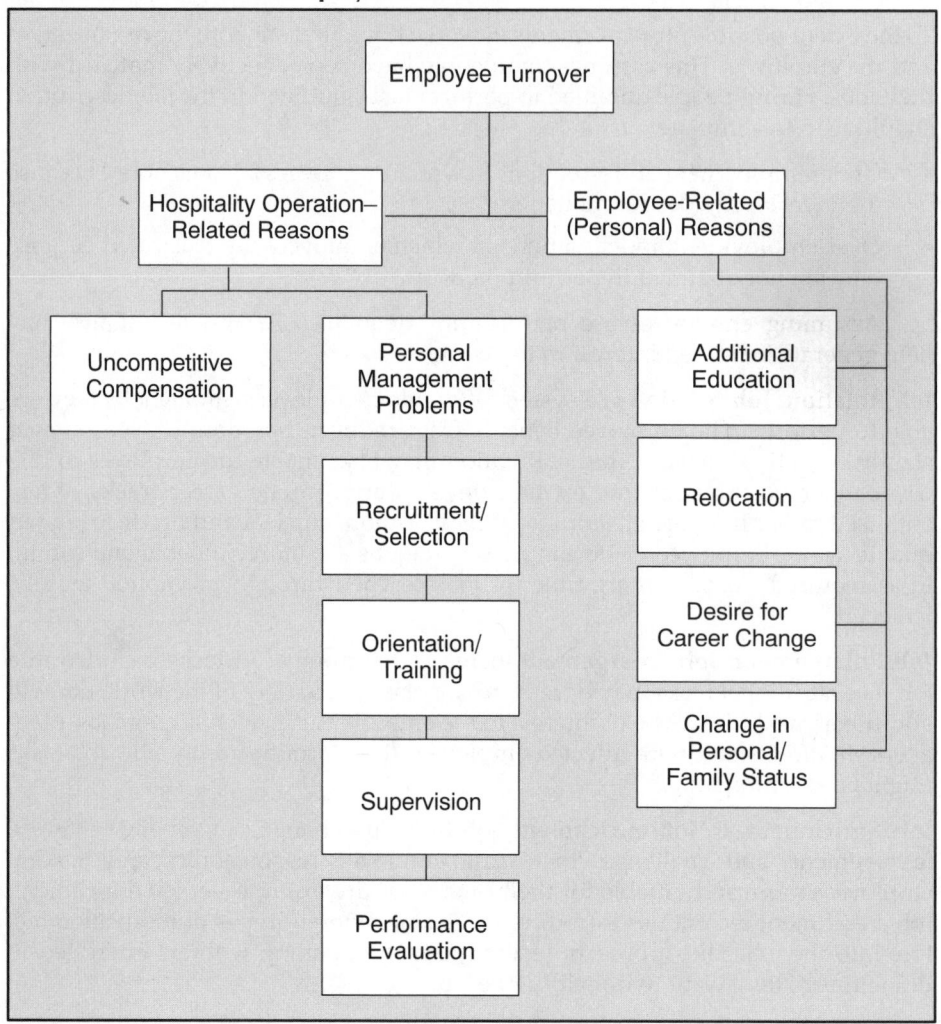

necessarily searching for a career, are likely candidates for these positions. The labor market of persons desiring these positions, then, contributes to the problem. Are tactics to address this problem within the manager's control?

As suggested in Exhibit 10, uncompetitive **compensation** is a reason for turnover and must be addressed. Increasingly, managers realize that:

- Compensation must be competitive not only with other hospitality businesses, but with other potential employers outside the hospitality industry.

- Compensation paid to entry-level restaurant employees is often among the lowest in a community, and, therefore, good employees may be attracted to positions paying significantly higher wage rates. (However, tips received by bartenders, servers, bellpersons, and others in service-related positions can significantly increase their compensation.)

- Benefits packages may also need to be examined to assess the role, if any, that they play in retaining employees.

Compensation (especially salaries and wages) is not always the only, or even the most important, factor that influences turnover. Pay must be satisfactory (as opposed to optimal), so the employee has a continuing interest in a position. However, what managers do (and do not do) as they supervise and interact with their employees is often a more important factor in the employee's decision to remain with or leave the organization.

Exhibit 10 notes another broad cause of employee turnover: personal reasons that relate to the employees themselves. For example, staff members may enroll for additional education and not have time to work during a busy school schedule. (Managers who permit staff members to work just a few hours or who can call on these persons for extra-busy occasions may still benefit from their contributions.)

Some staff members may relocate to other communities. In such cases, if they move to another location in which a chain restaurant has a unit, a good referral from the unit manager can help the individual remain with the organization.

Other employees may want a career change (which may or may not be prompted by a desire for increased compensation). Changes in personal/family status, including marriage, birth of children, and retirement, are still other reasons for employee resignations. These motives for employee turnover cannot be modified by management action. However, managers should still invite departing employees to consider future employment opportunities with the organization, especially if they are above-average employees.

Commonsense Tactics to Reduce Turnover. Hospitality managers make a significant investment in the recruitment and training of entry-level staff members. Resources resulting from this investment— including valuable knowledge, skills, and experience—are lost when employees leave. Turnover and low morale can be a challenge, but, fortunately, there are numerous tactics that can help improve retention rates. Exhibit 11 reviews some of these tactics. Note that, for most of the tactics, little time and money is required to implement them. Note also that you would probably like to work for an organization whose leadership consistently practiced these tactics. Their use can help move the food and beverage operation toward "employer of choice" status within the community, so all managers and supervisors should consider using them.

Human Resources and Multi-Unit Management

Area managers typically supervise between 2 and 15 unit managers. They serve as the "linking pins" between higher levels of management and individual unit managers in their multi-unit organizations. As the supervisors of unit managers, area managers must:

- Help unit managers to ensure that the chain's quality standards are consistently attained.

Exhibit 11   Commonsense Tactics for Reducing Turnover

Follow Sound Management Advice

Tactic One:	Serve first and lead second
Tactic Two:	Eliminate employees who won't
Tactic Three:	Eliminate supervisors who can't
Tactic Four:	Manage the guests

First Impressions Make a Difference

Tactic One:	Understand the role of starting wages
Tactic Two:	Inform employees about their total compensation
Tactic Three:	Explain the long-term benefits of staying
Tactic Four:	Share the vision
Tactic Five:	Motivate entry-level employees
Tactic Six:	Conduct entrance interviews
Tactic Seven:	Create a career ladder

Train! Train ! Train!—and Do It Correctly!

Tactic One:	Invest in training
Tactic Two:	Train trainers to train
Tactic Three:	Reward trainers
Tactic Four:	Relieve trainers of other jobs/duties
Tactic Five:	Conduct pre-shift training

Maintain a Professional Workplace

Tactic One:	Strictly enforce a zero-tolerance harassment policy
Tactic Two:	Create a culturally diverse workplace
Tactic Three:	Make employee safety a top priority
Tactic Four:	Ensure reasonable accommodations for disabled employees
Tactic Five:	Share financial numbers with employees
Tactic Six:	Conduct entrance interviews
Tactic Seven:	Create a career ladder

Supervise as You Would Like to Be Supervised

Tactic One:	Use on-time policies fairly and consistently
Tactic Two:	Be careful not to over-schedule
Tactic Three:	Give employees a personal copy of their work schedule
Tactic Four:	Know about employee assistance programs
Tactic Five:	Invite "fast-track" employees to attend management meetings
Tactic Six:	Implement a "catch the employee doing something right" program
Tactic Seven:	Conduct an exit interview with employees who leave

Encourage On-Going Communication

Tactic One:	Hold employee-focused meetings with non-management staff
Tactic Two:	Communicate the benefits of one's unique facility
Tactic Three:	Recognize employee birthdays
Tactic Four:	Make daily "howdy" rounds

Exhibit 11   *(Continued)*

Create a Friendly Workplace

Tactic One:	Use employee recognition programs
Tactic Two:	Build a great team and praise it often
Tactic Three:	Share scheduling responsibilities with employees
Tactic Four:	Reward employees who work on non-scheduled days
Tactic Five:	Invite family members of new employees to visit the workplace
Tactic Six:	Make the workplace fun

Help Your Employees to Succeed

Tactic One:	Reward success in each employee
Tactic Two:	Recognize employees' elder-care responsibilities
Tactic Three:	Do not punish your best for being good
Tactic Four:	Go to lunch
Tactic Five:	Help employees learn about public transportation systems

---

Source: Adapted from Jack Ninemeier and David Hayes, *50 One-Minute Tips for Retaining Employees* (Menlo Park, Calif.: Crisp Publications, Inc., 2001).

Management of Human Resources in Multi-Unit Organizations

The adage that "people are people" applies to interactions between managers and staff members working in single- as well as multi-unit food and beverage operations. What motivates (and frustrates) managers in terms of human resources issues is the same in both types of operations. However, managers of multi-unit properties often have a resource not available to their single-unit counterparts: a centralized human resources department that can provide them with a wealth of materials and programs that could be developed only by specialists who have time away from on-going operations to develop them. Examples include:

- Recruitment advertising.

- Professional development opportunities for the managers themselves to improve their supervisory skills.

- Orientation and training materials and programs.

- "Mechanics" and documentation for performance appraisal programs.

- Procedures to comply with ever-increasing legal issues related to employment (which can create employee dissatisfaction if not managed properly).

Multi-unit managers often have at least one additional advantage not enjoyed by single-unit managers: career opportunities that permit their best staff members to advance "up the organization" and throughout the country (and even internationally). These opportunities can help attract and retain employees who want to work effectively and creatively as they begin initial employment with the organization at the manager's unit.

- Provide clear parameters about the job to be done.

- Help the unit manager to implement (not create) policy.

- Motivate unit managers to excel.

- Utilize control procedures to ensure that goals are efficiently and effectively achieved. (This typically involves personal meetings to discuss issues and actions needed in response to control-related problems.)

Area managers typically meet with unit managers at least monthly, often more frequently. Some organizations hold teleconferences with unit personnel on a regularly scheduled basis, and there may be meetings of all unit managers several times yearly. With these relatively limited contact opportunities, unit managers, like their counterparts in other food services who work for absentee owners/investors, must work in situations without constant on-site supervision. While many managers prefer this work arrangement, some, especially those who are inexperienced, may desire expertise to be more readily available than merely by telephone or e-mail.

Area Manager Responsibilities

Area managers have a wide variety of responsibilities, among which are business development, employee development, and operational control. As part of their business development efforts, area managers must:

- Negotiate operating budgets and capital expenditure plans.

- Analyze financial performance.

- Provide advice about revenue, pricing, promotion, and merchandising issues.

- Ensure that each unit's products/services are consistent with those required by the brand.

    An area manager's employee development responsibilities include:

- Recruiting/selecting unit managers.

- Planning training for unit managers.

- Motivating and conducting performance appraisals for unit managers.

- Assisting with each unit's employee relations issues.

- Identifying/developing high-potential employees.

    An area manager's operational control responsibilities include:

- Checking/measuring the extent to which operating standards are met, and assisting in the development and implementation of corrective action tactics that address operating problems.

- Monitoring inventory procedures.

- Ensuring that planned maintenance schedules and capital investment projects are on track.

- Managing/monitoring the health, hygiene, and safety aspects of individual units.

Endnotes

1. For more information on training, see Debra F. Cannon and Catherine M. Gustafson, *Training and Development for the Hospitality Industry* (Lansing, Mich.: American Hotel & Lodging Educational Institute, 2002).

2. For more information on this subject, see Raphael R. Kavanaugh and Jack D. Ninemeier, *Supervision in the Hospitality Industry,* 4th ed. (Lansing, Mich.: American Hotel & Lodging Educational Institute, 2007).

3. First reported in Edward A. Kazarian, *Work Analysis and Design for Hotels, Restaurants, and Institutions* (Westport, Conn.: AVI, 1969), pp. 4–5.

4. Frederick Herzberg, Bernard Mausner, and Barbara Bloch Snyderman, *The Motivation to Work,* 2d ed. (New York: Wiley, 1959). The discussion that follows greatly simplifies the employee motivation concepts outlined in this classic text.

Key Terms

career ladder—A plan of advancement to positions of increasing responsibility, supported with training and professional development opportunities to prepare persons for new positions.

chain of command—The flow of authority (power) throughout management levels in an organization.

compensation—Pay or remuneration (typically in the form of wages and salaries) for work done. The term is commonly used today to include, in addition to wages and salaries, all fringe benefits that make up the "compensation—or pay—package."

job description—A written, detailed summary of duties, requirements, and supervisory relationships for each employee position within the hospitality operation.

job enlargement—Increasing the number of tasks included in a job.

job enrichment—Changing a job by adding motivational factors—such as responsibility, decision-making, variety, and challenge—to the job itself.

job rotation—A system of moving employees among jobs they are able to perform.

job specification—A selection tool that lists the personal qualities deemed necessary for an employee's successful performance on the job.

organization chart—A visual picture of the hierarchical structure of positions within a hospitality organization.

orientation program—A program used to provide information that must by known by all employees of a hospitality organization.

selection test—An examination requiring job applicants to demonstrate skills included in the job descriptions for the desired positions.

Review Questions

1. When should labor control begin? Why?

2. Is it always necessary to have job descriptions and job specifications? Why or why not?

3. What are the steps in the process of selecting a new employee? Why are these steps important?

4. Why is it important to properly orient and train new employees as soon as they are hired?

5. What are the steps in conducting an employee performance evaluation? Why are they important?

6. What are some factors that influence employee work performance and productivity?

7. What are some questions to ask when analyzing work procedures?

8. What can be done to increase an employee's interest in work?

9. What can supervisors do to increase employee productivity?

10. Why is it important that supervisors get to know their employees?

11. What are examples of ways that motivation theory can be used in interactions with food and beverage employees?

12. Why are employee turnover rates so high in many food and beverage operations? What can be done to reduce turnover rates?

Internet Sites

For more information, visit the following Internet sites. Remember that Internet addresses can change without notice. If the site is no longer there, you can use a search engine to look for additional sites.

Food Service Job Descriptions

Allfoodbusiness.com
www.allfoodbusiness.com/
restaurant_news.php

Job Genie
www.stepfour.com/genie

U.S. Department of Labor (Bureau of Labor Statistics)
www.bls.gov
(Enter desired position in the site's search box.)

Human Resources

About.com: Human Resources
www.humanresources.about.com

Free Management Library
www.managementhelp.org
(Click on "Human Resources Management" and related topics of interest.)

HR-Guide.com
www.hr-guide.com

International Association for Human Resources Information Management, Inc.
www.ihrim.org
(Click on "Learning Center.")

Personnel Recruiting Organizations

Adventures in Hospitality Careers
www.hospitalityadventures.com

Hospitality Career Services
www.foodheadhunters.com

Resources in Food
www.rifood.com

Restaurant Recruit
www.restaurantrecruit.com

Chapter 14 Outline

Establishing a Unit of Measurement for
    Labor Standards
Determining Productivity Rates
Constructing a Staffing Guide
    Fixed versus Variable Labor
    Staffing Guides and Budgets
The Staffing Guide as a Scheduling Tool
The Staffing Guide as a Control Tool
    Variance Analysis
    Comparing Actual Labor Costs to
        Budgeted Labor Costs
    Planning Corrective Action
Employee Scheduling in Multi-Unit
    Operations
Automated Labor and Payroll Information
    Systems
    Payroll Register File

Competencies

1. Explain how food and beverage managers determine labor standards. (pp. 445–449)

2. Identify factors food and beverage managers consider when constructing a staffing guide. (pp. 449–450)

3. Distinguish between fixed and variable labor in relation to food and beverage operations, and explain calculations managers can perform to reconcile budgeted labor costs with staffing guide productivity rates. (pp. 450–454)

4. Explain how food and beverage managers use staffing guides as labor scheduling tools. (pp. 454–458)

5. Explain how food and beverage managers use staffing guides as labor cost control tools. (pp. 458–463)

6. Discuss employee scheduling issues in multi-unit operations, and describe automated labor and payroll information systems. (pp. 463–475)

Implementing Labor
Cost Controls

Labor standards form the basis for effective labor control systems. However, before labor standards can be developed and implemented, managers must consider quality requirements. For example, labor standards for service staff depend on the level of service defined by management. The level of service is strongly influenced by the number of labor hours scheduled relative to the number of guests served. As more labor hours are scheduled for a constant number of guests, employees can give each guest more attention. Conversely, fewer scheduled labor hours could mean service that is lower in quality or at least different, because less attention can be given to each guest.

Labor standards for kitchen staff must consider the time necessary to produce food of the required quality, which is based on standard recipes. Elaborate buffet presentations, ice carvings, fancy cake decorating, and similar labor-intensive tasks require extra time, but quality should not be sacrificed.

Since quality requirements form the foundation of labor standards, training programs to provide employees with the knowledge and skills necessary to meet quality requirements are important.

The chapter begins by discussing how managers can measure labor activity in such a way that meaningful comparisons can be made between labor standards and actual labor costs. Next, labor standards are defined in relation to productivity rates established by managers. Once labor standards are determined, they can be used to construct a staffing guide. Much of this chapter focuses on how managers can use a staffing guide to implement labor cost controls consistent with budgeted goals.

The final sections of the chapter address special labor scheduling techniques used by some multi-unit operations and how labor cost control can be enhanced by automated labor and payroll information systems.

Establishing a Unit of Measurement for Labor Standards

When developing labor standards, managers must decide how labor activity will be measured and specify the level of detail needed to adequately control labor costs. Recall that standard cost information for food and beverage products is generally expressed in dollars and percentages. Actual food and beverage costs are then measured in the same way, so that comparisons can be made with standard cost information. But what unit of measurement applies to labor?

Several factors must be considered in choosing a measure for labor costs. First, the measurement must be used consistently. If number of guests per labor hour is used in developing labor standards, and another unit of measurement, such as labor cost percentage, is used to report actual labor costs, managers will be left comparing "apples to oranges." Second, the unit of measurement must be simple enough so that managers can readily explain it to staff members. Using a ratio of labor costs to total costs may be useful for management tasks, but is it easily understood by supervisors and other staff members who may work with it on a daily basis? Third, the unit of measurement must be compatible with the operation's accounting system and should incorporate information from the property's payroll and accounting systems.

Labor activity may be expressed in terms of labor dollars or labor hours. When dollars are used as the unit of measurement, managers may work with (be permitted to schedule) a designated number of labor dollars per day to achieve a predetermined labor cost percentage. Advantages of measuring labor standards in dollars include the following:

- Budgets are expressed in dollars, not hours.

- Financial operating statements are expressed in dollars, not hours.

- Labor costs can be separated by shift and position within each department.

Labor activity may also be measured in labor hours. For example, a unit of measurement might be based on the number of labor hours required to produce a given number of meals or generate a certain level of revenue. Reasons for measuring labor standards in hours, rather than dollars, include the following:

- When productivity is emphasized instead of labor cost reduction, it is easier to incorporate quality requirements into work tasks.

- Labor hours must be calculated for many staff members' wages even if labor cost measurements are used, since the number of hours determines wages.

- Systems to control labor dollars are often time-consuming and difficult to use. Different wages and salaries for personnel within each position make calculating labor standards in dollars a challenge if a manual scheduling system is used.

- Fixed labor costs (labor costs that do not vary with the volume of meals served or the amount of revenue produced) may distort labor costs as meal counts decrease or as revenue increases.

- Calculating labor hours rather than dollars keeps the measure from being affected during times of economic inflation.

The decision about whether to base labor measurement systems on labor dollars or labor hours is important. In many large food and beverage operations, a combined approach is practical and yields accurate and useful information. The approach used in the remainder of this chapter focuses on the control of labor hours. However, procedures to convert hours into dollars are included to facilitate the combined approach.

Determining Productivity Rates

Productivity can be measured by comparing the number of labor hours expended to the number of meals served or to the amount of revenue generated. Managers must decide whether to determine productivity rates by department, by shift, by position, or by position and shift. Use of automated technology makes it easy to assess these rates on the basis of each of these measures.

A detailed standard makes it easier to take corrective action when variances between standards and actual results occur. It is much better, for example, to know that excess hours (those worked above those scheduled) were worked in a specific department than to know that excess hours were expended "somewhere" in the operation. The greater usefulness of more specific information to the corrective action phase of the control system must be considered when assessing the trade-off between accuracy and the time required to collect information.

Determining productivity rates by position and shift yields the most accurate, detailed information. Suppose a food and beverage manager, after carefully studying the operation, determines that a productivity rate of 15 meals per labor hour is a desired efficiency level; that is, for every hour of labor (input), there should be 15 guests served (output). Let's assume that productivity rates for cooks, dishwashers, and service personnel were not considered separately. After a given meal period, the manager discovers that the actual productivity rate was only 13 meals per labor hour. Since the productivity rate was established without considering positions separately, the manager cannot pinpoint the cause of the lower overall productivity. If, however, the manager knew that the labor performance standard for cooks was 15 meals per labor hour, while the actual productivity rate was only 12, then at least part of the problem could have been immediately traced to the kitchen, and corrective action(s) could be more quickly taken.

Establishing productivity rates by position makes it easier to examine the efficiency of each staff member. Experienced food service managers realize that productivity rates for different positions (cooks versus dishwashers, for example) vary. These different rates must be determined and incorporated into labor standards.

After determining minimum quality requirements, the unit of measure to be assessed, and how productivity rates are to be measured, managers can develop labor standards by considering the number of labor hours required to perform assigned tasks. The following technique—position performance analysis—yields reasonably accurate results.

Position performance analysis is a subjective technique to determine labor standards for each position and shift. An observation period is set during which employees are instructed to carefully follow all established policies and procedures. They are closely supervised to ensure compliance. For example, a cook would be told to follow all standard recipes, and all staff would be instructed to observe rest breaks and to perform tasks at the required quality levels. No changes in employee scheduling are made. During the study period the manager closely observes and analyzes job performance.

Exhibit 1 presents a worksheet that a manager can use to determine a labor standard for food servers. The worksheet provides columns for recording data

Exhibit 1   Position Performance Analysis Form

Position Performance Analysis

Position: _____ *Service* _____   Name of Employee: _____ *Joyce* _____

Shift: _____ A.M.—*Lunch* _____

	4/14	4/15	4/16	4/17	4/18
No. of Guests Served	38	60	25	45	50
No. of Hours Worked	4	4	4	4	3.5
No. of Guests/Labor Hour	9.5	15	6.3	11.3	14.3
Review Comments	Even workflow; no problems	Was really rushed; could not provide adequate service	Too much "standing around"; very inefficient	No problems; handled everything well	Worked fast whole shift; better with fewer guests

General Comments

   Joyce is a better than average server; with all the tasks that service personnel must do in our restaurant, approximately 10 guests per labor hour can be served by one server. When the number of guests goes up, service quality decreases. When Joyce really had to rush, some guests waited longer than they should have had to. When the number of guests per labor hour dropped and Joyce was not busy, there was a lot of unproductive time.

Suggested Guests/Labor Hour
(for this position): _____ *10* _____   Performance Review by: _____ *W. Brown* _____
                                                                              Restaurant Manager

---

and observations on the work of a single server over five lunch shifts. For each lunch shift, the manager records the following data:

- Number of guests served
- Number of hours the server worked
- Number of guests the server served per hour worked
- Comments concerning how well the server performed

The exhibit shows that on April 14, Joyce served 38 guests during a four-hour shift. This resulted in 9.5 guests served per hour worked (38 guests divided by four hours of work). Over a five-day period, the manager observed her work and then recorded comments relating to her efficiency.

Before calculating a labor standard for this position, the manager would have completed worksheets for several trained servers who worked similar lunch shifts. In our example, the manager determined a labor standard of ten guests per labor hour. That is, in the manager's view, trained servers should be able to serve ten guests for each hour worked without sacrificing quality requirements.

With slight alterations, Exhibit 1 can be used to determine labor standards for other positions in the operation. For example, a worksheet for a lunch cook would have space to record the number of meals prepared, the number of hours the cook worked, and the number of meals prepared per hour worked. A position performance analysis should be completed for each position and shift. This is because productivity rates for positions are different for each meal period because of the different tasks required by the various menus, service styles, and guests' expectations.

Constructing a Staffing Guide

A **staffing guide** indicates the number of labor hours needed for each position and each shift to produce and serve a given number of meals, while maintaining at least minimum quality requirements. The staffing guide incorporates labor standards and tells managers the number of labor hours needed for each position according to the volume of business forecasted for any given meal period. By converting the labor hour information into labor dollars, the manager can also establish standard labor costs. Procedures for converting labor hours into labor dollars are discussed later in this chapter.

The staffing guide serves as a tool for both planning work schedules and controlling labor costs. When the number of actual labor hours exceeds the standard labor hours identified by the staffing guide, managers should consider the need, if any, to take corrective action(s).

A staffing guide can be developed either for each department or for each position within each department. If the staffing guide is developed for a department, first analyze and summarize each position within the department (such as cook, assistant cook, and kitchen helper in the food production department). Then, average the required labor hours. For example, suppose the standard labor hours for each position in the food production department (as determined by position performance analyses) are as follows:

Cook	30 meals/labor hour
Assistant cook	20 meals/labor hour
Kitchen helper	10 meals/labor hour
Total	60

$$\frac{\text{Total Meals per Labor Hour}}{\text{Number of Positions}} = \text{Average Meals per Labor Hour}$$

$$\frac{60}{3} = 20 \text{ Meals per Labor Hour (Average)}$$

In this example, when scheduling staff for the food production department, the manager should schedule one labor hour for every 20 meals forecasted. However, this standard does not indicate the number of labor hours that need to be scheduled for each position in the department. Moreover, if standard labor hours are exceeded, how can the manager identify which position (cook, assistant cook, or kitchen helper) is using the extra time?

A second method for developing a staffing guide separates hours worked by position. With this approach, the schedule maker can plan the number of labor hours needed for each position. If actual labor hours exceed standard labor hours, it becomes obvious which position incurred the additional hours. This procedure yields more accurate and useful labor control information both for scheduling and for assessing the need for corrective action.

When constructing staffing guides, managers should consider the following points:

- Each property must set specific labor standards. Standards developed by another operation are generally meaningless because different properties have different menus, equipment, quality standards, etc. An exception to this general rule might exist in multi-unit operations that feature the same menus, layout/design features, and operating procedures. (This is discussed in detail later in the chapter.)

- Use the productivity rates of good employees to set labor standards for average employees.

- As employees become more efficient through practice, work simplification initiatives, and other efficiency measures, update the staffing guide to reflect the higher productivity rates.

- The standard labor dollars resulting from following the staffing guide must be consistent with the standard labor dollars permitted by the operating budget. This point also is discussed later in the chapter.

Fixed versus Variable Labor

Before deciding on procedures for developing staffing guides, managers must understand the difference between fixed and variable labor. **Fixed labor** is the minimum labor required to operate the food and beverage operation regardless of the volume of business. For example, when a restaurant is open, at least one cook, server, and bartender may be needed, up to a certain volume of guests, before additional cooks, servers, and bartenders are required. This minimum amount of labor must be considered and incorporated into the staffing guide. Up to a certain volume of business (a point determined by management), no additional staff are necessary. Above this defined level, however, additional labor is needed. This additional labor is referred to as **variable labor**, which varies according to the volume of business activity. Therefore, as more guests are served or as more meals are produced, additional service and kitchen labor is needed.

Exhibit 2 provides a sample staffing guide format for variable labor positions. The hours noted in the guide include the fixed hours that are required regardless of business volume. To understand the staffing guide, look at the position of food server. When 50 dinners are forecasted, 8.5 food server labor hours should be scheduled. The 8.5 labor hours represent the standard of meals per labor hour based on a position performance analysis. That is, the labor standard (8.5 labor hours) equals the total hours that should normally be scheduled to serve 50 meals. The manager must decide how many and which food servers to schedule. The times listed (5:00 to 9:30 and 7:00 to 11:00) represent a staff schedule that incorporates typical peaks and valleys in business volume each shift.

Exhibit 2 Standard Labor Hour Staffing Guide: Dinner

		Standard Labor Hour Staffing Guide: Dinner			
			Number of Dinners		
	50	75	100	125	150
Position Food Server	8.5 5:00-9:30 7:00-11:00	9.5 5:00-9:30 6:30-11:30	16.0 5:00-9:30 6:30-10:00 7:00-10:00 7:30-12:30	16.0 5:00-9:30 6:30-10:00 7:00-10:00 7:30-12:30	19.0 5:00-10:00 6:00-11:00 6:00-11:00 7:30-11:30
Bartender	9.0 4:00-1:00	9.0 4:00-1:00	9.0 4:00-1:00	9.0 4:00-1:00	9.0 4:00-1:00
Cocktail Server	6.5 4:30-11:00	6.5 4:30-11:00	6.5 4:30-11:00	6.5 4:30-11:00	6.5 4:30-11:00
Cook	7 4:00-11:00	14 3:00-10:00 5:00-12:00	14 3:00-10:00 5:00-12:00	14 3:00-10:00 5:00-12:00	16 3:00-11:00 4:00-12:00
Steward	6.5 5:00-11:30	6.5 5:00-11:30	9.0 3:00-12:00	9.5 3:00-12:30	9.5 3:00-12:30
Busperson	—	2 7:30-9:30	4 7:30-9:30 7:30-9:30	5 7:00-9:30 7:30-10:00	7 7:00-9:30 7:30-10:00 7:30-9:30
Host (Manager serves as host on slow evenings)	—	3 6:00-9:00	3.5 6:00-9:30	4.0 6:00-10:00	4.0 6:00-10:00

Note: Labor hour standards are used for illustrative purposes only. Information must be developed for a specific property based upon factors that influence worker efficiency within that food and beverage operation.

Determining Fixed Labor Requirements. Remember that each food and beverage operation has fixed labor needs (the minimum amount of labor necessary regardless of business volume) that dictate, in effect, a minimum staffing level. The amount of fixed labor should be established on a by-department basis. Several times each year, managers should evaluate the amount of fixed labor recommended by department heads. Many factors affect the amount of fixed labor required, such as changes in quality requirements, operating procedures, the menu, and guest expectations.

The work performed by fixed labor staff must be analyzed to ensure that these employees are as productive as possible. During this analysis, managers may consider temporary actions to reduce labor expense during slow business periods. For example, it might be possible to reduce the hours of dining room service or valet parking service in a hotel. Also, the tasks performed by hourly fixed staff could be adjusted. For example, given the proper cross-training, a cook may be able to perform certain baking duties.

Controlling Salaried Labor Costs. Salaried labor costs do not increase or decrease according to the number of guests served. One manager, paid at a predetermined salary rate, creates a fixed labor cost. Normally, salaried personnel should be scheduled to perform only the work their job descriptions require. Management tasks such as recordkeeping, purchasing, and work scheduling should be scheduled during non-peak production periods. During busy times, managers should be available to perform supervisory and operational duties, including guest contact responsibilities.

During slow business periods, salaried staff could be assigned duties normally performed by hourly employees. For example, an assistant restaurant manager might be stationed at the host stand, seating guests and taking reservations. However, salaried staff should not be used indiscriminately to reduce hourly labor costs. Although management staff must know how to perform all the tasks in the operation, salaried staff members should not be the first chosen to replace hourly employees who fail to report to work. Efficiency, attitude, and ability decrease as the length of the workweek increases. Every hour spent by a salaried employee performing the unexpected work of another staff member adds an additional hour that the salaried manager must spend performing administrative duties. Management turnover often can be traced to overwork and poorly assigned work.

When developing the staffing guide, the tasks of salaried staff indicated on current job descriptions should be analyzed thoroughly. Schedules should allow enough time for salaried staff to do their required work. Also, the personal preferences of salaried staff should be considered when developing schedules. Managers often develop responsibilities, tasks, and the volume of work for salaried staff first, then schedule variable labor staff to perform the remaining tasks.

Staffing Guides and Budgets

When budgeted labor costs are based on the same productivity rates as the staffing guide, it is relatively easy for managers to keep labor costs in line with budgeted goals. When this is not the case, managers must ensure that standard labor hours permitted by the staffing guide remain within budgeted labor costs. Sometimes the staffing guide must be revised so that its use will allow labor costs to remain within operating budget limitations.

Let's assume that the manager of an operation constructed the staffing guide shown in Exhibit 2. Before scheduling employees according to the staffing guide, the manager wants to ensure that the resulting labor costs will be within the limits established by the operating budget. Assume that the current operating budget limits labor costs for variable labor to 18.9 percent of total food and beverage revenue. The manager must calculate a comparable labor cost percentage based on the labor hours expressed by the staffing guide. Therefore, for each level of business volume within the staffing guide, the manager must:

1. Convert labor hours into labor dollars.
2. Determine the total labor cost.
3. Estimate the total food and beverage revenue.
4. Determine a labor cost percentage.

Exhibit 3 Converting Standard Labor Hours into Standard Labor Dollars

Position	Number of Meals														
	50			75			100			125			150		
	Std. Labor Hours	Avg. Hourly Rate	Std. Labor Costs	Std. Labor Hours	Avg. Hourly Rate	Std. Labor Costs	Std. Labor Hours	Avg. Hourly Rate	Std. Labor Costs	Std. Labor Hours	Avg. Hourly Rate	Std. Labor Costs	Std. Labor Hours	Avg. Hourly Rate	Std. Labor Costs
Food Server	8.5/5.00		42.50	9.5/5.00		47.50	16.0/5.00		80.00	16.0/5.00		80.00	19.0/5.00		95.00
Bartender	9.0/8.00		72.00	9.00/8.00		72.00	9.0/8.00		72.00	9.0/8.00		72.00	9.0/8.00		72.00
Cocktail Server	6.5/5.00		32.50	6.5/5.00		32.50	6.5/5.00		32.50	6.5/5.00		32.50	6.5/5.00		32.50
Cook	7.0/11.00		77.00	14.0/11.00		154.00	14.0/11.00		154.00	14.0/11.00		154.00	16.0/11.00		176.00
Steward	6.5/6.50		42.25	6.5/6.50		42.25	9.0/6.50		58.50	9.5/6.50		61.75	9.5/6.50		61.75
Busperson	—		—	2.0/5.50		11.00	4.0/5.50		22.00	5.0/5.50		27.50	7.0/5.50		38.50
Host	—		—	—		—	—		—	—		—	—		—
Total Standard Labor Cost	$266.25			$359.25			$419.00			$427.75			$475.75		
Revenue (Meals × Avg. Checks)	$1,604.00			$2,406.00			$3,208.00			$4,010.00			$4,812.00		
Standard Labor Cost Percentage*	16.6%			14.9%			13%			10.7%			9.8%		

NOTE: Hourly rate and number of hours worked for varying numbers of meals are for illustrative purposes only. Food and beverage operations must develop this information based on factors that influence worker efficiency in their own specific properties.

*In no instance does the labor cost percentage exceed the allowable variable labor cost percentage (18.9 percent) as calculated for the operating budget.

Converting Labor Hours into Labor Dollars. Labor hours expressed by the staffing guide are converted into labor dollars by multiplying the number of hours allowed for each position by the average hourly rate for the position. For example, Exhibit 3 notes that 16 standard labor hours are allowed for the cook when 150 meals are served. The standard labor cost for the cook's position is calculated as follows: 16 standard labor hours × $11.00 average hourly rate = $176 standard labor cost. (Note that if labor cost calculations for the operating budget include employee benefits, the cost of employee benefits must also be added when converting labor hours into labor dollars; normally these are calculated separately on budgets and income statements.)

Determining a Total Labor Cost. Total labor cost is determined by adding the labor dollars for each position for each level of business volume. For example, Exhibit 3 shows that when 150 meals are served, the total variable labor cost for all employees in all positions is expected to be $475.75.

Estimating Total Food and Beverage Revenue. Estimates for total food and beverage revenue for each level of business volume can be made by multiplying the number of meals identified in the staffing guide by the guest check average. Let's assume that a review of current revenue information shows that the guest check average is $32.08 (total revenue ÷ number of guests = $32.08). When 150 meals are served, the total food and beverage revenue would be estimated at $4,812 (150 meals × $32.08).

Determining a Labor Cost Percentage. For each level of business volume identified in the staffing guide, a labor cost percentage can be determined by dividing the total labor cost by the estimated total of food and beverage revenue. Therefore, in Exhibit 3, when 150 meals are served, the labor cost is 9.8 percent ($475.75 total labor cost ÷ $4,812 total revenue × 100). Note that the labor cost percentage for each level of business volume remains within the limits established by the operating budget (18.9 percent). Note also that, as the number of meals served *increases*, the labor cost percentage *decreases*. This is generally the case, because production and service efficiencies can be built into the standards. (For example, it takes the same amount of time to clean a steam kettle if 100 or 150 portions were prepared.) This means that the manager can use the staffing guide to schedule employees and remain safely within budgeted labor cost standards if scheduled labor hours are not exceeded.

However, what would happen if the staffing guide yielded higher labor costs than those permitted by the operating budget? One course of action would be to revise the budget accordingly. If costs could not be reduced in other expense areas, or if revenue could not be increased, profit expectations would have to be lowered. Another option would be to revise the quality requirements and productivity rates on which the staffing guide is based. In this case, productivity might be increased and labor costs could be reduced through further position performance analyses to increase worker efficiency.

The Staffing Guide as a Scheduling Tool

The staffing guide and business volume forecasts are tools managers can use to schedule employees. In practice, it is much easier and more efficient to schedule employees on the basis of labor hours rather than to expect managers to consider specific hourly rates when developing work schedules.

Some managers schedule required labor hours during the midweek for the next workweek (Monday through Sunday). Others develop work schedules for longer or shorter time periods. In any case, the important point is to establish a routine scheduling procedure. Computerized systems are available to help managers more quickly and efficiently schedule employees (these systems will be discussed later in the chapter).

A schedule worksheet can be used to determine when employees are needed. For example, let's look at Exhibit 4. After receiving the forecast of 250 guests for Monday evening, the supervisor checked the staffing guide for the dinner meal period and found that 18 labor hours should be scheduled for assistant cooks. Knowing that the peak hours during the dinner period are between 7:30 P.M. and 9:30 P.M., the supervisor staggered the work schedules of three assistant cooks to cover these peak hours. Joe was scheduled to work earlier to perform duties at

Exhibit 4 Schedule Worksheet

	Day:	Monday	Estimated Guests:	Department: Food Service
	Date:	8/1/XX	A.M. / P.M. 250	Position: Assistant Cook
	Shift:	P.M.		

Employee	6:00 a	7:00 a	8:00 a	9:00 a	10:00 a	11:00 a	12:00 p	1:00 p	2:00 p	3:00 p	4:00 p	5:00 p	6:00 p	7:00 p	8:00 p	9:00 p	10:00 p	11:00 p	12:00 a	1:00 a	2:00 a	3:00 a	4:00 a	5:00 a	6:00 a	Planned Total Hours
Joe																										7.0
Sally																										6.5
Phyllis																										4.5
																										18.0

Position: Assistant Cook

Standard Labor Hours: 18

Planned Labor Hours: 18

Difference: 0

the beginning of the shift, and Phyllis was scheduled to work later to perform closing duties at the end of the shift. All three assistant cooks would be available for regular duties during the peak business hours. In some operations, managers rotate employees through "early" and "late" schedules to help balance work responsibilities.

There are times when managers or supervisors need to schedule more labor hours than those indicated by the staffing guide. Additional hours may be needed to train new staff members, introduce a new menu, or train experienced staff to operate newly installed equipment.

Before considering specific methods of employee scheduling, we will examine some principles relevant to all employee scheduling methods.

Staggered Work Schedules. In most food and beverage operations, the work flow is rarely constant throughout a shift. There is usually a mixture of rush, normal, and slow periods. Therefore, it is generally not useful for all staff members to begin and end work shifts at the same time. By staggering and overlapping work shifts, managers can ensure that the greatest number of employees are working during peak business hours.

For example, one server might begin work an hour before the dining room opens. The server can use this time to check or set up tables and perform other miscellaneous **mise-en-place** tasks. A second server could be scheduled to arrive one-half hour before opening to perform other pre-opening duties. Both employees can begin serving when needed. Staggered ending times are also encouraged to ensure maximum worker efficiency. The first employee to check in might be the first to leave. Of course, it is necessary to comply with property policies and applicable laws as scheduling decisions are made.

Full-Time versus Part-Time Staff. Part-time staff can be hired to work short shifts of, for example, three to five hours. If some of these employees want more hours, a split shift—two short shifts in one day separated by time off—may be possible. Since staggered scheduling often reduces labor hours, there may be less need for full-time personnel. However, full-time personnel will likely be needed to fill key administrative positions.

If there are not enough administrative tasks to justify certain full-time positions, some full-time jobs can be composed of management and nonmanagement tasks. For example, a full-time head bartender or head dishwasher position could be developed. The head dishwasher could handle management duties such as supervising personnel and developing cleaning schedules. However, the position might also include the nonmanagement task of dishwashing during busy times. With these types of arrangements, salaries or wages are set on the basis of reasonable pay for all work performed so that both the operation and its employees benefit.

Temporary Employees. Many properties keep a file of names of people who do not want steady work but like to work occasionally. A large banquet, employee illness, seasonal business fluctuations, or similar circumstances may create a need for temporary employees.

While scheduling principles are helpful, two of the most useful scheduling tools are the manager's experience in developing schedules and the manager's knowledge of the staff's capabilities. In many food and beverage operations, the pattern of business volume stabilizes, creating a recognizable pattern of labor requirements. The more experience the manager acquires in a specific operation, the easier it becomes to stagger work schedules, balance full-time and part-time employees, and effectively use temporary workers. Similarly, the better the manager understands the capabilities of the operation's staff, the easier it becomes to schedule the right employees for particular times and shifts. For example, some servers may work best when they are scheduled for the late dinner shift, or some cooks may not perform well during a dinner rush. These factors can be taken into account when planning work schedules.

Whenever possible, managers or supervisors with scheduling responsibilities should consider employees' preferences. Employees can be given schedule request forms to indicate which days or shifts they want off. These requests should be submitted by employees according to established policies and honored by management when possible.

Reports generated by software available today can help managers ensure that their schedules will be in concert with the hours permitted by the staffing guide. Exhibit 5 shows one such report. It shows, on a by-position basis (servers and hostess in this section of the report), the number of staff required ("Requirements Generation" per the staffing guide) and the number of employees actually scheduled, along with the variance, if any, between the two.

Exhibit 5 Staff Requirements vs. Actual Schedule

Staff Requirements vs. Actual Schedule

Report Date:

Filter: Jobs, Date Range

M. Bruno

	08/01/20XX	08/02/20XX	08/03/20XX	08/04/20XX	08/05/20XX	08/06/20XX	08/07/20XX
Servers							
Breakfast							
Requirements Generation	7	4	4	4	4	5	6
Actual Schedule	8	4	4	4	3	3	5
Variance	1	0	0	0	-1	-2	-1
Lunch							
Requirements Generation	6	3	3	4	5	5	5
Actual Schedule	6	4	3	3	4	5	5
Variance	0	1	0	-1	-1	0	0
Dinner							
Requirements Generation	6	3	3	4	5	5	5
Actual Schedule	6	4	3	3	4	5	5
Variance	0	1	0	-1	-1	0	0
Hostess							
Breakfast							
Requirements Generation	2	1	1	1	1	1	2
Actual Schedule	2	1	1	1	1	1	1
Variance	0	0	0	0	0	0	-1
Lunch							
Requirements Generation	2	1	1	1	2	2	3
Actual Schedule	2	1	1	1	1	2	2
Variance	0	0	0	0	-1	0	-1
Dinner							
Requirements Generation	2	2	2	2	3	4	4
Actual Schedule	2	1	2	2	3	5	4
Variance	0	-1	0	0	0	1	0

Courtesy of MICROS Systems, Inc., Columbia, Maryland (www.micros.com).

Exhibit 6   Sample Employee Schedule

	Week of:	7/14/XX					
Shift: P.M.					Supervisor: Julie		
Position: Cook							

Employee	7/14 Monday	7/15 Tuesday	7/16 Wednesday	7/17 Thursday	7/18 Friday	7/19 Saturday	7/20 Sunday
Syrus	12:00-7:00	—	12:00-7:00	1:00-7:30	—	12:00-7:00	—
Ann	—	12:00-7:00	1:00-7:30	12:00-7:00	—	—	12:00-7:00
Jean	3:00-8:00	1:00-5:00	3:00-8:00	—	—	1:00-7:30	1:00-7:30
Sue	—	3:00-8:30	12:30-8:30	12:30-7:30	12:00-7:00	—	—
Gabridle	12:30-6:30	12:30-6:00	—	—	3:00-7:00	3:00-8:00	3:00-8:00
Stacey	3:00-7:00	3:00-7:00	3:00-7:30	3:00-7:30	—	—	12:30-8:30
Phyllis	1:00-5:00	1:00-5:00	—	—	3:00-8:00	12:30-8:30	3:00-7:00
Andres	1:00-7:00	—	—	1:00-7:00	1:00-8:30	3:00-7:00	—
Sally	—	—	3:00-8:00	1:00-7:00	3:00-7:30	—	1:00-6:00
Karen	1:00-7:00	1:00-7:00	—	—	1:00-5:00	1:00-6:00	2:00-7:00
Bettina	—	—	3:00-7:00	3:00-8:00	3:00-7:00	2:00-7:00	—

Once the working hours for each employee are established, they should be combined in a schedule and made available to employees for review and use. Note that the sample employee schedule shown in Exhibit 6 indicates the days and hours of each shift that each cook is scheduled to work during the upcoming week. The schedule attempts to provide employees with the best possible advance notice of their work hours. Once developed, the schedule can be provided to employees in paycheck envelopes, for example, or posted in locker rooms, on bulletin boards, or at other appropriate locations. Some food service operations make schedules available on property intranet systems to which staff members have access.

Of course, schedule plans do not always work. Employees might call in sick or fail to show up without warning. Also, the number of actual guests and the volume of meals might differ from expectations. Therefore, it may be necessary to revise posted work schedules.

Managers must continually encourage employees to follow posted work schedules. Policies providing for on-call staff members may help protect the operation when the attendance problems of staff members result in a reduced number of employees. Managers must comply with all union, legal, and other restrictions regarding policies requiring employees to call in or be available for work on days when they are not scheduled.

The Staffing Guide as a Control Tool

Using a staffing guide and a reliable business volume forecast to develop employee work schedules does not guarantee that the hours employees actually work will equal the number of hours they were scheduled to work. Managers must monitor

---

Learn More on the Web

Want to learn how a point-of-sale (POS) system can help with labor scheduling? If so, review the Digital Dining website (www.digitaldining.com). When you reach the site, click on "Products," then "Back Office Solutions," and then "Labor Scheduling."

---

the scheduling process by comparing the actual hours each employee works with the number of hours the employee was scheduled to work. Information about actual hours worked is usually obtained from the accounting department or, increasingly, from a point-of-sale system. Managers using manual systems may find it practical to compare scheduled to actual hours on a weekly basis. Their counterparts using a computerized system can easily do so on a daily or even by-shift basis.

Exhibit 7 presents a sample weekly department labor hour report. Actual hours worked by each employee are recorded for each day of the week in columns 2 through 8. Actual total hours worked for each employee and for the position categories are totaled in column 9. These actual hours worked can be compared with the scheduled labor hours shown in column 10. Significant variances should be analyzed and corrective action taken when necessary.

Variance Analysis

Exhibit 7 shows that, during the week of July 14, 216.5 labor hours were scheduled for dining room employees; however, the actual hours worked totaled 224.5, a variance of 8 hours. Is this a significant variance? Should the manager investigate it? Let's do some quick calculations. Assuming that the average hourly wage for the staff is $10, including benefits, the variance of 8 hours costs the operation a total of $80 for the week of July 14. If actual hours worked differed from scheduled labor hours at this rate for the entire year, it would cost the operation a total of $4,160 ($80 weekly × 52 weeks = $4,160) in lost profits. Since no manager wants to lose any amount of potential profit, the variance is significant enough to warrant further investigation.

The remarks at the bottom of the report list reasons for the variances. If similar variances and remarks occur over a period of several weeks, corrective action may be necessary. For example, the manager or supervisor may need to do a better job of planning and scheduling necessary cleaning for the dining room and storage areas.

A weekly department labor hour report will almost always reveal differences between the hours scheduled and the actual hours worked. Generally, a small deviation is permitted. For example, if the labor performance standard for a position is 210 hours for the week, a variance of 2 percent, or approximately 4.2 hours, might be tolerated. So, if actual labor hours do not exceed 214.2 (210.00 + 4.2 = 214.2), no investigation is necessary. If actual labor hours increase beyond 214.2, analysis and corrective action may be required. Managers should determine the variance levels that, if exceeded, should be investigated.

Exhibit 7   Weekly Department Labor Hour Report

Weekly Department Labor Hour Report									
Week of: 7/14/XX	**Department:** *Food Service* **Supervisor:** *Sandra*								
	Shift: *P.M.*								
Actual Labor Hours Worked									
Position/ Employee	7/14 Mon	7/15 Tues	7/16 Wed	7/17 Thurs	7/18 Fri	7/19 Sat	7/20 Sun	Total Labor Hours Actual	Std.
DINING ROOM 1	2	3	4	5	6	7	8	9	10
Jennifer	7	—	7	6.5	7	6	—	33.5	31.0
Brenda	—	7	6.5	7	6.5	6.5	5	38.5	38.5
Sally	—	5	8	7	8	10	—	38.0	36.0
Patty	8	6	6	4.5	—	—	6	30.5	31.0
Anna	4	4	6.5	—	4.5	—	5	24.0	22.0
Thelma	6	5	5	5	5	—	—	26.0	24.0
Elsie	6	—	—	6	6	8	8	34.0	34.0
								224.5	216.5
COOK									
Peggy	4	4	4	4	4	—	—	20.0	20.0
Kathy	4	4	4	—	—	4	4	20.0	20.0
Tilly	4	—	—	4	4	4	4	20.0	18.0
Carlos	—	4	4	4	4	4	—	20.0	20.0
Sam	4	4	—	—	—	—	4	12.0	12.0
								92.0	90.0
DISHWASHING									
Terry	—	—	6	6	6	—	—	18.0	18.0
Andrew	6	6	—	—	8	5	5	30.0	30.0
Robert	8	8	8	8	—	—	6	38.0	38.0
Carl	5	—	5	5	5	6	—	26.0	26.0
								112.0	112.0
							Total (all personnel)	428.5	418.5
Remarks: 7/18 — Jennifer, Sally and Elsie given extra hours to learn tableside flaming 7/19 — Sally stayed 2 hours—special cleaning 7/20 — Tilly stayed 2 hours—cleaned storeroom shelves							Difference	+10.00	

There may be legitimate reasons for a difference between standard and actual results. Examples include:

- Hours worked by new employees and included in the weekly department labor hour report that represent training time rather than time spent on productive work.

- Out-of-order equipment that results in additional labor being necessary.

- New menu items or new work procedures that create a training or transitional period that increases labor hours.

- A rush of late-shift business that requires staff to remain on duty longer than scheduled.

If there are legitimate reasons for variances, corrective actions are not needed. The manager is aware of the problems and their causes, expected duration, and estimated economic costs.

Occasionally, problems may exist for which immediate causes or solutions are not apparent. In these situations, the manager could ask employees for ideas about the problem. Also, the manager could work in the affected position for a shift or two or, at least, could closely observe employees who work in the position. Unknown reasons for variances require high priority to ensure that the operation is in control of labor costs at all times.

The procedures discussed so far use one week as the time period for comparing labor standards and actual labor hours. If comparisons are made too infrequently, time is wasted, and labor dollars are lost before managers notice that a problem exists. On the other hand, if comparisons are made too frequently, excessive time and money is spent in assembling data, performing calculations, and making comparisons. Some time is necessary for labor hours and costs to average out. Obviously, labor hours can be higher than established labor standards on some days and lower on other days.

When a comparison of labor standards with actual labor results indicates unacceptable variances, finding answers to the following questions may be helpful:

- Are the labor standards established by position performance analyses (see Exhibit 1) correct? If they are incorrect, the staffing guide itself will be incorrect. A recurring problem may call for reviewing position performance analyses and evaluating the accuracy of the labor standards used to construct the staffing guide.

- How accurate are the forecasts used for scheduling staff? Additional labor hours may have been necessary if more meals were produced and served than forecasted. If this happens frequently, forecasting techniques should be evaluated.

- Are employees performing tasks not listed in their job descriptions? These tasks may not have been considered in the initial position performance analyses that established the labor standards.

- Are there new employees who do not perform as efficiently as employees did during the initial position performance analyses?

- Have factors affecting labor efficiency changed (such as menu revisions or new equipment purchases)? If so, updated position performance analyses leading to revised labor standards may be necessary.

- Are personal or professional problems among the staff affecting efficiency?

Comparing Actual Labor Costs to Budgeted Labor Costs

Information recorded in a weekly labor hour report must be consistent with information developed for other aspects of the labor control system. For example, the department weekly labor hour and cost report shown in Exhibit 8 provides the same information that appears in Exhibit 7, but also lists hourly rates for each employee and converts actual and standard labor hours into labor dollars. Labor dollars enable managers to compare actual labor costs with budgeted labor costs.

Exhibit 8   Department Weekly Labor Hour and Cost Report

Week of: _____ 7/14/XX _____

Department: _Food Service_   Supervisor: _____ Sandra _____

Shift: _____ P.M. _____

Actual Labor Hours Worked

Position/ Employee	Mon 7/14	Tues 7/15	Wed 7/16	Thurs 7/17	Fri 7/18	Sat 7/19	Sun 7/20	Total Labor Hours Actual	Standard	Hourly Rate	Total Labor Costs Actual	Standard
1	2	3	4	5	6	7	8	9	10	11	12	13
DINING ROOM												
Jennifer	7	—	7	6.5	7	6	—	33.5	31.0	$7.00	$234.50	$217.00
Brenda	—	7	6.5	7	6.5	6.5	5	38.5	38.5	7.15	275.28	275.28
Sally	—	5	8	7	8	10	—	38.0	36.0	7.25	275.50	261.00
Patty	8	6	6	4.5	—	—	6	30.5	31.0	7.10	216.55	220.10
Anna	4	4	6.5	—	4.5	—	5	24.0	22.0	7.10	170.40	156.20
Thelma	6	5	5	5	5	—	—	26.0	24.0	7.40	192.40	177.60
Elsie	6	—	—	6	6	8	8	34.0	34.0	7.05	239.70	239.70
								224.5	216.5		$1,604.33	$1,546.88
COOK												
Peggy	4	4	4	4	4	—	—	20.0	20.0	14.00	280.00	280.00
Kathy	4	4	4	—	—	4	4	20.0	20.0	14.15	283.00	283.00
Tilly	4	—	—	4	4	4	4	20.0	18.0	14.50	290.00	261.00
Carlos	—	4	4	4	4	4	—	20.0	20.0	14.00	280.00	280.00
Sam	4	4	—	—	—	—	4	12.0	12.0	14.10	169.20	169.20
								92.0	90.0		$1,302.20	$1,273.20
DISHWASHING												
Terry	—	—	6	6	6	—	—	18.0	18.0	9.50	171.00	171.00
Andrew	6	6	—	—	8	5	5	30.0	30.0	9.25	277.50	277.50
Robert	8	8	8	8	—	—	6	38.0	38.0	9.55	362.90	362.90
Carl	5	—	5	5	5	6	—	26.0	26.0	9.50	247.00	247.00
								112.0	112.0		$1,058.40	$1,058.40
											$3,964.93	$3,875.48

During the course of each month, the manager can determine the actual labor costs to date and subtract those costs from the total labor costs allowed by the operating budget for that month. The result indicates the amount of labor dollars left in the current month's budget. This helps managers plan future expenses and remain within the budgeted allowance for labor costs.

Alternatively, the manager can review the actual labor costs and food and beverage revenue to date. This yields a to-date actual labor cost percentage that can be compared with the budgeted labor cost percentage for the period.

The weekly labor hour and cost report can also be used to monitor **overtime** labor costs. Some companies use the term "overtime" to refer to a situation in which an employee has worked more than the time the staffing guide lists for his or her position. Federal guidelines specify that non-exempt employees who work in excess of the standard 40-hour workweek are generally entitled to receive overtime pay of one-and-one-half-times the hourly rate. Any number of situations may arise that force a supervisor to schedule overtime for some employees. However, most operations require management approval for scheduled overtime. Unscheduled and excessive overtime costs often are signs of poor forecasting and problems with scheduling.

The weekly labor hour and cost report in Exhibit 8 presents, on a by-employee basis, a detailed overview of scheduled (standard) and actual labor hours, hourly rates, and total costs. (Note: Hourly rates may include prorated benefits expenses if these are included in the budgeted labor cost goals.) The weekly labor hour and cost report alerts the manager to any instances in which an employee's actual labor hours worked exceed the number of hours for which that employee was scheduled. If previous approval of a variance was not granted, the discrepancy may signal a need for tighter controls, or even indicate an attempt by one or more dishonest employees to steal through payroll fraud.

Planning Corrective Action

A corrective action plan should follow a sequence that ensures important elements of the control system are not overlooked. Such a sequence should include:

1. Provisions for identification of variations between labor standards and actual labor results. The department supervisor should briefly explain these on the weekly department labor hour report (see the "Remarks" section at the bottom of Exhibit 7).

2. Analysis of the weekly department labor hour report by a senior manager.

3. Discussions between the supervisor and senior manager to determine and agree on corrective actions and a timeline by which the actual labor hours and costs should get back in line with the standards in the staffing guide.

4. Implementation procedures for corrective action(s). Both managers should closely monitor the effectiveness of the corrective action(s).

5. Review of the corrective action(s). After the time limit has elapsed, managers should again meet to review the effectiveness of the corrective action(s) they implemented. Any findings applicable to other positions or departments can be noted. The need for an updated position performance analysis can also be reviewed.

Developing the best corrective action plan is important. Managers must know exactly what the problems are, consider effective management strategies, supervise workers, and evaluate them to ensure that corrective action is successful. The checklist presented in Exhibit 9 can help managers spot potential labor problems and take corrective action.

Employee Scheduling in Multi-Unit Operations ⎯⎯⎯⎯⎯⎯

When developing labor standards, some multi-unit (especially fast-food) companies conduct relatively sophisticated time studies of trained employees in several operations. In a fast-food operation, where there is typically a limited variety of food products and a consistent repetition of procedures required to produce them, this system creates exciting possibilities.

The time study analysis used by some multi-unit food and beverage companies to develop labor standards is similar to procedures used in manufacturing industries where conveyer assembly lines or similar processes are studied. For

Exhibit 9   Checklist for Labor Control

Personnel Administration

☐ Job descriptions for all tasks performed by all positions in all sections of the operation are available, accurately reflect the positions, and are revised as necessary.

☐ Personnel are aware of tasks in job descriptions.

☐ Job specifications are available and are used in employee selection to ensure that properly qualified personnel are hired.

☐ A current organization chart shows relationships between and among departments and positions within the property.

☐ New employees are given copies of job descriptions, specifications, and an organization chart, along with other materials in an employee handbook, when hired. Orientation is completed.

☐ Supervisors, by interviewing applicants and participating in decisions, are involved in hiring for vacant positions in their sections.

☐ When possible, eligible current employees are promoted to fill vacant positions; there is a "career ladder" for employees.

☐ Supervisors are aware of and work with informal employee groups.

☐ Only qualified applicants are considered for vacant positions.

☐ An employee application form is the initial step in selecting employees.

☐ References on employee application forms are contacted for additional information.

☐ Food and beverage managers interview applicants.

☐ The supervisor/section head interviews the applicants.

☐ Top managers and the section supervisor discuss and make a joint decision regarding the applicant.

☐ Simple tests, such as extending a recipe or working the dishwashing machine, are used to ensure that experienced personnel have basic knowledge on which the facility can build through training.

☐ Several applicants are considered for each position; the best is selected.

☐ The selection process allows the applicant to learn about the facility, in addition to food service personnel learning about the applicant.

☐ New employees are given a tour of the property and introduced to other employees before being taken to the workstation.

☐ The formal work group is notified in advance of new employees' arrivals.

☐ Supervisors spend time with new employees on their first day, making them feel comfortable and answering basic questions.

☐ An experienced employee is assigned to the new employee to help with other questions and to begin on-the-job training.

☐ A planned training program ensures that the new employee can do required tasks according to required procedures.

☐ The trainer and supervisor formally discuss any need for additional training and evaluate the new employee's progress.

☐ Training is used to bring long-time employees up to minimum quality standards if they are not working according to required procedures.

Exhibit 9 *(continued)*

☐ A formal employee evaluation program allows the supervisor to inform employees about their strengths and weaknesses and permits employees to talk with supervisors about ways to improve their jobs.

☐ Employees know the job standards on which they will be evaluated and are trained to achieve these standards.

Labor Control System

☐ A standard labor hour staffing guide is available to help supervisors schedule variable labor employees.

☐ Salaried labor is scheduled according to need; salaried labor is not generally used to replace hourly employees; tasks performed by salaried personnel are in line with salaries.

☐ The supervisor and top management staff know, for each position in the department, the number of labor hours needed to produce minimum quality levels for varied revenue volumes.

☐ The department supervisor and other managers regularly observe personnel in all positions to ensure that the staffing guide accurately reflects the number of labor hours needed.

☐ There are separate staffing guides for each shift if different menus affect worker productivity.

☐ Supervisors use the standard labor hour staffing guide and schedule only the maximum number of labor hours judged necessary for each shift.

☐ Supervisors use split shifts, part-time personnel, and staggered scheduling to ensure that personnel are available only when needed.

☐ Employees are informed about their work schedules through a formal schedule posted in an employee area; schedules for at least one week are prepared one week in advance.

☐ Supervisors confirm the number of labor hours worked by hourly employees. A report, signed by each supervisor, indicating the number of labor hours worked by each employee is an integral part of the property's payroll system.

☐ Supervisors must explain the reasons when the actual number of labor hours worked by employees within a position exceeds the standard (allowable) number of labor hours.

☐ Top management officials carefully review all weekly reports to note trends and to take corrective action(s) when actual labor hours within a department consistently exceed standard labor hours.

☐ The reasons for excessive labor hours are known, and necessary corrective action is taken.

☐ Managers and supervisors jointly plan and monitor results of corrective actions.

☐ A standard labor hour cost control system is used to monitor and control labor costs; systems involving labor cost dollars and budget development and use are considered according to their applicability to the property.

(continued)

Exhibit 9 *(continued)*

Personnel Supervision

☐ Supervisors recognize that employee motivation and training are part of their jobs.

☐ Supervisors recognize that employee problems frequently result from improper supervisory techniques.

☐ Supervisors know how to give instructions properly; they seek cooperation and take time to explain, defend, and justify reasons for actions.

☐ Supervisors have been taught procedures for motivating and directing employees.

☐ Supervisors are aware of and attempt to provide those things that employees want from their jobs.

☐ Supervisors know what affects employee morale and constantly work to improve morale.

☐ Supervisors can make decisions and solve problems to do their jobs as effectively as possible.

☐ Supervisors solicit ideas from all affected parties when making decisions.

☐ Supervisors and top managers are aware that, in some instances, the supervisor is part of the problem. The supervisor as well as employees must sometimes change.

☐ Supervisors are fair and reasonable in disciplining employees; discipline is designed to create adherence to fair and reasonable procedures, rather than to punish.

☐ Supervisors help make decisions regarding promotion.

☐ Supervisors are involved in decisions regarding termination.

Work Simplification

☐ Supervisors know how to analyze jobs to improve the work performed.

☐ The philosophy of work simplification is an integral part of the supervisor's job.

☐ Supervisors are constantly reviewing work with the intent to eliminate, simplify, or combine tasks.

☐ Supervisors are alert to signs that examination of work tasks is in order.

☐ Supervisors know how to analyze a job for work simplification improvements.

☐ Supervisors can recognize problems and know how to correct them when jobs are examined.

☐ Supervisors encourage employees to help with work simplification.

---

example, employees may be videotaped while performing selected tasks. Careful analysis of the videotaped activity often suggests ways to simplify and speed work procedures. Such study also generates ideas for improved placement of equipment and for combining tasks within each job position. When the videotaped employees consistently use the standard operating procedures prescribed by the company, it becomes possible to determine the minimum amount of time needed for employees in each position to complete their work.

Exhibit 10   Sample Staffing Grid for a Pizza Operation

Position	Hourly Revenue						
	$0–$150	$151–$250	$251–$450	$451–$600	$601–$750	$751–$900	$901–$1,050
Manager	1	1	1	1	1	1	1
Delivery Person	2	3	3	4	4	5	6
Phone Operator	0	0	1	2	2	2	2
Cook	0	0	1	1	2	2	2
Total	3	4	6	8	9	10	11

Fast-food operations may base the allowable number of labor hours (or labor dollars) for each position on estimated revenue for the scheduling period. With many of these operations, it is even possible to use hourly revenue estimates as the basis for labor control and employee scheduling. Exhibit 10 illustrates a staffing plan for a pizza operation using this labor control system. Notice that when less than $150 will be generated during a specific hour of operation, one manager and two delivery persons should be scheduled. If, during a busy hour of operation, revenue levels are estimated at between $451 and $600, still only one manager is needed. However, four delivery persons, two phone operators, and one cook would be required.

According to this staffing grid, the lower the revenue levels, the more responsibilities must overlap from one position to the next. For example, the manager answers the phone and also cooks during slow periods. By contrast, a cook who only produces food is not required until revenue increases beyond $250 per hour. Also, as more pizzas are ordered, there is a greater likelihood that several orders will be delivered to the same area, and fewer delivery persons may be required on a per-unit (per-pizza) basis.

To use the staffing grid, the schedule planner can estimate hourly revenue for the scheduling period by averaging hourly revenue recorded for four or five previous weeks. For example, to estimate revenue to be generated on Monday from 11:00 A.M. to noon, a manager could review the revenue generated from 11:00 A.M. to noon on the previous five Mondays and divide that total by five (automated systems generate this data easily).

Once hourly revenue estimates are made, the manager of the pizza operation can schedule employees according to the procedures already described. This approach to scheduling tries to match input (number of employee hours) with output (amount of revenue generated). As pressures for reduced labor costs increase throughout the food and beverage industry, this approach may become more useful to managers in other types of food and beverage operations.

Hourly revenue forecasting and labor scheduling are accomplished easily by many automated fast-food operations. Exhibit 11 illustrates an **hourly revenue report** that tracks revenue and labor figures for each hour of a workday. These daily reports can be processed to project revenue for every hour of each day of the coming week or other planning period. Exhibit 12 depicts a **labor requirements report** that shows the amount of projected revenue and the number of sales

Exhibit 11   Hourly Revenue Report

Through Time	Revenue	Guests	Checks	Labor Hrs	Labor $$	Lbr/Rev
8:00 AM	0.00	0	0	0.00	0.00	0.00%
9:00 AM	0.00	0	0	0.13	0.70	0.00%
10:00 AM	0.00	0	0	5.52	27.46	0.00%
11:00 AM	0.00	1	1	10.28	47.68	0.00%
12:00 PM	100.45	12	5	16.30	65.98	65.68%
1:00 PM	93.40	7	8	17.78	67.81	72.60%
2:00 PM	139.05	14	13	18.00	67.81	48.77%
3:00 PM	76.80	6	10	18.00	67.81	88.29%
4:00 PM	615.89	86	56	17.67	64.42	10.46%
5:00 PM	240.55	7	12	25.17	85.85	35.69%
6:00 PM	609.85	48	28	39.73	137.82	22.60%
7:00 PM	1,319.29	141	89	45.42	160.94	12.20%
8:00 PM	1,573.40	167	131	52.70	190.49	12.11%
9:00 PM	1,815.77	92	169	56.95	213.66	11.77%
10:00 PM	1,376.40	67	213	57.50	229.18	16.65%
11:00 PM	1,317.80	159	237	51.53	203.61	15.45%
12.00 AM	1,281.95	34	237	47.18	181.08	14.13%
1:00 AM	1,220.30	22	231	38.62	152.32	12.48%
2:00 AM	791.30	122	161	32.97	128.98	16.30%
3:00 AM	2,575.50	3	3	20.90	78.13	3.03%
4:00 AM	0.00	0	0	6.73	11.67	0.00%
5:00 AM	0.00	0	0	0.00	0.00	0.00%
6:00 AM	0.00	0	0	0.00	0.00	0.00%
7:00 AM	0.00	0	0	0.00	0.00	0.00%
Total	15,147.70	988	1604	579.08	2,183.40	14.41%

counter employees required for every hour of each day of the coming week. The projections are calculated by averaging the revenue for each hour of the past four weeks. The labor standards specified by management are then used to arrive at the number of counter staff needed for each hour according to projected revenue.

Automated Labor and Payroll Information Systems

You've just seen how computerized systems can help managers use historic revenue data to forecast and schedule labor needs for subsequent time periods. These systems have numerous additional applications in the control of labor costs.[1]

Calculating each employee's pay, developing accounting records, and preparing the reports required by federal, state, and local governments are ongoing tasks carried out by every food service operation. Payroll activities can be time-consuming tasks in non-automated properties. Not only do pay rates vary with job classifications, but a single employee may work at different tasks over a number of work shifts, each of which may involve a separate pay rate. In addition, unlike many other accounting functions, payroll system requirements arise from sources other than property managers. Government agencies, unions, pension trust funds, credit unions, banks, and employees themselves often have input into how payroll information is stored and reported.

Many properties use a **computerized time-clock system** to record employees' log-in and log-out work times. Exhibit 13 illustrates a time card produced by a

Exhibit 12   Sample Labor Requirements Report

		...MONDAY...		...TUESDAY...		...WEDNESDAY...		...THURSDAY...		...FRIDAY...		...SATURDAY...		...SUNDAY...	
FROM	TO	SALES	PEOPLE	SALES	PEOPLE	SALES	PEOPLE	SALES	PEOPLE	SALES	PEOPLE	SALES	PEOPLE	SALES	PEOPLE
0 -	1 A.M.														
1 -	2														
2 -	3														
3 -	4														
4 -	5														
5 -	6														
6 -	7														
7 -	8														
8 -	9	37	5	37	5	39	5	42	7	55	8	55	8	55	8
9 -	10	61	8	61	8	61	8	61	8	79	9	79	9	79	9
10 -	11	85	9	85	9	85	9	85	9	111	9	111	9	111	9
11 -	NOON	97	9	99	9	99	9	100	9	127	10	127	10	130	10
12 -	1 P.M.	115	9	169	13	114	9	114	9	169	13	171	15	171	15
1 -	2	132	10	132	10	132	10	132	10	154	12	189	15	163	13
2 -	3	130	10	133	10	172	15	121	10	168	13	172	15	175	15
3 -	4	157	12	157	12	157	12	234	15	213	15	220	15	213	15
4 -	5	210	15	205	15	195	15	171	15	208	15	217	15	213	15
5 -	6	126	10	127	10	129	10	171	15	201	15	203	15	207	15
6 -	7	115	9	112	9	116	9	103	9	174	15	172	15	171	15
7 -	8	82	9	67	8	70	8	100	9	115	9	150	11	120	9
8 -	9	36	5	73	9	58	8	51	8	138	10	138	10	136	10
9 -	10														
10 -	11														
11 -	MID														

	MONDAY	TUESDAY	WEDNESDAY	THURSDAY	FRIDAY	SATURDAY	SUNDAY
TOTAL SALES	$1383.00	$1457.00	$1427.00	$1485.00	$1912.00	$2004.00	$1944.00
TOTAL HOURS	120.0	127.0	127.0	133.0	153.0	162.0	158.0
AVG. SALE PER HOUR	$ 11.53	$ 11.47	$ 11.23	$ 11.17	$ 12.50	$ 12.37	$ 12.30

```
01  -  CHICKEN DELICIOUS INC.            LABOR REQUIREMENTS          LS2043  PAGE     1
001 -  CHICKEN DELICIOUS #1           FOR WEEK BEGINNING 10/01/XX      17.44.00    10/01/XX
```

TOTAL PROJECTED WEEKLY SALES $11,613.00

TOTAL LABOR HOURS 980.0

AVERAGE SALE PER HOUR . . . . $ 11.85

computerized time-clock system. When a time-clock system is interfaced with a computer system, data can be transferred daily to the automated payroll system and the previous day's pay can be calculated for each employee. Clocking in may be done by a time-card punch, a touch screen selection, and even a biometric scan of an employee's finger, hand, or eye. Terminals for modern POS systems allow employees to check in and check out of work by entering an employee ID number (and perhaps other identifying information) directly into the system at many different locations. For example, servers, bartenders, buspersons, and other front-of-the-house employees can access POS systems in service areas. Cooks, dishwashers, and other back-of-the-house staff members can use a terminal in a kitchen area, the manager's office, or in a service area if it is conveniently located.

Exhibit 13   Sample Time Card from a Computerized Time-Clock System

TIMEKEEPER 35 FEATURES

- Employee Classification
- Department #
- Employee name
- Column headings
- Day or date (01–31)
- Automatic meal deduction
- Daily total
- Separation of hours into categories

- 9-digit employee number
- Pay period ending
- Automatic timecard preparation
- Automatic rounding of punches
- Weekly total breakout
- Hours/minutes or Hours/hundredths of hours

DAY	IN	OUT	DAILY	REG	OT
MO	7:30A	12:00P	4:30	4.50	0.00
MO	12:30P	4:00P	8:00	8.00	0.00
TU	7:23A	12:00P	4:30	12.50	0.00
TU	12:30P	4:05P	8:00	16.00	0.00
WE	7:30A	4:00P	8:00	24.00	0.00
TH	7:24A	4:07P	8:00	32.00	0.00
FR	7:30A	12:00P	4:30	36.50	0.00
FR	12:30P	6:00P	10:00	40.00	2.00

R= 40.00 OT= 2.00 P= 0.00 M= 0.00

PAT. 4,270,043; 4,361,082 & FOR. PRINTED IN U.S.A. © 1981–84, KRONOS

KRONOS INCORPORATED   **TIMEKEEPER**

Terminal systems may be used to communicate with employees. One type of system ensures that immediately after employees sign into the system, a message screen is displayed. This message screen enables management to deliver different messages to different categories of employees or to individual employees. For example, employees with job codes corresponding to food servers might receive messages about daily specials and prices. Or an individual employee might receive a message from a supervisor about work schedule changes or the work schedule for the following week. Since employees must touch the message screen to complete sign-in procedures, management is assured that employees have received their messages.

Sophisticated POS systems can maintain or be interfaced with an electronic file that contains a **labor master file** that stores individual employee data such as

Exhibit 14 Sample Payroll Withholdings and Deductions

TAXES
• Federal, state, and city withholding amounts for income taxes
• Federal Insurance Contribution Act tax (Social Security tax)
• State unemployment compensation (selected states)

OTHER

- Savings bonds
- Medical insurance
- Life insurance
- Retirement contribution
- Charitable contribution
- Capital stock purchase plan
- Savings plan, credit union
- Charge for meals
- Payroll advance
- Garnishment of wages
- Union dues

name, employee number, Social Security number, and authorized job codes and corresponding hourly wage rates. Other data may include the types and amounts of withholdings and deductions, requests for direct deposit of payroll checks, and time used for vacation, sick leave, training, etc.

The labor master file can be extensive. Appropriate deductions and withholding amounts are subtracted from each employee's gross pay to arrive at net pay. **Withholdings** are for income and Social Security taxes. Since federal tax regulations frequently change, and since state withholdings vary across the country, many payroll modules are designed so that the user is able to make the necessary programming adjustments. **Deductions** are usually voluntary and depend on the types of benefits available from the employer. Exhibit 14 lists some of the kinds of deductions made from the gross pay of employees.

This file may also contain data needed to produce labor reports. Data accumulated in individual records of the master file may include:

- Actual hours worked.
- Total hourly wages.
- Tips.
- Credits for employee meals.
- Number of guests served.
- Gross revenues.

Exhibit 15 illustrates a sample time card and job detail report that lists each employee's job number and name, hours worked (regular and overtime), wages earned, and wages declared for each employee on a given workday. This report

Exhibit 15   Employee Time Card and Job Detail Report

Employee Time Card And Job Detail
MICROS Systems - Mike Rose Cafe

Bruno The Manager
Printed on Thursday, October 03, 20XX - 11:09 AM

Employee # And Name					Payroll ID			

1 - Phoebe Kramer   123-46-6789

Job # and Name	Clock In/Out Date and Time		Hours	Status	Adjusted By	Reason		
401 - Servers	IN Tue 20XX/10/03 8:15am			No Schedule				
	OUT	10:44am	2.46	Not Scheduled				
401 - Servers	IN Tue 20XX/10/03 10:48am			On Time				
	OUT	2:50pm	4.04	On Time				

Total Hours Worked This Week:	6.52	Regular:	6.52	Overtime:	0.00			

Job Totals		Regular Hours	Overtime Hours	Regular Pay	Overtime Pay	Total Pay
Total Hours Worked This Pay Period:	6.52	6.52	0.00	27.71	0.00	27.71

2 - Dave Sherman   456-78-1235

Job # and Name	Clock In/Out Date and Time		Hours	Status	Adjusted By	Reason
401 - Servers	IN Tue 20XX/10/03 10:49am			On Time		
	OUT	2:51pm	4.03	Early		

Total Hours Worked This Week:	4.03	Regular:	4.03	Overtime:	0.00			

Job Totals		Regular Hours	Overtime Hours	Regular Pay	Overtime Pay	Total Pay
Total Hours Worked This Pay Period:	4.03	4.03	0.00	17.13	0.00	17.13

3 - Rachel Johnson   453-09-3412

Job # and Name	Clock In/Out Date and Time		Hours	Status	Adjusted By	Reason
401 - Servers	IN Tue 20XX/10/03 2:52pm			On Time		
	OUT	7:58pm	5.10	On Time		

Total Hours Worked This Week:	5.10	Regular:	5.10	Overtime:	0.00			

Job Totals		Regular Hours	Overtime Hours	Regular Pay	Overtime Pay	Total Pay
Total Hours Worked This Pay Period:	5.10	5.10	0.00	21.68	0.00	21.68

4 - John Mark   435-94-0923

Job # and Name	Clock In/Out Date and Time		Hours	Status	Adjusted By	Reason
401 - Servers	IN Tue 20XX/10/03 8:18am			No Schedule		
	OUT	10:46am	2.46	Not Scheduled		
401 - Servers	IN Tue 20XX/10/03 2:52pm			On Time		
	OUT	7:50pm	5.11	On Break		
401 - Servers	IN Tue 20XX/10/03 8:40pm			Late From Break		
	OUT	8:41pm	0.02	Not Scheduled		

Total Hours Worked This Week:	7.61	Regular:	7.61	Overtime:	0.00			

Job Totals		Regular Hours	Overtime Hours	Regular Pay	Overtime Pay	Total Pay
Total Hours Worked This Pay Period:	7.61	7.61	0.00	32.35	0.00	32.35

Courtesy of MICROS Systems, Inc., Columbia, Maryland (www.micros.com).

Exhibit 16   Weekly Consolidated Employee Job Summary

Weekly Consolidated Employee Job Summary
MICROS Systems - Bar & Grille

Sunday   Wednesday
Period From : 10/06/   To : 10/09/XX

Bruno The Manager
nted on Wednesday, October 09, XX   - 7:40 PM

	Hours Worked				Labor Cost			
	Regular	Overtime	Total	% of Ttl	Regular	Overtime	Total	% of Ttl
1 - Phoebe Ramierez 123-46-6789								
401 Servers	24.69	0.00	24.69	100.00%	104.95	0.00	104.95	100.00%
Total	24.69	0.00	24.69	14.84%	104.95	0.00	104.95	10.82%
11 - Lisa Sherman 765-00-9123								
501 Bartender	16.18	0.00	16.18	100.00%	0.00	0.00	0.00	0.00%
Total	16.18	0.00	16.18	9.73%	0.00	0.00	0.00	0.00%
13 - Asa Sessions 999-44-1111								
12 Hourly Mgr	50.44	0.00	50.44	100.00%	504.45	0.00	504.45	100.00%
Total	50.44	0.00	50.44	30.32%	504.45	0.00	504.45	52.01%
14 - Rick LaBlanc 345-94-0273								
602 Dishwasher	41.81	0.00	41.81	100.00%	177.73	0.00	177.73	100.00%
Total	41.81	0.00	41.81	25.14%	177.73	0.00	177.73	18.32%
15 - Jeff Schwimmer 321-54-9876								
603 Cook	33.22	0.00	33.22	100.00%	182.75	0.00	182.75	100.00%
Total	33.22	0.00	33.22	19.97%	182.75	0.00	182.75	18.84%
Grand Total	166.34	0.00	166.34		969.88	0.00	969.88	

Courtesy of MICROS Systems, Inc., Columbia, Maryland (www.micros.com).

also can be used in combination with another report—a consolidated employee job summary (Exhibit 16)—to consolidate information for a week or other time period.

Reports can summarize labor hour and cost information by position, shift, department, total operation, or by any level of data sorting that is helpful or deemed necessary by management.

Automated payroll systems must be flexible enough to meet all the demands placed on the system with a minimum of programming changes. In many cases, a utility program enables a property to define its own particular pay period (daily, weekly, biweekly, or monthly). Typically, automated payroll systems can:

- Maintain an employee master file.

- Calculate gross and net pay for salaried and hourly employees.

- Print paychecks.

- Produce payroll tax registers and reports.

- Prepare labor cost reports.

- Provide overtime warnings that alert employers to employees who are nearing the hour limit after which overtime pay will be required.

- Reduce lost time by not allowing an employee to check into the system before a certain number of minutes prior to his or her scheduled work time or to check out after a specified time beyond the scheduled shift. Some systems will only authorize wages to be paid during assigned (scheduled) times, so that, while an employee may check in earlier or check out later than scheduled, wages will not be paid for other than the employee's scheduled work hours without authorization by management.

Payroll Register File

To calculate gross and net pay for hourly employees, the payroll module relies on a payroll register file to access the number of hours each employee worked during the pay period and other data that may require special tax calculations, such as:

- Sick leave pay.

- Bonus pay.

- Tips.

- Expense reimbursements.

Automated payroll systems generally maintain a government reporting file for quarter-to-date and year-to-date federal and state tax histories. Deduction reports can be produced with year-to-date computations. Exhibit 17 illustrates a sample detailed check history produced by a back office accounting system. The check register summarizes important payroll information for each employee.

Automated payroll systems can accommodate manually written payroll checks and voided payroll checks. Systems typically reconcile outstanding paychecks (checks that have been issued) with paychecks that have cleared the bank and appear on bank statements. Generally, at the end of a check reconciliation routine, the system prints an updated list of outstanding checks.

Payroll modules typically calculate sick leave and vacation hours accrued (earned) by employees. This may be done by accruing hours each pay period,

Exhibit 17   Sample Payroll Check Register

UNIVERSITY CLUB OF MSU
EMPLOYEE SS# XXX-XX-XXXX
NAME: MARY ADAMS

PAYROLL
DETAILED CHECK HISTORY

CHECK #	DATE	REG GRAT (1)	OVT OTHER (2)	HOL HOLWK (3)	VAC XTIP (4)	SICK (5)	TIP WAGES TOTAL GROSS (6)	FIT SIT (7)	CITY #1 W/H CITY #2 W/H (8)	OTHER W/H SDI (9)	FICA TOTAL DED (10)
046713	10/19/XX	244.05	.00	.00	.00	.00	.00	51.22	4.43	.00	33.93
		199.44	.00	.00	.00	.00	443.49	18.63	.00	.00	.00
							TOTAL HOURS-			NET PAY-	46.63 ... 335.28
EMPLOYEE TOTAL		244.05	.00	.00	.00	.00	.00	51.22	4.43	.00	33.93
		199.44	.00	.00	.00	.00	443.49	18.63	.00	.00	.00
							TOTAL HOURS-			NET PAY-	46.63 ... 335.28
FINAL TOTALS		244.05	.00	.00	.00	.00	.00	51.22	4.43	.00	33.93
		199.44	.00	.00	.00	.00	443.49	18.63	.00	.00	.00
							TOTAL HOURS-			NET PAY-	46.63 ... 335.28

EXPLANATION OF COLUMN HEADERS

(1) Regular Wage
Gratutities

(2) Overtime
Other (such as bonus)

(3) Holiday Pay
Holiday Work
(Holiday Pay &
Hourly Compensation)

(4) Vacation
Extra Tip

(5) Sick Pay

(6) Tip Wages
Total Gross Wages

(7) Federal Income Tax
State Income Tax

(8) City #1 withholding tax
City #2 withholding tax

(9) Other withholding tax
State disability insurance

(10) Federal Insurance Contribution Act
(Social Security; includes Medicare)
Total Deductions
(Employee share of insurance, 401(k) plans, etc.)

Courtesy of The University Club, Michigan State University, East Lansing, Michigan.

periodically (for example, on the first pay period of the month), or yearly on the basis of the employee's anniversary date.

Based on each employee's hourly rate (previously stored in the system) and calculations of pay for salaried employees, payroll modules can generate departmental labor cost reports by department or job classification.

Endnote

1. For more information about automated payroll applications, see Michael L. Kasavana and John J. Cahill, *Managing Technology in the Hospitality Industry*, 5th ed. (Lansing, Mich.: American Hotel & Lodging Educational Institute, 2007), Chapter 9.

Key Terms

computerized time-clock system—Records time in and time out for employees as they enter and leave the work area; when interfaced with an automated payroll system, relevant data can be transferred each day and the previous day's pay calculated for each employee.

deductions—Subtractions from gross pay that are usually voluntary and depend on the types of benefits available from the employer.

fixed labor—The minimum amount and type of labor required to run the food and beverage operation regardless of business volume.

hourly revenue report—Shows revenue and labor figures for each hour of a day; used by some fast-food operations as the basis for scheduling employees.

labor master file—A file containing employee records and data used to produce labor-related reports.

labor requirements report—Shows the amount of projected revenue and the number of employees required for every hour of each day of the coming week; the projections are calculated by averaging the revenues for each hour of the past four weeks.

mise en place—A French phrase meaning "everything in its place"; it is necessary to stock workstations and do necessary preparation tasks before guests arrive.

overtime—Some companies use the term "overtime" to refer to situations in which employees work more than the time they were scheduled to work (a food server works five hours instead of the scheduled four hours, for example). Federal guidelines specify that non-exempt employees who work in excess of the standard 40-hour workweek are generally entitled to receive overtime pay of one-and-one-half-times the hourly rate.

position performance analysis—A technique for determining labor standards for each position and shift.

staffing guide—A labor scheduling and control tool that incorporates labor standards and tells managers the number of labor hours needed for each position according to the volume of business forecasted for any given meal period.

variable labor—Labor requirements that vary according to the volume of business activity; for example, as more guests are served or as more meals are produced, additional service and kitchen labor is needed.

withholdings—Subtractions from gross pay for income and Social Security taxes.

 Review Questions ————————————————————————

1. Why must managers consider quality requirements before developing labor standards?

2. What are the advantages of expressing labor standards in terms of labor dollars? In terms of labor hours?

3. How can managers use a position performance analysis to determine labor standards for each position and shift?

4. What are some factors managers must consider when constructing a staffing guide?

5. How is fixed labor different from variable labor?

6. How can managers evaluate a staffing guide in relation to budgeted goals?

7. How can managers use a staffing guide as a scheduling tool? As a control tool?

8. How do managers of fast-food operations schedule employees on the basis of estimated sales?

9. Why can payroll activities become time-consuming activities for managers of non-automated operations?

10. What functions can be performed by an automated payroll system?

 Internet Sites ————————————————————————

For more information, visit the following Internet sites. Remember that Internet addresses can change without notice. If the site is no longer there, you can use a search engine to look for additional sites.

Automated Labor Control Tools

Altametrics, Inc
www.erestaurantservices.com

Kronos, Inc.
www.kronos.com

Barrington Software, Inc.
www.cooken.com

MICROS Systems, Inc.
www.micros.com

Compeat Restaurant Systems
www.compeat.com

PriZem International, Inc.
www.prizem.com

Datavision Technologies, Inc.
www.datavisiontech.com

TimeManagement Corporation
www.timemgmt.com

Tracrite Software Inc.
www.tracrite.net

UniFocus
www.unifocus.com

Other Labor-Cost-Related Websites

Cost-Watch Restaurant Reports
www.cost-watch.com

The Restaurant Resource Group
www.rrgconsulting.com
(Click on "Tips & Articles.")

Problems

Problem 1

What is the standard labor cost percentage to serve 50, 75, and 100 lunches, given the following number of standard labor hours (assume a guest check average for lunch of $14.75)?

	Number of Lunches								
	50			75			100		
Position	Std. Labor Hours	Avg. Hourly Rate	Std. Labor Costs	Std. Labor Hours	Avg. Hourly Rate	Std. Labor Costs	Std. Labor Hours	Avg. Hourly Rate	Std. Labor Costs
Server	9.5	5.25	49.88	11.0	5.25	57.75	15.75	5.25	82.69
Bartender	4.75	7.75	36.81	4.75	7.55	35.66	4.75	7.75	36.81
Cook	12.0	11.50	138	16.0	11.50	184	19.0	11.50	218.50
Steward	9.5	6.75	64.12	9.5	6.75	64.12	11.0	6.25	68.75
Busperson	8.5	4.25	36.12	8.5	4.25	36.12	8.5	4.25	36.12
Host	4.0	.00	0	4.0	7.00	28.00	6.0	7.00	42
Total Standard Labor Cost		===			===			===	

Problem 2

Following is the hourly pay scale for the Southern Center Restaurant:

Cook	= $9.75
Food Server	= $5.50
Bartender	= $5.75
Dishwasher	= $6.85

The schedule for the upcoming week requires the following number of hours for each position:

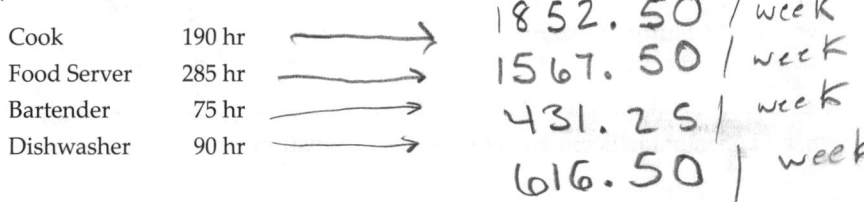

Cook	190 hr
Food Server	285 hr
Bartender	75 hr
Dishwasher	90 hr

1852.50 / week
1567.50 / week
431.25 / week
616.50 / week

a. If all persons work the number of hours on the schedule, what will be the expected wage for each position and for all positions for the workweek?

b. What is the average hourly labor cost for the Southern Center Restaurant, given the financial data above?

c. The manager of the Southern Center Restaurant wants to know the average hourly labor cost for back-of-the-house positions; what is that average hourly rate?

d. What is the average hourly rate for front-of-the-house positions in the Southern Center Restaurant?

e. Assume expected revenues are $14,725.00; what is the expected labor cost percentage?

f. Actual revenues for the period are very close to target ($14,650); however, for reasons that must be determined, the actual number of cooks' and servers' hours were 210 and 315, respectively. What is the actual labor cost percentage if the bartenders' and dishwashers' hours were as scheduled?

g. How much profit was lost because of this higher-than-expected labor cost?

Problem 3

Complete the weekly department labor hour report shown below for the cook's position.

Employee	7/16	7/17	7/18	Actual Hours 7/19	7/20	7/21	7/22	Total Actual	Standard
Bill	—	—	5	8	8	8	7		34
Phil	5	—	—	5	8	8	8		30
Latoya	8	4	—	—	8	7	8		32
Enid	8	8	8	—	—	8	8		40
Pasco	7	8	8	8	7	—	—		36
									172

What are your comments as you compare the actual to the standard (expected) number of hours worked?

Problem 4

Complete the weekly department labor hour and cost report for the cook's position.

Employee	7/14	7/15	7/16	7/17	7/18	7/19	7/20	Actual	Standard	Rate	Actual	Standard
Phyllis	8	—	8	7	8	—	8		40	$11.00		
Ahmed	7	8	7	8	—	8	—		35	$10.90		
Tom	8	8	7	8	—	—	8		35	$10.55		
Orlando	8	8	—	—	8	8	7		40	$11.25		
Moses	—	—	8	7	8	8	8		38	$9.95		
									188			

What comments would you make to the schedule planner?

Index